The New Oxford Book
of American Verse

The
New Oxford Book
of
American Verse

Chosen and Edited by

RICHARD ELLMANN

New York
OXFORD UNIVERSITY PRESS
1976

INTRODUCTION

American poetry, once an offshoot, now appears to be a parent stem. Speculative, daring, and sometimes melodious, it has become the register of some of the most independent minds. What they have written has urgency, sensitivity to contemporary conditions, force of utterance. That isolated figures should have achieved so much might be put down to chance. Beyond chance, however, these qualities have been sustained and fostered by many good poets as well as by a few great ones. Such clustered enterprise makes persuasive the claim of this poetry to have a distinctive and national character.

For the new settlers in North America, versifying was as natural as ploughing. Their early poems were usually prayers lauding the deity for enabling them to supersede the Indians, who themselves addressed poems in other languages to less responsive deities. Yet if writing English verse was a prevalent pastime in America from the sixteenth to the eighteenth centuries, it was hardly ever done well. The stronger talents, founding fathers or God's ministers, were more felicitous in prose.

Almost from the beginning there must have been a glimmer that new exploits might be hazarded in creative literature as in other kinds of endeavor. The colonists came, after all, from lands that were already storied and poemed, and there seemed no reason why the new country should not have its moments and places similarly memorialized. If memorialists were scarce, it is salutary to recognize, in an age of chairpersons, that the first American poet of consequence was a woman. Anne Bradstreet, born before Shakespeare died, belonged to a pious and workaday world as unlike his as possible.

She was modest about her poems,

> I am obnoxious to each carping tongue,
> Who sayes, my hand a needle better fits,

and about her sex,

> Men have precedency, and still excell. . .
> Men can doe best, and Women know it well. . .

But friends who were proud of her talent had her poems published in 1650 under the title, *The Tenth Muse Lately Sprung Up in America*. Nine European incumbents were displaced. If Anne Bradstreet's verse did not live up to this billing, even to the degree of parochialism (she had, after all, been born in England, and was devoted to the mother country), it has some elegance in its handling of simple themes such as the burning of her house or the absence of her loving husband. What her title suggested was true, that through her an upstart country was claiming audience.

Yet no one followed her, or so it seemed until, in the late 1930s, the discovery of Edward Taylor's poems indicated that she had in fact had a successor. Taylor, also born in England, thirty years after Anne Bradstreet, outrivaled her self-effacement by publishing nothing. It might be supposed that humility would also pervade his poems. They are humble enough before God, but Taylor has, even in abasement, a firm and often grand manner. He had as models the seventeenth-century English metaphysical poets, as Eliot would have after him; and like them, he is intricate even when testifying devotion, and sonorous as well:

> Oh! What a thing is Man? Lord, Who am I. . .
> Make me, O Lord, thy Spining Wheele compleate. . .
> I kening through Astronomy Divine
>   The Worlds bright Battlement, wherein I spy
> A Golden Path my Pensill cannot line,
>   From that bright Throne unto my Threshold ly.

Or he can ask like Blake,

> Who Lac'de and Fillitted the earth so fine,
> With Rivers like green Ribbons Smaragdine?

Taylor's force of utterance and homely figures have their precedents, and he does not mind being within a tradition. Nor did Philip Freneau, born a century later, who lacked Taylor's heights and depths and controlled a middle style closer to that of the Augustan poets. Some of his verse was satirical, and ably so, but he had a capacity also for tight declarative statement:

> The space between, is but an hour,
> The frail duration of a flower.
> There ages past have rolled away,
> And forests bloomed but to decay.

Not much is being said, but that little is said well.

What we usually think of as American verse is more freestepping than this. But in fact much American verse of good quality, including some of the most familiar poems, is in established forms and presents accustomed feelings. If poets who can be described as traditional seem less representative of the new country, they provide the setting for more spectacular excursions. And some of them wrote very well. William Cullen Bryant regarded his art as consolatory, and he found nature a consolation which he could celebrate. That it might be, as Wordsworth was attesting across the water, a transforming power as well, did not occur to him. He sought long-established truths which he could impressively reiterate. He informed the Waterfowl (in his poem to that bird) of what it presumably did not need to be told:

> There is a Power, whose care
> Teaches thy way along that pathless coast...

yet he could do better than that, in descriptive passages,

> All day thy wings have fanned,
> At that far height, the cold, thin atmosphere...

Longfellow had wider interests and keener melancholy than Bryant. He could write commonplaces too, but apart from moral uplift, he was 'one acquainted with the night.' So he could address the darkness.

> Peace! Peace! Orestes-like I breathe this prayer,

or sympathize with 'These Ishmaels and Hagars of mankind,' and he knew 'the first slight swerving of the heart' that heralds the end of friendship. He propounded several themes which gave impetus to Frost, whose first book gratefully borrowed its title, *A Boy's Will*, from Longfellow.

Whittier, unlike Longfellow, situated most of his poems in his own time. He had, in fact, a fierce political interest in the abolition of slavery, which animated many of his poems. But the poem which musters his best talent is his New England pastoral, *Snowbound*. The blinding storm of his childhood knits together his family and some of their friends. Whittier describes them with great fondness and yet an attentive eye, so that the poem is a domestic vignette of American life, sharpened by the fact that now all except the poet and his brother are dead and confined to memory. Conviviality masters the snow, but is itself mastered by time. It is not a poem to lead to other poems, yet it stands out as perfectly realized.

Alongside this group arose another with incompatible ambitions. In 1837 Emerson renewed the claim that had been made by Anne Bradstreet's *The Tenth Muse*. 'We have listened too long to the courtly muses of Europe,' he wrote in 'The American Scholar.' A courtless country demanded a new form of literary enterprise. His restless mind could not be satisfied with stereotyped lines or routine sentiments. His verse sought nothing less than to reconstitute the relation of man and the world about him. The old dualism between subject and object is erased, we become as Emerson declared a transparent eyeball, and in drawing the world into ourselves we and the world too are altered. As James Russell Lowell said, in polite mockery, Emerson was a man

> In whose mind all creation is duly respected
> As parts of himself—just a little projected...

The unexpectedness of theme is often matched in Emerson by an unexpectedness of diction:

> Daughters of Time, the hypocritic Days,

or

> In a tumultuous privacy of storm,

or

> Things are in the saddle,
> And ride mankind.

The density of these lines comes from his resolute sifting of intractable material and hard questions.

Important as he was in himself, Emerson also served as precursor, though an unwitting one, for Walt Whitman. He laid down his specifications for the poetry to come: 'I ask not for the great, the remote, the romantic; what is doing in Italy or Arabia; what is Greek art, or Provençal minstrelsy: I embrace the common, I explore and sit at the feet of the familiar, the low.' Commonness might now be a focus of interest rather than a derogatory epithet. All the details of living in America were suddenly eligible for inclusion in poetry, in the service of what Edward Dorn would later call 'a new look at man.'

Walt Whitman felt himself charged with the poetic mission as Emerson had defined it. 'I was simmering, simmering, simmering; Emerson brought me to a boil.' Politics and esthetics were one: individuality went hand in hand with equality. 'I speak the password primeval, I give the sign of democracy,' said Whitman in the long poem which he could appropriately entitle, 'Song of Myself.' Emerson had said that the poet 'unlocks our chains and admits us to a new scene.' Whitman subscribed to Emerson's word 'freedom,' and added to it 'variety'; these two words he saw as the vital attributes for poetry as well as for politics and for progress. He held that democracy could not prove itself beyond cavil until it evolved its own works of art, its own poets, and until it had displaced all that had been produced elsewhere under opposite influences. A class of native authors would affect politics 'far more than the popular superficial suffrage,' he insisted. As against W. H. Auden's conception that poetry makes nothing happen, Whitman held the conviction that poetry can make everything happen.

This message is at once grand and, like most grand messages, vague. It could best be defined by Whitman in terms of his own poems, which met Emerson's prophecy that the new state made inevitable a new poetry. 'Yet America is a poem in our eyes,' said Emerson, 'its ample geography dazzles the imagination, and it will not wait long for meters.' To this Whitman boomed in reply, 'The Americans of all nations at any time upon the earth have probably the fullest poetical nature. The United States themselves are essentially the great poem.' The claim of the fullest poetical nature might be made because of the freedom and variety which were hitherto unprecedented among peoples. The poem that the country itself comprised was the one that Whitman proposed to indite. Like Rimbaud, he could say, 'Et tout le reste est littérature.' The poem had only to be uttered, though without the meters Emerson imagined for it.

From this time on it begins to be possible to speak of American poetry, even if it can be defined better by its practitioners than by its tenets. Has it, as one critic has proposed, continuity? A common ideological concern, and one that is purely indigenous, is hard to substantiate. But if it has not the continuity of a single theme, it has lesser continuities of emphasis and of attitude. To a number of poets it seemed possible to evoke what Hart Crane would call 'new thresholds, new anatomies,' with an exhilaration that was not available in countries where literature prided itself on its antiquity and made constant allusion to Greek and Latin predecessors. In America the desire and the propensity to be first affected even poets who wrote conventionally. Phillis Wheatley had nothing new to say, but she was the first black slave poet and knew it.

Whitman's imitators were not to come until this century, but this common exhilaration was widespread. It lends even poets of no great talent an assurance out of keeping with their merits. The country demanded a new poetry, and the poetry demanded a new country. The geography of the United States was made up not only of loved spots that might have poems conferred upon them, but also of a national consciousness that found its reflection in large distances and unexpected vistas. The land became a new metaphor to be commandeered, the one amplitude evoked another; that is, the immensity of nature's work appeared to validate a great work of human art. Mileage became political became poetical. In a whole series of poets, Sandburg, Hart Crane, and Allen Ginsberg, for example, there can be seen a concerted effort to gather the whole massive country into their arms in a kind of continental embrace.

If this embrace had been indiscriminate, as in some earlier works such as Barlow's The Columbiad, the poets would be beyond credibility. But characteristically, they did not merely celebrate, they also criticized. No sooner had they discovered American innocence than they began to lament its loss. As Robert Frost would say wryly, 'The land was ours before we were the land's,' and 'The deed of gift was many deeds of war.' The issue was drawn early, in Emerson's 'Ode Inscribed to W. H. Channing,' which he wrote in 1846. No one had more sanguine hopes for his country than Emerson, but he was too intelligent and too honest not to testify to other feelings as well. In replying to a request from Channing that he take a public stand against slavery, Emerson indicated his awareness of his country's shortcomings. It was no use prating of culture when the United States was fighting an unjust war:

> Go, blindworm, go,
> Behold the famous States
> Harrying Mexico
> With rifle and with knife!

This political sensitivity is to be found also in Whitman, perhaps more unexpectedly in him because his tremendous affirmations are sometimes thought to leave no space for questionings. D. H. Lawrence accused Whitman of extolling 'an empty Allness,' and of failing to see that 'men are tricky-tricksy, and they shy all sorts of ways.' Whitman did in fact know this as well as Lawrence, and said so. In *Democratic Vistas* he wrote unhappily in prose, 'Never was there, perhaps, more hollowness at heart than at present, and here in the United States. . . The spectacle is appalling. We live in an atmosphere of hypocrisy throughout.' In verse he wrote, among other things, what he first entitled 'Poem of the Propositions of Nakedness' (later, 'Respondez'), which began:

> Stifled, O days! O lands! in every public and private corruption!
> Smother'd in thievery, impotence, shamelessness, mountain-high;
> Brazen effrontery, scheming, rolling like ocean's waves around
>   and upon you, O my days! my lands!
> For not even those thunderstorms, nor fiercest lightnings of the
>   war, have purified the atmosphere. . .

These poems confirm that the celebration of the new man in American poetry quickly became associated with dissent. The national idealism has continued to be checked by disquietude and even revulsion. As Hart Crane wrote in *The Bridge,*

> —Rush down the plenitude, and you shall see
> Isaiah counting famine on this lee!

Robinson Jeffers elegized corruption, 'Shine, perishing republic,' and predicted it would fall to 'some soft Sicilian tyrant.' Robert Lowell, observing the disappearance of the old Boston Aquarium, observed also that

> Everywhere
> giant-finned cars move forward like fish;
> a savage servility
> slides by on grease.

The tradition of dissent has not always been so fortunately sustained. Ezra Pound was determined to make a radical criticism of his country, but with rising hatred lost sight of the freedom and variety which were central in Whitman's and Emerson's visions of America. His zeal for a change in the economic system led him to endorse authoritarianism in the political system, and he began to see the cruelty and conformism of fascist Italy and Nazi Germany as good ways to implement change. He enlisted his great gifts in the propaganda service of government by terror, and escaped trial for treason only by pleading, with some justification, insanity. His later silence and sporadic bursts of remorse indicate that Pound too saw that he had lost his center 'fighting the world.'

Against Pound's receptivity to Nazi-Fascist repression, the Vietnam War proved an occasion for American poets to dissent for good reason. They protested in prose, and in person, as well as in verse. Some wrote strange and bitter poems, such as Robert Bly's visionary 'Johnson's Cabinet Watched by Ants':

> It is a clearing deep in a forest: overhanging boughs
> Make a low place. Here the citizens we knew during the day,
> The ministers, the department heads,
> Appear changed: the stockholders of large steel companies
> In small wooden shoes: here are the generals dressed as
> gamboling lambs.

Such works did not content themselves with simple indignation, but mustered irony and eerie fantasy to arouse horror and revulsion.

Not in politics alone, Whitman grows larger and larger with time. Under his eye books of verse reached out to be more than themselves. 'This is not a book,' he said in *Leaves of Grass*, 'Who touches this touches a man.' Through him there arose the blazing idea that to write a poem was not only to cultivate an art, it was also to perpetrate an act, and that act could be momentous in the life of a people as well as of a solitary poet. Emerson had celebrated in his 'Concord Hymn' the embattled farmer who once had stood at Concord and 'fired the shot heard round the world.' Whitman offered a comparable gesture when he wrote, 'I sound my barbaric yawp across the rooftops of the world.' The poetic act he undertook to perpetrate was on the grandest scale. He had read the epic poets, and he knew that Dante had discovered the vernacular, as opposed to Latin, for Italian verse. In a way he was out to discover the vernacular too, not in language alone—though a large proportion of his vocabulary had never before been the language of verse—but in people, places, incidents, symbols. A whole new area of expression, and so of mental experience, was now made available for poetry. The forms he hit upon suited his liberating theme. In this century Pound, who was wary of Whitman, would still salute him for his formal innovations, and say in one of the *Cantos*, 'Breaking the pentameter, that was the first heave.' But the heave was more than technical, more than the casting off of metrical bondage; it was the sensing of new rhythms made necessary by a new self and conception of self, and so it was the unfolding also of hitherto unregarded areas in the external world as human consciousness flowed into them and to some extent infused itself into them and changed them.

The example of Whitman was supported by the examples of other poets. Edgar Allan Poe regarded himself as Whitman's opposite, and—in the new dislocation of form and content—argued for form as did Whitman for content. Yet, if in no other way, they resemble each other in ambition: the world that Whitman was busy creating was the world that Poe was busy destroying. Poe's apocalyptic imagination saw love, the haunted palace of the mind, and the whole fabric of reality about to fall—like the house of Usher—into negativity. To Whitman's calls to awakening Poe responded with 'Nevermore.'

Emily Dickinson said she had not read Whitman, and probably she had not. But her conception of the poetic act as one that encompassed poet and reality,

> Inebriate of Air—am I—
> And Debauchee of Dew—

was parallel to his. 'If I read a book and it makes my whole body so cold no fire can ever warm me,' she said, 'I know *that* is poetry. If I feel physically as if the top of my head were taken off, I know *that* is poetry. These are the only ways I know it. Is there any other way?' In short lines and small stanzas she offered the second great innovative reinterpretation of life during the nineteenth century in America.

Emily Dickinson exerted no influence during her lifetime because, like Taylor's, her poems were unpublished, and little influence later, because imitating her was not easy. But Whitman's influence spread incalculably. In our own century only T. S. Eliot has had an effect in any way comparable to it. Whitman affected even poets who did not read him. Abroad two poets who were to lead the way for later verse, Yeats and Hopkins, found him electrifying. Not that he was emulated directly. Even in the United States few poets adopted free verse in the nineteenth century; they kept mostly to well-worn meters, following the more traveled road, but with, for the first time, a sense that an alternative to traditional prosody was open to them. At the end of the century Stephen Crane adopted free verse, not very satisfactorily; after 1910 Sandburg, Masters, Pound, Williams, and Jeffers did the same. After 1945 there was probably more free than metrical verse in the new poetry.

Whitman's attitude toward form continued to find disciples. 'Who troubles himself about his ornaments or fluency is lost,' he said in his 1855 Preface, and in 'A Backward Glance o'er Travel'd Roads,' he said, 'I round and finish little, if anything: and could not, consistently with my scheme. . . .' Melville kept to meters, but handled them with studied clumsiness, evidently convinced that a tortured idiom, an ill-tuned instrument, might better suit the mind in its processive unfolding of itself and its world than would more decorous methods. For the pivotal relationship between form and content had been irrevocably disturbed, and the result was to be, in our time, Robert Creeley's axiom, 'Form is never more than an extension of content,' and Lowell's remark, 'Imperfection is the language of art.'

Yet along with the urge to imitate Whitman's roughness went an opposite impulse, to improve upon him. It was easy though misguided to see him as Neanderthal. Ezra Pound felt initially a contempt for him, but at last came to acknowledge his value as ancestor:

> I come to you as a grown child
> Who has had a pig-headed father. . .
> It was you that broke the new wood,
> Now is a time for carving.

The prospect of achieving an innovative verse that would be subtler than Whitman's opened before the gifted poets who were born in the United States in the seventies and eighties of the last century. The most important of these were Robert Frost, born in 1874, Wallace Stevens, born in 1879, and William Carlos Williams, Ezra Pound, and T. S. Eliot, born respectively in 1883, 1885, and 1888. All came to maturity after 1910 and they held the stage until after the Second World War.

Together they might be imagined as making up a composite American twentieth-century poet to set against the image of Whitman as nineteenth-century exemplar. Frost and Stevens offer in American translation something of the contrast of Wordsworth and Keats. Frost, prompted by Robinson, and by Horace, sought to bring an urban subtlety to his rural New England characters, to assemble a manner and an authority based upon wry admissions, half tones, and ironic concessions rather than upon the forceful declarations which were almost habitual with Whitman. Sparse in expressing strong passion, Frost was free of fustian. He lived and liked living in an old and weatherbeaten world. But for Wallace Stevens the world was new: the old gods had left it, and man, on his own at last, could make of it what he chose. 'That gross universe' was at his disposal, and for the new dispensation Stevens offered a Florida to balance Frost's Vermont, something provisional rather than absolute, a profusion of sights and sounds, an opulence of feelings along with 'a drama of mental images' (in Paul Valéry's phrase). For Stevens as for Whitman, the poetic act could compound 'the imagination's Latin' with 'the gibberish of the vulgate' to discover 'new heaven, new earth.'

Stevens and Frost paid scant attention to each other; the other three poets were much more closely involved. Williams's verse derived some of its power from his disapproval of both Pound and Eliot. Roland to their Oliver, stay-at-home to their gadabout, he insisted on the necessity of writing 'in the American grain.' To him Eliot's *The Waste Land* was 'the great catastrophe' for American letters, because it interrupted the 'rediscovery of a primary impetus, the elementary principle of all art, in the local conditions.' While his long poem, *Paterson*, bore a resemblance to Pound's *Cantos*, Williams insisted that he had a different goal and method. He wished in his verse to capture the very breathing of Americans, the rhythms of speech which were different from those in England. Eliot and Pound were too myth-conscious and philosophical, as well as too international. Against what he regarded as their portentousness, Williams celebrated immediacy, 'contact' with 'those things which lie under the direct scrutiny of the senses, close to the nose.' Eventually he hit upon his famous if unworkable prescription, 'No ideas but in things.'

The precise degree of Americanism did not much occupy Pound, though he considered himself American, and certainly not Eliot, who increasingly considered himself English. But they met Williams on another ground, that they were equally concerned with speech. The diction which Eliot evolved may prove to have been his supreme accomplishment: his words had the sound of spoken English yet were extraordinarily resonant with undertones, and could express complicated ideas as well as barroom chatter. Pound's diction was based largely on a mélange of carved phrases and backroom colloquialisms, facilitating quick shifts from grand to casual and back again. The effect was, as Eliot once complained, 'quaint and archaic,' yet it was extremely versatile.

For their subject Pound and Eliot, like Williams, took the experience of their own time, not only American, however, but European or even Oriental. They saw familiar events such as the

First World War to be encrusted with myths and vestiges of past cultures. They were also unusually conscious of the past of literature and invoked other writers, whether Dante or Li Po, as precedents or foils for their own vision. The world around them was deeply dispiriting: Eliot followed Baudelaire in finding it a scene of horror; Pound saw it as wildly adrift but still salvageable. Both men aspired to make works that would somehow contain the modern sense of oneself in relation to history as well as to possible transcendence of time. Eliot's principal effort was *The Waste Land*, though his early work is preparatory to it and his later works effect a synthesis of elements that *The Waste Land* had portrayed as torn apart.

Pound's verse may seem, in relation to Eliot's, incoherent. In his poems up to and including *Hugh Selwyn Mauberley*, the objectives are somewhat diffuse. But in *The Cantos*, which he began in 1917 and continued until his death in 1972, by which time there were one hundred and twenty of them, he projected a poem of epic dimensions on a new principle, different from that of Eliot. For Eliot the modern scene was one of broken images which must be mended: otherwise no life was possible. He tried to reassemble them into a Christian framework somewhat updated by an infusion of Buddhism and vegetarian myths. But for Pound, after some initial hesitancy, it began to seem that the fragmentation of the modern world was precisely what gave it character. The poet might exploit that fragmentariness by a collage of disparate materials which could be allowed to check and balance each other. To do so he would have to remain out of sight, so that the material might seem to gather into patterns without outside control by properties inherent within it. From these reflections came the method which in later life Pound called 'spots and dots,' meaning that a miscellany of facts and images, set whirling in the mind, would gradually coalesce into, or otherwise bring to being, what Wordsworth called 'spots of time,' or what Pound described as 'magic moments,' of total insight. (Williams was later to formulate a comparable theory of 'radiant gists' also arising out of variegated sensations.) After his first thirty *Cantos* Pound, increasingly fanatical in political and economic formulation, lost the original purity of his design, and instead of letting the materials find their own level, he began to push them about with his didactic thumb. From seeming dispassionateness, the poem became overt special pleading. But the force of his innovation in structure remained a model almost in spite of him.

At first the influence of Eliot was by far the stronger. The gloom of *The Waste Land* could be recognized in every language, and for years the latest poem in Urdu or Swahili or Japanese was more likely to resemble that poem than to resemble previous poems written in those languages. But if young poets began by imitating Eliot, their next task was not to imitate him, to avoid his cadences and to see life without his spectacles. Poets like Hart Crane labored splendidly to free themselves. As for Pound, his influence was at first more personal than poetic. A generous man outside of politics, he aided a great many other writers to find themselves and then to find publishers. Only gradually did his influence, and that of Williams, prove to be more helpful guides for the young than that of Eliot.

In view of Eliot's decision to be naturalized a British subject and to be received in the Anglican Church, his status as American poet may seem jeopardized. Still, some claim to him may be made by the land where he was born and spent his first twenty-four years, especially since his later poetry draws heavily upon the Mississippi River and the Dry Salvages off Cape Ann just as his early poetry is often set in Boston. (W. H. Auden, though he became an American citizen as Eliot a British one, seems English to the bone.) More largely, Eliot's break with traditional forms was a much more conspicuous feature of American than of English poets of the time, and the same could be said of his attempt at radical criticism and large-scale synthesis.

These five poets, and several others, lesser perhaps but of exceptional ability, such as Robinson Jeffers, Marianne Moore, John Crowe Ransom, E. E. Cummings, and Hart Crane, were dominant into the fifties and sixties. Stevens died in 1953, Frost and Williams ten years later, Eliot in 1965, and Pound in 1972. New reputations were slow to form in their shadow. Some poets in later generations died before their seniors, several of them by their own hand. It seemed for a time that the great eminences of twentieth-century poetry were to be followed by low-lying plains. But as the century progressed, it became clear that younger poets had found their own recourse.

This began with a suspicion or even distaste for eminences. The immense conceptions of their predecessors seized large truths at the expense of small ones. The presuppositions which had been common about art, about poetry itself, now appeared to be dubiously élitist. The institution of literature was itself called into question. Black poets contended against artifact poems as though they were irremediably associated with white poets, but most white poets, disobligingly, now came to evince a similar bias. There was a sense that the earlier poets of the century had aimed to become modern classics, and in so doing had lost touch with the immediate and the unkempt, with the authentic and the imperfect, with the contemporary pungency.

The labels which many recent poets have adopted, such as Black Mountain, projectivist, New York, beat, are not likely to survive. Two directions have, however, become conspicuous in much recent poetry. One takes its point of departure from a late change in Eliot's conception of verse. Originally he insisted upon its impersonality, and found the test of a successful work to be the author's skill in finding an objective correlative for feelings. In later life, however, he acknowledged with needless embarrassment and humility that *The Waste Land* was for him only a 'personal and wholly insignificant grouse against life.' It was no longer impersonal, then. In his last work, *Four Quartets*, he wished to be understood as speaking in his own voice. Ezra Pound's *Cantos* went through a similar development, the earlier ones held away from the poet, the later ones sporadically autobiographical: 'From the wreckage of Europe ego scriptor.' The possibility of a more explicit autobiographical poetry, verging sometimes on confession, has attracted many recent poets. Robert Lowell's *Life Studies* in 1959, sacrificing many of the elaborations of his early verse for the sake of candor, marked a turn. But a similar development occurred in Berryman, Merwin, and others. If Allen Ginsberg was attempting to outconfess confession, in the service of new forms of ecstatic realization, these other poets had also their motives beyond autobiography. Sylvia Plath gathers the world into her account of private incidents and feelings. If Eliot and

Pound were covertly autobiographical when they pretended not to be, their more autobiographical descendants were covertly archetypal, as if the universe were confessing through them.

Another and almost opposite emphasis in much contemporary verse might be seen as a development from Pound and Williams, though averse to acknowledge the derivation. These poets mostly shun personality as egoistic, and seem concerned to extend the boundaries of verse by incorporating a surrealist strangeness into the familiar. Pound had spoken of a 'consciousness disjunct,' but Pound was not greatly interested in the unconscious or in the disjunctiveness between it and the conscious mind. For some poets this unconscious is rather the archaic survivals into the present: Olson justifies considering the geological remains that form Gloucester, as Snyder sees the temper of Oxford and Cambridge in terms of the strata that underlie them. Other poets, such as Denise Levertov, seek out the 'authentic' in the casual, or like Robert Duncan, the magical in the natural, and move toward a secular mysticism. Poets such as Robert Bly and John Ashbery find a certain logic, or at least a concord of discords, in disconnected or uncanny images. And of course there are excellent poets who successfully resist even these general classifications.

. . .

This volume begins with Anne Bradstreet, who died in 1672, and ends with Imamu Amiri Baraka (LeRoi Jones), born in 1934. In accommodating a group of new poets not included in the excellent compilation of my predecessor and friend, F. O. Matthiessen, I have reconsidered the old poets as well. A few ballads and folk songs, and one hymn, are also included. Most of the poets are represented with some amplitude so as to give a sense of their range and variety. A number of the choices, and of the exclusions, may be controversial. I have attempted to select poems on the basis of intrinsic merit rather than the tendencies they represent. Still, taken, as a whole, the book gives a broad indication of the principal directions of American poetry, and of its accomplishment.

CONTENTS

CONTENTS

CONTENTS

CONTENTS

CONTENTS

CONTENTS

CONTENTS

CONTENTS

CONTENTS

CONTENTS

CONTENTS

CONTENTS

CONTENTS

1

CONTENTS

lii

CONTENTS

CONTENTS

IMAMU AMIRI BARAKA (LEROI JONES), b. 1934

With a few exceptions, the poems of each poet are arranged
in the order of their first appearance in volume form.

The New Oxford Book
of American Verse

ANNE BRADSTREET

? 1612–1672

The Prologue

1

To sing of Wars, of Captaines, and of Kings,
Of Cities founded, Common-wealths begun,
For my mean Pen, are too superiour things,
And how they all, or each, their dates have run:
Let Poets, and Historians set these forth,
My obscure Verse, shal not so dim their worth.

2

But when my wondring eyes, and envious heart,
Great *Bartas* sugar'd lines doe but read o're;
Foole, *I* doe grudge, the Muses did not part
'Twixt him and me, that over-fluent store;
A *Bartas* can, doe what a *Bartas* wil,
But simple I, according to my skill.

3

From School-boyes tongue, no Rhethorick we expect,
Nor yet a sweet Confort, from broken strings,
Nor perfect beauty, where's a maine defect,
My foolish, broken, blemish'd Muse so sings;
And this to mend, alas, no Art is able,
'Cause Nature made it so irreparable.

4

Nor can I, like that fluent sweet tongu'd *Greek*
Who lisp'd at first, speake afterwards more plaine
By Art, he gladly found what he did seeke,
A full requitall of his striving paine:
Art can doe much, but this maxime's most sure,
A weake or wounded braine admits no cure.

5

I am obnoxious to each carping tongue,
Who sayes, my hand a needle better fits,
A Poets Pen, all scorne, I should thus wrong;
For such despight they cast on female wits:
If what I doe prove well, it wo'nt advance,
They'l say its stolne, or else, it was by chance.

6

But sure the antick *Greeks* were far more milde,
Else of our Sex, why feigned they those nine,
And poesy made, *Calliope's* owne childe,
So 'mongst the rest, they plac'd the Arts divine:
But this weake knot they will full soone untye,
The *Greeks* did nought, but play the foole and lye.

7

Let *Greeks* be *Greeks*, and Women what they are,
Men have precedency, and still excell,
It is but vaine, unjustly to wage war,
Men can doe best, and Women know it well;
Preheminence in each, and all is yours,
Yet grant some small acknowledgement of ours.

8

And oh, ye high flown quils, that soare the skies,
And ever with your prey, still catch your praise,
If e're you daigne these lowly lines, your eyes
Give wholsome Parsley wreath, I aske no Bayes:
This meane and unrefined stuffe of mine,
Will make your glistering gold but more to shine.

The Flesh and the Spirit

In secret place where once I stood
Close by the Banks of *Lacrim* flood,
I heard two sisters reason on
Things that are past, and things to come.
One Flesh was call'd, who had her eye
On worldly wealth and vanity;
The other Spirit, who did rear
Her thoughts unto a higher sphere:
Sister, quoth Flesh, what liv'st thou on —
Nothing but Meditation?
Doth Contemplation feed thee so
Regardlessly to let earth goe?
Can Speculation satisfy
Notion without Reality?
Dost dream of things beyond the Moon
And dost thou hope to dwell there soon?

2

Hast treasures there laid up in store
That all in th' world thou count'st but poor?
Art fancy sick, or turn'd a Sot
To catch at shadowes which are not?
Come, come, Ile shew unto thy sence
Industry hath its recompence.
What canst desire, but thou maist see
True substance in variety?
Dost honour like? Acquire the same,
As some to their immortal fame:
And trophyes to thy name erect
Which wearing time shall ne're deject.
For riches dost thou long full sore?
Behold enough of precious store.
Earth hath more silver, pearls and gold,
Than eyes can see, or hands can hold.
Affect'st thou pleasure? Take thy fill,
Earth hath enough of what you will.
Then let not goe what thou maist find
For things unknown, only in mind.

Spirit:
Be still thou unregenerate part,
Disturb no more my setled heart,
For I have vow'd (and so will doe)
Thee as a foe still to pursue.
And combate with thee will and must
Untill I see thee laid in th' dust.
Sisters we are, yea, twins we be,
Yet deadly feud 'twixt thee and me;
For from one father are we not,
Thou by old Adam wast begot,
But my arise is from above,
Whence my dear Father I do love.
Thou speak'st me fair, but hat'st me sore,
Thy flatt'ring shews Ile trust no more.
How oft thy slave hast thou me made
When I believ'd what thou hast said,
And never had more cause of woe
Than when I did what thou bad'st doe.
Ile stop mine ears at these thy charms,
And count them for my deadly harms.
Thy sinfull pleasures I doe hate,

3

Thy riches are to me no bait,
Thine honours doe nor will I love,
For my ambition lyes above.
My greatest honour it shall be
When I am victor over thee,
And triumph shall, with laurel head,
When thou my Captive shalt be led.
How I do live thou need'st not scoff,
For I have meat thou know'st not of:
The hidden Manna I doe eat,
The word of life it is my meat.
My thoughts do yield me more content
Than can thy hours in pleasure spent
Nor are they shadows which I catch,
Nor fancies vain at which I snatch,
But reach at things that are so high,
Beyond thy dull Capacity.
Eternal substance I do see,
With which inriched I would be;
Mine Eye doth pierce the heavens, and see
What is Invisible to thee.
My garments are not silk nor gold,
Nor such like trash which Earth doth hold,
But Royal Robes I shall have on,
More glorious than the glistring Sun;
My Crown not Diamonds, Pearls, and Gold,
But such as Angels heads infold.
The City where I hope to dwell,
There's none on Earth can parallel:
The stately Walls both high and strong,
Are made of pretious Jasper stone;
The Gates of Pearl, both rich and clear,
And Angels are for Porters there;
The Streets thereof transparent gold,
Such as no Eye did e're behold;
A Chrystal River there doth run,
Which doth proceed from the Lamb's Throne.
Of Life there are the waters sure,
Which shall remain for ever pure;
Nor Sun, nor Moon, they have no need,
For glory doth from God proceed;
No Candle there, nor yet Torch light,
For there shall be no darksome night.

From sickness and infirmity
For evermore they shall be free,
Nor withering age shall e're come there,
But beauty shall be bright and clear.
This City pure is not for thee,
For things unclean there shall not be.
If I of Heaven may have my fill,
Take thou the world, and all that will.

The Author to Her Book

Thou ill-formed offspring of my feeble brain,
Who after birth didst by my side remain,
Till snatched from thence by friends, less wise than true,
Who thee abroad, expos'd to publick view,
Made thee in raggs, halting to th' press to trudg,
Where errors were not lessened (all may judge).
At thy return my blushing was not small,
My rambling brat (in print) should mother call,
I cast thee by as one unfit for light,
Thy Visage was so irksome in my sight;
Yet being mine own, at length affection would
Thy blemishes amend, if so I could:
I wash'd thy face, but more defects I saw,
And rubbing off a spot still made a flaw.
I stretched thy joynts to make thee even feet,
Yet still thou run'st more hobling than is meet;
In better dress to trim thee was my mind,
But nought save homespun Cloth i' th' house I find[.]
In this array 'mongst Vulgars may'st thou roam[.]
In Criticks hands, beware thou dost not come;
And take thy way where yet thou art not known;
If for thy Father asked, say thou hadst none;
And for thy Mother, she alas is poor,
Which caus'd her thus to send thee out of door.

Before the Birth of One of Her Children

All things within this fading world hath end,
Adversity doth still our joys attend;
No ties so strong, no friends so dear and sweet,

But with death's parting blow is sure to meet.
The sentence past is most irrevocable,
A common thing, yet oh inevitable.
How soon, my Dear, death may my steps attend,
How soon't may be thy Lot to lose thy friend,
We are both ignorant, yet love bids me
These farewell lines to recommend to thee,
That when that knot's untied that made us one,
I may seem thine, who in effect am none.
And if I see not half my dayes that's due,
What nature would, God grant to yours and you;
The many faults that well you know I have
Let be interr'd in my oblivious grave;
If any worth or virtue were in me,
Let that live freshly in thy memory
And when thou feel'st no grief, as I no harms,
Yet love thy dead, who long lay in thine arms.
And when thy loss shall be repaid with gains
Look to my little babes[,] my dear remains.
And if thou love thyself, or loved'st me[,]
These o protect from step Dames injury.
And if chance to thine eyes shall bring this verse,
With some sad sighs honour my absent Herse;
And kiss this paper for thy loves dear sake,
Who with salt tears this last Farewel did take.

To My Dear and Loving Husband

If ever two were one, then surely we.
If ever man were lov'd by wife, then thee;
If ever wife was happy in a man,
Compare with me ye women if you can.
I prize thy love more than whole Mines of gold,
Or all the riches that the East doth hold.
My love is such that Rivers cannot quench,
Nor ought but love from thee, give recompense.
Thy love is such I can no way repay,
The heavens reward thee manifold, I pray.
Then while we live, in love lets so persever,
That when we live no more, we may live ever.

Some Verses upon the Burning
of Our House July 10th, 1666

In silent night when rest I took
For sorrow near I did not look
I waken'd was with thundring nois
And Piteous shrieks of dreadfull voice.
That fearfull sound of fire and fire,
Let no man know is my Desire.

I, starting up, the light did spye,
And to my God my heart did cry
To strengthen me in my Distresse
And not to leave me succorlesse.
Then coming out beheld a space,
The flame consume my dwelling place.

And when I could no longer look,
I blest his Name that gave and took,
That layd my goods now in the dust:
Yea so it was, and so 'twas just.
It was his own: it was not mine;
Far be it that I should repine;

He might of All justly bereft,
But yet sufficient for us left.
When by the Ruines oft I past,
My sorrowing eyes aside did cast,
And here and there the places spye
Where oft I sate and long did lye.

Here stood that Trunk, and there that chest;
There lay that store I counted best:
My pleasant things in ashes lye,
And them behold no more shall I.
Under thy roof no guest shall sitt,
Nor at thy Table eat a bitt.

No pleasant tale shall 'ere be told,
Nor things recounted done of old.
No candle 'ere shall shine in Thee,
Nor bridegroom's voice 'ere heard shall bee.
In silence ever shall thou lye;
Adieu, Adieu; All's vanity.

7

Then streight I 'gin my heart to chide,
And did thy wealth on earth abide?
Didst fix thy hope on mouldring dust,
The arm of flesh didst make thy trust?
Raise up thy thoughts above the skye
That dunghill mists away may fly.

Thou hast an house on high erect,
Fram'd by that mighty Architect,
With glory richly furnished,
Stands permanent though this be fled.
It's purchased and paid for too
By Him who hath enough to doe.

A prise so vast as is unknown,
Yet by his Gift, is made thine own.
There's wealth enough, I need no more;
Farewell my Pelf, farewell my Store.
The world no longer let me Love,
My hope and Treasure lyes Above.

PHILIP PAIN
c. 1666

Meditation 8

Scarce do I pass a day, but that I hear
Some one or other's dead; and to my ear
Me thinks it is no news: but Oh! did I
Think deeply on it, what it is to dye,
  My Pulses all would beat, I should not be
  Drown'd in this Deluge of Security.

Meditation 9

Man's life is like a Rose, that in the Spring
Begins to blossome, fragrant smells to bring:
Within a day or two, behold Death's sent,
A publick Messenger of discontent.
  Lord grant, that when my Rose begins to fade,
  I may behold an Everlasting shade.

8

Meditation 10

Alas, what is the *World?* a Sea of Glass.
Alas, what's *Earth?* it's but an Hower-glass.
The Sea dissolves; the Glass is quickly run:
Behold, with speed man's Life is quickly done.
   Let me so swim in this Sea, that I may
   With thee live happy in another day.

Meditation 29

How mutable is every thing that here
Below we do enjoy? with how much fear
And trouble are those gilded Vanities
Attended, that so captivate our eyes?
   Oh, who would trust this World, or prize what's in it,
   That gives, and takes, and changes in a minute?

Meditation 62

How is it that I am so careless here,
And never mind how I my Course do steer
For an Eternal Port? and never think
That at the last my leaky Ship will sink?
   Lord, guard me from those Pirats that would catch
   My Soul, do thou (Lord) be there over-match.

EDWARD TAYLOR
? 1644–1729

8. *Meditation. Joh. 6.51. I am the Living Bread*

I kening through Astronomy Divine
   The Worlds bright Battlement, wherein I spy
A Golden Path my Pensill cannot line,
   From that bright Throne unto my Threshold ly.
   And while my puzzled thoughts about it pore
   I finde the Bread of Life in't at my doore.

When that this Bird of Paradise put in
  This Wicker Cage (my Corps) to tweedle praise
Had peckt the Fruite forbad: and so did fling
  Away its Food; and lost its golden dayes;
  It fell into Celestiall Famine sore:
  And never could attain a morsell more.

Alas! alas! Poore Bird, what wilt thou doe?
  The Creatures field no food for Souls e're gave.
And if thou knock at Angells dores they show
  An Empty Barrell: they no soul bread have.
  Alas! Poore Bird, the Worlds White Loafe is done.
  And cannot yield thee here the smallest Crumb.

In this sad state, Gods Tender Bowells run
  Out streams of Grace: And he to end all strife
The Purest Wheate in Heaven, his deare-dear Son
  Grinds, and kneads up into this Bread of Life.
  Which Bread of Life from Heaven down came and stands
  Disht on thy Table up by Angells Hands.

Did God mould up this Bread in Heaven, and bake,
  Which from his Table came, and to thine goeth?
Doth he bespeake thee thus, This Soule Bread take.
  Come Eate thy fill of this thy Gods White Loafe?
  Its Food too fine for Angells, yet come, take
  And Eate thy fill. Its Heavens Sugar Cake.

What Grace is this knead in this Loafe? This thing
  Souls are but petty things it to admire.
Yee Angells, help: This fill would to the brim
  Heav'ns whelm'd-down Chrystall meele Bowle, yea and higher.
  This Bread of Life dropt in thy mouth, doth Cry.
  Eate, Eate me, Soul, and thou shalt never dy.

38. *Meditation.* 1 *Joh.* 2.1. *An Advocate with the Father*

  Oh! What a thing is Man? Lord, Who am I?
    That thou shouldst give him Law (Oh! golden Line)
  To regulate his Thoughts, Words, Life thereby.
    And judge him Wilt thereby too in thy time.
    A Court of Justice thou in heaven holdst
    To try his Case while he's here housd on mould.

How do thy Angells lay before thine eye
  My Deeds both White, and Black I dayly doe?
How doth thy Court thou Pannellst there them try?
  But flesh complains. What right for this? let's know.
  For right, or wrong I can't appeare unto't.
  And shall a sentence Pass on such a suite?

Soft; blemish not this golden Bench, or place.
  Here is no Bribe, nor Colourings to hide
Nor Pettifogger to befog the Case
  But Justice hath her Glory here well tri'de.
  Her spotless Law all spotted Cases tends.
  Without Respect or Disrespect them ends.

God's Judge himselfe: and Christ Atturny is,
  The Holy Ghost Regesterer is founde.
Angells the sergeants are, all Creatures kiss
  The booke, and doe as Evidences abounde.
  All Cases pass according to pure Law
  And in the sentence is no Fret, nor flaw.

What saist, my soule? Here all thy Deeds are tri'de.
  Is Christ thy Advocate to pleade thy Cause?
Art thou his Client? Such shall never slide.
  He never lost his Case: he pleads such Laws
  As Carry do the same, nor doth refuse
  The Vilest sinners Case that doth him Choose.

This is his Honour, not Dishonour: nay
  No Habeas-Corpus gainst his Clients came
For all their Fines his Purse doth make down pay.
  He Non-Suites Satan's Suite or Casts the Same.
  He'l plead thy Case, and not accept a Fee.
  He'l plead Sub Forma Pauperis for thee.

My Case is bad. Lord, be my Advocate.
  My sin is red: I'me under Gods Arrest.
Thou hast the Hint of Pleading; plead my State.
  Although it's bad thy Plea will make it best.
  If thou wilt plead my Case before the King:
  I'le Waggon Loads of Love, and Glory bring.

112. *Meditation. 2 Cor. 5.14. If one died for all then are all Dead*

Oh! Good, Good, Good, my Lord. What more Love yet.
   Thou dy for mee! What, am I dead in thee?
What did Deaths arrow shot at me thee hit?
     Didst slip between that flying shaft and mee?
     Didst make thyselfe Deaths marke shot at for mee?
     So that her Shaft shall fly no far than thee?

Di'dst dy for mee indeed, and in thy Death
   Take in thy Dying thus my death the Cause?
And lay I dying in thy Dying breath,
     According to Graces Redemption Laws?
     If one did dy for all, it needs must bee
     That all did dy in one, and from death free.

Infinities fierce firy arrow red
   Shot from the splendid Bow of Justice bright
Did smite thee down, for thine. Thou art their head.
     They di'de in thee. Their death did on thee light.
     They di'de their Death in thee, thy Death is theirs.
     Hence thine is mine, thy death my trespass clears.

How sweet is this: my Death lies buried
   Within thy Grave, my Lord, deep under ground,
It is unskin'd, as Carrion rotten Dead.
     For Grace's hand gave Death its deadly wound.
     Deaths no such terrour on th'Saints blesst Coast.
     Its but a harmless Shade: No walking Ghost.

The Painter lies: the Bellfrey Pillars weare
   A false Effigies now of Death, alas!
With empty Eyeholes, Butter teeth, bones bare
     And spraggling arms, having an Hour Glass
     In one grim paw. Th'other a Spade doth hold
     To shew deaths frightfull region under mould.

Whereas its Sting is gone: its life is lost.
   Though unto Christless ones it is most Grim
Its but a Shade to Saints whose path it Crosst,
     Or Shell or Washen face, in which she sings
     Their Bodies in her lap a Lollaboy
     And sends their Souls to sing their Masters joy.

Lord let me finde Sin, Curse and Death that doe
  Belong to me ly slain too in thy Grave.
And let thy law my clearing hence bestow
  And from these things let me acquittance have.
The Law suffic'de: and I discharg'd, Hence sing
Thy praise I will over Deaths Death, and Sin.

The Preface [to God's Determinations]

  Infinity, when all things it beheld
In Nothing, and of Nothing all did build,
Upon what Base was fixt the Lath, wherein
He turn'd this Globe, and riggalld it so trim?
Who blew the Bellows of his Furnace Vast?
Or held the Mould wherein the world was Cast?
Who laid its Corner Stone? Or whose Command?
Where stand the Pillars upon which it stands?
Who Lac'de and Fillitted the earth so fine,
With Rivers like green Ribbons Smaragdine?
Who made the Sea's its Selvedge, and it locks
Like a Quilt Ball within a Silver Box?
Who Spread its Canopy? Or Curtains Spun?
Who in this Bowling Alley bowld the Sun?
Who made it always when it rises set
To go at once both down, and up to get?
Who th'Curtain rods made for this Tapistry?
Who hung the twinckling Lanthorns in the Sky?
Who? who did this? or who is he? Why, know
Its Onely Might Almighty this did doe.
His hand hath made this noble worke which Stands
His Glorious Handywork not made by hands.
Who spake all things from nothing; and with ease
Can speake all things to nothing, if he please.
Whose Little finger at his pleasure Can
Out mete ten thousand worlds with halfe a Span:
Whose Might Almighty can by half a looks
Root up the rocks and rock the hills by th'roots.
Can take this mighty World up in his hande,
And shake it like a Squitchen or a Wand.
Whose single Frown will make the Heavens shake
Like as an aspen leafe the Winde makes quake.
Oh! what a might is this Whose single frown

Doth shake the world as it would shake it down?
Which All from Nothing fet, from Nothing, All:
Hath All on Nothing set, lets Nothing fall.
Gave All to nothing Man indeed, whereby
Through nothing man all might him Glorify.
In Nothing then imbosst the brightest Gem
More pretious than all pretiousness in them.
But Nothing man did throw down all by Sin:
And darkened that lightsom Gem in him.
That now his Brightest Diamond is grown
Darker by far than any Coalpit Stone.

Upon a Spider Catching a Fly

Thou sorrow, venom Elfe.
  Is this thy play,
To spin a web out of thyselfe
  To Catch a Fly?
    For Why?

I saw a pettish wasp
  Fall foule therein.
Whom yet thy Whorle pins did not clasp
  Lest he should fling
    His sting.

But as affraid, remote
  Didst stand hereat
And with thy little fingers stroke
  And gently tap
    His back.

Thus gently him didst treate
  Lest he should pet,
And in a froppish, waspish heate
  Should greatly fret
    Thy net.

Whereas the silly Fly,
  Caught by its leg
Thou by the throate tookst hastily
  And 'hinde the head
    Bite Dead.

This goes to pot, that not
   Nature doth call.
Strive not above what strength hath got
   Lest in the brawle
     Thou fall.

This Frey seems thus to us.
   Hells Spider gets
His intrails spun to whip Cords thus
   And wove to nets
     And sets.

To tangle Adams race
   In's stratigems
To their Destructions, spoil'd, made base
   By venom things
     Damn'd Sins.

But mighty, Gracious Lord
   Communicate
Thy Grace to breake the Cord, afford
   Us Glorys Gate
     And State.

We'l Nightingaile sing like
   When pearcht on high
In Glories Cage, thy glory, bright,
   And thankfully,
     For joy.

Huswifery

Make me, O Lord, thy Spining Wheele compleate.
   Thy Holy Worde my Distaff make for mee.
Make mine Affections thy Swift Flyers neate
   And make my Soule thy holy Spoole to bee.
   My Conversation make to be thy Reele
   And reele the yarn thereon spun of thy Wheele.

Make me thy Loome then, knit therein this Twine:
  And make thy Holy Spirit, Lord, winde quills:
Then weave the Web thyselfe. The yarn is fine.
  Thine Ordinances make my Fulling Mills.
  Then dy the same in Heavenly Colours Choice,
  All pinkt with Varnisht Flowers of Paradise.

Then cloath therewith mine Understanding, Will,
  Affections, Judgment, Conscience, Memory
My Words, and Actions, that their shine may fill
  My wayes with glory and thee glorify.
  Then mine apparell shall display before yee
  That I am Cloathd in Holy robes for glory.

Let by rain

Ye Flippering Soule,
  Why dost between the Nippers dwell?
Not stay, nor goe. Not yea, nor yet Controle.
  Doth this doe well?
    Rise journy'ng when the skies fall weeping Showers.
    Not o're nor under th'Clouds and Cloudy Powers.

Not yea, nor noe:
  On tiptoes thus? Why sit on thorns?
Resolve the matter: Stay thyselfe or goe.
  Be n't both wayes born.
    Wager thyselfe against thy surplice, see,
    And win thy Coate: or let thy Coate Win thee.

Is this th'Effect,
  To leaven thus my Spirits all?
To make my heart a Crabtree Cask direct?
  A Verjuicte Hall?
    As Bottle Ale, whose Spirits prisond nurst
    When jog'd, the bung with Violence doth burst?

Shall I be made
  A sparkling Wildfire Shop
Where my dull Spirits at the Fireball trade
  Do frisk and hop?
    And while the Hammer doth the Anvill pay,
    The fireball matter sparkles ery way.

One sorry fret,
  An anvill Sparke, rose higher
And in thy Temple falling almost set
  The house on fire.
    Such fireballs droping in the Temple Flame
    Burns up the building: Lord forbid the same.

Upon a Wasp Child with Cold

The Bare that breaths the Northern blast
Did numb, Torpedo like, a Wasp
Whose stiffend limbs encrampt, lay bathing
In Sol's warm breath and shine as saving,
Which with her hands she chafes and stands
Rubbing her Legs, Shanks, Thighs, and hands.
Her petty toes, and fingers ends
Nipt with this breath, she out extends
Unto the Sun, in greate desire
To warm her digits at that fire.
Doth hold her Temples in this state
Where pulse doth beate, and head doth ake.
Doth turn, and stretch her body small,
Doth Comb her velvet Capitall.
As if her little brain pan were
A Volume of Choice precepts cleare.
As if her sattin jacket hot
Contained Apothecaries Shop
Of Natures recepts, that prevails
To remedy all her sad ailes,
As if her velvet helmet high
Did turret rationality.
She fans her wing up to the Winde
As if her Pettycoate were lin'de,
With reasons fleece, and hoises sails
And hu'ming flies in thankfull gails
Unto her dun Curld palace Hall
Her warm thanks offering for all.
  Lord cleare my misted sight that I
May hence view thy Divinity.
Some sparkes whereof thou up dost hasp
Within this little downy Wasp
In whose small Corporation wee

A school and a schoolmaster see
Where we may learn, and easily finde
A nimble Spirit bravely minde
Her worke in e'ry limb: and lace
It up neate with a vitall grace,
Acting each part though ne'er so small
Here of this Fustian animall.
Till I enravisht Climb into
The Godhead on this Lather doe.
Where all my pipes inspir'de upraise
An Heavenly musick furrd with praise.

PHILIP FRENEAU
1752–1832

George the Third's Soliloquy

What mean these dreams, and hideous forms that rise
Night after night, tormenting to my eyes —
No real foes these horrid shapes can be,
But thrice as much they vex and torture me.
　　How cursed is he — how doubly cursed am I —
Who lives in pain, and yet who dares not die;
To him no joy this world of Nature brings,
In vain the wild rose blooms, the daisy springs.
Is this a prelude to some new disgrace,
Some baleful omen to my name and race! —
It may be so — ere mighty Caesar died
Presaging Nature felt his doom, and sighed;
A bellowing voice through midnight groves was heard,
And threatening ghosts at dusk of eve appeared —
Ere Brutus fell, to adverse fates a prey,
His evil genius met him on the way,
And so may mine! — but who would yield so soon
A prize, some luckier hour may make my own?
Shame seize my crown ere such a deed be mine —
No — to the last my squadrons shall combine,
And slay my foes, while foes remain to slay,
Or *heaven* shall grant me one successful day.
　　Is there a robber close in Newgate hemmed,
Is there a cut-throat, fettered and condemned?
Haste, loyal slaves, to George's standard come,

Attend his lectures when you hear the drum;
Your chains I break — for better days prepare,
Come out, my friends, from prison and from care,
Far to the west I plan your desperate sway,
There 'tis no sin to ravage, burn, and slay.
There, without fear, your bloody aims pursue,
And shew mankind what English thieves can do.
   That day, when first I mounted to the throne,
I swore to let all foreign foes alone.
Through love of peace to terms did I advance,
And made, they say, a shameful league with France.
But different scenes rise horrid to my view,
I charged my hosts to plunder and subdue —
At first, indeed, I thought short wars to wage
And sent some jail-birds to be led by *Gage*,
For 'twas but right, that those we marked for slaves
Should be reduced by cowards, fools, and knaves;
Awhile directed by his feeble hand,
Whose *troops* were kicked and pelted through the land,
Or starved in Boston, cursed the unlucky hour
They left their dungeons for that fatal shore.
   France aids them now, a desperate game I play,
And hostile Spain will do the same, they say;
My armies vanquished, and my heroes fled,
My people murmuring, and my commerce dead,
My shattered navy pelted, bruised, and clubbed,
By Dutchmen bullied, and by Frenchmen drubbed,
My name abhorred, my nation in disgrace,
How should I act in such a mournful case!
My hopes and joys are vanished with my coin,
My ruined army, and my lost Burgoyne!
What shall I do — confess my labours vain,
Or whet my tusks, and to the charge again!
But where's my force — my choicest troops are fled,
Some thousands crippled, and a myriad dead —
If I were owned the boldest of mankind,
And hell with all her flames inspired my mind,
Could I at once with Spain and France contend,
And fight the *rebels* on the world's green end? —
The pangs of *parting* I can ne'er endure,
Yet *part* we must, and part to meet no more!
Oh! blast this *Congress*, blast each upstart STATE,
On whose commands ten thousand captains wait;

From various climes that dire *Assembly* came,
True to their trust, as hostile to my fame,
'Tis these, ah these, have ruined half my sway,
Disgraced my arms, and led my slaves astray —
Cursed be the day, when first I saw the sun,
Cursed be the hour, when I these wars begun:
The fiends of darkness then possessed my mind,
And powers unfriendly to the human kind.
To wasting grief, and sullen rage a prey,
To *Scotland's* utmost verge I'll take my way,
There with eternal storms due concert keep
And while the billows rage, as fiercely weep —
Ye highland lads, my rugged fate bemoan,
Assist me with one sympathizing groan,
For late I find the nations are my foes,
I must submit, and that with bloody nose,
Or, like our James, fly basely from the state,
Or share, what still is worse — old *Charles's* fate.

The Wild Honey Suckle

Fair flower, that dost so comely grow,
Hid in this silent, dull retreat,
Untouched thy honied blossoms blow,
Unseen thy little branches greet:
   No roving foot shall crush thee here,
   No busy hand provoke a tear.

By Nature's self in white arrayed,
She bade thee shun the vulgar eye,
And planted here the guardian shade,
And sent soft waters murmuring by;
   Thus quietly thy summer goes,
   Thy days declining to repose.

Smit with those charms, that must decay,
I grieve to see your future doom;
They died — nor were those flowers more gay,
The flowers that did in Eden bloom;
   Unpitying frosts, and Autumn's power
   Shall leave no vestige of this flower.

From morning suns and evening dews
At first thy little being came:
If nothing once, you nothing lose,
For when you die you are the same;
 The space between, is but an hour,
 The frail duration of a flower.

To an Author

Your leaves bound up compact and fair,
In neat array at length prepare,
To pass their hour on learning's stage,
To meet the surly critic's rage;
The statesman's slight, the smatterer's sneer —
Were these, indeed, your only fear,
You might be tranquil and resigned:
What most should touch your fluttering mind;
Is that, few critics will be found
To sift your works, and deal the wound.

Thus, when one fleeting year is past
On some bye-shelf *your* book is cast —
Another comes, with *something new*,
And drives you fairly out of view:
With some to praise, *but more to blame*,
The mind returns to — whence it came;
And some alive, who *scarce could read*
Will publish satires on the dead.

Thrice happy Dryden, who could meet
Some rival bard in every street!
When all were bent on writing well
It was some credit to excel: —

Thrice happy Dryden, who could find
A *Milbourne* for his sport designed —
And *Pope*, who saw the harmless rage
Of *Dennis* bursting o'er his page
Might justly spurn the *critic's aim*,
Who only helped to swell his fame.

On these bleak climes by Fortune thrown,
Where rigid *Reason* reigns alone,
Where lovely *Fancy* has no sway,
Nor magic forms about us play —
Nor nature takes her summer hue
Tell me, what has the muse to do? —

An age employed in edging steel
Can no poetic raptures feel;
No solitude's attracting power,
No leisure of the noon day hour,
No shaded stream, no quiet grove
Can this fantastic century move;

The muse of love in no request —
Go — try your fortune with the rest,
One of the nine you should engage,
To meet the follies of the age: —

On *one*, we fear, your choice must fall —
The least engaging of them all —
Her visage stern — an angry style —
A clouded brow — malicious smile —
A mind on *murdered victims* placed —
She, only she, can please the taste!

The Indian Burying Ground

In spite of all the learned have said,
I still my old opinion keep;
The *posture*, that *we* give the dead,
Points out the soul's eternal sleep.

Not so the ancients of these lands —
The Indian, when from life released,
Again is seated with his friends,
And shares again the joyous feast.

His imaged birds, and painted bowl,
And venison, for a journey dressed.
Bespeak the nature of the soul,
ACTIVITY, that knows no rest.

His bow, for action ready bent,
And arrows, with a head of stone,
Can only mean that life is spent,
And not the old ideas gone.

Thou, stranger, that shalt come this way,
No fraud upon the dead commit —
Observe the swelling turf, and say
They do not *lie*, but here they *sit*,

Here still a lofty rock remains,
On which the curious eye may trace
(Now wasted, half, by wearing rains)
The fancies of a ruder race.

Here still an aged elm aspires,
Beneath whose far-projecting shade
(And which the shepherd still admires)
The children of the forest played!

There oft a restless Indian queen
(Pale *Shebah*, with her braided hair)
And many a barbarous form is seen
To chide the man that lingers there.

By midnight moons, o'er moistening dews,
In habit for the chase arrayed,
The hunter still the deer pursues,
The hunter and the deer, a shade!

And long shall timorous fancy see
The painted chief, and pointed spear,
And Reason's self shall bow the knee
To shadows and delusions here.

PHILLIS WHEATLEY
?1753–1784

On Being Brought from Africa to America

'Twas mercy brought me from my *Pagan* land,
Taught my benighted soul to understand
That there's a God, that there's a *Saviour* too:
Once I redemption neither sought nor knew.
Some view our sable race with scornful eye,
"Their colour is a diabolic die."
Remember, *Christians*, *Negroes*, black as *Cain*,
May be refin'd, and join th' angelic train.

JOEL BARLOW
1754–1812

The Hasty-Pudding
Canto I

Ye Alps audacious, thro' the Heavens that rise,
To cramp the day and hide me from the skies;
Ye Gallic flags, that o'er their heights unfurl'd,
Bear death to kings, and freedom to the world,
I sing not you. A softer theme I chuse,
A virgin theme, unconscious of the Muse,
But fruitful, rich, well suited to inspire
The purest frenzy of poetic fire.
　　Despise it not, ye Bards to terror steel'd,
Who hurl'd your thunders round the epic field;
Nor ye who strain your midnight throats to sing
Joys that the vineyard and the still-house bring;
Or on some distant fair your notes employ,
And speak of raptures that you ne'er enjoy.
I sing the sweets I know, the charms I feel,
My morning incense, and my evening meal,
The sweets of Hasty-Pudding. Come, dear bowl,
Glide o'er my palate, and inspire my soul.
The milk beside thee, smoking from the kine,
Its substance mingled, married in with thine,
Shall cool and temper thy superior heat,
And save the pains of blowing while I eat.

Oh! could the smooth, the emblematic song
Flow like thy genial juices o'er my tongue,
Could those mild morsels in my numbers chime,
And, as they roll in substance, roll in rhyme,
No more thy aukward unpoetic name
Should shun the Muse, or prejudice thy fame;
But rising grateful to the accustom'd ear,
All Bards should catch it, and all realms revere!
   Assist me first with pious toil to trace
Thro' wrecks of time thy lineage and thy race;
Declare what lovely squaw, in days of yore,
(Ere great Columbus sought thy native shore)
First gave thee to the world; her works of fame
Have liv'd indeed, but liv'd without a name.
Some tawny Ceres, goddess of her days,
First learn'd with stones to crack the well-dry'd maize,
Thro' the rough sieve to shake the golden show'r,
In boiling water stir the yellow flour.
The yellow flour, bestrew'd and stir'd with haste,
Swells in the flood and thickens to a paste,
Then puffs and wallops, rises to the brim,
Drinks the dry knobs that on the surface swim:
The knobs at last the busy ladle breaks,
And the whole mass its true consistence takes.
   Could but her sacred name, unknown so long,
Rise like her labors, to the sons of song,
To her, to them, I'd consecrate my lays,
And blow her pudding with the breath of praise.
If 'twas Oella, whom I sang before,
I here ascribe her one great virtue more.
Not thro' the rich Peruvian realms alone
The fame of Sol's sweet daughter should be known,
But o'er the world's wide climes should live secure,
Far as his rays extend, as long as they endure.
   Dear Hasty-Pudding, what unpromis'd joy
Expands my heart, to meet thee in Savoy!
Doom'd o'er the world thro' devious paths to roam,
Each clime my country, and each house my home,
My soul is sooth'd, my cares have found an end,
I greet my long-lost, unforgotten friend.
   For thee thro' Paris, that corrupted town,
How long in vain I wandered up and down,

Where shameless Bacchus, with his drenching hoard
Cold from his cave usurps the morning board.
London is lost in smoke and steep'd in tea;
No Yankey there can lisp the name of thee:
The uncouth word, a libel on the town,
Would call a proclamation from the crown.
For climes oblique, that fear the sun's full rays,
Chill'd in their fogs, exclude the generous maize;
A grain whose rich luxuriant growth requires
Short gentle showers, and bright etherial fires.
　But here tho' distant from our native shore,
With mutual glee we meet and laugh once more,
The same! I know thee by that yellow face,
That strong complexion of true Indian race,
Which time can never change, nor soil impair,
Nor Alpine snows, nor Turkey's morbid air;
For endless years, thro' every mild domain,
Where grows the maize, there thou art sure to reign.
　But man, more fickle, the bold licence claims,
In different realms to give thee different names.
Thee the soft nations round the warm Levant
Palanta call, the French of course *Polante*;
E'en in thy native regions, how I blush
To hear the Pennsylvanians call thee *Mush!*
On Hudson's banks, while men of Belgic spawn
Insult and eat thee by the name *suppawn*.
All spurious appellations, void of truth:
I've better known thee from my earliest youth,
Thy name is *Hasty-Pudding!* thus our sires
Were wont to greet thee fuming from their fires;
And while they argu'd in thy just defence
With logic clear, they thus explained the sense: —
"In *haste* the boiling cauldron o'er the blaze,
Receives and cooks the ready-powder'd maize;
In *haste* 'tis serv'd, and then in equal *haste*,
With cooling milk, we make the sweet repast.
No carving to be done, no knife to grate
The tender ear, and wound the stony plate;
But the smooth spoon, just fitted to the lip,
And taught with art the yielding mass to dip,
By frequent journies to the bowl well stor'd,
Performs the hasty honors of the board."

Such is thy name, significant and clear,
A name, a sound to every Yankey dear,
But most to me, whose heart and palate chaste
Preserve my pure hereditary taste.
   There are who strive to stamp with disrepute
The luscious food, because it feeds the brute;
In tropes of high-strain'd wit, while gaudy prigs
Compare thy nursling man to pamper'd pigs;
With sovereign scorn I treat the vulgar jest,
Nor fear to share thy bounties with the beast.
What though the generous cow gives me to quaff
The milk nutritious; am I then a calf?
Or can the genius of the noisy swine,
Tho' nurs'd on pudding, thence lay claim to mine?
Sure the sweet song, I fashion to thy praise,
Runs more melodious than the notes they raise.
   My song resounding in its grateful glee,
No merit claims; I praise myself in thee.
My father lov'd thee through his length of days:
For thee his fields were shaded o'er with maize;
From thee what health, what vigour he possest,
Ten sturdy freemen sprung from him attest;
Thy constellation rul'd my natal morn,
And all my bones were made of Indian corn.
Delicious grain! whatever form it take,
To roast or boil, to smother or to bake,
In every dish 'tis welcome still to me,
But most, my Hasty-Pudding, most in thee.
   Let the green Succatash with thee contend,
Let beans and corn their sweetest juices blend,
Let butter drench them in its yellow tide,
And a long slice of bacon grace their side;
Not all the plate, how fam'd soe'er it be,
Can please my palate like a bowl of thee.
   Some talk of Hoe-cake, fair Virginia's pride,
Rich Johnny-cake this mouth has often tri'd;
Both please me well, their virtues much the same;
Alike their fabric, as allied their fame,
Except in dear New-England, where the last
Receives a dash of pumpkin in the paste,
To give it sweetness and improve the taste.
But place them all before me, smoaking hot,

The big round dumplin rolling from the pot;
The pudding of the bag, whose quivering breast,
With suet lin'd leads on the Yankey feast;
The Charlotte brown, within whose crusty sides
A belly soft the pulpy apple hides;
The yellow bread, whose face like amber glows,
And all of Indian that the bake-pan knows —
You tempt me not — my fav'rite greets my eyes,
To that lov'd bowl my spoon by instinct flies.

Advice to a Raven in Russia

Black fool, why winter here? These frozen skies,
Worn by your wings and deafen'd by your cries,
Should warn you hence, where milder suns invite,
And day alternates with his mother night.
    You fear perhaps your food may fail you there —
Your human carnage, that delicious fare,
That lured you higher, following still your friend,
The great Napoleon to the world's bleak end.
You fear, because the southern climes pour'd forth
Their clustering nations to infest the north,
Bavarians, Austrians, those who drink the Po
And those who skirt the Tuscan seas below,
With all Germania, Neustria, Belgia, Gaul,
Doom'd here to wade thro slaughter to their fall,
You fear he left behind no wars, to feed
His feather'd cannibals and nurse the breed.
    Fear not, my screamer, call your greedy train,
Sweep over Europe, hurry back to Spain,
You'll find his legions there; the valiant crew
Please best their master when they toil for you.
Abundant there they spread the country o'er
And taint the breeze with every nation's gore,
Iberian, Lusian, British widely strown;
But still more wide and copious flows their own.
    Go where you will; Calabria, Malta, Greece,
Egypt and Syria still his fame increase,
Domingo's fatten'd isle and India's plains
Glow deep with purple drawn from Gallic veins.
No raven's wing can stretch the flight so far
As the torn bandrols of Napoleon's war.

Choose then your climate, fix your best abode,
He'll make you deserts and he'll bring you blood.
　　How could you fear a dearth? have not mankind,
Tho slain by millions, millions left behind?
Has not CONSCRIPTION still the power to wield
Her annual faulchion o'er the human field?
A faithful harvester! or if a man
Escape that gleaner, shall he scape the BAN?
The triple BAN, that like the hound of hell
Gripes with joles, to hold his victim well.
　　Fear nothing then, hatch fast your ravenous brood,
Teach them to cry to Buonaparte for food;
They'll be like you, of all his suppliant train,
The only class that never cries in vain.
For see what natural benefits you lend!
(The surest way to fix the mutual friend)
While on his slaughter'd troops are fed,
You cleanse his camp and carry off his dead.
Imperial scavenger! but now you know,
Your work is vain amid these hills of snow.
His tentless troops are marbled through with frost
And change to crystal when the breath is lost.
Mere trunks of ice, tho limb'd like human frames,
And lately warm'd with life's endearing flames.
They cannot taint the air, the world impest.
Nor can they tear one fiber from their breast.
No! from their visual sockets as they lie,
With beak and claw you cannot pluck an eye,
The frozen orb, preserving still its form,
Defies your talons as it braves the storm,
But stands and stares to God, as if to know
In what curst hands he leaves his world below.
　　Fly then, or starve; tho all the dreadful road
From Minsk to Moskow with their bodies strow'd
May count some Myriads, yet they can't suffice
To feed you more beneath these dreary skies.
Go back and winter in the wilds of Spain;
Feast there awhile, and in the next campaign
Rejoin your master; for you'll find him then,
With his new million of the race of men,
Clothed in his thunders, all his flags unfurl'd,
Raging and storming o'er the prostrate world!
　　War after war his hungry soul requires,

State after state shall sink beneath his fires,
Yet other Spains in victim smoke shall rise
And other Moskows suffocate the skies,
Each land lie reeking with its peoples slain
And not a stream run bloodless to the main.
Till men resume their souls, and dare to shed
Earth's total vengeance on the monster's head,
Hurl from his blood-built throne this king of woes,
Dash him to dust, and let the world repose.

WILLIAM CULLEN BRYANT
1794–1878

Thanatopsis

To him who in the love of Nature holds
Communion with her visible forms, she speaks
A various language; for his gayer hours
She has a voice of gladness, and a smile
And eloquence of beauty, and she glides
Into his darker musings, with a mild
And healing sympathy, that steals away
Their sharpness, ere he is aware. When thoughts
Of the last bitter hour come like a blight
Over thy spirit, and sad images
Of the stern agony, and shroud, and pall,
And breathless darkness, and the narrow house,
Make thee to shudder, and grow sick at heart; —
Go forth, under the open sky, and list
To Nature's teachings, while from all around —
Earth and her waters, and the depths of air —
Comes a still voice — Yet a few days, and thee
The all-beholding sun shall see no more
In all his course; nor yet in the cold ground,
Where thy pale form was laid, with many tears,
Nor in the embrace of ocean, shall exist
Thy image. Earth, that nourished thee, shall claim
Thy growth, to be resolved to earth again,
And, lost each human trace, surrendering up
Thine individual being, shalt thou go
To mix for ever with the elements,
To be a brother to the insensible rock

And to the sluggish clod, which the rude swain
Turns with his share, and treads upon. The oak
Shall send his roots abroad, and pierce thy mould.

   Yet not to thine eternal resting-place
Shalt thou retire alone, nor couldst thou wish
Couch more magnificent. Thou shalt lie down
With patriarchs of the infant world — with kings,
The powerful of the earth — the wise, the good,
Fair forms, and hoary seers of ages past,
All in one mighty sepulchre. The hills
Rock-ribbed and ancient as the sun, — the vales
Stretching in pensive quietness between;
The venerable woods — rivers that move
In majesty, and the complaining brooks
That make the meadows green; and, poured round all,
Old Ocean's gray and melancholy waste, —
Are but the solemn decorations all
Of the great tomb of man. The golden sun,
The planets, all the infinite host of heaven,
Are shining on the sad abodes of death,
Through the still lapse of ages. All that tread
The globe are but a handful to the tribes
That slumber in its bosom. — Take the wings
Of morning, pierce the Barcan wilderness,
Or lose thyself in the continuous woods
Where rolls the Oregon, and hears no sound,
Save his own dashings — yet the dead are there:
And millions in those solitudes, since first
The flight of years began, have laid them down
In their last sleep — the dead reign there alone.
So shalt thou rest, and what if thou withdraw
In silence from the living, and no friend
Take note of thy departure? All that breathe
Will share thy destiny. The gay will laugh
When thou art gone, the solemn brood of care
Plod on, and each one as before will chase
His favorite phantom; yet all these shall leave
Their mirth and their employments, and shall come
And make their bed with thee. As the long train
Of ages glide away, the sons of men,
The youth in life's green spring, and he who goes
In the full strength of years, matron and maid,

The speechless babe, and the gray-headed man —
Shall one by one be gathered to thy side,
By those, who in their turn shall follow them.

So live, that when thy summons comes to join
The innumerable caravan, which moves
To that mysterious realm, where each shall take
His chamber in the silent halls of death,
Thou go not, like the quarry-slave at night,
Scourged to his dungeon, but, sustained and soothed
By an unfaltering trust, approach thy grave,
Like one who wraps the drapery of his couch
About him, and lies down to pleasant dreams.

To a Waterfowl

Whither, midst falling dew,
While glow the heavens with the last steps of day,
Far, through their rosy depths, dost thou pursue
    Thy solitary way?

Vainly the fowler's eye
Might mark thy distant flight to do thee wrong,
As, darkly seen against the crimson sky,
    Thy figure floats along.

Seek'st thou the plashy brink
Of weedy lake, or marge of river wide,
Or where the rocking billows rise and sink
    On the chafed ocean-side?

There is a Power whose care
Teaches thy way along that pathless coast —
The desert and illimitable air —
    Lone wandering, but not lost.

All day thy wings have fanned,
At that far height, the cold, thin atmosphere,
Yet stoop not, weary, to the welcome land,
    Though the dark night is near.

And soon that toil shall end;
Soon shalt thou find a summer home, and rest,
And scream among thy fellows; reeds shall bend,
    Soon, o'er thy sheltered nest.

Thou'rt gone, the abyss of heaven
Hath swallowed up thy form; yet, on my heart
Deeply has sunk the lesson thou hast given,
    And shall not soon depart.

He who, from zone to zone,
Guides through the boundless sky thy certain flight,
In the long way that I must tread alone,
    Will lead my steps aright.

Green River

When breezes are soft and skies are fair,
I steal an hour from study and care,
And hie me away to the woodland scene,
Where wanders the stream with waters of green,
As if the bright fringe of herbs on its brink
Had given their stain to the waves they drink;
And they, whose meadows it murmurs through,
Have named the stream from its own fair hue.

Yet pure its waters — its shallows are bright
With colored pebbles and sparkles of light,
And clear the depths where its eddies play,
And dimples deepen and whirl away,
And the plane-tree's speckled arms o'ershoot
The swifter current that mines its root,
Through whose shifting leaves, as you walk the hill,
The quivering glimmer of sun and rill
With a sudden flash on the eye is thrown,
Like the ray that streams from the diamond-stone.
Oh, loveliest there the spring days come,
With blossoms, and birds, and wild-bees' hum;
The flowers of summer are fairest there,
And freshest the breath of the summer air;
And sweetest the golden autumn day
In silence and sunshine glides away.

Yet, fair as thou art, thou shunnest to glide,
Beautiful stream! by the village side;
But windest away from haunts of men,
To quiet valley and shaded glen;
And forest, and meadow, and slope of hill,
Around thee, are lonely, lovely, and still,
Lonely — save when, by thy rippling tides,
From thicket to thicket the angler glides;
Or the simpler comes, with basket and book,
For herbs of power on thy banks to look;
Or haply, some idle dreamer, like me,
To wander, and muse, and gaze on thee,
Still — save the chirp of birds that feed
On the river cherry and seedy reed,
And thy own wild music gushing out
With mellow murmur of fairy shout,
From dawn to the blush of another day,
Like traveller singing along his way.

That fairy music I never hear,
Nor gaze on those waters so green and clear,
And mark them winding away from sight,
Darkened with shade or flashing with light,
While o'er them the vine to its thicket clings,
And the zephyr stoops to freshen his wings,
But I wish that fate had left me free
To wander these quiet haunts with thee,
Till the eating cares of earth should depart,
And the peace of the scene pass into my heart;
And I envy thy stream, as it glides along
Through its beautiful banks in a trance of song.

Though forced to drudge for the dregs of men,
And scrawl strange words with the barbarous pen,
And mingle among the jostling crowd,
Where the sons of strife are subtle and loud —
I often come to this quiet place,
To breathe the airs that ruffle thy face,
And gaze upon thee in silent dream,
For in thy lonely and lovely stream
An image of that calm life appears
That won my heart in my greener years.

The Prairies

These are the gardens of the Desert, these
The unshorn fields, boundless and beautiful,
For which the speech of England has no name —
The Prairies. I behold them for the first,
And my heart swells, while the dilated sight
Takes in the encircling vastness. Lo! they stretch,
In airy undulations, far away,
As if the ocean, in his gentlest swell,
Stood still, with all his rounded billows fixed,
And motionless forever. — Motionless? —
No — they are all unchained again. The clouds
Sweep over with their shadows, and, beneath,
The surface rolls and fluctuates to the eye;
Dark hollows seem to glide along and chase
The sunny ridges. Breezes of the South!
Who toss the golden and the flame-like flowers,
And pass the prairie-hawk that, poised on high,
Flaps his broad wings, yet moves not — ye have played
Among the palms of Mexico and vines
Of Texas, and have crisped the limpid brooks
That from the fountains of Sonora glide
Into the calm Pacific — have ye fanned
A nobler or a lovelier scene than this?
Man hath no power in all this glorious work:
The hand that built the firmament hath heaved
And smoothed these verdant swells, and sown their slopes
With herbage, planted them with island groves,
And hedged them round with forests. Fitting floor
For this magnificent temple of the sky —
With flowers whose glory and whose multitude
Rival the constellations! The great heavens
Seem to stoop down upon the scene in love, —
A nearer vault, and of a tenderer blue,
Than that which bends above our eastern hills.

As o'er the verdant waste I guide my steed,
Among the high rank grass that sweeps his sides
The hollow beating of his footstep seems
A sacrilegious sound. I think of those
Upon whose rest he tramples. Are they here —
The dead of other days? — and did the dust

35

Of these fair solitudes once stir with life
And burn with passion? Let the mighty mounds
That overlook the rivers, or that rise
In the dim forest crowded with old oaks,
Answer. A race, that long has passed away,
Built them; — a disciplined and populous race
Heaped, with long toil, the earth, while yet the Greek
Was hewing the Pentelicus to forms
Of symmetry, and rearing on its rock
The glittering Parthenon. These ample fields
Nourished their harvests, here their herds were fed,
When haply by their stalls the bison lowed,
And bowed his manèd shoulder to the yoke.
All day this desert murmured with their toils,
Till twilight blushed, and lovers walked, and wooed
In a forgotten language, and old tunes,
From instruments of unremembered form,
Gave the soft winds a voice. The red man came —
The roaming hunter tribes, warlike and fierce,
And the mound-builders vanished from the earth.
The solitude of centuries untold
Has settled where they dwelt. The prairie-wolf
Hunts in their meadows, and his fresh-dug den
Yawns by my path. The gopher mines the ground
Where stood their swarming cities. All is gone;
All — save the piles of earth that hold their bones,
The platforms where they worshipped unknown gods,
The barriers which they builded from the soil
To keep the foe at bay — till o'er the walls
The wild beleaguerers broke, and, one by one,
The strongholds of the plain were forced, and heaped
With corpses. The brown vultures of the wood
Flocked to those vast uncovered sepulchres,
And sat unscared and silent at their feast.
Haply some solitary fugitive,
Lurking in marsh and forest, till the sense
Of desolation and of fear became
Bitterer than death, yielded himself to die.
Man's better nature triumphed then. Kind words
Welcomed and soothed him; the rude conquerors
Seated the captive with their chiefs; he chose
A bride among their maidens, and at length
Seemed to forget — yet ne'er forgot — the wife

Of his first love, and her sweet little ones,
Butchered, amid their shrieks, with all his race.

  Thus change the forms of being. Thus arise
Races of living things, glorious in strength,
And perish, as the quickening breath of God
Fills them, or is withdrawn. The red man, too,
Has left the blooming wilds he ranged so long,
And, nearer to the Rocky Mountains, sought
A wider hunting-ground. The beaver builds
No longer by these streams, but far away,
On waters whose blue surface ne'er gave back
The white man's face — among Missouri's springs,
And pools whose issues swell the Oregon,
He rears his little Venice. In these plains
The bison feeds no more. Twice twenty leagues
Beyond remotest smoke of hunter's camp,
Roams the majestic brute, in herds that shake
The earth with thundering steps — yet here I meet
His ancient footprints stamped beside the pool.

  Still this great solitude is quick with life.
Myriads of insects, gaudy as the flowers
They flutter over, gentle quadrupeds,
And birds, that scarce have learned the fear of man,
Are here, and sliding reptiles of the ground,
Startlingly beautiful. The graceful deer
Bounds to the wood at my approach. The bee,
A more adventurous colonist than man,
With whom he came across the eastern deep,
Fills the savannas with his murmurings,
And hides his sweets, as in the golden age,
Within the hollow oak. I listen long
To his domestic hum, and think I hear
The sound of that advancing multitude
Which soon shall fill these deserts. From the ground
Comes up the laugh of children, the soft voice
Of maidens, and the sweet and solemn hymn
Of Sabbath worshippers. The low of herds
Blends with the rustling of the heavy grain
Over the dark-brown furrows. All at once
A fresher wind sweeps by, and breaks my dream,
And I am in the wilderness alone.

RALPH WALDO EMERSON
1803–1882

Each and All

Little thinks, in the field, yon red-cloaked clown
Of thee from the hill-top looking down;
The heifer that lows in the upland farm,
Far-heard, lows not thine ear to charm;
The sexton, tolling his bell at noon,
Deems not that great Napoleon
Stops his horse, and lists with delight,
Whilst his files sweep round yon Alpine height;
Nor knowest thou what argument
Thy life to thy neighbor's creed has lent.
All are needed by each one;
Nothing is fair or good alone.
I thought the sparrow's note from heaven,
Singing at dawn on the alder bough;
I brought him home, in his nest, at even;
He sings the song, but it cheers not now,
For I did not bring home the river and sky; —
He sang to my ear, — they sang to my eye.
The delicate shells lay on the shore;
The bubbles of the latest wave
Fresh pearls to their enamel gave,
And the bellowing of the savage sea
Greeted their safe escape to me.
I wiped away the weeds and foam,
I fetched my sea-born treasures home;
But the poor, unsightly, noisome things
Had left their beauty on the shore
With the sun and the sand and the wild uproar.
The lover watched his graceful maid,
As 'mid the virgin train she strayed,
Nor knew her beauty's best attire
Was woven still by the snow-white choir.
At last she came to his hermitage,
Like the bird from the woodlands to the cage; —
The gay enchantment was undone,
A gentle wife, but fairy none.
Then I said, "I covet truth;
Beauty is unripe childhood's cheat;
I leave it behind with the games of youth:" —

As I spoke, beneath my feet
The ground-pine curled its pretty wreath,
Running over the club-moss burrs;
I inhaled the violet's breath;
Around me stood the oaks and firs;
Pine-cones and acorns lay on the ground;
Over me soared the eternal sky,
Full of light and of deity;
Again I saw, again I heard,
The rolling river, the morning bird; —
Beauty through my senses stole;
I yielded myself to the perfect whole.

The Problem

I like a church; I like a cowl;
I love a prophet of the soul;
And on my heart monastic aisles
Fall like sweet strains, or pensive smiles;
Yet not for all his faith can see
Would I that cowlèd churchman be.

Why should the vest on him allure,
Which I could not on me endure?

Not from a vain or shallow thought
His awful Jove young Phidias brought;
Never from lips of cunning fell
The thrilling Delphic oracle;
Out from the heart of nature rolled
The burdens of the Bible old;
The litanies of nations came,
Like the volcano's tongue of flame,
Up from the burning core below, —
The canticles of love and woe:
The hand that rounded Peter's dome
And groined the aisles of Christian Rome
Wrought in a sad sincerity;
Himself from God he could not free;
He builded better than he knew; —
The conscious stone to beauty grew.

Know'st thou what wove yon woodbird's nest
Of leaves, and feathers from her breast?
Or how the fish outbuilt her shell,
Painting with morn each annual cell?
Or how the sacred pine-tree adds
To her old leaves new myriads?
Such and so grew these holy piles,
Whilst love and terror laid the tiles.
Earth proudly wears the Parthenon,
As the best gem upon her zone,
And Morning opes with haste her lids
To gaze upon the Pyramids;
O'er England's abbeys bends the sky,
As on its friends, with kindred eye;
For out of Thought's interior sphere
These wonders rose to upper air;
And Nature gladly gave them place,
Adopted them into her race,
And granted them an equal date
With Andes and with Ararat.

These temples grew as grows the grass;
Art might obey, but not surpass.
The passive Master lent his hand
To the vast soul that o'er him planned;
And the same power that reared the shrine
Bestrode the tribes that knelt within.
Ever the fiery Pentecost
Girds with one flame the countless host,
Trances the heart through chanting choirs,
And through the priest the mind inspires.
The word unto the prophet spoken
Was writ on tables yet unbroken;
The word by seers or sibyls told,
In groves of oak, or fanes of gold,
Still floats upon the morning wind,
Still whispers to the willing mind.
One accent of the Holy Ghost
The heedless world hath never lost.
I know what say the fathers wise, —
The Book itself before me lies,
Old *Chrysostom*, best Augustine,

And he who blent both in his line,
The younger *Golden Lips* or mines,
Taylor, the Shakspeare of divines.
His words are music in my ear,
I see his cowlèd portrait dear;
And yet, for all his faith could see,
I would not the good bishop be.

The Visit

Askest, "How long thou shalt stay?"
Devastator of the day!
Know, each substance and relation,
Thorough nature's operation,
Hath its unit, bound and metre;
And every new compound
Is some product and repeater, —
Product of the earlier found.
But the unit of the visit,
The encounter of the wise, —
Say, what other metre is it
Than the meeting of the eyes?
Nature poureth into nature
Through the channels of that feature,
Riding on the ray of sight,
Fleeter far than whirlwinds go,
Or for service, or delight,
Hearts to hearts their meaning show,
Sum their long experience,
And import intelligence.
Single look has drained the breast;
Single moment years confessed.
The duration of a glance
Is the term of convenance,
And, though thy rede be church or state,
Frugal multiples of that.
Speeding Saturn cannot halt;
Linger, — thou shalt rue the fault:
If Love his moment overstay,
Hatred's swift repulsions play.

Uriel

It fell in the ancient periods
   Which the brooding soul surveys,
Or ever the wild Time coined itself
   Into calendar months and days.

This was the lapse of Uriel,
Which in Paradise befell.
Once, among the Pleiads walking,
Seyd overheard the young gods talking;
And the treason, too long pent,
To his ears was evident.
The young deities discussed
Laws of form, and metre just,
Orb, quintessence, and sunbeams,
What subsisteth, and what seems.
One, with low tones that decide,
And doubt and reverend use defied,
With a look that solved the sphere,
And stirred the devils everywhere,
Gave his sentiment divine
Against the being of a line.
"Line in nature is not found;
Unit and universe are round;
In vain produced, all rays return;
Evil will bless, and ice will burn."
As Uriel spoke with piercing eye,
A shudder ran around the sky;
The stern old war-gods shook their heads,
The seraphs frowned from myrtle-beds;
Seemed to the holy festival
The rash word boded ill to all;
The balance-beam of Fate was bent;
The bounds of good and ill were rent;
Strong Hades could not keep his own,
But all slid to confusion.

A sad self-knowledge, withering, fell
On the beauty of Uriel;
In heaven once eminent, the god
Withdrew, that hour, into his cloud;

Whether doomed to long gyration
In the sea of generation,
Or by knowledge grown too bright
To hit the nerve of feebler sight.
Straightway, a forgetting wind
Stole over the celestial kind,
And their lips the secret kept,
If in ashes the fire-seed slept.
But now and then, truth-speaking things
Shamed the angels' veiling wings;
And, shrilling from the solar course,
Or from fruit of chemic force,
Procession of a soul in matter,
Or the speeding change of water,
Or out of the good of evil born,
Came Uriel's voice of cherub scorn,
And a blush tinged the upper sky,
And the gods shook, they knew not why.

The Sphinx

The Sphinx is drowsy,
    Her wings are furled:
Her ear is heavy,
    She broods on the world.
"Who'll tell me my secret,
    The ages have kept? —
I awaited the seer
    While they slumbered and slept: —

"The fate of the man-child,
    The meaning of man;
Known fruit of the unknown;
    Dædalian plan;
Out of sleeping a waking,
    Out of waking a sleep;
Life death overtaking;
    Deep underneath deep?

"Erect as a sunbeam,
　　Upspringeth the palm;
The elephant browses,
　　Undaunted and calm;
In beautiful motion
　　The thrush plies his wings;
Kind leaves of his covert,
　　Your silence he sings.

"The waves, unashamèd,
　　In difference sweet,
Play glad with the breezes,
　　Old playfellows meet;
The journeying atoms,
　　Primordial wholes,
Firmly draw, firmly drive,
　　By their animate poles.

"Sea, earth, air, sound, silence,
　　Plant, quadruped, bird,
By one music enchanted,
　　One deity stirred, —
Each the other adorning,
　　Accompany still;
Night veileth the morning,
　　The vapor the hill.

"The babe by its mother
　　Lies bathèd in joy;
Glide its hours uncounted, —
　　The sun is its toy;
Shines the peace of all being,
　　Without cloud, in its eyes;
And the sum of the world
　　In soft miniature lies.

"But man crouches and blushes,
　　Absconds and conceals;
He creepeth and peepeth,
　　He palters and steals;
Infirm, melancholy,
　　Jealous glancing around,
An oaf, an accomplice,
　　He poisons the ground.

"Out spoke the great mother,
　　Beholding his fear; —
At the sound of her accents
　　Cold shuddered the sphere: —
'Who has drugged my boy's cup?
　　Who has mixed my boy's bread?
Who, with sadness and madness,
　　Has turned my child's head?' "

I heard a poet answer
　　Aloud and cheerfully,
"Say on, sweet Sphinx! thy dirges
　　Are pleasant songs to me.
Deep love lieth under
　　These pictures of time;
They fade in the light of
　　Their meaning sublime.

"The fiend that man harries
　　Is love of the Best;
Yawns the pit of the Dragon,
　　Lit by rays from the Blest.
The Lethe of Nature
　　Can't trance him again,
Whose soul sees the perfect,
　　Which his eyes seek in vain.

"To vision profounder,
　　Man's spirit must dive;
His aye-rolling orb
　　At no goal will arrive;
The heavens that now draw him
　　With sweetness untold,
Once found, — for new heavens
　　He spurneth the old.

"Pride ruined the angels,
　　Their shame them restores;
Lurks the joy that is sweetest
　　In stings of remorse.
Have I a lover
　　Who is noble and free? —
I would he were nobler
　　Than to love me.

"Eterne alternation
　　Now follows, now flies;
And under pain, pleasure, —
　　Under pleasure, pain lies.
Love works at the centre,
　　Heart-heaving alway;
Forth speed the strong pulses
　　To the borders of day.

"Dull Sphinx, Jove keep thy five wits;
　　Thy sight is growing blear;
Rue, myrrh and cummin for the Sphinx,
　　Her muddy eyes to clear!"
The old Sphinx bit her thick lip, —
　　Said, "Who taught thee me to name?
I am thy spirit, yoke-fellow;
　　Of thine eye I am eyebeam.

"Thou art the unanswered question;
　　Couldst see thy proper eye,
Alway it asketh, asketh;
　　And each answer is a lie.
So take thy quest through nature,
　　It through thousand natures ply;
Ask on, thou clothed eternity;
　　Time is the false reply."

Uprose the merry Sphinx,
　　And crouched no more in stone;
She melted into purple cloud,
　　She silvered in the moon;
She spired into a yellow flame;
　　She flowered in blossoms red;
She flowed into a foaming wave:
　　She stood Monadnoc's head.

Thorough a thousand voices
　　Spoke the universal dame;
"Who telleth one of my meanings
　　Is master of all I am."

46

Alphonso of Castile

I, Alphonso, live and learn,
Seeing Nature go astern.
Things deteriorate in kind;
Lemons run to leaves and rind;
Meagre crop of figs and limes;
Shorter days and harder times.
Flowering April cools and dies
In the insufficient skies.
Imps, at high midsummer, blot
Half the sun's disk with a spot:
'T will not now avail to tan
Orange cheek or skin of man.
Roses bleach, the goats are dry,
Lisbon quakes, the people cry.
Yon pale, scrawny fisher fools,
Gaunt as bitterns in the pools,
Are no brothers of my blood; —
They discredit Adamhood.
Eyes of gods! ye must have seen,
O'er your ramparts as ye lean,
The general debility;
Of genius the sterility;
Mighty projects countermanded;
Rash ambition, brokenhanded;
Puny man and scentless rose
Tormenting Pan to double the dose.
Rebuild or ruin: either fill
Of vital force the wasted rill,
Or tumble all again in heap
To weltering chaos and to sleep.

Say, Seigniors, are the old Niles dry,
Which fed the veins of earth and sky,
That mortals miss the loyal heats,
Which drove them erst to social feats;
Now, to a savage selfness grown,
Think nature barely serves for one;
With science poorly mask their hurt,
And vex the gods with question pert,
Immensely curious whether you
Still are rulers, or mildew?

Masters, I'm in pain with you;
Masters, I'll be plain with you;
In my palace of Castile,
I, a king, for kings can feel.
There my thoughts the matter roll,
And solve and oft resolve the whole.
And, for I'm styled Alphonse the Wise,
Ye shall not fail for sound advice.
Before ye want a drop of rain,
Hear the sentiment of Spain.

You have tried famine: no more try it;
Ply us now with a full diet;
Teach your pupils now with plenty;
For one sun supply us twenty.
I have thought it thoroughly over, —
State of hermit, state of lover;
We must have society,
We cannot spare variety.
Hear you, then, celestial fellows!
Fits not to be over-zealous;
Steads not to work on the clean jump,
Nor wine nor brains perpetual pump.
Men and gods are too extense;
Could you slacken and condense?
Your rank overgrowths reduce
Till your kinds abound with juice?
Earth, crowded, cries, "Too many men!"
My counsel is, kill nine in ten,
And bestow the shares of all
On the remnant decimal.
Add their nine lives to this cat;
Stuff their nine brains in his hat;
Make his frame and forces square
With the labours he must dare;
Thatch his flesh, and even his years
With the marble which he rears.
There, growing slowly old at ease,
No faster than his planted trees,
He may, by warrant of his age,
In schemes of broader scope engage.
So shall ye have a man of the sphere,
Fit to grace the solar year.

Mithridates

I cannot spare water or wine,
    Tobacco-leaf, or poppy, or rose;
From the earth-poles to the Line,
    All between that works or grows,
Every thing is kin of mine.

Give me agates for my meat;
· Give me cantharids to eat;
From air and ocean bring me foods,
From all zones and altitudes; —

From all natures, sharp and slimy,
    Salt and basalt, wild and tame:
Tree and lichen, ape, sea-lion,
    Bird, and reptile, be my game.
Ivy for my fillet band;
Blinding dog-wood in my hand;
Hemlock for my sherbet cull me,
And the prussic juice to lull me;
Swing me in the upas boughs,
Vampyre-fanned, when I carouse.

Too long shut in strait and few,
Thinly dieted on dew,
I will use the world, and sift it,
To a thousand humors shift it,
As you spin a cherry.
O doleful ghosts, and goblins merry!
O all you virtues, methods, mights,
Means, appliances, delights,
Reputed wrongs and braggart rights,
Smug routine, and things allowed,
Minorities, things under cloud!
Hither! take me, use me, fill me,
Vein and artery, though ye kill me!

Guy

Mortal mixed of middle clay,
Attempered to the night and day,
Interchangeable with things,
Needs no amulets nor rings.

Guy possessed the talisman
That all things from him began;
And as, of old, Polycrates
Chained the sunshine and the breeze,
So did Guy betimes discover
Fortune was his guard and lover;
In strange junctures, felt, with awe,
His own symmetry with law;
That no mixture could withstand
The virtue of his lucky hand.
He gold or jewel could not lose,
Nor not receive his ample dues.
Fearless Guy had never foes,
He did their weapons decompose.
Aimed at him, the blushing blade
Healed as fast the wounds it made.
If on the foeman fell his gaze,
Him it would straightway blind or craze:
In the street, if he turned round,
His eye the eye 'twas seeking found.
It seemed his Genius discreet
Worked on the Maker's own receipt,
And made each tide and element
Stewards of stipend and of rent;
So that the common waters fell
As costly wine into his well.
He had so sped his wise affairs
That he caught Nature in his snares.
Early or late, the falling rain
Arrived in time to swell his grain;
Stream could not so perversely wind
But corn of Guy's was there to grind:
The siroc found it on its way,
To speed his sails, to dry his hay;
And the world's sun seemed to rise
To drudge all day for Guy the wise.
In his rich nurseries, timely skill
Strong crab with nobler blood did fill;
The zephyr in his garden rolled
From plum-trees vegetable gold;
And all the hours of the year
With their own harvest honored were.
There was no frost but welcome came,

Nor freshet, nor midsummer flame.
Belonged to wind and world the toil
And venture, and to Guy the oil.

Hamatreya

Bulkeley, Hunt, Willard, Hosmer, Meriam, Flint,
Possessed the land which rendered to their toil
Hay, corn, roots, hemp, flax, apples, wool and wood.
Each of these landlords walked amidst his farm,
Saying, " 'T is mine, my children's and my name's.
How sweet the west wind sounds in my own trees!
How graceful climb those shadows on my hill!
I fancy these pure waters and the flags
Know me, as does my dog: we sympathize;
And, I affirm, my actions smack of the soil."

Where are these men? Asleep beneath their grounds:
And strangers, fond as they, their furrows plough.
Earth laughs in flowers, to see her boastful boys
Earth-proud, proud of the earth which is not theirs;
Who steer the plough, but cannot steer their feet
Clear of the grave.
They added ridge to valley, brook to pond,
And sighed for all that bounded their domain;
"This suits me for a pasture; that's my park;
We must have clay, lime, gravel, granite-ledge,
And misty lowland, where to go for peat.
The land is well, — lies fairly to the south.
'T is good, when you have crossed the sea and back,
To find the sitfast acres where you left them."
Ah! the hot owner sees not Death, who adds
Him to his land, a lump of mould the more.
Hear what the Earth says: —

Earth-Song

"Mine and yours;
Mine, not yours.
Earth endures;
Stars abide —
Shine down in the old sea;

Old are the shores;
But where are old men?
I who have seen much,
Such have I never seen.

"The lawyer's deed
Ran sure,
In tail,
To them, and to their heirs
Who shall succeed,
Without fail,
Forevermore.

"Here is the land,
Shaggy with wood,
With its old valley,
Mound and flood.
But the heritors? —
Fled like the flood's foam.
The lawyer, and the laws,
And the kingdom,
Clean swept herefrom.

"They called me theirs,
Who so controlled me;
Yet every one
Wished to stay, and is gone,
How am I theirs,
If they cannot hold me,
But I hold them?"

When I heard the Earth-song
I was no longer brave;
My avarice cooled
Like lust in the chill of the grave.

The Rhodora:

On being asked, whence is the flower?

In May, when sea-winds pierced our solitudes,
I found the fresh Rhodora in the woods,

Spreading its leafless blooms in a damp nook,
To please the desert and the sluggish brook.
The purple petals, fallen in the pool,
Made the black water with their beauty gay;
Here might the red-bird come his plumes to cool,
And court the flower that cheapens his array.
Rhodora! if the sages ask thee why
This charm is wasted on the earth and sky,
Tell them, dear, that if eyes were made for seeing,
Then Beauty is its own excuse for being:
Why thou wert there, O rival of the rose!
I never thought to ask, I never knew:
But, in my simple ignorance, suppose
The self-same Power that brought me there brought you.

The Humble-Bee

Burly, dozing humble-bee,
Where thou art is clime for me.
Let them sail for Porto Rique,
Far-off heats through seas to seek;
I will follow thee alone,
Thou animated torrid-zone!
Zigzag steerer, desert cheerer,
Let me chase thy waving lines;
Keep me nearer, me thy hearer,
Singing over shrubs and vines.

Insect lover of the sun,
Joy of thy dominion!
Sailor of the atmosphere;
Swimmer through the waves of air;
Voyager of light and noon;
Epicurean of June;
Wait, I prithee, till I come
Within earshot of thy hum, —
All without is martyrdom.

When the south wind, in May days,
With a net of shining haze
Silvers the horizon wall,
And with softness touching all,

Tints the human countenance
With a color of romance,
And infusing subtle heats,
Turns the sod to violets,
Thou, in sunny solitudes,
Rover of the underwoods,
The green silence dost displace
With thy mellow, breezy bass.

Hot midsummer's petted crone,
Sweet to me thy drowsy tone
Tells of countless sunny hours,
Long days, and solid banks of flowers;
Of gulfs of sweetness without bound
In Indian wildernesses found;
Of Syrian peace, immortal leisure,
Firmest cheer, and bird-like pleasure.

Aught unsavory or unclean
Hath my insect never seen;
But violets and bilberry bells,
Maple-sap and daffodels,
Grass with green flag half-mast high,
Succory to match the sky,
Columbine with horn of honey,
Scented fern, and agrimony,
Clover, catchfly, adder's-tongue
And brier-roses, dwelt among;
All beside was unknown waste,
All was picture as he passed.

Wiser far than human seer,
Yellow-breeched philosopher!
Seeing only what is fair,
Sipping only what is sweet,
Thou dost mock at fate and care,
Leave the chaff, and take the wheat.
When the fierce northwestern blast
Cools sea and land so far and fast,
Thou already slumberest deep;
Woe and want thou canst outsleep;
Want and woe, which torture us,
Thy sleep makes ridiculous.

The Snow-Storm

Announced by all the trumpets of the sky,
Arrives the snow, and, driving o'er the fields,
Seems nowhere to alight: the whited air
Hides hills and woods, the river, and the heaven,
And veils the farm-house at the garden's end.
The sled and traveller stopped, the courier's feet
Delayed, all friends shut out, the housemates sit
Around the radiant fireplace, enclosed
In a tumultuous privacy of storm.

Come see the north wind's masonry.
Out of an unseen quarry evermore
Furnished with tile, the fierce artificer
Curves his white bastions with projected roof
Round every windward stake, or tree, or door.
Speeding, the myriad-handed, his wild work
So fanciful, so savage, nought cares he
For number or proportion. Mockingly,
On coop or kennel he hangs Parian wreaths;
A swan-like form invests the hidden thorn;
Fills up the farmer's lane from wall to wall,
Maugre the farmer's sighs; and at the gate
A tapering turret overtops the work.
And when his hours are numbered, and the world
Is all his own, retiring, as he were not,
Leaves, when the sun appears, astonished Art
To mimic in slow structures, stone by stone,
Built in an age, the mad wind's night-work,
The frolic architecture of the snow.

Woodnotes I

1

When the pine tosses its cones
To the song of its waterfall tones,
Who speeds to the woodland walks?
To birds and trees who talks?
Cæsar of his leafy Rome,
There the poet is at home.
He goes to the river-side, —
Not hook nor line hath he;

He stands in the meadows wide, —
Nor gun nor scythe to see.
Sure some god his eye enchants:
What he knows nobody wants.
In the wood he travels glad,
Without better fortune had,
Melancholy without bad.
Knowledge this man prizes best
Seems fantastic to the rest:
Pondering shadows, colors, clouds,
Grass-buds and caterpillar-shrouds,
Boughs on which the wild bees settle,
Tints that spot the violet's petal,
Why Nature loves the number five,
And why the star-form she repeats:
Lover of all things alive,
Wonderer at all he meets,
Wonderer chiefly at himself,
Who can tell him what he is?
Or how meet in human elf
Coming and past eternities?

2

And such I knew, a forest seer,
A minstrel of the natural year,
Foreteller of the vernal ides,
Wise harbinger of spheres and tides,
A lover true, who knew by heart
Each joy the mountain dales impart;
It seemed that Nature could not raise
A plant in any secret place,
In quaking bog, on snowy hill,
Beneath the grass that shades the rill,
Under the snow, between the rocks,
In damp fields known to bird and fox.
But he would come in the very hour
It opened in its virgin bower,
As if a sunbeam showed the place,
And tell its long-descended race.
It seemed as if the breezes brought him,
It seemed as if the sparrows taught him;
As if by secret sight he knew
Where, in far fields, the orchis grew.

Many haps fall in the field
Seldom seen by wishful eyes,
But all her shows did Nature yield,
To please and win this pilgrim wise.
He saw the partridge drum in the woods;
He heard the woodcock's evening hymn;
He found the tawny thrushes' broods;
And the shy hawk did wait for him;
What others did at distance hear,
And guessed within the thicket's gloom,
Was shown to this philosopher,
And at his bidding seemed to come.

3

In unploughed Maine he sought the lumberers' gang
Where from a hundred lakes young rivers sprang;
He trode the unplanted forest floor, whereon
The all-seeing sun for ages hath not shone;
Where feeds the moose, and walks the surly bear,
And up the tall mast runs the woodpecker.
He saw beneath dim aisles, in odorous beds,
The slight Linnæa hang its twin-born heads,
And blessed the monument of the man of flowers,
Which breathes his sweet fame through the northern bowers.
He heard, when in the grove, at intervals,
With sudden roar the aged pine-tree falls, —
One crash, the death-hymn of the perfect tree,
Declares the close of its green century.
Low lies the plant to whose creation went
Sweet influence from every element;
Whose living towers the years conspired to build,
Whose giddy top the morning loved to gild.
Through these green tents, by eldest Nature dressed,
He roamed, content alike with man and beast.
Where darkness found him he lay glad at night;
There the red morning touched him with its light.
Three moons his great heart him a hermit made,
So long he roved at will the boundless shade.
The timid it concerns to ask their way,
And fear what foe in caves and swamps can stray,
To make no step until the event is known,
And ills to come as evils past bemoan.
Not so the wise; no coward watch he keeps

To spy what danger on his pathway creeps;
Go where he will, the wise man is at home,
His hearth the earth, — his hall the azure dome;
Where his clear spirit leads him, there's his road,
By God's own light illumined and foreshowed.

4
'Twas one of the charmèd days
When the genius of God doth flow,
The wind may alter twenty ways,
A tempest cannot blow;
It may blow north, it still is warm;
Or south, it still is clear;
Or east, it smells like a clover-farm;
Or west, no thunder fear.
The musing peasant lowly great
Beside the forest water sate;
The rope-like pine roots crosswise grown
Composed the network of his throne;
The wide lake, edged with sand and grass,
Was burnished to a floor of glass,
Painted with shadows green and proud
Of the tree and of the cloud.
He was the heart of all the scene;
On him the sun looked more serene;
To hill and cloud his face was known, —
It seemed the likeness of their own;
They knew by secret sympathy
The public child of earth and sky.
"You ask," he said, "what guide
Me through trackless thickets led,
Through thick-stemmed woodlands rough and wide.
I found the water's bed.
The watercourses were my guide;
I travelled grateful by their side,
Or through their channel dry;
They led me through the thicket damp,
Through brake and fern, the beavers' camp,
Through beds of granite cut my road,
And their resistless friendship showed:
The falling waters led me,
The foodful waters fed me,
And brought me to the lowest land,

Unerring to the ocean sand.
The moss upon the forest bark
Was pole-star when the night was dark;
The purple berries in the wood
Supplied me necessary food;
For Nature ever faithful is
To such as trust her faithfulness.
When the forest shall mislead me,
When the night and morning lie,
When sea and land refuse to feed me,
'T will be time enough to die;
Then will yet my mother yield
A pillow in her greenest field,
Nor the June flowers scorn to cover
The clay of their departed lover."

Woodnotes II

As sunbeams stream through liberal space
And nothing jostle or displace,
So waved the pine-tree through my thought
And fanned the dreams it never brought.

"Whether is better, the gift or the donor?
Come to me,"
Quoth the pine-tree,
"I am the giver of honor.
My garden is the cloven rock,
And my manure the snow;
And drifting sand-heaps feed my stock,
In summer's scorching glow.
He is great who can live by me:
The rough and bearded forester
Is better than the lord;
God fills the scrip and canister,
Sin piles the loaded board.
The lord is the peasant that was,
The peasant the lord that shall be;
The lord is hay, the peasant grass,
One dry, and one the living tree.
Who liveth by the ragged pine
Foundeth a heroic line;

Who liveth in the palace hall
Waneth fast and spendeth all.
He goes to my savage haunts,
With his chariot and his care;
My twilight realm he disenchants,
And finds his prison there.

"What prizes the town and the tower?
Only what the pine-tree yields;
Sinew that subdued the fields;
The wild-eyed boy, who in the woods
Chants his hymn to hills and floods,
Whom the city's poisoning spleen
Made not pale, or fat, or lean;
Whom the rain and the wind purgeth,
Whom the dawn and the day-star urgeth,
In whose cheek the rose-leaf blusheth,
In whose feet the lion rusheth,
Iron arms, and iron mould,
That know not fear, fatigue, or cold.
I give my rafters to his boat,
My billets to his boiler's throat,
And I will swim the ancient sea
To float my child to victory,
And grant to dwellers with the pine
Dominion o'er the palm and vine.
Who leaves the pine-tree, leaves his friend,
Unnerves his strength, invites his end.
Cut a bough from my parent stem,
And dip it in thy porcelain vase;
A little while each russet gem
Will swell and rise with wonted grace;
But when it seeks enlarged supplies,
The orphan of the forest dies.
Whoso walks in solitude
And inhabiteth the wood,
Choosing light, wave, rock and bird,
Before the money-loving herd,
Into that forester shall pass,
From these companions, power and grace.
Clean shall he be, without, within,
From the old adhering sin,
All ill dissolving in the light

Of his triumphant piercing sight:
Not vain, sour, nor frivolous;
Not mad, athirst, nor garrulous;
Grave, chaste, contented, though retired,
And of all other men desired.
On him the light of star and moon
Shall fall with purer radiance down;
All constellations of the sky
Shed their virtue through his eye.
Him Nature giveth for defence
His formidable innocence;
The mounting sap, the shells, the sea,
All spheres, all stones, his helpers be;
He shall meet the speeding year,
Without wailing, without fear;
He shall be happy in his love,
Like to like shall joyful prove;
He shall be happy whilst he wooes,
Muse-born, a daughter of the Muse.
But if with gold she bind her hair,
And deck her breast with diamond,
Take off thine eyes, thy heart forbear,
Though thou lie alone on the ground.

"Heed the old oracles,
Ponder my spells;
Song wakes in my pinnacles
When the wind swells.
Soundeth the prophetic wind,
The shadows shake on the rock behind,
And the countless leaves of the pine are strings
Tuned to the lay the wood-god sings.
    Hearken! Hearken!
If thou wouldst know the mystic song
Chanted when the sphere was young.
Aloft, abroad, the pæan swells;
O wise man! hear'st thou half it tells?
O wise man! hear'st thou the least part?
'T is the chronicle of art.
To the open ear it sings
Sweet the genesis of things,
Of tendency through endless ages,
Of star-dust, and star-pilgrimages,

Of rounded worlds, of space and time,
Of the old flood's subsiding slime,
Of chemic matter, force and form,
Of poles and powers, cold, wet, and warm:
The rushing metamorphosis
Dissolving all that fixture is,
Melts things that be to things that seem,
And solid nature to a dream.
O, listen to the undersong,
The ever old, the ever young;
And, far within those cadent pauses,
The chorus of the ancient Causes!
Delights the dreadful Destiny
To fling his voice into the tree,
And shock thy weak ear with a note
Breathed from the everlasting throat.
In music he repeats the pang
Whence the fair flock of Nature sprang.
O mortal! thy ears are stones;
These echoes are laden with tones
Which only the pure can hear;
Thou canst not catch what they recite
Of Fate and Will, of Want and Right,
Of man to come, of human life,
Of Death and Fortune, Growth and Strife."

    Once again the pine-tree sung: —
"Speak not thy speech my boughs among:
Put off thy years, wash in the breeze;
My hours are peaceful centuries.
Talk no more with feeble tongue;
No more the fool of space and time,
Come weave with mine a nobler rhyme.
Only thy Americans
Can read thy line, can meet thy glance,
But the runes that I rehearse
Understands the universe;
The least breath my boughs which tossed
Brings again the Pentecost;
To every soul resounding clear
In a voice of solemn cheer, —
'Am I not thine? Are not these thine?'
And they reply, 'Forever mine!'

My branches speak Italian,
English, German, Basque, Castilian,
Mountain speech to Highlanders,
Ocean tongues to islanders,
To Fin and Lap and swart Malay,
To each his bosom-secret say.

"Come learn with me the fatal song
Which knits the world in music strong,
Come lift thine eyes to lofty rhymes,
Of things with things, of times with times,
Primal chimes of sun and shade,
Of sound and echo, man and maid,
The land reflected in the flood,
Body with shadow still pursued.
For Nature beats in perfect tune,
And rounds with rhyme her every rune,
Whether she work in land or sea,
Or hide underground her alchemy.
Thou canst not wave thy staff in air,
Or dip thy paddle in the lake,
But it carves the bow of beauty there,
And the ripples in rhymes the oar forsake.
The wood is wiser far than thou;
The wood and wave each other know
Not unrelated, unaffied.
But to each thought and thing allied,
Is perfect Nature's every part,
Rooted in the mighty Heart.
But thou, poor child! unbound, unrhymed,
Whence camest thou, misplaced, mistimed,
Whence, O thou orphan and defrauded?
Is thy land peeled, thy realm marauded?
Who thee divorced, deceived and left?
Thee of thy faith who hath bereft,
And torn the ensigns from thy brow,
And sunk the immortal eye so low?
Thy cheek too white, thy form too slender,
Thy gait too slow, thy habits tender
For royal man; — they thee confess
An exile from the wilderness, —
The hills where health with health agrees,
And the wise soul expels disease.

Hark! in thy ear I will tell the sign
By which thy hurt thou may'st divine.
When thou shalt climb the mountain cliff,
Or see the wide shore from thy skiff,
To thee the horizon shall express
But emptiness on emptiness;
There lives no man of Nature's worth
In the circle of the earth;
And to thine eye the vast skies fall,
Dire and satirical,
On clucking hens and prating fools,
On thieves, on drudges and on dolls.
And thou shalt say to the Most High,
'Godhead! all this astronomy,
And fate and practice and invention,
Strong art and beautiful pretension,
This radiant pomp of sun and star,
Throes that were, and worlds that are,
Behold! were in vain and in vain; —
It cannot be, — I will look again.
Surely now will the curtain rise,
And earth's fit tenant me surprise; —
But the curtain doth *not* rise,
And Nature has miscarried wholly
Into failure, into folly.'

"Alas! thine is the bankruptcy,
Blessed Nature so to see.
Come, lay thee in my soothing shade,
And heal the hurts which sin has made.
I see thee in the crowd alone;
I will be thy companion.
Quit thy friends as the dead in doom,
And build to them a final tomb;
Let the starred shade that nightly falls
Still celebrate their funerals,
And the bell of beetle and of bee
Knell their melodious memory.
Behind thee leave thy merchandise,
Thy churches and thy charities;
And leave thy peacock wit behind;
Enough for thee the primal mind
That flows in streams, that breathes in wind:

Leave all thy pedant lore apart;
God hid the whole world in thy heart.
Love shuns the sage, the child it crowns,
Gives all to them who all renounce.
The rain comes when the wind calls;
The river knows the way to the sea;
Without a pilot it runs and falls,
Blessing all lands with its charity;
The sea tosses and foams to find
Its way up to the cloud and wind;
The shadow sits close to the flying ball;
The date fails not on the palm-tree tall;
And thou, — go burn thy wormy pages, —
Shalt outsee seers, and outwit sages.
Oft didst thou thread the woods in vain
To find what bird had piped the strain: —
Seek not, and the little eremite
Flies gayly forth and sings in sight.

"Hearken once more!
I will tell thee the mundane lore.
Older am I than thy numbers wot,
Change I may, but I pass not.
Hitherto all things fast abide,
And anchored in the tempest ride.
Trenchant time behoves to hurry
All to yean and all to bury:
All the forms are fugitive,
But the substances survive.
Ever fresh the broad creation,
A divine improvisation,
From the heart of God proceeds,
A single will, a million deeds.
Once slept the world an egg of stone,
And pulse, and sound, and light was none;
And God said, 'Throb!' and there was motion
And the vast mass became vast ocean.
Onward and on, the eternal Pan,
Who layeth the world's incessant plan,
Halteth never in one shape,
But forever doth escape,
Like wave or flame, into new forms
Of gem, and air, of plants, and worms.

I, that to-day am a pine,
Yesterday was a bundle of grass.
He is free and libertine,
Pouring of his power the wine
To every age, to every race;
Unto every race and age
He emptieth the beverage;
Unto each, and unto all,
Maker and original.
The world is the ring of his spells,
And the play of his miracles.
As he giveth to all to drink,
Thus or thus they are and think.
With one drop sheds form and feature;
With the next a special nature;
The third adds heat's indulgent spark;
The fourth gives light which eats the dark;
Into the fifth himself he flings,
And conscious Law is King of kings.
As the bee through the garden ranges,
From world to world the godhead changes;
As the sheep go feeding in the waste,
From form to form He maketh haste;
This vault which glows immense with light
Is the inn where he lodges for a night.
What recks such Traveller if the bowers
Which bloom and fade like meadow flowers.
A bunch of fragrant lilies be,
Or the stars of eternity?
Alike to him the better, the worse, —
The glowing angel, the outcast corse.
Thou metest him by centuries,
And lo! he passes like the breeze;
Thou seek'st in globe and galaxy,
He hides in pure transparency;
Thou askest in fountains and in fires,
He is the essence that inquires.
He is the axis of the star;
He is the sparkle of the spar;
He is the heart of every creature;
He is the meaning of each feature;
And his mind is the sky,
Than all it holds more deep, more high."

Ode

Inscribed to W. H. Channing

Though loath to grieve
The evil time's sole patriot,
I cannot leave
My honied thought
For the priest's cant,
Or statesman's rant.

If I refuse
My study for their politique,
Which at the best is trick,
The angry Muse
Puts confusion in my brain.

But who is he that prates
Of the culture of mankind,
Of better arts and life?
Go, blindworm, go,
Behold the famous States
Harrying Mexico
With rifle and with knife!

Or who, with accent bolder,
Dare praise the freedom-loving mountaineer?
I found by thee, O rushing Contoocook!
And in thy valleys, Agiochook!
The jackals of the negro-holder.

The God who made New Hampshire
Taunted the lofty land
With little men; —
Small bat and wren
House in the oak: —
If earth-fire cleave
The upheaved land, and bury the folk,
The southern crocodile would grieve.
Virtue palters; Right is hence;
Freedom praised, but hid;
Funeral eloquence
Rattles the coffin-lid.

What boots thy zeal,
O glowing friend,
That would indignant rend
The northland from the south?
Wherefore? to what good end?
Boston Bay and Bunker Hill
Would serve things still; —
Things are of the snake.

The horseman serves the horse,
The neatherd serves the neat,
The merchant serves the purse,
The eater serves his meat;
'T is the day of the chattel,
Web to weave, and corn to grind;
Things are in the saddle,
And ride mankind.

There are two laws discrete,
Not reconciled, —
Law for man, and law for thing;
The last builds town and fleet,
But it runs wild,
And doth the man unking.

'T is fit the forest fall,
The steep be graded,
The mountain tunnelled,
The sand shaded,
The orchard planted,
The glebe tilled,
The prairie granted,
The steamer built.

Let man serve law for man;
Live for friendship, live for love,
For truth's and harmony's behoof;
The state may follow how it can,
As Olympus follows Jove.

    Yet do not I implore
The wrinkled shopman to my sounding woods,
Nor bid the unwilling senator

Ask votes of thrushes in the solitudes.
Every one to his chosen work; —
Foolish hands may mix and mar;
Wise and sure the issues are.
Round they roll till dark is light,
Sex to sex, and even to odd; —
The over-god
Who marries Right to Might,
Who peoples, unpeoples, —
He who exterminates
Races by stronger races,
Black by white faces, —
Knows to bring honey
Out of the lion;
Grafts gentlest scion
On pirate and Turk.

The Cossack eats Poland,
Like stolen fruit;
Her last noble is ruined,
Her last poet mute:
Straight, into double band
The victors divide;
Half for freedom strike and stand; —
The astonished Muse finds thousands at her side.

Give All to Love

Give all to love;
Obey thy heart;
Friends, kindred, days,
Estate, good-fame,
Plans, credit and the Muse, —
Nothing refuse.

'T is a brave master;
Let it have scope:
Follow it utterly,
Hope beyond hope:
High and more high
It dives into noon,
With wing unspent,

Untold intent:
But it is a god,
Knows its own path
And the outlets of the sky.

It was never for the mean;
It requireth courage stout.
Souls above doubt,
Valor unbending,
It will reward, —
They shall return
More than they were,
And ever ascending.

Leave all for love;
Yet, hear me, yet,
One word more thy heart behoved,
One pulse more of firm endeavor, —
Keep thee to-day,
To-morrow, forever,
Free as an Arab
Of thy beloved.

Cling with life to the maid;
But when the surprise,
First vague shadow of surmise
Flits across her bosom young,
Of a joy apart from thee,
Free be she, fancy-free;
Nor thou detain her vesture's hem,
Nor the palest rose she flung
From her summer diadem.

Though thou loved her as thyself,
As a self of purer clay,
Though her parting dims the day,
Stealing grace from all alive;
Heartily know,
When half-gods go,
The gods arrive.

Thine Eyes Still Shined

Thine eyes still shined for me, though far
　　I lonely roved the land or sea:
As I behold yon evening star,
　　Which yet beholds not me.

This morn I climbed the misty hill
　　And roamed the pastures through;
How danced thy form before my path
　　Amidst the deep-eyed dew!

When the redbird spread his sable wing,
　　And showed his side of flame;
When the rosebud ripened to the rose,
　　In both I read thy name.

Merlin   I

Thy trivial harp will never please
Or fill my craving ear;
Its chords should ring as blows the breeze,
Free, peremptory, clear.
No jingling serenader's art,
Nor tinkle of piano strings,
Can make the wild blood start
In its mystic springs.
The kingly bard
Must smite the chords rudely and hard,
As with hammer or with mace;
That they may render back
Artful thunder, which conveys
Secrets of the solar track,
Sparks of the supersolar blaze.
Merlin's blows are strokes of fate,
Chiming with the forest tone,
When boughs buffet boughs in the wood;
Chiming with the gasp and moan
Of the ice-imprisoned flood;
With the pulse of manly hearts;
With the voice of orators;
With the din of city arts;
With the cannonade of wars;
With the marches of the brave;
And prayers of might from martyrs' cave.

Great is the art,
Great be the manners, of the bard.
He shall not his brain encumber
With the coil of rhythm and number;
But, leaving rule and pale forethought,
He shall aye climb
For his rhyme.
"Pass in, pass in," the angels say,
"In to the upper doors,
Nor count compartments of the floors,
But mount to paradise
By the stairway of surprise."

Blameless master of the games,
King of sport that never shames,
He shall daily joy dispense
Hid in song's sweet influence.
Forms more cheerly live and go,
What time the subtle mind
Sings aloud the tune whereto
Their purses beat,
And march their feet,
And their members are combined.

By Sybarites beguiled,
He shall no task decline;
Merlin's mighty line
Extremes of nature reconciled, —
Bereaved a tyrant of his will,
And made the lion mild.
Songs can the tempest still.
Scattered on the stormy air,
Mould the year to fair increase,
And bring in poetic peace.

He shall not seek to weave,
In weak, unhappy times,
Efficacious rhymes;
Wait his returning strength.
Bird that from the nadir's floor
To the zenith's top can soar, —
The soaring orbit of the muse exceeds that
        journey's length.

Nor profane affect to hit
Or compass that, by meddling wit,
Which only the propitious mind
Publishes when 't is inclined.
There are open hours
When the God's will sallies free,
And the dull idiot might see
The flowing fortunes of a thousand years; —
Sudden, at unawares,
Self-moved, fly-to the doors,
Nor sword of angels could reveal
What they conceal.

Merlin II

The rhyme of the poet
Modulates the king's affairs;
Balance-loving Nature
Made all things in pairs.
To every foot its antipode;
Each color with its counter glowed;
To every tone beat answering tones,
Higher or graver;
Flavor gladly blends with flavor;
Leaf answers leaf upon the bough;
And match the paired cotyledons.
Hands to hands, and feet to feet,
In one body grooms and brides;
Eldest rite, two married sides
In every mortal meet.
Light's far furnace shines,
Smelting balls and bars,
Forging double stars,
Glittering twins and trines.
The animals are sick with love,
Lovesick with rhyme;
Each with all propitious Time
Into chorus wove.
Like the dancers' ordered band,
Thoughts come also hand in hand;
In equal couples mated,
Or else alternated;

Adding by their mutual gage,
One to other, health and age.
Solitary fancies go
Short-lived wandering to and fro,
Most like to bachelors,
Or an ungiven maid,
Not ancestors,
With no posterity to make the lie afraid,
Or keep truth undecayed.
Perfect-paired as eagle's wings,
Justice is the rhyme of things;
Trade and counting use
The self-same tuneful muse;
And Nemesis,
Who with even matches odd,
Who athwart space redresses
The partial wrong,
Fills the just period,
And finishes the song.

Subtle rhymes, with ruin rife,
Murmur in the house of life,
Sung by the Sisters as they spin;
In perfect time and measure they
Build and unbuild our echoing clay.
As the two twilights of the day
Fold us music-drunken in.

Bacchus

Bring me wine, but wine which never grew
In the belly of the grape,
Or grew on vine whose tap-roots, reaching through
Under the Andes to the Cape,
Suffer no savor of the earth to scape.

Let its grapes the morn salute
From a nocturnal root,
Which feels the acrid juice
Of Styx and Erebus;
And turns the woe of Night,
By its own craft, to a more rich delight.

We buy ashes for bread;
We buy diluted wine;
Give me of the true, —
Whose ample leaves and tendrils curled
Among the silver hills of heaven
Draw everlasting dew;
Wine of wine,
Blood of the world,
Form of forms, and mould of statures,
That I intoxicated,
And by the draught assimilated,
May float at pleasure through all natures;
The bird-language rightly spell,
And that which roses say so well.

Wine that is shed
Like the torrents of the sun
Up the horizon walls,
Or like the Atlantic streams, which run
When the South Sea calls.

Water and bread,
Food which needs no transmuting,
Rainbow-flowering, wisdom-fruiting,
Wine which is already man,
Food which teach and reason can.

Wine which Music is, —
Music and wine are one, —
That I, drinking this,
Shall hear far Chaos talk with me;
Kings unborn shall walk with me;
And the poor grass shall plot and plan
What it will do when it is man.
Quickened so, will I unlock
Every crypt of every rock.

I thank the joyful juice
For all I know; —
Winds of remembering
Of the ancient being blow,
And seeming-solid walls of use
Open and flow.

Pour, Bacchus! the remembering wine;
Retrieve the loss of me and mine!
Vine for vine be antidote,
And the grape requite the lote!
Haste to cure the old despair, —
Reason in Nature's lotus drenched,
The memory of ages quenched;
Give them again to shine;
Let wine repair what this undid;
And where the infection slid,
A dazzling memory revive;
Refresh the faded tints,
Recut the aged prints,
And write my old adventures with the pen
Which on the first day drew,
Upon the tablets blue,
The dancing Pleiads and eternal men.

Xenophanes

By fate, not option, frugal Nature gave
One scent to hyson and to wall-flower,
One sound to pine-groves and to waterfalls,
One aspect to the desert and the lake.
It was her stern necessity: all things
Are of one pattern made; bird, beast and flower,
Song, picture, form, space, thought and character
Deceive us, seeming to be many things,
And are but one. Beheld far off, they part
As God and devil; bring them to the mind,
They dull its edge with their monotony.
To know one element, explore another,
And in the second reappears the first.
The specious panorama of a year
But multiplies the image of a day, —
A belt of mirrors round a taper's flame;
And universal Nature, through her vast
And crowded whole, an infinite paroquet,
Repeats one note.

Blight

Give me truths;
For I am weary of the surfaces,
And die of inanition. If I knew
Only the herbs and simples of the wood,
Rue, cinquefoil, gill, vervain and agrimony,
Blue-vetch and trillium, hawkweed, sassafras,
Milkweeds and murky brakes, quaint pipes and sundew,
And rare and virtuous roots, which in these woods
Draw untold juices from the common earth,
Untold, unknown, and I could surely spell
Their fragrance, and their chemistry apply
By sweet affinities to human flesh,
Driving the foe and stablishing the friend, —
O, that were much, and I could be a part
Of the round day, related to the sun
And planted world, and full executor
Of their imperfect functions.
But these young scholars, who invade our hills,
Bold as the engineer who fells the wood,
And travelling often in the cut he makes,
Love not the flower they pluck, and know it not,
And all their botany is Latin names.
The old men studied magic in the flowers,
And human fortunes in astronomy,
And an omnipotence in chemistry,
Preferring things to names, for these were men,
Were unitarians of the united world,
And, wheresoever their clear eye-beams fell,
They caught the footsteps of the SAME. Our eyes
Are armed, but we are strangers to the stars,
And strangers to the mystic beast and bird,
And strangers to the plant and to the mine.
The injured elements say, "Not in us;"
And night and day, ocean and continent,
Fire, plant and mineral say, "Not in us;"
And haughtily return us stare for stare.
For we invade them impiously for gain;
We devastate them unreligiously,
And coldly ask their pottage, not their love.
Therefore they shove us from them, yield to us
Only what to our griping toil is due;
But the sweet affluence of love and song,

The rich results of the divine consents
Of man and earth, of world beloved and lover,
The nectar and ambrosia, are withheld;
And in the midst of spoils and slaves, we thieves
And pirates of the universe, shut out
Daily to a more thin and outward rind,
Turn pale and starve. Therefore, to our sick eyes,
The stunted trees look sick, the summer short,
Clouds shade the sun, which will not tan our hay,
And nothing thrives to reach its natural term;
And life, shorn of its venerable length,
Even at its greatest space is a defeat,
And dies in anger that it was a dupe;
And, in its highest noon and wantonness,
Is early frugal, like a beggar's child;
Even in the hot pursuit of the best aims
And prizes of ambition, checks its hand,
Like Alpine cataracts frozen as they leaped,
Chilled with a miserly comparison
Of the toy's purchase with the length of life.

Concord Hymn

Sung at the completion of the Battle Monument, July 4, 1837

By the rude bridge that arched the flood,
    Their flag to April's breeze unfurled,
Here once the embattled farmers stood
    And fired the shot heard round the world.

The foe long since in silence slept;
    Alike the conqueror silent sleeps;
And Time the ruined bridge has swept
    Down the dark stream which seaward creeps.

On this green bank, by this soft stream,
    We set to-day a votive stone;
That memory may their deed redeem,
    When, like our sires, our sons are gone.

Spirit, that made those heroes dare
    To die, and leave their children free,
Bid Time and Nature gently spare
    The shaft we raise to them and thee.

Brahma

If the red slayer think he slays,
  Or if the slain think he is slain,
They know not well the subtle ways
  I keep, and pass, and turn again.

Far or forgot to me is near;
  Shadow and sunlight are the same;
The vanished gods to me appear;
  And one to me are shame and fame.

They reckon ill who leave me out;
  When me they fly, I am the wings;
I am the doubter and the doubt,
  And I the hymn the Brahmin sings.

The strong gods pine for my abode,
  And pine in vain the sacred Seven;
But thou, meek lover of the good!
  Find me, and turn thy back on heaven.

Nemesis

Already blushes on thy cheek
The bosom thought which thou must speak;
The bird, how far it haply roam
By cloud or isle, is flying home;
The maiden fears, and fearing runs
Into the charmed snare she shuns;
And every man, in love or pride,
Of his fate is never wide.

Will a woman's fan the ocean smooth?
Or prayers the stony Parcæ soothe,
Or coax the thunder from its mark?
Or tapers light the chaos dark?
In spite of Virtue and the Muse,
Nemesis will have her dues,
And all our struggles and our toils
Tighter wind the giant coils.

Two Rivers

Thy summer voice, Musketaquit,
Repeats the music of the rain;
But sweeter rivers pulsing flit
Through thee, as thou through Concord Plain.

Thou in thy narrow banks art pent:
The stream I love unbounded goes
Through flood and sea and firmament;
Through light, through life, it forward flows.

I see the inundation sweet,
I hear the spending of the stream
Through years, through men, through Nature fleet,
Through love and thought, through power and dream.

Musketaquit, a goblin strong,
Of shard and flint makes jewels gay;
They lose their grief who hear his song,
And where he winds is the day of day.

So forth and brighter fares my stream, —
Who drink it shall not thirst again;
No darkness stains its equal gleam,
And ages drop in it like rain.

Waldeinsamkeit

I do not count the hours I spend
In wandering by the sea;
The forest is my loyal friend,
Like God it useth me.

In plains that room for shadows make
Of skirting hills to lie,
Bound in by streams which give and take
Their colors from the sky;

Or on the mountain-crest sublime,
Or down the oaken glade,
O what have I to do with time?
For this the day was made.

Cities of mortals woe-begone
Fantastic care derides,
But in the serious landscape lone
Stern benefit abides.

Sheen will tarnish, honey cloy,
And merry is only a mask of sad,
But, sober on a fund of joy,
The woods at heart are glad.

There the great Planter plants
Of fruitful worlds the grain,
And with a million spells enchants
The souls that walk in pain.

Still on the seeds of all he made
The rose of beauty burns;
Through times that wear and forms that fade,
Immortal youth returns.

The black ducks mounting from the lake,
The pigeon in the pines,
The bittern's boom, a desert make
Which no false art refines.

Down in yon watery nook,
Where bearded mists divide,
The gray old gods whom Chaos knew,
The sires of Nature, hide.

Aloft, in secret veins of air,
Blows the sweet breath of song,
O, few to scale those uplands dare,
Though they to all belong!

See thou bring not to field or stone
The fancies found in books;
Leave authors' eyes, and fetch your own,
To brave the landscape's looks.

Oblivion here thy wisdom is,
Thy thrift, the sleep of cares;
For a proud idleness like this
Crowns all thy mean affairs.

Terminus

It is time to be old,
To take in sail: —
The god of bounds,
Who sets to seas a shore,
Came to me in his fatal rounds,
And said: "No more!
No farther shoot
Thy broad ambitious branches, and thy root.
Fancy departs; no more invent;
Contract thy firmament
To compass of a tent.
There's not enough for this and that,
Make thy option which of two;
Economize the failing river,
Not the less revere the Giver,
Leave the many and hold the few.
Timely wise accept the terms,
Soften the fall with wary foot;
A little while
Still plan and smile,
And, — fault of novel germs, —
Mature the unfallen fruit.
Curse, if thou wilt, thy sires,
Bad husbands of their fires,
Who, when they gave thee breath,
Failed to bequeath
The needful sinew stark as once,
The Baresark marrow to thy bones,
But left a legacy of ebbing veins,
Inconstant heat and nerveless reins, —
Amid the Muses, left thee deaf and dumb,
Amid the gladiators, halt and numb."

As the bird trims her to the gale,
I trim myself to the storm of time,
I man the rudder, reef the sail,
Obey the voice at eve obeyed at prime:
"Lowly faithful, banish fear,
Right onward drive unharmed;
The port, well worth the cruise, is near,
And every wave is charmed."

Compensation

The wings of Time are black and white,
Pied with morning and with night.
Mountain tall and ocean deep
Trembling balance duly keep.
In changing moon and tidal wave
Glows the feud of Want and Have.
Gauge of more and less through space,
Electric star or pencil plays,
The lonely Earth amid the balls
That hurry through the eternal halls,
A makeweight flying to the void,
Supplemental asteroid,
Or compensatory spark,
Shoots across the neutral Dark.

Man's the elm, and Wealth the vine;
Stanch and strong the tendrils twine:
Though the frail ringlets thee deceive,
None from its stock that vine can reave.
Fear not, then, thou child infirm,
There's no god dare wrong a worm;
Laurel crowns cleave to deserts,
And power to him who power exerts.
Hast not thy share? On winged feet,
Lo! it rushes thee to meet;
And all that Nature made thy own,
Floating in air or pent in stone,
Will rive the hills and swim the sea,
And, like thy shadow, follow thee.

Song of Seyd Nimetollah of Kuhistan

Spin the ball! I reel, I burn,
Nor head from foot can I discern,
Nor my heart from love of mine,
Nor the wine-cup from the wine.
All my doing, all my leaving,
Reaches not to my perceiving;
Lost in whirling spheres I rove,
And know only that I love.

I am seeker of the stone,
Living gem of Solomon;
From the shore of souls arrived,
In the sea of sense I dived;
But what is land, or what is wave,
To me who only jewels crave?
Love is the air-fed fire intense,
And my heart the frankincense;
As the rich aloe flames, I glow,
Yet the censer cannot know.
I'm all-knowing, yet unknowing;
Stand not, pause not, in my going.

Ask not me, as Muftis can,
To recite the Alcoran;
Well I love the meaning sweet, —
I tread the book beneath my feet.

Lo! the God's love blazes higher,
Till all difference expire.
What are Moslems? what are Giaours?
All are Love's, and all are ours.
I embrace the true believers,
But I reck not of deceivers.
Firm to Heaven my bosom clings,
Heedless of inferior things;
Down on earth there, underfoot,
What men chatter know I not.

Days

Daughters of Time, the hypocritic Days,
Muffled and dumb like barefoot dervishes,
And marching single in an endless file,
Bring diadems and fagots in their hands.
To each they offer gifts after his will,
Bread, kingdoms, stars, and sky that holds them all.
I, in my pleached garden, watched the pomp,
Forgot my morning wishes, hastily
Took a few herbs and apples, and the Day
Turned and departed silent. I, too late,
Under her solemn fillet saw the scorn.

HENRY WADSWORTH LONGFELLOW
1807–1882

Hymn to the Night

I heard the trailing garments of the Night
  Sweep through her marble halls!
I saw her sable skirts all fringed with light
  From the celestial walls!

I felt her presence, by its spell of might,
  Stoop o'er me from above;
The calm, majestic presence of the Night,
  As of the one I love.

I heard the sounds of sorrow and delight,
  The manifold, soft chimes,
That fill the haunted chambers of the Night,
  Like some old poet's rhymes.

From the cool cisterns of the midnight air
  My spirit drank repose;
The fountain of perpetual peace flows there, —
  From those deep cisterns flows.

O holy Night! from thee I learn to bear
  What man has borne before!
Thou layest thy finger on the lips of Care,
  And they complain no more.

Peace! Peace! Orestes-like I breathe this prayer!
  Descend with broad-winged flight,
The welcome, the thrice-prayed for, the most fair,
  The best-loved Night!

The Day Is Done

The day is done, and the darkness
  Falls from the wings of Night,
As a feather is wafted downward
  From an eagle in his flight.

I see the lights of the village
    Gleam through the rain and the mist,
And a feeling of sadness comes o'er me
    That my soul cannot resist:

A feeling of sadness and longing,
    That is not akin to pain,
And resembles sorrow only
    As the mist resembles the rain.

Come, read to me some poem,
    Some simple and heartfelt lay,
That shall soothe this restless feeling,
    And banish the thoughts of day.

Not from the grand old masters,
    Not from the bards sublime,
Whose distant footsteps echo
    Through the corridors of Time.

For, like strains of martial music,
    Their mighty thoughts suggest
Life's endless toil and endeavor;
    And to-night I long for rest.

Read from some humbler poet,
    Whose songs gushed from his heart,
As showers from the clouds of summer,
    Or tears from the eyelids start;

Who, through long days of labor,
    And nights devoid of ease,
Still heard in his soul the music
    Of wonderful melodies.

Such songs have power to quiet
    The restless pulse of care,
And come like the benediction
    That follows after prayer.

Then read from the treasured volume
    The poem of thy choice,
And lend to the rhyme of the poet
    The beauty of thy voice.

And the night shall be filled with music,
  And the cares, that infest the day,
Shall fold their tents, like the Arabs,
  And as silently steal away.

The Fire of Drift-wood

We sat within the farm-house old,
  Whose windows, looking o'er the bay,
Gave to the sea-breeze damp and cold,
  An easy entrance, night and day.

Not far away we saw the port,
  The strange, old-fashioned, silent town,
The lighthouse, the dismantled fort,
  The wooden houses, quaint and brown.

We sat and talked until the night,
  Descending, filled the little room;
Our faces faded from the sight,
  Our voices only broke the gloom.

We spake of many a vanished scene,
  Of what we once had thought and said,
Of what had been, and might have been,
  And who was changed, and who was dead;

And all that fills the hearts of friends,
  When first they feel, with secret pain,
Their lives thenceforth have separate ends,
  And never can be one again;

The first slight swerving of the heart,
  That words are powerless to express,
And leave it still unsaid in part,
  Or say it in too great excess.

The very tones in which we spake
  Had something strange, I could but mark;
The leaves of memory seemed to make
  A mournful rustling in the dark.

Oft died the words upon our lips,
   As suddenly, from out the fire
Built of the wreck of stranded ships,
   The flames would leap and then expire.

And, as their splendor flashed and failed,
   We thought of wrecks upon the main,
Of ships dismasted, that were hailed
   And sent no answer back again.

The windows, rattling in their frames,
   The ocean, roaring up the beach,
The gusty blast, the bickering flames,
   All mingled vaguely in our speech;

Until they made themselves a part
   Of fancies floating through the brain,
The long-lost ventures of the heart,
   That send no answers back again.

O flames that glowed! O hearts that yearned!
   They were indeed too much akin,
The drift-wood fire without that burned,
   The thoughts that burned and glowed within.

from The Song of Hiawatha

Introduction

Should you ask me, whence these stories?
Whence these legends and traditions,
With the odors of the forest,
With the dew and damp of meadows,
With the curling smoke of wigwams,
With the rushing of great rivers,
With their frequent repetitions,
And their wild reverberations,
As of thunder in the mountains?
   I should answer, I should tell you,
"From the forests and the prairies,
From the great lakes of the Northland,
From the land of the Ojibways,

88

From the land of the Dacotahs,
From the mountains, moors, and fen-lands
Where the heron, the Shuh-shuh-gah,
Feeds among the reeds and rushes.
I repeat them as I heard them
From the lips of Nawadaha,
The musician, the sweet singer."
    Should you ask where Nawadaha
Found these songs so wild and wayward,
Found these legends and traditions,
I should answer, I should tell you,
"In the bird's-nests of the forest,
In the lodges of the beaver,
In the hoof-prints of the bison,
In the eyry of the eagle!
    "All the wild-fowl sang them to him,
In the moorlands and the fen-lands,
In the melancholy marshes;
Chetowaik, the plover, sang them,
Mahng, the loon, the wild-goose, Wawa,
The blue heron, the Shuh-shuh-gah,
And the grouse, the Mushkodasa!"
    If still further you should ask me,
Saying, "Who was Nawadaha?
Tell us of this Nawadaha,"
I should answer your inquiries
Straightway in such words as follow.
    "In the vale of Tawasentha,
In the green and silent valley,
By the pleasant water-courses,
Dwelt the singer Nawadaha.
Round about the Indian village
Spread the meadows and the corn-fields,
And beyond them stood the forest,
Stood the groves of singing pine-trees,
Green in Summer, white in Winter,
Ever sighing, ever singing.
    "And the pleasant water-courses,
You could trace them through the valley,
By the rushing in the Spring-time,
By the alders in the Summer,
By the white fog in the Autumn,
By the black line in the Winter;

And beside them dwelt the singer,
In the vale of Tawasentha,
In the green and silent valley.
   "There he sang of Hiawatha,
Sang the Song of Hiawatha,
Sang his wondrous birth and being,
How he prayed and how he fasted,
How he lived, and toiled, and suffered,
That the tribes of men might prosper,
That he might advance his people!"
   Ye who love the haunts of Nature,
Love the sunshine of the meadow,
Love the shadow of the forest,
Love the wind among the branches,
And the rain-shower and the snow-storm,
And the rushing of great rivers
Through their palisades of pine-trees,
And the thunder in the mountains,
Whose innumerable echoes
Flap like eagles in their eyries; —
Listen to these wild traditions,
To this Song of Hiawatha!
   Ye who love a nation's legends,
Love the ballads of a people,
That like voices from afar off
Call to us to pause and listen,
Speak in tones so plain and childlike,
Scarcely can the ear distinguish
Whether they are sung or spoken; —
Listen to this Indian Legend,
To this Song of Hiawatha!
   Ye whose hearts are fresh and simple,
Who have faith in God and Nature,
Who believe that in all ages
Every human heart is human,
That in even savage bosoms
There are longings, yearnings, strivings
For the good they comprehend not,
That the feeble hands and helpless,
Groping blindly in the darkness,
Touch God's right hand in that darkness
And are lifted up and strengthened; —
Listen to this simple story,

To this Song of Hiawatha!
   Ye, who sometimes, in your rambles
Through the green lanes of the country,
Where the tangled barberry-bushes
Hang their tufts of crimson berries
Over stone walls gray with mosses,
Pause by some neglected graveyard,
For a while to muse, and ponder
On a half-effaced inscription
Written with little skill of song-craft,
Homely phrases, but each letter
Full of hope and yet of heart-break,
Full of all the tender pathos
Of the Here and the Hereafter; —
Stay and read this rude inscription,
Read this Song of Hiawatha!

The Jewish Cemetery at Newport

How strange it seems! These Hebrews in their graves,
   Close by the street of this fair seaport town,
Silent beside the never-silent waves,
   At rest in all this moving up and down!

The trees are white with dust, that o'er their sleep
   Wave their broad curtains in the south-wind's breath,
While underneath these leafy tents they keep
   The long, mysterious Exodus of Death.

And these sepulchral stones, so old and brown,
   That pave with level flags their burial-place,
Seem like the tablets of the Law, thrown down
   And broken by Moses at the mountain's base.

The very names recorded here are strange,
   Of foreign accent, and of different climes;
Alvares and Rivera interchange
   With Abraham and Jacob of old times.

"Blessed be God! for he created Death!"
   The mourners said, "and Death is rest and peace;"
Then added, in the certainty of faith,
   "And giveth Life that nevermore shall cease."

Closed are the portals of their Synagogue,
  No Psalms of David now the silence break,
No Rabbi reads the ancient Decalogue
  In the grand dialect the Prophets spake.

Gone are the living, but the dead remain,
  And not neglected; for a hand unseen,
Scattering its bounty, like a summer rain,
  Still keeps their graves and their remembrance green.

How came they here? What burst of Christian hate,
  What persecution, merciless and blind,
Drove o'er the sea — that desert desolate —
  These Ishmaels and Hagars of mankind?

They lived in narrow streets and lanes obscure,
  Ghetto and Judenstrass, in mirk and mire;
Taught in the school of patience to endure
  The life of anguish and the death of fire.

All their lives long, with the unleavened bread
  And bitter herbs of exile and its fears,
The wasting famine of the heart they fed,
  And slaked its thirst with marah of their tears.

Anathema maranatha! was the cry
  That rang from town to town, from street to street;
At every gate the accursed Mordecai
  Was mocked and jeered, and spurned by Christian feet.

Pride and humiliation hand in hand
  Walked with them through the world where'er they went;
Trampled and beaten were they as the sand,
  And yet unshaken as the continent.

For in the background figures vague and vast
  Of patriarchs and of prophets rose sublime,
And all the great traditions of the Past
  They saw reflected in the coming time.

And thus for ever with reverted look
  The mystic volume of the world they read,
Spelling it backward, like a Hebrew book,
  Till life became a Legend of the Dead.

But ah! what once has been shall be no more!
   The groaning earth in travail and in pain
Brings forth its races, but does not restore,
   And the dead nations never rise again.

My Lost Youth

Often I think of the beautiful town
   That is seated by the sea;
Often in thought go up and down
The pleasant streets of that dear old town,
   And my youth comes back to me.
     And a verse of a Lapland song
     Is haunting my memory still:
"A boy's will is the wind's will,
And the thoughts of youth are long, long thoughts."

I can see the shadowy lines of its trees,
   And catch, in sudden gleams,
The sheen of the far-surrounding seas,
And islands that were the Hesperides
   Of all my boyish dreams.
     And the burden of that old song,
     It murmurs and whispers still:
"A boy's will is the wind's will,
And the thoughts of youth are long, long thoughts."

I remember the black wharves and the slips,
   And the sea-tides tossing free;
And Spanish sailors with bearded lips,
And the beauty and mystery of the ships,
   And the magic of the sea.
     And the voice of that wayward song
     Is singing and saying still:
"A boy's will is the wind's will,
And the thoughts of youth are long, long thoughts."

I remember the bulwarks by the shore,
   And the fort upon the hill;
The sunrise gun, with its hollow roar,
The drum-beat repeated o'er and o'er,
   And the bugle wild and shrill.

And the music of that old song
    Throbs in my memory still:
"A boy's will is the wind's will,
And the thoughts of youth are long, long thoughts."

I remember the sea-fight far away,
    How it thundered o'er the tide!
And the dead captains, as they lay
In their graves, o'erlooking the tranquil bay,
    Where they in battle died.
        And the sound of that mournful song
        Goes through me with a thrill:
"A boy's will is the wind's will,
And the thoughts of youth are long, long thoughts."

I can see the breezy dome of groves,
    The shadows of Deering's Woods;
And the friendships old and the early loves
Come back with a Sabbath sound, as of doves
    In quiet neighborhoods.
        And the verse of that sweet old song,
        It flutters and murmurs still:
"A boy's will is the wind's will,
And the thoughts of youth are long, long thoughts."

I remember the gleams and glooms that dart
    Across the school-boy's brain;
The song and the silence in the heart,
That in part are prophecies, and in part
    Are longings wild and vain.
        And the voice of that fitful song
        Sings on, and is never still:
"A boy's will is the wind's will,
And the thoughts of youth are long, long thoughts."

There are things of which I may not speak;
    There are dreams that cannot die;
There are thoughts that make the strong heart weak,
And bring a pallor into the cheek,
    And a mist before the eye.
        And the words of that fatal song
        Come over me like a chill:
"A boy's will is the wind's will,   .
And the thoughts of youth are long, long thoughts."

Strange to me now are the forms I meet
  When I visit the dear old town;
But the native air is pure and sweet,
And the trees that o'ershadow each well-known street,
  As they balance up and down,
    Are singing the beautiful song,
    Are sighing and whispering still:
"A boy's will is the wind's will,
And the thoughts of youth are long, long thoughts."

And Deering's Woods are fresh and fair,
  And with joy that is almost pain
My heart goes back to wander there,
And among the dreams of the days that were,
  I find my lost youth again.
    And the strange and beautiful song,
    The groves are repeating it still:
"A boy's will is the wind's will,
And the thoughts of youth are long, long thoughts."

Snow-Flakes

Out of the bosom of the Air,
  Out of the cloud-folds of her garments shaken,
Over the woodlands brown and bare,
  Over the harvest-fields forsaken,
    Silent, and soft, and slow
    Descends the snow.

Even as our cloudy fancies take
  Suddenly shape in some divine expression,
Even as the troubled heart doth make
  In the white countenance confession,
    The troubled sky reveals
    The grief it feels.

This is the poem of the air,
  Slowly in silent syllables recorded;
This is the secret of despair,
  Long in its cloudy bosom hoarded,
    Now whispered and revealed
    To wood and field.

Aftermath

When the summer fields are mown,
When the birds are fledged and flown,
    And the dry leaves strew the path;
With the falling of the snow,
With the cawing of the crow,
Once again the fields we mow
    And gather in the aftermath.

Not the sweet, new grass with flowers
Is this harvesting of ours;
    Not the upland clover bloom;
But the rowen mixed with weeds,
Tangled tufts from marsh and meads,
Where the poppy drops its seeds
    In the silence and the gloom.

Chaucer

An old man in a lodge within a park;
    The chamber walls depicted all around
    With portraitures of huntsman, hawk, and hound,
    And the hurt deer. He listeneth to the lark.
Whose song comes with the sunshine through the dark
    Of painted glass in leaden lattice bound;
    He listeneth and he laugheth at the sound,
    Then writeth in a book like any clerk.
He is the poet of the dawn, who wrote
    The Canterbury Tales, and his old age
    Made beautiful with song; and as I read
I hear the crowing cock, I hear the note
    Of lark and linnet, and from every page
    Rise odors of ploughed field or flowery mead.

The Tide Rises, the Tide Falls

The tide rises, the tide falls,
    The twilight darkens, the curlew calls;
Along the sea-sands damp and brown
The traveller hastens toward the town,
    And the tide rises, the tide falls.

Darkness settles on roofs and walls,
But the sea, the sea in the darkness calls;
The little waves, with their soft, white hands,
Efface the footprints in the sands,
    And the tide rises, the tide falls.

The morning breaks; the steeds in their stalls
Stamp and neigh, as the hostler calls;
The day returns, but nevermore
Returns the traveller to the shore,
    And the tide rises, the tide falls.

The Cross of Snow

In the long, sleepless watches of the night,
  A gentle face — the face of one long dead —
  Looks at me from the wall, where round its head
  The night-lamp casts a halo of pale light.
Here in this room she died; and soul more white
  Never through martyrdom of fire was led
  To its repose; nor can in books be read
  The legend of a life more benedight.
There is a mountain in the distant West
  That, sun-defying, in its deep ravines
  Displays a cross of snow upon its side.
Such is the cross I wear upon my breast
  These eighteen years, through all the changing scenes
  And seasons, changeless since the day she died.

JOHN GREENLEAF WHITTIER
1807-1892

Ichabod

So fallen! so lost! the light withdrawn
    Which once he wore!
The glory from his gray hairs gone
    Forevermore!

Revile him not, the Tempter hath
    A snare for all;
And pitying tears, not scorn and wrath,
    Befit his fall!

Oh, dumb be passion's stormy rage,
    When he who might
Have lighted up and led his age,
    Falls back in night.

Scorn! would the angels laugh, to mark
    A bright soul driven,
Fiend-goaded, down the endless dark,
    From hope and heaven!

Let not the land once proud of him
    Insult him now,
Nor brand with deeper shame his dim,
    Dishonored brow.

But let its humbled sons, instead,
    From sea to lake,
A long lament, as for the dead,
    ·In sadness make.

Of all we loved and honored, naught
    Save power remains;
A fallen angel's pride of thought,
    Still strong in chains.

All else is gone; from those great eyes
    The soul has fled:
When faith is lost, when honor dies,
    The man is dead!

Then, pay the reverence of old days
    To his dead fame;
Walk backward, with averted gaze,
    And hide the shame!

To My Old Schoolmaster

An epistle not after the manner of Horace

Old friend, kind friend! lightly down
Drop time's snow-flakes on thy crown!
Never be thy shadow less,
Never fail thy cheerfulness;

Care, that kills the cat, may plough
Wrinkles in the miser's brow,
Deepen envy's spiteful frown,
Draw the mouths of bigots down,
Plague ambition's dream, and sit
Heavy on the hypocrite,
Haunt the rich man's door, and ride
In the gilded coach of pride; —
Let the fiend pass! — what can he
Find to do with such as thee?
Seldom comes that evil guest
Where the conscience lies at rest,
And brown health and quiet wit
Smiling on the threshold sit.

I, the urchin unto whom,
In that smoked and dingy room,
Where the district gave thee rule
O'er its ragged winter school,
Thou didst teach the mysteries
Of those weary A B C's, —
Where, to fill the every pause
Of thy wise and learned saws,
Through the cracked and crazy wall
Came the cradle-rock and squall,
And the goodman's voice, at strife
With his shrill and tipsy wife, —
Luring us by stories old,
With a comic unction told,
More than by the eloquence
Of terse birchen arguments
(Doubtful gain, I fear), to look
With complacence on a book! —
Where the genial pedagogue
Half forgot his rogues to flog,
Citing tale or apologue,
Wise and merry in its drift
As was Phædrus' twofold gift,
Had the little rebels known it,
Risum et prudentiam monet!
I, — the man of middle years,
In whose sable locks appears
Many a warning fleck of gray, —

Looking back to that far day,
And thy primal lessons, feel
Grateful smiles my lips unseal,
As, remembering thee, I blend
Olden teacher, present friend,
Wise with antiquarian search,
In the scrolls of State and Church:
Named on history's title-page,
Parish-clerk and justice sage;
For the ferule's wholesome awe
Wielding now the sword of law.

Threshing Time's neglected sheaves,
Gathering up the scattered leaves
Which the wrinkled sibyl cast
Careless from her as she passed, —
Twofold citizen art thou,
Freeman of the past and now.
He who bore thy name of old
Midway in the heavens did hold
Over Gibeon moon and sun;
Thou hast bidden them backward run;
Of to-day the present ray
Flinging over yesterday!

Let the busy ones deride
What I deem of right thy pride:
Let the fools their treadmills grind,
Look not forward nor behind,
Shuffle in and wriggle out,
Veer with every breeze about,
Turning like a windmill sail,
Or a dog that seeks his tail;
Let them laugh to see thee fast
Tabernacled in the Past,
Working out with eye and lip
Riddles of old penmanship,
Patient as Belzoni there
Sorting out, with loving care,
Mummies of dead questions stripped
From their sevenfold manuscript!

Dabbling, in their noisy way,
In the puddles of to-day,
Little know they of that vast
Solemn ocean of the past,
On whose margin, wreck-bespread,
Thou art walking with the dead,
Questioning the stranded years,
Waking smiles by turns, and tears,
As thou callest up again
Shapes the dust has long o'erlain, —
Fair-haired woman, bearded man,
Cavalier and Puritan;
In an age whose eager view
Seeks but present things, and new,
Mad for party, sect and gold,
Teaching reverence for the old.

On that shore, with fowler's tact,
Coolly bagging fact on fact,
Naught amiss to thee can float,
Tale, or song, or anecdote;
Village gossip, centuries old,
Scandals by our grandams told,
What the pilgrim's table spread,
Where he lived, and whom he wed,
Long-drawn bill of wine and beer
For his ordination cheer,
Or the flip that wellnigh made
Glad his funeral cavalcade;
Weary prose, and poet's lines,
Flavored by their age, like wines,
Eulogistic of some quaint,
Doubtful, Puritanic saint;
Lays that quickened husking jigs,
Jests that shook grave periwigs,
When the parson had his jokes
And his glass, like other folks;
Sermons that, for mortal hours,
Taxed our fathers' vital powers,
As the long nineteenthlies poured
Downward from the sounding-board,
And, for fire of Pentecost,
Touched their beards December's frost.

Time is hastening on, and we
What our fathers are shall be, —
Shadow-shapes of memory!
Joined to that vast multitude
Where the great are but the good,
And the mind of strength shall prove
Weaker than the heart of love;
Pride of graybeard wisdom less
Than the infant's guilelessness,
And his song of sorrow more
Than the crown the Psalmist wore!
Who shall then, with pious zeal,
At our moss-grown thresholds kneel,
From a stained and stony page
Reading to a careless age,
With a patient eye like thine,
Prosing tale and limping line,
Names and words the hoary rime
Of the Past has made sublime?
Who shall work for us as well
The antiquarian's miracle?
Who to seeming life recall
Teacher grave and pupil small?
Who shall give to thee and me
Freeholds in futurity?

Well, whatever lot be mine,
Long and happy days be thine,
Ere thy full and honored age
Dates of time its latest page!
Squire for master, State for school,
Wisely lenient, live and rule;
Over grown-up knave and rogue
Play the watchful pedagogue;
Or, while pleasure smiles on duty,
At the call of youth and beauty,
Speak for them the spell of law
Which shall bar and bolt withdraw,
And the flaming sword remove
From the Paradise of Love.
Still, with undimmed eyesight, pore
Ancient tome and record o'er;
Still thy week-day lyrics croon,

Pitch in church the Sunday tune,
Showing something, in thy part,
Of the old Puritanic art,
Singer after Sternhold's heart!
In thy pew, for many a year,
Homilies from Oldbug hear,
Who to wit like that of South,
And the Syrian's golden mouth,
Doth the homely pathos add
Which the pilgrim preachers had;
Breaking, like a child at play,
Gilded idols of the day,
Cant of knave and pomp of fool
Tossing with his ridicule,
Yet, in earnest or in jest,
Ever keeping truth abreast.
And, when thou art called, at last,
To thy townsmen of the past,
Not as stranger shalt thou come;
Thou shalt find thyself at home
With the little and the big,
Woollen cap and periwig,
Madam in her high-laced ruff,
Goody in her home-made stuff, —
Wise and simple, rich and poor,
Thou hast known them all before!

Skipper Ireson's Ride

Of all the rides since the birth of time,
Told in story or sung in rhyme, —
On Apuleius's Golden Ass,
Or one-eyed Calender's horse of brass,
Witch astride of a human back,
Islam's prophet on Al-Borák, —
The strangest ride that ever was sped
Was Ireson's, out from Marblehead!
  Old Floyd Ireson, for his hard heart,
    Tarred and feathered and carried in a cart
    By the women of Marblehead!

Body of turkey, head of owl,
Wings a-droop like a rained-on fowl,
Feathered and ruffled in every part,
Skipper Ireson stood in the cart.
Scores of women, old and young,
Strong of muscle, and glib of tongue,
Pushed and pulled up the rocky lane,
Shouting and singing the shrill refrain:
  "Here 's Flud Oirson, fur his horrd horrt,
    Torr'd an' futherr'd an' corr'd in a corrt
      By the women o' Morble'ead!"

Wrinkled scolds with hands on hips,
Girls in bloom of cheek and lips,
Wild-eyed, free-limbed, such as chase
Bacchus round some antique vase,
Brief of skirt, with ankles bare,
Loose of kerchief and loose of hair,
With conch-shells blowing and fish-horns' twang,
Over and over the Mænads sang:
  "Here's Flud Oirson, fur his horrd horrt,
    Torr'd an' futherr'd an' corr'd in a corrt
      By the women o' Morble'ead!"

Small pity for him! — He sailed away
From a leaking ship in Chaleur Bay, —
Sailed away from a sinking wreck,
With his own town's-people on her deck!
"Lay by! lay by!" they called to him.
Back he answered, "Sink or swim!
Brag of your catch of fish again!"
And off he sailed through the fog and rain!
  Old Floyd Ireson, for his hard heart,
    Tarred and feathered and carried in a cart
      By the women of Marblehead!

Fathoms deep in dark Chaleur
That wreck shall lie forevermore.
Mother and sister, wife and maid,
Looked from the rocks of Marblehead
Over the moaning and rainy sea, —
Looked for the coming that might not be!

What did the winds and the sea-birds say
Of the cruel captain who sailed away? —
  Old Floyd Ireson, for his hard heart,
  Tarred and feathered and carried in a cart
    By the women of Marblehead!

Through the street, on either side,
Up flew windows, doors swung wide;
Sharp-tongued spinsters, old wives gray,
Treble lent the fish-horn's bray.
Sea-worn grandsires, cripple-bound,
Hulks of old sailors run aground,
Shook head, and fist, and hat, and cane,
And cracked with curses the hoarse refrain:
  "Here's Flud Oirson, fur his horrd horrt,
  Torr'd an' futherr'd an' corr'd in a corrt
    By the women o' Morble'ead!"

Sweetly along the Salem road
Bloom of orchard and lilac showed.
Little the wicked skipper knew
Of the fields so green and the sky so blue.
Riding there in his sorry trim,
Like an Indian idol glum and grim,
Scarcely he seemed the sound to hear
Of voices shouting, far and near:
  "Here's Flud Oirson, fur his horrd horrt,
  Torr'd an' futherr'd an' corr'd in a corrt
    By the women o' Morble'ead!"

"Hear me, neighbors!" at last he cried, —
"What to me is this noisy ride?
What is the shame that clothes the skin
To the nameless horror that lives within?
Waking or sleeping, I see a wreck,
And hear a cry from a reeling deck!
Hate me and curse me, — I only dread
The hand of God and the face of the dead!"
  Said old Floyd Ireson, for his hard heart,
  Tarred and feathered and carried in a cart
    By the women of Marblehead!

Then the wife of the skipper lost at sea
Said, "God has touched him! why should we!"
Said an old wife mourning her only son,
"Cut the rogue's tether and let him run!"
So with soft relentings and rude excuse,
Half scorn, half pity, they cut him loose,
And gave him a cloak to hide him in,
And left him alone with his shame and sin.
  Poor Floyd Ireson, for his hard heart,
  Tarred and feathered and carried in a cart
  By the women of Marblehead!

Telling the Bees

Here is the place; right over the hill
  Runs the path I took;
You can see the gap in the old wall still,
  And the stepping-stones in the shallow brook.

There is the house, with the gate red-barred,
  And the poplars tall;
And the barn's brown length, and the cattle-yard,
  And the white horns tossing above the wall.

There are the beehives ranged in the sun;
  And down by the brink
Of the brook are her poor flowers, weed-o'errun,
  Pansy and daffodil, rose and pink.

A year has gone, as the tortoise goes,
  Heavy and slow;
And the same rose blows, and the same sun glows,
  And the same brook sings of a year ago.

There's the same sweet clover-smell in the breeze;
  And the June sun warm
Tangles his wings of fire in the trees,
  Setting, as then, over Fernside farm.

I mind me how with a lover's care
  From my Sunday coat
I brushed off the burrs, and smoothed my hair,
  And cooled at the brookside my brow and throat.

Since we parted, a month had passed, —
    To love, a year;
Down through the beeches I looked at last
    On the little red gate and the well-sweep near.

I can see it all now, — the slantwise rain
    Of light through the leaves,
The sundown's blaze on her window-pane,
    The bloom of her roses under the eaves.

Just the same as a month before, —
    The house and the trees,
The barn's brown gable, the vine by the door, —
    Nothing changed but the hives of bees.

Before them, under the garden wall,
    Forward and back,
Went drearily singing the chore-girl small,
    Draping each hive with a shred of black.

Trembling, I listened: the summer sun
    Had the chill of snow;
For I knew she was telling the bees of one
    Gone on the journey we all must go!

Then I said to myself, "My Mary weeps
    For the dead to-day:
Haply her blind old grandsire sleeps
    The fret and the pain of his age away."

But her dog whined low; on the doorway sill,
    With his cane to his chin,
The old man sat; and the chore-girl still
    Sang to the bees stealing out and in.

And the song she was singing ever since
    In my ear sounds on: —
"Stay at home, pretty bees, fly not hence!
    Mistress Mary is dead and gone!"

My Playmate

The pines were dark on Ramoth hill,
　Their song was soft and low;
The blossoms in the sweet May wind
　Were falling like the snow.

The blossoms drifted at our feet,
　The orchard birds sang clear;
The sweetest and the saddest day
　It seemed of all the year.

For, more to me than birds or flowers,
　My playmate left her home,
And took with her the laughing spring,
　The music and the bloom.

She kissed the lips of kith and kin,
　She laid her hand in mine:
What more could ask the bashful boy
　Who fed her father's kine?

She left us in the bloom of May:
　The constant years told o'er
Their seasons with as sweet May morns,
　But she came back no more.

I walk, with noiseless feet, the round
　Of uneventful years;
Still o'er and o'er I sow the spring
　And reap the autumn ears.

She lives where all the golden year
　Her summer roses blow;
The dusky children of the sun
　Before her come and go.

There haply with her jewelled hands
　She smooths her silken gown, —
No more the homespun lap wherein
　I shook the walnuts down.

The wild grapes wait us by the brook,
　The brown nuts on the hill,
And still the May-day flowers make sweet
　The woods of Follymill.

The lilies blossom in the pond,
    The bird builds in the tree,
The dark pines sing on Ramoth hill
    The slow song of the sea.

I wonder if she thinks of them,
    And how the old time seems, —
If ever the pines of Ramoth wood
    Are sounding in her dreams.

I see her face, I hear her voice;
    Does she remember mine?
And what to her is now the boy
    Who fed her father's kine?

What cares she that the orioles build
    For other eyes than ours, —
That other hands with nuts are filled,
    And other laps with flowers?

O playmate in the golden time!
    Our mossy seat is green,
Its fringing violets blossom yet,
    The old trees o'er it lean.

The winds so sweet with birch and fern
    A sweeter memory blow;
And there in spring the veeries sing
    The song of long ago.

And still the pines of Ramoth wood
    Are moaning like the sea, —
The moaning of the sea of change
    Between myself and thee!

Barbara Frietchie

Up from the meadows rich with corn,
Clear in the cool September morn,

The clustered spires of Frederick stand
Green-walled by the hills of Maryland.

Round about them orchards sweep,
Apple and peach trees fruited deep,

Fair as the garden of the Lord
To the eyes of the famished rebel horde,

On that pleasant morn of the early fall
When Lee marched over the mountain-wall;

Over the mountains winding down,
Horse and foot, into Frederick town.

Forty flags with their silver stars,
Forty flags with their crimson bars,

Flapped in the morning wind: the sun
Of noon looked down, and saw not one.

Up rose old Barbara Frietchie then,
Bowed with her fourscore years and ten;

Bravest of all in Frederick town,
She took up the flag the men hauled down;

In her attic window the staff she set,
To show that one heart was loyal yet.

Up the street came the rebel tread,
Stonewall Jackson riding ahead.

Under his slouched hat left and right
He glanced; the old flag met his sight.

"Halt!" — the dust-brown ranks stood fast.
"Fire!" — out blazed the rifle-blast.

It shivered the window, pane and sash;
It rent the banner with seam and gash.

Quick, as it fell, from the broken staff
Dame Barbara snatched the silken scarf.

She leaned far out on the window-sill,
And shook it forth with a royal will.

"Shoot, if you must, this old gray head,
But spare your country's flag," she said.

A shade of sadness, a blush of shame,
Over the face of the leader came;

The nobler nature within him stirred
To life at that woman's deed and word;

"Who touches a hair of yon gray head
Dies like a dog! March on!" he said.

All day long through Frederick street
Sounded the tread of marching feet:

All day long that free flag tost
Over the heads of the rebel host.

Ever its torn folds rose and fell
On the loyal winds that loved it well;

And through the hill-gaps sunset light
Shone over it with a warm good-night.

Barbara Frietchie's work is o'er,
And the Rebel rides on his raids no more.

Honor to her! and let a tear
Fall, for her sake, on Stonewall's bier.

Over Barbara Frietchie's grave,
Flag of Freedom and Union, wave!

Peace and order and beauty draw
Round thy symbol of light and law;

And ever the stars above look down
On thy stars below in Frederick town!

Snow-Bound

A *winter idyl*

The sun that brief December day
Rose cheerless over hills of gray,
And, darkly circled, gave at noon
A sadder light than waning moon.
Slow tracing down the thickening sky
Its mute and ominous prophecy,
A portent seeming less than threat,
It sank from sight before it set.
A chill no coat, however stout,
Of homespun stuff could quite shut out,
A hard, dull bitterness of cold,
That checked, mid-vein, the circling race
Of life-blood in the sharpened face,
The coming of the snow-storm told.
The wind blew east; we heard the roar
Of Ocean on his wintry shore,
And felt the strong pulse throbbing there
Beat with low rhythm our inland air.

Meanwhile we did our nightly chores, —
Brought in the wood from out of doors,
Littered the stalls, and from the mows
Raked down the herd's-grass for the cows:
Heard the horse whinnying for his corn;
And, sharply clashing horn on horn,
Impatient down the stanchion rows
The cattle shake their walnut bows;
While, peering from his early perch
Upon the scaffold's pole of birch,
The cock his crested helmet bent
And down his querulous challenge sent.

Unwarmed by any sunset light
The gray day darkened into night,
A night made hoary with the swarm
And whirl-dance of the blinding storm,
As zigzag, wavering to and fro,
Crossed and recrossed the wingëd snow:
And ere the early bedtime came
The white drift piled the window-frame,

And through the glass the clothes-line posts
Looked in like tall and sheeted ghosts.

So all night long the storm roared on:
The morning broke without a sun;
In tiny spherule traced with lines
Of Nature's geometric signs,
In starry flake, and pellicle,
All day the hoary meteor fell;
And, when the second morning shone,
We looked upon a world unknown,
On nothing we could call our own.
Around the glistening wonder bent
The blue walls of the firmament,
No cloud above, no earth below, —
A universe of sky and snow!
The old familiar sights of ours
Took marvellous shapes; strange domes and towers
Rose up where sty or corn-crib stood,
Or garden-wall, or belt of wood;
A smooth white mound the brush-pile showed,
A fenceless drift what once was road;
The bridle-post an old man sat
With loose-flung coat and high cocked hat;
The well-curb had a Chinese roof;
And even the long sweep, high aloof,
In its slant splendor, seemed to tell
Of Pisa's leaning miracle.

A prompt, decisive man, no breath
Our father wasted: "Boys, a path!"
Well pleased, (for when did farmer boy
Count such a summons less than joy?)
Our buskins on our feet we drew;
With mittened hands, and caps drawn low,
To guard our necks and ears from snow,
We cut the solid whiteness through.
And, where the drift was deepest, made
A tunnel walled and overlaid
With dazzling crystal: we had read
Of rare Aladdin's wondrous cave,
And to our own his name we gave,

With many a wish the luck were ours
To test his lamp's supernal powers.
We reached the barn with merry din,
And roused the prisoned brutes within.
The old horse thrust his long head out,
And grave with wonder gazed about;
The cock his lusty greeting said,
And forth his speckled harem led;
The oxen lashed their tails, and hooked,
And mild reproach of hunger looked;
The hornëd patriarch of the sheep,
Like Egypt's Amun roused from sleep,
Shook his sage head with gesture mute,
And emphasized with stamp of foot.

All day the gusty north-wind bore
The loosening drift its breath before;
Low circling round its southern zone,
The sun through dazzling snow-mist shone.
No church-bell lent its Christian tone
To the savage air, no social smoke
Curled over woods of snow-hung oak.
A solitude made more intense
By dreary-voicëd elements,
The shrieking of the mindless wind,
The moaning tree-boughs swaying blind,
And on the glass the unmeaning beat
Of ghostly finger-tips of sleet.
Beyond the circle of our hearth
No welcome sound of toil or mirth
Unbound the spell, and testified
Of human life and thought outside.
We minded that the sharpest ear
The buried brooklet could not hear,
The music of whose liquid lip
Had been to us companionship,
And, in our lonely life, had grown
To have an almost human tone.

As night drew on, and, from the crest
Of wooded knolls that ridged the west,
The sun, a snow-blown traveller, sank
From sight beneath the smothering bank,

We piled, with care, our nightly stack
Of wood against the chimney-back, —
The oaken log, green, huge, and thick,
And on its top the stout back-stick;
The knotty forestick laid apart,
And filled between with curious art
The ragged brush; then, hovering near,
We watched the first red blaze appear,
Heard the sharp crackle, caught the gleam
On whitewashed wall and sagging beam,
Until the old, rude-furnished room
Burst, flower-like, into rosy bloom;
While radiant with a mimic flame
Outside the sparkling drift became,
And through the bare-boughed lilac-tree
Our own warm hearth seemed blazing free.
The crane and pendent trammels showed,
The Turks' heads on the andirons glowed;
While childish fancy, prompt to tell
The meaning of the miracle,
Whispered the old rhyme: *"Under the tree,*
When fire outdoors burns merrily,
There the witches are making tea."

The moon above the eastern wood
Shone at its full; the hill-range stood
Transfigured in the silver flood,
Its blown snows flashing cold and keen,
Dead white, save where some sharp ravine
Took shadow, or the sombre green
Of hemlocks turned to pitchy black
Against the whiteness at their back.
For such a world and such a night
Most fitting that unwarming light,
Which only seemed where'er it fell
To make the coldness visible.

Shut in from all the world without,
We sat the clean-winged hearth about,
Content to let the north-wind roar
In baffled rage at pane and door,
While the red logs before us beat
The frost-line back with tropic heat;

And ever, when a louder blast
Shook beam and rafter as it passed,
The merrier up its roaring draught
The great throat of the chimney laughed;
The house-dog on his paws outspread
Laid to the fire his drowsy head,
The cat's dark silhouette on the wall
A couchant tiger's seemed to fall;
And, for the winter fireside meet,
Between the andirons' straddling feet,
The mug of cider simmered slow,
The apples sputtered in a row,
And, close at hand, the basket stood
With nuts from brown October's wood.

What matter how the night behaved?
What matter how the north-wind raved?
Blow high, blow low, not all its snow
Could quench our hearth-fire's ruddy glow.
O Time and Change! — with hair as gray
As was my sire's that winter day,
How strange it seems, with so much gone
Of life and love, to still live on!
Ah, brother! only I and thou
Are left of all that circle now, —
The dear home faces whereupon
That fitful firelight paled and shone.
Henceforward, listen as we will,
The voices of that hearth are still;
Look where we may, the wide earth o'er,
Those lighted faces smile no more.
We tread the paths their feet have worn,
    We sit beneath their orchard trees,
    We hear, like them, the hum of bees
And rustle of the bladed corn;
We turn the pages that they read,
    Their written words we linger o'er,
But in the sun they cast no shade,
No voice is heard, no sign is made,
    No step is on the conscious floor!
Yet Love will dream, and Faith will trust,
(Since He who knows our need is just,)
That somehow, somewhere, meet we must.

Alas for him who never sees
The stars shine through his cypress-trees!
Who, hopeless, lays his dead away,
Nor looks to see the breaking day
Across the mournful marbles play!
Who hath not learned, in hours of faith,
    The truth to flesh and sense unknown,
That Life is ever lord of Death,
    And Love can never lose its own!

We sped the time with stories old,
Wrought puzzles out, and riddles told,
Or stammered from our school-book lore
"The Chief of Gambia's golden shore."
How often since, when all the land
Was clay in Slavery's shaping hand,
As if a far-blown trumpet stirred
The languorous sin-sick air, I heard:
"Does not the voice of reason cry,
    Claim the first right which Nature gave,
From the red scourge of bondage fly,
    Nor deign to live a burdened slave!"
Our father rode again his ride
On Memphremagog's wooded side;
Sat down again to moose and samp
In trapper's hut and Indian camp;
Lived o'er the old idyllic ease
Beneath St. François' hemlock-trees;
Again for him the moonlight shone
On Norman cap and bodiced zone;
Again he heard the violin play
Which led the village dance away.
And mingled in its merry whirl
The grandam and the laughing girl.
Or, nearer home, our steps he led
Where Salisbury's level marshes spread
    Mile-wide as flies the laden bee;
Where merry mowers, hale and strong,
Swept, scythe on scythe, their swaths along
    The low green prairies of the sea.
We share the fishing off Boar's Head,
    And round the rocky Isles of Shoals
    The hake-broil on the drift-wood coals;

The chowder on the sand-beach made,
Dipped by the hungry, steaming hot,
With spoons of clam-shell from the pot.
We heard the tales of witchcraft old,
And dream and sign and marvel told
To sleepy listeners as they lay
Stretched idly on the salted hay,
Adrift along the winding shores,
When favoring breezes deigned to blow
The square sail of the gundelow
And idle lay the useless oars.

Our mother, while she turned her wheel
Or run the new-knit stocking-heel,
Told how the Indian hordes came down
At midnight on Cocheco town,
And how her own great-uncle bore
His cruel scalp-mark to fourscore.
Recalling, in her fitting phrase,
    So rich and picturesque and free,
    (The common unrhymed poetry
Of simple life and country ways,)
The story of her early days, —
She made us welcome to her home;
Old hearths grew wide to give us room;
We stole with her a frightened look
At the gray wizard's conjuring-book,
The fame whereof went far and wide
Through all the simple country side;
We heard the hawks at twilight play,
The boat-horn on Piscataqua,
The loon's weird laughter far away;
We fished her little trout-brook, knew
What flowers in wood and meadow grew,
What sunny hillsides autumn-brown
She climbed to shake the ripe nuts down,
Saw where in sheltered cove and bay
The ducks' black squadron anchored lay,
And heard the wild-geese calling loud
Beneath the gray November cloud.

Then, haply, with a look more grave,
And soberer tone, some tale she gave

From painful Sewel's ancient tome,
Beloved in every Quaker home,
Of faith fire-winged by martyrdom,
Or Chalkley's Journal, old and quaint, —
Gentlest of skippers, rare sea-saint! —
Who, when the dreary calms prevailed,
And water-butt and bread-cask failed,
And cruel, hungry eyes pursued
His portly presence mad for food,
With dark hints muttered under breath
Of casting lots for life or death,
Offered, if Heaven withheld supplies,
To be himself the sacrifice.
Then, suddenly, as if to save
The good man from his living grave,
A ripple on the water grew,
A school of porpoise flashed in view.
"Take, eat," he said, "and be content;
These fishes in my stead are sent
By Him who gave the tangled ram
To spare the child of Abraham."

Our uncle, innocent of books,
Was rich in lore of fields and brooks,
The ancient teachers never dumb
Of Nature's unhoused lyceum.
In moons and tides and weather wise,
He read the clouds as prophecies,
And foul or fair could well divine,
By many an occult hint and sign,
Holding the cunning-warded keys
To all the woodcraft mysteries;
Himself to Nature's heart so near
That all her voices in his ear
Of beast or bird had meanings clear,
Like Apollonius of old,
Who knew the tales the sparrows told,
Or Hermes who interpreted
What the sage cranes of Nilus said;
A simple, guileless, childlike man,
Content to live where life began;
Strong only on his native grounds,
The little world of sights and sounds

Whose girdle was the parish bounds,
Whereof his fondly partial pride
The common features magnified,
As Surrey hills to mountains grew
In White of Selborne's loving view, —
He told how teal and loon he shot,
And how the eagle's eggs he got,
The feats on pond and river done,
The prodigies of rod and gun;
Till, warming with the tales he told,
Forgotten was the outside cold,
The bitter wind unheeded blew,
From ripening corn the pigeons flew,
The partridge drummed i' the wood, the mink
Went fishing down the river-brink.
In fields with bean or clover gay,
The woodchuck, like a hermit gray,
  Peered from the doorway of his cell:
The muskrat plied the mason's trade,
And tier by tier his mud-walls laid;
And from the shagbark overhead
  The grizzled squirrel dropped his shell.

Next, the dear aunt, whose smile of cheer
And voice in dreams I see and hear, —
The sweetest woman ever Fate
Perverse denied a household mate,
Who, lonely, homeless, not the less
Found peace in love's unselfishness,
And welcome wheresoe'er she went,
A calm and gracious element,
Whose presence seemed the sweet income
And womanly atmosphere of home, —
Called up her girlhood memories,
The huskings and the apple-bees,
The sleigh-rides and the summer sails.
Weaving through all the poor details
And homespun warp of circumstance
A golden woof-thread of romance.
For well she kept her genial mood
And simple faith of maidenhood;
Before her still a cloud-land lay,
The mirage loomed across her way;

The morning dew, that dries so soon
With others, glistened at her noon;
Through years of toil and soil and care,
From glossy tress to thin gray hair,
All unprofaned she held apart
The virgin fancies of the heart.
Be shame to him of woman born
Who hath for such but thought of scorn.

There, too, our elder sister plied
Her evening task the stand beside;
A full, rich nature, free to trust,
Truthful and almost sternly just,
Impulsive, earnest, prompt to act,
And make her generous thought a fact,
Keeping with many a light disguise
The secret of self-sacrifice.
O heart sore-tried! thou hast the best
That Heaven itself could give thee, — rest,
Rest from all bitter thoughts and things!
    How many a poor one's blessing went
    With thee beneath the low green tent
Whose curtain never outward swings!

As one who held herself a part
Of all she saw, and let her heart
    Against the household bosom lean,
Upon the motley-braided mat
Our youngest and our dearest sat,
Lifting her large, sweet, asking eyes,
    Now bathed in the unfading green
And holy peace of Paradise.
Oh, looking from some heavenly hill,
    Or from the shade of saintly palms,
    Or silver reach of river calms,
Do those large eyes behold me still?
With me one little year ago: —
The chill weight of the winter snow
    For months upon her grave has lain;
And now, when summer south-winds blow
    And brier and harebell bloom again,
I tread the pleasant paths we trod,
I see the violet-sprinkled sod

Whereon she leaned, too frail and weak
The hillside flowers she loved to seek,
Yet following me where'er I went
With dark eyes full of love's content.
The birds are glad; the brier-rose fills
The air with sweetness; all the hills
Stretch green to June's unclouded sky;
But still I wait with ear and eye
For something gone which should be nigh,
A loss in all familiar things,
In flower that blooms, and bird that sings.
And yet, dear heart! remembering thee,
   Am I not richer than of old?
Safe in thy immortality,
   What change can reach the wealth I hold?
   What chance can mar the pearl and gold
Thy love hath left in trust with me?
And while in life's late afternoon,
   Where cool and long the shadows grow,
I walk to meet the night that soon
   Shall shape and shadow overflow,
I cannot feel that thou art far,
Since near at need the angels are;
And when the sunset gates unbar,
   Shall I not see thee waiting stand,
And, white against the evening star,
   The welcome of thy beckoning hand?

Brisk wielder of the birch and rule,
The master of the district school
Held at the fire his favored place,
Its warm glow lit a laughing face
Fresh-hued and fair, where scarce appeared
The uncertain prophecy of beard.
He teased the mitten-blinded cat,
Played cross-pins on my uncle's hat,
Sang songs, and told us what befalls
In classic Dartmouth's college halls.
Born the wild Northern hills among,
From whence his yeoman father wrung
By patient toil subsistence scant,
Not competence and yet not want,
He early gained the power to pay

His cheerful, self-reliant way;
Could doff at ease his scholar's gown
To peddle wares from town to town:
Or through the long vacation's reach
In lonely lowland districts teach,
Where all the droll experience found
At stranger hearths in boarding round,
The moonlit skater's keen delight,
The sleigh-drive through the frosty night,
The rustic-party, with its rough
Accompaniment of blind-man's-buff,
And whirling-plate, and forfeits paid,
His winter task a pastime made.
Happy the snow-locked homes wherein
He tuned his merry violin,
Or played the athlete in the barn,
Or held the good dame's winding-yarn,
Or mirth-provoking versions told
Of classic legends rare and old,
Wherein the scenes of Greece and Rome
Had all the commonplace of home,
And little seemed at best the odds
'Twixt Yankee pedlers and old gods;
Where Pindus-born Arachthus took
The guise of any grist-mill brook,
And dread Olympus at his will
Became a huckleberry hill.

A careless boy that night he seemed;
    But at his desk he had the look
And air of one who wisely schemed,
    And hostage from the future took
    In trainèd thought and lore of book.
Large-brained, clear-eyed, of such as he
Shall Freedom's young apostles be,
Who, following in War's bloody trail,
Shall every lingering wrong assail;
All chains from limb and spirit strike,
Uplift the black and white alike;
Scatter before their swift advance
The darkness and the ignorance,
The pride, the lust, the squalid sloth,
Which nurtured Treason's monstrous growth,

Made murder pastime, and the hell
Of prison-torture possible;
The cruel lie of caste refute,
Old forms remould, and substitute
For Slavery's lash the freeman's will,
For blind routine, wise-handed skill;
A school-house plant on every hill,
Stretching in radiate nerve-lines thence
The quick wires of intelligence;
Till North and South together brought
Shall own the same electric thought,
In peace a common flag salute,
And, side by side in labor's free
And unresentful rivalry,
Harvest the fields wherein they fought.

Another guest that winter night
Flashed back from lustrous eyes the light.
Unmarked by time, and yet not young,
The honeyed music of her tongue
And words of meekness scarcely told
A nature passionate and bold,
Strong, self-concentred, spurning guide,
Its milder features dwarfed beside
Her unbent will's majestic pride.
She sat among us, at the best,
A not unfeared, half-welcome guest,
Rebuking with her cultured phrase
Our homeliness of words and ways.
A certain pard-like, treacherous grace
Swayed the lithe limbs and drooped the lash,
Lent the white teeth their dazzling flash;
And under low brows, black with night,
Rayed out at times a dangerous light;
The sharp heat-lightnings of her face
Presaging ill to him whom Fate
Condemned to share her love or hate.
A woman tropical, intense
In thought and act, in soul and sense,
She blended in a like degree
The vixen and the devotee,
Revealing with each freak or feint
    The temper of Petruchio's Kate,

The raptures of Siena's saint.
Her tapering hand and rounded wrist
Had facile power to form a fist;
The warm, dark languish of her eyes
Was never safe from wrath's surprise.
Brows saintly calm and lips devout
Knew every change of scowl and pout;
And the sweet voice had notes more high
And shrill for social battle-cry.

Since then what old cathedral town
Has missed her pilgrim staff and gown,
What convent-gate has held its lock
Against the challenge of her knock!
Through Smyrna's plague-hushed thoroughfares,
Up sea-set Malta's rocky stairs,
Gray olive slopes of hills that hem
Thy tombs and shrines, Jerusalem,
Or startling on her desert throne
The crazy Queen of Lebanon
With claims fantastic as her own,
Her tireless feet have held their way;
And still, unrestful, bowed, and gray,
She watches under Eastern skies,
    With hope each day renewed and fresh,
    The Lord's quick coming in the flesh,
Whereof she dreams and prophesies!

Where'er her troubled path may be,
    The Lord's sweet pity with her go!
The outward wayward life we see,
    The hidden springs we may not know.
Nor is it given us to discern
    What threads the fatal sisters spun,
    Through what ancestral years has run
The sorrow with the woman born,
What forged her cruel chain of moods,
What set her feet in solitudes,
    And held the love within her mute,
What mingled madness in the blood,
    A life-long discord and annoy,
    Water of tears with oil of joy,
And hid within the folded bud

Perversities of flower and fruit.
It is not ours to separate
The tangled skein of will and fate,
To show what metes and bounds should stand
Upon the soul's debatable land,
And between choice and Providence
Divide the circle of events;
But He who knows our frame is just,
Merciful and compassionate,
And full of sweet assurances
And hope for all the language is,
That He remembereth we are dust!

At last the great logs, crumbling low,
Sent out a dull and duller glow,
The bull's-eye watch that hung in view,
Ticking its weary circuit through,
Pointed with mutely warning sign
Its black hand to the hour of nine.
That sign the pleasant circle broke:
My uncle ceased his pipe to smoke,
Knocked from its bowl the refuse gray,
And laid it tenderly away;
Then roused himself to safely cover
The dull red brands with ashes over.
And while, with care, our mother laid
The work aside, her steps she stayed
One moment, seeking to express
Her grateful sense of happiness
For food and shelter, warmth and health,
And love's contentment more than wealth,
With simple wishes (not the weak,
Vain prayers which no fulfilment seek,
But such as warm the generous heart,
O'er-prompt to do with Heaven its part)
That none might lack, that bitter night,
For bread and clothing, warmth and light.

Within our beds awhile we heard
The wind that round the gables roared,
With now and then a ruder shock,
Which made our very bedsteads rock.
We heard the loosened clapboards tost,

The board-nails snapping in the frost;
And on us, through the unplastered wall,
Felt the light sifted snow-flakes fall.
But sleep stole on, as sleep will do
When hearts are light and life is new;
Faint and more faint the murmurs grew,
Till in the summer-land of dreams
They softened to the sound of streams,
Low stir of leaves, and dip of oars,
And lapsing waves on quiet shores.

Next morn we wakened with the shout
Of merry voices high and clear;
And saw the teamsters drawing near
To break the drifted highways out.
Down the long hillside treading slow
We saw the half-buried oxen go,
Shaking the snow from heads uptost,
Their straining nostrils white with frost.
Before our door the straggling train
Drew up, an added team to gain.
The elders threshed their hands a-cold,
    Passed, with the cider-mug, their jokes
    From lip to lip; the younger folks
Down the loose snow-banks, wrestling, rolled,
Then toiled again the cavalcade
    O'er windy hill, through clogged ravine,
    And woodland paths that wound between
Low drooping pine-boughs winter-weighed.
From every barn a team afoot,
At every house a new recruit,
Where, drawn by Nature's subtlest law,
Haply the watchful young men saw
Sweet doorway pictures of the curls
And curious eyes of merry girls,
Lifting their hands in mock defence
Again the snow-ball's compliments,
And reading in each missive tost
The charm with Eden never lost.

We heard once more the sleigh-bells' sound;
    And, following where the teamsters led,
The wise old Doctor went his round,

Just pausing at our door to say,
In the brief autocratic way
Of one who, prompt at Duty's call,
. Was free to urge her claim on all,
 That some poor neighbor sick abed
At night our mother's aid would need.
For, one in generous thought and deed,
 What mattered in the sufferer's sight
 The Quaker matron's inward light,
The Doctor's mail of Calvin's creed?
All hearts confess the saints elect
 Who, twain in faith, in love agree,
And melt not in an acid sect
 The Christian pearl of charity!

So days went on: a week had passed
Since the great world was heard from last.
The Almanac we studied o'er,
Read and reread our little store
Of books and pamphlets, scarce a score;
One harmless novel, mostly hid
From younger eyes, a book forbid,
And poetry, (or good or bad,
A single book was all we had,)
Where Ellwood's meek, drab-skirted Muse,
 A stranger to the heathen Nine,
 Sang, with a somewhat nasal whine,
The wars of David and the Jews.
At last the floundering carrier bore
The village paper to our door.
Lo! broadening outward as we read,
To warmer zones the horizon spread
In panoramic length unrolled
We saw the marvels that it told.
Before us passed the painted Creeks,
 And daft McGregor on his raids
 In Costa Rica's everglades.
And up Taygetos winding slow
Rode Ypsilanti's Mainote Greeks,
A Turk's head at each saddle-bow!
Welcome to us its week-old news,
Its corner for the rustic Muse,
 Its monthly gauge of snow and rain,

Its record, mingling in a breath
The wedding bell and dirge of death:
Jest, anecdote, and love-lorn tale,
The latest culprit sent to jail;
Its hue and cry of stolen and lost,
Its vendue sales and goods at cost,
    And traffic calling loud for gain.
We felt the stir of hall and street,
The pulse of life that round us beat;
The chill embargo of the snow
Was melted in the genial glow;
Wide swung again our ice-locked door,
And all the world was ours once more!

Clasp, Angel of the backward look
    And folded wings of ashen gray
    And voice of echoes far away,
The brazen covers of thy book;
The weird palimpsest old and vast,
Wherein thou hid'st the spectral past;
Where, closely mingling, pale and glow
The characters of joy and woe;
The monographs of outlived years,
Or smile-illumed or dim with tears,
    Green hills of life that slope to death,
And haunts of home, whose vistaed trees
Shade off to mournful cypresses
    With the white amaranths underneath
Even while I look, I can but heed
    The restless sands' incessant fall,
Importunate hours that hours succeed,
Each clamorous with its own sharp need,
    And duty keeping pace with all.
Shut down and clasp the heavy lids;
I hear again the voice that bids
The dreamer leave his dream midway
For larger hopes and graver fears:
Life greatens in these later years,
The century's aloe flowers to-day!

Yet, haply, in some lull of life,
Some Truce of God which breaks its strife,
The worldling's eyes shall gather dew,

Dreaming in throngful city ways
Of winter joys his boyhood knew;
And dear and early friends — the few
Who yet remain — shall pause to view
  These Flemish pictures of old days;
Sit with me by the homestead hearth,
And stretch the hands of memory forth
  To warm them at the wood-fire's blaze!
And thanks untraced to lips unknown
Shall greet me like the odors blown
From unseen meadows newly mown,
Or lilies floating in some pond,
Wood-fringed, the wayside gaze beyond;
The traveller owns the grateful sense
Of sweetness near, he knows not whence,
And, pausing, takes with forehead bare
The benediction of the air.

What the Birds Said

The birds against the April wind
  Flew northward, singing as they flew;
They sang, "The land we leave behind
  Has swords for corn-blades, blood for dew."

"O wild-birds, flying from the South,
  What saw and heard ye, gazing down?"
"We saw the mortar's upturned mouth,
  The sickened camp, the blazing town!

"Beneath the bivouac's starry lamps,
  We saw your march-worn children die;
In shrouds of moss, in cypress swamps,
  We saw your dead uncoffined lie.

"We heard the starving prisoner's sighs,
  And saw, from line and trench, your sons
Follow our flight with home-sick eyes
  Beyond the battery's smoking guns."

"And heard and saw ye only wrong
  And pain," I cried, "O wing-worn flocks?"
"We heard," they sang, "the freedman's song,
  The crash of Slavery's broken locks!

"We saw from new, uprising States
    The treason-nursing mischief spurned,
As, crowding Freedom's ample gates,
    The long-estranged and lost returned.

"O'er dusky faces, seamed and old,
    And hands horn-hard with unpaid toil,
With hope in every rustling fold,
    We saw your star-dropt flag uncoil.

"And struggling up through sounds accursed,
    A grateful murmur clomb the air;
A whisper scarcely heard at first,
    It filled the listening heavens with prayer.

"And sweet and far, as from a star,
    Replied a voice which shall not cease,
Till, drowning all the noise of war,
    It sings the blessed song of peace!"

So to me, in a doubtful day
    Of chill and slowly greening spring,
Low stooping from the cloudy gray,
    The wild-birds sang or seemed to sing.

They vanished in the misty air,
    The song went with them in their flight;
But lo! they left the sunset fair,
    And in the evening there was light.

My Triumph

The autumn-time has come;
On woods that dream of bloom,
And over purpling vines,
The low sun fainter shines.

The aster-flower is failing,
The hazel's gold is paling;
Yet overhead more near
The eternal stars appear!

And present gratitude
Insures the future's good,
And for the things I see
I trust the things to be;

That in the paths untrod,
And the long days of God,
My feet shall still be led,
My heart be comforted.

O living friends who love me!
O dear ones gone above me!
Careless of other fame,
I leave to you my name.

Hide it from idle praises,
Save it from evil phrases:
Why, when dear lips that spake it
Are dumb, should strangers wake it?

Let the thick curtain fall;
I better know than all
How little I have gained,
How vast the unattained.

Not by the page word-painted
Let life be banned or sainted:
Deeper than written scroll
The colors of the soul.

Sweeter than any sung
My songs that found no tongue;
Nobler than any fact
My wish that failed of act.

Others shall sing the song,
Others shall right the wrong, —
Finish what I begin,
And all I fail of win.

What matter, I or they?
Mine or another's day,
So the right word be said
And life the sweeter made?

Hail to the coming singers!
Hail to the brave light-bringers!
Forward I reach and share
All that they sing and dare.

The airs of heaven blow o'er me;
A glory shines before me
Of what mankind shall be, —
Pure, generous, brave, and free.

A dream of man and woman
Diviner but still human,
Solving the riddle old,
Shaping the Age of Gold!

The love of God and neighbor;
An equal-handed labor;
The richer life, where beauty
Walks hand in hand with duty.

Ring, bells in unreared steeples,
The joy of unborn peoples!
Sound, trumpets far off blown,
Your triumph is my own!

Parcel and part of all,
I keep the festival,
Fore-reach the good to be,
And share the victory.

I feel the earth more sunward,
I join the great march onward,
And take, by faith, while living,
My freehold of thanksgiving.

The Lost Occasion

Some die too late and some too soon,
At early morning, heart of noon,
Or the chill evening twilight. Thou,
Whom the rich heavens did so endow
With eyes of power and Jove's own brow,

With all the massive strength that fills
Thy home-horizon's granite hills,
With rarest gifts of heart and head
From manliest stock inherited,
New England's stateliest type of man,
In port and speech Olympian;
Whom no one met, at first, but took
A second awed and wondering look
(As turned, perchance, the eyes of Greece
On Phidias' unveiled masterpiece);
Whose words in simplest homespun clad,
The Saxon strength of Cædmon's had,
With power reserved at need to reach
The Roman forum's loftiest speech,
Sweet with persuasion, eloquent
In passion, cool in argument,
Or, ponderous, falling on thy foes
As fell the Norse god's hammer blows,
Crushing as if with Talus' flail
Through Error's logic-woven mail,
And failing only when they tried
The adamant of the righteous side, —
Thou, foiled in aim and hope, bereaved
Of old friends, by the new deceived,
Too soon for us, too soon for thee,
Beside thy lonely Northern sea,
Where long and low the marsh-lands spread,
Laid wearily down thy august head.

Thou shouldst have lived to feel below
Thy feet Disunion's fierce upthrow;
The late-sprung mine that underlaid
Thy sad concessions vainly made.
Thou shouldst have seen from Sumter's wall
The star-flag of the Union fall,
And armed rebellion pressing on
The broken lines of Washington!
No stronger voice than thine had then
Called out the utmost might of men,
To make the Union's charter free
And strengthen law by liberty.
How had that stern arbitrament
To thy gray age youth's vigor lent,

Shaming ambition's paltry prize
Before thy disillusioned eyes;
Breaking the spell about thee wound
Like the green withes that Samson bound;
Redeeming in one effort grand,
Thyself and thy imperilled land!
Ah, cruel fate, that closed to thee,
O sleeper by the Northern sea,
The gates of opportunity!
God fills the gaps of human need,
Each crisis brings its word and deed.
Wise men and strong we did not lack;
But still, with memory turning back,
In the dark hours we thought of thee,
And thy lone grave beside the sea.

Above that grave the east winds blow,
And from the marsh-lands drifting slow
The sea-fog comes, with evermore
The wave-wash of a lonely shore,
And sea-bird's melancholy cry,
As Nature fain would typify
The sadness of a closing scene,
The loss of that which should have been.
But, where thy native mountains bare
Their foreheads to diviner air,
Fit emblem of enduring fame,
One lofty summit keeps thy name.
For thee the cosmic forces did
The rearing of that pyramid,
The prescient ages shaping with
Fire, flood, and frost thy monolith.
Sunrise and sunset lay thereon
With hands of light their benison,
The stars of midnight pause to set
Their jewels in its coronet.
And evermore that mountain mass
Seems climbing from the shadowy pass
To light, as if to manifest
Thy nobler self, thy life at best!

OLIVER WENDELL HOLMES
1809–1894

The Deacon's Masterpiece

Or, the wonderful "One-Hoss Shay"
A logical story

Have you heard of the wonderful one-hoss shay,
That was built in such a logical way
It ran a hundred years to a day,
And then, of a sudden, it — ah, but stay,
I'll tell you what happened without delay,
Scaring the parson into fits,
Frightening people out of their wits, —
Have you ever heard of that, I say?

Seventeen hundred and fifty-five.
Georgius Secundus was then alive, —
Snuffy old drone from the German hive.
That was the year when Lisbon-town
Saw the earth open and gulp her down,
And Braddock's army was done so brown,
Left without a scalp to its crown.
It was on the terrible Earthquake-day
That the Deacon finished the one-hoss shay.

Now in building of chaises, I tell you what,
There is always *somewhere* a weakest spot, —
In hub, tire, felloe, in spring or thill,
In panel, or crossbar, or floor, or sill,
In screw, bolt, thoroughbrace, — lurking still,
Find it somewhere you must and will, —
Above or below, or within or without, —
And that's the reason, beyond a doubt,
That a chaise *breaks down*, but does n't *wear out*.

But the Deacon swore (as Deacons do,
With an "I dew vum," or an "I tell *yeou*")
He would build one shay to beat the taown
N' the keounty 'n' all the kentry raoun';
It should be so built that it *could n'* break daown;
"Fur," said the Deacon, " 't's mighty plain

Thut the weakes' place mus' stan' the strain;
'N' the way t' fix it, uz I maintain, is only jest
T' make that place uz strong uz the rest."

So the Deacon inquired of the village folk
Where he could find the strongest oak,
That could n't be split nor bent nor broke, —
That was for spokes and floor and sills;
He sent for lancewood to make the thills;
The crossbars were ash, from the straightest trees,
The panels of white-wood, that cuts like cheese,
But lasts like iron for things like these;
The hubs of logs from the "Settler's ellum," —
Last of its timber, — they could n't sell 'em,
Never an axe had seen their chips,
And the wedges flew from between their lips,
Their blunt ends frizzled like celery-tips;
Step and prop-iron, bolt and screw,
Spring, tire, axle, and linchpin too,
Steel of the finest, bright and blue;
Thoroughbrace bison-skin, thick and wide;
Boot, top, dasher, from tough old hide
Found in the pit when the tanner died.
That was the way he "put her through."
"There!" said the Deacon, "naow she'll dew!"

Do! I tell you, I rather guess
She was a wonder, and nothing less!
Colts grew horses, beards turned gray,
Deacon and deaconess dropped away,
Children and grandchildren — where were they?
But there stood the stout old one-hoss shay
As fresh as on Lisbon-earthquake day!

EIGHTEEN HUNDRED; — It came and found
The Deacon's masterpiece strong and sound.
Eighteen hundred increased by ten; —
"Hahnsum kerridge" they called it then.
Eighteen hundred and twenty came; —
Running as usual; much the same.
Thirty and forty at last arrive,
And then come fifty, and FIFTY-FIVE.

Little of all we value here
Wakes on the morn of its hundredth year
Without both feeling and looking queer.
In fact, there's nothing that keeps its youth,
So far as I know, but a tree and truth.
(This is a moral that runs at large;
Take it. — You're welcome. — No extra charge.)

FIRST OF NOVEMBER, — the Earthquake day, —
There are traces of age in the one-hoss shay,
A general flavor of mild decay,
But nothing local, as one may say.
There could n't be, — for the Deacon's art
Had made it so like in every part
That there wasn't a chance for one to start.
For the wheels were just as strong as the thills,
And the floor was just as strong as the sills,
And the panels just as strong as the floor,
And the whipple-tree neither less nor more,
And the back crossbar as strong as the fore,
And spring and axle and hub *encore*.
And yet, *as a whole*, it is past a doubt
In another hour it will be *worn out!*

First of November, 'Fifty-five!
This morning the parson takes a drive.
Now, small boys, get out of the way!
Here comes the wonderful one-hoss shay,
Drawn by a rat-tailed, ewe-necked bay.
"Huddup!" said the parson. — Off went they.
The parson was working his Sunday's text, —
Had got to *fifthly*, and stopped perplexed
At what the — Moses — was coming next.
All at once the horse stood still.
Close by the meet'n'-house on the hill.
First a shiver, and then a thrill,
Then something decidedly like a spill, —
And the parson was sitting upon a rock,
At half past nine by the meet'n'-house clock, —
Just the hour of the Earthquake shock!
What do you think the parson found,
When he got up and stared around?
The poor old chaise in a heap or mound,

As if it had been to the mill and ground!
You see, of course, if you're not a dunce,
How it went to pieces all at once, —
All at once, and nothing first, —
Just as bubbles do when they burst.

End of the wonderful one-hoss shay.
Logic is logic. That's all I say.

The Chambered Nautilus

This is the ship of pearl, which, poets feign,
   Sails the unshadowed main, —
   The venturous bark that flings
On the sweet summer wind its purpled wings
In gulfs enchanted, where the Siren sings,
   And coral reefs lie bare,
Where the cold sea-maids rise to sun their streaming hair.

Its webs of living gauze no more unfurl;
   Wrecked is the ship of pearl!
   And every chambered cell,
Where its dim dreaming life was wont to dwell,
As the frail tenant shaped his growing shell,
   Before thee lies revealed, —
Its irised ceiling rent, its sunless crypt unsealed!

Year after year beheld the silent toil
   That spread his lustrous coil;
   Still, as the spiral grew,
He left the past year's dwelling for the new,
Stole with soft step its shining archway through,
   Built up its idle door,
Stretched in his last-found home, and knew the old no more.

Thanks for the heavenly message brought by thee,
   Child of the wandering sea,
   Cast from her lap, forlorn!
From thy dead lips a clearer note is born
Than ever Triton blew from wreathèd horn!
   While on mine ear it rings,
Through the deep caves of thought I hear a voice that sings: —

Build thee more stately mansions, O my soul,
  As the swift seasons roll!
  Leave thy low-vaulted past!
Let each new temple, nobler than the last,
Shut thee from heaven with a dome more vast,
  Till thou at length art free,
Leaving thine outgrown shell by life's unresting sea!

Dorothy Q.

A *family portrait*

Grandmother's mother: her age, I guess,
Thirteen summers, or something less;
Girlish bust, but womanly air;
Smooth, square forehead with uprolled hair;
Lips that lover has never kissed;
Taper fingers and slender wrist;
Hanging sleeves of stiff brocade;
So they painted the little maid.

On her hand a parrot green
Sits unmoving and broods serene.
Hold up the canvas full in view, —
Look! there's a rent the light shines through,
Dark with a century's fringe of dust, —
That was a Red-Coat's rapier-thrust!
Such is the tale the lady old,
Dorothy's daughter's daughter, told.

Who the painter was none may tell, —
One whose best was not over well;
Hard and dry, it must be confessed,
Flat as a rose that has long been pressed;
Yet in her cheek the hues are bright,
Dainty colors of red and white,
And in her slender shape are seen
Hint and promise of stately mien.

Look not on her with eyes of scorn, —
Dorothy Q. was a lady born!
Ay! since the galloping Normans came,

England's annals have known her name;
And still to the three-hilled rebel town
Dear is that ancient name's renown,
For many a civic wreath they won,
The youthful sire and the gray-haired son.

O Damsel Dorothy! Dorothy Q.!
Strange is the gift that I owe to you;
Such a gift as never a king
Save to daughter or son might bring, —
All my tenure of heart and hand,
All my title to house and land;
Mother and sister and child and wife
And joy and sorrow and death and life!

What if a hundred years ago
Those close-shut lips had answered No,
When forth the tremulous question came
That cost the maiden her Norman name,
And under the folds that look so still
The bodice swelled with the bosom's thrill?
Should I be I, or would it be
One tenth another, to nine tenths me?

Soft is the breath of a maiden's YES:
Not the light gossamer stirs with less;
But never a cable that holds so fast
Through all the battles of wave and blast,
And never an echo of speech or song
That lives in the babbling air so long!
There were tones in the voice that whispered then
You may hear to-day in a hundred men.

O lady and lover, how faint and far
Your images hover, — and here we are,
Solid and stirring in flesh and bone, —
Edward's and Dorothy's — all their own, —
A goodly record for Time to show
Of a syllable spoken so long ago! —
Shall I bless you, Dorothy, or forgive
For the tender whisper that bade me live?

It shall be a blessing, my little maid!
I will heal the stab of the Red-Coat's blade,
And freshen the gold of the tarnished frame,
And gild with a rhyme your household name;
So you shall smile on us brave and bright
As first you greeted the morning's light,
And live untroubled by woes and fears
Through a second youth of a hundred years.

EDGAR ALLAN POE
1809–1849

A Dream within a Dream

Take this kiss upon the brow!
And, in parting from you now,
Thus much let me avow —
You are not wrong, who deem
That my days have been a dream;
Yet if hope has flown away
In a night, or in a day,
In a vision, or in none,
Is it therefore the less *gone?*
All that we see or seem
Is but a dream within a dream.

I stand amid the roar
Of a surf-tormented shore,
And I hold within my hand
Grains of the golden sand —
How few! yet how they creep
Through my fingers to the deep,
While I weep — while I weep!
O God! can I not grasp
Them with a tighter clasp?
O God! can I not save
One from the pitiless wave?
Is *all* that we see or seem
But a dream within a dream?

Song from Al Aaraaf

Young flowers were whispering in melody
To happy flowers that night — and tree to tree;
Fountains were gushing music as they fell
In many a star-lit grove, or moon-lit dell;
Yet silence came upon material things —
Fair flowers, bright waterfalls and angel wings —
And sound alone that from the spirit sprang
Bore burthen to the charm the maiden sang:
" 'Neath blue-bell or streamer —
   Or tufted wild spray
That keeps, from the dreamer,
   The moonbeam away —
Bright beings! that ponder,
   With half closing eyes,
On the stars which your wonder
   Hath drawn from the skies,
Till they glance thro' the shade, and
   Come down to your brow
Like — eyes of the maiden
   Who calls on you now —
Arise! from your dreaming
   In violet bowers,
To duty beseeming
   These star-litten hours —
And shake from your tresses
   Encumber'd with dew
The breath of those kisses
   That cumber them too —
(O! how, without you, Love!
   Could angels be blest?)
Those kisses of true love
   That lull'd ye to rest!
Up! — shake from your wing
   Each hindering thing:
The dew of the night —
   It would weigh down your flight;
And true love caresses —
   O! leave them apart!
They are light on the tresses,
   But lead on the heart.

Ligeia! Ligeia!
  My beautiful one!
Whose harshest idea
  Will to melody run,
O! is it thy will
  On the breezes to toss?
Or, capriciously still,
  Like the lone Albatross,
Incumbent on night
  (As she on the air)
To keep watch with delight
  On the harmony there?

Ligeia! wherever
  Thy image may be,
No magic shall sever
  Thy music from thee.
Thou hast bound many eyes
  In a dreamy sleep —
But the strains still arise
  Which *thy* vigilance keep —
The sound of the rain
  Which leaps down to the flower,
And dances again
  In the rhythm of the shower —
The murmur that springs
  From the growing of grass
Are the music of things —
  But are modell'd, alas! —
Away, then my dearest,
  O! hie thee away
To springs that lie clearest
  Beneath the moon-ray —
To lone lake that smiles,
  In its dream of deep rest,
At the many star-isles
  That enjewel its breast —
Where wild flowers, creeping,
  Have mingled their shade,
On its margin is sleeping
  Full many a maid —
Some have left the cool glade, and
  Have slept with the bee —

Arouse them my maiden,
    On moorland and lea —
Go! breathe on their slumber,
    All softly in ear,
The musical number
    They slumber'd to hear —
For what can awaken
    An angel so soon
Whose sleep hath been taken
    Beneath the cold moon,
As the spell which no slumber
    Of witchery may test,
The rhythmical number
    Which lull'd him to rest?"

Introduction [*to* Poems, *1831*]

Romance, who loves to nod and sing,
With drowsy head and folded wing,
Among the green leaves as they shake
Far down within some shadowy lake,
To me a painted paroquet
Hath been — a most familiar bird —
Taught me my alphabet to say —
To lisp my very earliest word
While in the wild-wood I did lie
A child — with a most knowing eye.

Succeeding years, too wild for song,
Then roll'd like tropic storms along,
Where, tho' the garish lights that fly
Dying along the troubled sky,
Lay bare, thro' vistas thunder-riven,
The blackness of the general Heaven,
That very blackness yet doth fling
Light on the lightning's silver wing.

For, being an idle boy lang syne,
Who read Anacreon, and drank wine,
I early found Anacreon rhymes
Were almost passionate sometimes —
And by strange alchemy of brain

His pleasures always turn'd to pain —
His naivete to wild desire —
His wit to love — his wine to fire —
And so, being young and dipt in folly
I fell in love with melancholy,
And used to throw my earthly rest
And quiet all away in jest —
I could not love except where Death
Was mingling his with Beauty's breath —
Or Hymen, Time, and Destiny
Were stalking between her and me.

O, then the eternal Condor years
So shook the very Heavens on high,
With tumult as they thunder'd by;
I had no time for idle cares,
Thro' gazing on the unquiet sky!
Or if an hour with calmer wing
Its down did on my spirit fling,
That little hour with lyre and rhyme
To while away — forbidden thing!
My heart half fear'd to be a crime
Unless it trembled with the string.

But *now* my soul hath too much room —
Gone are the glory and the gloom —
The black hath mellow'd into grey,
And all the fires are fading away.

My draught of passion hath been deep —
I revell'd, and I now would sleep —
And after-drunkenness of soul
Succeeds the glories of the bowl —
An idle longing night and day
To dream my very life away.

But dreams — of those who dream as I,
Aspiringly, are damned, and die:
Yet should I swear I mean alone,
By notes so very shrilly blown,
To break upon Time's monotone,
While yet my vapid joy and grief
Are tintless of the yellow leaf —

Why not an imp the greybeard hath,
Will shake his shadow in my path —
And even the greybeard will o'erlook
Connivingly my dreaming-book.

To Helen

Helen, thy beauty is to me
   Like those Nicéan barks of yore,
That gently, o'er a perfumed sea,
    The weary, way-worn wanderer bore
   To his own native shore.

On desperate seas long wont to roam,
   Thy hyacinth hair, thy classic face,
Thy Naiad airs have brought me home
    To the glory that was Greece,
And the grandeur that was Rome.

Lo! in yon brilliant window-niche
   How statue-like I see thee stand,
    The agate lamp within thy hand!
Ah, Psyche, from the regions which
   Are Holy-Land!

Israfel

*And the angel Israfel, whose heart-strings are a lute, and
who has the sweetest voice of all God's creatures.*   KORAN

In Heaven a spirit doth dwell
   "Whose heart-strings are a lute;"
None sing so wildly well
As the angel Israfel,
And the giddy stars (so legends tell)
Ceasing their hymns, attend the spell
   Of his voice, all mute.

Tottering above
   In her highest noon,
   The enamoured moon
Blushes with love,

While, to listen, the red levin
(With the rapid Pleiads, even,
Which were seven,)
Pauses in Heaven.

And they say (the starry choir
    And the other listening things)
That Israfeli's fire
Is owing to that lyre
    By which he sits and sings —
The trembling living wire
Of those unusual strings.

But the skies that angel trod,
    Where deep thoughts are a duty —
Where Love's a grown-up God —
    Where the Houri glances are
Imbued with all the beauty
    Which we worship in a star.

Therefore, thou art not wrong,
    Israfeli, who despisest
An unimpassioned song;
To thee the laurels belong,
    Best bard, because the wisest!
Merrily live, and long!

The ecstasies above
    With thy burning measures suit —
Thy grief, thy joy, thy hate, thy love,
    With the fervour of thy lute —
    Well may the stars be mute!

Yes, Heaven is thine; but this
    Is a world of sweets and sours;
    Our flowers are merely — flowers,
And the shadow of thy perfect bliss
    Is the sunshine of ours.

If I could dwell
Where Israfel
    Hath dwelt, and he where I,
He might not sing so wildly well

A mortal melody,
While a bolder note than this might swell
From my lyre within the sky.

The City in the Sea

Lo! Death has reared himself a throne
In a strange city lying alone
Far down within the dim West,
Where the good and the bad and the worst and the best
Have gone to their eternal rest.
There shrines and palaces and towers
(Time-eaten towers that tremble not!)
Resemble nothing that is ours.
Around, by lifting winds forgot,
Resignedly beneath the sky
The melancholy waters lie.

No rays from the holy heaven come down
On the long night-time of that town;
But light from out the lurid sea
Streams up the turrets silently —
Gleams up the pinnacles far and free
Up domes — up spires — up kingly halls —
Up fanes — up Babylon-like walls —
Up shadowy long-forgotten bowers
Of sculptured ivy and stone flowers —
Up many and many a marvellous shrine
Whose wreathéd friezes intertwine
The viol, the violet, and the vine.

Resignedly beneath the sky
The melancholy waters lie.
So blend the turrets and shadows there
That all seem pendulous in air,
While from a proud tower in the town
Death looks gigantically down.

There open fanes and gaping graves
Yawn level with the luminous waves;
But not the riches there that lie
In each idol's diamond eye —

Not the gaily-jewelled dead
Tempt the waters from their bed;
For no ripples curl, alas!
Along that wilderness of glass —
No swellings tell that winds may be
Upon some far-off happier sea —
No heavings hint that winds have been
On seas less hideously serene.

But lo, a stir is in the air!
The wave — there is a movement there!
As if the towers had thrust aside,
In slightly sinking, the dull tide —
As if their tops had feebly given
A void within the filmy Heaven.
The waves have now a redder glow —
The hours are breathing faint and low —
And when, amid no earthly moans,
Down, down that town shall settle hence,
Hell, rising from a thousand thrones,
Shall do it reverence.

The Sleeper

At midnight, in the month of June,
I stand beneath the mystic moon.
An opiate vapour, dewy, dim,
Exhales from out her golden rim,
And, softly dripping, drop by drop,
Upon the quiet mountain top,
Steals drowsily and musically
Into the universal valley.
The rosemary nods upon the grave;
The lily lolls upon the wave;
Wrapping the fog about its breast,
The ruin moulders into rest;
Looking like Lethë, see! the lake
A conscious slumber seems to take,
And would not, for the world, awake.
All Beauty sleeps! — and lo! where lies
Irenë, with her Destinies!

Oh, lady bright! can it be right —
This window open to the night?
The wanton airs, from the tree-top,
Laughingly through the lattice drop —
The bodiless airs, a wizard rout,
Flit through thy chamber in and out,
And wave the curtain canopy
So fitfully — so fearfully —
Above the closed and fringéd lid
'Neath which thy slumb'ring soul lies hid,
That, o'er the floor and down the wall,
Like ghosts the shadows rise and fall!
Oh, lady dear, hast thou no fear?
Why and what art thou dreaming here?
Sure thou art come o'er far-off seas,
A wonder to these garden trees!
Strange is thy pallor! strange thy dress!
Strange, above all, thy length of tress,
And this all solemn silentness!

The lady sleeps! Oh, may her sleep,
Which is enduring, so be deep!
Heaven have her in its sacred keep!
This chamber changed for one more holy,
This bed for one more melancholy,
I pray to God that she may lie
Forever with unopened eye,
While the pale sheeted ghosts go by!

My love, she sleeps! Oh, may her sleep,
As it is lasting, so be deep!
Soft may the worms about her creep!
Far in the forest, dim and old,
For her may some tall vault unfold —
Some vault that oft hath flung its black
And wingéd pannels fluttering back,
Triumphant, o'er the crested palls,
Of her grand family funerals —
Some sepulchre, remote, alone,
Against whose portal she hath thrown,
In childhood, many an idle stone —
Some tomb from out whose sounding door

She ne'er shall force an echo more,
Thrilling to think, poor child of sin!
It was the dead who groaned within.

The Haunted Palace

In the greenest of our valleys
    By good angels tenanted,
Once a fair and stately palace —
    Radiant palace — reared its head.
In the monarch Thought's dominion —
    It stood there!
Never seraph spread a pinion
    Over fabric half so fair!

Banners yellow, glorious, golden,
    On its roof did float and flow —
(This — all this — was in the olden
    Time long ago)
And every gentle air that dallied,
    In that sweet day,
Along the ramparts plumed and pallid,
    A wingéd odor went away.

Wanderers in that happy valley,
    Through two luminous windows, saw
Spirits moving musically,
    To a lute's well-tunéd law,
Round about a throne where, sitting,
    Porphyrogene,
In state his glory well befitting
    The ruler of the realm was seen.

And all with pearl and ruby glowing
    Was the fair palace door,
Through which came flowing, flowing flowing,
    And sparkling evermore,
A troop of Echoes whose sweet duty
    Was but to sing,
In voices of surpassing beauty,
    The wit and wisdom of their king.

But evil things, in robes of sorrow,
   Assailed the monarch's high estate.
(Ah, let us mourn! — for never morrow
   Shall dawn upon him, desolate!)
And round about his home the glory
   That blushed and bloomed,
Is but a dim-remembered story
   Of the old-time entombed.

And travellers, now, within that valley,
   Through the encrimsoned windows see
Vast forms that move fantastically
   To a discordant melody,
While, like a ghastly rapid river,
   Through the pale door
A hideous throng rush out forever
   And laugh — but smile no more.

The Coliseum

Type of the antique Rome! Rich reliquary
Of lofty contemplation left to Time
By buried centuries of pomp and power!
At length — at length — after so many days
Of weary pilgrimage and burning thirst,
(Thirst for the springs of lore that in thee lie,)
I kneel, an altered and an humble man,
Amid thy shadows, and so drink within
My very soul thy grandeur, gloom, and glory!

Vastness! and Age! and Memories of Eld!
Silence! and Desolation! and dim Night!
I feel ye now — I feel ye in your strength —
O spells more sure than e'er Judæan king
Taught in the gardens of Gethsemane
O charms more potent than the rapt Chaldee
Ever drew down from out the quiet stars!

Here, where a hero fell, a column falls!
Here, where the mimic eagle glared in gold,
A midnight vigil holds the swarthy bat!
Here, where the dames of Rome their gilded hair

Waved to the wind, now wave the reed and thistle!
Here, where on golden throne the monarch lolled,
Glides, spectre-like, unto his marble home,
Lit by the wan light of the hornéd moon,
The swift and silent lizard of the stones!

But stay! these walls — these ivy-clad arcades —
These mouldering plinths — these sad and blackened shafts —
These vague entablatures — this crumbling frieze —
These shattered cornices — this wreck — this ruin —
All of the famed, and the colossal left
By the corrosive Hours to Fate and me?

"Not all" — the Echoes answer me — "not all!
Prophetic sounds and loud, arise forever
From us, and from all Ruin, unto the wise,
As melody from Memnon to the Sun.
We rule the hearts of mightiest men — we rule
With a despotic sway all giant minds.
We are not impotent — we pallid stones.
Not all our power is gone — not all our fame —
Not all the magic of our high renown —
Not all the wonder that encircles us —
Not all the mysteries that in us lie —
Not all the memories that hang upon
And cling around about us as a garment,
Clothing us in a robe of more than glory."

Sonnet — Silence

There are some qualities — some incorporate things,
   That have a double life, which thus is made
A type of that twin entity which springs
   From matter and light, evinced in solid and shade.
There is a two-fold *Silence* — sea and shore —
   Body and Soul. One dwells in lonely places,
   Newly with grass o'ergrown; some solemn graces,
Some human memories and tearful lore,
Render him terrorless: his name's "No more."
He is the corporate Silence: dread him not!
   No power hath he of evil in himself;
But should some urgent fate (untimely lot!)

Bring thee to meet his shadow (nameless elf,
That haunteth the lone regions where hath trod
No foot of man,) commend thyself to God!

The Conqueror Worm

Lo! 'tis a gala night
   Within the lonesome latter years!
An angel throng, bewinged, bedight
   In veils, and drowned in tears,
Sit in a theatre, to see
   A play of hopes and fears,
While the orchestra breathes fitfully
   The music of the spheres.

Mimes, in the form of God on high.
   Mutter and mumble low,
And hither and thither fly —
   Mere puppets they, who come and go
At bidding of vast formless things
   That shift the scenery to and fro,
Flapping from out their Condor wings
   Invisible Woe!

That motley drama — oh, be sure
   It shall not be forgot!
With its Phantom chased for evermore,
   By a crowd that seize it not,
Through a circle that ever returneth in
   To the self-same spot.
And much of Madness, and more of Sin,
   And Horror the soul of the plot.

But see, amid the mimic rout
   A crawling shape intrude!
A blood-red thing that writhes from out
   The scenic solitude!
It writhes! — it writhes! — with mortal pangs
   The mimes become its food,
And seraphs sob at vermin fangs
   In human gore imbued.

Out — out are the lights — out all!
    And, over each quivering form,
The curtain, a funeral pall,
    Comes down with the rush of a storm,
While the angels, all pallid and wan,
    Uprising, unveiling, affirm
That the play is the tragedy, "Man,"
    And its hero the Conqueror Worm.

Dream-Land

By a route obscure and lonely,
Haunted by ill angels only,
Where an Eidolon, named Night,
On a black throne reigns upright,
I have reached these lands but newly
From an ultimate dim Thule —
From a wild weird clime that lieth, sublime,
    Out of Space — out of Time.

Bottomless vales and boundless floods,
And chasms, and caves, and Titan woods,
With forms that no man can discover
For the dews that drip all over;
Mountains toppling evermore
Into seas without a shore;
Seas that restlessly aspire,
Surging, unto skies of fire;
Lakes that endlessly outspread
Their lone waters — lone and dead, —
Their still waters — still and chilly
With the snows of the lolling lily.

By the lakes that thus outspread
Their lone waters, lone and dead, —
Their sad waters, sad and chilly
With the snows of the lolling lily, —
By the mountains — near the river
Murmuring lowly, murmuring ever, —
By the grey woods, — by the swamp

Where the toad and the newt encamp, —
By the dismal tarns and pools
   Where dwell the Ghouls, —
By each spot the most unholy —
In each nook most melancholy, —
There the traveller meets aghast
Sheeted Memories of the Past —
Shrouded forms that start and sigh
As they pass the wanderer by —
White-robed forms of friends long given,
In agony, to the Earth — and Heaven.

For the heart whose woes are legion
'Tis a peaceful, soothing region —
For the spirit that walks in shadow
O! it is an Eldorado!
But the traveller, travelling through it,
May not — dare not openly view it;
Never its mysteries are exposed
To the weak human eye unclosed;
So wills its King, who hath forbid
The uplifting of the fringed lid;
And thus the sad Soul that here passes
Beholds it but through darkened glasses.

By a route obscure and lonely,
Haunted by ill angels only,
Where an Eidolon, named Night,
On a black throne reigns upright,
I have wandered home but newly
From this ultimate dim Thule.

The Raven

Once upon a midnight dreary, while I pondered, weak and weary,
Over many a quaint and curious volume of forgotten lore —
While I nodded, nearly napping, suddenly there came a tapping,
As of some one gently rapping, rapping at my chamber door —
" 'Tis some visiter," I muttered, "tapping at my chamber door —
     Only this and nothing more."

Ah, distinctly I remember it was in the bleak December;
And each separate dying ember wrought its ghost upon the floor.
Eagerly I wished the morrow; — vainly I had sought to borrow
From my books surcease of sorrow — sorrow for the lost Lenore —
For the rare and radiant maiden whom the angels name Lenore —
      Nameless *here* for evermore.

And the silken, sad, uncertain rustling of each purple curtain
Thrilled me — filled me with fantastic terrors never felt before;
So that now, to still the beating of my heart, I stood repeating,
" 'Tis some visiter entreating entrance at my chamber door —
Some late visiter entreating entrance at my chamber door; —
      This it is and nothing more."

Presently my soul grew stronger; hesitating then no longer,
"Sir," said I, "or Madam, truly your forgiveness I implore;
But the fact is I was napping, and so gently you came rapping,
And so faintly you came tapping, tapping at my chamber door,
That I scarce was sure I heard you" — here I opened wide the door; ——
      Darkness there and nothing more.

Deep into that darkness peering, long I stood there wondering, fearing,
Doubting, dreaming dreams no mortal ever dared to dream before;
But the silence was unbroken, and the stillness gave no token,
And the only word there spoken was the whispered word, "Lenore?"
This I whispered, and an echo murmured back the word "Lenore!"
      Merely this and nothing more.

Back into the chamber turning, all my soul within me burning,
Soon again I heard a tapping somewhat louder than before.
"Surely," said I, "surely that is something at my window lattice;
Let me see, then, what thereat is, and this mystery explore —
Let my heart be still a moment and this mystery explore; —
      'Tis the wind and nothing more!"

Open here I flung the shutter, when, with many a flirt and flutter,
In there stepped a stately Raven of the saintly days of yore:
Not the least obeisance made he; not a minute stopped or stayed he;
But, with mien of lord or lady, perched above my chamber door —
Perched upon a bust of Pallas just above my chamber door —
      Perched, and sat, and nothing more.

Then this ebony bird beguiling my sad fancy into smiling,
By the grave and stern decorum of the countenance it wore:
"Though thy crest be shorn and shaven, thou," I said, "art sure no
       craven,
Ghastly grim and ancient Raven wandering from the Nightly shore —
Tell me what thy lordly name is on the Night's Plutonian shore!"
      Quoth the Raven "Nevermore."

Much I marvelled this ungainly fowl to hear discourse so plainly,
Though its answer little meaning — little relevancy bore:
For we cannot help agreeing that no living human being
Ever yet was blessed with seeing bird above his chamber door —
Bird or beast upon the sculptured bust above his chamber door,
      With such name as "Nevermore."

But the Raven, sitting lonely on the placid bust, spoke only
That one word, as if his soul in that one word he did outpour.
Nothing farther then he uttered — not a feather then he fluttered —
Till I scarcely more than muttered "Other friends have flown before —
On the morrow *he* will leave me, as my Hopes have flown before."
      Then the bird said "Nevermore."

Startled at the stillness broken by reply so aptly spoken,
"Doubtless," said I, "what it utters is its only stock and store
Caught from some unhappy master whom unmerciful Disaster
Followed fast and followed faster till his songs one burden bore —
Till the dirges of his Hope that melancholy burden bore
      Of 'Never — nevermore.' "

But the Raven still beguiling my sad fancy into smiling,
Straight I wheeled a cushioned seat in front of bird, and bust and door;
Then, upon the velvet sinking, I betook myself to linking
Fancy unto fancy, thinking what this ominous bird of yore —
What this grim, ungainly, ghastly, gaunt, and ominous bird of yore
      Meant in croaking "Nevermore."

This I sat engaged in guessing, but no syllable expressing
To the fowl whose fiery eyes now burned into my bosom's core;
This and more I sat divining, with my head at ease reclining
On the cushion's velvet lining that the lamp-light gloated o'er,
But whose velvet-violet lining with the lamp-light gloating o'er,
      She shall press, ah, nevermore!

Then, methought, the air grew denser, perfumed from an unseen censer
Swung by seraphim whose foot-falls tinkled on the tufted floor.
"Wretch," I cried, "thy God hath lent thee — by these angels he hath
   sent thee
Respite — respite and nepenthe from thy memories of Lenore;
Quaff, oh quaff this kind nepenthe and forget this lost Lenore!"
   Quoth the Raven "Nevermore."

"Prophet!" said I, "thing of evil! — prophet still, if bird or devil! —
Whether Tempter sent, or whether tempest tossed thee here ashore,
Desolate yet all undaunted, on this desert land enchanted —
On this home by Horror haunted — tell me truly, I implore —
Is there — is there balm in Gilead? — tell me — tell me, I implore!"
   Quoth the Raven "Nevermore."

"Prophet!" said I, "thing of evil! — prophet still, if bird or devil! —
By that Heaven that bends above us — by that God we both adore —
Tell this soul with sorrow laden if, within the distant Aidenn,
It shall clasp a sainted maiden whom the angels name Lenore —
Clasp a rare and radiant maiden whom the angels name Lenore."
   Quoth the Raven "Nevermore."

"Be that word our sign of parting, bird or fiend!" I shrieked, upstarting —
"Get thee back into the tempest and the Night's Plutonian shore!
Leave no black plume as a token of that lie thy soul hath spoken!
Leave my loneliness unbroken! — quit the bust above my door!
Take thy beak from out my heart, and take thy form from off my door!"
   Quoth the Raven "Nevermore."

And the Raven, never flitting, still is sitting, *still* is sitting
On the pallid bust of Pallas just above my chamber door;
And his eyes have all the seeming of a demon's that is dreaming,
And the lamp-light o'er him streaming throws his shadow on the floor;
And my soul from out that shadow that lies floating on the floor
   Shall be lifted — nevermore!

Ulalume — A Ballad

  The skies they were ashen and sober;
   The leaves they were crispéd and sere —
   The leaves they were withering and sere:
  It was night, in the lonesome October

Of my most immemorial year:
It was hard by the dim lake of Auber,
   In the misty mid region of Weir: —
It was down by the dank tarn of Auber,
   In the ghoul-haunted woodland of Weir.

Here once, through an alley Titanic,
   Of cypress, I roamed with my Soul —
   Of cypress, with Psyche, my Soul.
These were days when my heart was volcanic
   As the scoriac rivers that roll —
   As the lavas that restlessly roll
Their sulphurous currents down Yaanek,
   In the ultimate climes of the Pole —
That groan as they roll down Mount Yaanek,
   In the realms of the Boreal Pole.

Our talk had been serious and sober,
   But our thoughts they were palsied and sere —
   Our memories were treacherous and sere;
For we knew not the month was October,
   And we marked not the night of the year —
   (Ah, night of all nights in the year!)
We noted not the dim lake of Auber,
   (Though once we had journeyed down here)
We remembered not the dank tarn of Auber,
   Nor the ghoul-haunted woodland of Weir.

And now, as the night was senescent,
   And star-dials pointed to morn —
   As the star-dials hinted of morn —
At the end of our path a liquescent
   And nebulous lustre was born,
Out of which a miraculous crescent
   Arose with a duplicate horn —
Astarte's bediamonded crescent,
   Distinct with its duplicate horn.

And I said — "She is warmer than Dian;
   She rolls through an ether of sighs —
   She revels in a region of sighs.
She has seen that the tears are not dry on
   These cheeks where the worm never dies,

And has come past the stars of the Lion,
   To point us the path to the skies —
   To the Lethean peace of the skies —
Come up, in despite of the Lion,
   To shine on us with her bright eyes —
Come up, through the lair of the Lion,
   With love in her luminous eyes."

But Psyche, uplifting her finger,
   Said — "Sadly this star I mistrust —
   Her pallor I strangely mistrust —
Ah, hasten! — ah, let us not linger!
   Ah, fly! — let us fly! — for we must."
In terror she spoke; letting sink her
   Wings till they trailed in the dust —
In agony sobbed; letting sink her
   Plumes till they trailed in the dust —
   Till they sorrowfully trailed in the dust.

I replied — "This is nothing but dreaming.
   Let us on, by this tremulous light!
   Let us bathe in this crystalline light!
Its Sibyllic splendor is beaming
   With Hope and in Beauty to-night —
   See! — it flickers up the sky through the night!
Ah, we safely may trust to its gleaming
   And be sure it will lead us aright —
We surely may trust to a gleaming
   That cannot but guide us aright
Since it flickers up to Heaven through the night."

Thus I pacified Psyche and kissed her,
   And tempted her out of her gloom —
   And conquered her scruples and gloom;
And we passed to the end of the vista —
   But were stopped by the door of a tomb, —
   By the door of a legended tomb: —
And I said — "What is written, sweet sister,
   On the door of this legended tomb?"
   She replied — "Ulalume — Ulalume! —
   'T is the vault of thy lost Ulalume!"

Then my heart it grew ashen and sober
  As the leaves that were crispéd and sere —
  As the leaves that were withering and sere —
And I cried — "It was surely October,
  On *this* very night of last year,
  That I journeyed — I journeyed down here! —
  That I brought a dread burden down here —
  On this night, of all nights in the year,
  Ah, what demon hath tempted me here?
Well I know, now, this dim lake of Auber —
  This misty mid region of Weir: —
Well I know, now, this dank tarn of Auber —
  This ghoul-haunted woodland of Weir.". . .

Eldorado

    Gaily bedight,
    A gallant knight,
In sunshine and in shadow,
    Had journeyed long,
    Singing a song,
In search of Eldorado.

    But he grew old —
    This knight so bold —
And o'er his heart a shadow
    Fell, as he found
    No spot of ground
That looked like Eldorado.

    And, as his strength
    Failed him at length
He met a pilgrim shadow —
    "Shadow," said he,
    "Where can it be —
This land of Eldorado?"

    "Over the Mountains
    Of the Moon,
Down the Valley of the Shadow,
    Ride, boldly ride,"
    The shade replied, —
"If you seek for Eldorado!"

For Annie

Thank Heaven! the crisis —
  The danger is past,
And the lingering illness
  Is over at last —
And the fever called "Living"
  Is conquered at last.

Sadly, I know
  I am shorn of my strength,
And no muscle I move
  As I lie at full length —
But no matter! — I feel
  I am better at length.

And I rest so composedly,
  Now, in my bed,
That any beholder
  Might fancy me dead —
Might start at beholding me,
  Thinking me dead.

The moaning and groaning,
  The sighing and sobbing,
Are quieted now,
  With that horrible throbbing
At heart: — ah, that horrible,
  Horrible throbbing!

The sickness — the nausea —
  The pitiless pain —
Have ceased, with the fever
  That maddened my brain —
With the fever called "Living"
  That burned in my brain.

And oh! of all tortures
  That torture the worst
Has abated — the terrible
  Torture of thirst
For the napthaline river
  Of Passion accurst: —
I have drank of a water
  That quenches all thirst: —

Of a water that flows,
  With a lullaby sound,
From a spring but a very few
  Feet under ground —
From a cavern not very far
  Down under ground.

And ah! let it never
  Be foolishly said
That my room it is gloomy
  And narrow my bed;
For man never slept
  In a different bed —
And, to *sleep*, you must slumber
  In just such a bed.

My tantalized spirit
  Here blandly reposes,
Forgetting, or never
  Regretting its roses —
Its old agitations
  Of myrtles and roses:

For now, while so quietly
  Lying, it fancies
A holier odor
  About it, of pansies —
A rosemary odor,
  Commingled with pansies —
With rue and the beautiful
  Puritan pansies.

And so it lies happily,
  Bathing in many
A dream of the truth
  And the beauty of Annie —
Drowned in a bath
  Of the tresses of Annie.

She tenderly kissed me,
  She fondly caressed,
And then I fell gently
  To sleep on her breast —
Deeply to sleep
  From the heaven of her breast. ☛

When the light was extinguished,
  She covered me warm,
And she prayed to the angels
  To keep me from harm —
To the queen of the angels
  To shield me from harm.

And I lie so composedly,
  Now, in my bed,
(Knowing her love)
  That you fancy me dead —
And I rest so contentedly,
  Now in my bed,
(With her love at my breast)
  That you fancy me dead —
That you shudder to look at me,
  Thinking me dead: —

But my heart it is brighter
  Than all of the many
Stars in the sky,
  For it sparkles with Annie —
It glows with the light
  Of the love of my Annie —
With the thought of the light
  Of the eyes of my Annie.

Annabel Lee

It was many and many a year ago,
  In a kingdom by the sea,
That a maiden there lived whom you may know
  By the name of Annabel Lee; —
And this maiden she lived with no other thought
  Than to love and be loved by me.

She was a child and *I* was a child,
   In this kingdom by the sea,
But we loved with a love that was more than love —
   I and my Annabel Lee —
With a love that the wingéd seraphs of Heaven
   Coveted her and me.

And this was the reason that, long ago,
   In this kingdom by the sea,
A wind blew out of a cloud by night
   Chilling my Annabel Lee;
So that her highborn kinsmen came
   And bore her away from me,
To shut her up in a sepulchre
   In this kingdom by the sea.

The angels, not half so happy in Heaven,
   Went envying her and me: —
Yes! that was the reason (as all men know,
   In this kingdom by the sea)
That the wind came out of the cloud, chilling
   And killing my Annabel Lee.

But our love it was stronger by far than the love
   Of those who were older than we —
   Of many far wiser than we —
And neither the angels in Heaven above
   Nor the demons down under the sea
Can ever dissever my soul from the soul
   Of the beautiful Annabel Lee: —

For the moon never beams without bringing me dreams
   Of the beautiful Annabel Lee;
And the stars never rise but I see the bright eyes
   Of the beautiful Annabel Lee;
And so, all the night-tide, I lie down by the side
Of my darling, my darling, my life and my bride
   In her sepulchre there by the sea —
   In her tomb by the side of the sea.

JONES VERY
1813–1880

The Columbine

Still, still my eye will gaze long fixed on thee,
Till I forget that I am called a man,
And at thy side fast-rooted seem to be,
And the breeze comes my cheek with thine to fan.
Upon this craggy hill our life shall pass,
A life of summer days and summer joys,
Nodding our honey-bells mid pliant grass
In which the bee half hid his time employs;
And here we'll drink with thirsty pores the rain,
And turn dew-sprinkled to the rising sun,
And look when in the flaming west again
His orb across the heaven its path has run;
Here left in darkness on the rocky steep,
My weary eyes shall close like folding flowers in sleep.

The New Birth

'Tis a new life; — thoughts move not as they did
With slow uncertain steps across my mind,
In thronging haste fast pressing on they bid
The portals open to the viewless wind
That comes not save when in the dust is laid
The crown of pride that gilds each mortal brow,
And from before man's vision melting fade
The heavens and earth; — their walls are falling now. —
Fast crowding on, each thought asks utterance strong;
Storm-lifted waves swift rushing to the shore,
On from the sea they send their shouts along,
Back through the cave-worn rocks their thunders roar;
And I a child of God by Christ made free
Start from death's slumbers to Eternity.

The Dead

I see them, — crowd on crowd they walk the earth
Dry leafless trees to autumn wind laid bare;
And in their nakedness find cause for mirth,

And all unclad would winter's rudeness dare;
No sap doth through their clattering branches flow,
Whence springing leaves and blossoms bright appear;
Their hearts the living God have ceased to know
Who gives the spring time to th' expectant year;
They mimic life, as if from him to steal
His glow of health to paint the livid cheek;
They borrow words for thoughts they cannot feel,
That with a seeming heart their tongue may speak;
And in their show of life more dead they live
Than those that to the earth with many tears they give.

The Grave-Yard

My heart grows sick before the wide-spread death
That walks and speaks in seeming life around;
And I would love the corse without a breath,
That sleeps forgotten 'neath the cold, cold ground;
For these do tell the story of decay,
The worm and rotten flesh hide not nor lie;
But this, though dying too from day to day,
With a false show doth cheat the longing eye;
And hide the worm that gnaws the core of life,
With painted cheek and smooth deceitful skin;
Covering a grave with sights of darkness rife,
A secret cavern filled with death and sin;
And men walk o'er these graves and know it not,
For in the body's health the soul's forgot.

Thy Brother's Blood

I have no Brother, — they who meet me now
Offer a hand with their own wills defiled,
And, while they wear a smooth unwrinkled brow,
Know not that Truth can never be beguiled;
Go wash the hand that still betrays thy guilt; —
Before the spirit's gaze what stain can hide?
Abel's red blood upon the earth is spilt,
And by thy tongue it cannot be denied;
I hear not with the ear, — the heart doth tell
Its secret deeds to me untold before;

Go, all its hidden plunder quickly sell,
Then shalt thou cleanse thee from thy brother's gore,
Then will I take thy gift; — that bloody stain
Shall not be seen upon thy hand again.

The New Man

The hands must touch and handle many things,
The eyes long waste their glances all in vain;
The feet course still in idle, mazy rings,
Ere man himself, the lost, shall back regain
The hand that ever moves, the eyes that see,
While day holds out his shining lamp on high,
And, strait as flies the honey-seeking bee,
Direct the feet to unseen flowers they spy;
These, when they come, the man revealed from heaven,
Shall labor all the day in quiet rest,
And find at eve the covert duly given,
Where with the bird they find sweet sleep and rest,
That shall their wasted strength to health restore,
And bid them seek with morn the hills and fields once more.

The Clouded Morning

The morning comes, and thickening clouds prevail,
    Hanging like curtains all the horizon round,
Or overhead in heavy stillness sail;
    So still is day, it seems like night profound;
Scarce by the city's din the air is stirred,
    And dull and deadened comes its every sound;
The cock's shrill, piercing voice subdued is heard,
    By the thick folds of muffling vapors drowned.
Dissolved in mists the hills and trees appear,
    Their outlines lost and blended with the sky;
And well-known objects, that to all are near,
    No longer seem familiar to the eye,
But with fantastic forms they mock the sight,
As when we grope amid the gloom of night.

The Trees of Life

For those who worship Thee there is no death,
For all they do is but with Thee to dwell;
Now while I take from Thee this passing breath,
It is but of Thy glorious name to tell;
Nor words nor measured sounds have I to find,
But in them both my soul doth ever flow;
They come as viewless as the unseen wind,
And tell Thy noiseless steps where'er I go;
The trees that grow along Thy living stream,
And from its springs refreshment ever drink,
Forever glittering in Thy morning beam
They bend them o'er the river's grassy brink.
And as more high and wide their branches grow
They look more fair within the depths below.

I Was Sick and in Prison

Thou hast not left the rough-barked tree to grow
Without a mate upon the river's bank;
Nor dost Thou on one flower the rain bestow,
But many a cup the glittering drops has drank;
The bird must sing to one who sings again,
Else would her note less welcome be to hear;
Nor hast Thou bid thy word descend in vain,
But soon some answering voice shall reach my ear;
Then shall the brotherhood of peace begin,
And the new song be raised that never dies,
That shall the soul from death and darkness win,
And burst the prison where the captive lies;
And one by one new-born shall join the strain,
Till earth restores her sons to heaven again.

Yourself

'T is to yourself I speak; you cannot know
Him whom I call in speaking such an one,
For thou beneath the earth liest buried low,
Which he alone as living walks upon;
Thou mayst at times have heard him speak to you,
And often wished perchance that you were he;

And I must ever wish that it were true,
For then thou couldst hold fellowship with me;
But now thou hear'st us talk as strangers, met
Above the room wherein thou liest abed;
A word perhaps loud spoken thou mayst get,
Or hear our feet when heavily they tread;
But he who speaks, or him who's spoken to,
Must both remain as strangers still to you.

The Lost

The fairest day that ever yet has shone
Will be when thou the day within shalt see;
The fairest rose that ever yet has blown,
When thou the flower thou lookest on shalt be;
But thou art far away amidst Time's toys;
Thyself the day thou lookest for in them,
Thyself the flower that now thine eye enjoys;
But wilted now thou hang'st upon thy stem;
The bird thou hearest on the budding tree
Thou hast made sing with thy forgotten voice;
But when it swells again to melody,
The song is thine in which thou wilt rejoice;
And thou new risen 'midst these wonders live,
That now to them dost all thy substance give.

The Fair Morning

The clear bright morning, with its scented air
    And gaily waving flowers, is here again;
Man's heart is lifted with the voice of prayer,
    And peace descends, as falls the gentle rain;
The tuneful birds, that all the night have slept,
    Take up at dawn the evening's dying lay,
When sleep upon their eyelids gently crept
    And stole with stealthy craft their song away.
High overhead the forest's swaying boughs
    Sprinkle with drops the traveler on his way;
He hears far off the tinkling bells of cows
    Driven to pasture at the break of day;
With vigorous step he passes swift along,
Making the woods reëcho with his song.

The Day of Denial

Are there not twelve whole hours in every day
The sun upon thy dial marks for toil;
How is it some but five, some seven say,
And some among you of the whole make spoil?
Think'st thou to gain by taking from your life,
By dying many hours to live the more?
Dost thou not see the suicidal knife,
Made hour by hour yet redder in thy gore?
The day! the living day! how soon 't is night,
With him who rises not till near its noon;
His candle lit for many hours to light,
Put out ere yet he learned to prize the boon;
How dark his darkness, who till latest eve
Still slumbers on, nor then his couch will leave!

The Lament of the Flowers

I looked to find Spring's early flowers,
  In spots where they were wont to bloom;
But they had perished in their bowers;
  The haunts they loved had proved their tomb!

The alder, and the laurel green,
  Which sheltered them, had shared their fate;
And but the blackened ground was seen,
  Where hid their swelling buds of late.

From the bewildered, homeless bird,
  Whose half-built nest the flame destroys,
A low complaint of wrong I heard,
  Against the thoughtless, ruthless boys.

Sadly I heard its notes complain,
  And ask the young its haunts to spare;
Prophetic seemed the sorrowing strain,
  Sung o'er its home, but late so fair!

"No more with hues like ocean shell
  The delicate wind-flower here shall blow;
The spot that loved its form so well
  Shall ne'er again its beauty know.

"Or, if it bloom, like some pale ghost
    'T will haunt the black and shadeless dell,
Where once it bloomed a numerous host,
    Of its once pleasant bowers to tell.

"And coming years no more shall find
    The laurel green upon the hills;
The frequent fire leaves naught behind,
    But e'en the very roots it kills.

"No more upon the turnpike's side
    The rose shall shed its sweet perfume;
The traveler's joy, the summer's pride,
    Will share with them a common doom.

"No more shall these returning fling
    Round childhood's home a heavenly charm,
With song of bird in early spring,
    To glad the heart and save from harm."

The Sumach Leaves

Some autumn leaves a painter took,
    And with his colors caught their hues;
So true to nature did they look
    That none to praise them could refuse.

The yellow mingling with the red
    Shone beauteous in their bright decay,
And round a golden radiance shed,
    Like that which hangs o'er parting day.

Their sister leaves, that, fair as these,
    Thus far had shared a common lot,
All soiled and scattered by the breeze
    Are now by every one forgot.

Soon, trodden under foot of men,
    Their very forms will cease to be,
Nor they remembered be again,
    Till Autumn decks once more the tree.

But these shall still their beauty boast,
   To praise the painter's wondrous art,
When Autumn's glories all are lost
   And with the fading year depart;

And through the wintry months so pale
   The sumach's brilliant hues recall;
Where, waving over hill and vale,
   They gave its splendor to our fall.

HENRY DAVID THOREAU
1817–1862

I am a Parcel of Vain Strivings Tied

I am a parcel of vain strivings tied
   By a chance bond together,
Dangling this way and that, their links
   Were made so loose and wide,
     Methinks,
   For milder weather.

A bunch of violets without their roots,
   And sorrel intermixed,
Encircled by a wisp of straw
   Once coiled about their shoots,
     The law
   By which I'm fixed.

A nosegay which Time clutched from out
   Those fair Elysian fields,
With weeds and broken stems, in haste,
   Doth make the rabble rout
     That waste
   The day he yields.

And here I bloom for a short hour unseen,
   Drinking my juices up,
With no root in the land
   To keep my branches green,
     But stand
   In a bare cup.

Some tender buds were left upon my stem
    In mimicry of life,
But ah! the children will not know,
    Till time has withered them,
        The woe
      With which they're rife.

But now I see I was not plucked for naught,
    And after in life's vase
Of glass set while I might survive,
    But by a kind hand brought
        Alive
      To a strange place.

That stock thus thinned will soon redeem its hours,
    And by another year,
Such as God knows, with freer air,
    More fruits and fairer flowers
        Will bear,
      While I droop here.

Light-Winged Smoke, Icarian Bird

Light-winged Smoke, Icarian bird,
Melting thy pinions in thy upward flight,
Lark without song, and messenger of dawn,
Circling above the hamlets as thy nest;
Or else, departing dream, and shadowy form
Of midnight vision, gathering up thy skirts;
By night star-veiling, and by day
Darkening the light and blotting out the sun;
Go thou my incense upward from this hearth,
And ask the gods to pardon this clear flame.

Inspiration

Whate'er we leave to God, God does,
    And blesses us;
The work we choose should be our own,
    God lets alone.

If with light head erect I sing,
   Though all the muses lend their force,
From my poor love of anything,
   The verse is weak and shallow as its source.

But if with bended neck I grope,
   Listening behind me for my wit,
With faith superior to hope,
   More anxious to keep back than forward it,

Making my soul accomplice there
   Unto the flame my heart hath lit,
Then will the verse forever wear, —
   Time cannot bend the line which God hath writ.

Always the general show of things
   Floats in review before my mind,
And such true love and reverence brings,
   That sometimes I forget that I am blind.

But now there comes unsought, unseen,
   Some clear, divine electuary,
And I who had but sensual been,
   Grow sensible, and as God is, am wary.

I hearing get who had but ears,
   And sight, who had but eyes before,
I moments live who lived but years,
   And truth discern who knew but learning's lore.

I hear beyond the range of sound,
   I see beyond the range of sight,
New earths and skies and seas around,
   And in my day the sun doth pale his light.

A clear and ancient harmony
   Pierces my soul through all its din,
As through its utmost melody, —
   Farther behind than they — farther within.

More swift its bolt than lightning is,
   Its voice than thunder is more loud,
It doth expand my privacies
   To all, and leave me single in the crowd.

It speaks with such authority,
   With so serene and lofty tone,
That idle Time runs gadding by,
   And leaves me with Eternity alone.

Then chiefly is my natal hour,
   And only then my prime of life,
Of manhood's strength it is the flower,
   'Tis peace's end and war's beginning strife.

'T 'hath come in summer's broadest noon,
   By a grey wall or some chance place,
Unseasoned time, insulted June,
   And vexed the day with its presuming face.

Such fragrance round my couch it makes,
   More rich than are Arabian drugs,
That my soul scents its life and wakes
   The body up beneath its perfumed rugs.

Such is the Muse — the heavenly maid,
   The star that guides our mortal course,
Which shows where life's true kernel's laid,
   Its wheat's fine flower, and its undying force.

She with one breath attunes the spheres,
   And also my poor human heart,
With one impulse propels the years
   Around, and gives my throbbing pulse its start.

I will not doubt forever more,
   Nor falter from a steadfast faith,
For though the system be turned o'er,
   God takes not back the word which once he saith.

I will then trust the love untold
   Which not my worth nor want has bought,
Which wooed me young and woos me old,
   And to this evening hath me brought.

My memory I'll educate
   To know the one historic truth,
Remembering to the latest date
   The only true and sole immortal youth.

Be but thy inspiration given,
  No matter through what danger sought,
I'll fathom hell or climb to heaven,
  And yet esteem that cheap which love has bought.

———————

Fame cannot tempt the bard
  Who's famous with his God,
Nor laurel him reward
  Who hath his Maker's nod.

Within the Circuit of this Plodding Life

Within the circuit of this plodding life
There enter moments of an azure hue,
Untarnished fair as is the violet
Or anemone, when the spring strews them
By some meandering rivulet, which make
The best philosophy untrue that aims
But to console man for his grievances.
I have remembered when the winter came,
High in my chamber in the frosty nights,
When in the still light of the cheerful moon,
On every twig and rail and jutting spout,
The icy spears were adding to their length
Against the arrows of the coming sun,
How in the shimmering noon of summer past
Some unrecorded beam slanted across
The upland pastures where the Johnswort grew;
Or heard, amid the verdure of my mind,
The bee's long smothered hum, on the blue flag
Loitering amidst the mead; or busy rill,
Which now through all its course stands still and dumb
Its own memorial, — purling at its play
Along the slopes, and through the meadows next,
Until its youthful sound was hushed at last
In the staid current of the lowland stream;
Or seen the furrows shine but late upturned,
And where the fieldfare followed in the rear,
When all the fields around lay bound and hoar
Beneath a thick integument of snow.
So by God's cheap economy made rich
To go upon my winter's task again.

The River Swelleth More and More

The river swelleth more and more,
Like some sweet influence stealing o'er
The passive town; and for a while
Each tussuck makes a tiny isle,
Where, on some friendly Ararat,
Resteth the weary water-rat.

No ripple shows Musketaquid,
Her very current e'en is hid,
As deepest souls do calmest rest,
When thoughts are swelling in the breast,
And she that in the summer's drought
Doth make a rippling and a rout,
Sleeps from Nahshawtuck to the Cliff,
Unruffled by a single skiff.
But by a thousand distant hills
The louder roar a thousand rills,
And many a spring which now is dumb,
And many a stream with smothered hum,
Doth swifter well and faster glide,
Though buried deep beneath the tide.

Our village shows a rural Venice,
Its broad lagoons where yonder fen is;
As lovely as the Bay of Naples
Yon placid cove amid the maples;
And in my neighbor's field of corn
I recognise the Golden Horn.
Here Nature taught from year to year,
When only red men came to hear,
Methinks 'twas in this school of art
Venice and Naples learned their part,
But still their mistress, to my mind,
Her young disciples leaves behind.

Great God, I Ask Thee for No Meaner Pelf

Great God, I ask thee for no meaner pelf
Than that I may not disappoint myself,
That in my action I may soar as high,
As I can now discern with this clear eye.

And next in value, which thy kindness lends,
That I may greatly disappoint my friends,
Howe'er they think or hope that it may be,
They may not dream how thou'st distinguished me.

That my weak hand may equal my firm faith,
And my life practice more than my tongue saith;
That my low conduct may not show,
Nor my relenting lines,
That I thy purpose did not know,
Or overrated thy designs.

JULIA WARD HOWE
1819–1910

The Battle Hymn of the Republic

Mine eyes have seen the glory of the coming of the Lord:
He is trampling out the vintage where the grapes of wrath are stored;
He hath loosed the fatal lightning of His terrible swift sword:
    His truth is marching on.

I have seen Him in the watch-fires of a hundred circling camps,
They have builded Him an altar in the evening dews and damps;
I can read His righteous sentence by the dim and flaring lamps:
    His day is marching on.

I have read a fiery gospel writ in burnished rows of steel:
"As ye deal with my contemners, so with you my grace shall deal;
Let the Hero, born of woman, crush the serpent with his heel,
    Since God is marching on."

He has sounded forth the trumpet that shall never call retreat;
He is sifting out the hearts of men before His judgement seat:
Oh, be swift, my soul, to answer Him! Be jubilant, my feet!
    Our God is marching on.

In the beauty of the lilies Christ was born across the sea,
With a glory in his bosom that transfigures you and me:
As he died to make men holy, let us die to make men free,
    While God is marching on.

JAMES RUSSELL LOWELL
1819–1891

from A Fable for Critics

[*Emerson*]

"There comes Emerson first, whose rich words, every one,
Are like gold nails in temples to hang trophies on,
Whose prose is grand verse, while his verse, the Lord knows,
Is some of it pr— No, 't is not even prose;
I'm speaking of metres; some poems have welled
From those rare depths of soul that have ne'er been excelled;
They're not epics, but that doesn't matter a pin,
In creating, the only hard thing's to begin;
A grass-blade's no easier to make than an oak;
If you've once found the way, you've achieved the grand stroke;
In the worst of his poems are mines of rich matter,
But thrown in a heap with a crash and a clatter;
Now it is not one thing nor another alone
Makes a poem, but rather the general tone,
The something pervading, uniting the whole,
The before unconceived, unconceivable soul,
So that just in removing this trifle or that, you
Take away, as it were, a chief limb of the statue;
Roots, wood, bark, and leaves singly perfect may be,
But, clapt hodge-podge together, they don't make a tree.

"But, to come back to Emerson (whom by the way,
I believe we left waiting), — his is, we may say,
A Greek head on right Yankee shoulders, whose range
Has Olympus for one pole, for t'other the Exchange;
He seems, to my thinking (although I'm afraid
The comparison must, long ere this, have been made),
A Plotinus-Montaigne, where the Egyptian's gold mist
And the Gascon's shrewd wit cheek-by-jowl coexist;
All admire, and yet scarcely six converts he's got
To I don't (nor they either) exactly know what;
For though he builds glorious temples, 't is odd
He leaves never a doorway to get in a god.
'T is refreshing to old-fashioned people like me
To meet such a primitive Pagan as he,
In whose mind all creation is duly respected
As parts of himself — just a little projected;

And who's willing to worship the stars and the sun,
A convert to — nothing but Emerson.
So perfect a balance there is in his head,
That he talks of things sometimes as if they were dead;
Life, nature, love, God, and affairs of that sort,
He looks at as merely ideas; in short,
As if they were fossils stuck round in a cabinet,
Of such vast extent that our earth's a mere dab in it;
Composed just as he is inclined to conjecture her,
Namely, one part pure earth, ninety-nine parts pure lecturer;
You are filled with delight at his clear demonstration,
Each figure, word, gesture, just fits the occasion,
With the quiet precision of science he'll sort 'em,
But you can't help suspecting the whole a *post mortem*.

"There are persons, mole-blind to the soul's make and style,
Who insist on a likeness 'twixt him and Carlyle;
To compare him with Plato would be vastly fairer,
Carlyle's the more burly, but E. is the rarer;
He sees fewer objects, but clearlier, truelier,
If C.'s as original, E.'s more peculiar;
That he's more of a man you might say of the one,
Of the other he's more of an Emerson;
C.'s the Titan, as shaggy of mind as of limb, —
E. the clear-eyed Olympian, rapid and slim;
The one's two thirds Norseman, the other half Greek,
Where the one's most abounding, the other's to seek;
C.'s generals require to be seen in the mass, —
E.'s specialties gain if enlarged by the glass;
C. gives nature and God his fits of the blues,
And rims common-sense things with mystical hues, —
E. sits in a mystery calm and intense,
And looks coolly around him with sharp common-sense;
C. shows you how every-day matters unite
With the dim transdiurnal recesses of night, —
While E., in a plain, preternatural way,
Makes mysteries matters of mere every day;
C. draws all his characters quite *à la* Fuseli, —
No sketching their bundles of muscles and thews illy,
He paints with a brush so untamed and profuse,
They seem nothing but bundles of muscles and thews;
E. is rather like Flaxman, lines strait and severe,
And a colorless outline, but full, round, and clear; —

To the men he thinks worthy he frankly accords
The design of a white marble statue in words.
C. labors to get at the centre, and then
Take a reckoning from there of his actions and men;
E. calmly assumes the said centre as granted,
And, given himself, has whatever is wanted.

"He has imitators in scores, who omit
No part of the man but his wisdom and wit, —
Who go carefully o'er the sky-blue of his brain,
And when he has skimmed it once, skim it again;
If at all they resemble him, you may be sure it is
Because their shoals mirror his mists and obscurities,
As a mud-puddle seems deep as heaven for a minute,
While a cloud that floats o'er is reflected within it.

"There comes ——, for instance; to see him 's rare sport,
Tread in Emerson's tracks with legs painfully short;
How he jumps, how he strains, and gets red in the face,
To keep step with the mystagogue's natural pace!
He follows as close as a stick to a rocket,
His fingers exploring the prophet's each pocket.
Fie, for shame, brother bard; with good fruit of your own,
Can't you let Neighbor Emerson's orchards alone?
Besides, 't is no use, you'll not find e'en a core, —
—— has picked up all the windfalls before.
They might strip every tree, and E. never would catch 'em,
His Hesperides have no rude dragon to watch 'em;
When they send him a dishful, and ask him to try 'em,
He never suspects how the sly rogues came by 'em;
He wonders why 't is there are none such his trees on,
And thinks 'em the best he has tasted this season.

. . .

[Bryant]

"There is Bryant, as quiet, as cool, and as dignified,
As a smooth, silent iceberg, that never is ignified,
Save when by reflection 't is kindled o' nights
With a semblance of flame by the chill Northern Lights.
He may rank (Griswold says so) first bard of your nation
(There's no doubt that he stands in supreme iceolation),
Your topmost Parnassus he may set his heel on,

But no warm applauses come, peal following peal on, —
He's too smooth and too polished to hang any zeal on:
Unqualified merits, I'll grant, if you choose, he has 'em,
But he lacks the one merit of kindling enthusiasm;
If he stir you at all, it is just, on my soul,
Like being stirred up with the very North Pole.

"He is very nice reading in summer, but *inter
Nos*, we don't want *extra* freezing in winter;
Take him up in the depth of July, my advice is,
When you feel an Egyptian devotion to ices.
But, deduct all you can, there's enough that's right good in him,
He has a true soul for field, river, and wood in him;
And his heart, in the midst of brick walls, or where'er it is,
Glows, softens, and thrills with the tenderest charities —
To you mortals that delve in this trade-ridden planet?
No, to old Berkshire's hills, with their limestone and granite.
If you're one who *in loco* (add *foco* here) *desipis*,
You will get of his outermost heart (as I guess) a piece;
But you'd get deeper down if you came as a precipice,
And would break the last seal of its inwardest fountain,
If you only could palm yourself off for a mountain.
Mr. Quivis, or somebody quite as discerning,
Some scholar who's hourly expecting his learning,
Calls B. the American Wordsworth; but Wordsworth
May be rated at more than your whole tuneful herd's worth.
No, don't be absurd, he's an excellent Bryant;
But, my friends, you 'll endanger the life of your client,
By attempting to stretch him up into a giant:
If you choose to compare him, I think there are two per-
-sons fit for a parallel — Thomson and Cowper;
I don't mean exactly, — there 's something of each,
There 's T.'s love of nature, C.'s penchant to preach;
Just mix up their minds so that C.'s spice of craziness
Shall balance and neutralize T.'s turn for laziness,
And it gives you a brain cool, quite frictionless, quiet,
Whose internal police nips the buds of all riot, —
A brain like a permanent strait-jacket put on
The heart that strives vainly to burst off a button, —
A brain which, without being slow or mechanic,
Does more than a larger less drilled, more volcanic;
He's a Cowper condensed, with no craziness bitten,
And the advantage that Wordsworth before him had written.

"But, my dear little bardlings, don't prick up your ears
Nor suppose I would rank you and Bryant as peers;
If I call him an iceberg, I don't mean to say
There is nothing in that which is grand in its way;
He is almost the one of your poets that knows
How much grace, strength, and dignity lie in Repose;
If he sometimes fall short, he is too wise to mar
His thought's modest fulness by going too far;
'T would be well if your authors should all make a trial
Of what virtue there is in severe self-denial,
And measure their writings by Hesiod's staff,
Which teaches that all has less value than half.

[Whittier]

"There is Whittier, whose swelling and vehement heart
Strains the strait-breasted drab of the Quaker apart,
And reveals the live Man, still supreme and erect,
Underneath the bemummying wrappers of sect;
There was ne'er a man born who had more of the swing
Of the true lyric bard and all that kind of thing;
And his failures arise (though he seem not to know it)
From the very same cause that has made him a poet, —
A fervor of mind which knows no separation
'Twixt simple excitement and pure inspiration,
As my Pythoness erst sometimes erred from not knowing
If 't were I or mere wind through her tripod was blowing;
Let his mind once get head in its favorite direction
And the torrent of verse bursts the dams of reflection,
While, borne with the rush of the metre along,
The poet may chance to go right or go wrong,
Content with the whirl and delirium of song;
Then his grammar's not always correct, nor his rhymes,
And he 's prone to repeat his own lyrics sometimes,
Not his best, though, for those are struck off at white-heats
When the heart in his breast like a trip-hammer beats,
And can ne'er be repeated again any more
Than they could have been carefully plotted before:
Like old what 's-his-name there at the battle of Hastings
(Who, however, gave more than mere rhythmical bastings),
Our Quaker leads off metaphorical fights
For reform and whatever they call human rights,
Both singing and striking in front of the war,

And hitting his foes with the mallet of Thor;
Anne haec, one exclaims, on beholding his knocks,
Vestis filii tui, O leather-clad Fox?
Can that be thy son, in the battle's mid din,
Preaching brotherly love and then driving it in
To the brain of the tough old Goliath of sin,
With the smoothest of pebbles from Castaly's spring
Impressed on his hard moral sense with a sling?

   "All honor and praise to the right-hearted bard
Who was true to The Voice when such service was hard,
Who himself was so free he dared sing for the slave
When to look but a protest in silence was brave;
All honor and praise to the women and men
Who spoke out for the dumb and the down-trodden then!
It needs not to name them, already for each
I see History preparing the statue and niche;
They were harsh, but shall *you* be so shocked at hard words
Who have beaten your pruning-hooks up into swords,
Whose rewards and hurrahs men are surer to gain
By the reaping of men and of women than grain?
Why should *you* stand aghast at their fierce wordy war, if
You scalp one another for Bank or for Tariff?
Your calling them cut-throats and knaves all day long
Does n't prove that the use of hard language is wrong;
While the World's heart beats quicker to think of such men
As signed Tyranny's doom with a bloody steel-pen,
While on Fourth-of-Julys beardless orators fright one
With hints at Harmodius and Aristogeiton,
You need not look shy at your sisters and brothers
Who stab with sharp words for the freedom of others; —
No, a wreath, twine a wreath for the loyal and true
Who, for sake of the many, dared stand with the few,
Not of blood-spattered laurel for enemies braved,
But of broad, peaceful oak-leaves for citizens saved!

      .   .   .

[Hawthorne]

   "There is Hawthorne, with genius so shrinking and rare
That you hardly at first see the strength that is there;
A frame so robust, with a nature so sweet,
So earnest, so graceful, so lithe and so fleet,

Is worth a descent from Olympus to meet;
'T is as if a rough oak that for ages had stood,
With his gnarled bony branches like ribs of the wood,
Should bloom, after cycles of struggle and scathe,
With a single anemone trembly and rathe;
His strength is so tender, his wildness so meek,
That a suitable parallel sets one to seek, —
He's a John Bunyan Fouqué, a Puritan Tieck;
When Nature was shaping him, clay was not granted
For making so full-sized a man as she wanted,
So, to fill out her model, a little she spared
From some finer-grained stuff for a woman prepared,
And she could not have hit a more excellent plan
For making him fully and perfectly man.
The success of her scheme gave her so much delight,
That she tried it again, shortly after, in Dwight;
Only, while she was kneading and shaping the clay,
She sang to her work in her sweet childish way,
And found, when she'd put the last touch to his soul,
That the music had somehow got mixed with the whole.

[*Cooper*]

"Here's Cooper, who's written six volumes to show
He's as good as a lord: well, let's grant that he's so;
If a person prefer that description of praise,
Why, a coronet's certainly cheaper than bays;
But he need take no pains to convince us he's not
(As his enemies say) the American Scott.
Choose any twelve men, and let C. read aloud
That one of his novels of which he 's most proud,
And I'd lay any bet that, without ever quitting
Their box, they'd be all, to a man, for acquitting.
He has drawn you one character, though, that is new,
One wildflower he's plucked that is wet with the dew
Of this fresh Western world, and the thing not to mince,
He has done naught but copy it ill ever since;
His Indians, with proper respect be it said,
Are just Natty Bumppo, daubed over with red,
And his very Long Toms are the same useful Nat,
Rigged up in duck pants and a sou'wester hat
(Though once in a Coffin, a good chance was found
To have slipped the old fellow away underground).

All his other men-figures are clothes upon sticks,
The *dernière chemise* of a man in a fix
(As a captain besieged, when his garrison's small,
Sets up caps upon poles to be seen o'er the wall);
And the women he draws from one model don't vary,
All sappy as maples and flat as a prairie.
When a character 's wanted, he goes to the task
As a cooper would do in composing a cask;
He picks out the staves, of their qualities heedful,
Just hoops them together as tight as is needful,
And, if the best fortune should crown the attempt, he
Has made at the most something wooden and empty.

"Don't suppose I would underrate Cooper's abilities;
If I thought you'd do that, I should feel very ill at ease;
The men who have given to *one* character life
And objective existence are not very rife;
You may number them all, both prose-writers and singers,
Without overrunning the bounds of your fingers,
And Natty won't go to oblivion quicker
Than Adams the parson or Primrose the vicar.

"There is one thing in Cooper I like, too, and that is
That on manners he lectures his countrymen gratis;
Not precisely so either, because, for a rarity,
He is paid for his tickets in unpopularity.
Now he may overcharge his American pictures,
But you 'll grant there 's a good deal of truth in his structures;
And I honor the man who is willing to sink
Half his present repute for the freedom to think,
And, when he has thought, be his cause strong or weak,
Will risk t' other half for the freedom to speak,
Caring naught for what vengeance the mob has in store,
Let that mob be the upper ten thousand or lower.

"There are truths you Americans need to be told,
And it never 'll refute them to swagger and scold;
John Bull, looking o'er the Atlantic, in choler
At your aptness for trade, says you worship the dollar;
But to scorn such eye-dollar-try's what very few do,
And John goes to that church as often as you do.
No matter what John says, don't try to outcrow him,
'T is enough to go quietly on and outgrow him;

Like most fathers, Bull hates to see Number One
Displacing himself in the mind of his son,
And detests the same faults in himself he 'd neglected
When he sees them again in his child's glass reflected;
To love one another you're too like by half;
If he is a bull, you're a pretty stout calf,
And tear your own pasture for naught but to show
What a nice pair of horns you're beginning to grow.

"There are one or two things I should just like to hint,
For you don't often get the truth told you in print;
The most of you (this is what strikes all beholders)
Have a mental and physical stoop in the shoulders;
Though you ought to be free as the winds and the waves,
You've the gait and the manners of runaway slaves;
Though you brag of your New World, you don't half believe in it;
And as much of the Old as is possible weave in it;
Your goddess of freedom, a tight, buxom girl,
With lips like a cherry and teeth like a pearl,
With eyes bold as Herë's, and hair floating free,
And full of the sun as the spray of the sea,
Who can sing at a husking or romp at a shearing,
Who can trip through the forests alone without fearing,
Who can drive home the cows with a song through the grass,
Keeps glancing aside into Europe's cracked glass,
Hides her red hands in gloves, pinches up her lithe waist,
And makes herself wretched with transmarine taste;
She loses her fresh country charm when she takes
Any mirror except her own rivers and lakes.

"You steal Englishmen's books and think Englishmen's thought,
With their salt on her tail your wild eagle is caught;
Your literature suits its each whisper and motion
To what will be thought of it over the ocean;
The cast clothes of Europe your statesmanship tries
And mumbles again the old blarneys and lies; —
Forget Europe wholly, your veins throb with blood,
To which the dull current in hers is but mud:
Let her sneer, let her say your experiment fails,
In her voice there's a tremble e'en now while she rails,
And your shore will soon be in the nature of things
Covered thick with gilt drift-wood of castaway kings,
Where alone, as it were in a Longfellow's Waif,

Her fugitive pieces will find themselves safe.
O my friends, thank your god, if you have one, that he
'Twixt the Old World and you set the gulf of a sea;
Be strong-backed, brown-handed, upright as your pines,
By the scale of a hemisphere shape your designs,
Be true to yourselves and this new nineteenth age,
As a statue by Powers, or a picture by Page,
Plough, sail, forge, build, carve, paint, make all over new,
To your own New-World instincts contrive to be true,
Keep your ears open wide to the Future's first call,
Be whatever you will, but yourselves first of all,
Stand fronting the dawn on Toil's heaven-scaling peaks,
And become my new race of more practical Greeks. —
Hem ! your likeness at present, I shudder to tell o't,
Is that you have your slaves, and the Greek had his helot."

.   .   .

[Poe and Longfellow]

"There comes Poe, with his raven, like Barnaby Rudge,
Three fifths of him genius and two fifths sheer fudge,
Who talks like a book of iambs and pentameters,
In a way to make people of common sense damn metres,
Who has written some things quite the best of their kind,
But the heart somehow seems all squeezed out by the mind,
Who — But hey-day! What's this? Messieurs Mathews and Poe,
You must n't fling mud-balls at Longfellow so,
Does it make a man worse that his character's such
As to make his friends love him (as you think) too much?
Why, there is not a bard at this moment alive
More willing than he that his fellows should thrive;
While you are abusing him thus, even now
He would help either one of you out of a slough;
You may say that he's smooth and all that till you're hoarse,
But remember that elegance also is force;
After polishing granite as much as you will,
The heart keeps its tough old persistency still;
Deduct all you can, *that* still keeps you at bay;
Why, he'll live till men weary of Collins and Gray.
I 'm not over-fond of Greek metres in English,
To me rhyme's a gain, so it be not too jinglish,
And your modern hexameter verses are no more
Like Greek ones than sleek Mr. Pope is like Homer;

As the roar of the sea to the coo of a pigeon is,
So, compared to your moderns, sounds old Melesigenes;
I may be too partial, the reason, perhaps, o't is
That I 've heard the old blind man recite his own rhapsodies,
And my ear with that music impregnate may be,
Like the poor exiled shell with the soul of the sea,
Or as one can't bear Strauss when his nature is cloven
To its deeps within deeps by the stroke of Beethoven;
But, set that aside, and 't is truth that I speak,
Had Theocritus written in English, not Greek,
I believe that his exquisite sense would scarce change a line
In that rare, tender, virgin-like pastoral Evangeline.
That 's not ancient nor modern, its place is apart
Where time has no sway, in the realm of pure Art,
'T is a shrine of retreat from Earth's hubbub and strife
As quiet and chaste as the author's own life.

. . .

[Holmes]

"There's Holmes, who is matchless among you for wit;
A Leyden-jar always full-charged, from which flit
The electrical tingles of hit after hit;
In long poem 't is painful sometimes, and invites
A thought of the way the new Telegraph writes,
Which pricks down its little sharp sentences spitefully
As if you got more than you 'd title to rightfully,
And you find yourself hoping its wild father Lightning
Would flame in for a second and give you a fright'ning.
He has perfect sway of what I call a sham metre,
But many admire it, the English pentameter,
And Campbell, I think, wrote most commonly worse,
With less nerve, swing, and fire in the same kind of verse,
Nor e'er achieved aught in 't so worthy of praise
As the tribute of Holmes to the grand *Marseillaise*.
You went crazy last year over Bulwer's New Timon; —
Why, if B., to the day of his dying, should rhyme on,
Heaping verses on verses and tomes upon tomes,
He could ne'er reach the best point and vigor of Holmes.
His are just the fine hands, too, to weave you a lyric
Full of fancy, fun, feeling, or spiced with satiric
In a measure so kindly, you doubt if the toes
That are trodden upon are your own or your foes'.

[*Lowell*]

"There is Lowell, who 's striving Parnassus to climb
With a whole bale of *isms* tied together with rhyme,
He might get on alone, spite of brambles and boulders,
But he can't with that bundle he has on his shoulders,
The top of the hill he will ne'er come nigh reaching
Till he learns the distinction 'twixt singing and preaching;
His lyre has some chords that would ring pretty well,
But he 'd rather by half make a drum of the shell,
And rattle away till he 's old as Methusalem,
At the head of a march to the last new Jerusalem.

from The Biglow Papers

The Courtin'

God makes sech nights, all white an' still
    Fur 'z you can look or listen,
Moonshine an' snow on field an' hill,
    All silence an' all glisten.

Zekle crep' up quite unbeknown
    An' peeked in thru' the winder,
An' there sot Huldy all alone,
    'ith no one nigh to hender.

A fireplace filled the room's one side
    With half a cord o' wood in —
There war n't no stoves (tell comfort died)
    To bake ye to a puddin'.

The wa'nut logs shot sparkles out
    Towards the pootiest, bless her,
An' leetle flames danced all about
    The chiny on the dresser.

Agin the chimbley crook-necks hung,
    An' in amongst 'em rusted
The ole queen's-arm thet gran'ther Young
    Fetched back f'om Concord busted.

The very room, coz she was in,
    Seemed warm f'om floor to ceilin',
An' she looked full ez rosy agin
    Ez the apples she was peelin'.

'T was kin' o' kingdom-come to look
    On sech a blessed cretur,
A dogrose blushin' to a brook
    Ain't modester nor sweeter.

He was six foot o' man, A 1,
    Clear grit an' human natur',
None could n't quicker pitch a ton
    Nor dror a furrer straighter.

He 'd sparked it with full twenty gals,
    He'd squired 'em, danced 'em, druv 'em,
Fust this one, an' then thet, by spells —
    All is, he could n't love 'em.

But long o' her his veins 'ould run
    All crinkly like curled maple,
The side she breshed felt full o' sun
    Ez a south slope in Ap'il.

She thought no v'ice hed sech a swing
    Ez hisn in the choir;
My! when he made Ole Hunderd ring,
    She *knowed* the Lord was nigher.

An' she 'd blush scarlit, right in prayer,
    When her new meetin'-bunnet
Felt somehow thru' its crown a pair
    O' blue eyes sot upon it.

Thet night, I tell ye, she looked *some!*
    She seemed to 've gut a new soul,
For she felt sartin-sure he 'd come,
    Down to her very shoe-sole.

She heered a foot, an' knowed it tu,
    A-raspin' on the scraper, —
All ways to once her feelins flew
    Like sparks in burnt-up paper.

He kin' o' l'itered on the mat,
    Some doubtfle o' the sekle,
His heart kep' goin' pity-pat,
    But hern went pity Zekle.

An' yit she gin her cheer a jerk
    Ez though she wished him furder,
An' on her apples kep' to work,
    Parin' away like murder.

"You want to see my Pa, I s'pose?"
    "Wal . . . no . . . I come dasignin' " —
"To see my Ma? She 's sprinklin' clo'es
    Agin to-morrer's i'nin'."

To say why gals acts so or so,
    Or don't, 'ould be persumin';
Mebby to mean *yes* an' say *no*
    Comes nateral to women.

He stood a spell on one foot fust,
    Then stood a spell on t' other,
An' on which one he felt the wust
    He could n't ha' told ye nuther.

Says he, "I 'd better call agin;"
    Says she, "Think likely, Mister:"
Thet last word pricked him like a pin,
    An' . . . Wal, he up an' kist her.

When Ma bimeby upon 'em slips,
    Huldy sot pale ez ashes,
All kin' o' smily roun' the lips
    An' teary roun' the lashes.

For she was jes' the quiet kind
    Whose naturs never vary,
Like streams that keep a summer mind
    Snowhid in Jenooary.

The blood clost roun' her heart felt glued
    Too tight for all expressin',
Tell mother see how metters stood,
    An' gin 'em both her blessin'.

Then her red come back like the tide
Down to the Bay o' Fundy,
An' all I know is they was cried
In meetin' come nex' Sunday.

Ode Recited at the Harvard Commemoration

I

Weak-winged is song,
Nor aims at that clear-ethered height
Whither the brave deed climbs for light:
We seem to do them wrong,
Bringing our robin's-leaf to deck their hearse
Who in warm life-blood wrote their nobler verse,
Our trivial song to honor those who come
With ears attuned to strenuous trump and drum,
And shaped in squadron-strophes their desire,
Live battle-odes whose lines were steel and fire:
Yet sometimes feathered words are strong,
A gracious memory to buoy up and save
From Lethe's dreamless ooze, the common grave
Of the unventurous throng.

II

To-day our Reverend Mother welcomes back
Her wisest Scholars, those who understood
The deeper teaching of her mystic tome,
And offered their fresh lives to make it good:
No lore of Greece or Rome,
No science peddling with the names of things,
Or reading stars to find inglorious fates,
Can lift our life with wings
Far from Death's idle gulf that for the many waits,
And lengthen out our dates
With that clear fame whose memory sings
In manly hearts to come, and nerves them and dilates:
Nor such thy teaching, Mother of us all!
Not such the trumpet-call
Of thy diviner mood,
That could thy sons entice
From happy homes and toils, the fruitful nest
Of those half-virtues which the world calls best,

Into War's tumult rude;
 But rather far that stern device
The sponsors chose that round thy cradle stood
 In the dim, unventured wood,
 The VERITAS that lurks beneath
 The letter's unprolific sheath,
 Life of whate'er makes life worth living,
Seed-grain of high emprise, immortal food,
 One heavenly thing whereof earth hath the giving.

III

Many loved Truth, and lavished life's best oil
 Amid the dust of books to find her,
Content at last, for guerdon of their toil,
 With the cast mantle she hath left behind her.
 Many in sad faith sought for her,
 Many with crossed hands sighed for her;
 But these, our brothers, fought for her,
 At life's dear peril wrought for her,
 So loved her that they died for her,
 Tasting the raptured fleetness
 Of her divine completeness:
 Their higher instinct knew
Those love her best who to themselves are true,
And what they dare to dream of, dare to do;
 They followed her and found her
 Where all may hope to find,
Not in the ashes of the burnt-out mind,
But beautiful, with danger's sweetness round her.
 Where faith made whole with deed
 Breathes its awakening breath
 Into the lifeless creed,
 They saw her plumed and mailed,
 With sweet, stern face unveiled,
And all-repaying eyes, look proud on them in death.

IV

Our slender life runs rippling by, and glides
 Into the silent hollow of the past;
 What is there that abides
 To make the next age better for the last?
 Is earth too poor to give us
 Something to live for here that shall outlive us?

Some more substantial boon
Than such as flows and ebbs with Fortune's fickle moon?
 The little that we see
 From doubt is never free;
 The little that we do
 Is but half-nobly true;
 With our laborious hiving
What men call treasure, and the gods call dross,
 Life seems a jest of Fate's contriving,
 Only secure in every one's conniving,
A long account of nothings paid with loss,
Where we poor puppets, jerked by unseen wires,
 After our little hour of strut and rave,
With all our pasteboard passions and desires,
Loves, hates, ambitions, and immortal fires,
 Are tossed pell-mell together in the grave.
 But stay! no age was e'er degenerate,
 Unless men held it at too cheap a rate,
 For in our likeness still we shape our fate.
  Ah, there is something here
 Unfathoned by the cynic's sneer,
 Something that gives our feeble light
 A high immunity from Night,
 Something that leaps life's narrow bars
To claim its birthright with the hosts of heaven;
 A seed of sunshine that can leaven
 Our earthly dullness with the beams of stars,
  And glorify our clay
 With light from fountains elder than the Day;
 A conscience more divine than we,
 A gladness fed with secret tears,
 A vexing, forward-reaching sense
 Of some more noble permanence;
  A light across the sea,
Which haunts the soul and will not let it be,
Still beaconing from the heights of undegenerate years.

   V
 Whither leads the path
 To ampler fates that leads?
 Not down through flowery meads,
 To reap an aftermath
Of youth's vainglorious weeds,

But up the steep, amid the wrath
And shock of deadly-hostile creeds,
Where the world's best hope and stay
By battle's flashes gropes a desperate way,
And every turf the fierce foot clings to bleeds.
Peace hath her not ignoble wreath,
Ere yet the sharp, decisive word
Light the black lips of cannon, and the sword
Dreams in its easeful sheath;
But some day the live coal behind the thought,
Whether from Baäl's stone obscene,
Or from the shrine serene
Of God's pure altar brought,
Bursts up in flame; the war of tongue and pen
Learns with what deadly purpose it was fraught,
And, helpless in the fiery passion caught,
Shakes all the pillared state with shock of men:
Some day the soft Ideal that we wooed
Confronts us fiercely, foe-beset, pursued,
And cries reproachful: "Was it, then, my praise,
And not myself was loved? Prove now thy truth;
I claim of thee the promise of thy youth;
Give me thy life, or cower in empty phrase,
The victim of the genius, not its mate!"
Life may be given in many ways,
And loyalty to Truth be sealed
As bravely in the closet as the field,
So bountiful is Fate;
But then to stand beside her,
When craven churls deride her,
To front a lie in arms and not to yield,
This shows, methinks, God's plan
And measure of a stalwart man,
Limbed like the old heroic breeds,
Who stands self-poised on manhood's solid earth,
Not forced to frame excuses for his birth,
Fed from within with all the strength he needs.

VI

Such was he, our Martyr-Chief,
Whom late the Nation he had led,
With ashes on her head,
Wept with the passion of an angry grief:

Forgive me, if from present things I turn
To speak what in my heart will beat and burn,
And hang my wreath on his world-honored urn.
  Nature, they say, doth dote,
  And cannot make a man
  Save on some worn-out plan,
  Repeating us by rote:
For him her Old-World moulds aside she threw,
  And, choosing sweet clay from the breast
  Of the unexhausted West,
With stuff untainted shaped a hero new,
Wise, steadfast in the strength of God, and true.
  How beautiful to see
Once more a shepherd of mankind indeed,
Who loved his charge, but never loved to lead;
One whose meek flock the people joyed to be,
  Not lured by any cheat of birth,
  But by his clear-grained human worth,
And brave old wisdom of sincerity!
  They knew that outward grace is dust;
  They could not choose but trust
In that sure-footed mind's unfaltering skill,
  And supple-tempered will
That bent like perfect steel to spring again and thrust.
  His was no lonely mountain-peak of mind,
  Thrusting to thin air o'er our cloudy bars,
  A sea-mark now, now lost in vapors blind;
  Broad prairie rather, genial, level-lined,
  Fruitful and friendly for all human kind,
Yet also nigh to heaven and loved of loftiest stars.
   Nothing of Europe here,
Or, then, of Europe fronting mornward still,
  Ere any names of Serf and Peer
  Could Nature's equal scheme deface
  And thwart her genial will;
  Here was a type of the true elder race,
And one of Plutarch's men talked with us face to face.
  I praise him not; it were too late;
And some innative weakness there must be
In him who condescends to victory
Such as the Present gives, and cannot wait,
  Safe in himself as in a fate.
   So always firmly he:

He knew to bide his time,
And can his fame abide,
Still patient in his simple faith sublime,
Till the wise years decide.
Great captains, with their guns and drums,
Disturb our judgment for the hour,
But at last silence comes;
These all are gone, and, standing like a tower,
Our children shall behold his fame.
The kindly-earnest, brave, foreseeing man,
Sagacious, patient, dreading praise, not blame,
New birth of our new soil, the first American.

VII
Long as man's hope insatiate can discern
Or only guess some more inspiring goal
Outside of Self, enduring as the pole,
Along whose course the flying axles burn
Of spirits bravely-pitched, earth's manlier brood;
Long as below we cannot find
The need that stills the inexorable mind;
So long this faith to some ideal Good,
Under whatever mortal names it masks,
Freedom, Law, Country, this ethereal mood
That thanks the Fates for their severer tasks,
Feeling its challenged pulses leap,
While others skulk in subterfuges cheap,
And, set in Danger's van, has all the boon it asks,
Shall win man's praise and woman's love,
Shall be a wisdom that we set above
All other skills and gifts to culture dear,
A virtue round whose forehead we inwreathe
Laurels that with a living passion breathe
When other crowns grow, while we twine them, sear.
What brings us thronging these high rites to pay,
And seal these hours the noblest of our year,
Save that our brothers found this better way?

VIII
We sit here in the Promised Land
That flows with Freedom's honey and milk;
But 't was they won it, sword in hand,
Making the nettle danger soft for us as silk.

We welcome back our bravest and our best; —
Ah me! not all! some come not with the rest,
Who went forth brave and bright as any here!
I strive to mix some gladness with my strain,
But the sad strings complain,
And will not please the ear:
I sweep them for a pæan, but they wane
Again and yet again
Into a dirge, and die away, in pain.
In these brave ranks I only see the gaps,
Thinking of dear ones whom the dumb turf wraps,
Dark to the triumph which they died to gain:
Fitlier may others greet the living,
For me the past is unforgiving;
I with uncovered head
Salute the sacred dead,
Who went, and who return not. — Say not so!
'T is not the grapes of Canaan that repay,
But the high faith that failed not by the way;
Virtue treads paths that end not in the grave;
No ban of endless night exiles the brave;
And to the saner mind
We rather seem the dead that stayed behind.
Blow, trumpets, all your exultations blow!
For never shall their aureoled presence lack:
I see them muster in a gleaming row,
With ever-youthful brows that nobler show;
We find in our dull road their shining track;
In every nobler mood
We feel the orient of their spirit glow,
Part of our life's unalterable good,
Of all our saintlier aspiration;
They come transfigured back,
Secure from change in their high-hearted ways,
Beautiful evermore, and with the rays
Of morn on their white Shields of Expectation!

IX

But is there hope to save
Even this ethereal essence from the grave?
What ever 'scaped Oblivion's subtle wrong
Save a few clarion names, or golden threads of song?
Before my musing eye

The mighty ones of old sweep by,
Disvoicëd now and insubstantial things,
Shadows of empire wholly gone to dust,
And many races, nameless long ago,
To darkness driven by that imperious gust
Of ever-rushing Time that here doth blow:
O visionary world, condition strange,
Where naught abiding is but only Change,
Where the deep-bolted stars themselves still shift and range!
Shall we to more continuance make pretence?
Renown builds tombs; a life-estate is Wit;
　　　And, bit by bit,
The cunning years steal all from us but woe;
Leaves are we, whose decays no harvest sow.
　　　But, when we vanish hence,
Shall they lie forceless in the dark below,
Save to make green their little length of sods,
Or deepen pansies for a year or two,
Who now to us are shining-sweet as gods?
Was dying all they had the skill to do?
That were not fruitless: but the Soul resents
Such short-lived service, as if blind events
Ruled without her, or earth could so endure;
She claims a more divine investiture
Of longer tenure than Fame's airy rents;
Whate'er she touches doth her nature share;
Her inspiration haunts the ennobled air,
　　　Gives eyes to mountains blind,
Ears to the deaf earth, voices to the wind,
And her clear trump sings succor everywhere
By lonely bivouacs to the wakeful mind;
For soul inherits all that soul could dare:
　　　Yea, Manhood hath a wider span
And larger privilege of life than man.
The single deed, the private sacrifice,
So radiant now through proudly-hidden tears,
Is covered up erelong from mortal eyes
With thoughtless drift of the deciduous years;
But that high privilege that makes all men peers,
That leap of heart whereby a people rise
　　　Up to a noble anger's height,
And, flamed on by the Fates, not shrink, but grow more bright,
　　That swift validity in noble veins,

Of choosing danger and disdaining shame,
Of being set on flame
By the pure fire that flies all contact base
But wraps its chosen with angelic might,
These are imperishable gains,
Sure as the sun, medicinal as light,
These hold great futures in their lusty reins
And certify to earth a new imperial race.

X
Who now shall sneer?
Who dare again to say we trace
Our lines to a plebeian race?
Roundhead and Cavalier!
Dumb are those names erewhile in battle loud;
Dream-footed as the shadow of a cloud,
They flit across the ear:
That is best blood that hath most iron in 't.
To edge resolve with, pouring without stint
For what makes manhood dear.
Tell us not of Plantagenets,
Hapsburgs, and Guelfs, whose thin bloods crawl
Down from some victor in a border-brawl!
How poor their outworn coronets,
Matched with one leaf of that plain civic wreath
Our brave for honor's blazon shall bequeath,
Through whose desert a rescued Nation sets
Her heel on treason, and the trumpet hears
Shout victory, tingling Europe's sullen ears
With vain resentments and more vain regrets!

XI
Not in anger, not in pride,
Pure from passion's mixture rude
Ever to base earth allied,
But with far-heard gratitude,
Still with heart and voice renewed,
To heroes living and dear martyrs dead,
The strain should close that consecrates our brave.
Lift the heart and lift the head!
Lofty be its mood and grave,
Not without a martial ring,
Not without a prouder tread

And a peal of exultation:
Little right has he to sing
Through whose heart in such an hour
Beats no march of conscious power,
Sweeps no tumult of elation!
'T is no Man we celebrate,
By his country's victories great,
A hero half, and half the whim of Fate,
But the pith and marrow of a Nation
Drawing force from all her men,
Highest, humblest, weakest, all,
For her time of need, and then
Pulsing it again through them,
Till the basest can no longer cower,
Feeling his soul spring up divinely tall,
Touched but in passing by her mantlehem.
Come back, then, noble pride, for 't is her dower!
How could poet ever tower,
If his passions, hopes, and fears,
If his triumphs and his tears,
Kept not measure with his people?
Boom, cannon, boom to all the winds and waves!
Clash out, glad bells, from every rocking steeple!
Banners, adance with triumph, bend your staves!
And from every mountain-peak
Let beacon-fire to answering beacon speak,
Katahdin tell Monadnock, Whiteface he,
And so leap on in light from sea to sea,
Till the glad news be sent
Across a kindling continent,
Making earth feel more firm and air breathe braver:
"Be proud! for she is saved, and all have helped to save her!
She that lifts up the manhood of the poor,
She of the open soul and open door,
With room about her hearth for all mankind!
The fire is dreadful in her eyes no more;
From her bold front the helm she doth unbind,
Sends all her handmaid armies back to spin,
And bids her navies, that so lately hurled
Their crashing battle, hold their thunders in,
Swimming like birds of calm along the unharmful shore.
No challenge sends she to the elder world,
That looked askance and hated; a light scorn

Plays o'er her mouth, as round her mighty knees
She calls her children back, and waits the morn
Of nobler day, enthroned between her subject seas."

XII

Bow down, dear Land, for thou hast found release!
   Thy God, in these distempered days,
    Hath taught thee the sure wisdom of His ways,
And through thine enemies hath wrought thy peace!
    Bow down in prayer and praise!
No poorest in thy borders but may now
Lift to the juster skies a man's enfranchised brow.
O Beautiful! my Country! ours once more!
Smoothing thy gold of war-dishevelled hair
O'er such sweet brows as never other wore,
    And letting thy set lips,
    Freed from wrath's pale eclipse,
The rosy edges of their smile lay bare,
What words divine of lover or of poet
Could tell our love and make thee know it,
Among the Nations bright beyond compare?
    What were our lives without thee?
    What all our lives to save thee?
    We reck not what we gave thee;
    We will not dare to doubt thee,
But ask whatever else, and we will dare!

WALT WHITMAN
1819–1892

Come, Said My Soul

Come, said my Soul,
Such verses for my Body let us write, (for we are one,)
That should I after death invisibly return,
Or, long, long hence, in other spheres,
There to some group of mates the chants resuming,
(Tallying Earth's soil, trees, winds, tumultuous waves,)
Ever with pleas'd smile I may keep on,
Ever and ever yet the verses owning — as, first, I here and now,
Signing for Soul and Body, set to them my name,

Walt Whitman

Song of Myself

1

I celebrate myself, and sing myself,
And what I assume you shall assume,
For every atom belonging to me as good belongs to you.

I loafe and invite my soul,
I lean and loafe at my ease observing a spear of summer grass.

My tongue, every atom of my blood, form'd from this soil, this air,
Born here of parents born here from parents the same, and their parents
    the same,
I, now thirty-seven years old in perfect health begin,
Hoping to cease not till death.

Creeds and schools in abeyance,
Retiring back a while sufficed at what they are, but never forgotten,
I harbor for good or bad, I permit to speak at every hazard,
Nature without check with original energy.

2

Houses and rooms are full of perfumes, the shelves are crowded with
    perfumes,
I breathe the fragrance myself and know it and like it,
The distillation would intoxicate me also, but I shall not let it.

The atmosphere is not a perfume, it has no taste of the distillation, it is
    odorless,
It is for my mouth forever, I am in love with it,
I will go to the bank by the wood and become undisguised and naked,
I am mad for it to be in contact with me.
The smoke of my own breath,
Echoes, ripples, buzz'd whispers, love-root, silk-thread, crotch and vine,
My respiration and inspiration, the beating of my heart, the passing of
    blood and air through my lungs,
The sniff of green leaves and dry leaves, and of the shore and dark-
    color'd sea-rocks, and of hay in the barn,
The sound of the belch'd words of my voice loos'd to the eddies of the
    wind,
A few light kisses, a few embraces, a reaching around of arms,
The play of shine and shade on the trees as the supple boughs wag,

The delight alone or in the rush of the streets, or along the fields and
    hill-sides,
The feeling of health, the full-noon trill, the song of me rising from bed
    and meeting the sun.

Have you reckon'd a thousand acres much? have you reckon'd the earth
    much?
Have you practis'd so long to learn to read?
Have you felt so proud to get at the meaning of poems?

Stop this day and night with me and you shall possess the origin of all
    poems,
You shall possess the good of the earth and sun, (there are millions of
    suns left,)
You shall no longer take things at second or third hand, nor look
    through the eyes of the dead, nor feed on the spectres in books,
You shall not look through my eyes either, nor take things from me,
You shall listen to all sides and filter them from your self.

3
I have heard what the talkers were talking, the talk of the beginning and
    the end,
But I do not talk of the beginning or the end.

There was never any more inception than there is now,
Nor any more youth or age than there is now,
And will never be any more perfection than there is now,
Nor any more heaven or hell than there is now.

Urge and urge and urge,
Always the procreant urge of the world.

Out of the dimness opposite equals advance, always substance and
    increase, always sex,
Always a knit of identity, always distinction, always a breed of life.

To elaborate is no avail, learn'd and unlearn'd feel that it is so.

Sure as the most certain sure, plumb in the uprights, well entretied,
    braced in the beams,
Stout as a horse, affectionate, haughty, electrical,
I and this mystery here we stand.

Clear and sweet is my soul, and clear and sweet is all that is not my soul.

Lack one lacks both, and the unseen is proved by the seen,
Till that becomes unseen and receives proof in its turn.

Showing the best and dividing it from the worst age vexes age,
Knowing the perfect fitness and equanimity of things, while they discuss
    I am silent, and go bathe and admire myself.

Welcome is every organ and attribute of me, and of any man hearty and
    clean,
Not an inch nor a particle of an inch is vile, and none shall be less
    familiar than the rest.

I am satisfied — I see, dance, laugh, sing;
As the hugging and loving bed-fellow sleeps at my side through the
    night, and withdraws at the peep of the day with stealthy tread,
Leaving me baskets cover'd with white towels swelling the house with
    their plenty,
Shall I postpone my acceptation and realization and scream at my eyes,
That they turn from gazing after and down the road,
And forthwith cipher and show me to a cent,
Exactly the value of one and exactly the value of two, and which is
    ahead?

4

Trippers and askers surround me,
People I meet, the effect upon me of my early life or the ward and city
    I live in, or the nation,
The latest dates, discoveries, inventions, societies, authors old and new,
My dinner, dress, associates, looks, compliments, dues,
The real or fancied indifference of some man or woman I love,
The sickness of one of my folks or of myself, or ill-doing or loss or lack
    of money, or depressions or exaltations,
Battles, the horrors of fratricidal war, the fever of doubtful news, the
    fitful events;
These come to me days and nights and go from me again,
But they are not the Me myself.

Apart from the pulling and hauling stands what I am,
Stands amused, complacent, compassionating, idle, unitary,
Looks down, is erect, or bends an arm on an impalpable certain rest,
Looking with side-curved head curious what will come next,
Both in and out of the game and watching and wondering at it.

Backward I see in my own days where I sweated through fog with
    linguists and contenders,
I have no mockings or arguments, I witness and wait.

5

I believe in you my soul, the other I am must not abase itself to you,
And you must not be abased to the other.

Loafe with me on the grass, loose the stop from your throat,
Not words, not music or rhyme I want, not custom or lecture, not even
    the best,
Only the lull I like, the hum of your valvèd voice.

I mind how once we lay such a transparent summer morning,
How you settled your head athwart my hips and gently turn'd over upon
    me,
And parted the shirt from my bosom-bone, and plunged your tongue to
    my bare-stript heart,
And reach'd till you felt my beard, and reach'd till you held my feet.

Swiftly arose and spread around me the peace and knowledge that pass
    all the argument of the earth,
And I know that the hand of God is the promise of my own,
And I know that the spirit of God is the brother of my own,
And that all the men ever born are also my brothers, and the women
    my sisters and lovers,
And that a kelson of the creation is love,
And limitless are leaves stiff or drooping in the fields,
And brown ants in the little wells beneath them,
And mossy scabs of the worm fence, heap'd stones, elder, mullein and
    poke-weed.

6

A child said *What is the grass?* fetching it to me with full hands,
How could I answer the child? I do not know what it is any more than
    he.

I guess it must be the flag of my disposition, out of hopeful green stuff
    woven.

Or I guess it is the handkerchief of the Lord,
A scented gift and remembrancer designedly dropt,
Bearing the owner's name someway in the corners, that we may see and
    remark, and say *Whose?*

Or I guess the grass is itself a child, the produced babe of the vegetation.

Or I guess it is a uniform hieroglyphic;
And it means, Sprouting alike in broad zones and narrow zones,
Growing among black folks as among white,
Kanuck, Tuckahoe, Congressman, Cuff, I give them the same, I receive
   them the same.

And now it seems to me the beautiful uncut hair of graves.

Tenderly will I use you curling grass,
It may be you transpire from the breasts of young men,
It may be if I had known them I would have loved them,
It may be you are from old people, or from offspring taken soon out of
   their mothers' laps,
And here you are the mothers' laps.

This grass is very dark to be from the white heads of old mothers,
Darker than the colorless beards of old men,
Dark to come from under the faint red roofs of mouths.

O I perceive after all so many uttering tongues,
·And I perceive they do not come from the roofs of mouths for nothing.

I wish I could translate the hints about the dead young men and women,
And the hints about old men and mothers, and the offspring taken soon
   out of their laps.

What do you think has become of the young and old men?
And what do you think has become of the women and children?

They are alive and well somewhere,
The smallest sprout shows there is really no death,
And if there was it led forward life, and does not wait at the end to
   arrest it,
And ceas'd the moment life appear'd.

All goes onward and outward, nothing collapses,
And to die is different from what any one supposed, and luckier.

7
Has any one supposed it lucky to be born?
I hasten to inform him or her it is just as lucky to die, and I know it.

I pass death with the dying and birth with the new-wash'd babe, and
am not contain'd between my hat and boots,
And peruse manifold objects, no two alike and every one good,
The earth good and the stars good, and their adjuncts all good.

I am not an earth nor an adjunct of an earth,
I am the mate and companion of people, all just as immortal and
fathomless as myself,
(They do not know how immortal, but I know.)

Every kind for itself and its own, for me mine male and female,
For me those that have been boys and that love women,
For me the man that is proud and feels how it stings to be slighted,
For me the sweet-heart and the old maid, for me mothers and the
mothers of mothers,
For me lips that have smiled, eyes that have shed tears,
For me children and the begetters of children.

Undrape! you are not guilty to me, nor stale nor discarded,
I see through the broadcloth and gingham whether or no,
And am around, tenacious, acquisitive, tireless, and cannot be shaken
away.

8

The little one sleeps in its cradle,
I lift the gauze and look a long time, and silently brush away flies with
my hand.

The youngster and the red-faced girl turn aside up the busy hill,
I peeringly view them from the top.

The suicide sprawls on the bloody floor of the bedroom,
I witness the corpse with its dabbled hair, I note where the pistol has
fallen.

The blab of the pave, tires of carts, sluff of boot-soles, talk of the
promenaders,
The heavy omnibus, the driver with his interrogating thumb, the clank
of the shod horses on the granite floor,
The snow-sleighs, clinking, shouted jokes, pelts of snow-balls,
The hurrahs for popular favorites, the fury of rous'd mobs,
The flap of the curtain'd litter, a sick man inside borne to the hospital,
The meeting of enemies, the sudden oath, the blows and fall,

The excited crowd, the policeman with his star quickly working his
    passage to the centre of the crowd,
The impassive stones that receive and return so many echoes,
What groans of over-fed or half-starv'd who fall sunstruck or in fits,
What exclamation of women taken suddenly who hurry home and give
    birth to babes,
What living and buried speech is always vibrating here, what howls
    restrain'd by decorum,
Arrests of criminals, slights, adulterous offers made, acceptances, rejec-
    tions with convex lips,
I mind them or the show or resonance of them — I come and I depart.

9

The big doors of the country barn stand open and ready,
The dried grass of the harvest-time loads the slow-drawn wagon,
The clear light plays on the brown gray and green intertinged,
The armfuls are pack'd to the sagging mow.

I am there, I help, I came stretch'd atop of the load,
I felt its soft jolts, one leg reclined on the other,
I jump from the cross-beams and seize the clover and timothy,
And roll head over heels and tangle my hair full of wisps.

10

Alone far in the wilds and mountains I hunt,
Wandering amazed at my own lightness and glee,
In the late afternoon choosing a safe spot to pass the night,
Kindling a fire and broiling the fresh-kill'd game,
Falling asleep on the gather'd leaves with my dog and gun by my side.

The Yankee clipper is under her sky-sails, she cuts the sparkle and scud,
My eyes settle the land, I bend at her prow or shout joyously from the
    deck.

The boatmen and clam-diggers arose early and stopt for me,
I tuck'd my trowser-ends in my boots and went and had a good time;
You should have been with us that day round the chowder-kettle.

I saw the marriage of the trapper in the open air in the far west, the
    bride was a red girl,
Her father and his friends sat near cross-legged and dumbly smoking,
    they had moccasins to their feet and large thick blankets hanging
    from their shoulders,

On a bank lounged the trapper, he was drest mostly in skins, his
luxuriant beard and curls protected his neck, he held his bride by
the hand,
She had long eyelashes, her head was bare, her coarse straight locks
descended upon her voluptuous limbs and reach'd to her feet.

The runaway slave came to my house and stopt outside,
I heard his motions crackling the twigs of the woodpile,
Through the swung half-door of the kitchen I saw him limpsy and weak,
And went where he sat on a log and led him in and assured him,
And brought water and fill'd a tub for his sweated body and bruis'd feet,
And gave him a room that enter'd from my own, and gave him some
coarse clean clothes,
And remember perfectly well his revolving eyes and his awkwardness,
And remember putting plasters on the galls of his neck and ankles;
He staid with me a week before he was recuperated and pass'd north,
I had him sit next me at table, my fire-lock lean'd in the corner.

11

Twenty-eight young men bathe by the shore,
Twenty-eight young men and all so friendly;
Twenty-eight years of womanly life and all so lonesome.

She owns the fine house by the rise of the bank,
She hides handsome and richly drest aft the blinds of the window.

Which of the young men does she like the best?
Ah the homeliest of them is beautiful to her.

Where are you off to, lady? for I see you,
You splash in the water there, yet stay stock still in your room.

Dancing and laughing along the beach came the twenty-ninth bather,
The rest did not see her, but she saw them and loved them.

The beards of the young men glisten'd with wet, it ran from their long
hair,
Little streams pass'd all over their bodies.

An unseen hand also pass'd over their bodies,
It descended tremblingly from their temples and ribs.

The young men float on their backs, their white bellies bulge to the sun,
   they do not ask who seizes fast to them,
They do not know who puffs and declines with pendant and bending
   arch,
They do not think whom they souse with spray.

12

The butcher-boy puts off his killing-clothes, or sharpens his knife at the
   stall in the market,
I loiter enjoying his repartee and his shuffle and break-down.

Blacksmiths with grimed and hairy chests environ the anvil,
Each has his main-sledge, they are all out, there is a great heat in the
   fire.

From the cinder-strew'd threshold I follow their movements,
The lithe sheer of their waists plays even with their massive arms,
Overhand the hammers swing, overhand so slow, overhand so sure,
They do not hasten, each man hits in his place.

13

The negro holds firmly the reins of his four horses, the block swags
   underneath on its tied-over chain,
The negro that drives the long dray of the stone-yard, steady and tall
   he stands pois'd on one leg on the string-piece,
His blue shirt exposes his ample neck and breast and loosens over his
   hip-band,
His glance is calm and commanding, he tosses the slouch of his hat
   away from his forehead,
The sun falls on his crispy hair and mustache, falls on the black of his
   polish'd and perfect limbs.

I behold the picturesque giant and love him, and I do not stop there,
I go with the team also.

In me the caresser of life wherever moving, backward as well as forward
   sluing,
To niches aside and junior bending, not a person or object missing,
Absorbing all to myself and for this song.

Oxen that rattle the yoke and chain or halt in the leafy shade, what is
   that you express in your eyes?
It seems to me more than all the print I have read in my life.

My tread scares the wood-drake and wood-duck on my distant and day-
long ramble,
They rise together, they slowly circle around.

I believe in those wing'd purposes,
And acknowledge red, yellow, white, playing within me,
And consider green and violet and the tufted crown intentional,
And do not call the tortoise unworthy because she is not something else,
And the jay in the woods never studied the gamut, yet trills pretty well
to me,
And the look of the bay mare shames silliness out of me.

14

The wild gander leads his flock through the cool night,
Ya-honk he says, and sounds it down to me like an invitation,
The pert may suppose it meaningless, but I listening close,
Find its purpose and place up there toward the wintry sky.

The sharp-hoof'd moose of the north, the cat on the house-sill, the
chickadee, the prairie-dog,
The litter of the grunting sow as they tug at her teats,
The brood of the turkey-hen and she with her half-spread wings,
I see in them and myself the same old law.

The press of my foot to the earth springs a hundred affections,
They scorn the best I can do to relate them.

I am enamour'd of growing out-doors,
Of men that live among cattle or taste of the ocean or woods,
Of the builders and steerers of ships and the wielders of axes and mauls,
and the drivers of horses,
I can eat and sleep with them week in and week out.

What is commonest, cheapest, nearest, easiest, is Me,
Me going in for my chances, spending for vast returns,
Adorning myself to bestow myself on the first that will take me,
Not asking the sky to come down to my good will,
Scattering it freely forever.

15

The pure contralto sings in the organ loft,
The carpenter dresses his plank, the tongue of his foreplane whistles its
wild ascending lisp,

The married and unmarried children ride home to their Thanksgiving
    dinner,
The pilot seizes the king-pin, he heaves down with a strong arm,
The mate stands braced in the whale-boat, lance and harpoon are ready,
The duck-shooter walks by silent and cautious stretches,
The deacons are ordain'd with cross'd hands at the altar,
The spinning-girl retreats and advances to the hum of the big wheel,
The farmer stops by the bars as he walks on a First-day loafe and looks
    at the oats and rye,
The lunatic is carried at last to the asylum a confirm'd case,
(He will never sleep any more as he did in the cot in his mother's bed-
    room;)
The jour printer with gray head and gaunt jaws works at his case,
He turns his quid of tobacco while his eyes blurr with the manuscript;
The malform'd limbs are tied to the surgeon's table,
What is removed drops horribly in a pail;
The quadroon girl is sold at the auction-stand, the drunkard nods by the
    bar-room stove,
The machinist rolls up his sleeves, the policeman travels his beat, the
    gate-keeper marks who pass,
The young fellow drives the express-wagon, (I love him, though I do
    not know him;)
The half-breed straps on his light boots to compete in the race,
The western turkey-shooting draws old and young, some lean on their
    rifles, some sit on logs,
Out from the crowd steps the marksman, takes his position, levels his
    piece;
The groups of newly-come immigrants cover the wharf or levee,
As the woolly-pates hoe in the sugar-field, the overseer views them from
    his saddle,
The bugle calls in the ball-room, the gentlemen run for their partners,
    the dancers bow to each other,
The youth lies awake in the cedar-roof'd garret and harks to the musical
    rain,
The Wolverine sets traps on the creek that helps fill the Huron,
The squaw wrapt in her yellow-hemm'd cloth is offering moccasins and
    bead-bags for sale,
The connoisseur peers along the exhibition-gallery with half-shut eyes
    bent sideways,
As the deck-hands make fast the steamboat the plank is thrown for the
    shore-going passengers,
The young sister holds out the skein while the elder sister winds it off
    in a ball, and stops now and then for the knots,

The one-year wife is recovering and happy having a week ago borne her
first child,

The clean-hair'd Yankee girl works with her sewing-machine or in the
factory or mill,

The paving-man leans on his two-handed rammer, the reporter's lead
flies swiftly over the note-book, the sign-painter is lettering with
blue and gold,

The canal boy trots on the tow-path, the book-keeper counts at his desk,
the shoemaker waxes his thread,

The conductor beats time for the band and all the performers follow
him,

The child is baptized, the convert is making his first professions,

The regatta is spread on the bay, the race is begun, (how the white sails
sparkle!)

The drover watching his drove sings out to them that would stray,

The pedler sweats with his pack on his back, (the purchaser higgling
about the odd cent;)

The bride unrumples her white dress, the minute-hand of the clock
moves slowly,

The opium-eater reclines with rigid head and just-open'd lips,

The prostitute draggles her shawl, her bonnet bobs on her tipsy and
pimpled neck,

The crowd laugh at her backguard oaths, the men jeer and wink to each
other,

(Miserable! I do not laugh at your oaths nor jeer you;)

The President holding a cabinet council is surrounded by the great
Secretaries,

On the piazza walk three matrons stately and friendly with twined arms,

The crew of the fish-smack pack repeated layers of halibut in the hold,

The Missourian crosses the plains toting his wares and his cattle,

As the fare-collector goes through the train he gives notice by the
jingling of loose change,

The floor-men are laying the floor, the tinners are tinning the roof, the
masons are calling for mortar,

In single file each shouldering his hod pass onward the laborers;

Seasons pursuing each other the indescribable crowd is gather'd, it is
the fourth of Seventh-month, (what salutes of cannon and small
arms!)

Seasons pursuing each other the plougher ploughs, the mower mows,
and the winter-grain falls in the ground;

Off on the lakes the pike-fisher watches and waits by the hole in the
frozen surface,

The stumps stand thick round the clearing, the squatter strikes deep
with his axe,
Flatboatmen make fast towards dusk near the cotton-wood or pecan-
trees,
Coon-seekers go through the regions of the Red river or through those
drain'd by the Tennessee, or through those of the Arkansas,
Torches shine in the dark that hangs on the Chattahooche or Altamahaw,
Patriarchs sit at supper with sons and grandsons and great-grandsons
around them,
In walls of adobe, in canvas tents, rest hunters and trappers after their
day's sport,
The city sleeps and the country sleeps,
The living sleep for their time, the dead sleep for their time,
The old husband sleeps by his wife and the young husband sleeps by his
wife;
And these tend inward to me, and I tend outward to them,
And such as it is to be of these more or less I am,
And of these one and all I weave the song of myself.

16

I am of old and young, of the foolish as much as the wise,
Regardless of others, ever regardful of others,
Maternal as well as paternal, a child as well as a man,
Stuff'd with the stuff that is coarse and stuff'd with the stuff that is fine,
One of the Nation of many nations, the smallest the same and the
largest the same,
A Southerner soon as a Northerner, a planter nonchalant and hospitable
down by the Oconee I live,
A Yankee bound my own way ready for trade, my joints the limberest
joints on earth and the sternest joints on earth,
A Kentuckian walking the vale of the Elkhorn in my deer-skin leggings,
a Louisianian or Georgian,
A boatman over lakes or bays or along coasts, a Hoosier, Badger, Buckeye;
At home on Kanadian snow-shoes or up in the bush, or with fishermen
off Newfoundland,
At home in the fleet of ice-boats, sailing with the rest and tacking,
At home on the hills of Vermont or in the woods of Maine, or the
Texan ranch,
Comrade of Californians, comrade of free North-Westerners, (loving
their big proportions,)
Comrade of raftsmen and coalmen, comrade of all who shake hands
and welcome to drink and meat,

A learner with the simplest, a teacher of the thoughtfullest,
A novice beginning yet experient of myriads of seasons,
Of every hue and caste am I, of every rank and religion,
A farmer, mechanic, artist, gentleman, sailor, quaker,
Prisoner, fancy-man, rowdy, lawyer, physician, priest.

I resist any thing better than my own diversity,
Breathe the air but leave plenty after me,
And am not stuck up, and am in my place.

(The moth and the fish-eggs are in their place,
The bright suns I see and the dark suns I cannot see are in their place,
The palpable is in its place and the impalpable is in its place.)

17

These are really the thoughts of all men in all ages and lands, they are
    not original with me,
If they are not yours as much as mine they are nothing, or next to
    nothing,
If they are not the riddle and the untying of the riddle they are nothing,
If they are not just as close as they are distant they are nothing.

This is the grass that grows wherever the land is and the water is,
This the common air that bathes the globe.

18

With music strong I come, with my cornets and my drums,
I play not marches for accepted victors only, I play marches for con-
    quer'd and slain persons.

Have you heard that it was good to gain the day?
I also say it is good to fall, battles are lost in the same spirit in which
    they are won.

I beat and pound for the dead,
I blow through my embouchures my loudest and gayest for them.

Vivas to those who have fail'd!
And to those whose war-vessels sank in the sea!
And to those themselves who sank in the sea!
And to all generals that lost engagements, and all overcome heroes!
And the numberless unknown heroes equal to the greatest heroes known!

19

This is the meal equally set, this the meat for natural hunger,
It is for the wicked just the same as the righteous, I make appointments
    with all,
I will not have a single person slighted or left away,
The kept-woman, sponger, thief, are hereby invited,
The heavy-lipp'd slave is invited, the venerealee is invited,
There shall be no difference between them and the rest.

This is the press of a bashful hand, this the float and odor of hair,
This the touch of my lips to yours, this the murmur of yearning,
This the far-off depth and height reflecting my own face,
This the thoughtful merge of myself, and the outlet again.

Do you guess I have some intricate purpose?
Well I have, for the Fourth-month showers have, and the mica on the
    side of a rock has.

Do you take it I would astonish?
Does the daylight astonish? does the early redstart twittering through
    the woods?
Do I astonish more than they?

This hour I tell things in confidence,
I might not tell everybody, but I will tell you.

20

Who goes there? hankering, gross, mystical, nude;
How is it I extract strength from the beef I eat?

What is a man anyhow? what am I? what are you?

All I mark as my own you shall offset it with your own,
Else it were time lost listening to me.

I do not snivel that snivel the world over,
That months are vacuums and the ground but wallow and filth.

Whimpering and truckling fold with powders for invalids, conformity,
    goes to the fourth-remov'd,
I wear my hat as I please indoors or out.

Why should I pray? why should I venerate and be ceremonious?

Having pried through the strata, analyzed to a hair, counsel'd with doctors and calculated close,
I find no sweeter fat than sticks to my own bones.

In all people I see myself, none more and not one a barley-corn less,
And the good or bad I say of myself I say of them.

I know I am solid and sound,
To me the converging objects of the universe perpetually flow,
All are written to me, and I must get what the writing means.

I know I am deathless,
I know this orbit of mine cannot be swept by a carpenter's compass,
I know I shall not pass like a child's carlacue cut with a burnt stick at night.

I know I am august,
I do not trouble my spirit to vindicate itself or be understood,
I see that the elementary laws never apologize,
(I reckon I behave no prouder than the level I plant my house by, after all.)

I exist as I am, that is enough,
If no other in the world be aware I sit content,
And if each and all be aware I sit content.

One world is aware and by far the largest to me, and that is myself,
And whether I come to my own to-day or in ten thousand or ten million years,
I can cheerfully take it now, or with equal cheerfulness I can wait.

My foothold is tenon'd and mortis'd in granite,
I laugh at what you call dissolution,
And I know the amplitude of time.

21

I am the poet of the Body and I am the poet of the Soul,
The pleasures of heaven are with me and the pains of hell are with me,
The first I graft and increase upon myself, the latter I translate into a new tongue.

I am the poet of the woman the same as the man,
And I say it is as great to be a woman as to be a man,
And I say there is nothing greater than the mother of men.

I chant the chant of dilation or pride,
We have had ducking and deprecating about enough,
I show that size is only development.

Have you outstript the rest? are you the President?
It is a trifle, they will more than arrive there every one, and still pass on.

I am he that walks with the tender and growing night,
I call to the earth and sea half-held by the night.

Press close bare-bosom'd night — press close magnetic nourishing night!
Night of south winds — night of the large few stars!
Still nodding night — mad naked summer night.

Smile O voluptuous cool-breath'd earth!
Earth of the slumbering and liquid trees!
Earth of departed sunset — earth of the mountains misty-topt!
Earth of the vitreous pour of the full moon just tinged with blue!
Earth of shine and dark mottling the tide of the river!
Earth of the limpid gray of clouds brighter and clearer for my sake!
Far-swooping elbow'd earth — rich apple-blossom'd earth!
Smile, for your lover comes.

Prodigal, you have given me love — therefore I to you give love!
O unspeakable passionate love.

22

You sea! I resign myself to you also — I guess what you mean,
I behold from the beach your crooked inviting fingers,
I believe you refuse to go back without feeling of me,
We must have a turn together, I undress, hurry me out of sight of the
     land,
Cushion me soft, rock me in billowy drowse,
Dash me with amorous wet, I can repay you.

Sea of stretch'd ground-swells,
Sea breathing broad and convulsive breaths,
Sea of the brine of life and of unshovell'd yet always-ready graves,
Howler and scooper of storms, capricious and dainty sea,
I am integral with you, I too am of one phase and of all phases.

Partaker of influx and efflux I, extoller of hate and conciliation,
Extoller of amies and those that sleep in each others' arms.

I am he attesting sympathy,
(Shall I make my list of things in the house and skip the house that
     supports them?)

I am not the poet of goodness only, I do not decline to be the poet of
     wickedness also.

What blurt is this about virtue and about vice?
Evil propels me and reform of evil propels me, I stand indifferent,
My gait is no fault-finder's or rejecter's gait,
I moisten the roots of all that has grown.

Did you fear some scrofula out of the unflagging pregnancy?
Did you guess the celestial laws are yet to be work'd over and rectified?

I find one side a balance and the antipodal side a balance,
Soft doctrine as steady help as stable doctrine,
Thoughts and deeds of the present our rouse and early start.

This minute that comes to me over the past decillions,
There is no better than it and now.

What behaved well in the past or behaves well to-day is not such a
     wonder,
The wonder is always and always how there can be a mean man or an
     infidel.

23

Endless unfolding of words of ages!
And mine a word of the modern, the word En-Masse.

A word of the faith that never balks,
Here or henceforward it is all the same to me, I accept Time absolutely.

It alone is without flaw, it alone rounds and completes all,
That mystic baffling wonder alone completes all.

I accept Reality and dare not question it,
Materialism first and last imbuing.

Hurrah for positive science! long live exact demonstration!
Fetch stonecrop mixt with cedar and branches of lilac,

This is the lexicographer, this the chemist, this made a grammar of the old cartouches,
These mariners put the ship through dangerous unknown seas,
This is the geologist, this works with the scalpel, and this is a mathematician.

Gentlemen, to you the first honors always!
Your facts are useful, and yet they are not my dwelling,
I but enter by them to an area of my dwelling.

Less the reminders of properties told my words,
And more the reminders they of life untold, and of freedom and extrication,
And make short account of neuters and geldings, and favor men and women full equipt,
And beat the gong of revolt, and stop with fugitives and them that plot and conspire.

24

Walt Whitman, a kosmos, of Manhattan the son,
Turbulent, fleshy, sensual, eating, drinking and breeding,
No sentimentalist, no stander above men and women or apart from them,
No more modest than immodest.

Unscrew the locks from the doors!
Unscrew the doors themselves from their jambs!

Whoever degrades another degrades me,
And whatever is done or said returns at last to me.

Through me the afflatus surging and surging, through me the current and index.

I speak the pass-word primeval, I give the sign of democracy,
By God! I will accept nothing which all cannot have their counterpart of on the same terms.

Through me many long dumb voices,
Voices of the interminable generations of prisoners and slaves,
Voices of the diseas'd and despairing and of thieves and dwarfs,
Voices of cycles of preparation and accretion,

And of the threads that connect the stars, and of wombs and of the
father-stuff,
And of the rights of them the others are down upon,
Of the deform'd, trivial, flat, foolish, despised,
Fog in the air, beetles rolling balls of dung.

Through me forbidden voices,
Voices of sexes and lusts, voices veil'd and I remove the veil,
Voices indecent by me clarified and transfigur'd.

I do not press my fingers across my mouth,
I keep as delicate around the bowels as around the head and heart,
Copulation is no more rank to me than death is.

I believe in the flesh and the appetites.
Seeing, hearing, feeling, are miracles, and each part and tag of me is a
miracle.

Divine am I inside and out, and make holy whatever I touch or am
touch'd from,
The scent of these arm-pits aroma finer than prayer,
This head more than churches, bibles, and all the creeds.

If I worship one thing more than another it shall be the spread of my
own body, or any part of it,
Translucent mould of me it shall be you!
Shaded ledges and rests it shall be you!
Firm masculine colter it shall be you!
Whatever goes to the tilth of me it shall be you!
You my rich blood! your milky stream pale strippings of my life!
Breast that presses against other breasts it shall be you!
My brain it shall be your occult convolutions!
Root of wash'd sweet-flag! timorous pond-snipe! nest of guarded dupli-
cate eggs! it shall be you!
Mix'd tussled hay of head, beard, brawn, it shall be you!
Trickling sap of maple, fibre of manly wheat, it shall be you!
Sun so generous it shall be you!
Vapors lighting and shading my face it shall be you!
You sweaty brooks and dews it shall be you!
Winds whose soft-tickling genitals rub against me it shall be you!
Broad muscular fields, branches of live oak, loving lounger in my wind-
ing paths, it shall be you!
Hands I have taken, face I have kiss'd, mortal I have ever touch'd, it
shall be you.

I dote on myself, there is that lot of me and all so luscious,
Each moment and whatever happens thrills me with joy,
I cannot tell how my ankles bend, nor whence the cause of my faintest
wish,
Nor the cause of the friendship I emit, nor the cause of the friendship
I take again.

That I walk up my stoop, I pause to consider if it really be,
A morning-glory at my window satisfies me more than the metaphysics
of books.

To behold the day-break!
The little light fades the immense and diaphanous shadows,
The air tastes good to my palate.

Hefts of the moving world at innocent gambols silently rising freshly
exuding,
Scooting obliquely high and low.

Something I cannot see puts upward libidinous prongs,
Seas of bright juice suffuse heaven.

The earth by the sky staid with, the daily close of their junction,
The heav'd challenge from the east that moment over my head,
The mocking taunt, See then whether you shall be master!

25
Dazzling and tremendous how quick the sun-rise would kill me,
If I could not now and always send sun-rise out of me.

We also ascend dazzling and tremendous as the sun,
We found our own O my soul in the calm and cool of the daybreak.

My voice goes after what my eyes cannot reach,
With the twirl of my tongue I encompass worlds and volumes of worlds.

Speech is the twin of my vision, it is unequal to measure itself,
It provokes me forever, it says sarcastically,
Walt you contain enough, why don't you let it out then?

Come now I will not be tantalized, you conceive too much of articulation,
Do you not know O speech how the buds beneath you are folded?
Waiting in gloom, protected by frost,

The dirt receding before my prophetical screams,
I underlying causes to balance them at last,
My knowledge my live parts, it keeping tally with the meaning of all
    things,
Happiness, (which whoever hears me let him or her set out in search of
    this day.)

My final merit I refuse you, I refuse putting from me what I really am,
Encompass worlds, but never try to encompass me,
I crowd your sleekest and best by simply looking toward you.

Writing and talk do not prove me,
I carry the plenum of proof and every thing else in my face,
With the hush of my lips I wholly confound the skeptic.

26

Now I will do nothing but listen,
To accrue what I hear into this song, to let sounds contribute toward it.

I hear bravuras of birds, bustle of growing wheat, gossip of flames, clack
    of sticks cooking my meals,
I hear the sound I love, the sound of the human voice,
I hear all sounds running together, combined, fused or following,
Sounds of the city and sounds out of the city, sounds of the day and
    night,
Talkative young ones to those that like them, the loud laugh of work-
    people at their meals,
The angry base of disjointed friendship, the faint tones of the sick,
The judge with hands tight to the desk, his pallid lips pronouncing a
    death-sentence,
The heave'e'yo of stevedores unlading ships by the wharves, the refrain
    of the anchor-lifters,
The ring of alarm-bells, the cry of fire, the whirr of swift-streaking
    engines and hose-carts with premonitory tinkles and color'd lights,
The steam-whistle, the solid roll of the train of approaching cars,
The slow march play'd at the head of the association marching two and
    two,
(They go to guard some corpse, the flag-tops are draped with black
    muslin.)

I hear the violoncello, ('tis the young man's heart's complaint,)
I hear the key'd cornet, it glides quickly in through my ears,
It shakes mad-sweet pangs through my belly and breast.

I hear the chorus, it is a grand opera,
Ah this indeed is music — this suits me.

A tenor large and fresh as the creation fills me,
The orbic flex of his mouth is pouring and filling me full.

I hear the train'd soprano (what work with hers is this?)
The orchestra whirls me wider than Uranus flies,
It wrenches such ardors from me I did not know I possess'd them,
It sails me, I dab with bare feet, they are lick'd by the indolent waves,
I am cut by bitter and angry hail, I lose my breath,
Steep'd amid honey'd morphine, my windpipe throttled in fakes of
    death,
At length let up again to feel the puzzle of puzzles,
And that we call Being.

27

To be in any form, what is that?
(Round and round we go, all of us, and ever come back thither,)
If nothing lay more develop'd the quahaug in its callous shell were
    enough.

Mine is no callous shell,
I have instant conductors all over me whether I pass or stop,
They seize every object and lead it harmlessly through me.

I merely stir, press, feel with my fingers, and am happy,
To touch my person to some one else's is about as much as I can stand.

28

Is this then a touch? quivering me to a new identity,
Flames and ether making a rush for my veins,
Treacherous tip of me reaching and crowding to help them,
My flesh and blood playing out lightning to strike what is hardly dif-
    ferent from myself,
On all sides prurient provokers stiffening my limbs,
Straining the udder of my heart for its withheld drip,
Behaving licentious toward me, taking no denial,
Depriving me of my best as for a purpose,
Unbuttoning my clothes, holding me by the bare waist,
Deluding my confusion with the calm of the sunlight and pasture-fields,
Immodestly sliding the fellow-senses away,
They bribed to swap off with touch and go and graze at the edges of me,

No consideration, no regard for my draining strength or my anger,
Fetching the rest of the herd around to enjoy them a while,
Then all uniting to stand on a headland and worry me.

The sentries desert every other part of me,
They have left me helpless to a red marauder,
They all come to the headland to witness and assist against me.

I am given up by traitors,
I talk wildly, I have lost my wits, I and nobody else am the greatest
    traitor,
I went myself first to the headland, my own hands carried me there.

You villain touch! what are you doing? my breath is tight in its throat,
Unclench your floodgates, you are too much for me.

29
Blind loving wrestling touch, sheath'd hooded sharp-tooth'd touch!
Did it make you ache so, leaving me?

Parting track'd by arriving, perpetual payment of perpetual loan,
Rich showering rain, and recompense richer afterward.

Sprouts take and accumulate, stand by the curb prolific and vital,
Landscapes projected masculine, full-sized and golden.

30
All truths wait in all things,
They neither hasten their own delivery nor resist it,
They do not need the obstetric forceps of the surgeon,
The insignificant is as big to me as any,
(What is less or more than a touch?)

Logic and sermons never convince,
The damp of the night drives deeper into my soul.

(Only what proves itself to every man and woman is so,
Only what nobody denies is so.)

A minute and a drop of me settle my brain,
I believe the soggy clods shall become lovers and lamps,
And a compend of compends is the meat of a man or woman,
And a summit and flower there is the feeling they have for each other,

And they are to branch boundlessly out of that lesson until it becomes
omnific,
And until one and all shall delight us, and we them.

31

I believe a leaf of grass is no less than the journey-work of the stars,
And the pismire is equally perfect, and a grain of sand, and the egg of
the wren,
And the tree-toad is a chef-d'œuvre for the highest,
And the running blackberry would adorn the parlors of heaven,
And the narrowest hinge in my hand puts to scorn all machinery,
And the cow crunching with depress'd head surpasses any statue,
And a mouse is miracle enough to stagger sextillions of infidels.

I find I incorporate gneiss, coal, long-threaded moss, fruits, grains,
esculent roots,
And am stucco'd with quadrupeds and birds all over,
And have distanced what is behind me for good reasons,
But call any thing back again when I desire it.

In vain the speeding or shyness,
In vain the plutonic rocks send their old heat against my approach,
In vain the mastodon retreats beneath its own powder'd bones,
In vain objects stand leagues off and assume manifold shapes,
In vain the ocean settling in hollows and the great monsters lying low,
In vain the buzzard houses herself with the sky,
In vain the snake slides through the creepers and logs,
In vain the elk takes to the inner passes of the woods,
In vain the razor-bill'd auk sails far north to Labrador,
I follow quickly, I ascend to the nest in the fissure of the cliff.

32

I think I could turn and live with animals, they are so placid and self-
contain'd,
I stand and look at them long and long.

They do not sweat and whine about their condition,
They do not lie awake in the dark and weep for their sins,
They do not make me sick discussing their duty to God,
Not one is dissatisfied, not one is demented with the mania of owning
things,
Not one kneels to another, nor to his kind that lived thousands of years
ago,
Not one is respectable or unhappy over the whole earth.

So they show their relations to me and I accept them,
They bring me tokens of myself, they evince them plainly in their
    possession.

I wonder where they get those tokens,
Did I pass that way huge times ago and negligently drop them?

Myself moving forward then and now and forever,
Gathering and showing more always and with velocity,
Infinite and omnigenous, and the like of these among them,
Not too exclusive toward the reachers of my remembrancers,
Picking out here one that I love, and now go with him on brotherly
    terms.

A gigantic beauty of a stallion, fresh and responsive to my caresses,
Head high in the forehead, wide between the ears,
Limbs glossy and supple, tail dusting the ground,
Eyes full of sparkling wickedness, ears finely cut, flexibly moving.

His nostrils dilate as my heels embrace him,
His well-built limbs tremble with pleasure as we race around and return.

I but use you a minute, then I resign you, stallion,
Why do I need your paces when I myself out-gallop them?
Even as I stand or sit passing faster than you.

33
Space and Time! now I see it is true, what I guess'd at,
What I guess'd when I loaf'd on the grass,
What I guess'd while I lay alone in my bed,
And again as I walk'd the beach under the paling stars of the morning.

My ties and ballasts leave me, my elbows rest in sea-gaps,
I am sierras, my palms cover continents,
I am afoot with my vision.

By the city's quadrangular houses — in log huts, camping with lumber-
    men,
Along the ruts of the turnpike, along the dry gulch and rivulet bed,
Weeding my onion-patch or hoeing rows of carrots and parsnips, cross-
    ing savannas, trailing in forests,
Prospecting, gold-digging, girdling the trees of a new purchase,

Scorch'd ankle-deep by the hot sand, hauling by boat down the shallow
river,
Where the panther walks to and fro on a limb overhead, where the
buck turns furiously at the hunter,
Where the rattlesnake suns his flabby length on a rock, where the otter
is feeding on fish,
Where the alligator in his tough pimples sleeps by the bayou,
Where the black bear is searching for roots or honey, where the beaver
pats the mud with his paddle-shaped tail;
Over the growing sugar, over the yellow-flower'd cotton plant, over the
rice in its low moist field,
Over the sharp-peak'd farm house, with its scallop'd scum and slender
shoots from the gutters,
Over the western persimmon, over the long-leav'd corn, over the delicate
blue-flower flax,
Over the white and brown buckwheat, a hummer and buzzer there with
the rest,
Over the dusky green of the rye as it ripples and shades in the breeze;
Scaling mountains, pulling myself cautiously up, holding on by low
scragged limbs,
Walking the path worn in the grass and beat through the leaves of the
brush,
Where the quail is whistling betwixt the woods and the wheat-lot,
Where the bat flies in the Seventh-month eve, where the great goldbug
drops through the dark,
Where the brook puts out of the roots of the old tree and flows to the
meadow,
Where cattle stand and shake away flies with the tremulous shuddering
of their hides,
Where the cheese-cloth hangs in the kitchen, where andirons straddle
the hearth-slab, where cobwebs fall in festoons from the rafters;
Where trip-hammers crash, where the press is whirling its cylinders,
Wherever the human heart beats with terrible throes under its ribs,
Where the pear-shaped balloon is floating aloft, (floating in it myself
and looking composedly down,)
Where the life-car is drawn on the slip-noose, where the heat hatches
pale-green eggs in the dented sand,
Where the she-whale swims with her calf and never forsakes it,
Where the steam-ship trails hind-ways its long pennant of smoke,
Where the fin of the shark cuts like a black chip out of the water,
Where the half-burn'd brig is riding on unknown currents,
Where shells grow to her slimy deck, where the dead are corrupting
below;

Where the dense-starr'd flag is borne at the head of the regiments,
Approaching Manhattan up by the long-stretching island,
Under Niagara, the cataract falling like a veil over my countenance,
Upon a door-step, upon the horse-block of hard wood outside,
Upon the race-course, or enjoying picnics or jigs or a good game of
  baseball,
At he-festivals, with blackguard gibes, ironical license, bull-dances, drink-
  ing, laughter,
At the cider-mill tasting the sweets of the brown mash, sucking the
  juice through a straw,
At apple-peelings wanting kisses for all the red fruit I find,
At musters, beach-parties, friendly bees, huskings, house-raisings;
Where the mocking-bird sounds his delicious gurgles, cackles, screams,
  weeps,
Where the hay-rick stands in the barn-yard, where the dry-stalks are
  scatter'd, where the brood-cow waits in the hovel,
Where the bull advances to do his masculine work, where the stud to
  the mare, where the cock is treading the hen,
Where the heifers browse, where geese nip their food with short jerks,
Where sun-down shadows lengthen over the limitless and lonesome
  prairie,
Where herds of buffalo make a crawling spread of the square miles far
  and near,
Where the humming-bird shimmers, where the neck of the long-lived
  swan is curving and winding,
Where the laughing-gull scoots by the shore, where she laughs her near-
  human laugh,
Where bee-hives range on a gray bench in the garden half hid by the
  high weeds,
Where band-neck'd partridges roost in a ring on the ground with their
  heads out,
Where burial coaches enter the arch'd gates of a cemetery,
Where winter wolves bark amid wastes of snow and icicled trees,
Where the yellow-crown'd heron comes to the edge of the marsh at
  night and feeds upon small crabs,
Where the splash of swimmers and divers cools the warm noon,
Where the katy-did works her chromatic reed on the walnut-tree over
  the well,
Through patches of citrons and cucumbers with silver-wired leaves,
Through the salt-lick or orange glade, or under conical firs,
Through the gymnasium, through the curtain'd saloon, through the
  office or public hall;

Pleas'd with the native and pleas'd with the foreign, pleas'd with the
new and old,
Pleas'd with the homely woman as well as the handsome,
Pleas'd with the quakeress as she puts off her bonnet and talks
melodiously,
Pleas'd with the tune of the choir of the whitewash'd church,
Pleas'd with the earnest words of the sweating Methodist preacher,
impress'd seriously at the camp-meeting;
Looking in at the shop windows of Broadway the whole forenoon,
flatting the flesh of my nose on the thick plate glass,
Wandering the same afternoon with my face turn'd up to the clouds,
or down a lane or along the beach,
My right and left arms round the sides of two friends, and I in the
middle;
Coming home with the silent and dark-cheek'd bush-boy, (behind me
he rides at the drape of the day,)
Far from the settlements studying the print of animals' feet, or the
moccasin print,
By the cot in the hospital reaching lemonade to a feverish patient,
Nigh the coffin'd corpse when all is still, examining with a candle;
Voyaging to every port to dicker and adventure,
Hurrying with the modern crowd as eager and fickle as any,
Hot toward one I hate, ready in my madness to knife him,
Solitary at midnight in my back yard, my thoughts gone from me a
long while,
Walking the old hills of Judæa with the beautiful gentle God by my
side,
Speeding through space, speeding through heaven and the stars,
Speeding amid the seven satellites and the broad ring, and the diameter
of eighty thousand miles,
Speeding with tail'd meteors, throwing fire-balls like the rest,
Carrying the crescent child that carries its own full mother in its belly,
Storming, enjoying, planning, loving, cautioning,
Backing and filling, appearing and disappearing.
I tread day and night such roads.

I visit the orchards of spheres and look at the product,
And look at quintillions ripen'd and look at quintillions green.

I fly those flights of a fluid and swallowing soul,
My course runs below the soundings of plummets.

I help myself to material and immaterial,
No guard can shut me off, no law prevent me.

I anchor my ship for a little while only,
My messengers continually cruise away or bring their returns to me.

I go hunting polar furs and the seal, leaping chasms with a pike-pointed
staff, clinging to topples of brittle and blue.

I ascend to the foretruck,
I take my place late at night in the crow's-nest,
We sail the arctic sea, it is plenty light enough,
Through the clear atmosphere I stretch around on the wonderful beauty,
The enormous masses of ice pass me and I pass them, the scenery is
plain in all directions,
The white-topt mountains show in the distance, I fling out my fancies
toward them,
We are approaching some great battle-field in which we are soon to be
engaged,
We pass the colossal outposts of the encampment, we pass with still feet
and caution,
Or we are entering by the suburbs some vast and ruin'd city,
The blocks and fallen architecture more than all the living cities of the
globe.

I am a free companion, I bivouac by invading watchfires,
I turn the bridegroom out of bed and stay with the bride myself,
I tighten her all night to my thighs and lips.

My voice is the wife's voice, the screech by the rail of the stairs,
They fetch my man's body up dripping and drown'd.

I understand the large hearts of heroes,
The courage of present times and all times,
How the skipper saw the crowded and rudderless wreck of the steam-
ship, and Death chasing it up and down the storm,
How he knuckled tight and gave not back an inch, and was faithful of
days and faithful of nights,
And chalk'd in large letters on a board, *Be of good cheer, we will not
desert you;*
How he follow'd with them and tack'd with them three days and would
not give it up,

How he saved the drifting company at last,
How the lank loose-grown'd women look'd when boated from the side
of their prepared graves,
How the silent old-faced infants and the lifted sick, and the sharp-lipp'd
unshaved men;
All this I swallow, it tastes good, I like it well, it becomes mine,
I am the man, I suffer'd, I was there.

The disdain and calmness of martyrs,
The mother of old, condemn'd for a witch, burnt with dry wood, her
children gazing on,
The hounded slave that flags in the race, leans by the fence, blowing,
cover'd with sweat,
The twinges that sting like needles his legs and neck, the murderous
buckshot and the bullets,
All these I feel or am.

I am the hounded slave, I wince at the bite of the dogs,
Hell and despair are upon me, crack and again crack the marksmen,
I clutch the rails of the fence, my gore dribs, thinn'd with the ooze of
my skin,
I fall on the weeds and stones,
The riders spur their unwilling horses, haul close,
Taunt my dizzy ears and beat me violently over the head with whip-
stocks.

Agonies are one of my changes of garments,
I do not ask the wounded person how he feels, I myself become the
wounded person,
My hurts turn livid upon me as I lean on a cane and observe.

I am the mash'd fireman with breast-bone broken,
Tumbling walls buried me in their debris,
Heat and smoke I inspired, I heard the yelling shouts of my comrades,
I heard the distant click of their picks and shovels,
They have clear'd the beams away, they tenderly lift me forth.

I lie in the night air in my red shirt, the pervading hush is for my sake,
Painless after all I lie exhausted but not so unhappy,
White and beautiful are the faces around me, the heads are bared of
their fire-caps,
The kneeling crowd fades with the light of the torches.

Distant and dead resuscitate,
They show as the dial or move as the hands of me, I am the clock
    myself.

I am an old artillerist, I tell of my fort's bombardment,
I am there again.

Again the long roll of the drummers,
Again the attacking cannon, mortars,
Again to my listening ears the cannon responsive.

I take part, I see and hear the whole,
The cries, curses, roar, the plaudits for well-aim'd shots,
The ambulanza slowly passing trailing its red drip,
Workmen searching after damages, making indispensable repairs,
The fall of grenades through the rent roof, the fan-shaped explosion,
The whizz of limbs, heads, stone, wood, iron, high in the air.

Again gurgles the mouth of my dying general, he furiously waves with
    his hand,
He gasps through the clot *Mind not me — mind — the entrenchments.*

34

Now I tell what I knew in Texas in my early youth,
(I tell not the fall of Alamo,
Not one escaped to tell the fall of Alamo,
The hundred and fifty are dumb yet at Alamo,)
'Tis the tale of the murder in cold blood of four hundred and twelve
    young men.

Retreating they had form'd in a hollow square with their baggage for
    breastworks,
Nine hundred lives out of the surrounding enemy's, nine times their
    number, was the price they took in advance,
Their colonel was wounded and their ammunition gone,
They treated for an honorable capitulation, receiv'd writing and seal,
    gave up their arms and march'd back prisoners of war.

They were the glory of the race of rangers,
Matchless with horse, rifle, song, supper, courtship,
Large, turbulent, generous, handsome, proud, and affectionate,
Bearded, sunburnt, drest in the free costume of hunters,
Not a single one over thirty years of age.

The second First-day morning they were brought out in squads and
    massacred, it was beautiful early summer,
The work commenced about five o'clock and was over by eight.

None obey'd the command to kneel,
Some made a mad and helpless rush, some stood stark and straight,
A few fell at once, shot in the temple or heart, the living and dead lay
    together,
The maim'd and mangled dug in the dirt, the new-comers saw them
    there,
Some half-kill'd attempted to crawl away,
These were despatch'd with bayonets or batter'd with the blunts of
    muskets,
A youth not seventeen years old seiz'd his assassin till two more came
    to release him,
The three were all torn and cover'd with the boy's blood.

At eleven o'clock began the burning of the bodies;
That is the tale of the murder of the four hundred and twelve young
    men.

35

Would you hear of an old-time sea fight?
Would you learn who won by the light of the moon and stars?
List to the yarn, as my grandmother's father the sailor told it to me.

Our foe was no skulk in his ship I tell you, (said he,)
His was the surly English pluck, and there is no tougher or truer, and
    never was, and never will be;
Along the lower'd eve he came horribly raking us.

We closed with him, the yards entangled, the cannon touch'd,
My captain lash'd fast with his own hands.

We had receiv'd some eighteen pound shots under the water,
On our lower-gun-deck two large pieces had burst at the first fire, killing
    all around and blowing up overhead.

Fighting at sun-down, fighting at dark,
Ten o'clock at night, the full moon well up, our leaks on the gain, and
    five feet of water reported,
The master-at-arms loosing the prisoners confined in the after-hold to
    give them a chance for themselves.

The transit to and from the magazine is now stopt by the sentinels,
They see so many strange faces they do not know whom to trust.

Our frigate takes fire,
The other asks if we demand quarter?
If our colors are struck and the fighting done?

Now I laugh content, for I hear the voice of my little captain,
We have not struck, he composedly cries, *we have just begun our part
of the fighting.*

Only three guns are in use,
One is directed by the captain himself against the enemy's mainmast,
Two well serv'd with grape and canister silence his musketry and clear
his decks.

The tops alone second the fire of this little battery, especially the main-
top,
They hold out bravely during the whole of the action.

Not a moment's cease,
The leaks gain fast on the pumps, the fire eats toward the powder-
magazine.

One of the pumps has been shot away, it is generally thought we are
sinking.

Serene stands the little captain,
He is not hurried, his voice is neither high nor low,
His eyes give more light to us than our battle-lanterns.

Toward twelve there in the beams of the moon they surrender to us.

36

Stretch'd and still lies the midnight,
Two great hulls motionless on the breast of the darkness,
Our vessel riddled and slowly sinking, preparations to pass to the one
we have conquer'd,
The captain on the quarter-deck coldly giving his orders through a
countenance white as a sheet,
Near by the corpse of the child that serv'd in the cabin,
The dead face of an old salt with long white hair and carefully curl'd
whiskers,

The flames spite of all that can be done flickering aloft and below,
The husky voices of the two or three officers yet fit for duty,
Formless stacks of bodies and bodies by themselves, dabs of flesh upon
    the masts and spars,
Cut of cordage, dangle.of rigging, slight shock of the soothe of waves,
Black and impassive guns, litter of powder-parcels, strong scent,
A few large stars overhead, silent and mournful shining,
Delicate sniffs of sea-breeze, smells of sedgy grass and fields by the shore,
    death-messages given in charge to survivors,
The hiss of the surgeon's knife, the gnawing teeth of his saw,
Wheeze, cluck, swash of falling blood, short wild scream, and long dull,
    tapering groan,
These so, these irretrievable.

37

You laggards there on guard! look to your arms!
In at the conquer'd doors they crowd! I am possess'd!
Embody all presences outlaw'd or suffering,
See myself in prison shaped like another man,
And feel the dull unintermitted pain.

For me the keepers of convicts shoulder their carbines and keep watch,
It is I let out in the morning and barr'd at night.

Not a mutineer walks handcuff'd to jail but I am handcuff'd to him and
    walk by his side,
(I am less the jolly one there, and more the silent one with sweat on
    my twitching lips.)

Not a youngster is taken for larceny but I go up too, and am tried and
    sentenced.

Not a cholera patient lies at the last gasp but I also lie at the last gasp,
My face is ash-color'd, my sinews gnarl, away from me people retreat.

Askers embody themselves in me and I am embodied in them,
I project my hat, sit shame-faced, and beg.

38

Enough! enough! enough!
Somehow I have been stunn'd. Stand back!
Give me a little time beyond my cuff'd head, slumbers, dreams, gaping,
I discover myself on the verge of a usual mistake.

That I could forget the mockers and insults!
That I could forget the trickling tears and the blows of the bludgeons
and hammers!
That I could look with a separate look on my own crucifixion and
bloody crowning.

I remember now,
I resume the overstaid fraction,
The grave of rock multiplies what has been confided to it, or to any
graves,
Corpses rise, gashes heal, fastenings roll from me.

I troop forth replenish'd with supreme power, one of an average unend-
ing procession,
Inland and sea-coast we go, and pass all boundary lines,
Our swift ordinances on their way over the whole earth,
The blossoms we wear in our hats the growth of thousands of years.

Eleves, I salute you! come forward!
Continue your annotations, continue your questionings.

39

The friendly and flowing savage, who is he?
Is he waiting for civilization, or past it and mastering it?

Is he some Southwesterner rais'd out-doors? is he Kanadian?
Is he from the Mississippi country? Iowa, Oregon, California?
The mountains? prairie-life, bush-life? or sailor from the sea?

Wherever he goes men and women accept and desire him,
They desire he should like them, touch them, speak to them, stay with
them.

Behavior lawless as snow-flakes, words simple as grass, uncomb'd head,
laughter, and naivetè,
Slow-stepping feet, common features common modes and emanations,
They descend in new forms from the tips of his fingers,
They are wafted with the odor of his body or breath, they fly out of the
glance of his eyes.

40

Flaunt of the sunshine I need not your bask — lie over!
You light surfaces only, I force surfaces and depths also.

Earth! you seem to look for something at my hands,
Say, old top-knot, what do you want?

Man or woman, I might tell how I like you, but cannot,
And might tell what it is in me and what it is in you, but cannot,
And might tell that pining I have, that pulse of my nights and days.

Behold, I do not give lectures or a little charity,
When I give I give myself.

You there, impotent, loose in the knees,
Open your scarf'd chops till I blow grit within you,
Spread your palms and lift the flaps of your pockets,
I am not to be denied, I compel, I have stores plenty and to spare,
And any thing I have I bestow.

I do not ask who you are, that is not important to me,
You can do nothing and be nothing but what I will infold you.

To cotton-field drudge or cleaner of privies I lean,
On his right cheek I put the family kiss,
And in my soul I swear I never will deny him.

On women fit for conception I start bigger and nimbler babes,
(This day I am jetting the stuff of far more arrogant republics.)

To any one dying, thither I speed and twist the knob of the door,
Turn the bed-clothes toward the foot of the bed,
Let the physician and the priest go home.

I seize the descending man and raise him with resistless will,
O despairer, here is my neck,
By God, you shall not go down! hang your whole weight upon me.

I dilate you with tremendous breath, I buoy you up,
Every room of the house do I fill with an arm'd force,
Lovers of me, bafflers of graves.

Sleep — I and they keep guard all night,
Not doubt, not decease shall dare to lay finger upon you,
I have embraced you, and henceforth possess you to myself,
And when you rise in the morning you will find what I tell you is so.

41

I am he bringing help for the sick as they pant on their backs,
And for strong upright men I bring yet more needed help.
I heard what was said of the universe,
Heard it and heard it of several thousand years;
It is middling well as far as it goes — but is that all?

Magnifying and applying come I,
Outbidding at the start the old cautious hucksters,
Taking myself the exact dimensions of Jehovah,
Lithographing Kronos, Zeus his son, and Hercules his grandson,
Buying drafts of Osiris, Isis, Belus, Brahma, Buddha,
In my portfolio placing Manito loose, Allah on a leaf, the crucifix
    engraved,
With Odin and the hideous-faced Mexitli and every idol and image,
Taking them all for what they are worth and not a cent more,
Admitting they were alive and did the work of their days,
(They bore mites as for unfledg'd birds who have now to rise and fly
    and sing for themselves,)
Accepting the rough deific sketches to fill out better in myself, bestow-
    ing them freely on each man and woman I see,
Discovering as much or more in a framer framing a house,
Putting higher claims for him there with his roll'd-up sleeves driving
    the mallet and chisel,
Not objecting to special revelations, considering a curl of smoke or a hair
    on the back of my hand just as curious as any revelation,
Lads ahold of fire-engines and hook-and-ladder ropes no less to me than
    the gods of the antique wars,
Minding their voices peal through the crash of destruction,
Their brawny limbs passing safe over charr'd laths, their white fore-
    heads whole and unhurt out of the flames;
By the mechanic's wife with her babe at her nipple interceding for every
    person born,
Three scythes at harvest whizzing in a row from three lusty angels with
    shirts bagg'd out at their waists,
The snag-tooth'd hostler with red hair redeeming sins past and to come,
Selling all he possesses, traveling on foot to fee lawyers for his brother
    and sit by him while he is tried for forgery;
What was strewn in the amplest strewing the square rod about me, and
    not filling the square rod then,
The bull and the bug never worshipp'd half enough,
Dung and dirt more admirable than was dream'd,

The supernatural of no account, myself waiting my time to be one of
   the supremes,
The day getting ready for me when I shall do as much good as the best,
   and be as prodigious;
By my life-lumps! becoming already a creator,
Putting myself here and now to the ambush'd womb of the shadows.

42

A call in the midst of the crowd,
My own voice, orotund sweeping and final.

Come my children,
Come my boys and girls, my women, household and intimates,
Now the performer launches his nerve, he has pass'd his prelude on the
   reeds within.

Easily written loose-finger'd chords — I feel the thrum of your climax
   and close.

My head slues round on my neck,
Music rolls, but not from the organ,
Folks are around me, but they are no household of mine.

Ever the hard unsunk ground,
Ever the eaters and drinkers, ever the upward and downward sun, ever
   the air and the ceaseless tides,
Ever myself and my neighbors, refreshing, wicked, real,
Ever the old inexplicable query, ever that thorn'd thumb, that breath
   of itches and thirsts,
Ever the vexer's *hoot! hoot!* till we find where the sly one hides and
   bring him forth,
Ever love, ever the sobbing liquid of life,
Ever the bandage under the chin, ever the trestles of death.

Here and there with dimes on the eyes walking,
To feed the greed of the belly the brains liberally spooning,
Tickets buying, taking, selling, but in to the feast never once going,
Many sweating, ploughing, thrashing, and then the chaff for payment
   receiving,
A few idly owning, and they the wheat continually claiming.

This is the city and I am one of the citizens,
Whatever interests the rest interests me, politics, wars, markets, news-
    papers, schools,
The mayor and councils, banks, tariffs, steamships, factories, stocks,
    stores, real estate and personal estate.

The little plentiful manikins skipping around in collars and tail'd coats,
I am aware who they are, (they are positively not worms or fleas,)
I acknowledge the duplicates of myself, the weakest and shallowest is
    deathless with me,
What I do and say the same waits for them,
Every thought that flounders in me the same flounders in them.

I know perfectly well my own egotism,
Know my omnivorous lines and must not write any less,
And would fetch you whoever you are flush with myself.

Not words of routine this song of mine,
But abruptly to question, to leap beyond yet nearer bring;
This printed and bound book — but the printer and the printing-office
    boy?
The well-taken photographs — but your wife or friend close and solid
    in your arms?
The black ship mail'd with iron, her mighty guns in her turrets — but
    the pluck of the captain and engineers?
In the houses the dishes and fare and furniture — but the host and
    hostess, and the look out of their eyes?
The sky up there — yet here or next door, or across the way?
The saints and sages in history — but you yourself?
Sermons, creeds, theology — but the fathomless human brain,
And what is reason? and what is love? and what is life?

43
I do not despise you priests, all time, the world over,
My faith is the greatest of faiths and the least of faiths,
Enclosing worship ancient and modern and all between ancient and
    modern,
Believing I shall come again upon the earth after five thousand years,
Waiting responses from oracles, honoring the gods, saluting the sun,
Making a fetich of the first rock or stump, powowing with sticks in the
    circle of obis,
Helping the llama or brahmin as he trims the lamps of the idols,

Dancing yet through the streets in a phallic procession, rapt and austere in the woods a gymnosophist,
Drinking mead from the skull-cup, to Shastas and Vedas admirant, minding the Koran,
Walking the teokallis, spotted with gore from the stone and knife, beating the serpent-skin drum,
Accepting the Gospels, accepting him that was crucified, knowing assuredly that he is divine,
To the mass kneeling or the puritan's prayer rising, or sitting patiently in a pew,
Ranting and frothing in my insane crisis, or waiting dead-like till my spirit arouses me,
Looking forth on pavement and land, or outside of pavement and land,
Belonging to the winders of the circuit of circuits.

One of that centripetal and centrifugal gang I turn and talk like a man leaving charges before a journey.

Down-hearted doubters dull and excluded,
Frivolous, sullen, moping, angry, affected, dishearten'd, atheistical,
I know every one of you, I know the sea of torment, doubt, despair and unbelief.

How the flukes splash!
How they contort rapid as lightning, with spasms and spouts of blood!

Be at peace bloody flukes of doubters and sullen mopers,
I take my place among you as much as among any,
The past is the push of you, me, all, precisely the same,
And what is yet untried and afterward is for you, me, all, precisely the same.

I do not know what is untried and afterward,
But I know it will in its turn prove sufficient, and cannot fail.

Each who passes is consider'd, each who stops is consider'd, not a single one can it fail.

It cannot fail the young man who died and was buried,
Nor the young woman who died and was put by his side,
Nor the little child that peep'd in at the door, and then drew back and was never seen again,

Nor the old man who has lived without purpose, and feels it with bitter-
  ness worse than gall,
Nor him in the poor house tubercled by rum and the bad disorder,
Nor the numberless slaughter'd and wreck'd, nor the brutish koboo
  call'd the ordure of humanity,
Nor the sacs merely floating with open mouths for food to slip in,
Nor any thing in the earth, or down in the oldest graves of the earth,
Nor any thing in the myriads of spheres, nor the myriads of myriads that
  inhabit them,
Nor the present, nor the least wisp that is known.

44
It is time to explain myself — let us stand up.

What is known I strip away,
I launch all men and women forward with me into the Unknown.

The clock indicates the moment — but what does eternity indicate?

We have thus far exhausted trillions of winters and summers,
There are trillions ahead, and trillions ahead of them.

Births have brought us richness and variety,
And other births will bring us richness and variety.

I do not call one greater and one smaller,
That which fills its period and place is equal to any.

Were mankind murderous or jealous upon you, my brother, my sister?
I am sorry for you, they are not murderous or jealous upon me,
All has been gentle with me, I keep no account with lamentation,
(What have I to do with lamentation?)

I am an acme of things accomplish'd, and I am encloser of things to be.

My feet strike an apex of the apices of the stairs,
On every step bunches of ages, and larger bunches between the steps,
All below duly travel'd, and still I mount and mount.

Rise after rise bow the phantoms behind me,
Afar down I see the huge first Nothing, I know I was even there,
I waited unseen and always, and slept through the lethargic mist,
And took my time, and took no hurt from the fetid carbon.

Long I was hugg'd close — long and long.

Immense have been the preparations for me,
Faithful and friendly the arms that have help'd me.

Cycles ferried my cradle, rowing and rowing like cheerful boatmen,
For room to me stars kept aside in their own rings,
They sent influences to look after what was to hold me.

Before I was born out of my mother generations guided me,
My embryo has never been torpid, nothing could overlay it.

For it the nebula cohered to an orb,
The long slow strata piled to rest it on,
Vast vegetables gave it sustenance,
Monstrous sauroids transported it in their mouths and deposited it with
    care.

All forces have been steadily employ'd to complete and delight me,
Now on this spot I stand with my robust soul.

45

O span of youth! ever-push'd elasticity!
O manhood, balanced, florid and full.

My lovers suffocate me,
Crowding my lips, thick in the pores of my skin,
Jostling me through streets and public halls, coming naked to me at
    night,
Crying by day *Ahoy!* from the rocks of the river, swinging and chirping
    over my head,
Calling my name from flower-beds, vines, tangled underbrush,
Lighting on every moment of my life,
Bussing my body with soft balsamic busses,
Noiseless passing handfuls out of their hearts and giving them to be
    mine.

Old age superbly rising! O welcome, ineffable grace of dying days!

Every condition promulges not only itself, it promulges what grows after
    and out of itself,
And the dark hush promulges as much as any.

I open my scuttle at night and see the far-sprinkled systems,
And all I see multiplied as high as I can cipher edge but the rim of the
farther systems.

Wider and wider they spread, expanding, always expanding,
Outward and outward and forever outward.

My sun has his sun and round him obediently wheels,
He joins with his partners a group of superior circuit,
And greater sets follow, making specks of the greatest inside them.

There is no stoppage and never can be stoppage,
If I, you, and the worlds, and all beneath or upon their surfaces, were
this moment reduced back to a pallid float, it would not avail in
the long run,
We should surely bring up again where we now stand,
And surely go as much farther, and then farther and farther.

A few quadrillions of eras, a few octillions of cubic leagues, do not
hazard the span or make it impatient,
They are but parts, any thing is but a part.

See ever so far, there is limitless space outside of that,
Count ever so much, there is limitless time around that.

My rendezvous is appointed, it is certain,
The Lord will be there and wait till I come on perfect terms,
The great Camerado, the lover true for whom I pine will be there.

46

I know I have the best of time and space, and was never measured and
never will be measured.

I tramp a perpetual journey, (come listen all!)
My signs are a rain-proof coat, good shoes, and a staff cut from the
woods,
No friend of mine takes his ease in my chair,
I have no chair, no church, no philosophy,
I lead no man to a dinner-table, library, exchange,
But each man and each woman of you I lead upon a knoll,
My left hand hooking you round the waist,
My right hand pointing to landscapes of continents and the public road.

Not I, not any one else can travel that road for you,
You must travel it for yourself.

It is not far, it is within reach,
Perhaps you have been on it since you were born and did not know,
Perhaps it is everywhere on water and on land.

Shoulder your duds dear son, and I will mine, and let us hasten forth,
Wonderful cities and free nations we shall fetch as we go.

If you tire, give me both burdens, and rest the chuff of your hand on
    my hip,
And in due time you shall repay the same service to me,
For after we start we never lie by again.

This day before dawn I ascended a hill and look'd at the crowded heaven,
And I said to my spirit *When we become the enfolders of those orbs, and*
    the pleasure and knowledge of every thing in them, shall we be
    fill'd and satisfied then?
And my spirit said *No, we but level that lift to pass and continue beyond.*

You are also asking me questions and I hear you,
I answer that I cannot answer, you must find out for yourself.

Sit a while dear son,
Here are biscuits to eat and here is milk to drink,
But as soon as you sleep and renew yourself in sweet clothes, I kiss you
    with a good-by kiss and open the gate for your egress hence.

Long enough have you dream'd contemptible dreams,
Now I wash the gum from your eyes,
You must habit yourself to the dazzle of the light and of every moment
    of your life.

Long have you timidly waded holding a plank by the shore,
Now I will you to be a bold swimmer,
To jump off in the midst of the sea, rise again, nod to me, shout, and
    laughingly dash with your hair.

47

I am the teacher of athletes,
He that by me spreads a wider breast than my own proves the width of
    my own,
He most honors my style who learns under it to destroy the teacher.

The boy I love, the same becomes a man not through derived power,
    but in his own right,
Wicked rather than virtuous out of conformity or fear,
Fond of his sweetheart, relishing well his steak,
Unrequited love or a slight cutting him worse than sharp steel cuts,
First-rate to ride, to fight, to hit the bull's eye, to sail a skiff, to sing a
    song or play on the banjo,
Preferring scars and the beard and faces pitted with small-pox over all
    latherers,
And those well-tann'd to those that keep out of the sun.

I teach straying from me, yet who can stray from me?
I follow you whoever you are from the present hour,
My words itch at your ears till you understand them.

I do not say these things for a dollar or to fill up the time while I wait
    for a boat,
(It is you talking just as much as myself, I act as the tongue of you,
Tied in your mouth, in mine it begins to be loosen'd.)

I swear I will never again mention love or death inside a house,
And I swear I will never translate myself at all, only to him or her who
    privately stays with me in the open air.

If you would understand me go to the heights or water-shore,
The nearest gnat is an explanation, and a drop or motion of waves a key,
The maul, the oar, the hand-saw, second my words.

No shutter'd room or school can commune with me,
But roughs and little children better than they.

The young mechanic is closest to me, he knows me well,
The woodman that takes his axe and jug with him shall take me with
    him all day,
The farm-boy ploughing in the field feels good at the sound of my voice,
In vessels that sail my words sail, I go with fishermen and seamen and
    love them.

The soldier camp'd or upon the march is mine,
On the night ere the pending battle many seek me, and I do not fail
    them,
On that solemn night (it may be their last) those that know me seek
    me.

My face rubs to the hunter's face when he lies down alone in his blanket,
The driver thinking of me does not mind the jolt of his wagon,
The young mother and old mother comprehend me,
The girl and the wife rest the needle a moment and forget where they
    are,
They and all would resume what I have told them.

48

I have said that the soul is not more than the body,
And I have said that the body is not more than the soul,
And nothing, not God, is greater to one than one's self is,
And whoever walks a furlong without sympathy walks to his own funeral
    drest in his shroud,
And I or you pocketless of a dime may purchase the pick of the earth,
And to glance with an eye or show a bean in its pod confounds the
    learning of all times,
And there is no trade or employment but the young man following it
    may become a hero,
And there is no object so soft but it makes a hub for the wheel'd
    universe,
And I say to any man or woman, Let your soul stand cool and composed
    before a million universes.

And I say to mankind, Be not curious about God,
For I who am curious about each am not curious about God,
(No array of terms can say how much I am at peace about God and
    about death.)

I hear and behold God in every object, yet understand God not in the
    least,
Nor do I understand who there can be more wonderful than myself.

Why should I wish to see God better than this day?
I see something of God each hour of the twenty-four, and each moment
    then,
In the faces of men and women I see God, and in my own face in the
    glass,

I find letters from God dropt in the street, and every one is sign'd by
  God's name,
And I leave them where they are, for I know that wheresoe'er I go,
Others will punctually come for ever and ever.

49

And as to you Death, and you bitter hug of mortality, it is idle to try
  to alarm me.

To his work without flinching the accoucheur comes,
I see the elder-hand pressing receiving supporting,
I recline by the sills of the exquisite flexible doors,
And mark the outlet, and mark the relief and escape.

And as to you Corpse I think you are good manure, but that does not
  offend me,
I smell the white roses sweet-scented and growing,
I reach to the leafy lips, I reach to the polish'd breasts of melons.

And as to you Life I reckon you are the leavings of many deaths,
(No doubt I have died myself ten thousand times before.)

I hear you whispering there O stars of heaven,
O suns — O grass of graves — O perpetual transfers and promotions,
If you do not say any thing how can I say any thing?

Of the turbid pool that lies in the autumn forest,
Of the moon that descends the steeps of the soughing twilight,
Toss, sparkles of day and dusk — toss on the black stems that decay in
  the muck,
Toss to the moaning gibberish of the dry limbs.

I ascend from the moon, I ascend from the night,
I perceive that the ghastly glimmer is noonday sunbeams reflected,
And debouch to the steady and central from the offspring great or small.

50

There is that in me — I do not know what it is — but I know it is in
  me.

Wrench'd and sweaty — calm and cool then my body becomes,
I sleep — I sleep long.

I do not know it — it is without name — it is a word unsaid,
It is not in any dictionary, utterance, symbol.

Something it swings on more than the earth I swing on,
To it the creation is the friend whose embracing awakes me.

Perhaps I might tell more. Outlines! I plead for my brothers and sisters.

Do you see O my brothers and sisters?
It is not chaos or death — it is form, union, plan — it is eternal life —
    it is Happiness.

51

The past and present wilt — I have fill'd them, emptied them,
And proceed to fill my next fold of the future.

Listener up there! what have you to confide to me?
Look in my face while I snuff the sidle of evening,
(Talk honestly, no one else hears you, and I stay only a minute longer.)

Do I contradict myself?
Very well then I contradict myself,
(I am large, I contain multitudes.)

I concentrate toward them that are nigh, I wait on the door-slab.

Who has done his day's work? who will soonest be through with his
    supper?
Who wishes to walk with me?

Will you speak before I am gone? will you prove already too late?

52

The spotted hawk swoops by and accuses me, he complains of my gab
    and my loitering.

I too am not a bit tamed, I too am untranslatable,
I sound my barbaric yawp over the roofs of the world.

The last scud of day holds back for me,
It flings my likeness after the rest and true as any on the shadow'd wilds,
It coaxes me to the vapor and the dusk.

I depart as air, I shake my white locks at the runaway sun,
I effuse my flesh in eddies, and drift it in lacy jags.

I bequeath myself to the dirt to grow from the grass I love,
If you want me again look for me under your boot-soles.

You will hardly know who I am or what I mean,
But I shall be good health to you nevertheless,
And filter and fibre your blood.

Failing to fetch me at first keep encouraged,
Missing me one place search another,
I stop somewhere waiting for you.

A Woman Waits for Me

A woman waits for me, she contains all, nothing is lacking,
Yet all were lacking if sex were lacking, or if the moisture of the right
    man were lacking.

Sex contains all, bodies, souls,
Meanings, proofs, purities, delicacies, results, promulgations,
Songs, commands, health, pride, the maternal mystery, the seminal milk,
All hopes, benefactions, bestowals, all the passions, loves, beauties,
    delights of the earth,
All the governments, judges, gods, follow'd persons of the earth,
These are contain'd in sex as parts of itself and justifications of itself.

Without shame the man I like knows and avows the deliciousness of
    his sex,
Without shame the woman I like knows and avows hers.

Now I will dismiss myself from impassive women,
I will go stay with her who waits for me, and with those women that
    are warm-blooded and sufficient for me,
I see that they understand me and do not deny me,
I see that they are worthy of me, I will be the robust husband of those
    women.

They are not one jot less than I am,
They are tann'd in the face by shining suns and blowing winds,
Their flesh has the old divine suppleness and strength,

They know how to swim, row, ride, wrestle, shoot, run, strike, retreat,
    advance, resist, defend themselves,
They are ultimate in their own right — they are calm, clear, well-
    possess'd of themselves.

I draw you close to me, you women,
I cannot let you go, I would do you good,
I am for you, and you are for me, not only for our own sake, but for
    others' sakes,
Envelop'd in you sleep great heroes and bards,
They refuse to awake at the touch of any man but me.

It is I, you women, I make my way,
I am stern, acrid, large, undissuadable, but I love you,
I do not hurt you any more than is necessary for you,
I pour the stuff to start sons and daughters fit for these States, I press
    with slow rude muscle,
I brace myself effectually, I listen to no entreaties,
I dare not withdraw till I deposit what has so long accumulated within me.

Through you I drain the pent-up rivers of myself,
In you I wrap a thousand onward years,
On you I graft the grafts of the best-beloved of me and America,
The drops I distil upon you shall grow fierce and athletic girls, new
    artists, musicians, and singers,
The babes I beget upon you are to beget babes in their turn,
I shall demand perfect men and women out of my love-spendings,
I shall expect them to interpenetrate with others, as I and you inter-
    penetrate now,
I shall count on the fruits of the gushing showers of them, as I count
    on the fruits of the gushing showers I give now,
I shall look for loving crops from the birth, life, death, immortality, I
    plant so lovingly now.

Song of the Open Road

1

Afoot and light-hearted I take to the open road,
Healthy, free, the world before me,
The long brown path before me leading wherever I choose.

Henceforth I ask not good-fortune, I myself am good-fortune,
Henceforth I whimper no more, postpone no more, need nothing,
Done with indoor complaints, libraries, querulous criticisms,
Strong and content I travel the open road.

The earth, that is sufficient,
I do not want the constellations any nearer,
I know they are very well where they are,
I know they suffice for those who belong to them.

(Still here I carry my old delicious burdens,
I carry them, men and women, I carry them with me wherever I go,
I swear it is impossible for me to get rid of them,
I am fill'd with them, and I will fill them in return.)

2

You road I enter upon and look around, I believe you are not all that
    is here,
I believe that much unseen is also here.

Here the profound lesson of reception, nor preference nor denial,
The black with his woolly head, the felon, the diseas'd, the illiterate
    person, are not denied;
The birth, the hasting after the physician; the beggar's tramp, the
    drunkard's stagger, the laughing party of mechanics,
The escaped youth, the rich person's carriage, the fop, the eloping
    couple,
The early market-man, the hearse, the moving of furniture into the
    town, the return back from the town,
They pass, I also pass, any thing passes, none can be interdicted,
None but are accepted, none but shall be dear to me.

3

You air that serves me with breath to speak!
You objects that call from diffusion my meanings and give them shape!
You light that wraps me and all things in delicate equable showers!
You paths worn in the irregular hollows by the roadsides!
I believe you are latent with unseen existences, you are so dear to me.

You flagg'd walks of the cities! you strong curbs at the edges!
You ferries! you planks and posts of wharves! you timber-lined sides!
    you distant ships!
You rows of houses! you window-pierc'd façades! you roofs!

You porches and entrances! you copings and iron guards!
You windows whose transparent shells might expose so much!
You doors and ascending steps! you arches!
You gray stones of interminable pavements! you trodden crossings!
From all that has touch'd you I believe you have imparted to yourselves,
    and now would impart the same secretly to me,
From the living and the dead you have peopled your impassive surfaces,
    and the spirits thereof would be evident and amicable with me.

4

The earth expanding right hand and left hand,
The picture alive, every part in its best light,
The music falling in where it is wanted, and stopping where it is not
    wanted,
The cheerful voice of the public road, the gay fresh sentiment of the
    road.

O highway I travel, do you say to me *Do not leave me?*
Do you say *Venture not — if you leave me you are lost?*
Do you say *I am already prepared, I am well-beaten and undenied,
adhere to me?*

O public road, I say back I am not afraid to leave you, yet I love you,
You express me better than I can express myself,
You shall be more to me than my poem.

I think heroic deeds were all conceiv'd in the open air, and all free
    poems also,
I think I could stop here myself and do miracles,
I think whatever I shall meet on the road I shall like, and whoever
    beholds me shall like me,
I think whoever I see must be happy.

5

From this hour I ordain myself loos'd of limits and imaginary lines,
Going where I list, my own master total and absolute,
Listening to others, considering well what they say,
Pausing, searching, receiving, contemplating,
Gently, but with undeniable will, divesting myself of the holds that
    would hold me.

I inhale great draughts of space,
The east and the west are mine, and the north and the south are mine.

I am larger, better than I thought,
I did not know I held so much goodness.

All seems beautiful to me,
I can repeat over to men and women You have done such good to me
    I would do the same to you,
I will recruit for myself and you as I go,
I will scatter myself among men and women as I go,
I will toss a new gladness and roughness among them,
Whoever denies me it shall not trouble me,
Whoever accepts me he or she shall be blessed and shall bless me.

6

Now if a thousand perfect men were to appear it would not amaze me,
Now if a thousand beautiful forms of women appear'd it would not
    astonish me.

Now I see the secret of the making of the best persons,
It is to grow in the open air and to eat and sleep with the earth.

Here a great personal deed has room,
(Such a deed seizes upon the hearts of the whole race of men,
Its effusion of strength and will overwhelms law and mocks all authority
    and all argument against it.)

Here is the test of wisdom,
Wisdom is not finally tested in schools,
Wisdom cannot be pass'd from one having it to another not having it,
Wisdom is of the soul, is not susceptible of proof, is its own proof,
Applies to all stages and objects and qualities and is content,
Is the certainty of the reality and immortality of things, and the excel-
    lence of things;
Something there is in the float of the sight of things that provokes it out
    of the soul.

Now I re-examine philosophies and religions,
They may prove well in lecture-rooms, yet not prove at all under the
    spacious clouds and along the landscape and flowing currents.

Here is realization,
Here is a man tallied — he realizes here what he has in him,
The past, the future, majesty, love — if they are vacant of you, you are
    vacant of them.

Only the kernel of every object nourishes;
Where is he who tears off the husks for you and me?
Where is he that undoes stratagems and envelopes for you and me?

Here is adhesiveness, it is not previously fashion'd, it is apropos;
Do you know what it is as you pass to be loved by strangers?
Do you know the talk of those turning eye-balls?

7

Here is the efflux of the soul,
The efflux of the soul comes from within through embower'd gates,
    ever provoking questions,
These yearnings why are they? these thoughts in the darkness why are
    they?
Why are there men and women that while they are nigh me the sunlight
    expands my blood?
Why when they leave me do my pennants of joy sink flat and lank?
Why are there trees I never walk under but large and melodious
    thoughts descend upon me?
(I think they hang there winter and summer on those trees and always
    drop fruit as I pass;)
What is it I interchange so suddenly with strangers?
What with some driver as I ride on the seat by his side?
What with some fisherman drawing his seine by the shore as I walk
    by and pause?
What gives me to be free to a woman's and man's good-will? what
    gives them to be free to mine?

8

The efflux of the soul is happiness, here is happiness,
I think it pervades the open air, waiting at all times,
Now it flows unto us, we are rightly charged.

Here rises the fluid and attaching character,
The fluid and attaching character is the freshness and sweetness of
    man and woman,
(The herbs of the morning sprout no fresher and sweeter every day
    out of the roots of themselves, than it sprouts fresh and sweet
    continually out of itself.)

Toward the fluid and attaching character exudes the sweat of the love
    of young and old,
From it falls distill'd the charm that mocks beauty and attainments,
Toward it heaves the shuddering longing ache of contact.

9

Allons! whoever you are come travel with me!
Traveling with me you find what never tires.

The earth never tires,
The earth is rude, silent, incomprehensible at first, Nature is rude and
    incomprehensible at first,
Be not discouraged, keep on, there are divine things well envelop'd,
I swear to you there are divine things more beautiful than words can tell.

Allons! we must not stop here,
However sweet these laid-up stores, however convenient this dwelling
    we cannot remain here,
However shelter'd this port and however calm these waters we must
    not anchor here,
However welcome the hospitality that surrounds us we are permitted
    to receive it but a little while.

10

Allons! the inducements shall be greater,
We will sail pathless and wild seas,
We will go where winds blow, waves dash, and the Yankee clipper
    speeds by under full sail.

Allons! with power, liberty, the earth, the elements,
Health, defiance, gayety, self-esteem, curiosity;
Allons! from all formules!
From your formules, O bat-eyed and materialistic priests.

The stale cadaver blocks up the passage — the burial waits no longer.

Allons! yet take warning!
He traveling with me needs the best blood, thews, endurance,
None may come to the trial till he or she bring courage and health,
Come not here if you have already spent the best of yourself,
Only those may come who come in sweet and determin'd bodies,
No diseas'd person, no rum drinker or venereal taint is permitted here.

(I and mine do not convince by arguments, similes, rhymes,
We convince by our presence.)

11

Listen! I will be honest with you,
I do not offer the old smooth prizes, but offer rough new prizes,

These are the days that must happen to you:
You shall not heap up what is call'd riches,
You shall scatter with lavish hand all that you earn or achieve,
You but arrive at the city to which you were destin'd, you hardly settle
yourself to satisfaction before you are call'd by an irresistible call to
depart,
You shall be treated to the ironical smiles and mockings of those who
remain behind you,
What beckonings of love you receive you shall only answer with pas-
sionate kisses of parting,
You shall not allow the hold of those who spread their reach'd hands
toward you.

12

Allons! after the great Companions, and to belong to them!
They too are on the road — they are the swift and majestic men —
they are the greatest women,
Enjoyers of calms of seas and storms of seas,
Sailors of many a ship, walkers of many a mile of land,
Habituès of many distant countries, habituès of far-distant dwellings,
Trusters of men and women, observers of cities, solitary toilers,
Pausers and contemplators of tufts, blossoms, shells of the shore,
Dancers at wedding-dances, kissers of brides, tender helpers of children,
bearers of children,
Soldiers of revolts, standers by gaping graves, lowerers-down of coffins,
Journeyers over consecutive seasons, over the years, the curious years
each emerging from that which preceded it,
Journeyers as with companions, namely their own diverse phases,
Forth-steppers from the latent unrealized baby-days,
Journeyers gayly with their own youth, journeyers with their bearded
and well-grain'd manhood,
Journeyers with their womanhood, ample, unsurpass'd, content,
Journeyers with their own sublime old age of manhood or womanhood,
Old age, calm, expanded, broad with the haughty breadth of the
universe,
Old age, flowing free with the delicious near-by freedom of death.

13

Allons! to that which is endless as it was beginningless,
To undergo much, tramps of days, rests of nights,
To merge all in the travel they tend to, and the days and nights they
tend to,
Again to merge them in the start of superior journeys,

To see nothing anywhere but what you may reach it and pass it,
To conceive no time, however distant, but what you may reach it and
pass it,
To look up or down no road but it stretches and waits for you, however
long but it stretches and waits for you,
To see no being, not God's or any, but you also go thither,
To see no possession but you may possess it, enjoying all without labor
or purchase, abstracting the feast yet not abstracting one particle
of it,
To take the best of the farmer's farm and the rich man's elegant
villa, and the chaste blessings of the well-married couple, and the
fruit of orchards and flowers of gardens,
To take to your use out of the compact cities as you pass through,
To carry buildings and streets with you afterward wherever you go,
To gather the minds of men out of their brains as you encounter them,
to gather the love out of their hearts,
To take your lovers on the road with you, for all that you leave them
behind you,
To know the universe itself as a road, as many roads, as roads for
traveling souls.

All parts away for the progress of souls,
All religion, all solid things, arts, governments — all that was or is
apparent upon this globe or any globe, falls into niches and corners
before the procession of souls along the grand roads of the universe.

Of the progress of the souls of men and women along the grand roads
of the universe, all other progress is the needed emblem and
sustenance.

Forever alive, forever forward,
Stately, solemn, sad, withdrawn, baffled, mad, turbulent, feeble, dis-
satisfied,
Desperate, proud, fond, sick, accepted by men, rejected by men,
They go! they go! I know that they go, but I know not where they go,
But I know that they go toward the best — toward something great.

Whoever you are, come forth! or man or woman come forth!
You must not stay sleeping and dallying there in the house, though
you built it, or though it has been built for you.

Out of the dark confinement! out from behind the screen!
It is useless to protest, I know all and expose it.

Behold through you as bad as the rest,
Through the laughter, dancing, dining, supping, of people,
Inside of dresses and ornaments, inside of those wash'd and trimm'd
    faces,
Behold a secret silent loathing and despair.

No husband, no wife, no friend, trusted to hear the confession,
Another self, a duplicate of every one, skulking and hiding it goes,
Formless and wordless through the streets of the cities, polite and bland
    in the parlors,
In the cars of railroads, in steamboats, in the public assembly,
Home to the houses of men and women, at the table, in the bedroom,
    everywhere,
Smartly attired, countenance smiling, form upright, death under the
    breast-bones, hell under the skull-bones,
Under the broadcloth and gloves, under the ribbons and artificial flowers,
Keeping fair with the customs, speaking not a syllable of itself,
Speaking of any thing else but never of itself.

14

Allons! through struggles and wars!
The goal that was named cannot be countermanded.

Have the past struggles succeeded?
What has succeeded? yourself? your nation? Nature?
Now understand me well — it is provided in the essence of things that
    from any fruition of success, no matter what, shall come forth
    something to make a greater struggle necessary.

My call is the call of battle, I nourish active rebellion,
He going with me must go well arm'd,
He going with me goes often with spare diet, poverty, angry enemies,
    desertions.

15

Allons! the road is before us!
It is safe — I have tried it — my own feet have tried it well — be not
    detain'd!
Let the paper remain on the desk unwritten, and the book on the shelf
    unopen'd!
Let the tools remain in the workshop! let the money remain unearn'd!
Let the school stand! mind not the cry of the teacher!
Let the preacher preach in his pulpit! let the lawyer plead in the court,
    and the judge expound the law.

Camerado, I give you my hand!
I give you my love more precious than money,
I give you myself before preaching or law;
Will you give me yourself? will you come travel with me?
Shall we stick by each other as long as we live?

Crossing Brooklyn Ferry

1

Flood-tide below me! I see you face to face!
Clouds of the west — sun there half an hour high — I see you also
    face to face.

Crowds of men and women attired in the usual costumes, how curious
    you are to me!
On the ferry-boats the hundreds and hundreds that cross, returning
    home, are more curious to me than you suppose,
And you that shall cross from shore to shore years hence are more to
    me, and more in my meditations, than you might suppose.

2

The impalpable sustenance of me from all things at all hours of the day,
The simple, compact, well-join'd scheme, myself disintegrated, every
    one disintegrated yet part of the scheme,
The similitudes of the past and those of the future,
The glories strung like beads on my smallest sights and hearings, on the
    walk in the street and the passage over the river,
The current rushing so swiftly and swimming with me far away,
The others that are to follow me, the ties between me and them,
The certainty of others, the life, love, sight, hearing of others.

Others will enter the gates of the ferry and cross from shore to shore,
Others will watch the run of the flood-tide,
Others will see the shipping of Manhattan north and west, and the
    heights of Brooklyn to the south and east,
Others will see the islands large and small;
Fifty years hence, others will see them as they cross, the sun half an
    hour high,
A hundred years hence, or ever so many hundred years hence, others
    will see them,
Will enjoy the sunset, the pouring-in of the flood-tide, the falling-back
    to the sea of the ebb-tide.

3

It avails not, time nor place — distance avails not,
I am with you, you men and women of a generation, or ever so many
    generations hence,
Just as you feel when you look on the river and sky, so I felt,
Just as any of you is one of a living crowd, I was one of a crowd,
Just as you are refresh'd by the gladness of the river and the bright
    flow, I was refresh'd,
Just as you stand and lean on the rail, yet hurry with the swift current,
    I stood yet was hurried,
Just as you look on the numberless masts of ships and the thick-stemm'd
    pipes of steamboats, I look'd.

I too many and many a time cross'd the river of old,
Watched the Twelfth-month sea-gulls, saw them high in the air floating
    with motionless wings, oscillating their bodies,
Saw how the glistening yellow lit up parts of their bodies and left the
    rest in strong shadow,
Saw the slow-wheeling circles and the gradual edging toward the south,
Saw the reflection of the summer sky in the water,
Had my eyes dazzled by the shimmering track of beams,
Look'd at the fine centrifugal spokes of light round the shape of my
    head in the sunlit water,
Look'd on the haze on the hills southward and south-westward,
Look'd on the vapor as it flew in fleeces tinged with violet,
Look'd toward the lower bay to notice the vessels arriving,
Saw their approach, saw aboard those that were near me,
Saw the white sails of schooners and sloops, saw the ships at anchor,
The sailors at work in the rigging or out astride the spars,
The round masts, the swinging motion of the hulls, the slender ser-
    pentine pennants,
The large and small steamers in motion, the pilots in their pilot-houses,
The white wake left by the passage, the quick tremulous whirl of the
    wheels,
The flags of all nations, the falling of them at sunset,
The scallop-edged waves in the twilight, the ladled cups, the frolicsome
    crests and glistening,
The stretch afar growing dimmer and dimmer, the gray walls of the
    granite storehouses by the docks,
On the river the shadowy group, the big steam-tug closely flank'd on
    each side by the barges, the hay-boat, the belated lighter,
On the neighboring shore the fires from the foundry chimneys burning
    high and glaringly into the night,

Casting their flicker of black contrasted with wild red and yellow light
over the tops of houses, and down into the clefts of streets.

4

These and all else were to me the same as they are to you,
I loved well those cities, loved well the stately and rapid river,
The men and women I saw were all near to me,
Others the same — others who look back on me because I look'd forward
to them,
(The time will come, though I stop here to-day and to-night.)

5

What is it then between us?
What is the count of the scores or hundreds of years between us?

Whatever it is, it avails not — distance avails not, and place avails not,
I too lived, Brooklyn of ample hills was mine,
I too walk'd the streets of Manhattan island, and bathed in the waters
around it,
I too felt the curious abrupt questionings stir within me,
In the day among crowds of people sometimes they came upon me,
In my walks home late at night or as I lay in my bed they came upon
me,
I too had been struck from the float forever held in solution,
I too had receiv'd identity by my body,
That I was I knew was of my body, and what I should be I knew I
should be of my body.

6

It is not upon you alone the dark patches fall,
The dark threw its patches down upon me also,
The best I had done seem'd to me blank and suspicious,
My great thoughts as I supposed them, were they not in reality meagre?
Nor is it you alone who know what it is to be evil,
I am he who knew what it was to be evil,
I too knitted the old knot of contrariety,
Blabb'd, blush'd, resented, lied, stole, grudg'd,
Had guile, anger, lust, hot wishes I dared not speak,
Was wayward, vain, greedy, shallow, sly, cowardly, malignant,
The wolf, the snake, the hog, not wanting in me,
The cheating look, the frivolous word, the adulterous wish, not wanting,
Refusals, hates, postponements, meanness, laziness, none of these
wanting,

Was one with the rest, the days and haps of the rest,
Was call'd by my nighest name by clear loud voices of young men as
they saw me approaching or passing,
Felt their arms on my neck as I stood, or the negligent leaning of their
flesh against me as I sat,
Saw many I loved in the street or ferry-boat or public assembly, yet
never told them a word,
Lived the same life with the rest, the same old laughing, gnawing,
sleeping,
Play'd the part that still looks back on the actor or actress,
The same old role, the role that is what we make it, as great as we like,
Or as small as we like, or both great and small.

7

Closer yet I approach you,
What thought you have of me now, I had as much of you — I laid in
my stores in advance,
I consider'd long and seriously of you before you were born.

Who was to know what should come home to me?
Who knows but I am enjoying this?
Who knows, for all the distance, but I am as good as looking at you
now, for all you cannot see me?

8

Ah, what can ever be more stately and admirable to me than mast-
hemm'd Manhattan?
River and sunset and scallop-edg'd waves of flood-tide?
The sea-gulls oscillating their bodies, the hay-boat in the twilight, and
the belated lighter?
What gods can exceed these that clasp me by the hand, and with
voices I love call me promptly and loudly by my nighest name as
I approach?
What is more subtle than this which ties me to the woman or man that
looks in my face?
Which fuses me into you now, and pours my meaning into you?

We understand then do we not?
What I promis'd without mentioning it, have you not accepted?
What the study could not teach — what the preaching could not accom-
plish is accomplish'd, it is not?

9

Flow on, river! flow with the flood-tide, and ebb with the ebb-tide!

Frolic on, crested and scallop-edg'd waves!

Gorgeous clouds of the sunset! drench with your splendor me, or the
men or women generations after me!

Cross from shore to shore, countless crowds of passengers!

Stand up, tall masts of Mannahatta! stand up, beautiful hills of
Brooklyn!

Throb, baffled and curious brain! throw out questions and answers!

Suspend here and everywhere, eternal float of solution!

Gaze, loving and thirsting eyes, in the house or street or public assembly!

Sound out, voices of young men! loudly and musically call me by my
nighest name!

Live, old life! play the part that looks back on the actor or actress!

Play the old role, the role that is great or small according as one makes it!

Consider, you who peruse me, whether I may not in unknown ways
be looking upon you;

Be firm, rail over the river, to support those who lean idly, yet haste
with the hasting current;

Fly on, sea-birds! fly sideways, or wheel in large circles high in the air;

Receive the summer sky, you water, and faithfully hold it till all down-
cast eyes have time to take it from you!

Diverge, fine spokes of light, from the shape of my head, or any one's
head, in the sunlit water!

Come on, ships from the lower bay! pass up or down, white-sail'd
schooners, sloops, lighters!

Flaunt away, flags of all nations! be duly lower'd at sunset!

Burn high your fires, foundry chimneys! cast black shadows at nightfall!
cast red and yellow light over the tops of the houses!

Appearances, now or henceforth, indicate what you are,

You necessary film, continue to envelop the soul,

About my body for me, and your body for you, be hung our divinest
aromas,

Thrive, cities — bring your freight, bring your shows, ample and suf-
ficient rivers,

Expand, being than which none else is perhaps more spiritual,

Keep your places, objects than which none else is more lasting.

You have waited, you always wait, you dumb, beautiful ministers,

We receive you with free sense at last, and are insatiate hence-
forward,

Not you any more shall be able to foil us, or withhold yourselves from us,

We use you, and do not cast you aside — we plant you permanently
    within us,
We fathom you not — we love you — there is perfection in you also,
You furnish your parts toward eternity,
Great or small, you furnish your parts toward the soul.

On the Beach at Night

On the beach at night,
Stands a child with her father,
Watching the east, the autumn sky.

Up through the darkness,
While ravening clouds, the burial clouds, in black masses spreading,
Lower sullen and fast athwart and down the sky,
Amid a transparent clear belt of ether yet left in the east,
Ascends large and calm the lord-star Jupiter,
And nigh at hand, only a very little above,
Swim the delicate sisters the Pleiades.

From the beach the child holding the hand of her father,
Those burial-clouds that lower victorious soon to devour all,
Watching, silently weeps.

Weep not, child,
Weep not, my darling,
With these kisses let me remove your tears,
The ravening clouds shall not long be victorious,
They shall not long possess the sky, they devour the stars only in
    apparition,
Jupiter shall emerge, be patient, watch again another night, the Pleiades
    shall emerge,
They are immortal, all those stars both silvery and golden shall shine
    out again,
The great stars and the little ones shall shine out again, they endure,
The vast immortal suns and the long-enduring pensive moons shall
    again shine.

Then dearest child mournest thou only for Jupiter?
Considerest thou alone the burial of the stars?.

Something there is,
(With my lips soothing thee, adding I whisper,
I give thee the first suggestion, the problem and indirection,)
Something there is more immortal even than the stars,
(Many the burials, many the days and nights, passing away,)
Something that shall endure longer even than lustrous Jupiter,
Longer than sun or any revolving satellite,
Or the radiant sisters the Pleiades.

Me Imperturbe

Me imperturbe, standing at ease in Nature,
Master of all or mistress of all, aplomb in the midst of irrational things,
Imbued as they, passive, receptive, silent as they,
Finding my occupation, poverty, notoriety, foibles, crimes, less important
than I thought,
Me toward the Mexican sea, or in the Mannahatta or the Tennessee, or
far north or inland,
A river man, or a man of the woods, or of any farm-life of these States
or of the coast, or the lakes or Kanada,
Me wherever my life is lived, O to be self-balanced for contingencies,
To confront night, storms, hunger, ridicule, accidents, rebuffs, as the
trees and animals do.

From Pent-up Aching Rivers

From pent-up aching rivers,
From that of myself without which I were nothing,
From what I am determin'd to make illustrious, even if I stand sole
among men,
From my own voice resonant, singing the phallus,
Singing the song of procreation,
Singing the need of superb children and therein superb grown people,
Singing the muscular urge and the blending,
Singing the bedfellow's song, (O resistless yearning!
O for any and each the body correlative attracting!
O for you whoever you are your correlative body! O it, more than all
else, you delighting!)
From the hungry gnaw that eats me night and day,
From native moments, from bashful pains, singing them,

Seeking something yet unfound though I have diligently sought it many
    a long year,
Singing the true song of the soul fitful at random,
Renascent with grossest Nature or among animals,
Of that, of them and what goes with them my poems informing,
Of the smell of apples and lemons, of the pairing of birds,
Of the wet of woods, of the lapping of waves,
Of the mad pushes of waves upon the land, I them chanting,
The overture lightly sounding, the strain anticipating,
The welcome nearness, the sight of the perfect body,
The swimmer swimming naked in the bath, or motionless on his back
    lying and floating,
The female form approaching, I pensive, love-flesh tremulous aching,
The divine list for myself or you or for any one making,
The face, the limbs, the index from head to foot, and what it arouses,
The mystic deliria, the madness amorous, the utter abandonment,
(Hark close and still what I now whisper to you,
I love you, O you entirely possess me,
O that you and I escape from the rest and go utterly off, free and lawless,
Two hawks in the air, two fishes swimming in the sea not more lawless
    than we;)
The furious storm through me careering, I passionately trembling,
The oath of the inseparableness of two together, of the woman that
    loves me and whom I love more than my life, that oath swearing,
(O I willingly stake all for you,
O let me be lost if it must be so!
O you and I! what is it to us what the rest do or think?
What is all else to us? only that we enjoy each other and exhaust each
    other if it must be so;)
From the master, the pilot I yield the vessel to,
The general commanding me, commanding all, from him permission
    taking,
From time the programme hastening, (I have loiter'd too long as it is,)
From sex, from the warp and from the woof,
From privacy, from frequent repinings alone,
From plenty of persons near and yet the right person not near,
From the soft sliding of hands over me and thrusting of fingers through
    my hair and beard,
From the long sustain'd kiss upon the mouth or bosom,
From the close pressure that makes me or any man drunk, fainting with
    excess,
From what the divine husband knows, from the work of fatherhood,

From exultation, victory and relief, from the bedfellow's embrace in the
    night,
From the act-poems of eyes, hands, hips and bosoms,
From the cling of the trembling arm,
From the bending curve and the clinch,
From side by side the pliant coverlet off-throwing,
From the one so unwilling to have me leave, and me just as unwilling
    to leave,
(Yet a moment O tender waiter, and I return,)
From the hour of shining stars and dropping dews,
From the night a moment I emerging flitting out,
Celebrate you act divine and you children prepared for,
And you stalwart loins.

In Paths Untrodden

In paths untrodden,
In the growth by margins of pond-waters,
Escaped from the life that exhibits itself,
From all the standards hitherto publish'd, from the pleasures, profits,
    conformities,
Which too long I was offering to feed my soul,
Clear to me now standards not yet publish'd, clear to me that my soul,
That the soul of the man I speak for rejoices in comrades,
Here by myself away from the clank of the world,
Tallying and talk'd to here by tongues aromatic,
No longer abash'd, (for in this secluded spot I can respond as I would
    not dare elsewhere,)
Strong upon me the life that does not exhibit itself, yet contains all the
    rest,
Resolv'd to sing no songs to-day but those of manly attachment,
Projecting them along that substantial life,
Bequeathing hence types of athletic love,
Afternoon this delicious Ninth-month in my forty-first year,
I proceed for all who are or have been young men,
To tell the secret of my nights and days,
To celebrate the need of comrades.

I Saw in Louisiana a Live-Oak Growing

I saw in Louisiana a live-oak growing,
All alone stood it and the moss hung down from the branches,
Without any companion it grew there uttering joyous leaves of dark
    green,
And its look, rude, unbending, lusty, made me think of myself,
But I wonder'd how it could utter joyous leaves standing alone there
    without its friend near, for I knew I could not,
And I broke off a twig with a certain number of leaves upon it, and
    twined around it a little moss,
And brought it away, and I have placed it in sight in my room,
It is not needed to remind me as of my own dear friends,
(For I believe lately I think of little else than of them,)
Yet it remains to me a curious token, it makes me think of manly love;
For all that, and though the live-oak glistens there in Louisiana solitary
    in a wide flat space,
Uttering joyous leaves all its life without a friend a lover near,
I know very well I could not.

Out of the Cradle Endlessly Rocking

Out of the cradle endlessly rocking,
Out of the mocking-bird's throat, the musical shuttle,
Out of the Ninth-month midnight,
Over the sterile sands and the fields beyond, where the child leaving his
    bed wander'd alone, bareheaded, barefoot,
Down from the shower'd halo,
Up from the mystic play of shadows twining and twisting as if they
    were alive,
Out from the patches of briers and blackberries,
From the memories of the bird that chanted to me,
From your memories sad brother, from the fitful risings and fallings I
    heard,
From under that yellow half-moon late-risen and swollen as if with tears,
From those beginning notes of yearning and love there in the mist,
From the thousand responses of my heart never to cease,
From the myriad thence-arous'd words,
From the word stronger and more delicious than any,
From such as now they start the scene revisiting,
As a flock, twittering, rising, or overhead passing,
Borne hither, ere all eludes me, hurriedly,
A man, yet by these tears a little boy again,

Throwing myself on the sand, confronting the waves,
I, chanter of pains and joys, uniter of here and hereafter,
Taking all hints to use them, but swiftly leaping beyond them,
A reminiscence sing.

Once Paumanok,
When the lilac-scent was in the air and Fifth-month grass was growing,
Up this seashore in some briers,
Two feather'd guests from Alabama, two together,
And their nest, and four light-green eggs spotted with brown,
And every day the he-bird to and fro near at hand,
And every day the she-bird crouch'd on her nest, silent, with bright eyes,
And every day I, a curious boy, never too close, never disturbing them,
Cautiously peering, absorbing, translating.

Shine! shine! shine!
Pour down your warmth, great sun!
While we bask, we two together.

Two together!
Winds blow south, or winds blow north,
Day come white, or night come black,
Home, or rivers and mountains from home,
Singing all time, minding no time,
While we two keep together.

Till of a sudden,
May-be kill'd, unknown to her mate,
One forenoon the she-bird crouch'd not on the nest,
Nor return'd that afternoon, nor the next,
Nor ever appear'd again.

And thenceforward all summer in the sound of the sea,
And at night under the full of the moon in calmer weather,
Over the hoarse surging of the sea,
Or flitting from brier to brier by day,
I saw, I heard at intervals the remaining one, the he-bird,
The solitary guest from Alabama.

Blow! blow! blow!
Blow up sea-winds along Paumanok's shore;
I wait and I wait till you blow my mate to me.

Yes, when the stars glisten'd,
All night long on the prong of a moss-scallop'd stake,
Down almost amid the slapping waves,
Sat the lone singer wonderful causing tears.

He call'd on his mate,
He pour'd forth the meanings which I of all men know.

Yes my brother I know,
The rest might not, but I have treasur'd every note,
For more than once dimly down to the beach gliding,
Silent, avoiding the moonbeams, blending myself with the shadows,
Recalling now the obscure shapes, the echoes, the sounds and sights
　　after their sorts,
The white arms out in the breakers tirelessly tossing,
I, with bare feet, a child, the wind wafting my hair, ⹁
Listen'd long and long.

Listen'd to keep, to sing, now translating the notes,
Following you my brother.

Soothe! soothe! soothe!
Close on its wave soothes the wave behind,
And again another behind embracing and lapping, every one close,
But my love soothes not me, not me.

Low hangs the moon, it rose late,
It is lagging — O I think it is heavy with love, with love.

O madly the sea pushes upon the land,
With love, with love.

O night! do I not see my love fluttering out among the breakers?
What is that little black thing I see there in the white?

Loud! loud! loud!
Loud I call to you, my love!

High and clear I shoot my voice over the waves,
Surely you must know who is here, is here,
You must know who I am, my love.

Low-hanging moon!
What is that dusky spot in your brown yellow?
O it is the shape, the shape of my mate!
O moon do not keep her from me any longer.

Land! land! O land!
Whichever way I turn, O I think you could give me my mate back again
*   if you only would,*
For I am almost sure I see her dimly whichever way I look.

O rising stars!
Perhaps the one I want so much will rise, will rise with some of you.

O throat! O trembling throat!
Sound clearer through the atmosphere!
Pierce the woods, the earth,
Somewhere listening to catch you must be the one I want.

Shake out carols!
Solitary here, the night's carols!
Carols of lonesome love! death's carols!
Carols under that lagging, yellow, waning moon!
O under that moon where she droops almost down into the sea!
O reckless despairing carols.

But soft! sink low!
Soft! let me just murmur,
And do you wait a moment you husky-nois'd sea,
For somewhere I believe I heard my mate responding to me,
So faint, I must be still, be still to listen,
But not altogether still, for then she might not come immediately to me.

Hither my love!
Here I am! here!
With this just-sustain'd note I announce myself to you,
This gentle call is for you my love, for you.

Do not be decoy'd elsewhere,
That is the whistle of the wind, it is not my voice,
That is the fluttering, the fluttering of the spray,
Those are the shadows of leaves.

O darkness! O in vain!
O I am very sick and sorrowful.

O brown halo in the sky near the moon, drooping upon the sea!
O troubled reflection in the sea!
O throat! O throbbing heart!
And I singing uselessly, uselessly all the night.

O past! O happy life! O songs of joy!
In the air, in the woods, over fields,
Loved! loved! loved! loved! loved!
But my mate no more, no more with me!
We two together no more.

The aria sinking,
All else continuing, the stars shining,
The winds blowing, the notes of the bird continuous echoing,
With angry moans the fierce old mother incessantly moaning,
On the sands of Paumanok's shore gray and rustling,
The yellow half-moon enlarged, sagging down, drooping, the face of the
    sea almost touching,
The boy ecstatic, with his bare feet the waves, with his hair the atmos-
    phere dallying,
The love in the heart long pent, now loose, now at last tumultuously
    bursting,
The aria's meaning, the ears, the soul, swiftly depositing,
The strange tears down the cheeks coursing,
The colloquy there, the trio, each uttering,
The undertone, the savage old mother incessantly crying,
To the boy's soul's questions sullenly timing, some drown'd secret
    hissing,
To the outsetting bard.

Demon or bird (said the boy's soul,)
Is it indeed toward your mate you sing? or is it really to me?
For I, that was a child, my tongue's use sleeping, now I have heard you,
Now in a moment I know what I am for, I awake,
And already a thousand singers, a thousand songs, clearer, louder and
    more sorrowful than yours,
A thousand warbling echoes have started to life within me, never to die.

O you singer solitary, singing by yourself, projecting me,
O solitary me listening, never more shall I cease perpetuating you,
Never more shall I escape, never more the reverberations,
Never more the cries of unsatisfied love be absent from me,
Never again leave me to be the peaceful child I was before what there
    in the night,
By the sea under the yellow and sagging moon,
The messenger there arous'd, the fire, the sweet hell within,
The unknown want, the destiny of me.

O give me the clew! (it lurks in the night here somewhere,)
O if I am to have so much, let me have more!

A word then, (for I will conquer it,)
The word final, superior to all,
Subtle, sent up — what is it? — I listen;
Are you whispering it, and have been all the time, you sea-waves?
Is that it from your liquid rims and wet sands?

Whereto answering, the sea,
Delaying not, hurrying not,
Whisper'd me through the night, and very plainly before daybreak,
Lisp'd to me the low and delicious word death,
And again death, death, death, death,
Hissing melodious, neither like the bird nor like my arous'd child's heart,
But edging near as privately for me rustling at my feet,
Creeping thence steadily up to my ears and laving me softly all over,
Death, death, death, death, death.

Which I do not forget,
But fuse the song of my dusky demon and brother,
That he sang to me in the moonlight on Paumanok's gray beach,
With the thousand responsive songs at random,
My own songs awaked from that hour,
And with them the key, the word up from the waves,
The word of the sweetest song and all songs,
That strong and delicious word which, creeping to my feet,
(Or like some old crone rocking the cradle, swathed in sweet garments,
    bending aside,)
The sea whisper'd me.

As I Ebb'd with the Ocean of Life

1

As I ebb'd with the ocean of life,
As I wended the shores I know,
As I walk'd where the ripples continually wash you Paumanok,
Where they rustle up hoarse and sibilant,
Where the fierce old mother endlessly cries for her castaways,
I musing late in the autumn day, gazing off southward,
Held by this electric self out of the pride of which I utter poems,
Was seiz'd by the spirit that trails in the lines underfoot,
The rim, the sediment that stands for all the water and all the land of
    the globe.

Fascinated, my eyes reverting from the south, dropt, to follow those
    slender windrows,
Chaff, straw, splinters of wood, weeds, and the sea-gluten,
Scum, scales from shining rocks, leaves of salt-lettuce, left by the tide,
Miles walking, the sound of breaking waves the other side of me,
Paumanok there and then as I thought the old thought of likenesses,
These you presented to me you fish-shaped island,
As I wended the shores I know,
As I walk'd with that electric self seeking types.

2

As I wend to the shores I know not,
As I list to the dirge, the voices of men and women wreck'd,
As I inhale the impalpable breezes that set in upon me,
As the ocean so mysterious rolls toward me closer and closer,
I too but signify at the utmost a little wash'd-up drift,
A few sands and dead leaves to gather,
Gather, and merge myself as part of the sands and drift.

O baffled, balk'd, bent to the very earth,
Oppress'd with myself that I have dared to open my mouth,
Aware now that amid all that blab whose echoes recoil upon me I have
    not once had the least idea who or what I am,
But that before all my arrogant poems the real Me stands yet untouch'd,
    untold, altogether unreach'd,
Withdrawn far, mocking me with mock-congratulatory signs and bows,
With peals of distant ironical laughter at every word I have written,
Pointing in silence to these songs, and then to the sand beneath.

I perceive I have not really understood any thing, not a single object,
    and that no man ever can,
Nature here in sight of the sea taking advantage of me to dart upon me
    and sting me,
Because I have dared to open my mouth to sing at all.

3

You oceans both, I close with you,
We murmur alike reproachfully rolling sands and drift, knowing not
    why,
These little shreds indeed standing for you and me and all.

You friable shore with trails of debris,
You fish-shaped island, I take what is underfoot,
What is yours is mine my father.

I too Paumanok,
I too have bubbled up, floated the measureless float, and been wash'd
    on your shores,
I too am but a trail of drift and debris,
I too leave little wrecks upon you, you fish-shaped island.

I throw myself upon your breast my father,
I cling to you so that you cannot unloose me,
I hold you so firm till you answer me something.
Kiss me my father,
Touch me with your lips as I touch those I love,
Breathe to me while I hold you close the secret of the murmuring I envy.

4

Ebb, ocean of life, (the flow will return,)
Cease not your moaning you fierce old mother,
Endlessly cry for your castaways, but fear not, deny not me,
Rustle not up so hoarse and angry against my feet as I touch you or
    gather from you.

I mean tenderly by you and all,
I gather for myself and for this phantom looking down where we lead,
    and following me and mine.

Me and mine, loose windrows, little corpses,
Froth, snowy white, and bubbles,
(See, from my dead lips the ooze exuding at last,
See, the prismatic colors glistening and rolling,)

Tufts of straw, sands, fragments,
Buoy'd hither from many moods, one contradicting another,
From the storm, the long calm, the darkness, the swell,
Musing, pondering, a breath, a briny tear, a dab of liquid or soil,
Up just as much out of fathomless workings fermented and thrown,
A limp blossom or two, torn, just as much over waves floating, drifted
    at random,
Just as much for us that sobbing dirge of Nature,
Just as much whence we come that blare of the cloud-trumpets,
We, capricious, brought hither we know not whence, spread out before
    you,
You up there walking or sitting,
Whoever you are, we too lie in drifts at your feet.

Long I Thought That Knowledge Alone Would Suffice

Long I thought that knowledge alone would suffice me — O if I could
    but obtain knowledge!
Then my lands engrossed me — Lands of the prairies, Ohio's land, the
    southern savannas, engrossed me — For them I would live — I
    would be their orator;
Then I met the examples of old and new heroes — I heard of warriors,
    sailors, and all dauntless persons — And it seemed to me that I too
    had it in me to be as dauntless as any — and would be so;
And then, to enclose all, it came to me to strike up the songs of the
    New World — And then I believed my life must be spent in
    singing;
But now take notice, land of the prairies, land of the south savannas,
    Ohio's land,
Take notice, you Kanuck woods — and you Lake Huron — and all that
    with you roll toward Niagara — and you Niagara also,
And you, Californian mountains — That you each and all find somebody
    else to be your singer of songs,
For I can be your singer of songs no longer — One who loves me is
    jealous of me, and withdraws me from all but love,
With the rest I dispense — I sever from what I thought would suffice
    me, for it does not — it is now empty and tasteless to me,
I heed knowledge, and the grandeur of The States, and the example
    of heroes, no more,
I am indifferent to my own songs — I will go with him I love,
It is to be enough for us that we are together — We never separate
    again.

O Living Always, Always Dying

O living always, always dying!
O the burials of me past and present,
O me while I stride ahead, material, visible, imperious as ever;
O me, what I was for years, now dead, (I lament not, I am content;)
O to disengage myself from those corpses of me, which I turn and look
    at where I cast them,
To pass on, (O living! always living!) and leave the corpses behind.

Shut Not Your Doors

Shut not your doors to me proud libraries,
For that which was lacking on all your well-fill'd shelves, yet needed
    most, I bring,
Forth from the war emerging, a book I have made,
The words of my book nothing, the drift of it every thing,
A book separate, not link'd with the rest nor felt by the intellect,
But you ye untold latencies will thrill to every page.

Vigil Strange I Kept on the Field One Night

Vigil strange I kept on the field one night;
When you my son and my comrade dropt at my side that day,
One look I but gave which your dear eyes return'd with a look I shall
    never forget,
One touch of your hand to mine O boy, reach'd up as you lay on the
    ground,
Then onward I sped in the battle, the even-contested battle,
Till late in the night reliev'd to the place at last again I made my way,
Found you in death so cold dear comrade, found your body son of
    responding kisses, (never again on earth responding,)
Bared your face in the starlight, curious the scene, cool blew the
    moderate night-wind,
Long there and then in vigil I stood, dimly around me the battlefield
    spreading,
Vigil wondrous and vigil sweet there in the fragrant silent night,
But not a tear fell, not even a long-drawn sigh, long, long I gazed,
Then on the earth partially reclining sat by your side leaning my chin
   ᐟ in my hands,
Passing sweet hours, immortal and mystic hours with you dearest com-
    rade — not a tear, not a word,

Vigil of silence, love and death, vigil for you my son and my soldier,
As onward silently stars aloft, eastward new ones upward stole,
Vigil final for you brave boy, (I could not save you, swift was your death,
I faithfully loved you and cared for you living, I think we shall surely
    meet again,)
Till at latest lingering of the night, indeed just as the dawn appear'd,
My comrade I wrapt in his blanket, envelop'd well his form,
Folded the blanket well, tucking it carefully over head and carefully
    under feet,
And there and then and bathed by the rising sun, my son in his grave,
    in his rude-dug grave I deposited,
Ending my vigil strange with that, vigil of night and battle-field dim,
Vigil for boy of responding kisses, (never again on earth responding,)
Vigil for comrade swiftly slain, vigil I never forget, how as day brighten'd,
I rose from the chill ground and folded my soldier well in his blanket,
And buried him where he fell.

The Wound-Dresser

1

An old man bending I come among new faces,
Years looking backward resuming in answer to children,
Come tell us old man, as from young men and maidens that love me,
(Arous'd and angry, I'd thought to beat the alarum, and urge relentless
    war,
But soon my fingers fail'd me, my face droop'd and I resign'd myself,
To sit by the wounded and soothe them, or silently watch the dead;)
Years hence of these scenes, of these furious passions, these chances,
Of unsurpass'd heroes, (was one side so brave? the other was equally
    brave;)
Now be witness again, paint the mightiest armies of earth,
Of those armies so rapid so wondrous what saw you to tell us?
What stays with you latest and deepest? of curious panics,
Of hard-fought engagements or sieges tremendous what deepest remains?

2

O maidens and young men I love and that love me,
What you ask of my days those the strangest and sudden your talking
    recalls,
Soldier alert I arrive after a long march cover'd with sweat and dust,
In the nick of time I come, plunge in the fight, loudly shout in the rush
    of successful charge,

Enter the captur'd works — yet lo, like a swift-running river they fade,
Pass and are gone they fade — I dwell not on soldiers' perils or soldiers'
   joys,
(Both I remember well — many the hardships, few the joys, yet I was
   content.)

But in silence, in dreams' projections,
While the world of gain and appearance and mirth goes on,
So soon what is over forgotten, and waves wash the imprints off the sand,
With hinged knees returning I enter the doors, (while for you up there,
Whoever you are, follow without noise and be of strong heart.)

Bearing the bandages, water and sponge,
Straight and swift to my wounded I go,
Where they lie on the ground after the battle brought in,
Where their priceless blood reddens the grass the ground,
Or to the rows of the hospital tent, or under the roof'd hospital,
To the long rows of cots up and down each side I return,
To each and all one after another I draw near, not one do I miss,
An attendant follows holding a tray, he carries a refuse pail,
Soon to be fill'd with clotted rags and blood, emptied and fill'd again.

I onward go, I stop,
With hinged knees and steady hand to dress wounds,
I am firm with each, the pangs are sharp yet unavoidable,
One turns to me his appealing eyes — poor boy! I never knew you,
Yet I think I could not refuse this moment to die for you, if that would
   save you.

3

On, on I go, (open doors of time! open hospital doors!)
The crush'd head I dress, (poor crazed hand tear not the bandage away,)
The neck of the cavalry-man with the bullet through and through I
   examine,
Hard the breathing rattles, quite glazed already the eye, yet life struggles
   hard,
(Come sweet death! be persuaded O beautiful death!
In mercy come quickly.)

From the stump of the arm, the amputated hand,
I undo the clotted lint, remove the slough, wash off the matter and
   blood,

Back on his pillow the soldier bends with curv'd neck and side-falling
    head,
His eyes are closed, his face is pale, he dares not look on the bloody
    stump,
And has not yet look'd on it.

I dress a wound in the side, deep, deep,
But a day or two more, for see the frame all wasted and sinking,
And the yellow-blue countenance see.

I dress the perforated shoulder, the foot with the bullet-wound,
Cleanse the one with a gnawing and putrid gangrene, so sickening, so
    offensive,
While the attendant stands behind aside me holding the tray and pail.

I am faithful, I do not give out,
The fractur'd thigh, the knee, the wound in the abdomen,
These and more I dress with impassive hand, (yet deep in my breast a
    fire, a burning flame.)

4

Thus in silence in dreams' projections,
Returning, resuming, I thread my way through the hospitals,
The hurt and wounded I pacify with soothing hand,
I sit by the restless all the dark night, some are so young,
Some suffer so much, I recall the experience sweet and sad,
(Many a soldier's loving arms about this neck have cross'd and rested,
Many a soldier's kiss dwells on these bearded lips.)

Give Me the Splendid Silent Sun

1

Give me the splendid silent sun with all his beams full-dazzling,
Give me juicy autumnal fruit ripe and red from the orchard,
Give me a field where the unmow'd grass grows,
Give me an arbor, give me the trellis'd grape,
Give me fresh corn and wheat, give me serene-moving animals teaching
    content,
Give me nights perfectly quiet as on high plateaus west of the Missis-
    sippi, and I looking up at the stars,
Give me odorous at sunrise a garden of beautiful flowers where I can
    walk undisturb'd,

Give me for marriage a sweet-breath'd woman of whom I should never
    tire,
Give me a perfect child, give me away aside from the noise of the world
    a rural domestic life,
Give me to warble spontaneous songs recluse by myself, for my own
    ears only,
Give me solitude, give me Nature, give me again O Nature your primal
    sanities!

These demanding to have them, (tired with ceaseless excitement, and
    rack'd by the war-strife,)
These to procure incessantly asking, rising in cries from my heart,
While yet incessantly asking still I adhere to my city,
Day upon day and year upon year O city, walking your streets,
Where you hold me enchain'd a certain time refusing to give me up,
Yet giving to make me glutted, enrich'd of soul, you give me forever
    faces;
(O I see what I sought to escape, confronting, reversing my cries,
I see my own soul trampling down what it ask'd for.)

2

Keep your splendid silent sun,
Keep your woods O Nature, and the quiet places by the woods,
Keep your fields of clover and timothy, and your corn-fields and orchards,
Keep the blossoming buckwheat fields where the Ninth-month bees
    hum;
Give me faces and streets — give me these phantoms incessant and
    endless along the trottoirs!
Give me interminable eyes — give me women — give me comrades and
    lovers by the thousand!
Let me see new ones every day — let me hold new ones by the hand
    every day!
Give me such shows — give me the streets of Manhattan!
Give me Broadway, with the soldiers marching — give me the sound of
    the trumpets and drums!
(The soldiers in companies or regiments — some starting away, flush'd
    and reckless,
Some, their time up, returning with thinn'd ranks, young, yet very old,
    worn, marching, noticing nothing;)
Give me the shores and wharves heavy-fringed with black ships!
O such for me! O an intense life, full to repletion and varied!
The life of the theatre, bar-room, huge hotel, for me!

The saloon of the steamer! the crowded excursion for me! the torchlight
    procession!
The dense brigade bound for the war, with high piled military wagons
    following;
People, endless, streaming, with strong voices, passions, pageants,
Manhattan streets with their powerful throbs, with beating drums as
    now,
The endless and noisy chorus, the rustle and clank of muskets, (even
    the sight of the wounded,)
Manhattan crowds, with their turbulent musical chorus!
Manhattan faces and eyes forever for me.

When Lilacs Last in the Dooryard Bloom'd

1

When lilacs last in the dooryard bloom'd,
And the great star early droop'd in the western sky in the night,
I mourn'd, and yet shall mourn with ever-returning spring.

Ever-returning spring, trinity sure to me you bring,
Lilac blooming perennial and drooping star in the west,
And thought of him I love.

2

O powerful western fallen star!
O shades of night — O moody, tearful night!
O great star disappear'd — O the black murk that hides the star!
O cruel hands that hold me powerless — O helpless soul of me!
O harsh surrounding cloud that will not free my soul.

3

In the dooryard fronting an old farm-house near the white-wash'd
    palings,
Stands the lilac-bush tall-growing with heart-shaped leaves of rich green,
With many a pointed blossom rising delicate, with the perfume strong
    I love,
With every leaf a miracle — and from this bush in the dooryard,
With delicate-color'd blossoms and heart-shaped leaves of rich green,
A sprig with its flower I break.

4

In the swamp in secluded recesses,
A shy and hidden bird is warbling a song.

Solitary the thrush,
The hermit withdrawn to himself, avoiding the settlements,
Sings by himself a song.

Song of the bleeding throat,
Death's outlet song of life, (for well dear brother I know,
If thou wast not granted to sing thou would'st surely die.)

5

Over the breast of the spring, the land, amid cities,
Amid lanes and through old woods, where lately the voilets peep'd from
    the ground, spotting the gray debris,
Amid the grass in the fields each side of the lanes, passing the endless
    grass,
Passing the yellow-spear'd wheat, every grain from its shroud in the dark-
    brown fields uprisen,
Passing the apple-tree blows of white and pink in the orchards,
Carrying a corpse to where it shall rest in the grave,
Night and day journeys a coffin.

6

Coffin that passes through lanes and streets,
Through day and night with the great cloud darkening the land,
With the pomp of the inloop'd flags with the cities draped in black,
With the show of the States themselves as of crape-veil'd women
    standing,
With processions long and winding and the flambeaus of the night,
With the countless torches lit, with the silent sea of faces and the
    unbared heads,
With the waiting depot, the arriving coffin, and the sombre faces,
With dirges through the night, with the thousand voices rising strong
    and solemn,
With all the mournful voices of the dirges pour'd around the coffin,
The dim-lit churches and the shuddering organs — where amid these
    you journey,
With the tolling tolling bells' perpetual clang,
Here, coffin that slowly passes,
I give you my sprig of lilac.

7

(Nor for you, for one alone,
Blossoms and branches green to coffins all I bring,
For fresh as the morning, thus would I chant a song for you O sane and
    sacred death.

All over bouquets of roses,
O death, I cover you over with roses and early lilies,
But mostly and now the lilac that blooms the first,
Copious I break, I break the sprigs from the bushes,
With loaded arms I come, pouring for you,
For you and the coffins all of you O death.)

8

O western orb sailing the heaven,
Now I know what you must have meant as a month since I walk'd,
As I walk'd in silence the transparent shadowy night,
As I saw you had something to tell as you bent to me night after night,
As you droop'd from the sky low down as if to my side, (while the
    other stars all look'd on,)
As we wander'd together the solemn night, (for something I know not
    what kept me from sleep,)
As the night advanced, and I saw on the rim of the west how full you
    were of woe,
As I stood on the rising ground in the breeze in the cool transparent
    night,
As I watch'd where you pass'd and was lost in the netherward black of
    the night,
As my soul in its trouble dissatisfied sank, as where you sad orb,
Concluded, dropt in the night, and was gone.

9

Sing on there in the swamp,
O singer bashful and tender, I hear your notes, I hear your call,
I hear, I come presently, I understand you,
But a moment I linger, for the lustrous star has detain'd me,
The star my departing comrade holds and detains me.

10

O how shall I warble myself for the dead one there I loved?
And how shall I deck my song for the large sweet soul that has gone?
And what shall my perfume be for the grave of him I love?

Sea-winds blown from east and west,
Blown from the Eastern sea and blown from the Western sea, till there
    on the prairies meeting,
These and with these and the breath of my chant,
I'll perfume the grave of him I love.

11

O what shall I hang on the chamber walls?
And what shall the pictures be that I hang on the walls,
To adorn the burial-house of him I love?

Pictures of growing spring and farms and homes,
With the Fourth-month eve at sundown, and the gray smoke lucid and
    bright,
With floods of the yellow gold of the gorgeous, indolent, sinking sun,
    burning, expanding the air,
With the fresh sweet herbage under foot, and the pale green leaves of
    the trees prolific,
In the distance the flowing glaze, the breast of the river, with a wind-
    dapple here and there,
With ranging hills on the banks, with many a line against the sky, and
    shadows,
And the city at hand with dwellings so dense, and stacks of chimneys,
And all the scenes of life and the workshops, and the workmen home-
    ward returning.

12

Lo, body and soul — this land,
My own Manhattan with spires, and the sparkling and hurrying tides,
    and the ships,
The varied and ample land, the South and the North in the light, Ohio's
    shores and flashing Missouri,
And ever the far-spreading prairies cover'd with grass and corn.

Lo, the most excellent sun so calm and haughty,
The violet and purple morn with just-felt breezes,
The gentle soft-born measureless light,
The miracle spreading bathing all, the fulfill'd noon,
The coming eve delicious, the welcome night and the stars,
Over my cities shining all, enveloping man and land.

13

Sing on, sing on you gray-brown bird,
Sing from the swamps, the recesses, pour your chant from the bushes,
Limitless out of the dusk, out of the cedars and pines.

Sing on dearest brother, warble your reedy song,
Loud human song, with voice of uttermost woe.

O liquid and free and tender!
O wild and loose to my soul — O wondrous singer!
You only I hear — yet the star holds me, (but will soon depart,)
Yet the lilac with mastering odor holds me.

14

Now while I sat in the day and look'd forth,
In the close of the day with its light and the fields of spring, and the
    farmers preparing their crops,
In the large unconscious scenery of my land with its lakes and forests,
In the heavenly aerial beauty, (after the perturb'd winds and the
    storms,)
Under the arching heavens of the afternoon swift passing, and the voices
    of children and women,
The many-moving sea-tides, and I saw the ships how they sail'd,
And the summer approaching with richness, and the fields all busy with
    labor,
And the infinite separate houses, how they all went on, each with its
    meals and minutia of daily usages,
And the streets how their throbbings throbb'd, and the cities pent —
    lo, then and there,
Falling upon them all and among them all, enveloping me with the rest,
Appear'd the cloud, appear'd the long black trail,
And I knew death, its thought, and the sacred knowledge of death.

Then with the knowledge of death as walking one side of me,
And the thought of death close-walking the other side of me,
And I in the middle as with companions, and as holding the hands of
    companions,
I fled forth to the hiding receiving night that talks not,
Down to the shores of the water, the path by the swamp in the dimness,
To the solemn shadowy cedars and ghostly pines so still.

And the singer so shy to the rest receiv'd me,
The gray-brown bird I know receiv'd us comrades three,
And he sang the carol of death, and a verse for him I love.

From deep secluded recesses,
From the fragrant cedars and the ghostly pines so still,
Came the carol of the bird.

And the charm of the carol rapt me,
As I held as if by their hands my comrades in the night,
And the voice of my spirit tallied the song of the bird.

Come lovely and soothing death,
Undulate round the world, serenely arriving, arriving,
In the day, in the night, to all, to each,
Sooner or later delicate death.

Prais'd be the fathomless universe,
For life and joy, and for objects and knowledge curious,
And for love, sweet love — but praise! praise! praise!
For the sure-enwinding arms of cool-enfolding death.

Dark mother always gliding near with soft feet,
Have none chanted for thee a chant of fullest welcome?
Then I chant it for thee, I glorify thee above all,
I bring thee a song that when thou must indeed come, come unfal-
  teringly.

Approach strong deliveress,
When it is so, when thou hast taken them I joyously sing the dead,
Lost in the loving floating ocean of thee,
Laved in the flood of thy bliss O death.

From me to thee glad serenades,
Dances for thee I propose saluting thee, adornments and feastings for
  thee,
And the sights of the open landscape and the high-spread sky are fitting,
And life and the fields, and the huge and thoughtful night.

The night in silence under many a star,
The ocean shore and the husky whispering wave whose voice I know,
And the soul turning to thee O vast and well-veil'd death,
And the body gratefully nestling close to thee.

Over the tree-tops I float thee a song,
Over the rising and sinking waves, over the myriad fields and the prairies
wide,
Over the dense-pack'd cities all and the teeming wharves and ways,
I float this carol with joy, with joy to thee O death.

15

To the tally of my soul,
Loud and strong kept up the gray-brown bird,
With pure deliberate notes spreading filling the night.

Loud in the pines and cedars dim,
Clear in the freshness moist and the swamp-perfume,
And I with my comrades there in the night.

While my sight that was bound in my eyes unclosed,
As to long panoramas of visions.

And I saw askant the armies,
I saw as in noiseless dreams hundreds of battle-flags,
Borne through the smoke of the battles and pierc'd with missiles I saw
them,
And carried hither and yon through the smoke, and torn and bloody,
And at last but a few shreds left on the staffs, (and all in silence,)
And the staffs all splinter'd and broken.

I saw battle-corpses, myriads of them,
And the white skeletons of young men, I saw them,
I saw the debris and debris of all the slain soldiers of the war,
But I saw they were not as was thought,
They themselves were fully at rest, they suffer'd not,
The living remain'd and suffer'd, the mother suffer'd,
And the wife and the child and the musing comrade suffer'd,
And the armies that remain'd suffer'd.

16

Passing the visions, passing the night,
Passing, unloosing the hold of my comrades' hands,
Passing the song of the hermit bird and the tallying song of my soul,
Victorious song, death's outlet song, yet varying ever-altering song,
As low and wailing, yet clear the notes, rising and falling, flooding the
night,
Sadly sinking and fainting, as warning and warning, and yet again burst-
ing with joy,

Covering the earth and filling the spread of the heaven,
As that powerful psalm in the night I heard from recesses,
Passing, I leave thee lilac with heart-shaped leaves,
I leave thee there in the door-yard, blooming, returning with spring.

I cease from my song for thee,
From my gaze on thee in the west, fronting the west, communing with
　　thee,
O comrade lustrous with silver face in the night.

Yet each to keep and all, retrievements out of the night,
The song, the wondrous chant of the gray-brown bird,
And the tallying chant, the echo arous'd in my soul,
With the lustrous and drooping star with the countenance full of woe,
With the holders holding my hand nearing the call of the bird,
Comrades mine and I in the midst, and their memory ever to keep,
　　for the dead I loved so well,
For the sweetest, wisest soul of all my days and lands — and this for his
　　dear sake,
Lilac and star and bird twined with the chant of my soul,
There in the fragrant pines and the cedars dusk and dim.

One's-Self I Sing

One's-Self I sing, a simple separate person,
Yet utter the word Democratic, the word En-Masse.

Of physiology from top to toe I sing,
Not physiognomy alone nor brain alone is worthy for the Muse, I say
　　the Form complete is worthier far,
The Female equally with the Male I sing.

Of Life immense in passion, pulse, and power,
Cheerful, for freest action form'd under the laws divine,
The Modern Man I sing.

To a Stranger

Passing stranger! you do not know how longingly I look upon you,
You must be he I was seeking, or she I was seeking, (it comes to me
　　as of a dream,)
I have somewhere surely lived a life of joy with you,
All is recall'd as we flit by each other, fluid, affectionate, chaste, matured,

You grew up with me, were a boy with me or a girl with me,
I ate with you and slept with you, your body has become not yours only
  nor left my body mine only,
You give me the pleasure of your eyes, face, flesh, as we pass, you take
  of my beard, breast, hands, in return,
I am not to speak to you, I am to think of you when I sit alone or wake
  at night alone,
I am to wait, I do not doubt I am to meet you again,
I am to see to it that I do not lose you.

Aboard at a Ship's Helm

Aboard at a ship's helm,
A young steersman steering with care.

Through fog on a sea-coast dolefully ringing,
An ocean-bell — O a warning bell, rock'd by the waves.

O you give good notice indeed, you bell by the sea-reefs ringing,
Ringing, ringing, to warn the ship from its wreck-place.

For as on the alert O steersman, you mind the loud admonition,
The bows turn, the freighted ship tacking speeds away under her gray
  sails,
The beautiful and noble ship with all her precious wealth speeds away
  gayly and safe.

But O the ship, the immortal ship! O ship aboard the ship!
Ship of the body, ship of the soul, voyaging, voyaging, voyaging.

A Noiseless Patient Spider

A noiseless patient spider,
I mark'd where on a little promontory it stood isolated,
Mark'd how to explore the vacant vast surrounding,
It launch'd forth filament, filament, filament, out of itself,
Ever unreeling them, ever tirelessly speeding them.

And you O my soul where you stand,
Surrounded, detached, in measureless oceans of space,
Ceaselessly musing, venturing, throwing, seeking the spheres to connect
  them,
Till the bridge you will need be form'd, till the ductile anchor hold,
Till the gossamer thread you fling catch somewhere, O my soul.

HERMAN MELVILLE
1819–1891

The Portent

Hanging from the beam,
 Slowly swaying (such the law),
Gaunt the shadow on your green,
 Shenandoah!
The cut is on the crown
(Lo, John Brown),
And the stabs shall heal no more.

Hidden in the cap
 Is the anguish none can draw;
So your future veils its face,
 Shenandoah!
But the streaming beard is shown
(Weird John Brown),
The meteor of the war.

Misgivings

When ocean-clouds over inland hills
 Sweep storming in late autumn brown,
And horror the sodden valley fills,
 And the spire falls crashing in the town,
I muse upon my country's ills —
The tempest bursting from the waste of Time
On the world's fairest hope linked with man's foulest crime.

Nature's dark side is heeded now —
 (Ah! optimist-cheer disheartened flown) —
A child may read the moody brow
 Of yon black mountain lone.
With shouts the torrents down the gorges go,
And storms are formed behind the storm we feel:
The hemlock shakes in the rafter, the oak in the driving keel.

The Conflict of Convictions

On starry heights
  A bugle wails the long recall;
Derision stirs the deep abyss,
  Heaven's ominous silence over all.
Return, return, O eager Hope,
  And face man's latter fall.
Events, they make the dreamers quail;
Satan's old age is strong and hale,
A disciplined captain, gray in skill,
And Raphael a white enthusiast still;
Dashed aims, at which Christ's martyrs pale,
Shall Mammon's slaves fulfill?

      (Dismantle the fort,
      Cut down the fleet —
      Battle no more shall be!
      While the fields for fight in æons to come
      Congeal beneath the sea.)

The terrors of truth and dart of death
  To faith alike are vain;
Though comets, gone a thousand years,
  Return again,
Patient she stands — she can no more —
And waits, nor heeds she waxes hoar.

      (At a stony gate,
      A statue of stone,
      Weed overgrown —
      Long 'twill wait!)

But God His former mind retains,
  Confirms his old decree;
The generations are inured to pains,
  And strong Necessity
Surges, and heaps Time's strand with wrecks.
  The People spread like a weedy grass,
  The thing they will they bring to pass,
And prosper to the apoplex.
The rout it herds around the heart,
  The ghost is yielded in the gloom;
Kings wag their heads — Now save thyself
  Who wouldst rebuild the world in bloom.

(Tide-mark
And top of the age's strife,
Verge where they called the world to come,
The last advance of life —
Ha ha, the rust on the Iron Dome!)

Nay, but revere the hid event;
   In the cloud a sword is girded on,
I mark a twinkling in the tent
   Of Michael the warrior one.
Senior wisdom suits not now,
The light is on the youthful brow.

     (Ay, in caves the miner see:
     His forehead bears a blinking light;
     Darkness so he feebly braves
     A meagre wight!)

But He who rules is old — is old;
Ah! faith is warm, but heaven with age is cold.

     (Ho ho, ho ho,
     The cloistered doubt
     Of olden times
     Is blurted out!)

The Ancient of Days forever is young,
   Forever the scheme of Nature thrives;
I know a wind in purpose strong —
   It spins *against* the way it drives.
What if the gulfs their slimed foundations bare?
So deep must the stones be hurled
Whereon the throes of ages rear
The final empire and the happier world.

     (The poor old Past,
     The Future's slave,
     She drudged through pain and crime
     To bring about the blissful Prime,
     Then — perished. There's a grave!)

Power unanointed may come —
Dominion (unsought by the free)
    And the Iron Dome,
Stronger for stress and strain,
Fling her huge shadow athwart the main;
But the Founders' dream shall flee.
Age after age shall be
As age after age has been,
(From man's changeless heart their way they win);
And death be busy with all who strive —
Death, with silent negative.

YEA AND NAY —
EACH HATH HIS SAY;
BUT GOD HE KEEPS THE MIDDLE WAY.
NONE WAS BY
WHEN HE SPREAD THE SKY;
WISDOM IS VAIN, AND PROPHESY.

Shiloh

A Requiem

Skimming lightly, wheeling still,
    The swallows fly low
Over the field in clouded days,
    The forest-field of Shiloh —
Over the field where April rain
Solaced the parched ones stretched in pain
Through the pause of night
That followed the Sunday fight
    Around the church of Shiloh —
The church so lone, the log-built one,
That echoed to many a parting groan
        And natural prayer
    Of dying foemen mingled there —
Foemen at morn, but friends at eve —
    Fame or country least their care:
(What like a bullet can undeceive!)
    But now they lie low,
While over them the swallows skim,
    And all is hushed at Shiloh.

The House-top
A Night Piece

No sleep. The sultriness pervades the air
And binds the brain — a dense oppression, such
As tawny tigers feel in matted shades,
Vexing their blood and making apt for ravage.
Beneath the stars the roofy desert spreads
Vacant as Libya. All is hushed near by.
Yet fitfully from far breaks a mixed surf
Of muffled sound, the Atheist roar of riot.
Yonder, where parching Sirius set in drought,
Balefully glares red Arson — there — and there.
The Town is taken by its rats — ship-rats
And rats of the wharves. All civil charms
And priestly spells which late held hearts in awe —
Fear-bound, subjected to a better sway
Than sway of self; these like a dream dissolve,
And man rebounds whole æons back in nature.
Hail to the low dull rumble, dull and dead,
And ponderous drag that shakes the wall.
Wise Draco comes, deep in the midnight roll
Of black artillery; he comes, though late;
In code corroborating Calvin's creed
And cynic tyrannies of honest kings;
He comes, nor parlies; and the Town, redeemed,
Gives thanks devout; nor, being thankful, heeds
The grimy slur on the Republic's faith implied,
Which holds that Man is naturally good,
And — more — is Nature's Roman, never to be scourged.

The Maldive Shark

About the Shark, phlegmatical one,
Pale sot of the Maldive sea,
The sleek little pilot-fish, azure and slim,
How alert in attendance be.
From his saw-pit of mouth, from his charnel of maw
They have nothing of harm to dread,
But liquidly glide on his ghastly flank
Or before his Gorgonian head;
Or lurk in the port of serrated teeth
In white triple tiers of glittering gates,

And there find a haven when peril's abroad,
An asylum in jaws of the Fates!
They are friends; and friendly they guide him to prey,
Yet never partake of the treat —
Eyes and brains to the dotard lethargic and dull,
Pale ravener of horrible meat.

To Ned

Where is the world we roved, Ned Bunn?
   Hollows thereof lay rich in shade
By voyagers old inviolate thrown
   Ere Paul Pry cruised with Pelf and Trade.
To us old lads some thoughts come home
Who roamed a world young lads no more shall roam.

Nor less the satiate year impends
   When, wearying of routine-resorts,
The pleasure-hunter shall break loose,
   Ned, for our Pantheistic ports: —
Marquesas and glenned isles that be
Authentic Edens in a Pagan sea.

The charm of scenes untried shall lure,
   And, Ned, a legend urge the flight —
The Typee-truants under stars
   Unknown to Shakespere's *Midsummer-Night*;
And man, if lost to Saturn's Age,
Yet feeling life no Syrian pilgrimage.

But, tell, shall he, the tourist, find
   Our isles the same in violet-glow
Enamoring us what years and years —
   Ah, Ned, what years and years ago!
Well, Adam advances, smart in pace,
But scarce by violets that advance you trace.

But we, in anchor-watches calm,
   The Indian Psyche's languor won,
And, musing, breathed primeval balm
   From Edens ere yet over-run;
Marvelling mild if mortal twice,
Here and hereafter, touch a Paradise.

The Berg

(A Dream)

I saw a ship of martial build
(Her standards set, her brave apparel on)
Directed as by madness mere
Against a stolid iceberg steer,
Nor budge it, though the infatuate ship went down.
The impact made huge ice-cubes fall
Sullen, in tons that crashed the deck;
But that one avalanche was all —
No other movement save the foundering wreck.

Along the spurs of ridges pale,
Not any slenderest shaft and frail,
A prism over glass-green gorges lone,
Toppled; nor lace of traceries fine,
Nor pendant drops in grot or mine
Were jarred, when the stunned ship went down.
Nor sole the gulls in cloud that wheeled
Circling one snow-flanked peak afar,
But nearer fowl the floes that skimmed
And crystal beaches, felt no jar.
No thrill transmitted stirred the lock
Of jack-straw needle-ice at base;
Towers undermined by waves — the block
Atilt impending — kept their place.
Seals, dozing sleek on sliddery ledges
Slipt never, when by loftier edges
Through very inertia overthrown,
The impetuous ship in bafflement went down.

Hard Berg (methought), so cold, so vast,
With mortal damps self-overcast;
Exhaling still thy dankish breath —
Adrift dissolving, bound for death;
Though lumpish thou, a lumbering one —
A lumbering lubbard loitering slow,
Impingers rue thee and go down,
Sounding thy precipice below,
Nor stir the slimy slug that sprawls
Along thy dead indifference of walls.

The Ravaged Villa

In shards the sylvan vases lie,
   Their links of dance undone,
And brambles wither by thy brim,
   Choked fountain of the sun!
The spider in the laurel spins,
   The weed exiles the flower:
And, flung to kiln, Apollo's bust
   Makes lime for Mammon's tower.

Art

In placid hours well-pleased we dream
Of many a brave unbodied scheme.
But form to lend, pulsed life create,
What unlike things must meet and mate:
A flame to melt — a wind to freeze;
Sad patience — joyous energies;
Humility — yet pride and scorn;
Instinct and study; love and hate;
Audacity — reverence. These must mate,
And fuse with Jacob's mystic heart,
To wrestle with the angel — Art.

Fragments of a Lost Gnostic Poem of the 12th Century

*   *   *   *   *

Found a family, build a state,
The pledged event is still the same:
Matter in end will never abate
His ancient brutal claim.

*   *   *   *   *

Indolence is heaven's ally here,
And energy the child of hell:
The Good Man pouring from his pitcher clear,
But brims the poisoned well.

The Attic Landscape

Tourist, spare the avid glance
　　That greedy roves the sight to see:
Little here of "Old Romance,"
　　Or Picturesque of Tivoli.

No flushful tint the sense to warm —
Pure outline pale, a linear charm.
The clear-cut hills carved temples face,
Respond, and share their sculptural grace.

'Tis Art and Nature lodged together,
　　Sister by sister, cheek to cheek;
Such Art, such Nature, and such weather
　　The All-in-All seems here a Greek.

The Return of the Sire de Nesle
A.D. 16—

My towers at last! These rovings end,
Their thirst is slaked in larger dearth:
The yearning infinite recoils,
　　For terrible is earth.

Kaf thrusts his snouted crags through fog:
Araxes swells beyond his span,
And knowledge poured by pilgrimage
　　Overflows the banks of man.

But thou, my stay, thy lasting love
One lonely good, let this but be!
Weary to view the wide world's swarm,
　　But blest to fold but thee.

The Blue-Bird

Beneath yon Larkspur's azure bells
That sun their bees in balmy air
In mould no more the Blue-Bird dwells
Though late he found interment there.

All stiff he lay beneath the Fir
When shrill the March piped overhead,
And Pity gave him sepulchre
Within the Garden's sheltered bed.

And soft she sighed — Too soon he came;
On wings of hope he met the knell;
His heavenly tint the dust shall tame;
Ah, some misgiving had been well!

But, look, the clear etherial hue
In June it makes the Larkspur's dower;
It is the self-same welkin-blue —
The Bird's transfigured in the Flower.

Pontoosuce

Crowning a bluff where gleams the lake below,
Some pillared pines in well-spaced order stand
And like an open temple show,
And here in best of seasons bland,
Autumnal noon-tide, I look out
From dusk arcades on sunshine all about.

Beyond the Lake, in upland cheer
Fields, pastoral fields, and barns appear,
They skirt the hills where lonely roads
Revealed in links thro' tiers of woods
Wind up to indistinct abodes
And faery-peopled neighborhoods;
While further fainter mountains keep
Hazed in romance impenetrably deep.

Look, corn in stacks, on many a farm,
And orchards ripe in languorous charm,
As dreamy Nature, feeling sure
Of all her genial labor done,
And the last mellow fruitage won,
Would idle out her term mature;
Reposing like a thing reclined
In kinship with man's meditative mind.

For me, within the brown arcade —
Rich life, methought; sweet here in shade
And pleasant abroad in air! — But, nay,
A counter thought intrusive played,
A thought as old as thought itself,
And who shall lay it on the shelf! —
I felt the beauty bless the day
In opulence of autumn's dower;
But evanescence will not stay!
A year ago was such an hour,
As this, which but foreruns the blast
Shall sweep these live leaves to the dead leaves past.

All dies! —
           I stood in revery long.
Then, to forget death's ancient wrong,
I turned me in the brown arcade,
And there by chance in lateral glade
I saw low tawny mounds in lines
Relics of trunks of stately pines
Ranked erst in colonnades where, lo!
Erect succeeding pillars show!

All dies! and not alone
The aspiring trees and men and grass;
The poet's forms of beauty pass,
And noblest deeds they are undone.

All dies!
The workman dies, and after him, the work;
Like to these pines whose graves I trace,
Statue and statuary fall upon their face:
In very amaranths the worm doth lurk;
Even stars, Chaldæans say, fade from the starry space.
Andes and Apalachee tell
Of havoc ere our Adam fell,
And present Nature as a moss doth show
On the ruins of the Nature of the æons of long ago.

But look — and hark!
           Adown the glade,
Where light and shadow sport at will,
Who cometh vocal, and arrayed

As in the first pale tints of morn —
So pure, rose-clear, and fresh and chill!
Some ground-pine sprigs her brow adorn,
The earthy rootlets tangled clinging.
Over tufts of moss which dead things made,
Under vital twigs which danced or swayed,
Along she floats, and lightly singing:

"Dies, all dies!
The grass it dies, but in vernal rain
Up it springs and it lives again;
Over and over, again and again
It lives, it dies and it lives again.
Who sighs that all dies?
Summer and winter, and pleasure and pain
And everything everywhere in God's reign,
They end, and anon they begin again:
Wane and wax, wax and wane:
Over and over and over amain
End, ever end, and begin again —
End, ever end, and forever and ever begin again!"

She ceased, and nearer slid, and hung
In dewy guise; then softlier sung:
"Since light and shade are equal set
And all revolves, nor more ye know;
Ah, why should tears the pale cheek fret
For aught that waneth here below.
Let go, let go!"

With that, her warm lips thrilled me through,
She kissed me, while her chaplet cold
Its rootlets brushed against my brow
With all their humid clinging mould.
She vanished, leaving fragrant breath
And warmth and chill of wedded life and death.

Billy in the Darbies

Good of the Chaplain to enter Lone Bay
And down on his marrow-bones here and pray
For the likes just o' me, Billy Budd. — But, look:

Through the port comes the moon-shine astray!
It tips the guard's cutlass and silvers this nook;
But 'twill die in the dawning of Billy's last day.
A jewel-block they'll make of me tomorrow,
Pendant pearl from the yard-arm-end
Like the ear-drop I gave to Bristol Molly —
O, 'tis me, not the sentence they'll suspend.
Ay, Ay, all is up; and I must up too
Early in the morning, aloft from alow.
On an empty stomach, now, never it would do.
They'll give me a nibble — bit o' biscuit ere I go.
Sure, a messmate will reach me the last parting cup;
But, turning heads away from the hoist and the belay,
Heaven knows who will have the running of me up!
No pipe to those halyards. — But aren't it all sham?
A blur's in my eyes; it is dreaming that I am.
A hatchet to my hawser? All adrift to go?
The drum roll to grog, and Billy never know?
But Donald he has promised to stand by the plank;
So I'll shake a friendly hand ere I sink.
But — no! It is dead then I'll be, come to think. —
I remember Taff the Welshman when he sank.
And his cheek it was like the budding pink[.]
But me they'll lash in hammock, drop me deep.
Fathoms down, fathoms down, how I'll dream fast asleep.
I feel it stealing now. Sentry, are you there?
Just ease these darbies at the wrist, and roll me over fair,
I am sleepy, and the oozy weeds about me twist.

FREDERICK GODDARD TUCKERMAN
1821–1873

An upper chamber in a darkened house

An upper chamber in a darkened house,
Where, ere his footsteps reached ripe manhood's brink,
Terror and anguish were his lot to drink;
I cannot rid the thought nor hold it close
But dimly dream upon that man alone:
Now though the autumn clouds most softly pass,
The cricket chides beneath the doorstep stone
And greener than the season grows the grass.

Nor can I drop my lids nor shade my brows,
But there he stands beside the lifted sash;
And with a swooning of the heart, I think
Where the black shingles slope to meet the boughs
And, shattered on the roof like smallest snows,
The tiny petals of the mountain ash.

Still pressing through these weeping solitudes

Still pressing through these weeping solitudes,
Perchance I snatch a beam of comfort bright
And pause to fix the gleam or lose it quite
That darkens as I move or but intrudes
To baffle and forelay: as sometimes here,
When late at night the waried engineer
Driving his engine up through Whately woods
Sees on the track a glimmering lantern light
And checks his crashing speed, with hasty hand
Revering and retarding; — but again,
Look where it burns, a furlong on before!
The witchlight of the reedy rivershore,
The pilot of the forest and the fen,
Not to be left, but with the waste woodland.

And change with hurried hand has swept these scenes

And change with hurried hand has swept these scenes:
The woods have fallen, across the meadow-lot
The hunter's trail and trap-path is forgot,
And fire has drunk the swamps of evergreens,
Yet for a moment let my fancy plant
These autumn hills again: the wild dove's haunt,
The wild deer's walk. In golden umbrage shut,
The Indian river runs, Quonecktacut!
Here, but a lifetime back, where falls tonight
Behind the curtained pane a sheltered light
On buds of rose or vase of violet
Aloft upon the marble mantel set,
Here in the forest-heart, hung blackening
The wolfbait on the bush beside the spring.

Sometimes I walk where the deep water dips

Sometimes I walk where the deep water dips
Against the land. Or on where fancy drives
I walk and muse aloud, like one who strives
To tell his half-shaped thought with stumbling lips,
And view the ocean sea, the ocean ships,
With joyless heart: still but myself I find
And restless phantoms of my restless mind:
Only the moaning of my wandering words,
Only the wailing of the wheeling plover,
And this high rock beneath whose base the sea
Has wormed long caverns, like my tears in me:
And hard like this I stand, and beaten and blind,
This desolate rock with lichens rusted over,
Hoar with salt-sleet and chalkings of the birds.

Here, where the red man swept the leaves away

Here, where the red man swept the leaves away
To dig for cordial bark or cooling root,
The wayside apple drops its surly fruit.
Right through the deep heart of his midmost wood,
Through range and river and swampy solitude,
The common highway landward runs today,
The train booms by with long derisive hoot
And, following fast, rise factory, school, and forge.
I heed them not; but where yon alders shoot,
Searching strange plants to medicine my mood —
With a quick savage sense I stop, or stray
Through the brush pines and up the mountain gorge:
With patient eye, and with as safe a foot,
As though I walked the wood with sagamore George.

Hast thou seen reversed the prophet's miracle

Hast thou seen reversed the prophet's miracle —
The worm that, touched, a twig-like semblance takes?
Or hast thou mused what giveth the craft that makes
The twirling spider at once invisible,
And the spermal odor to the barberry flower,
Or heard the singing sand by the cold coast foam,
Or late — in inland autumn groves afar —

312

Hast thou ever plucked the little chick-wintergreen star
And tasted the sour of its leaf? Then come
With me betimes, and I will show thee more
Than these, of nature's secrecies the least:
In the first morning, overcast and chill,
And in the day's young sunshine, seeking still
For earliest flowers and gathering to the east.

November

Oh! who is there of us that has not felt
The sad decadence of the failing year,
And marked the lesson still with grief and fear
Writ in the rolled leaf and widely dealt?
When now no longer burns yon woodland belt
Bright with disease; no tree in glowing death
Leans forth a cheek of flame to fade and melt
In the warm current of the west wind's breath;
Nor yet through low blue mist on slope and plain
Droops the red sunlight in a dream of day;
But from that lull the winds of change have burst
And dashed the drowsy leaf with shattering rain,
And swung the groves, and roared; and wreaked their worst
Till all the world is harsh and cold and gray.

Under the Locust Blossoms

Under the locust blossoms
That hung and smelt like grapes:
Under the honey-locust blossoms, —
Faintly their breath escapes
And smites my heart; though years have passed since I
Beheld those clusters swinging silently,
Silver racemes against that sunset sky:

A sky all over rosy.
I waited for the night
Till the crickets tinkled drowsy
In their beds of clover white
Or fell silent at my footfall, one by one.
Did I wait? Did I wander there alone,
Under shadow, in that garden not my own?

'Tis but a shade of odour,
A recollected breath,
And I stand, a dark intruder
The swaying flowers beneath,
Alone, and peering on through anxious gloom
For a motion, for a glimmer; did it come?
Oh that moment! Oh that breath of locust bloom!

The Cricket

I

The humming bee purrs softly o'er his flower;
    From lawn and thicket
The dogday locust singeth in the sun
    From hour to hour:
Each has his bard, and thou, ere day be done,
    Shalt have no wrong.
So bright that murmur mid the insect crowd,
Muffled and lost in bottom-grass, or loud
    By pale and picket:
Shall I not take to help me in my song
    A little cooing cricket?

II

The afternoon is sleepy; let us lie
Beneath these branches whilst the burdened brook,
Muttering and moaning to himself, goes by,
And mark our minstrel's carol whilst we look
Toward the faint horizon swooning blue.
    Or in a garden bower,
Trellised and trammeled with deep drapery
    Of hanging green,
    Light glimmering through —
There let the dull hop be,
Let bloom, with poppy's dark refreshing flower:
Let the dead fragrance round our temples beat,
Stunning the sense to slumber, whilst between
The falling water and fluttering wind
    Mingle and meet,
    Murmur and mix,
No few faint pipings from the glades behind,
    Or alder-thicks:

But louder as the day declines,
From tingling tassel, blade, and sheath,
Rising from nets of river vines,
   Winrows and ricks,
   Above, beneath,
   At every breath,
At hand, around, illimitably
Rising and falling like the sea,
   Acres of cricks!

III

Dear to the child who hears thy rustling voice
Cease at his footstep, though he hears thee still,
Cease and resume with vibrance crisp and shrill,
Thou sittest in the sunshine to rejoice.
Night lover too; bringer of all things dark
And rest and silence; yet thou bringest to me
Always that burthen of the unresting Sea,
The moaning cliffs, the low rocks blackly stark;
These upland inland fields no more I view,
But the long flat seaside beach, the wild seamew,
   And the overturning wave!
Thou bringest too, dim accents from the grave
To him who walketh when the day is dim,
Dreaming of those who dream no more of him,
With edged remembrances of joy and pain;
And heyday looks and laughter come again:
Forms that in happy sunshine lie and leap,
With faces where but now a gap must be,
Renunciations, and partitions deep
And perfect tears, and crowning vacancy!
And to thy poet at the twilight's hush,
No chirping touch of lips with laugh and blush,
But wringing arms, hearts wild with love and woe,
Closed eyes, and kisses that would not let go!

IV

So wert thou loved in that old graceful time
   When Greece was fair,
While god and hero hearkened to thy chime;
   Softly astir
Where the long grasses fringed Caÿster's lip;
Long-drawn, with glimmering sails of swan and ship,

And ship and swan;
Or where
Reedy Eurotas ran.
Did that low warble teach thy tender flute
   Xenaphyle?
Its breathings mild? say! did the grasshopper
Sit golden in thy purple hair
   O Psammathe?
   Or wert thou mute,
Grieving for Pan amid the alders there?
And by the water and along the hill
That thirsty tinkle in the herbage still,
Though the lost forest wailed to horns of Arcady?

V

Like the Enchanter old —
Who sought mid the dead water's weeds and scum
For evil growths beneath the moonbeam cold,
   Or mandrake or dorcynium;
And touched the leaf that opened both his ears,
So that articulate voices now he hears
In cry of beast, or bird, or insect's hum, —
Might I but find thy knowledge in thy song!
   That twittering tongue,
Ancient as light, returning like the years.
   So might I be,
Unwise to sing, thy true interpreter
Through denser stillness and in sounder dark,
Than ere thy notes have pierced to harrow me.
   So might I stir
   The world to hark
   To thee my lord and lawgiver,
   And cease my quest:
Content to bring my wisdom to the world;
Content to gain at last some low applause,
   Now low, now lost
Like thine from mossy stone, amid the stems and straws,
   Or garden gravemound tricked and dressed —
   Powdered and pearled
   By stealing frost —
In dusky rainbow beauty of euphorbias!
For larger would be less indeed, and like
The ceaseless simmer in the summer grass

To him who toileth in the windy field,
　　Or where the sunbeams strike,
Naught in innumerable numerousness.
　　So might I much possess,
　　So much must yield;
But failing this, the dell and grassy dike,
The water and the waste shall still be dear,
And all the pleasant plots and places
　　Where thou hast sung, and I have hung
　　To ignorantly hear.
Then Cricket, sing thy song! or answer mine!
Thine whispers blame, but mine has naught but praises.
It matters not. Behold! the autumn goes,
　　The shadow grows,
The moments take hold of eternity;
Even while we stop to wrangle or repine
　　Our lives are gone —
　　Like thinnest mist,
Like yon escaping color in the tree;
Rejoice! rejoice! whilst yet the hours exist —
Rejoice or mourn, and let the world swing on
Unmoved by cricket song of thee or me.

HENRY TIMROD
1828–1867

Charleston

Calm as that second summer which precedes
　　The first fall of the snow,
In the broad sunlight of heroic deeds,
　　The City bides the foe.

As yet, behind their ramparts stern and proud,
　　Her bolted thunders sleep —
Dark Sumter, like a battlemented cloud,
　　Looms o'er the solemn deep.

No Calpe frowns from lofty cliff or scar
　　To guard the holy strand;
But Moultrie holds in leash her dogs of war
　　Above the level sand.

And down the dunes a thousand guns lie couched,
  Unseen, beside the flood —
Like tigers in some Orient jungle crouched
  That wait and watch for blood.

Meanwhile, through streets still echoing with trade,
  Walk grave and thoughtful men,
Whose hands may one day wield the patriot's blade
  As lightly as the pen.

And maidens, with such eyes as would grow dim
  Over a bleeding hound,
Seem each one to have caught the strength of him
  Whose sword she sadly bound.

Thus girt without and garrisoned at home,
  Day patient following day,
Old Charleston looks from roof, and spire, and dome,
  Across her tranquil bay.

Ships, through a hundred foes, from Saxon lands
  And spicy Indian ports,
Bring Saxon steel and iron to her hands,
  And Summer to her courts.

But still, along yon dim Atlantic line,
  The only hostile smoke
Creeps like a harmless mist above the brine,
  From some frail, floating oak.

Shall the Spring dawn, and she still clad in smiles,
  And with an unscathed brow,
Rest in the strong arms of her palm-crowned isles,
  As fair and free as now?

We know not; in the temple of the Fates
  God has inscribed her doom;
And, all untroubled in her faith, she waits
  The triumph or the tomb.

Ethnogenesis

I

Hath not the morning dawned with added light?
And shall not evening call another star
Out of the infinite regions of the night,
To mark this day in Heaven? At last, we are
A nation among nations; and the world
Shall soon behold in many a distant port
      Another flag unfurled!
Now come what may, whose favor need we court?
And, under God, whose thunder need we fear?
    Thank Him who placed us here
Beneath so kind a sky — the very sun
Takes part with us; and on our errands run
All breezes of the ocean; dew and rain
Do noiseless battle for us; and the Year,
And all the gentle daughters in her train,
March in our ranks, and in our service wield
      Long spears of golden grain!
A yellow blossom as her fairy shield,
June flings her azure banner to the wind,
    While in the order of their birth
Her sisters pass, and many an ample field
Grows white beneath their steps, till now, behold,
     Its endless sheets unfold
THE SNOW OF SOUTHERN SUMMERS! Let the earth
Rejoice! beneath those fleeces soft and warm
     Our happy land shall sleep
     In a repose as deep
   As if we lay intrenched behind
Whole leagues of Russian ice and Arctic storm!

II

And what if, mad with wrongs themselves have wrought,
    In their own treachery caught,
    By their own fears made bold,
    And leagued with him of old,
Who long since in the limits of the North
Set up his evil throne, and warred with God —
What if, both mad and blinded in their rage,
Our foes should fling us down their mortal gage,
And with a hostile step profane our sod!
We shall not shrink, my brothers, but go forth

To meet them, marshalled by the Lord of Hosts,
And overshadowed by the mighty ghosts
Of Moultrie and of Eutaw — who shall foil
Auxiliars such as these? Nor these alone,
  But every stock and stone
  Shall help us; but the very soil,
And all the generous wealth it gives to toil,
And all for which we love our noble land,
Shall fight beside, and through us; sea and strand,
  The heart of woman, and her hand,
Tree, fruit, and flower, and every influence,
  Gentle, or grave, or grand;
  The winds in our defence
Shall seem to blow; to us the hills shall lend
  Their firmness and their calm;
And in our stiffened sinews we shall blend
  The strength of pine and palm!

III

Nor would we shun the battle-ground,
  Though weak as we are strong;
Call up the clashing elements around,
  And test the right and wrong!
On one side, creeds that dare to teach
What Christ and Paul refrained to preach;
Codes built upon a broken pledge,
And Charity that whets a poniard's edge;
Fair schemes that leave the neighboring poor
To starve and shiver at the schemer's door,
While in the world's most liberal ranks enrolled,
He turns some vast philanthropy to gold;
Religion, taking every mortal form
But that a pure and Christian faith makes warm,
Where not to vile fanatic passion urged,
Or not in vague philosophies submerged,
Repulsive with all Pharisaic leaven,
And making laws to stay the laws of Heaven!
And on the other, scorn of sordid gain,
Unblemished honor, truth without a stain,
Faith, justice, reverence, charitable wealth,
And, for the poor and humble, laws which give,
Not the mean right to buy the right to live,
  But life, and home, and health!

To doubt the end were want of trust in God,
    Who, if he has decreed
  That we must pass a redder sea
Than that which rang to Miriam's holy glee,
    Will surely raise at need
    A Moses with his rod!

IV

But let our fears — if fears we have — be still,
And turn us to the future! Could we climb
Some mighty Alp, and view the coming time,
  The rapturous sight would fill
    Our eyes with happy tears!
Not only for the glories which the years
Shall bring us; not for lands from sea to sea,
And wealth, and power, and peace, though these shall be;
But for the distant peoples we shall bless,
And the hushed murmurs of a world's distress:
For, to give labor to the poor,
    The whole sad planet o'er,
And save from want and crime the humblest door,
Is one among the many ends for which
    God makes us great and rich!
The hour perchance is not yet wholly ripe
When all shall own it, but the type
Whereby we shall be known in every land
Is that vast gulf which lips our Southern strand,
And through the cold, untempered ocean pours
Its genial streams, that far off Arctic shores
May sometimes catch upon the softened breeze
Strange tropic warmth and hints of summer seas.

Ode

Sung on the occasion of decorating the graves
of the Confederate dead, at Magnolia Cemetery,
Charleston, S. C., 1867.

I

Sleep sweetly in your humble graves,
    Sleep, martyrs of a fallen cause;
Though yet no marble column craves
    The pilgrim here to pause.

II

In seeds of laurel in the earth
    The blossom of your fame is blown,
And somewhere, waiting for its birth,
    The shaft is in the stone!

III

Meanwhile, behalf the tardy years
    Which keep in trust your storied tombs,
Behold! your sisters bring their tears,
    And these memorial blooms.

IV

Small tributes! but your shades will smile
    More proudly on these wreaths to-day,
Than when some cannon-moulded pile
    Shall overlook this bay.

V

Stoop, angels, hither from the skies!
    There is no holier spot of ground
Than where defeated valor lies,
    By mourning beauty crowned!

EMILY DICKINSON
1830–1886

I never lost as much but twice (49)

I never lost as much but twice,
And that was in the sod.
Twice have I stood a beggar
Before the door of God!

Angels — twice descending
Reimbursed my store —
Burglar! Banker — Father!
I am poor once more!

Success is counted sweetest (67)

Success is counted sweetest
By those who ne'er succeed.
To comprehend a nectar
Requires sorest need.

Not one of all the purple Host
Who took the Flag today
Can tell the definition
So clear of Victory

As he defeated — dying —
On whose forbidden ear
The distant strains of triumph
Burst agonized and clear!

"Arcturus" is his other name (70)

"Arcturus" is his other name —
I'd rather call him "Star."
It's very mean of Science
To go and interfere!

I slew a worm the other day —
A "Savan" passing by
Murmured "Resurgam" — "Centipede"!
"Oh Lord — how frail are we"!

I pull a flower from the woods —
A monster with a glass
Computes the stamens in a breath —
And has her in a "class"!

Whereas I took the Butterfly
Aforetime in my hat —
He sits erect in "Cabinets" —
The Clover bells forgot.

What once was "Heaven"
Is "*Zenith*" now —
Where I proposed to go
When Time's brief masquerade was done
Is mapped and charted too.

What if the poles sh'd frisk about
And stand upon their heads!
I hope I'm ready for "the worst" —
Whatever prank betides!

Perhaps the "Kingdom of Heaven's" changed —
I hope the "Children" there
Wont be "new fashioned" when I come —
And laugh at me — and stare —

I hope the Father in the skies
Will lift his little girl —
Old fashioned — naughty — everything —
Over the stile of "Pearl".

I never hear the word "escape" (77)

I never hear the word "escape"
Without a quicker blood,
A sudden expectation,
A flying attitude!

I never hear of prisons broad
By soldiers battered down,
But I tug childish at my bars
Only to fail again!

Our lives are Swiss (80)

Our lives are Swiss —
So still — so Cool —
Till some odd afternoon
The Alps neglect their Curtains
And we look farther on!

Italy stands the other side!
While like a guard between —
The solemn Alps —
The siren Alps
Forever intervene!

Just lost, when I was saved! (160)

Just lost, when I was saved!
Just felt the world go by!
Just girt me for the onset with Eternity,
When breath blew back,
And on the other side
I heard recede the disappointed tide!

Therefore, as One returned, I feel,
Odd secrets of the line to tell!
Some Sailor, skirting foreign shores —
Some pale Reporter, from the awful doors
Before the Seal!

Next time, to stay!
Next time, the things to see
By Ear unheard,
Unscrutinized by Eye —

Next time, to tarry,
While the Ages steal —
Slow tramp the Centuries,
And the Cycles wheel!

Ah, Necromancy Sweet! (177)

Ah, Necromancy Sweet!
Ah, Wizard erudite!
Teach me the skill,

That I instil the pain
Surgeons assuage in vain,
Nor Herb of all the plain
Can heal!

"Faith" is a fine invention (185)

"Faith" is a fine invention
When Gentlemen can *see* —
But *Microscopes* are prudent
In an Emergency.

I taste a liquor never brewed (214)

I taste a liquor never brewed —
From Tankards scooped in Pearl —
Not all the Frankfort Berries
Yield such an Alcohol!

Inebriate of Air — am I —
And Debauchee of Dew —
Reeling — thro endless summer days —
From inns of Molten Blue —

When "Landlords" turn the drunken Bee
Out of the Foxglove's door —
When Butterflies — renounce their "drams" —
I shall but drink the more!

Till Seraphs swing their snowy Hats —
And Saints — to windows run —
To see the little Tippler
From Manzanilla come!

Safe in their Alabaster Chambers (216)

Safe in their Alabaster Chambers —
Untouched by Morning
And untouched by Noon —
Sleep the meek members of the Resurrection —
Rafter of satin,
And Roof of stone.

Light laughs the breeze
In her Castle above them —
Babbles the Bee in a stolid Ear,
Pipe the Sweet Birds in ignorant cadence —
Ah, what sagacity perished here!

version of 1859

Safe in their Alabaster Chambers —
Untouched by Morning —
And untouched by Noon —
Lie the meek members of the Resurrection —
Rafter of Satin — and Roof of Stone!

Grand go the Years — in the Crescent — above them —
Worlds scoop their Arcs —
And Firmaments — row —
Diadems — drop — and Doges — surrender —
Soundless as dots — on a Disc of Snow —

version of 1861

Wild Nights — Wild Nights! (249)

Wild Nights — Wild Nights!
Were I with thee
Wild Nights should be
Our luxury!

Futile — the Winds —
To a Heart in port —
Done with the Compass —
Done with the Chart!

Rowing in Eden —
Ah, the Sea!
Might I but moor — Tonight —
In Thee!

I can wade Grief (252)

I can wade Grief —
Whole Pools of it —
I'm used to that —
But the least push of Joy
Breaks up my feet —
And I tip — drunken —
Let no Pebble — smile —
'Twas the New Liquor —
That was all!

Power is only Pain —
Stranded, thro' Discipline,
Till Weights — will hang —
Give Balm — to Giants —
And they'll wilt, like Men —
Give Himmaleh —
They'll Carry — Him!

"Hope" is the thing with feathers (254)

"Hope" is the thing with feathers —
That perches in the soul —
And sings the tune without the words —
And never stops — at all —

And sweetest — in the Gale — is heard —
And sore must be the storm —
That could abash the little Bird
That kept so many warm —

I've heard it in the chillest land —
And on the strangest Sea —
Yet, never, in Extremity,
It asked a crumb — of Me.

There's a certain Slant of light (258)

There's a certain Slant of light,
Winter Afternoons —
That oppresses, like the Heft
Of Cathedral Tunes —

Heavenly Hurt, it gives us —
We can find no scar,
But internal difference,
Where the Meanings, are —

None may teach it — Any —
'Tis the Seal Despair —
An imperial affliction
Sent us of the Air —

When it comes, the Landscape listens —
Shadows — hold their breath —
When it goes, 'tis like the Distance
On the look of Death —

I felt a Funeral, in my Brain (280)

I felt a Funeral, in my Brain,
And Mourners to and fro
Kept treading — treading — till it seemed
That Sense was breaking through —

And when they all were seated,
A Service, like a Drum —
Kept beating — beating — till I thought
My Mind was going numb —

And then I heard them lift a Box
And creak across my Soul
With those same Boots of Lead, again,
Then Space — began to toll,

As all the Heavens were a Bell,
And Being, but an Ear,
And I, and Silence, some strange Race
Wrecked, solitary, here —

And then a Plank in Reason, broke,
And I dropped down, and down —
And hit a World, at every plunge,
And Finished knowing — then —

I'm Nobody! Who are you? (288)

I'm Nobody! Who are you?
Are you — Nobody — too?
Then there's a pair of us!
Dont tell! they'd banish us — you know!

How dreary — to be — Somebody!
How public — like a Frog —
To tell your name — the livelong June —
To an admiring Bog!

The Soul selects her own Society (303)

The Soul selects her own Society —
Then — shuts the Door —
To her divine Majority —
Present no more —

Unmoved — she notes the Chariots — pausing —
At her low Gate —
Unmoved — an Emperor be kneeling
Upon her Mat —

I've known her — from an ample nation —
Choose One —
Then — close the Valves of her attention —
Like Stone —

There came a Day at Summer's full (322)

There came a Day at Summer's full,
Entirely for me —
I thought that such were for the Saints,
Where Resurrections — be —

The Sun, as common, went abroad,
The flowers, accustomed, blew,
As if no soul the solstice passed
That maketh all things new —

The time was scarce profaned, by speech —
The symbol of a word
Was needless, as at Sacrament,
The Wardrobe — of our Lord —

Each was to each The Sealed Church,
Permitted to commune this — time —
Lest we too awkward show
At Supper of the Lamb.

The Hours slid fast — as Hours will,
Clutched tight, by greedy hands —
So faces on two Decks, look back,
Bound to opposing lands —

And so when all the time had leaked,
Without external sound
Each bound the Other's Crucifix —
We gave no other Bond —

Sufficient troth, that we shall rise —
Deposed — at length, the Grave —
To that new Marriage,
Justified — through Calvaries of Love —

A Bird came down the Walk (328)

A Bird came down the Walk —
He did not know I saw —
He bit an Angleworm in halves
And ate the fellow, raw,

And then he drank a Dew
From a convenient Grass —
And then hopped sidewise to the Wall
To let a Beetle pass —

He glanced with rapid eyes
That hurried all around —
They looked like frightened Beads, I thought —
He stirred his Velvet Head

Like one in danger, Cautious,
I offered him a Crumb
And he unrolled his feathers
And rowed him softer home —

Than Oars divide the Ocean,
Too silver for a seam —
Or Butterflies, off Banks of Noon
Leap, plashless as they swim.

After great pain, a formal feeling comes (341)

After great pain, a formal feeling comes —
The Nerves sit ceremonious, like Tombs —
The stiff Heart questions was it He, that bore,
And Yesterday, or Centuries before?

The Feet, mechanical, go round —
Of Ground, or Air, or Ought —
A Wooden way
Regardless grown,
A Quartz contentment, like a stone —

This is the Hour of Lead —
Remembered, if outlived,
As Freezing persons, recollect the Snow —
First — Chill — then Stupor — then the letting go —

Did Our Best Moment last (393)

Did Our Best Moment last —
'Twould supersede the Heaven —
A few — and they by Risk — procure —
So this Sort — are not given —

Except as stimulants — in
Cases of Despair —
Or Stupor — The Reserve —
These Heavenly Moments are —

A Grant of the Divine —
That Certain as it Comes —
Withdraws — and leaves the dazzled Soul
In her unfurnished Rooms —

Much Madness is divinest Sense (435)

Much Madness is divinest Sense —
To a discerning Eye —
Much Sense — the starkest Madness —
'Tis the Majority
In this, as All, prevail —
Assent — and you are sane —
Demur — you're straightway dangerous —
And handled with a Chain —

This is my letter to the World (441)

This is my letter to the World
That never wrote to Me —
The simple News that Nature told —
With tender Majesty

Her Message is committed
To Hands I cannot see —
For love of Her — Sweet — countrymen —
Judge tenderly — of Me

This was a Poet — It is That (448)

This was a Poet — It is That
Distills amazing sense
From ordinary Meanings —
And Attar so immense

From the familiar species
That perished by the Door —
We wonder it was not Ourselves
Arrested it — before —

Of Pictures, the Discloser —
The Poet — it is He —
Entitles Us — by Contrast —
To ceaseless Poverty —

Of Portion — so unconscious —
The Robbing — could not harm —
Himself — to Him — a Fortune —
Exterior — to Time —

I died for Beauty — but was scarce (449)

I died for Beauty — but was scarce
Adjusted in the Tomb
When One who died for Truth, was lain
In an adjoining Room —

He questioned softly "Why I failed"?
"For Beauty", I replied —
"And I — for Truth — Themself are One —
We Bretheren, are", He said —

And so, as Kinsmen, met a Night —
We talked between the Rooms —
Until the Moss had reached our lips —
And covered up — our names —

I heard a Fly buzz — when I died (465)

I heard a Fly buzz — when I died —
The Stillness in the Room
Was like the Stillness in the Air —
Between the Heaves of Storm —

The Eyes around — had wrung them dry —
And Breaths were gathering firm
For that last Onset — when the King
Be witnessed — in the Room —

I willed my Keepsakes — Signed away
What portion of me be
Assignable — and then it was
There interposed a Fly —

With Blue — uncertain stumbling Buzz —
Between the light — and me —
And then the Windows failed — and then
I could not see to see —

I am alive — I guess (470)

I am alive —I guess —
The Branches on my Hand
Are full of Morning Glory —
And at my finger's end —

The Carmine — tingles warm —
And if I hold a Glass
Across my Mouth — it blurs it —
Physician's — proof of Breath —

I am alive — because
I am not in a Room —
The Parlor — Commonly — it is —
So Visitors may come —

And lean — and view it sidewise —
And add "How cold — it grew" —
And "Was it conscious — when it stepped
In Immortality?"

I am alive — because
I do not own a House —
Entitled to myself — precise —
And fitting no one else —

And marked my Girlhood's name —
So Visitors may know
Which Door is mine — and not mistake —
And try another Key —

I would not paint — a picture (505)

I would not paint — a picture —
I'd rather be the One
It's bright impossibility
To dwell — delicious — on —
And wonder how the fingers feel
Whose rare — celestial — stir —
Evokes so sweet a Torment —
Such sumptuous — Despair —

I would not talk, like Cornets —
I'd rather be the One
Raised softly to the Ceilings —
And out, and easy on —
Through Villages of Ether —
Myself endued Balloon
By but a lip of Metal —
The pier to my Pontoon —

Nor would I be a Poet —
It's finer — own the Ear —
Enamored — impotent — content —
The License to revere,
A privilege so awful
What would the Dower be,
Had I the Art to stun myself
With Bolts of Melody!

It was not Death, for I stood up (510)

It was not Death, for I stood up,
And all the Dead, lie down —
It was not Night, for all the Bells
Put out their Tongues, for Noon.

It was not Frost, for on my Flesh
I felt Siroccos — crawl —
Nor Fire — for just my Marble feet
Could keep a Chancel, cool —

And yet, it tasted, like them all,
The Figures I have seen
Set orderly, for Burial,
Reminded me, of mine —

As if my life were shaven,
And fitted to a frame,
And could not breathe without a key,
And 'twas like Midnight, some —

When everything that ticked — has stopped —
And Space stares all around —
Or Grisly frosts — first Autumn morns,
Repeal the Beating Ground —

But, most, like Chaos — Stopless — cool —
Without a Chance, or Spar —
Or even a Report of Land —
To justify — Despair.

If you were coming in the Fall (511)

If you were coming in the Fall,
I'd brush the Summer by
With half a smile, and half a spurn,
As Housewives do, a Fly.

If I could see you in a year,
I'd wind the months in balls —
And put them each in separate Drawers,
For fear the numbers fuse —

If only Centuries, delayed,
I'd count them on my Hand,
Subtracting, till my fingers dropped
Into Van Dieman's Land.

If certain, when this life was out —
That your's and mine, should be —
I'd toss it yonder, like a Rind,
And take Eternity —

But, now, uncertain of the length
Of this, that is between,
It goads me, like the Goblin Bee —
That will not state — it's sting.

The Heart asks Pleasure — first (536)

The Heart asks Pleasure — first —
And then — Excuse from Pain —
And then — those little Anodynes
That deaden suffering —

And then — to go to sleep —
And then — if it should be
The will of it's Inquisitor
The privilege to die —

I've seen a Dying Eye (547)

I've seen a Dying Eye
Run round and round a Room —
In search of Something — as it seemed —
Then Cloudier become —
And then — obscure with Fog —
And then — be soldered down
Without disclosing what it be
'Twere blessed to have seen —

The Brain, within it's Groove (556)

The Brain, within it's Groove
Runs evenly — and true —
But let a Splinter swerve —
'Twere easier for You —

To put a Current back —
When Floods have slit the Hills —
And scooped a Turnpike for Themselves —
And trodden out the Mills —

I like to see it lap the Miles (585)

I like to see it lap the Miles —
And lick the Valleys up —
And stop to feed itself at Tanks
And then — prodigious step

Around a Pile of Mountains —
And supercilious peer
In Shanties — by the sides of Roads
And then a Quarry pare

To fit it's sides
And crawl between
Complaining all the while
In horrid — hooting stanza —
Then chase itself down Hill —

And neigh like Boanerges —
Then — prompter than a Star
Stop — docile and omnipotent
At it's own stable door —

There is a pain — so utter (599)

There is a pain — so utter —
It swallows substance up —
Then covers the Abyss with Trance —
So Memory can step
Around — across — upon it —
As one within a Swoon —
Goes safely — where an open eye —
Would drop Him — Bone by Bone.

I Years had been from Home (609)

I Years had been from Home
And now before the Door
I dared not enter, lest a Face
I never saw before

Stare stolid into mine
And ask my Business there —
"My Business but a Life I left
Was such remaining there?"

I leaned upon the Awe —
I lingered with Before —
The Second like an Ocean rolled
And broke against my ear —

I laughed a crumbling Laugh
That I could fear a Door
Who Consternation compassed
And never winced before.

I fitted to the Latch
My Hand, with trembling care
Lest back the awful Door should spring
And leave me in the Floor —

Then moved my Fingers off
As cautiously as Glass
And held my ears, and like a Thief
Fled gasping from the House —

They shut me up in Prose (613)

They shut me up in Prose —
As when a little Girl
They put me in the Closet —
Because they liked me "still" —

Still! Could themself have peeped —
And seen my Brain — go round —
They might as wise have lodged a Bird
For Treason — in the Pound —

Himself has but to will
And easy as a Star
Look down upon Captivity —
And laugh — No more have I —

I asked no other thing (621)

I asked no other thing —
No other — was denied —
I offered Being — for it —
The Mighty Merchant sneered —

Brazil? He twirled a Button —
Without a glance my way —
"But — Madam — is there nothing else —
That We can show — Today?"

I cannot live with You (640)

I cannot live with You —
It would be Life —
And Life is over there —
Behind the Shelf

The Sexton keeps the Key to —
Putting up
Our Life — His Porcelain —
Like a Cup —

Discarded of the Housewife —
Quaint — or Broke —
A newer Sevres pleases —
Old Ones crack —

I could not die — with You —
For One must wait
To shut the Other's Gaze down —
You — could not —

And I — Could I stand by
And see You — freeze —
Without my Right of Frost —
Death's privilege?

Nor could I rise — with You —
Because Your Face
Would put out Jesus' —
That New Grace

Glow plain — and foreign
On my homesick Eye —
Except that You than He
Shone closer by —

They'd judge Us — How —
For You — served Heaven — You know,
Or sought to —
I could not —

Because You saturated Sight —
And I had no more Eyes
For sordid excellence
As Paradise

And were You lost, I would be —
Though My Name
Rang loudest
On the Heavenly fame —

And were You — saved —
And I — condemned to be
Where You were not —
That self — were Hell to Me —

So We must meet apart —
You there — I — here —
With just the Door ajar
That Oceans are — and Prayer —
And that White Sustenance —
Despair —

I dwell in Possibility (657)

I dwell in Possibility —
A fairer House than Prose —
More numerous of Windows —
Superior — for Doors —

Of Chambers as the Cedars —
Impregnable of Eye —
And for an Everlasting Roof
The Gambrels of the Sky —

Of Visiters — the fairest —
For Occupation — This —
The spreading wide my narrow Hands
To gather Paradise —

Because I could not stop for Death (712)

Because I could not stop for Death —
He kindly stopped for me —
The Carriage held but just Ourselves —
And Immortality.

We slowly drove — He knew no haste
And I had put away
My labor and my leisure too,
For His Civility —

We passed the School, where Children strove
At Recess — in the Ring —
We passed the Fields of Gazing Grain —
We passed the Setting Sun —

Or rather — He passed Us —
The Dews drew quivering and chill —
For only Gossamer, my Gown —
My Tippet — only Tulle —

We paused before a House that seemed
A Swelling of the Ground —
The Roof was scarcely visible —
The Cornice — in the Ground —

Since then — 'tis Centuries — and yet
Feels shorter than the Day
I first surmised the Horses Heads
Were toward Eternity —

Drama's Vitallest Expression is the Common Day (741)

Drama's Vitallest Expression is the Common Day
That arise and set about Us —
Other Tragedy

Perish in the Recitation —
This — the best enact
When the Audience is scattered
And the Boxes shut —

"Hamlet" to Himself were Hamlet —
Had not Shakespeare wrote —
Though the "Romeo" left no Record
Of his Juliet,

It were infinite enacted
In the Human Heart —
Only Theatre recorded
Owner cannot shut —

Remorse — is Memory — awake (744)

Remorse — is Memory — awake —
Her Parties all astir —
A Presence of Departed Acts —
At window — and at Door —

It's Past — set down before the Soul
And lighted with a Match —
Perusal — to facilitate —
And help Belief to stretch —

Remorse is cureless — the Disease
Not even God — can heal —
For 'tis His institution — and
The Adequate of Hell —

A Light exists in Spring (812)

A Light exists in Spring
Not present on the Year
At any other period —
When March is scarcely here

A Color stands abroad
On Solitary Fields
That Science cannot overtake
But Human Nature feels.

It waits upon the Lawn,
It shows the furthest Tree
Upon the furthest Slope you know
It almost speaks to you.

Then as Horizons step
Or Noons report away
Without the Formula of sound
It passes and we stay —

A quality of loss
Affecting our Content
As Trade had suddenly encroached
Upon a Sacrament.

Finding is the first Act (870)

Finding is the first Act
The second, loss,
Third, Expedition for
the "Golden Fleece"

Fourth, no Discovery —
Fifth, no Crew —
Finally, no Golden Fleece —
Jason — sham — too.

I stepped from Plank to Plank (875)

I stepped from Plank to Plank
A slow and cautious way
The Stars about my Head I felt
About my Feet the Sea.

I knew not but the next
Would be my final inch —
This gave me that precarious Gait
Some call Experience.

We outgrow love, like other things (887)

We outgrow love, like other things
And put it in the Drawer —
Till it an Antique fashion shows —
Like Costumes Grandsires wore.

I felt a Cleaving in my Mind (937)

I felt a Cleaving in my Mind —
As if my Brain had split —
I tried to match it — Seam by Seam —
But could not make them fit.

The thought behind, I strove to join
Unto the thought before —
But Sequence ravelled out of Sound
Like Balls — upon a Floor.

A *narrow Fellow in the Grass* (986)

A narrow Fellow in the Grass
Occasionally rides —
You may have met Him — did you not
His notice sudden is —

The Grass divides as with a Comb —
A spotted shaft is seen —
And then it closes at your feet
And opens further on —

He likes a Boggy Acre
A Floor too cool for Corn —
Yet when a Boy, and Barefoot —
I more than once at Noon

Have passed, I thought, a Whip lash
Unbraiding in the Sun
When stooping to secure it
It wrinkled, and was gone —

Several of Nature's People
I know, and they know me —
I feel for them a transport
Of cordiality —

But never met this Fellow
Attended, or alone
Without a tighter breathing
And Zero at the Bone —

Crumbling is not an instant's Act (997)

Crumbling is not an instant's Act
A fundamental pause
Delapidation's processes
Are organized Decays.

'Tis first a Cobweb on the Soul
A Cuticle of Dust
A Borer in the Axis
An Elemental Rust —

Ruin is formal — Devils work
Consecutive and slow —
Fail in an instant, no man did
Slipping — is Crashe's law.

Satisfaction — is the Agent (1036)

Satisfaction — is the Agent
Of Satiety —
Want — a quiet Comissary
For Infinity.

To possess, is past the instant
We achieve the Joy —
Immortality contented
Were Anomaly.

Reportless Subjects, to the Quick (1048)

Reportless Subjects, to the Quick
Continual addressed —
But foreign as the Dialect
Of Danes, unto the rest.

Reportless Measures, to the Ear
Susceptive — stimulus —
But like an Oriental Tale
To others, fabulous —

Further in Summer than the Birds (1068)

Further in Summer than the Birds
Pathetic from the Grass
A minor Nation celebrates
It's unobtrusive Mass.

No Ordinance be seen
So gradual the Grace
A pensive Custom it becomes
Enlarging Loneliness.

Antiquest felt at Noon
When August burning low
Arise this spectral Canticle
Repose to typify

Remit as yet no Grace
No Furrow on the Glow
Yet a Druidic Difference
Enhances Nature now

Perception of an object costs (1071)

Perception of an object costs
Precise the Object's loss —
Perception in itself a Gain
Replying to it's Price —
The Object Absolute — is nought —
Perception sets it fair
And then upbraids a Perfectness
That situates so far —

Title divine — is mine! (1072)

Title divine — is mine!
The Wife — without the Sign!
Acute Degree — conferred on me —
Empress of Calvary!
Royal — all but the Crown!
Betrothed — without the swoon
God sends us Women —
When you — hold — Garnet to Garnet —
Gold — to Gold —
Born — Bridalled — Shrouded —
In a Day —
Tri Victory

"My Husband" — women say —
Stroking the Melody —
Is *this* — the way?

Tell all the Truth but tell it slant (1129)

Tell all the Truth but tell it slant —
Success in Circuit lies
Too bright for our infirm Delight
The Truth's superb surprise
As Lightning to the Children eased
With explanation kind
The Truth must dazzle gradually
Or every man be blind —

So proud she was to die (1272)

So proud she was to die
It made us all ashamed
That what we cherished, so unknown
To her desire seemed —
So satisfied to go
Where none of us should be
Immediately — that Anguish stooped
Almost to Jealousy —

Until the Desert knows (1291)

Until the Desert knows
That Water grows
His Sands suffice
But let him once suspect
That Caspian Fact
Sahara dies

Utmost is relative —
Have not or Have
Adjacent sums
Enough — the first Abode
On the familiar Road
Galloped in Dreams —

A *Bee his burnished Carriage* (1339)

A Bee his burnished Carriage
Drove boldly to a Rose —
Combinedly alighting —
Himself — his Carriage was —
The Rose received his visit
With frank tranquility
Witholding not a Crescent
To his Cupidity —
Their Moment consummated —
Remained for him — to flee —
Remained for her — of rapture
But the humility.

As *imperceptibly as Grief* (1540)

As imperceptibly as Grief
The Summer lapsed away —
Too imperceptible at last
To seem like Perfidy —
A Quietness distilled
As Twilight long begun,
Or Nature spending with herself
Sequestered Afternoon —
The Dusk drew earlier in —
The Morning foreign shone —
A courteous, yet harrowing Grace,
As Guest, that would be gone —
And thus, without a Wing
Or service of a Keel
Our Summer made her light escape
Into the Beautiful.

There *came a Wind like a Bugle* (1593)

There came a Wind like a Bugle —
It quivered through the Grass
And a Green Chill upon the Heat
So ominous did pass
We barred the Windows and the Doors

As from an Emerald Ghost —
The Doom's electric Moccasin
That very instant passed —
On a strange Mob of panting Trees
And Fences fled away
And Rivers where the Houses ran
Those looked that lived — that Day —
The Bell within the steeple wild
The flying tidings told —
How much can come
And much can go,
And yet abide the World!

There are two Mays (1618)

There are two Mays
And then a Must
And after that a Shall.
How infinite the compromise
That indicates I will!

The pedigree of Honey (1627)

The pedigree of Honey
Does not concern the Bee,
Nor lineage of Ecstasy
Delay the Butterfly
On spangled journeys to the peak
Of some perceiveless thing —
The right of way to Tripoli
A more essential thing. -

In Winter in my Room (1670)

In Winter in my Room
I came upon a Worm
Pink lank and warm
But as he was a worm
And worms presume

Not quite with him at home
Secured him by a string
To something neighboring
And went along.

A Trifle afterward
A thing occurred
I'd not believe it if I heard
But state with creeping blood
A snake with mottles rare
Surveyed my chamber floor
In feature as the worm before

But ringed with power
The very string with which
I tied him — too
When he was mean and new
That string was there —

I shrank — "How fair you are"!
Propitiation's claw —
"Afraid he hissed
Of me"?
"No cordiality" —
He fathomed me —
Then to a Rhythm *Slim*
Secreted in his Form
As Patterns swim
Projected him.

That time I flew
Both eyes his way
Lest he pursue
Nor ever ceased to run
Till in a distant Town
Towns on from mine
I set me down
This was a dream —

God is indeed a jealous God (1719)

God is indeed a jealous God —
He cannot bear to see
That we had rather not with Him
But with each other play.

My life closed twice before its close (1732)

My life closed twice before its close;
It yet remains to see
If Immortality unveil
A third event to me,

So huge, so hopeless to conceive
As these that twice befel.
Parting is all we know of heaven,
And all we need of hell.

Softened by Time's consummate plush (1738)

Softened by Time's consummate plush,
How sleek the woe appears
That threatened childhood's citadel
And undermined the years.

Bisected now, by bleaker griefs,
We envy the despair
That devastated childhood's realm,
So easy to repair.

That it will never come again (1741)

That it will never come again
Is what makes life so sweet.
Believing what we don't believe
Does not exhilarate.

That if it be, it be at best
An ablative estate —
This instigates an appetite
Precisely opposite.

That Love is all there is (1765)

That Love is all there is,
Is all we know of Love;
It is enough, the freight should be
Proportioned to the groove.

Too happy Time dissolves itself (1774)

Too happy Time dissolves itself
And leaves no remnant by —
'Tis Anguish not a Feather hath
Or too much weight to fly —

FOLK SONGS AND BALLADS

Go Down Moses

1

When Israel was in Egypt land,
Let my people go,
Oppressed so hard they could not stand,
Let my people go.
Go down, Moses,
Way-down in Egypt land,
Tell old Pharaoh
To let my people go.

2

'Thus spoke the Lord' bold Moses said,
'Let my people go,
If not, I'll smite your first-born dead,
Let my people go.' (*Chorus*)

3
'Your foes shall not before you stand,
Let my people go,
And you'll possess fair Canaan's land,
Let my people go.' *(Chorus)*

4
'You'll not get lost in the wilderness,
Let my people go,
With a lighted candle in your breast,
Let my people go.' *(Chorus)*

Frankie and Johnny

1
Frankie and Johnny were lovers,
Lordy, how they could love,
Swore to be true to each other,
True as the stars above,
    He was her man, but he done her wrong.

2
Little Frankie was a good gal,
As everybody knows,
She did all the work around the house,
And pressed her Johnny's clothes,
    He was her man, but he done her wrong.

3
Johnny was a yeller man,
With coal black, curly hair,
Everyone up in St. Louis
Thought he was a millionaire,
    He was her man, but he done her wrong.

4
Frankie went down to the bar-room,
Called for a bottle of beer,
Says, "Looky here, Mister Bartender,
Has my lovin' Johnny been here?
    He is my man, and he's doin' me wrong."

5

"I will not tell you no story,
I will not tell you no lie,
Johnny left here about an hour ago,
With a gal named Nelly Bly,
He is your man and he's doing you wrong."

6

Little Frankie went down Broadway,
With her pistol in her hand,
Said, "Stand aside you chorus gals,
I'm lookin' for my man,
He is my man, and he's doin' me wrong."

7

The first time she shot him, he staggered,
The next time she shot him, he fell,
The last time she shot, O Lawdy,
There was a new man's face in hell,
She shot her man, for doin' her wrong.

8

"Turn me over doctor,
Turn me over slow,
I got a bullet in my left hand side,
Great God, it's hurtin' me so.
I was her man, but I done her wrong."

9

It was a rubber-tyred buggy,
Decorated hack,
Took poor Johnny to the graveyard,
Brought little Frankie back,
He was her man, but he done her wrong.

10

It was not murder in the first degree,
It was not murder in the third.
A woman simply dropped her man
Like a hunter drops his bird,
She shot her man, for doin' her wrong.

11

The last time I saw Frankie,
She was sittin' in the 'lectric chair,
Waitin' to go and meet her God
With the sweat runnin' out of her hair,
  She shot her man, for doin' her wrong.

12

Walked on down Broadway,
As far as I could see,
All I could hear was a two string bow
Playin' *"Nearer my God to thee,"*
  He was her man, and he done her wrong.

Take a Whiff on Me

1

Goin' up State Street, comin' down Main,
Lookin' for the woman that use cocaine.
  Hi, Hi, baby, take a sniff on me,
  All you bummers take a sniff on me,
  *Take a *! on me, take a *! on me,*
  *An' a Hi, Hi, honey take a *! on me.*

2

Woke up this mornin' by the courthouse bell,
Boys uptown givin' cocaine hell. *(Chorus)*

3

Went to Mister Lehman's on a lope,
Sign in the window said *No mo coke. (Chorus)*

4

You bring a nickel and I'll bring a dime,
You buy the coke and I'll buy the wine. *(Chorus)*

5

I chew my tobacco and I spit my juice,
And I love my baby till it ain't no use. *(Chorus)*

*Sing it or sniff it.

6

Cocaine's for horses and not for men,
The doctors say it'll kill you, but they don't say when. *(Chorus)*

7

Whifforee and a whifforye,
Gonna keep a-whiffin' boys, till I die. *(Chorus)*

8

Now the cocaine habit is mighty bad,
It kill everybody I know it to have had. *(Chorus)*

The Big Rock Candy Mountains

Introduction
On a summer day in the month of May,
A burly little bum come a-hikin',
He was travelin' down that lonesome road,
A-lookin' for his likin'.
He was headed for a land that's far away,
Beside those crystal fountains,
"I'll see you all, this comin' fall
In the Big Rock Candy Mountains."

1

In the Big Rock Candy Mountains
You never change your socks,
And the little streams of alkyhol
Come a-tricklin' down the rocks.
Where the shacks all have to tip their hats,
And the railroad bulls* are blind,
There's a lake of stew, and whiskey, too,
And you can paddle all around 'em in your big canoe,
In the Big Rock Candy Mountains.
            O ... the ... buzzin' of the bees
            In the cigarette trees,
            Round the sodawater fountains,
            Near the lemonade springs,
            Where the whangdoodle sings
            In the Big Rock Candy Mountains.

*Railroad guards.

358

2

In the Big Rock Candy Mountains,
There's a land that's fair and bright,
Where the handouts grow on bushes,
And you sleep out every night.
Where the box cars are all empty
And the sun shines every day,
O I'm bound to go, where there ain't no snow,
Where the rain don't fall and the wind don't blow,
In the Big Rock Candy Monutains. *(Chorus)*

3

In the Big Rock Candy Mountains,
The jails are made of tin,
And you can bust right out again
As soon as they put you in.
The farmers' trees are full of fruit,
The barns are full of hay,
I'm goin' to stay where you sleep all day,
Where they boiled in oil the inventor of toil,
In the Big Rock Candy Mountains. *(Chorus)*

De Ballit of de Boll Weevil

Oh, have you heard de lates',
De lates' of de songs?
It's about dem little Boll Weevils,
Dey's picked up bofe feet an' gone
A-lookin' for a home,
Jes a-lookin' for a home.

De Boll Weevil is a little bug
F'um Mexico, dey say,
He come to try dis Texas soil
En thought he better stay,
A-lookin' for a home,
Jes a-lookin' for a home.

359

De nigger say to de Boll Weevil
"Whut makes yo' head so red?"
"I's been wanderin' de whole worl' ovah
Till it's a wonder I ain't dead,
A-lookin' for a home,
Jes a-lookin' for a home."

First time I saw Mr. Boll Weevil,
He wuz on de western plain;
Next time I saw him,
He wuz ridin' on a Memphis train,
A-lookin' for a home,
Jes a-lookin' for a home.

De nex' time I saw him,
He was runnin' a spinnin' wheel;
De nex' time I saw him,
He was ridin' in an automobile,
A-lookin' for a home,
Jes a-lookin' for a home.

De fus' time I saw de Boll Weevil
He wuz settin' on de square,
De nex' time I saw de Boll Weevil
He had all his family dere —
Dey's lookin' for a home,
Jes a-lookin' for a home.

Then the Farmer got angry,
Sent him up in a balloon;
"Good-by, Mr. Farmer;
I'll see you again next June.
A-lookin' for a home,
Jes a-lookin' for a home."

De Farmer took de Boll Weevil
An' buried him in hot san';
De Boll Weevil say to de Farmer,
"I'll stan' it like a man,
Fur it is my home,
It is my home."

Den de Farmer took de Boll Weevil
An' lef' him on de ice;
Says de Boll Weevil to de Farmer,
"Dis is mighty cool an' nice.
Oh, it is my home,
It is my home."

Mr. Farmer took little Weevil
And put him in Paris Green;
"Thank you, Mr. Farmer;
It's the best I ever seen.
It is my home,
It's jes my home."

Den de Farmer say to de Merchant:
"We's in an awful fix;
De Boll Weevil's et all de cotton up
An' lef' us only sticks.
We's got no home,
Oh, we's got no home."

Den de Merchant say to de Farmer,
"Whut do you tink o' dat?
Ef you kin kill de Boll Weevil
I'll give you a bran-new Stetson hat,
A Stetson hat,
Oh, a Stetson hat."

Oh, de Farmer say to de Merchant,
"I ain't made but only one bale,
An' befo' I bring yo' dat one
I'll fight an' go to jail,
I'll have a home,
I'll have a home."

De Sharpshooter say to de Boll Weevil,
"What you doin' in dis square?"
An' the Boll Weevil say to de Sharpshooter,
"Ise makin' my home in here,
Here in dis square,
Here in dis square."

Oh, de Boll Weevil say to de Dutchman,
"Jes' poison me ef yo' dare,
An' when yo' come to make yo' crop
I'll punch out every square,
When de sun gits hot,
When de sun gits hot."

De Boll Weevil say to de Farmer,
"You better lemme alone,
I've et up all yo' cotton
An' now I'll begin on de co'n,
I'll have a home,
I'll have a home."

Boll Weevil say to de Doctor,
"Better po' out all yo' pills,
When I git through wid de Farmer,
He cain't pay no doctor's bills.
He'll have no home,
He'll have no home."

Boll Weevil say to de Preacher,
"You better close yo' church do',
When I git through wid de Farmer,
He cain't pay de Preacher no mo',
Won't have no home,
Won't have no home."

De Merchant got half de cotton,
De Boll Weevil got de res';
Didn't leave de nigger's wife
But one old cotton dress.
And it's full of holes,
Oh, it's full of holes.

Rubber-tired buggy,
Decorated hack,
Took dem Boll Weevils to de graveyard,
An' ain't goin' to bring 'em back.
Dey gone at las',
Oh, dey gone at las'.

Ef anybody axes you
Who wuz it writ dis song,
Tell 'em 'twuz a dark-skinned nigger
Wid a pair o' blue duckins on,
A-lookin' for a home,
Jes a-lookin' for a home.

John Henry

John Henry was a li'l baby, uh-huh,*
Sittin' on his mama's knee, oh, yeah,*
Said: "De Big Bend Tunnel on de C. & O. road
Gonna cause de death of me,
Lawd, Lawd, gonna cause de death of me."

John Henry, he had a woman,
Her name was Mary Magdalene,
She would go to de tunnel and sing for John,
Jes' to hear John Henry's hammer ring,
Lawd, Lawd, jes' to hear John Henry's hammer ring.

John Henry had a li'l woman,
Her name was Lucy Ann,
John Henry took sick an' had to go to bed,
Lucy Ann drove steel like a man,
Lawd, Lawd, Lucy Ann drove steel like a man.

Cap'n says to John Henry,
"Gonna bring me a steam drill 'round,
Gonna take dat steam drill out on de job,
Gonna whop dat steel on down,
Lawd, Lawd, gonna whop dat steel on down."

John Henry tol' his cap'n,
Lightnin' was in his eye:
"Cap'n, bet yo' las' red cent on me,
Fo' I'll beat it to de bottom or I'll die,
Lawd, Lawd, I'll beat it to de bottom or I'll die."

*These exclamatory phrases are repeated in each stanza.

Sun shine hot an' burnin',
Wer'n't no breeze a-tall,
Sweat ran down like water down a hill,
Dat day John Henry let his hammer fall,
Lawd, Lawd, dat day John Henry let his hammer fall.

John Henry went to de tunnel,
An' dey put him in de lead to drive;
De rock so tall an' John Henry so small,
Dat he lied down his hammer an' he cried,
Lawd, Lawd, dat he lied down his hammer an' he cried.

John Henry started on de right hand,
De steam drill started on de lef' —
"Before I'd let dis steam drill beat me down,
I'd hammer my fool self to death,
Lawd, Lawd, I'd hammer my fool self to death."

White man tol' John Henry,
"Nigger, damn yo' soul,
You might beat dis steam an' drill of mine,
When de rocks in dis mountain turn to gol',
Lawd, Lawd, when de rocks in dis mountain turn to gol'."

John Henry said to his shaker,
"Nigger, why don' you sing?
I'm throwin' twelve poun's from my hips on down,
Jes' listen to de col' steel ring,
Lawd, Lawd, jes' listen to de col' steel ring."

Oh, de captain said to John Henry,
"I b'lieve this mountain's sinkin' in."
John Henry said to his captain, oh my!
"Ain' nothin' but my hammer suckin' win',
Lawd, Lawd, ain' nothin' but my hammer suckin' win'."

John Henry tol' his shaker,
"Shaker, you better pray,
For, if I miss dis six-foot steel,
Tomorrow'll be yo' buryin' day,
Lawd, Lawd, tomorrow'll be yo' buryin' day."

John Henry tol' his captain,
"Looka yonder what I see —
Yo' drill's done broke an' yo' hole's done choke,
An' you cain' drive steel like me,
Lawd, Lawd, an' you cain' drive steel like me."

De man dat invented de steam drill,
Thought he was mighty fine.
John Henry drove his fifteen feet,
An' de steam drill only made nine,
Lawd, Lawd, an' de steam drill only made nine.

De hammer dat John Henry swung,
It weighed over nine pound;
He broke a rib in his lef'-han' side,
An' his intrels fell on de groun',
Lawd, Lawd, an' his intrels fell on de groun'.

John Henry was hammerin' on de mountain,
An' his hammer was strikin' fire,
He drove so hard till he broke his pore heart,
An' he lied down his hammer an' he died,
Lawd, Lawd, he lied down his hammer an' he died.

All de womens in de Wes',
When dey heared of John Henry's death,
Stood in de rain, flagged de eas'-boun' train,
Goin' where John Henry fell dead,
Lawd, Lawd, goin' where John Henry fell dead.

John Henry's li'l mother,
She was all dressed in red,
She jumped in bed, covered up her head,
Said she didn' know her son was dead,
Lawd, Lawd, didn' know her son was dead.

John Henry had a pretty li'l woman,
An' de dress she wo' was blue,
An' de las' words she said to him:
"John Henry, I've been true to you,
Lawd, Lawd, John Henry, I've been true to you."

"Oh, who's gonna shoe yo' lil feetses,
 An' who's gonna glub yo' han's,
 An' who's gonna kiss yo' rosy, rosy lips,
 An' who's gonna be yo' man,
 Lawd, Lawd, an' who's gonna be yo' man?"

"Oh, my mama's gonna shoe my lil feetses,
 An' my papa's gonna glub my lil han's,
 An' my sister's gonna kiss my rosy, rosy lips,
 An' I don' need no man,
 Lawd, Lawd, an' I don' need no man."

Dey took John Henry to de graveyard,
 An' dey buried him in de san',
 An' every locomotive come roarin' by,
 Says, "Dere lays a steel-drivin' man,
 Lawd, Lawd, dere lays a steel-drivin' man."

Joshua Fit de Battle ob Jerico

Joshua fit de battle ob Jerico, Jerico, Jerico,
Joshua fit de battle ob Jerico,
An' de walls come tumblin' down.

You may talk about yo' king ob Gideon,
You may talk about yo' man ob Saul,
Dere's none like good ole Joshua
At de battle ob Jerico.

Up to de walls ob Jerico,
He marched with spear in han',
"Go blow dem ram horns" Joshua cried,
"Kase de battle am in my han'."

Den de lam'ram sheep horns begin to blow, trumpets begin to soun',
Joshua commanded de chillen to shout,
An' de walls come tumblin' down.

Dat mornin' Joshua fit de battle ob Jerico, Jerico, Jerico,
Joshua fit de battle ob Jerico,
An' de walls come tumblin' down.

SIDNEY LANIER
1842–1881

From the Flats

What heartache — ne'er a hill!
Inexorable, vapid, vague, and chill
The drear sand-levels drain my spirit low.
With one poor word they tell me all they know;
Whereat their stupid tongues, to tease my pain,
Do drawl it o'er again and o'er again.
They hurt my heart with griefs I cannot name:
    Always the same, the same.

Nature hath no surprise,
No ambuscade of beauty 'gainst mine eyes
From brake or lurking dell or deep defile;
No humors, frolic forms — this mile, that mile;
No rich reserves or happy-valley hopes
Beyond the bends of roads, the distant slopes.
Her fancy fails, her wild is all run tame:
    Ever the same, the same.

Oh, might I through these tears
But glimpse some hill my Georgia high uprears,
Where white the quartz and pink the pebble shine,
The hickory heavenward strives, the muscadine
Swings o'er the slope, the oak's far-falling shade
Darkens the dogwood in the bottom glade,
And down the hollow from a ferny nook
    Bright leaps a living brook!

The Marshes of Glynn

Glooms of the live-oaks, beautiful-braided and woven
With intricate shades of the vines that myriad-cloven
  Clamber the forks of the multiform boughs, —
    Emerald twilights, —
    Virginal shy lights,
Wrought of the leaves to allure to the whisper of vows,
When lovers pace timidly down through the green colonnades
  Of the dim sweet woods, of the dear dark woods,

Of the heavenly woods and glades,
That run to the radiant marginal sand-beach within
        The wide sea-marshes of Glynn; —

Beautiful glooms, soft dusks in the noon-day fire, —
Wildwood privacies, closets of lone desire,
Chamber from chamber parted with wavering arras of leaves, —
Cells for the passionate pleasure of prayer to the soul that grieves,
    Pure with a sense of the passing of saints through the wood,
    Cool for the dutiful weighing of ill with good; —
O braided dusks of the oak and woven shades of the vine,
While the riotous noon-day sun of the June-day long did shine,
Ye held me fast in your heart and I held you fast in mine;
    But now when the noon is no more, and riot is rest,
    And the sun is a-wait at the ponderous gate of the West,
        And the slant yellow beam down the wood-aisle doth seem
        Like a lane into heaven that leads from a dream, —
Ay, now, when my soul all day hath drunken the soul of the oak,
And my heart is at ease from men, and the wearisome sound of the stroke
    Of the scythe of time and the trowel of trade is low,
    And belief overmasters doubt, and I know that I know,
    And my spirit is grown to a lordly great compass within,
    That the length and the breadth and the sweep of the marshes of
            Glynn
    Will work me no fear like the fear they have wrought me of yore
    When length was fatigue, and when breadth was but bitterness sore,
    And when terror and shrinking and dreary unnamable pain
    Drew over me out of the merciless miles of the plain, —
        Oh, now, unafraid, I am fain to face
        The vast sweet visage of space.
    To the edge of the wood I am drawn, I am drawn,
Where the gray beach glimmering runs, as a belt of the dawn,
        For a mete and a mark
        To the forest-dark: —
            So:
    Affable live-oak, leaning low, —
Thus — with your favor — soft, with a reverent hand,
(Not lightly touching your person, Lord of the land!)
Bending your beauty aside, with a step I stand
        On the firm-packed sand,
            Free
By a world of marsh that borders a world of sea.
Sinuous southward and sinuous northward the shimmering band

Of the sand-beach fastens the fringe of the marsh to the folds of the
          land.
Inward and outward to northward and southward the beachlines linger
          and curl
As a silver-wrought garment that clings to and follows the firm sweet
          limbs of a girl.
Vanishing, swerving, evermore curving again into sight,
Softly the sand-beach wavers away to a dim gray looping of light.
And what if behind me to westward the wall of the woods stands
          high?
The world lies east: how ample, the marsh and the sea and the sky!
A league and a league of marsh-grass, waist-high, broad in the blade,
Green, and all of a height, and unflecked with a light or a shade,
    Stretch leisurely off, in a pleasant plain,
    To the terminal blue of the main.

    Oh, what is abroad in the marsh and the terminal sea?
        Somehow my soul seems suddenly free
From the weighing of fate and the sad discussion of sin,
    By the length and the breadth and the sweep of the marshes of Glynn,
Ye marshes, how candid and simple and nothing-withholding and free
Ye publish yourselves to the sky and offer yourselves to the sea!
Tolerant plains, that suffer the sea and the rains and the sun,
Ye spread and span like the catholic man who hath mightily won
    God out of knowledge and good out of infinite pain
    And sight out of blindness and purity out of a stain.

    As the marsh-hen secretly builds on the watery sod,
    Behold I will build me a nest on the greatness of God:
    I will fly in the greatness of God as the marsh-hen flies
    In the freedom that fills all the space 'twixt the marsh and the skies:
    By so many roots as the marsh-grass sends in the sod
    I will heartily lay me a-hold on the greatness of God:
    Oh, like to the greatness of God is the greatness within
    The range of the marshes, the liberal marshes of Glynn.
And the sea lends large, as the marsh: lo, out of his plenty the sea
    Pours fast: full soon the time of the flood-tide must be:
        Look how the grace of the sea doth go
    About and about through the intricate channels that flow
        Here and there,
        Everywhere,
Till his waters have flooded the uttermost creeks and the low-lying lanes,
    And the marsh is meshed with a million veins,

That like as with rosy and silvery essences flow
  In the rose-and-silver evening glow.
      Farewell, my lord Sun!
The creeks overflow: a thousand rivulets run
'Twixt the roots of the sod; the blades of the marsh-grass stir;
Passeth a hurrying sound of wings that westward whirr;
Passeth, and all is still; and the currents cease to run;
      And the sea and the marsh are one.

    How still the plains of the waters be!
    The tide is in his ecstasy.
    The tide is at his highest height:
        And it is night.

And now from the Vast of the Lord will the waters of sleep
    Roll in on the souls of men,
  But who will reveal to our waking ken
  The forms that swim and the shapes that creep
    Under the waters of sleep?
And I would I could know what swimmeth below when the tide comes in
On the length and the breadth of the marvellous marshes of Glynn.

Marsh Song — At Sunset

  Over the monstrous shambling sea,
      Over the Caliban sea,
  Bright Ariel-cloud, thou lingerest:
  Oh wait, oh wait, in the warm red West, —
      Thy Prospero I'll be.

  Over the humped and fishy sea,
      Over the Caliban sea,
  O cloud in the West, like a thought in the heart
  Of pardon, loose thy wing and start,
      And do a grace for me.

  Over the huge and huddling sea,
      Over the Caliban sea,
  Bring hither my brother Antonio, — Man, —
  My injurer: night breaks the ban;
      Brother, I pardon thee.

A Ballad of Trees and the Master

Into the woods my Master went,
    Clean forspent, forspent.
Into the woods my Master came,
    Forspent with love and shame.
But the olives they were not blind to Him,
The little gray leaves were kind to Him:
The thorn-tree had a mind to Him
    When into the woods He came.

Out of the woods my Master went,
    And He was well content.
Out of the woods my Master came,
    Content with death and shame.
When Death and Shame would woo Him last,
From under the trees they drew Him last:
'Twas on a tree they slew Him — last
    When out of the woods He came.

Thar's More in the Man Than Thar Is in the Land

I knowed a man, which he lived in Jones,
Which Jones is a county of red hills and stones,
And he lived pretty much by gittin' of loans,
And his mules was nuthin' but skin and bones,
And his hogs was flat as his corn-bread pones,
And he had 'bout a thousand acres o' land.

This man — which his name it was also Jones —
He swore that he'd leave them old red hills and stones,
Fur he couldn't make nuthin' but yallerish cotton,
And little o' *that*, and his fences was rotten,
And what little corn he had, *hit* was boughten,
And dinged ef a livin' was in the land.

And the longer he swore the madder he got,
And he riz and he walked to the stable lot,
And he hollered to Tom to come thar and hitch,
Fur to emigrate somewhar whar land was rich,
And to quit rasin' cock-burrs, thistles and sich,
And a wastin' ther time on the cussed land.

371

So him and Tom they hitched up the mules,
Pertestin' that folks was mighty big fools
That 'ud stay in Georgy ther lifetime out,
Jest scratchin' a livin' when all of 'em mought
Git places in Texas whar cotton would sprout
By the time you could plant it in the land.

And he driv by a house whar a man named Brown
Was a livin', not fur from the edge o' town,
And he bantered Brown fur to buy his place,
And said that bein' as money was skace,
And bein' as sheriffs was hard to face,
Two dollars an acre would git the land.

They closed at a dollar and fifty cents,
And Jones he bought him a waggin and tents,
And loaded his corn, and his wimmin, and truck,
And moved to Texas, which it tuck
His entire pile, with the best of luck,
To git thar and git him a little land.

But Brown moved out on the old Jones farm,
And he rolled up his breeches and bared his arm,
And he picked all the rocks from off'n the groun',
And he rooted it up and he plowed it down,
Then he sowed his corn and his wheat in the land.

Five years glid by, and Brown, one day
(Which he'd got so fat that he wouldn't weigh),
Was a settin' down, sorter lazily,
To the bulliest dinner you ever see,
When one o' the children jumped on his knee
And says, "Yan's Jones, which you bought his land."

And thar was Jones, standin' out at the fence,
And he hadn't no waggin, nor mules, nor tents,
Fur he had left Texas afoot and cum
To Georgy to see if he couldn't git sum
Employment, and he was a lookin' as hum-
Ble as ef he had never owned any land.

But Brown he axed him in, and he sot
Him down to his vittles smokin' hot,
And when he had filled hisself and the floor
Brown looked at him sharp and riz and swore
That, "whether men's land was rich or poor
Thar was more in the *man* than thar was in the *land*."

EDGAR LEE MASTERS
1868–1950

The Hill

Where are Elmer, Herman, Bert, Tom and Charley,
The weak of will, the strong of arm, the clown, the boozer, the fighter?
All, all, are sleeping on the hill.

One passed in a fever,
One was burned in a mine,
One was killed in a brawl,
One died in a jail,
One fell from a bridge toiling for children and wife —
All, all are sleeping, sleeping, sleeping on the hill.

Where are Ella, Kate, Mag, Lizzie and Edith,
The tender heart, the simple soul, the loud, the proud, the happy
    one? —
All, all, are sleeping on the hill.

One died in shameful child-birth,
One of a thwarted love,
One at the hands of a brute in a brothel,
One of a broken pride, in the search for heart's desire,
One after life in far-away London and Paris
Was brought to her little space by Ella and Kate and Mag —
All, all are sleeping, sleeping, sleeping on the hill.

Where are Uncle Isaac and Aunt Emily,
And old Towny Kincaid and Sevigne Houghton,
And Major Walker who had talked
With venerable men of the revolution? —
All, all, are sleeping on the hill.

They brought them dead sons from the war,
And daughters whom life had crushed,
And their children fatherless, crying —
All, all are sleeping, sleeping, sleeping on the hill.

Where is Old Fiddler Jones
Who played with life all his ninety years,
Braving the sleet with bared breast,
Drinking, rioting, thinking neither of wife nor kin,
Nor gold, nor love, nor heaven?
Lo! he babbles of the fish-frys of long ago,
Of the horse-races of long ago at Clary's Grove,
Of what Abe Lincoln said
One time at Springfield.

Petit, the Poet

Seeds in a dry pod, tick, tick, tick,
Tick, tick, tick, like mites in a quarrel —
Faint iambics that the full breeze wakens —
But the pine tree makes a symphony thereof.
Triolets, villanelles, rondels, rondeaus,
Ballades by the score with the same old thought:
The snows and the roses of yesterday are vanished;
And what is love but a rose that fades?
Life all around me here in the village:
Tragedy, comedy, valor and truth,
Courage, constancy, heroism, failure —
All in the loom, and oh what patterns!
Woodlands, meadows, streams and rivers —
Blind to all of it all my life long.
Triolets, villanelles, rondels, rondeaus,
Seeds in a dry pod, tick, tick, tick,
Tick, tick, tick, what little iambics,
While Homer and Whitman roared in the pines?

Editor Whedon

To be able to see every side of every question;
To be on every side, to be everything, to be nothing long;
To pervert truth, to ride it for a purpose,

To use great feelings and passions of the human family
For base designs, for cunning ends;
To wear a mask like the Greek actors —
Your eight-page paper — behind which you huddle,
Bawling through the megaphone of big type;
"This is I, the giant."
Thereby also living the life of a sneak-thief,
Poisoned with the anonymous words
Of your clandestine soul.
To scratch dirt over scandal for money,
And exhume it to the winds for revenge,
Or to sell papers,
Crushing reputations, or bodies, if need be;
To win at any cost, save your own life.
To glory in demoniac power, ditching civilization,
As a paranoiac boy puts a log on the track
And derails the express train.
To be an editor, as I was.
Then to lie here close by the river over the place
Where the sewage flows from the village,
And the empty cans and garbage are dumped,
And abortions are hidden.

Anne Rutledge

Out of me unworthy and unknown
The vibrations of deathless music;
"With malice toward none, with charity for all."
Out of me the forgiveness of millions toward millions,
And the beneficent face of a nation
Shining with justice and truth.
I am Anne Rutledge who sleep beneath these weeds,
Beloved in life of Abraham Lincoln,
Wedded to him, not through union,
But through separation.
Bloom forever, O Republic,
From the dust of my bosom!

Lucinda Matlock

I went to the dances at Chandlerville,
And played snap-out at Winchester
One time we changed partners,
Driving home in the moonlight of middle June,
And then I found Davis.
We were married and lived together for seventy years,
Enjoying, working, raising the twelve children,
Eight of whom we lost
Ere I had reached the age of sixty.
I spun, I wove, I kept the house, I nursed the sick,
I made the garden, and for holiday
Rambled over the fields where sang the larks,
And by Spoon River gathering many a shell,
And many a flower and medicinal weed —
Shouting to the wooded hills, singing to the green valleys.
At ninety-six I had lived enough, that is all,
And passed to a sweet repose.
What is this I hear of sorrow and weariness,
Anger, discontent and drooping hopes?
Degenerate sons and daughters,
Life is too strong for you —
It takes life to love Life.

WILLIAM VAUGHAN MOODY
1869–1910

Gloucester Moors

A mile behind is Gloucester town
Where the fishing fleets put in,
A mile ahead the land dips down
And the woods and farms begin.
Here, where the moors stretch free
In the high blue afternoon,
Are the marching sun and talking sea,
And the racing winds that wheel and flee
On the flying heels of June.

Jill-o'-er-the-ground is purple blue,
Blue is the quaker-maid,
The wild geranium holds its dew

Long in the boulder's shade.
Wax-red hangs the cup
From the huckleberry boughs,
In barberry bells the grey moths sup,
Or where the choke-cherry lifts high up
Sweet bowls for their carouse.

Over the shelf of the sandy cove
Beach-peas blossom late.
By copse and cliff the swallows rove
Each calling to his mate.
Seaward the sea-gulls go,
And the land-birds all are here;
That green-gold flash was a vireo,
And yonder flame where the marsh-flags grow
Was a scarlet tanager.

This earth is not the steadfast place
We landsmen build upon;
From deep to deep she varies pace,
And while she comes is gone.
Beneath my feet I feel
Her smooth bulk heave and dip;
With velvet plunge and soft upreel
She swings and steadies to her keel
Like a gallant, gallant ship.

These summer clouds she sets for sail,
The sun is her masthead light,
She tows the moon like a pinnace frail
Where her phosphor wake churns bright.
Now hid, now looming clear,
On the face of the dangerous blue
The star fleets tack and wheel and veer,
But on, but on does the old earth steer
As if her port she knew.

God, dear God! Does she know her port,
Though she goes so far about?
Or blind astray, does she make her sport
To brazen and chance it out?
I watched when her captains passed:
She were better captainless.

Men in the cabin, before the mast,
But some were reckless and some aghast,
And some sat gorged at mess.

By her battened hatch I leaned and caught
Sounds from the noisome hold, —
Cursing and sighing of souls distraught
And cries too sad to be told.
Then I strove to go down and see;
But they said, "Thou art not of us!"
I turned to those on the deck with me
And cried, "Give help!" But they said, "Let be:
Our ship sails faster thus."

Jill-o'-er-the-ground is purple blue,
Blue is the quaker-maid,
The alder-clump where the brook comes through
Breeds cresses in its shade.
To be out of the moiling street
With its swelter and its sin!
Who has given to me this sweet,
And given my brother dust to eat?
And when will his wage come in?

Scattering wide or blown in ranks,
Yellow and white and brown,
Boats and boats from the fishing banks
Come home to Gloucester town.
There is cash to purse and spend,
There are wives to be embraced,
Hearts to borrow and hearts to lend,
And hearts to take and keep to the end, —
O little sails, make haste!

But thou, vast outbound ship of souls,
What harbor town for thee?
What shapes, when thy arriving tolls,
Shall crowd the banks to see?
Shall all the happy shipmates then
Stand singing brotherly?
Or shall a haggard ruthless few
Warp her over and bring her to,

While the many broken souls of men
Fester down in the slaver's pen,
And nothing to say or do?

On a Soldier Fallen in the Philippines

Streets of the roaring town,
Hush for him, hush, be still!
He comes, who was stricken down
Doing the word of our will.
Hush! Let him have his state,
Give him his soldier's crown.
The grists of trade can wait
Their grinding at the mill,
But he cannot wait for his honor, now the trumpet has been blown;
Wreathe pride now for his granite brow, lay love on his breast of stone.

Toll! Let the great bells toll
Till the clashing air is dim.
Did we wrong this parted soul?
We will make up it to him.
Toll! Let him never guess
What work we set him to.
Laurel, laurel, yes;
He did what we bade him do.
Praise, and never a whispered hint but the fight he fought was good;
Never a word that the blood on his sword was his country's own heart's-
blood.

A flag for the soldier's bier
Who dies that his land may live;
O, banners, banners here,
That he doubt not nor misgive!
That he heed not from the tomb
The evil days draw near
When the nation, robed in gloom,
With its faithless past shall strive.
Let him never dream that his bullet's scream went wide of its island
mark,
Home to the heart of his darling land where she stumbled and sinned
in the dark.

EDWIN ARLINGTON ROBINSON
1869–1935

Luke Havergal

Go to the western gate, Luke Havergal,
There where the vines cling crimson on the wall,
And in the twilight wait for what will come.
The leaves will whisper there of her, and some,
Like flying words, will strike you as they fall;
But go, and if you listen she will call.
Go to the western gate, Luke Havergal —
Luke Havergal.

No, there is not a dawn in eastern skies
To rift the fiery night that's in your eyes;
But there, where western glooms are gathering,
The dark will end the dark, if anything:
God slays Himself with every leaf that flies,
And hell is more than half of paradise.
No, there is not a dawn in eastern skies —
In eastern skies.

Out of a grave I come to tell you this,
Out of a grave I come to quench the kiss
That flames upon your forehead with a glow
That blinds you to the way that you must go.
Yes, there is yet one way to where she is,
Bitter, but one that faith may never miss.
Out of a grave I come to tell you this —
To tell you this.

There is the western gate, Luke Havergal,
There are the crimson leaves upon the wall.
Go, for the winds are tearing them away, —
Nor think to riddle the dead words they say,
Nor any more to feel them as they fall;
But go, and if you trust her she will call.
There is the western gate, Luke Havergal —
Luke Havergal.

Richard Cory

Whenever Richard Cory went down town,
We people on the pavement looked at him:
He was a gentleman from sole to crown,
Clean favored, and imperially slim.

And he was always quietly arrayed,
And he was always human when he talked;
But still he fluttered pulses when he said,
"Good-morning," and he glittered when he walked.

And he was rich — yes, richer than a king —
And admirably schooled in every grace:
In fine, we thought that he was everything
To make us wish that we were in his place.

So on we worked, and waited for the light,
And went without the meat, and cursed the bread;
And Richard Cory, one calm summer night,
Went home and put a bullet through his head.

Reuben Bright

Because he was a butcher and thereby
Did earn an honest living (and did right),
I would not have you think that Reuben Bright
Was any more a brute than you or I:
For when they told him that his wife must die,
He stared at them, and shook with grief and fright,
And cried like a great baby half that night,
And made the women cry to see him cry.

And after she was dead, and he had paid
The singers and the sexton and the rest,
He packed a lot of things that she had made
Most mournfully away in an old chest
Of hers, and put some chopped-up cedar boughs
In with them, and tore down the slaughter house.

George Crabbe

Give him the darkest inch your shelf allows,
Hide him in lonely garrets, if you will, —
But his hard, human pulse is throbbing still
With the sure strength that fearless truth endows.
In spite of all fine science disavows,
Of his plain excellence and stubborn skill
There yet remains what fashion cannot kill,
Though years have thinned the laurel from his brows.

Whether or not we read him, we can feel
From time to time the vigor of his name
Against us like a finger for the shame
And emptiness of what our souls reveal
In books that are as altars where we kneel
To consecrate the flicker, not the flame.

How Annandale Went Out

"They called it Annandale — and I was there
  To flourish, to find words, and to attend:
  Liar, physician, hypocrite, and friend,
  I watched him; and the sight was not so fair
  As one or two that I have seen eleswhere:
  An apparatus not for me to mend —
  A wreck, with hell between him and the end,
  Remained of Annandale; and I was there.

"I knew the ruin as I knew the man;
  So put the two together, if you can,
  Remembering the worst you know of me.
  Now view yourself as I was, on the spot —
  With a slight kind of engine. Do you see?
  Like this . . . You wouldn't hang me? I thought not."

Miniver Cheevy

Miniver Cheevy, child of scorn,
  Grew lean while he assailed the seasons;
He wept that he was ever born,
  And he had reasons.

Miniver loved the days of old
    When swords were bright and steeds were prancing;
The vision of a warrior bold
    Would set him dancing.

Miniver sighed for what was not,
    And dreamed, and rested from his labors;
He dreamed of Thebes and Camelot,
    And Priam's neighbors.

Miniver mourned the ripe renown
    That made so many a name so fragrant;
He mourned Romance, now on the town,
    And Art, a vagrant.

Miniver loved the Medici,
    Albeit he had never seen one;
He would have sinned incessantly
    Could he have been one.

Miniver cursed the commonplace
    And eyed a khaki suit with loathing;
He missed the mediæval grace
    Of iron clothing.

Miniver scorned the gold he sought,
    But sore annoyed was he without it;
Miniver thought, and thought, and thought,
    And thought about it.

Miniver Cheevy, born too late,
    Scratched his head and kept on thinking;
Miniver coughed, and called it fate,
    And kept on drinking.

For a Dead Lady

No more with overflowing light
Shall fill the eyes that now are faded,
Nor shall another's fringe with night
Their woman-hidden world as they did.

No more shall quiver down the days
The flowing wonder of her ways,
Whereof no language may requite
The shifting and the many-shaded.

The grace, divine, definitive,
Clings only as a faint forestalling;
The laugh that love could not forgive
Is hushed, and answers to no calling;
The forehead and the little ears
Have gone where Saturn keeps the years;
The breast where roses could not live
Has done with rising and with falling.

The beauty, shattered by the laws
That have creation in their keeping,
No longer trembles at applause,
Or over children that are sleeping;
And we who delve in beauty's lore
Know all that we have known before
Of what inexorable cause
Makes Time so vicious in his reaping.

Eros Turannos

She fears him, and will always ask
   What fated her to choose him;
She meets in his engaging mask
   All reasons to refuse him;
But what she meets and what she fears
Are less than are the downward years,
Drawn slowly to the foamless weirs
   Of age, were she to lose him.

Between a blurred sagacity
   That once had power to sound him,
And Love, that will not let him be
   The Judas that she found him,
Her pride assuages her almost,
As if it were alone the cost. —
He sees that he will not be lost,
   And waits and looks around him.

A sense of ocean and old trees
   Envelops and allures him;
Tradition, touching all he sees,
   Beguiles and reassures him;
And all her doubts of what he says
Are dimmed with what she knows of days —
Till even prejudice delays
   And fades, and she secures him.

The falling leaf inaugurates
   The reign of her confusion:
The pounding wave reverberates
   The dirge of her illusion;
And home, where passion lived and died,
Becomes a place where she can hide,
While all the town and harbor side
   Vibrate with her seclusion.

We tell you, tapping on our brows,
   The story as it should be, —
As if the story of a house
   Were told, or ever could be;
We'll have no kindly veil between
Her visions and those we have seen, —
As if we guessed what hers have been,
   Or what they are or would be.

Meanwhile we do no harm; for they
   That with a god have striven,
Not hearing much of what we say,
   Take what the god has given;
Though like waves breaking it may be
Or like a changed familiar tree,
Or like a stairway to the sea
   Where down the blind are driven.

Veteran Sirens

The ghost of Ninon would be sorry now
To laugh at them, were she to see them here,
So brave and so alert for learning how
To fence with reason for another year.

Age offers a far comelier diadem
Than theirs; but anguish has no eye for grace,
When time's malicious mercy cautions them
To think a while of number and of space.

The burning hope, the worn expectancy,
The martyred humor, and the maimed allure,
Cry out for time to end his levity,
And age to soften its investiture;

But they, though others fade and are still fair,
Defy their fairness and are unsubdued;
Although they suffer, they may not forswear
The patient ardor of the unpursued.

Poor flesh, to fight the calendar so long;
Poor vanity, so quaint and yet so brave;
Poor folly, so deceived and yet so strong,
So far from Ninon and so near the grave.

Mr. Flood's Party

Old Eben Flood, climbing alone one night
Over the hill between the town below
And the forsaken upland hermitage
That held as much as he should ever know
On earth again of home, paused warily.
The road was his with not a native near;
And Eben, having leisure, said aloud,
For no man else in Tilbury Town to hear:

"Well, Mr. Flood, we have the harvest moon
Again, and we may not have many more;
The bird is on the wing, the poet says,
And you and I have said it here before.
Drink to the bird." He raised up to the light
The jug that he had gone so far to fill,
And answered huskily: "Well, Mr. Flood,
Since you propose it, I believe I will."

Alone, as if enduring to the end
A valiant armor of scarred hopes outworn,
He stood there in the middle of the road
Like Roland's ghost winding a silent horn.
Below him, in the town among the trees,
Where friends of other days had honored him,
A phantom salutation of the dead
Rang thinly till old Eben's eyes were dim.

Then, as a mother lays her sleeping child
Down tenderly, fearing it may awake,
He set the jug down slowly at his feet
With trembling care, knowing that most things break;
And only when assured that on firm earth
It stood, as the uncertain lives of men
Assuredly did not, he paced away,
And with his hand extended paused again:

"Well, Mr. Flood, we have not met like this
In a long time; and many a change has come
To both of us, I fear, since last it was
We had a drop together. Welcome home!"
Convivially returning with himself,
Again he raised the jug up to the light;
And with an acquiescent quaver said:
"Well, Mr. Flood, if you insist, I might.

"Only a very little, Mr. Flood —
For auld lang syne. No more, sir; that will do."
So, for the time, apparently it did,
And Eben evidently thought so too;
For soon amid the silver loneliness
Of night he lifted up his voice and sang,
Secure, with only two moons listening,
Until the whole harmonious landscape rang —

"For auld lang syne." The weary throat gave out,
The last word wavered, and the song was done.
He raised again the jug regretfully
And shook his head, and was again alone.
There was not much that was ahead of him,
And there was nothing in the town below —
Where strangers would have shut the many doors
That many friends had opened long ago.

The Sheaves

Where long the shadows of the wind had rolled,
Green wheat was yieding to the change assigned;
And as by some vast magic undivined
The world was turning slowly into gold.
Like nothing that was ever bought or sold
It waited there, the body and the mind;
And with a mighty meaning of a kind
That tells the more the more it is not told.

So in a land where all days are not fair,
Fair days went on till on another day
A thousand golden sheaves were lying there,
Shining and still, but not for long to stay —
As if a thousand girls with golden hair
Might rise from where they slept and go away.

Why He Was There

Much as he left it when he went from us
Here was the room again where he had been
So long that something of him should be seen,
Or felt — and so it was. Incredulous,
I turned about, loath to be greeted thus,
And there he was in his old chair, serene
As ever, and as laconic and as lean
As when he lived, and as cadaverous.

Calm as he was of old when we were young,
He sat there gazing at the pallid flame
Before him. "And how far will this go on?"
I thought. He felt the failure of my tongue,
And smiled: "I was not here until you came;
And I shall not be here when you are gone."

New England

Here where the wind is always north-north-east
And children learn to walk on frozen toes,
Wonder begets an envy of all those
Who boil elsewhere with such a lyric yeast

Of love that you will hear them at a feast
Where demons would appeal for some repose,
Still clamoring where the chalice overflows
And crying wildest who have drunk the least.

Passion is here a soilure of the wits,
We're told, and Love a cross for them to bear;
Joy shivers in the corner where she knits
And Conscience always has the rocking-chair,
Cheerful as when she tortured into fits
The first cat that was ever killed by Care.

Reunion

By some derision of wild circumstance
Not then our pleasure somehow to perceive,
Last night we fell together to achieve
A light eclipse of years. But the pale chance
Of youth resumed was lost. Time gave a glance
At each of us, and there was no reprieve;
And when there was at last a way to leave,
Farewell was a foreseen extravagance.

Tonight the west has yet a failing red,
While silence whispers of all things not here;
And round there where the fire was that is dead,
Dusk-hidden tenants that are chairs appear.
The same old stars will soon be overhead,
But not so friendly and not quite so near.

STEPHEN CRANE
1871–1900

In the desert

In the desert
I saw a creature, naked, bestial,
Who, squatting upon the ground,
Held his heart in his hands,
And ate of it.
I said: "Is it good, friend?"

"It is bitter — bitter," he answered;
"But I like it
    Because it is bitter,
    And because it is my heart."

I saw a man pursuing the horizon

I saw a man pursuing the horizon;
Round and round they sped.
I was disturbed at this;
I accosted the man.
"It is futile," I said,
"You can never —"

"You lie," he cried,
    And ran on.

Do not weep, maiden, for war is kind

Do not weep, maiden, for war is kind.
Because your lover threw wild hands toward the sky
And the affrighted steed ran on alone,
Do not weep.
War is kind.

    Hoarse, booming drums of the regiment,
    Little souls who thirst for fight,
    These men were born to drill and die.
    The unexplained glory flies above them,
    Great is the Battle-God, great, and his Kingdom —
    A field where a thousand corpses lie.

Do not weep, babe, for war is kind.
Because your father tumbled in the yellow trenches,
Raged at his breast, gulped and died,
Do not weep.
War is kind.

Swift blazing flag of the regiment,
Eagle with crest of red and gold,
These men were born to drill and die.
Point for them the virtue of slaughter,
Make plain to them the excellence of killing
And a field where a thousand corpses lie.

Mother whose heart hung humble as a button
On the bright splendid shroud of your son,
Do not weep.
War is kind.

TRUMBULL STICKNEY
1874–1904

In the Past

There lies a somnolent lake
Under a noiseless sky,
Where never the mornings break
Nor the evenings die.

Mad flakes of colour
Whirl on its even face
Iridescent and streaked with pallour;
And, warding the silent place,

The rocks rise sheer and gray
From the sedgeless brink to the sky
Dull-lit with the light of pale half-day
Thro' a void space and dry.

And the hours lag dead in the air
With a sense of coming eternity
To the heart of the lonely boatman there:
That boatman am I,

I, in my lonely boat,
A waif on the somnolent lake,
Watching the colours creep and float
With the sinuous track of a snake.

Now I lean o'er the side
And lazy shades in the water see,
Lapped in the sweep of a sluggish tide
Crawled in from the living sea;

And next I fix mine eyes,
So long that the heart declines,
On the changeless face of the open skies
Where no star shines;

And now to the rocks I turn,
To the rocks, around
That lie like walls of a circling urn
Wherein lie bound

The waters that feel my powerless strength
And meet my homeless oar
Labouring over their ashen length
Never to find a shore.

But the gleam still skims
At times on the somnolent lake,
And a light there is that swims
With the whirl of a snake;

And tho' dead be the hours i' the air,
And dayless the sky,
The heart is alive of the boatman there:
That boatman am I.

Mnemosyne

It's autumn in the country I remember.

How warm a wind blew here about the ways!
And shadows on the hillside lay to slumber
During the long sun-sweetened summer-days.

It's cold abroad the country I remember.

The swallows veering skimmed the golden grain
At midday with a wing aslant and limber;
And yellow cattle browsed upon the plain.

It's empty down the country I remember.

I had a sister lovely in my sight:
Her hair was dark, her eyes were very sombre;
We sang together in the woods at night.

It's lonely in the country I remember.

The babble of our children fills my ears,
And on our hearth I stare the perished ember
To flames that show all starry thro' my tears.

It's dark about the country I remember.

There are the mountains where I lived. The path
Is slushed with cattle-tracks and fallen timber,
The stumps are twisted by the tempests' wrath.

But that I knew these places are my own,
I'd ask how came such wretchedness to cumber
The earth, and I to people it alone.

It rains across the country I remember.

ROBERT FROST
1874–1963

The Pasture

I'm going out to clean the pasture spring;
I'll only stop to rake the leaves away
(And wait to watch the water clear, I may):
I shan't be gone long. — You come too.

I'm going out to fetch the little calf
That's standing by the mother. It's so young
It totters when she licks it with her tongue.
I shan't be gone long. — You come too.

Mowing

There was never a sound beside the wood but one,
And that was my long scythe whispering to the ground.
What was it it whispered? I knew not well myself;
Perhaps it was something about the heat of the sun,
Something, perhaps, about the lack of sound —
And that was why it whispered and did not speak.
It was no dream of the gift of idle hours,
Or easy gold at the hand of fay or elf:
Anything more than the truth would have seemed too weak
To the earnest love that laid the swale in rows,
Not without feeble-pointed spikes of flowers
(Pale orchises), and scared a bright green snake.
The fact is the sweetest dream that labor knows.
My long scythe whispered and left the hay to make.

Reluctance

Out through the fields and the woods
    And over the walls I have wended;
I have climbed the hills of view
    And looked at the world, and descended;
I have come by the highway home,
    And lo, it is ended.

The leaves are all dead on the ground,
    Save those that the oak is keeping
To ravel them one by one
    And let them go scraping and creeping
Out over the crusted snow,
    When others are sleeping.

And the dead leaves lie huddled and still,
    No longer blown hither and thither;
The last lone aster is gone;
    The flowers of the witch hazel wither;
The heart is still aching to seek,
    But the feet question "Whither?"

Ah, when to the heart of man
    Was it ever less than a treason
To go with the drift of things,
    To yield with a grace to reason,
And bow and accept the end
    Of a love or a season?

Mending Wall

Something there is that doesn't love a wall,
That sends the frozen-ground-swell under it
And spills the upper boulders in the sun,
And makes gaps even two can pass abreast.
The work of hunters is another thing:
I have come after them and made repair
Where they have left not one stone on a stone,
But they would have the rabbit out of hiding,
To please the yelping dogs. The gaps I mean,
No one has seen them made or heard them made,
But at spring mending-time we find them there.
I let my neighbor know beyond the hill;
And on a day we meet to walk the line
And set the wall between us once again.
We keep the wall between us as we go.
To each the boulders that have fallen to each.
And some are loaves and some so nearly balls
We have to use a spell to make them balance:
"Stay where you are until our backs are turned!"
We wear our fingers rough with handling them.
Oh, just another kind of outdoor game,
One on a side. It comes to little more:
There where it is we do not need the wall:
He is all pine and I am apple orchard.
My apple trees will never get across
And eat the cones under his pines, I tell him.
He only says, "Good fences make good neighbors."
Spring is the mischief in me, and I wonder
If I could put a notion in his head:
"Why do they make good neighbors? Isn't it
Where there are cows? But here there are no cows.
Before I built a wall I'd ask to know
What I was walling in or walling out,

And to whom I was like to give offense.
Something there is that doesn't love a wall,
That wants it down." I could say "Elves" to him,
But it's not elves exactly, and I'd rather
He said it for himself. I see him there,
Bringing a stone grasped firmly by the top
In each hand, like an old-stone savage armed.
He moves in darkness as it seems to me,
Not of woods only and the shade of trees.
He will not go behind his father's saying,
And he likes having thought of it so well
He says again, "Good fences make good neighbors."

After Apple-Picking

My long two-pointed ladder's sticking through a tree
Toward heaven still,
And there's a barrel that I didn't fill
Beside it, and there may be two or three
Apples I didn't pick upon some bough.
But I am done with apple-picking now.
Essence of winter sleep is on the night,
The scent of apples: I am drowsing off.
I cannot rub the strangeness from my sight
I got from looking through a pane of glass
I skimmed this morning from the drinking trough
And held against the world of hoary grass.
It melted, and I let it fall and break.
But I was well
Upon my way to sleep before it fell,
And I could tell
What form my dreaming was about to take.
Magnified apples appear and disappear,
Stem end and blossom end,
And every fleck of russet showing clear.
My instep arch not only keeps the ache,
It keeps the pressure of a ladder-round.
I feel the ladder sway as the boughs bend.
And I keep hearing from the cellar bin
The rumbling sound
Of load on load of apples coming in.
For I have had too much

Of apple-picking: I am overtired
Of the great harvest I myself desired.
There were ten thousand thousand fruit to touch,
Cherish in hand, lift down, and not let fall.
For all
That struck the earth,
No matter if not bruised or spiked with stubble,
Went surely to the cider-apple heap
As of no worth.
One can see what will trouble
This sleep of mine, whatever sleep it is.
Were he not gone,
The woodchuck could say whether it's like his
Long sleep, as I describe its coming on,
Or just some human sleep.

The Oven Bird

There is a singer everyone has heard,
Loud, a mid-summer and a mid-wood bird,
Who makes the solid tree trunks sound again.
He says that leaves are old and that for flowers
Mid-summer is to spring as one to ten.
He says the early petal-fall is past,
When pear and cherry bloom went down in showers
On sunny days a moment overcast;
And comes that other fall we name the fall.
He says the highway dust is over all.
The bird would cease and be as other birds
But that he knows in singing not to sing.
The question that he frames in all but words
Is what to make of a diminished thing.

from Two Witches

The Witch of Coös

I stayed the night for shelter at a farm
Behind the mountain, with a mother and son,
Two old-believers. They did all the talking.

Mother.   Folks think a witch who has familiar spirits
She could call up to pass a winter evening,
But won't, should be burned at the stake or something.
Summoning spirits isn't "Button, button,
Who's got the button," I would have them know.

Son.   Mother can make a common table rear
And kick with two legs like an army mule.

Mother.   And when I've done it, what good have I done?
Rather than tip a table for you, let me
Tell you what Ralle the Sioux Control once told me.
He said the dead had souls, but when I asked him
How could that be — I thought the dead were souls —
He broke my trance. Don't that make you suspicious
That there's something the dead are keeping back?
Yes, there's something the dead are keeping back.

Son.   You wouldn't want to tell him what we have
Up attic, mother?

Mother.   Bones — a skeleton.

Son.   But the headboard of mother's bed is pushed
Against the attic door: the door is nailed.
It's harmless. Mother hears it in the night,
Halting perplexed behind the barrier
Of door and headboard. Where it wants to get
Is back into the cellar where it came from.

Mother.   We'll never let them, will we, son? We'll never!

Son.   It left the cellar forty years ago
And carried itself like a pile of dishes
Up one flight from the cellar to the kitchen,
Another from the kitchen to the bedroom,
Another from the bedroom to the attic,
Right past both father and mother, and neither stopped it.
Father had gone upstairs; mother was downstairs.
I was a baby: I don't know where I was.

Mother.   The only fault my husband found with me —
I went to sleep before I went to bed,
Especially in winter when the bed

Might just as well be ice and the clothes snow.
The night the bones came up the cellar stairs
Toffile had gone to bed alone and left me,
But left an open door to cool the room off
So as to sort of turn me out of it.
I was just coming to myself enough
To wonder where the cold was coming from,
When I heard Toffile upstairs in the bedroom
And thought I heard him downstairs in the cellar.
The board we had laid down to walk dry-shod on
When there was water in the cellar in spring
Struck the hard cellar bottom. And then someone
Began the stairs, two footsteps for each step,
The way a man with one leg and a crutch,
Or a little child, comes up. It wasn't Toffile:
It wasn't anyone who could be there.
The bulkhead double doors were double-locked
And swollen tight and buried under snow.
The cellar windows were banked up with sawdust
And swollen tight and buried under snow.
It was the bones. I knew them — and good reason.
My first impulse was to get to the knob
And hold the door. But the bones didn't try
The door; they halted helpless on the landing,
Waiting for things to happen in their favor.
The faintest restless rustling ran all through them.
I never could have done the thing I did
If the wish hadn't been too strong in me
To see how they were mounted for this walk.
I had a vision of them put together
Not like a man, but like a chandelier.
So suddenly I flung the door wide on him.
A moment he stood balancing with emotion,
And all but lost himself. (A tongue of fire
Flashed out and licked along his upper teeth.
Smoke rolled inside the sockets of his eyes.)
Then he came at me with one hand outstretched,
The way he did in life once; but this time
I struck the hand off brittle on the floor,
And fell back from him on the floor myself.
The finger-pieces slid in all directions.
(Where did I see one of those pieces lately?
Hand me my button box — it must be there.)

I sat up on the floor and shouted, "Toffile,
It's coming up to you." It had its choice
Of the door to the cellar or the hall.
It took the hall door for the novelty,
And set off briskly for so slow a thing,
Still going every which way in the joints, though,
So that it looked like lightning or a scribble,
From the slap I had just now given its hand.
I listened till it almost climbed the stairs
From the hall to the only finished bedroom,
Before I got up to do anything;
Then ran and shouted, "Shut the bedroom door,
Toffile, for my sake!" "Company?" he said,
"Don't make me get up; I'm too warm in bed."
So lying forward weakly on the handrail
I pushed myself upstairs, and in the light
(The kitchen had been dark) I had to own
I could see nothing. "Toffile, I don't see it.
It's with us in the room, though. It's the bones."
"What bones?" "The cellar bones — out of the grave."
That made him throw his bare legs out of bed
And sit up by me and take hold of me.
I wanted to put out the light and see
If I could see it, or else mow the room,
With our arms at the level of our knees,
And bring the chalk-pile down. "I'll tell you what —
It's looking for another door to try.
The uncommonly deep snow has made him think
Of his old song, 'The Wild Colonial Boy,'
He always used to sing along the tote road.
He's after an open door to get outdoors.
Let's trap him with an open door up attic."
Toffile agreed to that, and sure enough,
Almost the moment he was given an opening,
The steps began to climb the attic stairs.
I heard them. Toffile didn't seem to hear them.
"Quick!" I slammed to the door and held the knob.
"Toffile, get nails." I made him nail the door shut
And push the headboard of the bed against it.
Then we asked was there anything
Up attic that we'd ever want again.
The attic was less to us than the cellar.
If the bones liked the attic, let them have it.

Let them stay in the attic. When they sometimes
Come down the stairs at night and stand perplexed
Behind the door and headboard of the bed,
Brushing their chalky skull with chalky fingers,
With sounds like the dry rattling of a shutter,
That's what I sit up in the dark to say —
To no one anymore since Toffile died.
Let them stay in the attic since they went there.
I promised Toffile to be cruel to them
For helping them be cruel once to him.

Son.   We think they had a grave down in the cellar.

Mother.   We know they had a grave down in the cellar.

Son.   We never could find out whose bones they were.

Mother.   Yes, we could too, son. Tell the truth for once.
They were a man's his father killed for me.
I mean a man he killed instead of me.
The least I could do was help dig their grave.
We were about it one night in the cellar.
Son knows the story: but 'twas not for him
To tell the truth, suppose the time had come.
Son looks surprised to see me end a lie
We'd kept up all these years between ourselves
So as to have it ready for outsiders.
But tonight I don't care enough to lie —
I don't remember why I ever cared.
Toffile, if he were here, I don't believe
Could tell you why he ever cared himself. . . .

She hadn't found the finger-bone she wanted
Among the buttons poured out in her lap.
I verified the name next morning: Toffile.
The rural letter box said Toffile Lajway.

Fire and Ice

Some say the world will end in fire,
Some say in ice.
From what I've tasted of desire

I hold with those who favor fire.
But if it had to perish twice,
I think I know enough of hate
To say that for destruction ice
Is also great
And would suffice.

Nothing Gold Can Stay

Nature's first green is gold,
Her hardest hue to hold.
Her early leaf's a flower;
But only so an hour.
Then leaf subsides to leaf.
So Eden sank to grief,
So dawn goes down to day.
Nothing gold can stay.

Stopping by Woods on a Snowy Evening

Whose woods these are I think I know.
His house is in the village, though;
He will not see me stopping here
To watch his woods fill up with snow.

My little horse must think it queer
To stop without a farmhouse near
Between the woods and frozen lake
The darkest evening of the year.

He gives his harness bells a shake
To ask if there is some mistake.
The only other sound's the sweep
Of easy wind and downy flake.

The woods are lovely, dark, and deep,
But I have promises to keep,
And miles to go before I sleep,
And miles to go before I sleep.

For Once, Then, Something

Others taunt me with having knelt at well-curbs
Always wrong to the light, so never seeing
Deeper down in the well than where the water
Gives me back in a shining surface picture
Me myself in the summer heaven, godlike,
Looking out of a wreath of fern and cloud puffs.
Once, when trying with chin against a well-curb,
I discerned, as I thought, beyond the picture,
Through the picture, a something white, uncertain,
Something more of the depths — and then I lost it.
Water came to rebuke the too clear water.
One drop fell from a fern, and lo, a ripple
Shook whatever it was lay there at bottom,
Blurred it, blotted it out. What was that whiteness?
Truth? A pebble of quartz? For once, then, something.

To Earthward

Love at the lips was touch
As sweet as I could bear;
And once that seemed too much;
I lived on air

That crossed me from sweet things,
The flow of — was it musk
From hidden grapevine springs
Downhill at dusk?

I had the swirl and ache
From sprays of honeysuckle
That when they're gathered shake
Dew on the knuckle.

I craved strong sweets, but those
Seemed strong when I was young;
The petal of the rose
It was that stung.

Now no joy but lacks salt,
That is not dashed with pain
And weariness and fault;
I crave the stain

Of tears, the aftermark
Of almost too much love,
The sweet of bitter bark
And burning clove.

When stiff and sore and scarred
I take away my hand
From leaning on it hard
In grass and sand,

The hurt is not enough:
I long for weight and strength
To feel the earth as rough
To all my length.

The Lockless Door

It went many years,
But at last came a knock,
And I thought of the door
With no lock to lock.

I blew out the light,
I tiptoed the floor,
And raised both hands
In prayer to the door.

But the knock came again.
My window was wide;
I climbed on the sill
And descended outside.

Back over the sill
I bade a "Come in"
To whatever the knock
At the door may have been.

So at a knock
I emptied my cage
To hide in the world
And alter with age.

The Need of Being Versed in Country Things

The house had gone to bring again
To the midnight sky a sunset glow.
Now the chimney was all of the house that stood,
Like a pistil after the petals go.

The barn opposed across the way,
That would have joined the house in flame
Had it been the will of the wind, was left
To bear forsaken the place's name.

No more it opened with all one end
For teams that came by the stony road
To drum on the floor with scurrying hoofs
And brush the mow with the summer load.

The birds that came to it through the air
At broken windows flew out and in,
Their murmur more like the sigh we sigh
From too much dwelling on what has been.

Yet for them the lilac renewed its leaf,
And the aged elm, though touched with fire;
And the dry pump flung up an awkward arm;
And the fence post carried a strand of wire.

For them there was really nothing sad.
But though they rejoiced in the nest they kept,
One had to be versed in country things
Not to believe the phoebes wept.

Spring Pools

These pools that, though in forests, still reflect
The total sky almost without defect,
And like the flowers beside them, chill and shiver,
Will like the flowers beside them soon be gone,
And yet not out by any brook or river,
But up by roots to bring dark foliage on.

The trees that have it in their pent-up buds
To darken nature and be summer woods —
Let them think twice before they use their powers
To blot out and drink up and sweep away
These flowery waters and these watery flowers
From snow that melted only yesterday.

Once by the Pacific

The shattered water made a misty din.
Great waves looked over others coming in,
And thought of doing something to the shore
That water never did to land before.
The clouds were low and hairy in the skies,
Like locks blown forward in the gleam of eyes.
You could not tell, and yet it looked as if
The shore was lucky in being backed by cliff,
The cliff in being backed by continent;
It looked as if a night of dark intent
Was coming, and not only a night, an age.
Someone had better be prepared for rage.
There would be more than ocean-water broken
Before God's last *Put out the Light* was spoken.

Acquainted with the Night

I have been one acquainted with the night.
I have walked out in rain — and back in rain.
I have outwalked the furthest city light.

I have looked down the saddest city lane.
I have passed by the watchman on his beat
And dropped my eyes, unwilling to explain.

I have stood still and stopped the sound of feet
When far away an interrupted cry
Came over houses from another street,

But not to call me back or say good-by;
And further still at an unearthly height
One luminary clock against the sky

Proclaimed the time was neither wrong nor right.
I have been one acquainted with the night.

The Lovely Shall Be Choosers

The Voice said, "Hurl her down!"

The Voices, "How far down?"

"Seven levels of the world."

"How much time have we?"

"Take twenty years.
She *would* refuse love safe with wealth and honor!
The lovely shall be choosers, shall they?
Then let them choose!"

"Then we shall let her choose?"

"Yes, let her choose.
Take up the task beyond her choosing."

Invisible hands crowded on her shoulder
In readiness to weigh upon her.
But she stood straight still,
In broad round earrings, gold and jet with pearls,
And broad round suchlike brooch,
Her cheeks high-colored,
Proud and the pride of friends.

The voice asked, "You can let her choose?"

"Yes, we can let her and still triumph."

"Do it by joys, and leave her always blameless.
Be her first joy her wedding,
That though a wedding,
Is yet — well, something they know, he and she.
And after that her next joy
That though she grieves, her grief is secret:
Those friends know nothing of her grief to make it shameful.

Her third joy that though now they cannot help but know,
They move in pleasure too far off
To think much or much care.
Give her a child at either knee for fourth joy
To tell once and once only, for them never to forget,
How once she walked in brightness,
And make them see it in the winter firelight.
But give her friends, for then she dare not tell
For their foregone incredulousness.
And be her next joy this:
Her never having deigned to tell them.
Make her among the humblest even
Seem to them less than they are.
Hopeless of being known for what she has been,
Failing of being loved for what she is,
Give her the comfort for her sixth of knowing
She fails from strangeness to a way of life
She came to from too high too late to learn.
Then send some *one* with eyes to see
And wonder at her where she is,
And words to wonder in her hearing how she came there,
But without time to linger for her story.
Be her last joy her heart's going out to this one
So that she almost speaks.
You know them — seven in all."

"Trust us," the Voices said.

West-Running Brook

"Fred, where is north?"

　　　　　　　　　　"North? North is there, my love.
　　　The brook runs west."

　　　　　　　　　　"West-Running Brook then call it."
(West-Running Brook men call it to this day.)
"What does it think it's doing running west
When all the other country brooks flow east
To reach the ocean? It must be the brook
Can trust itself to go by contraries

The way I can with you — and you with me —
Because we're — we're — I don't know what we are.
What are we?"

   "Young or new?"

      "We must be something.
We've said we two. Let's change that to we three.
As you and I are married to each other,
We'll both be married to the brook. We'll build
Our bridge across it, and the bridge shall be
Our arm thrown over it asleep beside it.
Look, look, it's waving to us with a wave
To let us know it hears me."

     "Why, my dear,
That wave's been standing off this jut of shore — "
(The black stream, catching on a sunken rock,
Flung backward on itself in one white wave,
And the white water rode the black forever,
Not gaining but not losing, like a bird
White feathers from the struggle of whose breast
Flecked the dark stream and flecked the darker pool
Below the point, and were at last driven wrinkled
In a white scarf against the far-shore alders.)
"That wave's been standing off this jut of shore
Ever since rivers, I was going to say,
Were made in heaven. It wasn't waved to us."

"It wasn't, yet it was. If not to you,
It was to me — in an annunciation."

"Oh, if you take it off to lady-land,
As 't were the country of the Amazons
We men must see you to the confines of
And leave you there, ourselves forbid to enter —
It is your brook! I have no more to say."

"Yes, you have, too. Go on. You thought of something."

"Speaking of contraries, see how the brook
In that white wave runs counter to itself.
It is from that in water we were from

409

Long, long before we were from any creature.
Here we, in our impatience of the steps,
Get back to the beginning of beginnings,
The stream of everything that runs away.
Some say existence like a Pirouot
And Pirouette, forever in one place,
Stands still and dances, but it runs away;
It seriously, sadly, runs away
To fill the abyss's void with emptiness.
It flows beside us in this water brook,
But it flows over us. It flows between us
To separate us for a panic moment.
It flows between us, over us, and *with* us.
And it is time, strength, tone, light, life, and love —
And even substance lapsing unsubstantial;
The universal cataract of death
That spends to nothingness — and unresisted,
Save by some strange resistance in itself,
Not just a swerving, but a throwing back,
As if regret were in it and were sacred.
It has this throwing backward on itself
So that the fall of most of it is always
Raising a little, sending up a little.
Our life runs down in sending up the clock.
The brook runs down in sending up our life.
The sun runs down in sending up the brook.
And there is something sending up the sun.
It is this backward motion toward the source,
Against the stream, that most we see ourselves in,
The tribute of the current to the source.
It is from this in nature we are from.
It is most us."

                "Today will be the day
You said so."

           "No, today will be the day
You said the brook was called West-Running Brook."

"Today will be the day of what we both said."

A Drumlin Woodchuck

One thing has a shelving bank,
Another a rotting plank,
To give it cozier skies
And make up for its lack of size.

My own strategic retreat
Is where two rocks almost meet,
And still more secure and snug,
A two-door burrow I dug.

With those in mind at my back
I can sit forth exposed to attack,
As one who shrewdly pretends
That he and the world are friends.

All we who prefer to live
Have a little whistle we give,
And flash, at the least alarm
We dive down under the farm.

We allow some time for guile
And don't come out for a while,
Either to eat or drink.
We take occasion to think.

And if after the hunt goes past
And the double-barreled blast
(Like war and pestilence
And the loss of common sense),

If I can with confidence say
That still for another day,
Or even another year,
I will be there for you, my dear,

It will be because, though small
As measured against the All,
I have been so instinctively thorough
About my crevice and burrow.

Departmental

An ant on the tablecloth
Ran into a dormant moth
Of many times his size.
He showed not the least surprise.
His business wasn't with such.
He gave it scarcely a touch,
And was off on his duty run.
Yet if he encountered one
Of the hive's enquiry squad
Whose work is to find out God
And the nature of time and space,
He would put him onto the case.
Ants are a curious race;
One crossing with hurried tread
The body of one of their dead
Isn't given a moment's arrest —
Seems not even impressed.
But he no doubt reports to any
With whom he crosses antennae,
And they no doubt report
To the higher-up at court.
Then word goes forth in Formic:
"Death's come to Jerry McCormic,
Our selfless forager Jerry.
With the special Janizary
Whose office it is to bury
The dead of the commissary
Go bring him home to his people.
Lay him in state on a sepal.
Wrap him for shroud in a petal.
Embalm him with ichor of nettle.
This is the word of your Queen."
And presently on the scene
Appears a solemn mortician;
And taking formal position,
With feelers calmly atwiddle,
Seizes the dead by the middle,
And heaving him high in air,
Carries him out of there.
No one stands round to stare.
It is nobody else's affair.

It couldn't be called ungentle.
But how thoroughly departmental.

Desert Places

Snow falling and night falling fast, oh, fast
In a field I looked into going past,
And the ground almost covered smooth in snow,
But a few weeds and stubble showing last.

The woods around it have it — it is theirs.
All animals are smothered in their lairs.
I am too absent-spirited to count;
The loneliness includes me unawares.

And lonely as it is, that loneliness
Will be more lonely ere it will be less —
A blanker whiteness of benighted snow
With no expression, nothing to express.

They cannot scare me with their empty spaces
Between stars — on stars where no human race is.
I have it in me so much nearer home
To scare myself with my own desert places.

Leaves Compared with Flowers

A tree's leaves may be ever so good,
So may its bark, so may its wood;
But unless you put the right thing to its root
It never will show much flower or fruit.

But I may be one who does not care
Ever to have tree bloom or bear.
Leaves for smooth and bark for rough,
Leaves and bark may be tree enough.

Some giant trees have bloom so small
They might as well have none at all.
Late in life I have come on fern.
Now lichens are due to have their turn.

I bade men tell me which in brief,
Which is fairer, flower or leaf.
They did not have the wit to say,
Leaves by night and flowers by day.

Leaves and bark, leaves and bark,
To lean against and hear in the dark.
Petals I may have once pursued.
Leaves are all my darker mood.

Neither Out Far Nor In Deep

The people along the sand
All turn and look one way.
They turn their back on the land.
They look at the sea all day.

As long as it takes to pass
A ship keeps raising its hull;
The wetter ground like glass
Reflects a standing gull.

The land may vary more;
But wherever the truth may be —
The water comes ashore,
And the people look at the sea.

They cannot look out far.
They cannot look in deep.
But when was that ever a bar
To any watch they keep?

Design

I found a dimpled spider, fat and white,
On a white heal-all, holding up a moth
Like a white piece of rigid satin cloth —
Assorted characters of death and blight
Mixed ready to begin the morning right,
Like the ingredients of a witches' broth —
A snow-drop spider, a flower like a froth,
And dead wings carried like a paper kite.

What had that flower to do with being white,
The wayside blue and innocent heal-all?
What brought the kindred spider to that height,
Then steered the white moth thither in the night?
What but design of darkness to appall? —
If design govern in a thing so small.

Provide, Provide

The witch that came (the withered hag)
To wash the steps with pail and rag
Was once the beauty Abishag,

The picture pride of Hollywood.
Too many fall from great and good
For you to doubt the likelihood.

Die early and avoid the fate.
Or if predestined to die late,
Make up your mind to die in state.

Make the whole stock exchange your own!
If need be occupy a throne,
Where nobody can call *you* crone.

Some have relied on what they knew,
Others on being simply true.
What worked for them might work for you.

No memory of having starred
Atones for later disregard
Or keeps the end from being hard.

Better to go down dignified
With boughten friendship at your side
Than none at all. Provide, provide!

The Silken Tent

She is as in a field a silken tent
At midday when a sunny summer breeze
Has dried the dew and all its ropes relent,

So that in guys it gently sways at ease,
And its supporting central cedar pole,
That is its pinnacle to heavenward
And signifies the sureness of the soul,
Seems to owe naught to any single cord,
But strictly held by none, is loosely bound
By countless silken ties of love and thought
To everything on earth the compass round,
And only by one's going slightly taut
In the capriciousness of summer air
Is of the slightest bondage made aware.

Come In

As I came to the edge of the woods,
Thrush music — hark!
Now if it was dusk outside,
Inside it was dark.

Too dark in the woods for a bird
By sleight of wing
To better its perch for the night,
Though it still could sing.

The last of the light of the sun
That had died in the west
Still lived for one song more
In a thrush's breast.

Far in the pillared dark
Thrush music went —
Almost like a call to come in
To the dark and lament.

But no, I was out for stars:
I would not come in.
I meant not even if asked,
And I hadn't been.

The Subverted Flower

She drew back; he was calm:
"It is this that had the power."
And he lashed his open palm
With the tender-headed flower.
He smiled for her to smile,
But she was either blind
Or willfully unkind.
He eyed her for a while
For a woman and a puzzle.
He flicked and flung the flower,
And another sort of smile
Caught up like fingertips
The corners of his lips
And cracked his ragged muzzle.
She was standing to the waist
In goldenrod and brake,
Her shining hair displaced.
He stretched her either arm
As if she made it ache
To clasp her — not to harm;
As if he could not spare
To touch her neck and hair.
"If this has come to us
And not to me alone ——"
So she thought she heard him say;
Though with every word he spoke
His lips were sucked and blown
And the effort made him choke
Like a tiger at a bone.
She had to lean away.
She dared not stir a foot,
Lest movement should provoke
The demon of pursuit
That slumbers in a brute.
It was then her mother's call
From inside the garden wall
Made her steal a look of fear
To see if he could hear
And would pounce to end it all
Before her mother came.
She looked and saw the shame:

417

A hand hung like a paw,
An arm worked like a saw
As if to be persuasive,
An ingratiating laugh
That cut the snout in half,
An eye become evasive.
A girl could only see
That a flower had marred a man,
But what she could not see
Was that the flower might be
Other than base and fetid:
That the flower had done but part,
And what the flower began
Her own too meager heart
Had terribly completed.
She looked and saw the worst.
And the dog or what it was,
Obeying bestial laws,
A coward save at night,
Turned from the place and ran.
She heard him stumble first
And use his hands in flight.
She heard him bark outright.
And oh, for one so young
The bitter words she spit
Like some tenacious bit
That will not leave the tongue.
She plucked her lips for it,
And still the horror clung.
Her mother wiped the foam
From her chin, picked up her comb,
And drew her backward home.

The Gift Outright

The land was ours before we were the land's.
She was our land more than a hundred years
Before we were her people. She was ours
In Massachusetts, in Virginia,
But we were England's, still colonials,
Possessing what we still were unpossessed by,
Possessed by what we now no more possessed.

Something we were withholding made us weak
Until we found out that it was ourselves
We were withholding from our land of living,
And forthwith found salvation in surrender.
Such as we were we gave ourselves outright
(The deed of gift was many deeds of war)
To the land vaguely realizing westward,
But still unstoried, artless, unenhanced,
Such as she was, such as she would become.

Directive

Back out of all this now too much for us,
Back in a time made simple by the loss
Of detail, burned, dissolved, and broken off
Like graveyard marble sculpture in the weather,
There is a house that is no more a house
Upon a farm that is no more a farm
And in a town that is no more a town.
The road there, if you'll let a guide direct you
Who only has at heart your getting lost,
May seem as if it should have been a quarry —
Great monolithic knees the former town
Long since gave up pretense of keeping covered.
And there's a story in a book about it:
Besides the wear of iron wagon wheels
The ledges show lines ruled southeast-northwest,
The chisel work of an enormous Glacier
That braced his feet against the Arctic Pole.
You must not mind a certain coolness from him
Still said to haunt this side of Panther Mountain.
Nor need you mind the serial ordeal
Of being watched from forty cellar holes
As if by eye pairs out of forty firkins.
As for the woods' excitement over you
That sends light rustle rushes to their leaves,
Charge that to upstart inexperience.
Where were they all not twenty years ago?
They think too much of having shaded out
A few old pecker-fretted apple trees.
Make yourself up a cheering song of how
Someone's road home from work this once was,
Who may be just ahead of you on foot

Or creaking with a buggy load of grain.
The height of the adventure is the height
Of country where two village cultures faded
Into each other. Both of them are lost.
And if you're lost enough to find yourself
By now, pull in your ladder road behind you
And put a sign up CLOSED to all but me.
Then make yourself at home. The only field
Now left's no bigger than a harness gall.
First there's the children's house of make-believe,
Some shattered dishes underneath a pine,
The playthings in the playhouse of the children.
Weep for what little things could make them glad.
Then for the house that is no more a house,
But only a belilaced cellar hole,
Now slowly closing like a dent in dough.
This was no playhouse but a house in earnest.
Your destination and your destiny's
A brook that was the water of the house,
Cold as a spring as yet so near its source,
Too lofty and original to rage.
(We know the valley streams that when aroused
Will leave their tatters hung on barb and thorn.)
I have kept hidden in the instep arch
Of an old cedar at the waterside
A broken drinking goblet like the Grail
Under a spell so the wrong ones can't find it,
So can't get saved, as Saint Mark says they mustn't.
(I stole the goblet from the children's playhouse.)
Here are your waters and your watering place.
Drink and be whole again beyond confusion.

The Middleness of the Road

The road at the top of the rise
Seems to come to an end
And take off into the skies.
So at the distant bend

It seems to go into a wood,
The place of standing still
As long the trees have stood.
But say what Fancy will,

420

The mineral drops that explode
To drive my ton of car
Are limited to the road.
They deal with near and far,

But have almost nothing to do
With the absolute flight and rest
The universal blue
And local green suggest.

Away!

Now I out walking
The world desert,
And my shoe and my stocking
Do me no hurt.

I leave behind
Good friends in town.
Let them get well-wined
And go lie down.

Don't think I leave
For the outer dark
Like Adam and Eve
Put out of the Park.

Forget the myth.
There is no one I
Am put out with
Or put out by.

Unless I'm wrong
I but obey
The urge of a song:
"I'm — bound — away!"

And I may return
If dissatisfied
With what I learn
From having died.

CARL SANDBURG
1878–1967

Chicago

Hog Butcher for the World,
Tool Maker, Stacker of Wheat,
Player with Railroads and the Nation's Freight Handler;
Stormy, husky, brawling,
City of the Big Shoulders:

They tell me you are wicked and I believe them, for I have seen your
painted women under the gas lamps luring the farm boys.
And they tell me you are crooked and I answer: Yes, it is true I have
seen the gunman kill and go free to kill again.
And they tell me you are brutal and my reply is: On the faces of women
and children I have seen the marks of wanton hunger.
And having answered so I turn once more to those who sneer at this my
city, and I give them back the sneer and say to them:
Come and show me another city with lifted head singing so proud to be
alive and coarse and strong and cunning.
Flinging magnetic curses amid the toil of piling job on job, here is a tall
bold slugger set vivid against the little soft cities;
Fierce as a dog with tongue lapping for action, cunning as a savage pitted
against the wilderness,
  Bareheaded,
  Shoveling,
  Wrecking,
  Planning,
  Building, breaking, rebuilding,
Under the smoke, dust all over his mouth, laughing with white teeth,
Under the terrible burden of destiny laughing as a young man laughs,
Laughing even as an ignorant fighter laughs who has never lost a battle,
Bragging and laughing that under his wrist is the pulse, and under his
ribs the heart of the people,
              Laughing!
Laughing the stormy, husky, brawling laughter of Youth, half-naked,
sweating, proud to be Hog Butcher, Tool Maker, Stacker of Wheat,
Player with Railroads and Freight Handler to the Nation.

Gone

Everybody loved Chick Lorimer in our town.
              Far off
              Everybody loved her.
So we all love a wild girl keeping a hold
              On a dream she wants.
Nobody knows now where Chick Lorimer went.
Nobody knows why she packed her trunk . . . a few old things
And is gone,
                        Gone with her little chin
                        Thrust ahead of her
                        And her soft hair blowing careless
                        From under a wide hat,
Dancer, singer, a laughing passionate lover.

Were there ten men or a hundred hunting Chick?
Were there five men or fifty with aching hearts?
              Everybody loved Chick Lorimer.
              Nobody knows where she's gone.

Cool Tombs

When Abraham Lincoln was shoveled into the tombs, he forgot the copperheads and the assassin . . . in the dust, in the cool tombs.

And Ulysses Grant lost all thought of con men and Wall Street, cash and collateral turned ashes . . . in the dust, in the cool tombs.

Pocahontas' body, lovely as a poplar, sweet as a red haw in November or a pawpaw in May, did she wonder? does she remember? . . . in the dust, in the cool tombs?

Take any streetful of people buying clothes and groceries, cheering a hero or throwing confetti and blowing tin horns . . . tell me if the lovers are losers . . . tell me if any get more than the lovers . . . in the dust . . . in the cool tombs.

Grass

              Pile the bodies high at Austerlitz and Waterloo.
              Shovel them under and let me work —
                        I am the grass; I cover all.

And pile them high at Gettysburg
And pile them high at Ypres and Verdun.
Shovel them under and let me work.
Two years, ten years, and passengers ask the conductor:
What place is this?
Where are we now?

I am the grass.
Let me work.

Gargoyle

I saw a mouth jeering. A smile of melted red iron ran over it. Its laugh
was full of nails rattling. It was a child's dream of a mouth.
A fist hit the mouth: knuckles of gun-metal driven by an electric wrist
and shoulder. It was a child's dream of an arm.
The fist hit the mouth over and over, again and again. The mouth bled
melted iron, and laughed its laughter of nails rattling.
And I saw the more the fist pounded the more the mouth laughed. The
fist is pounding and pounding, and the mouth answering.

They All Want to Play Hamlet

They all want to play Hamlet.
They have not exactly seen their fathers killed
Nor their mothers in a frame-up to kill,
Nor an Ophelia dying with a dust gagging the heart,
Not exactly the spinning circles of singing golden spiders,
Not exactly this have they got at nor the meaning of flowers — O
flowers, flowers slung by a dancing girl — in the saddest play the
inkfish, Shakespeare, ever wrote;
Yet they all want to play Hamlet because it is sad like all actors are sad
and to stand by an open grave with a joker's skull in the hand and
then to say over slow and say over slow wise, keen, beautiful words
masking a heart that's breaking, breaking,
This is something that calls and calls to their blood.
They are acting when they talk about it and they know it is acting to be
particular about it and yet: They all want to play Hamlet.

424

Soup

I saw a famous man eating soup.
I say he was lifting a fat broth
Into his mouth with a spoon.
His name was in the newspapers that day
Spelled out in tall black headlines
And thousands of people were talking about him.

When I saw him,
He sat bending his head over a plate
Putting soup in his mouth with a spoon.

Aprons of Silence

Many things I might have said today.
And I kept my mouth shut.
So many times I was asked
To come and say the same things
Everybody was saying, no end
To the yes-yes, yes-yes,
      me-too, me-too.

The aprons of silence covered me.
A wire and hatch held my tongue.
I spit nails into an abyss and listened.
I shut off the gabble of Jones, Johnson, Smith,
All whose names take pages in the city directory.

I fixed up a padded cell and lugged it around.
I locked myself in and nobody knew it.
Only the keeper and the kept in the hoosegow
Knew it — on the streets, in the post office,
On the cars, into the railroad station
Where the caller was calling, "All a-board,
All a-board for . . . Blaa-blaa . . . Blaa-blaa,
Blaa-blaa . . . and all points northwest . . . all a-board."
Here I took along my own hoosegow
And did business with my own thoughts.
Do you see? It must be the aprons of silence.

Four Preludes on Playthings of the Wind
The past is a bucket of ashes.

1

The woman named Tomorrow
sits with a hairpin in her teeth
and takes her time
and does her hair the way she wants it
and fastens at last the last braid and coil
and puts the hairpin where it belongs
and turns and drawls: Well, what of it?
My grandmother, Yesterday, is gone.
What of it? Let the dead be dead.

2

The doors were cedar
and the panels strips of gold
and the girls were golden girls
and the panels read and the girls chanted:
    We are the greatest city,
    the greatest nation:
    nothing like us ever was.
The doors are twisted on broken hinges.
Sheets of rain swish through on the wind
    where the golden girls ran and the panels read:
    We are the greatest city,
    the greatest nation,
    nothing like us ever was.

3

It has happened before.
Strong men put up a city and got
    a nation together,
And paid singers to sing and women
    to warble: We are the greatest city,
    the greatest nation,
    nothing like us ever was.

And while the singers sang
and the strong men listened
and paid the singers well
and felt good about it all,
    there were rats and lizards who listened
    . . . and the only listeners left now
    . . . are . . . the rats . . . and the lizards.

And there are black crows
crying, "Caw, caw,"
bringing mud and sticks
building a nest
over the words carved
on the doors where the panels were cedar
and the strips on the panels were gold
and the golden girls came singing:
> We are the greatest city,
> the greatest nation:
> nothing like us ever was.

The only singers now are crows crying, "Caw, caw,"
And the sheets of rain whine in the wind and doorways.
And the only listeners now are . . . the rats . . . and the lizards.

4

The feet of the rats
scribble on the doorsills;
the hieroglyphs of the rat footprints
chatter the pedigrees of the rats
and babble of the blood
and gabble of the breed
of the grandfathers and the great-grandfathers
of the rats.

And the wind shifts
and the dust on a doorsill shifts
and even the writing of the rat footprints
tells us nothing, nothing at all
about the greatest city, the greatest nation
where the strong men listened
and the women warbled: Nothing like us ever was.

from The People, Yes

107

The people will live on.
The learning and blundering people will live on.
They will be tricked and sold and again sold
And go back to the nourishing earth for rootholds,
The people so peculiar in renewal and comeback,

You can't laugh off their capacity to take it.
The mammoth rests between his cyclonic dramas.

The people so often sleepy, weary, enigmatic,
is a vast huddle with many units saying:
    "I earn my living.
    I make enough to get by
    and it takes all my time.
    If I had more time
    I could do more for myself
    and maybe for others.
    I could read and study
    and talk things over
    and find out about things.
    It takes time.
    I wish I had the time."
The people is a tragic and comic two-face:
hero and hoodlum: phantom and gorilla twist-
ing to moan with a gargoyle mouth: "They
buy me and sell me . . . it's a game . . .
sometime I'll break loose . . ."

    Once having marched
Over the margins of animal necessity,
Over the grim line of sheer subsistence
    Then man came
To the deeper rituals of his bones,
To the lights lighter than any bones,
To the time for thinking things over,
To the dance, the song, the story,
Or the hours given over to dreaming,
    Once having so marched.

Between the finite limitations of the five senses
and the endless yearnings of man for the beyond
the people hold to the humdrum bidding of work and food
while reaching out when it comes their way
for lights beyond the prisms of the five senses,
for keepsakes lasting beyond any hunger or death.
    This reaching is alive.
The panderers and liars have violated and smutted it.
    Yet this reaching is alive yet
    for lights and keepsakes.

The people know the salt of the sea
and the strength of the winds
lashing the corners of the earth.
The people take the earth
as a tomb of rest and a cradle of hope.
Who else speaks for the Family of Man?
They are in tune and step
with constellations of universal law.

The people is a polychrome,
a spectrum and a prism
held in a moving monolith,
a console organ of changing themes,
a clavilux of color poems
wherein the sea offers fog
and the fog moves off in rain
and the labrador sunset shortens
to a nocturne of clear stars
serene over the shot spray
of northern lights.

The steel mill sky is alive.
The fire breaks white and zigzag
shot on a gun-metal gloaming.
Man is a long time coming.
Man will yet win.
Brother may yet line up with brother:

This old anvil laughs at many broken hammers.
There are men who can't be bought.
The fireborn are at home in fire.
The stars make no noise.
You can't hinder the wind from blowing.
Time is a great teacher.
Who can live without hope?

In the darkness with a great bundle of grief
the people march.
In the night, and overhead a shovel of stars for
keeps, the people march:
                    "Where to? what next?"

VACHEL LINDSAY
1879–1931

General William Booth
Enters into Heaven

(To be sung to the tune of "The Blood of the Lamb"
with indicated instrument)

I

(Bass drum beaten loudly.)
Booth led boldly with his big bass drum —
(Are you washed in the blood of the Lamb?)
The Saints smiled gravely and they said: "He's come."
(Are you washed in the blood of the Lamb?)
Walking lepers followed, rank on rank,
Lurching bravos from the ditches dank,
Drabs from the alleyways and drug fiends pale —
Minds still passion-ridden, soul-powers frail: —
Vermin-eaten saints with moldy breath,
Unwashed legions with the ways of Death —
(Are you washed in the blood of the Lamb?)

(Banjos.)
Every slum had sent its half-a-score
The round world over. (Booth had groaned for more.)
Every banner that the wide world flies
Bloomed with glory and transcendent dyes.
Big-voiced lasses made their banjos bang,
Tranced, fanatical they shrieked and sang: —
"Are you washed in the blood of the Lamb?"
Hallelujah! It was queer to see
Bull-necked convicts with that land make free.
Loons with trumpets blowed a blare, blare, blare
On, on upward thro' the golden air!
(Are you washed in the blood of the Lamb?)

II

(Bass drum slower and softer.)
Booth died blind and still by faith he trod,
Eyes still dazzled by the ways of God.
Booth led boldly, and he looked the chief
Eagle countenance in sharp relief,
Beard a-flying, air of high command
Unabated in that holy land.

430

(*Sweet flute music.*)
Jesus came from out the court-house door,
Stretched his hands above the passing poor.
Booth saw not, but led his queer ones there
Round and round the mighty court-house square.
Then, in an instant all that blear review
Marched on spotless, clad in raiment new.
The lame were straightened, withered limbs uncurled
And blind eyes opened on a new, sweet world.

(*Bass drum louder.*)
Drabs and vixens in a flash made whole!
Gone was the weasel-head, the snout, the jowl!
Sages and sibyls now, and athletes clean,
Rulers of empires, and of forests green!

(*Grand chorus of all instruments. Tambourines to the
foreground.*)
The hosts were sandalled, and their wings were fire!
(Are you washed in the blood of the Lamb?)
But their noise played havoc with the angel-choir.
(Are you washed in the blood of the Lamb?)
Oh, shout Salvation! It was good to see
Kings and Princes by the Lamb set free.
The banjos rattled and the tambourines
Jing-jing-jingled in the hands of Queens.

(*Reverently sung, no instruments.*)
And when Booth halted by the curb for prayer
He saw his Master thro' the flag-filled air.
Christ came gently with a robe and crown
For Booth the soldier, while the throng knelt down.
He saw King Jesus. They were face to face,
And he knelt a-weeping in that holy place.
Are you washed in the blood of the Lamb?

The Eagle That Is Forgotten

(John P. Altgeld. Born December 30, 1847; died March 12, 1902)

Sleep softly . . . eagle forgotten . . . under the stone.
Time has its way with you there, and the clay has its own.

431

"We have buried him now," thought your foes, and in secret rejoiced.
They made a brave show of their mourning, their hatred unvoiced.

They had snarled at you, barked at you, foamed at you day after day.
Now you were ended. They praised you, . . . and laid you away.

The others that mourned you in silence and terror and truth,
The widow bereft of her crust, and the boy without youth,
The mocked and the scorned and the wounded, the lame and the poor
That should have remembered forever, . . . remember no more.

Where are those lovers of yours, on what name do they call
The lost, that in armies wept over your funeral pall?
They call on the names of a hundred high-valiant ones,
A hundred white eagles have risen the sons of your sons,
The zeal in their wings is a zeal that your dreaming began
The valor that wore out your soul in the service of man.

Sleep softly, . . . eagle forgotten, . . . under the stone,
Time has its way with you there and the clay has its own.
Sleep on, O brave-hearted, O wise man, that kindled the flame —
To live in mankind is far more than to live in a name,
To live in mankind, far, far more . . . than to live in a name.

The Congo

A Study of the Negro Race

(Being a memorial to Ray Eldred, a Disciple missionary of
the Congo River)

I. Their Basic Savagery

Fat black bucks in a wine-barrel room,
Barrel-house kings, with feet unstable,

A deep rolling bass.   Sagged and reeled and pounded on the table,
Pounded on the table,
Beat an empty barrel with the handle of a broom,
Hard as they were able,
Boom, boom, Boom,
With a silk umbrella and the handle of a broom,
Boomlay, boomlay, boomlay, Boom.
Then I had religion, Then I had a vision.

I could not turn from their revel in derision.

More deliberate. Solemnly chanted. THEN I SAW THE CONGO, CREEPING THROUGH THE BLACK,
CUTTING THROUGH THE FOREST WITH A GOLDEN TRACK.
Then along that riverbank
A thousand miles
Tattooed cannibals danced in files;
Then I heard the boom of the blood-lust song

A rapidly piling climax of speed and racket. And a thigh-bone beating on a tin-pan gong.
And "BLOOD" screamed the whistles and the fifes of the warriors,
"BLOOD" screamed the skull-faced, lean witch-doctors,
"Whirl ye the deadly voo-doo rattle,
Harry the uplands,
Steal all the cattle,
Rattle-rattle, rattle-rattle,
Bing.
Boomlay, boomlay, boomlay, BOOM,"

With a philosophic pause. A roaring, epic, rag-time tune
From the mouth of the Congo
To the Mountains of the Moon.
Death is an Elephant,

Shrilly and with a heavily accented metre. Torch-eyed and horrible,
Foam-flanked and terrible.
BOOM, steal the pygmies,
BOOM, kill the Arabs,
BOOM, kill the white men,
HOO, HOO, HOO.

Like the wind in the chimney. Listen to the yell of Leopold's ghost
Burning in Hell for his hand-maimed host.
Hear how the demons chuckle and yell
Cutting his hands off, down in Hell.
Listen to the creepy proclamation,
Blown through the lairs of the forest-nation,
Blown past the white-ants' hill of clay,
Blown past the marsh where the butterflies play: —
"Be careful what you do,

All the "o" sounds very golden. Heavy accents very heavy. Light accents very light. Last line whispered. Or Mumbo-Jumbo, God of the Congo,
And all of the other
Gods of the Congo,
Mumbo-Jumbo will hoo-doo you,
Mumbo-Jumbo will hoo-doo you,
Mumbo-Jumbo will hoo-doo you."

II. *Their Irrepressible High Spirits*

<table>
<tr><td>

Rather shrill
and high.
</td><td>

Wild crap-shooters with a whoop and a call
Danced the juba in their gambling hall
And laughed fit to kill, and shook the town,
And guyed the policemen and laughed them down
With a boomlay, boomlay, boomlay, Boom.
</td></tr>
</table>

Rather shrill
and high.

Wild crap-shooters with a whoop and a call
Danced the juba in their gambling hall
And laughed fit to kill, and shook the town,
And guyed the policemen and laughed them down
With a boomlay, boomlay, boomlay, Boom.

Read exactly
as in first
section.

THEN I SAW THE CONGO, CREEPING THROUGH THE BLACK,
CUTTING THROUGH THE FOREST WITH A GOLDEN TRACK.
A Negro fairyland swung into view,

Lay emphasis
on the delicate
ideas. Keep as
light-footed as
possible.

A minstrel river
Where dreams come true.
The ebony palace soared on high
Through the blossoming trees to the evening sky.
The inlaid porches and casements shone
With gold and ivory and elephant-bone.
And the black crowd laughed till their sides were sore
At the baboon butler in the agate door,
And the well-known tunes of the parrot band
That trilled on the bushes of that magic land.

With
pomposity.

A troupe of skull-faced witch-men came
Through the agate doorway in suits of flame,
Yea, long-tailed coats with a gold-leaf crust
And hats that were covered with diamond-dust.
And the crowd in the court gave a whoop and a call
And danced the juba from wall to wall.

With a great
deliberation
and ghostliness.

But the witch-men suddenly stilled the throng
With a stern cold glare, and a stern old song: —
"Mumbo-Jumbo will hoo-doo you.". . .

With
overwhelming
assurance, good
cheer, and
pomp.

Just then from the doorway, as fat as shotes,
Came the cake-walk princes in their long red coats,
Canes with a brilliant lacquer shine,
And tall silk hats that were red as wine.

With growing
speed and
sharply marked
dance-rhythm.

And they pranced with their butterfly partners there,
Coal-black maidens with pearls in their hair,
Knee-skirts trimmed with the jassamine sweet,
And bells on their ankles and little black-feet.
And the couples railed at the chant and the frown
Of the witch-men lean, and laughed them down.
(Oh, rare was the revel, and well worth while
That made those glowing witch-men smile.)

With a touch
of negro dialect,
and as rapidly as
possible toward
the end.

The cake-walk royalty then began
To walk for a cake that was tall as a man
To the tune of "Boomlay, boomlay, BOOM,"
While the witch-men laughed, with a sinister air,
And sang with the scalawags prancing there: —
"Walk with care, walk with care,
Or Mumbo-Jumbo, God of the Congo,
And all of the other Gods of the Congo,
Mumbo-Jumbo will hoo-doo you.
Beware, beware, walk with care,
Boomlay, boomlay, boomlay, boom.
Boomlay, boomlay, boomlay, boom.
Boomlay, boomlay, boomlay, boom.
Boomlay, boomlay, boomlay,
BOOM."

Slow
philosophic
calm.

(Oh, rare was the revel, and well worth while
That made those glowering witch-men smile.)

III. *The Hope of Their Religion*

Heavy bass.
With a literal
imitation of
camp-meeting
racket, and
trance.

A good old Negro in the slums of the town
Preached at a sister for her velvet gown.
Howled at a brother for his low-down ways,
His prowling, guzzling, sneak-thief days.
Beat on the Bible till he wore it out
Starting the jubilee revival shout.
And some had visions, as they stood on chairs,
And sang of Jacob, and the golden stairs,
And they all repented, a thousand strong
From their stupor and savagery and sin and wrong
And slammed with their hymn books till they shook the
    room
With "glory, glory, glory,"
And "Boom, boom, BOOM."

Exactly as in
the first
section.
Begin with
terror and
power, end
with joy.

THEN I SAW THE CONGO, CREEPING THROUGH THE BLACK,
CUTTING THROUGH THE JUNGLE WITH A GOLDEN TRACK.
And the gray sky opened like a new-rent veil
And showed the Apostles with their coats of mail.
In bright white steel they were seated round
And their fire-eyes watched where the Congo wound.
And the twelve Apostles, from their thrones on high
Thrilled all the forest with their heavenly cry: —

Sung to the
tune of "Hark,
ten thousand
harps and
voices."

"Mumbo-Jumbo will die in the jungle.
Never again will he hoo-doo you,
Never again will he hoo-doo you.

With growing
deliberation
and joy.

Then along that river, a thousand miles
The vine-snared trees fell down in files.
Pioneer angels cleared the way
For a Congo paradise, for babes at play,
For sacred capitals, for temples clean.
Gone were the skull-faced witch-men lean.

In a rather
high key — as
delicately as
possible.

There, where the wild ghost-gods had wailed
A million boats of the angels sailed
With oars of silver, and prows of blue
And silken pennants that the sun shone through.
'Twas a land transfigured, 'twas a new creation.
Oh, a singing wind swept the negro nation
And on through the backwoods clearing flew: —

To the tune of
"Hark, ten
thousand harps
and voices."

"Mumbo-Jumbo is dead in the jungle.
Never again will he hoo-doo you.
Never again will he hoo-doo you."

Redeemed were the forests, the beasts and the men,
And only the vulture dared again
By the far, lone mountains of the moon

Dying down
into a
penetrating,
terrified
whisper.

To cry, in the silence, the Congo tune: —
"Mumbo-Jumbo will hoo-doo you,
Mumbo-Jumbo will hoo-doo you.
Mumbo . . . Jumbo . . .will . . . hoo-doo . . . you."

Abraham Lincoln Walks at Midnight

It is portentous, and a thing of state
That here at midnight, in our little town
A mourning figure walks, and will not rest,
Near the old court-house pacing up and down,

Or by his homestead, or in shadowed yards
He lingers where his children used to play,
Or through the market, on the well-worn stones
He stalks until the dawn-stars burn away.

A bronzed, lank man! His suit of ancient black,
A famous high top-hat and plain worn shawl
Make him the quaint great figure that men love,
The prairie-lawyer, master of us all.

He cannot sleep upon his hillside now.
He is among us: — as in times before!
And we who toss and lie awake for long
Breathe deep, and start, to see him pass the door.

His head is bowed. He thinks on men and kings.
Yea, when the sick world cries, how can he sleep?
Too many peasants fight, they know not why,
Too many homesteads in black terror weep.

The sins of all the war-lords burn his heart.
He sees the dreadnaughts scouring every main.
He carries on his shawl-wrapped shoulders now
The bitterness, the folly and the pain.

He cannot rest until a spirit-dawn
Shall come; — the shining hope of Europe free:
The league of sober folk, the Workers' Earth,
Bringing long peace to Cornland, Alp and Sea.

It breaks his heart that kings must murder still,
That all his hours of travail here for men
Seem yet in vain. And who will bring white peace
That he may sleep upon his hill again?

The Flower-fed Buffaloes

The flower-fed buffaloes of the spring
In the days of long ago,
Ranged where the locomotives sing
And the prairie flowers lie low: —
The tossing, blooming, perfumed grass
Is swept away by the wheat,
Wheels and wheels and wheels spin by
In the spring that still is sweet.
But the flower-fed buffaloes of the spring
Left us, long ago.

They gore no more, they bellow no more,
They trundle around the hills no more: —
With the Blackfeet, lying low,
With the Pawnees, lying low,
Lying low.

WALLACE STEVENS
1879–1955

Peter Quince at the Clavier

I

Just as my fingers on these keys
Make music, so the selfsame sounds
On my spirit make a music, too.

Music is feeling, then, not sound;
And thus it is that what I feel,
Here in this room, desiring you,

Thinking of your blue-shadowed silk,
Is music. It is like the strain
Waked in the elders by Susanna.

Of a green evening, clear and warm,
She bathed in her still garden, while
The red-eyed elders watching, felt

The basses of their beings throb
In witching chords, and their thin blood
Pulse pizzicati of Hosanna.

II

In the green water, clear and warm,
Susanna lay.
She searched
The touch of springs,
And found
Concealed imaginings.
She sighed,
For so much melody.

Upon the bank, she stood
In the cool
Of spent emotions.
She felt, among the leaves,
The dew
Of old devotions.

She walked upon the grass,
Still quavering.
The winds were like her maids,
On timid feet,
Fetching her woven scarves,
Yet wavering.

A breath upon her hand
Muted the night.
She turned —
A cymbal crashed,
And roaring horns.

III

Soon, with a noise like tambourines,
Came her attendant Byzantines.

They wondered why Susanna cried
Against the elders by her side;

And as they whispered, the refrain
Was like a willow swept by rain.

Anon, their lamps' uplifted flame
Revealed Susanna and her shame.

And then, the simpering Byzantines
Fled, with a noise like tambourines.

IV

Beauty is momentary in the mind —
The fitful tracing of a portal;
But in the flesh it is immortal.
The body dies; the body's beauty lives.
So evenings die, in their green going,
A wave, interminably flowing.

So gardens die, their meek breath scenting
The cowl of winter, done repenting.
So maidens die, to the auroral
Celebration of a maiden's choral.
Susanna's music touched the bawdy strings
Of those white elders; but, escaping,
Left only Death's ironic scraping.
Now, in its immortality, it plays
On the clear viol of her memory,
And makes a constant sacrament of praise.

Thirteen Ways of Looking at a Blackbird

I

Among twenty snowy mountains,
The only moving thing
Was the eye of the blackbird.

II

I was of three minds,
Like a tree
In which there are three blackbirds.

III

The blackbird whirled in the autumn winds.
It was a small part of the pantomime.

IV

A man and a woman
Are one.
A man and a woman and a blackbird
Are one.

V

I do not know which to prefer,
The beauty of inflections
Or the beauty of innuendoes,
The blackbird whistling
Or just after.

VI

Icicles filled the long window
With barbaric glass.

The shadow of the blackbird
Crossed it, to and fro.
The mood
Traced in the shadow
An indecipherable cause.

VII
O thin men of Haddam,
Why do you imagine golden birds?
Do you not see how the blackbird
Walks around the feet
Of the women about you?

VIII
I know noble accents
And lucid, inescapable rhythms;
But I know, too,
That the blackbird is involved
In what I know.

IX
When the blackbird flew out of sight,
It marked the edge
Of one of many circles.

X
At the sight of blackbirds
Flying in a green light,
Even the bawds of euphony
Would cry out sharply.

XI
He rode over Connecticut
In a glass coach.
Once, a fear pierced him,
In that he mistook
The shadow of his equipage
For blackbirds.

XII
The river is moving.
The blackbird must be flying.

XIII

It was evening all afternoon.
It was snowing
And it was going to snow.
The blackbird sat
In the cedar-limbs.

Sunday Morning

I

Complacencies of the peignoir, and late
Coffee and oranges in a sunny chair,
And the green freedom of a cockatoo
Upon a rug mingle to dissipate
The holy hush of ancient sacrifice.
She dreams a little, and she feels the dark
Encroachment of that old catastrophe,
As a calm darkens among water-lights.
The pungent oranges and bright, green wings
Seem things in some procession of the dead,
Winding across wide water, without sound.
The day is like wide water, without sound,
Stilled for the passing of her dreaming feet
Over the seas, to silent Palestine,
Dominion of the blood and sepulchre.

II

Why should she give her bounty to the dead?
What is divinity if it can come
Only in silent shadows and in dreams?
Shall she not find in comforts of the sun,
In pungent fruit and bright, green wings, or else
In any balm or beauty of the earth,
Things to be cherished like the thought of heaven?
Divinity must live within herself:
Passions of rain, or moods in falling snow;
Grievings in loneliness, or unsubdued
Elations when the forest blooms; gusty
Emotions on wet roads on autumn nights;
All pleasures and all pains, remembering
The bough of summer and the winter branch.
These are the measures destined for her soul.

III

Jove in the clouds had his inhuman birth.
No mother suckled him, no sweet land gave
Large-mannered motions to his mythy mind.
He moved among us, as a muttering king,
Magnificent, would move among his hinds,
Until our blood, commingling, virginal,
With heaven, brought such requital to desire
The very hinds discerned it, in a star.
Shall our blood fail? Or shall it come to be
The blood of paradise? And shall the earth
Seem all of paradise that we shall know?
The sky will be much friendlier then than now,
A part of labor and a part of pain,
And next in glory to enduring love,
Not this dividing and indifferent blue.

IV

She says, "I am content when wakened birds,
Before they fly, test the reality
Of misty fields, by their sweet questionings;
But when the birds are gone, and their warm fields
Return no more, where, then, is paradise?"
There is not any haunt of prophecy,
Nor any old chimera of the grave,
Neither the golden underground, nor isle
Melodious, where spirits gat'them home,
Nor visionary south, nor cloudy palm
Remote on heaven's hill, that has endured
As April's green endures; or will endure
Like her remembrance of awakened birds,
Or her desire for June and evening, tipped
By the consummation of the swallow's wings.

V

She says, "But in contentment I still feel
The need of some imperishable bliss."
Death is the mother of beauty; hence from her,
Alone, shall come fulfilment to our dreams
And our desires. Although she strews the leaves
Of sure obliteration on our paths,
The path sick sorrow took, the many paths
Where triumph rang its brassy phrase, or love

Whispered a little out of tenderness,
She makes the willow shiver in the sun
For maidens who were wont to sit and gaze
Upon the grass, relinquished to their feet.
She causes boys to pile new plums and pears
On disregarded plate. The maidens taste
And stray impassioned in the littering leaves.

VI

Is there no change of death in paradise?
Does ripe fruit never fall? Or do the boughs
Hang always heavy in that perfect sky,
Unchanging, yet so like our perishing earth,
With rivers like our own that seek for seas
They never find, the same receding shores
That never touch with inarticulate pang?
Why set the pear upon those river-banks
Or spice the shores with odors of the plum?
Alas, that they should wear our colors there,
The silken weavings of our afternoons,
And pick the strings of our insipid lutes!
Death is the mother of beauty, mystical,
Within whose burning bosom we devise
Our earthly mothers waiting, sleeplessly.

VII

Supple and turbulent, a ring of men
Shall chant in orgy on a summer morn
Their boisterous devotion to the sun,
Not as a god, but as a god might be,
Naked among them, like a savage source.
Their chant shall be a chant of paradise,
Out of their blood, returning to the sky;
And in their chant shall enter, voice by voice,
The windy lake wherein their lord delights,
The trees, like serafin, and echoing hills,
That choir among themselves long afterward.
They shall know well the heavenly fellowship
Of men that perish and of summer morn.
And whence they came and whither they shall go
The dew upon their feet shall manifest.

VIII

She hears, upon that water without sound,
A voice that cries, "The tomb in Palestine
Is not the porch of spirits lingering.
It is the grave of Jesus, where he lay."
We live in an old chaos of the sun,
Or old dependency of day and night,
Or island solitude, unsponsored, free,
Of that wide water, inescapable.
Deer walk upon our mountains, and the quail
Whistle about us their spontaneous cries;
Sweet berries ripen in the wilderness;
And, in the isolation of the sky,
At evening, casual flocks of pigeons make
Ambiguous undulations as they sink,
Downward to darkness, on extended wings.

A High-Toned Old Christian Woman

Poetry is the supreme fiction, madame.
Take the moral law and make a nave of it
And from the nave build haunted heaven. Thus,
The conscience is converted into palms,
Like windy citherns hankering for hymns.
We agree in principle. That's clear. But take
The opposing law and make a peristyle,
And from the peristyle project a masque
Beyond the planets. Thus, our bawdiness,
Unpurged by epitaph, indulged at last,
Is equally converted into palms,
Squiggling like saxophones. And palm for palm,
Madame, we are where we began. Allow,
Therefore, that in the planetary scene
Your disaffected flagellants, well-stuffed,
Smacking their muzzy bellies in parade,
Proud of such novelties of the sublime,
Such tink and tank and tunk-a-tunk-tunk,
May, merely may, madame, whip from themselves
A jovial hullabaloo among the spheres.
This will make widows wince. But fictive things
Wink as they will. Wink most when widows wince.

The Emperor of Ice-Cream

Call the roller of big cigars,
The muscular one, and bid him whip
In kitchen cups concupiscent curds.
Let the wenches dawdle in such dress
As they are used to wear, and let the boys
Bring flowers in last month's newspapers.
Let be be finale of seem.
The only emperor is the emperor of ice-cream.

Take from the dresser of deal,
Lacking the three glass knobs, that sheet
On which she embroidered fantails once
And spread it so as to cover her face.
If her horny feet protrude, they come
To show how cold she is, and dumb.
Let the lamp affix its beam.
The only emperor is the emperor of ice-cream.

Bantams in Pine-Woods

Chieftain Iffucan of Azcan in caftan
Of tan with henna hackles, halt!

Damned universal cock, as if the sun
Was blackamoor to bear your blazing tail.

Fat! Fat! Fat! Fat! I am the personal.
Your world is you. I am my world.

You ten-foot poet among inchlings. Fat!
Begone! An inchling bristles in these pines,

Bristles, and points their Appalachian tangs,
And fears not portly Azcan nor his hoos.

Anecdote of the Jar

I placed a jar in Tennessee,
And round it was, upon a hill.
It made the slovenly wilderness
Surround that hill.

The wilderness rose up to it,
And sprawled around, no longer wild
The jar was round upon the ground
And tall and of a port in air.

It took dominion everywhere.
The jar was gray and bare.
It did not give of bird or bush,
Like nothing else in Tennessee.

Dance of the Macabre Mice

In the land of turkeys in turkey weather
At the base of the statue, we go round and round.
What a beautiful history, beautiful surprise!
Monsieur is on horseback. The horse is covered with mice.

This dance has no name. It is a hungry dance.
We dance it out to the tip of Monsieur's sword,
Reading the lordly language of the inscription,
Which is like zithers and tambourines combined:

The Founder of the State. Whoever founded
A state that was free, in the dead of winter, from mice?
What a beautiful tableau tinted and towering,
The arm of bronze outstretched against all evil!

The Idea of Order at Key West

She sang beyond the genius of the sea.
The water never formed to mind or vice,
Like a body wholly body, fluttering
Its empty sleeves; and yet its mimic motion
Made constant cry, caused constantly a cry,
That was not ours although we understood,
Inhuman, of the veritable ocean.

The sea was not a mask. No more was she.
The song and water were not medleyed sound
Even if what she sang was what she heard,
Since what she sang was uttered word by word.

It may be that in all her phrases stirred
The grinding water and the gasping wind;
But it was she and not the sea we heard.

For she was the maker of the song she sang.
The ever-hooded, tragic-gestured sea
Was merely a place by which she walked to sing.
Whose spirit is this? we said, because we knew
It was the spirit that we sought and knew
That we should ask this often as she sang.

If it was only the dark voice of the sea
That rose, or even colored by many waves;
If it was only the outer voice of sky
And cloud, of the sunken coral water-walled,
However clear, it would have been deep air,
The heaving speech of air, a summer sound
Repeated in a summer without end
And sound alone. But it was more than that,
More even than her voice, and ours, among
The meaningless plungings of water and the wind,
Theatrical distances, bronze shadows heaped
On high horizons, mountainous atmospheres
Of sky and sea.
         It was her voice that made
The sky acutest at its vanishing.
She measured to the hour its solitude.
She was the single artificer of the world
In which she sang. And when she sang, the sea,
Whatever self it had, became the self
That was her song, for she was the maker. Then we,
As we beheld her striding there alone,
Knew that there never was a world for her
Except the one she sang and, singing, made.

Ramon Fernandez, tell me, if you know,
Why, when the singing ended and we turned
Toward the town, tell why the glassy lights,
The lights in the fishing boats at anchor there,
As the night descended, tilting in the air,
Mastered the night and portioned out the sea,
Fixing emblazoned zones and fiery poles,
Arranging, deepening, enchanting night.

Oh! Blessed rage for order, pale Ramon,
The maker's rage to order words of the sea,
Words of the fragrant portals, dimly-starred,
And of ourselves and of our origins,
In ghostlier demarcations, keener sounds.

Dry Loaf

It is equal to living in a tragic land
To live in a tragic time.
Regard now the sloping, mountainous rocks
And the river that batters its way over stones,
Regard the hovels of those that live in this land.

That was what I painted behind the loaf,
The rocks not even touched by snow,
The pines along the river and the dry men blown
Brown as the bread, thinking of birds
Flying from burning countries and brown sand shores,

Birds that came like dirty water in waves
Flowing above the rocks, flowing over the sky,
As if the sky was a current that bore them along,
Spreading them as waves spread flat on the shore,
One after another washing the mountains bare.

It was the battering of drums I heard.
It was hunger, it was the hungry that cried
And the waves, the waves were soldiers moving,
Marching and marching in a tragic time
Below me, on the asphalt, under the trees.

It was soldiers went marching over the rocks
And still the birds came, came in watery flocks,
Because it was spring and the birds had to come.
No doubt that soldiers had to be marching
And that drums had to be rolling, rolling, rolling.

The Sense of the Sleight-of-hand Man

One's grand flights, one's Sunday baths,
One's tootings at the weddings of the soul
Occur as they occur. So bluish clouds
Occurred above the empty house and the leaves
Of the rhododendrons rattled their gold,
As if someone lived there. Such floods of white
Came bursting from the clouds. So the wind
Threw its contorted strength around the sky.

Could you have said the bluejay suddenly
Would swoop to earth? It is a wheel, the rays
Around the sun. The wheel survives the myths.
The fire eye in the clouds survives the gods.
To think of a dove with an eye of grenadine
And pines that are comets, so it occurs,
And a little island full of geese and stars:
It may be that the ignorant man, alone,
Has any chance to mate his life with life
That is the sensual, pearly spouse, the life
That is fluent in even the wintriest bronze.

from Notes Toward a Supreme Fiction

To Henry Church

And for what, except for you, do I feel love?
Do I press the extremest book of the wisest man
Close to me, hidden in me day and night?
In the uncertain light of single, certain truth,
Equal in living changingness to the light
In which I meet you, in which we sit at rest,
For a moment in the central of our being,
The vivid transparence that you bring is peace.

It Must Be Abstract

I

Begin, ephebe, by perceiving the idea
Of this invention, this invented world,
The inconceivable idea of the sun.

You must become an ignorant man again
And see the sun again with an ignorant eye
And see it clearly in the idea of it.

Never suppose an inventing mind as source
Of this idea nor for that mind compose
A voluminous master folded in his fire.

How clean the sun when seen in its idea,
Washed in the remotest cleanliness of a heaven
That has expelled us and our images . . .

The death of one god is the death of all.
Let purple Phoebus lie in umber harvest,
Let Phoebus slumber and die in autumn umber,

Phoebus is dead, ephebe. But Phoebus was
A name for something that never could be named.
There was a project for the sun and is.

There is a project for the sun. The sun
Must bear no name, gold flourisher, but be
In the difficulty of what it is to be.

IV

The first idea was not our own. Adam
In Eden was the father of Descartes
And Eve made air the mirror of herself,

Of her sons and of her daughters. They found themselves
In heaven as in a glass; a second earth;
And in the earth itself they found a green —

The inhabitants of a very varnished green.
But the first idea was not to shape the clouds
In imitation. The clouds preceded us

There was a muddy centre before we breathed.
There was a myth before the myth began,
Venerable and articulate and complete.

From this the poem springs: that we live in a place
That is not our own and, much more, not ourselves
And hard it is in spite of blazoned days.

We are the mimics. Clouds are pedagogues
The air is not a mirror but bare board,
Coulisse bright-dark, tragic chiaroscuro

And comic color of the rose, in which
Abysmal instruments make sounds like pips
Of the sweeping meanings that we add to them.

VII

It feels good as it is without the giant,
A thinker of the first idea. Perhaps
The truth depends on a walk around a lake,

A composing as the body tires, a stop
To see hepatica, a stop to watch
A definition growing certain and

A wait within that certainty, a rest
In the swags of pine-trees bordering the lake.
Perhaps there are times of inherent excellence,

As when the cock crows on the left and all
Is well, incalculable balances,
At which a kind of Swiss perfection comes

And a familiar music of the machine
Sets up its Schwärmerei, not balances
That we achieve but balances that happen,

As a man and woman meet and love forthwith.
Perhaps there are moments of awakening,
Extreme, fortuitous, personal, in which

We more than awaken, sit on the edge of sleep,
As on an elevation, and behold
The academies like structures in a mist.

X

The major abstraction is the idea of man
And major man is its exponent, abler
In the abstract than in his singular,

More fecund as principle than particle,
Happy fecundity, flor-abundant force,
In being more than an exception, part,

Though an heroic part, of the commonal.
The major abstraction is the commonal,
The inanimate, difficult visage. Who is it?

What rabbi, grown furious with human wish,
What chieftain, walking by himself, crying
Most miserable, most victorious,

Does not see these separate figures one by one,
And yet see only one, in his old coat,
His slouching pantaloons, beyond the town,

Looking for what was, where it used to be?
Cloudless the morning. It is he. The man
In that old coat, those sagging pantaloons,

It is of him, ephebe, to make, to confect
The final elegance, not to console
Nor sanctify, but plainly to propound.

. . .

Soldier, there is a war between the mind
And sky, between thought and day and night. It is
For that the poet is always in the sun,

Patches the moon together in his room
To his Virgilian cadences, up down,
Up down. It is a war that never ends.

Yet it depends on yours. The two are one.
They are a plural, a right and left, a pair,
Two parallels that meet if only in

The meeting of their shadows or that meet
In a book in a barrack, a letter from Malay.
But your war ends. And after it you return

With six meats and twelve wines or else without
To walk another room . . . Monsieur and comrade,
The soldier is poor without the poet's lines,

His petty syllabi, the sounds that stick,
Inevitably modulating, in the blood.
And war for war, each has its gallant kind.

How simply the fictive hero becomes the real;
How gladly with proper words the soldier dies,
If he must, or lives on the bread of faithful speech.

from Esthétique du Mal

I

He was at Naples writing letters home
And, between his letters, reading paragraphs
On the sublime. Vesuvius had groaned
For a month. It was pleasant to be sitting there,
While the sultriest fulgurations, flickering,
Cast corners in the glass. He could describe
The terror of the sound because the sound
Was ancient. He tried to remember the phrases: pain
Audible at noon, pain torturing itself,
Pain killing pain on the very point of pain.
The volcano trembled in another ether,
As the body trembles at the end of life.

It was almost time for lunch. Pain is human.
There were roses in the cool café. His book
Made sure of the most correct catastrophe.
Except for us, Vesuvius might consume
In solid fire the utmost earth and know
No pain (ignoring the cocks that crow us up
To die). This is a part of the sublime

From which we shrink. And yet, except for us,
The total past felt nothing when destroyed.

VI

The sun, in clownish yellow, but not a clown,
Brings the day to perfection and then fails. He dwells
In a consummate prime, yet still desires
A further consummation. For the lunar month
He makes the tenderest research, intent
On a transmutation which, when seen, appears
To be askew. And space is filled with his
Rejected years. A big bird pecks at him
For food. The big bird's bony appetite
Is as insatiable as the sun's. The bird
Rose from an imperfection of its own
To feed on the yellow bloom of the yellow fruit
Dropped down from turquoise leaves. In the landscape of
The sun, its grossest appetite becomes less gross,
Yet, when corrected, has its curious lapses,
Its glitters, its divinations of serene
Indulgence out of all celestial sight.

The sun is the country wherever he is. The bird
In the brightest landscape downwardly revolves
Disdaining each astringent ripening,
Evading the point of redness, not content
To repose in an hour or season or long era
Of the country colors crowding against it, since
The yellow grassman's mind is still immense,
Still promises perfections cast away.

VII

How red the rose that is the soldier's wound,
The wounds of many soldiers, the wounds of all
The soldiers that have fallen, red in blood,
The soldier of time grown deathless in great size.

A mountain in which no ease is ever found,
Unless indifference to deeper death
Is ease, stands in the dark, a shadows' hill,
And there the soldier of time has deathless rest.

Concentric circles of shadows, motionless
Of their own part, yet moving on the wind,
Form mystical convolutions in the sleep
Of time's red soldier deathless on his bed.

The shadows of his fellows ring him round
In the high night, the summer breathes for them
Its fragrance, a heavy somnolence, and for him,
For the soldier of time, it breathes a summer sleep,

In which his wound is good because life was.
No part of him was ever part of death.
A woman smoothes her forehead with her hand
And the soldier of time lies calm beneath that stroke.

So-and-so Reclining on her Couch

On her side, reclining on her elbow,
This mechanism, this apparition,
Suppose we call it Projection A.

She floats in air at the level of
The eye, completely anonymous,
Born, as she was, at twenty-one,

Without lineage or language, only
The curving of her hip, as motionless gesture,
Eyes dripping blue, so much to learn.

If just above her head there hung,
Suspended in air, the slightest crown
Of Gothic prong and practick bright,

The suspension, as in solid space,
The suspending hand withdrawn, would be
An invisible gesture. Let this be called

Projection B. To get at the thing
Without gestures is to get at it as
Idea. She floats in the contention, the flux

Between the thing as idea and
The idea as thing. She is half who made her.
This is the final Projection, C.

The arrangement contains the desire of
The artist. But one confides in what has no
Concealed creator. One walks easily

The unpainted shore, accepts the world
As anything but sculpture. Good-bye,
Mrs. Pappadopoulos, and thanks.

Men Made Out of Words

What should we be without the sexual myth,
The human revery or poem of death?

Castratos of moon-mash — Life consists
Of propositions about life. The human

Revery is a solitude in which
We compose these propositions, torn by dreams,

By the terrible incantations of defeats
And by the fear that defeats and dreams are one.

The whole race is a poet that writes down
The eccentric propositions of its fate.

A Primitive Like an Orb

I

The essential poem at the centre of things,
The arias that spiritual fiddlings make,
Have gorged the cast-iron of our lives with good
And the cast-iron of our works. But it is, dear sirs,
A difficult apperception, this gorging good,
Fetched by such slick-eyed nymphs, this essential gold,
This fortune's finding, disposed and re-disposed
By such slight genii in such pale air.

II

We do not prove the existence of the poem.
It is something seen and known in lesser poems.
It is the huge, high harmony that sounds
A little and a little, suddenly,
By means of a separate sense. It is and it
Is not and, therefore, is. In the instant of speech,
The breadth of an accelerando moves,
Captives the being, widens — and was there.

III

What milk there is in such captivity,
What wheaten bread and oaten cake and kind,
Green guests and table in the woods and songs
At heart, within an instant's motion, within
A space grown wide, the inevitable blue
Of secluded thunder, an illusion, as it was,
Oh as, always too heavy for the sense
To seize, the obscurest as, the distant was . . .

IV

One poem proves another and the whole,
For the clairvoyant men that need no proof:
The lover, the believer and the poet.
Their words are chosen out of their desire,
The joy of language, when it is themselves.
With these they celebrate the central poem,
The fulfillment of fulfillments, in opulent,
Last terms, the largest, bulging still with more,

V

Until the used-to earth and sky, and the tree
And cloud, the used-to tree and used-to cloud,
Lose the old uses that they made of them,
And they: these men, and earth and sky, inform
Each other by sharp informations, sharp,
Free knowledges, secreted until then,
Breaches of that which held them fast. It is
As if the central poem became the world,

VI

And the world the central poem, each one the mate
Of the other, as if summer was a spouse,

Espoused each morning, each long afternoon,
And the mate of summer: her mirror and her look,
Her only place and person, a self of her
That speaks, denouncing separate selves, both one.
The essential poem begets the others. The light
Of it is not a light apart, up-hill.

VII

The central poem is the poem of the whole,
The poem of the composition of the whole,
The composition of blue sea and of green,
Of blue light and of green, as lesser poems,
And the miraculous multiplex of lesser poems,
Not merely into a whole, but a poem of
The whole, the essential compact of the parts,
The roundness that pulls tight the final ring

VIII

And that which in an altitude would soar,
A vis, a principle or, it may be,
The meditation of a principle,
Or else an inherent order active to be
Itself, a nature to its natives all
Beneficence, a repose, utmost repose,
The muscles of a magnet aptly felt,
A giant, on the horizon, glistening,

IX

And in bright excellence adorned, crested
With every prodigal, familiar fire,
And unfamiliar escapades: whirroos
And scintillant sizzlings such as children like,
Vested in the serious folds of majesty,
Moving around and behind, a following
A source of trumpeting seraphs in the eye,
A source of pleasant outbursts on the ear.

X

It is a giant, always, that is evolved,
To be in scale, unless virtue cuts him, snips
Both size and solitude or thinks it does,
As in a signed photograph on a mantelpiece.
But the virtuoso never leaves his shape,

Still on the horizon elongates his cuts,
And still angelic and still plenteous,
Imposes power by the power of his form.

XI

Here, then, is an abstraction given head,
A giant on the horizon, given arms,
A massive body and long legs, stretched out,
A definition with an illustration, not
Too exactly labelled, a large among the smalls
Of it, a close, parental magnitude,   .
At the centre on the horizon, concentrum, grave
And prodigious person, patron of origins.

XII

That's it. The lover writes, the believer hears,
The poet mumbles and the painter sees,
Each one, his fated eccentricity,
As a part, but part, but tenacious particle,
Of the skeleton of the ether, the total
Of letters, prophecies, perceptions, clods
Of color, the giant of nothingness, each one
And the giant ever changing, living in change.

The River of Rivers in Connecticut

There is a great river this side of Stygia,
Before one comes to the first black cataracts
And trees that lack the intelligence of trees.

In that river, far this side of Stygia,
The mere flowing of the water is a gayety,
Flashing and flashing in the sun. On its banks,

No shadow walks. The river is fateful,
Like the last one. But there is no ferryman,
He could not bend against its propelling force.

It is not to be seen beneath the appearances
That tell of it. The steeple at Farmington
Stands glistening and Haddam shines and sways.

It is the third commonness with light and air,
A curriculum, a vigor, a local abstraction . . .
Call it, once more, a river, an unnamed flowing,

Space-filled, reflecting the seasons, the folk-lore
Of each of the senses; call it, again and again,
The river that flows nowhere, like a sea.

The Irish Cliffs of Moher

Who is my father in this world, in this house,
At the spirit's base?

My father's father, his father's father, his —
Shadows like winds

Go back to a parent before thought, before speech,
At the head of the past.

They go to the cliffs of Moher rising out of the mist,
Above the real,

Rising out of present time and place, above
The wet, green grass.

This is not landscape, full of the somnambulations
Of poetry

And the sea. This is my father or, maybe,
It is as he was,

A likeness, one of the race of fathers: earth
And sea and air.

To an Old Philosopher in Rome

On the threshold of heaven, the figures in the street
Become the figures of heaven, the majestic movement
Of men growing small in the distances of space,
Singing, with smaller and still smaller sound,
Unintelligible absolution and an end —

The threshold, Rome, and that more merciful Rome
Beyond, the two alike in the make of the mind.
It is as if in a human dignity
Two parallels become one, a perspective, of which
Men are part both in the inch and in the mile.

- How easily the blown banners change to wings . . .
Things dark on the horizons of perception,
Become accompaniments of fortune, but
Of the fortune of the spirit, beyond the eye,
Not to its sphere, and yet not far beyond,

The human end in the spirit's greatest reach,
The extreme of the known in the presence of the extreme
Of the unknown. The newsboys' muttering
Becomes another murmuring; the smell
Of medicine, a fragrantness not to be spoiled . . .

The bed, the books, the chair, the moving nuns,
The candle as it evades the sight, these are
The sources of happiness in the shape of Rome,
A shape within the ancient circles of shapes,
And these beneath the shadow of a shape

In a confusion on bed and books, a portent
On the chair, a moving transparence on the nuns,
A light on the candle tearing against the wick
To join a hovering excellence, to escape
From fire and be part only of that of which

Fire is the symbol: the celestial possible.
Speak to your pillow as if it was yourself.
Be orator but with an accurate tongue
And without eloquence, O, half-asleep,
Of the pity that is the memorial of this room,

So that we feel, in this illumined large,
The veritable small, so that each of us
Beholds himself in you, and hears his voice
In yours, master and commiserable man,
Intent on your particles of nether-do,

Your dozing in the depths of wakefulness,
In the warmth of your bed, at the edge of your chair, alive
Yet living in two worlds, impenitent
As to one, and, as to one, most penitent,
Impatient for the grandeur that you need

In so much misery; and yet finding it
Only in misery, the afflatus of ruin,
Profound poetry of the poor and of the dead,
As in the last drop of the deepest blood,
As it falls from the heart and lies there to be seen,

Even as the blood of an empire, it might be,
For a citizen of heaven though still of Rome.
It is poverty's speech that seeks us out the most.
It is older than the oldest speech of Rome.
This is the tragic accent of the scene.

And you — it is you that speak it, without speech,
The loftiest syllables among loftiest things,
The one invulnerable man among
Crude captains, the naked majesty, if you like,
Of bird-nest arches and of rain-stained-vaults.

The sounds drift in. The buildings are remembered.
The life of the city never lets go, nor do you
Ever want it to. It is part of the life in your room.
Its domes are the architecture of your bed.
The bells keep on repeating solemn names

In choruses and choirs of choruses,
Unwilling that mercy should be a mystery
Of silence, that any solitude of sense
Should give you more than their peculiar chords
And reverberations clinging to whisper still.

It is a kind of total grandeur at the end,
With every visible thing enlarged and yet
No more than a bed, a chair and moving nuns,
The immensest theatre, the pillared porch,
The book and candle in your ambered room,

Total grandeur of a total edifice,
Chosen by an inquisitor of structures
For himself. He stops upon this threshold,
As if the design of all his words takes form
And frame from thinking and is realized.

WILLIAM CARLOS WILLIAMS
1883–1963

Tract

I will teach you my townspeople
how to perform a funeral
for you have it over a troop
of artists —
unless one should scour the world —
you have the ground sense necessary.

See! the hearse leads.
I begin with a design for a hearse.
For Christ's sake not black —
nor white either — and not polished!
Let it be weathered — like a farm wagon —
with gilt wheels (this could be
applied fresh at small expense)
or no wheels at all:
a rough dray to drag over the ground.

Knock the glass out!
My God — glass, my townspeople!
For what purpose? Is it for the dead
to look out or for us to see
how well he is housed or to see
the flowers or the lack of them —
or what?
To keep the rain and snow from him?
He will have a heavier rain soon:
pebbles and dirt and what not.
Let there be no glass —
and no upholstery, phew!

and no little brass rollers
and small easy wheels on the bottom —
my townspeople what are you thinking of?

A rough plain hearse then
with gilt wheels and no top at all.
On this the coffin lies
by its own weight.

              No wreaths please —
especially no hot house flowers.
Some common memento is better,
something he prized and is known by:
his old clothes — a few books perhaps —
God knows what! You realize
how we are about these things
my townspeople —
something will be found — anything
even flowers if he had come to that.
So much for the hearse.

For heaven's sake though see to the driver!
Take off the silk hat! In fact
that's no place at all for him —
up there unceremoniously
dragging our friend out to his own dignity!
Bring him down — bring him down!
Low and inconspicuous! I'd not have him ride
on the wagon at all — damn him —
the undertaker's understrapper!
Let him hold the reins
and walk at the side
and inconspicuously too!

Then briefly as to yourselves:
Walk behind — as they do in France,
seventh class, or if you ride
Hell take curtains! Go with some show
of inconvenience; sit openly —
to the weather as to grief.

Or do you think you can shut grief in?
What — from us? We who have perhaps
nothing to lose? Share with us
share with us — it will be money
in your pockets.

                  Go now
I think you are ready.

Danse Russe

If when my wife is sleeping
and the baby and Kathleen
are sleeping
and the sun is a flame-white disc
in silken mists
above shining trees, —
if I in my north room
dance naked, grotesquely
before my mirror
waving my shirt round my head
and singing softly to myself:
"I am lonely, lonely.
I was born to be lonely,
I am best so!"
If I admire my arms, my face,
my shoulders, flanks, buttocks
against the yellow drawn shades, —

Who shall say I am not
the happy genius of my household?

Queen-Ann's-Lace

Her body is not so white as
anemone petals nor so smooth — nor
so remote a thing. It is a field
of the wild carrot taking
the field by force; the grass
does not raise above it.
Here is no question of whiteness,
white as can be, with a purple mole
at the center of each flower.

Each flower is a hand's span
of her whiteness. Wherever
his hand has lain there is
a tiny purple blemish. Each part
is a blossom under his touch
to which the fibres of her being
stem one by one, each of its end,
until the whole field is a
white desire, empty, a single stem,
a cluster, flower by flower,
a pious wish to whiteness gone over —
or nothing.

The Widow's Lament in Springtime

Sorrow is my own yard
where the new grass
flames as it has flamed
often before but not
with the cold fire
that closes round me this year.
Thirtyfive years
I lived with my husband.
The plumtree is white today
with masses of flowers.
Masses of flowers
load the cherry branches
and color some bushes
yellow and some red
but the grief in my heart
is stronger than they
for though they were my joy
formerly, today I notice them
and turned away forgetting.
Today my son told me
that in the meadows,
at the edge of the heavy woods
in the distance, he saw
trees of white flowers.
I feel that I would like
to go there
and fall into those flowers
and sink into the marsh near them.

Spring and All

By the road to the contagious hospital
under the surge of the blue
mottled clouds driven from the
northeast — a cold wind. Beyond, the
waste of broad, muddy fields
brown with dried weeds, standing and fallen

patches of standing water
the scattering of tall trees

All along the road the reddish
purplish, forked, upstanding, twiggy
stuff of bushes and small trees
with dead, brown leaves under them
leafless vines —

Lifeless in appearance, sluggish
dazed spring approaches —

They enter the new world naked,
cold, uncertain of all
save that they enter. All about them
the cold, familiar wind —

Now the grass, tomorrow
the stiff curl of wildcarrot leaf
One by one objects are defined —
It quickens: clarity, outline of leaf

But now the stark dignity of
entrance — Still, the profound change
has come upon them: rooted, they
grip down and begin to awaken

The Red Wheelbarrow

so much depends
upon

a red wheel
barrow

glazed with rain
water

beside the white
chickens.

To Elsie

The pure products of America
go crazy —
mountain folk from Kentucky

or the ribbed north end of
Jersey
with its isolate lakes and

valleys, its deaf-mutes, thieves
old names
and promiscuity between

devil-may-care men who have taken
to railroading
out of sheer lust of adventure —

and young slatterns, bathed
in filth
from Monday to Saturday

to be tricked out that night
with gauds
from imaginations which have no

peasant traditions to give them
character
but flutter and flaunt

sheer rags — succumbing without
emotion
save numbed terror

under some hedge of choke-cherry
or viburnum —
which they cannot express —

Unless it be that marriage
perhaps
with a dash of Indian blood

will throw up a girl so desolate
so hemmed round
with disease or murder

that she'll be rescued by an
agent —
reared by the state and

sent out at fifteen to work in
some hard-pressed
house in the suburbs —

some doctor's family, some Elsie —
voluptuous water
expressing with broken

brain the truth about us —
her great
ungainly hips and flopping breasts

addressed to cheap
jewelry
and rich young men with fine eyes

as if the earth under our feet
were
an excrement of some sky

and we degraded prisoners
destined
to hunger until we eat filth

while the imagination strains
after deer
going by fields of goldenrod in

the stifling heat of September
Somehow
it seems to destroy us

It is only in isolate flecks that
something
is given off

No one
to witness
and adjust, no one to drive the car

At the Ball Game

The crowd at the ball game
is moved uniformly

by a spirit of uselessness
which delights them —

all the exciting detail
of the chase

and the escape, the error
the flash of genius —

all to no end save beauty
the eternal —

So in detail they, the crowd,
are beautiful

for this
to be warned against

saluted and defied —
It is alive, venomous

it smiles grimly
its words cut —

The flashy female with her
mother, gets it —

The Jew gets it straight — it
is deadly, terrifying —

It is the Inquisition, the
Revolution

It is beauty itself
that lives

day by day in them
idly —

This is
the power of their faces

It is summer, it is the solstice
the crowd is

cheering, the crowd is laughing
in detail

permanently, seriously
without thought

To Mark Anthony in Heaven

This quiet morning light
reflected, how many times
from grass and trees and clouds
enters my north room
touching the walls with
grass and clouds and trees.
Anthony,
trees and grass and clouds.
Why did you follow
that beloved body

with your ships at Actium?
I hope it was because
you knew her inch by inch
from slanting feet upward
to the roots of her hair
and down again and that
you saw her
above the battle's fury —
clouds and trees and grass —

For then you are
listening in heaven.

Portrait of a Lady

Your thighs are appletrees
whose blossoms touch the sky.
Which sky? The sky
where Watteau hung a lady's
slipper. Your knees
are a southern breeze — or
a gust of snow. Agh! what
sort of man was Fragonard?
— as if that answered
anything. Ah, yes — below
the knees, since the tune
drops that way, it is
one of those white summer days,
the tall grass of your ankles
flickers upon the shore —
Which shore? —
the sand clings to my lips —
Which shore?
Agh, petals maybe. How
should I know?
Which shore? Which shore?
I said petals from an appletree.

This Is Just To Say

I have eaten
the plums
that were in
the icebox

and which
you were probably
saving
for breakfast

Forgive me
they were delicious
so sweet
and so cold

The Yachts

contend in a sea which the land partly encloses
shielding them from the too-heavy blows
of an ungoverned ocean which when it chooses

tortures the biggest hulls, the best man knows
to pit against its beatings, and sinks them pitilessly.
Mothlike in mists, scintillant in the minute

brilliance of cloudless days, with broad bellying sails
they glide to the wind tossing green water
from their sharp prows while over them the crew crawls

ant-like, solicitously grooming them, releasing,
making fast as they turn, lean far over and having
caught the wind again, side by side, head for the mark.

In a well guarded arena of open water surrounded by
lesser and greater craft which, sycophant, lumbering
and flittering follow them, they appear youthful, rare

as the light of a happy eye, live with the grace
of all that in the mind is feckless, free and
naturally to be desired. Now the sea which holds them

is moody, lapping their glossy sides, as if feeling
for some slightest flaw but fails completely.
Today no race. Then the wind comes again. The yachts

move, jockeying for a start, the signal is set and they
are off. Now the waves strike at them but they are too
well made, they slip through, though they take in canvas.

Arms with hands grasping seek to clutch at the prows.
Bodies thrown recklessly in the way are cut aside.
It is a sea of faces about them in agony, in despair

until the horror of the race dawns staggering the mind,
the whole sea become an entanglement of watery bodies
lost to the world bearing what they cannot hold. Broken,

beaten, desolate, reaching from the dead to be taken up
they cry out, failing, failing! their cries rising
in waves still as the skillful yachts pass over.

The Catholic Bells

Tho' I'm no Catholic
I listen hard when the bells
in the yellow-brick tower
of their new church

ring down the leaves
ring in the frost upon them
and the death of the flowers
ring out the grackle

toward the south, the sky
darkened by them, ring in
the new baby of Mr. and Mrs.
Krantz which cannot

for the fat of its cheeks
open well its eyes, ring out
the parrot under its hood
jealous of the child

ring in Sunday morning
and old age which adds as it
takes away. Let them ring
only ring! over the oil

painting of a young priest
on the church wall advertising
last week's Novena to St.
Anthony, ring for the lame

young man in black with
gaunt cheeks and wearing a
Derby hat, who is hurrying
to 11 o'clock Mass (the

grapes still hanging to
the vine along the nearby
Concordia Halle like broken
teeth in the head of an

old man) Let them ring
for the eyes and ring for
the hands and ring for
the children of my friend

who no longer hears
them ring but with a smile
and in a low voice speaks
of the decisions of her

daughter and the proposals
and betrayals of her
husband's friends. O bells
ring for the ringing!

the beginning and the end
of the ringing! Ring ring
ring ring ring ring ring!
Catholic bells — !

These

are the desolate, dark weeks
when nature in its barrenness
equals the stupidity of man.

The year plunges into night
and the heart plunges
lower than night

to an empty, windswept place
without sun, stars or moon
but a peculiar light as of thought

that spins a dark fire —
whirling upon itself until,
in the cold, it kindles

to make a man aware of nothing
that he knows, not loneliness
itself — Not a ghost but

would be embraced — emptiness,
despair — (They
whine and whistle) among

the flashes and booms of war;
houses of whose rooms
the cold is greater than can be thought,

the people gone that we loved,
the beds lying empty, the couches
damp, the chairs unused —

Hide it away somewhere
out of the mind, let it get roots
and grow, unrelated to jealous

ears and eyes — for itself.
In this mine they come to dig — all.
Is this the counterfoil to sweetest

music? The source of poetry that
seeing the clock stopped, says,
The clock has stopped

that ticked yesterday so well?
and hears the sound of lakewater
splashing — that is now stone.

The Dance

In Breughel's great picture, The Kermess,
the dancers go round, they go round and
around, the squeal and the blare and the
tweedle of bagpipes, a bugle and fiddles
tipping their bellies (round as the thick-
sided glasses whose wash they impound)
their hips and their bellies off balance
to turn them. Kicking and rolling about
the Fair Grounds, swinging their butts, those
shanks must be sound to bear up under such
rollicking measures, prance as they dance
in Breughel's great picture, The Kermess.

Burning the Christmas Greens

Their time past, pulled down
cracked and flung to the fire
— go up in a roar

All recognition lost, burnt clean
clean in the flame, the green
dispersed, a living red,
flame red, red as blood wakes
on the ash —

and ebbs to a steady burning
the rekindled bed become
a landscape of flame

At the winter's midnight
we went to the trees, the coarse
holly, the balsam and
the hemlock for their green

At the thick of the dark
the moment of the cold's
deepest plunge we brought branches
cut from the green trees

to fill our need, and over
doorways, about paper Christmas
bells covered with tinfoil
and fastened by red ribbons

we stuck the green prongs
in the windows hung
woven wreaths and above pictures
the living green. On the

mantle we built a green forest
and among those hemlock
sprays put a herd of small
white deer as if they

were walking there. All this!
and it seemed gentle and good
to us. Their time past,
relief! The room bare. We

stuffed the dead grate
with them upon the half burnt out
log's smoldering eye, opening
red and closing under them

and we stood there looking down.
Green is a solace
a promise of peace, a fort
against the cold (though we

did not say so) a challenge
above the snow's
hard shell. Green (we might
have said) that, where

small birds hide and dodge
and lift their plaintive
rallying cries, blocks for them
and knocks down

the unseeing bullets of
the storm. Green spruce boughs
pulled down by a weight of
snow — Transformed!

Violence leaped and appeared.
Recreant! roared to life
as the flame rose through and
our eyes recoiled from it.

In the jagged flames green
to red, instant and alive. Green!
those sure abutments . . . Gone!
lost to mind

and quick in the contracting
tunnel of the grate
appeared a world! Black
mountains, black and red — as

yet uncolored — and ash white,
an infant landscape of shimmering
ash and flame and we, in
that instant, lost,

breathless to be witnesses,
as if we stood
ourselves refreshed among
the shining fauna of that fire.

To Ford Madox Ford in Heaven

Is it any better in Heaven, my friend Ford,
    than you found it in Provence?

I don't think so for you made Provence a
    heaven by your praise of it
to give a foretaste of what might be
    your joy in the present circumstances.
It was Heaven you were describing there
    transubstantiated from its narrowness
to resemble the paths and gardens of a
    greater world where you now reside.
But, dear man, you have taken a major
    part of it from us.
          Provence that you
praised so well will never be the same
    Provence to us
          now you are gone.

A heavenly man you seem to me now, never
    having been for me a saintly one.
It lived about you, a certain grossness that
    was not like the world.
The world is cleanly, polished and well
    made but heavenly man
is filthy with his flesh and corrupt that
    loves to eat and drink and whore —
to laugh at himself and not be afraid of
    himself knowing well he has
no possessions and opinions that are worth
    caring a broker's word about
and that all he is, but one thing, he feeds
    as one will feed a pet dog.

So roust and love and dredge the belly full
    in Heaven's name!
I laugh to think of you wheezing in Heaven.
    Where is Heaven? But why
do I ask that, since you showed the way?
    I don't care a damn for it
other than for that better part lives beside
    me here so long as I

live and remember you. Thank God you
    were not delicate, you let the world in
and lied! damn it you lied grossly
    sometimes. But it was all, I
see now, a carelessness, the part of a man
    that is homeless here on earth.

Provence, the fat assed Ford will never
    again strain the chairs of your cafés
pull and pare for his dish your sacred garlic,
    grunt and sweat and lick
his lips. Gross as the world he has left to
    us he has become
a part of that of which you were the known
    part, Provence, he loved so well.

The Rose

The stillness of the rose
in time of war
reminds me of
the long sleep just begun
of that sparrow
his head pillowed unroughed
and unalarmed upon
the polished pavement or
of voluptuous hours
with some
breathless book when
stillness was an eternity
long since begun

The Semblables

The red brick monastery in
the suburbs over against the dust-
hung acreage of the unfinished
and all but subterranean

munitions plant: those high
brick walls behind which at Easter
the little orphans and bastards
in white gowns sing their Latin

responses to the hoary ritual
while frankincense and myrrh
round out the dark chapel making
an enclosed sphere of it

of which they are the worm:
that cell outside the city beside
the polluted stream and dump
heap, uncomplaining, and the field

of upended stones with a photo
under glass fastened here and there
to one of them near the deeply
carved name to distinguish it:

that trinity of slate gables
the unembellished windows piling
up, the chapel with its round
window between the dormitories

peaked by the bronze belfry
peaked in turn by the cross,
verdegris — faces all silent
that miracle that has burst sexless

from between the carrot rows.
Leafless white birches, their
empty tendrils swaying in
the all but no breeze guard

behind the spiked monastery fence
the sacred statuary. But ranks
of brilliant car-tops row on row
give back in all his glory the

late November sun and hushed
attend, before that tumbled
ground, those sightless walls
and shovelled entrances where no

one but a lonesome cop swinging
his club gives sign, that agony
within where the wrapt machines
are praying. . . .

from Paterson: Book I

Preface

"Rigor of beauty is the quest. But how will you find
beauty when it is locked in the mind past all remon-
strance?"

To make a start,
out of particulars
and make them general, rolling
up the sum, by defective means —
Sniffing the trees,
just another dog
among a lot of dogs. What
else is there? And to do?
The rest have run out —
after the rabbits.
Only the lame stands — on
three legs. Scratch front and back.
Deceive and eat. Dig
a musty bone

For the beginning is assuredly
the end — since we know nothing, pure
and simple, beyond
our own complexities.

                        Yet there is
no return: rolling up out of chaos,
a nine months' wonder, the city
the man, an identity — it can't be
otherwise — an
interpenetration, both ways. Rolling
up! obverse, reverse;
the drunk the sober; the illustrious
the gross; one. In ignorance
a certain knowledge and knowledge,
undispersed, its own undoing.

                        (The multiple seed,
packed tight with detail, soured,
is lost in the flux and the mind,
distracted, floats off in the same
scum)

Rolling up, rolling up heavy with
numbers.

                    It is the ignorant sun
rising in the slot of
hollow suns risen, so that never in this
world will a man live well in his body
save dying — and not know himself
dying; yet that is
the design. Renews himself
thereby, in addition and subtraction,
walking up and down.

               and the craft,
subverted by thought, rolling up, let
him beware lest he turn to no more than
the writing of stale poems . . .
Minds like beds always made up,
                  (more stony than a shore)
unwilling or unable.

                 Rolling in, top up,
under, thrust and recoil, a great clatter:
lifted as air, boated, multicolored, a
wash of seas —
from mathematics to particulars —

                divided as the dew,
floating mists, to be rained down and
regathered into a river that flows
and encircles:

                shells and animalcules
generally and so to man,

             to Paterson.

Ol' Bunk's Band

These are men! the gaunt, unfore-
      sold, the vocal,
blatant, Stand up, stand up! the
      slap of a bass-string.

485

Pick, ping! The horn, the
    hollow horn
long drawn out, a hound deep
    tone —
Choking, choking! while the
    treble reed
races — alone, ripples, screams
    slow to fast —
to second to first! These are men!

Drum, drum, drum, drum, drum
    drum, drum! the
ancient cry, escaping crapulence
    eats through
transcendent — torn, tears, term
    town, tense,
turns and back off whole, leaps
    up, stomps down,
rips through! These are men
    beneath
whose force the melody limps —
    to
proclaim, proclaims — Run and
    lie down,
in slow measures, to rest and
    not never
need no more! These are men!
    Men!

Lear

When the world takes over for us
and the storm in the trees
replaces our brittle consciences
(like ships, female to all seas)
when the few last yellow leaves
stand out like flags on tossed ships
at anchor —`our minds are rested

Yesterday we sweated and dreamed
or sweated in our dreams walking
at a loss through the bulk of figures

that appeared solid, men or women,
but as we approached down the paved
corridor melted — Was it I? — like
smoke from bonfires blowing away

Today the storm, inescapable, has
taken the scene and we return
our hearts to it, however made, made
wives by it and though we secure
ourselves for a dry skin from the drench
of its passionate approaches we
yield and are made quiet by its fury

Pitiful Lear, not even you could
out-shout the storm — to make a fool
cry! Wife to its power might you not
better have yielded earlier? as on ships
facing the seas were carried once
the figures of women at repose to
signify the strength of the waves' lash.

A Unison

The grass is very green, my friend,
and tousled, like the head of —
your grandson, yes? And the mountain,
the mountain we climbed
twenty years since for the last
time (I write this thinking
of you) is saw-horned as then
upon the sky's edge — an old barn
is peaked there also, fatefully,
against the sky. And there it is
and we can't shift it or change
it or parse it or alter it
in any way. *Listen! Do you not hear
them? the singing?* There it is and
we'd better acknowledge it and
write it down, not otherwise.
Not twist the words to mean
what we should have said but to mean
— what cannot be escaped: the

mountain riding the afternoon as
it does, the grass matted green,
green underfoot and the air —
rotten wood. *Hear! Hear them!
the Undying.* The hill slopes away,
then rises in the middleground,
you remember, with a grove of gnarled
maples centering the bare pasture,
sacred, surely — for what reason?
I cannot say? Idyllic!
a shrine cinctured there by
the trees, a certainty of music!
a unison and a dance, joined
at this death's festival: Something
of a shed snake's skin, the beginning
goldenrod. Or, best, a white stone,
you have seen it: *Mathilda Maria
Fox* — and near the ground's lip,
all but undecipherable, *Aet Suae
Anno* 9 — still there, the grass
dripping of last night's rain — and
welcome! The thin air, the near,
clear brook water! — and could not,
and died, unable; to escape
what the air and the wet grass —
through which, tomorrow, bejeweled,
the great sun will rise — the
unchanging mountains, forced on them —
and they received, willingly!
Stones, stones of a difference
joining the others, at pace. *Hear!
Hear the unison of their voices.* . . . .

The Horse Show

Constantly near you, I never in my entire
sixty-four years knew you so well as yesterday
or half so well. We talked. You were never
so lucid, so disengaged from all exigencies
of place and time. We talked of ourselves,
intimately, a thing never heard of between us.
How long have we waited? almost a hundred years.

You said, Unless there is some spark, some
spirit we keep within ourselves, life, a
continuing life's impossible — and it is all
we have. There is no other life, only the one.
The world of the spirits that comes afterward
is the same as our own, just like you sitting
there they come and talk to me, just the same.

They come to bother us. Why? I said. I don't
know. Perhaps to find out what we are doing.
Jealous, do you think? I don't know. I
don't know why they should want to come back.
I was reading about some men who had been
buried under a mountain, I said to her, and
one of them came back after two months,

digging himself out. It was in Switzerland,
you remember? Of course I remember. The
villagers tho't it was a ghost coming down
to complain. They were frightened. They
do come, she said, what you call
my "visions." I talk to them just as I
am talking to you. I see them plainly.

Oh if I could only read! You don't know
what adjustments I have made. All
I can do is to try to live over again
what I knew when your brother and you
were children — but I can't always succeed.
Tell me about the horse show. I have
been waiting all week to hear about it.

Mother darling, I wasn't able to get away.
Oh that's too bad. It was just a show;
they make the horses walk up and down
to judge them by their form. Oh is that
all? I tho't it was something else. Oh
they jump and run too. I wish you had been
there, I was so interested to hear about it.

Coda

Inseparable from the fire
    its light
        takes precedence over it.
Then follows
    what we have dreaded —
        but it can never
overcome what has gone before.
    In the huge gap
        between the flash
and the thunderstroke
    spring has come in
        or a deep snow fallen.
Call it old age.
    In that stretch
        we have lived to see
a colt kick up his heels.
    Do not hasten
        laugh and play
in an eternity
    the heat will not overtake the light.
        That's sure.
That gelds the bomb,
    permitting
        that the mind contain it.
This is that interval,
    that sweetest interval,
        when love will blossom,
come early, come late
    and give itself to the lover.
Only the imagination is real!
    I have declared it
        time without end.
If a man die
    it is because death
        has first
possessed his imagination.
    But if he refuse death —
        no greater evil
can befall him
    unless it be the death of love
        meet him

in full career.
        Then indeed
               for him
the light has gone out.
But love and the imagination
        are of a piece,
               swift as the light
to avoid destruction.
        So we come to watch time's flight
               as we might watch
summer lightning
        or fireflies, secure,
               by grace of the imagination,
safe in its care.
        For if
               the light itself
has escaped,
        the whole edifice opposed to it
               goes down.
Light, the imagination
        and love,
               in our age,
by natural law,
        which we worship,
               maintain
all of a piece
        their dominance.
So let us love
        confident as is the light
               in its struggle with darkness
that there is as much to say
        and more
               for the one side
and that not the darker
        which John Donne
               for instance
among many men
        presents to us.
               In the controversy
touching the younger
        and the older Tolstoi,
               Villon, St. Anthony, Kung,

Rimbaud, Buddha
     and Abraham Lincoln
          the palm goes
always to the light;
     Who most shall advance the light —
          call it what you may!
The light
     for all time shall outspeed
          the thunder crack.
Medieval pageantry
     is human and we enjoy
          the rumor of it
as in our world we enjoy
     the reading of Chaucer,
          likewise
a priest's raiment
     (or that of a savage chieftain).
          It is all
a celebration of the light.
     All the pomp and ceremony
          of weddings,
"Sweet Thames, run softly
     till I end
          my song," —
are of an equal sort.
For our wedding, too,
     the light was wakened
          and shone. The light!
the light stood before us
     waiting!
          I thought the world
stood still.
     At the altar
          so intent was I
before my vows,
     so moved by your presence
          a girl so pale
and ready to faint
     that I pitied
          and wanted to protect you.
As I think of it now,
     after a lifetime,
          it is as if

a sweet-scented flower
        were poised
                and for me did open.
Asphodel
       has no odor
              save to the imagination
but it too
       celebrates the light.
             It is late
but an odor
       as from our wedding
             has revived for me
and begun again to penetrate
       into all crevices
            of my world.

At Kenneth Burke's Place

And "the earth under our feet,"
we say glibly, hating
the "Esoteric" which is not
to be included in our anthologies, the
unthinkable: the younger generation
the colored (unless marketable)
and — Plato was no different — the
"private language."
                  But
the earth also is a "private language"
barring, barring — Well,
principally cash, our one link,
says K. B., with the universal — the
steps, the first step out of
domesticity, the familial. Cash. The
first nickel is the first defiance.
But the earth under our feet is
the singing, the winds, the snow —
the surge and slosh of the sea. It's
the indecisive, the rare occurrence
of the expected. The earth
is the esoteric to our dullness,
it opens caves, it distils dews:
the furry root of the fern.

493

Catalogues are not its business.
Its business, its business is
external to anthologies, outside the
orthodoxy of plotted murders.
It is
the green apple smudged with
a sooty life that clings, also,
with the skin: the small green apple
still fast here and there
to the leafless brush of unpruned
twigs sprouting from old knees
and elbows upon the tree
that was cleared of undergrowth about
it and still stands.
There is a basketful
of them half rotted on the half rotten
bench. Take up one
and bite into it. It is still good
even unusual compared with the usual,
as if a taste long lost and regretted
had in the end, finally,
been brought to life again.

EZRA POUND

1885–1972

Sestina: *Altaforte*

Loquitur: *En* Bertrans de Born.
  Dante Alighieri put this man in hell for that he was a
stirrer-up of strife.
  Eccovi!
  Judge ye!
  Have I dug him up again?
The scene is at his castle, Altaforte. "Papiols" is his jongleur.
"The Leopard," the *device* of Richard (Cœur de Lion).

I

Damn it all! all this our South stinks peace.
You whoreson dog, Papiols, come! Let's to music!
I have no life save when the swords clash.
But ah! when I see the standards gold, vair, purple, opposing
And the broad fields beneath them turn crimson,
Then howl I my heart nigh mad with rejoicing.

II

In hot summer have I great rejoicing
When the tempests kill the earth's foul peace,
And the lightnings from black heav'n flash crimson,
And the fierce thunders roar me their music
And the winds shriek through the clouds mad, opposing,
And through all the riven skies God's swords clash.

III

Hell grant soon we hear again the swords clash!
And the shrill neighs of destriers in battle rejoicing,
Spiked breast to spiked breast opposing!
Better one hour's stour than a year's peace
With fat boards, bawds, wine and frail music!
Bah! there's no wine like the blood's crimson!

IV

And I love to see the sun rise blood-crimson.
And I watch his spears through the dark clash
And it fills all my heart with rejoicing
And pries wide my mouth with fast music
When I see him so scorn and defy peace,
His lone might 'gainst all darkness opposing.

V

The man who fears war and squats opposing
My words for stour, hath no blood of crimson
But is fit only to rot in womanish peace
Far from where worth's won and the swords clash
For the death of such sluts I go rejoicing;
Yea, I fill all the air with my music.

VI

Papiols, Papiols, to the music!
There's no sound like to swords swords opposing,
No cry like the battle's rejoicing
When our elbows and swords drip the crimson
And our charges 'gainst "The Leopard's" rush clash.
May God damn for ever all who cry "Peace!"

VII

And let the music of the swords make them crimson!
Hell grant soon we hear again the swords clash!
Hell blot black for always the thought "Peace!"

Portrait d'une Femme

Your mind and you are our Sargasso Sea,
London has swept about you this score years
And bright ships left you this or that in fee:
Ideas, old gossip, oddments of all things,
Strange spars of knowledge and dimmed wares of price.
Great minds have sought you — lacking someone else.
You have been second always. Tragical?
No. You preferred it to the usual thing:
One dull man, dulling and uxorious,
One average mind — with one thought less, each year.
Oh, you are patient, I have seen you sit
Hours, where something might have floated up.
And now you pay one. Yes, you richly pay.
You are a person of some interest, one comes to you
And takes strange gain away:
Trophies fished up; some curious suggestion;
Fact that leads nowhere; and a tale or two,
Pregnant with mandrakes, or with something else
That might prove useful and yet never proves,
That never fits a corner or shows use,
Or finds its hour upon the loom of days:
The tarnished, gaudy, wonderful old work;
Idols and ambergris and rare inlays,
These are your riches, your great store; and yet
For all this sea-hoard of deciduous things,
Strange woods half sodden, and new brighter stuff:
In the slow float of differing light and deep;
No! there is nothing! In the whole and all,
Nothing that's quite your own.
                    Yet this is you.

A Virginal

No, no! Go from me. I have left her lately.
I will not spoil my sheath with lesser brightness,
For my surrounding air hath a new lightness;
Slight are her arms, yet they have bound me straitly
And left me cloaked as with a gauze of æther;
As with sweet leaves; as with subtle clearness.
Oh, I have picked up magic in her nearness
To sheathe me half in half the things that sheathe her.

No, no! Go from me. I have still the flavour,
Soft as spring wind that's come from birchen bowers.
Green come the shoots, aye April in the branches,
As winter's wound with her sleight hand she staunches,
Hath of the trees a likeness of the savour:
As white their bark, so white this lady's hours.

The Return

See, they return; ah, see the tentative
    Movements, and the slow feet,
      The trouble in the pace and the uncertain
    Wavering!

See, they return, one, and by one,
With fear, as half-awakened;
As if the snow should hesitate
And murmur in the wind,
        and half turn back;
These were the "Wing'd-with-Awe,"
    Inviolable.

Gods of the wingèd shoe!
With them the silver hounds,
      sniffing the trace of air!

Haie! Haie!
    These were the swift to harry;
These the keen-scented;
These were the souls of blood.

Slow on the leash,
      pallid the leash-men!

An Immorality

Sing we for love and idleness,
Naught else is worth the having.

Though I have been in many a land,
There is naught else in living.

And I would rather have my sweet,
Though rose-leaves die of grieving,

Than do high deeds in Hungary
To pass all men's believing.

The River-Merchant's Wife:
A Letter

While my hair was still cut straight across my forehead
I played about the front gate, pulling flowers.
You came by on bamboo stilts, playing horse,
You walked about my seat, playing with blue plums.
And we went on living in the village of Chokan:
Two small people, without dislike or suspicion.

At fourteen I married My Lord you.
I never laughed, being bashful.
Lowering my head, I looked at the wall.
Called to, a thousand times, I never looked back.

At fifteen I stopped scowling,
I desired my dust to be mingled with yours
Forever and forever and forever.
Why should I climb the look out?

At sixteen you departed,
You went into far Ku-to-yen, by the river of swirling eddies,
And you have been gone five months.
The monkeys make sorrowful noise overhead.

You dragged your feet when you went out.
By the gate now, the moss is grown, the different mosses,
Too deep to clear them away!
The leaves fall early this autumn, in wind.
The paired butterflies are already yellow with August
Over the grass in the West garden;
They hurt me. I grow older.
If you are coming down through the narrows of the river Kiang,
Please let me know beforehand,
And I will come out to meet you
                    As far as Cho-fu-Sa.

                                        By Rihaku

The Jewel Stairs' Grievance

The jewelled steps are already quite white with dew,
It is so late that the dew soaks my gauze stockings,
And I let down the crystal curtain
And watch the moon through the clear autumn.

By Rihaku

Salutation

O generation of the thoroughly smug
    and thoroughly uncomfortable,
I have seen fishermen picnicking in the sun,
I have seen them with untidy families,
I have seen their smiles full of teeth
    and heard ungainly laughter.
And I am happier than you are,
And they were happier than I am;
And the fish swim in the lake
    and do not even own clothing.

Salutation The Second

You were praised, my books,
    because I had just come from the country;
I was twenty years behind the times
    so you found an audience ready.
I do not disown you,
    do not you disown your progeny.
Here they stand without quaint devices,
Here they are with nothing archaic about them.
Observe the irritation in general:

"Is this," they say, "the nonsense
    that we expect of poets?"
"Where is the Picturesque?"
    "Where is the vertigo of emotion?"
"No! his first work was the best."
    "Poor Dear! he has lost his illusions."

Go, little naked and impudent songs,
Go with a light foot!
(Or with two light feet, if it please you!)
Go and dance shamelessly!
Go with an impertinent frolic!

Greet the grave and the stodgy,
Salute them with your thumbs at your noses.

Here are your bells and confetti.
Go! rejuvenate things!
Rejuvenate even "The Spectator."
      Go! and make cat calls!
Dance and make people blush,
Dance the dance of the phallus
      and tell anecdotes of Cybele!
Speak of the indecorous conduct of the Gods!

Ruffle the skirts of prudes,
      speak of their knees and ankles.
But, above all, go to practical people —
Say that you do no work
      and that you will live forever.

A Pact

I make a pact with you, Walt Whitman —
I have detested you long enough.
I come to you as a grown child
Who has had a pig-headed father;
I am old enough now to make friends.
It was you that broke the new wood,
Now is a time for carving.
We have one sap and one root —
Let there be commerce between us.

The Rest

O helpless few in my country,
O remnant enslaved!

Artists broken against her,
A-stray, lost in the villages,
Mistrusted, spoken-against,

Lovers of beauty, starved,
Thwarted with systems,
Helpless against the control;

You who can not wear yourselves out
By persisting to successes,
You who can only speak,
Who can not steel yourselves into reiteration;

You of the finer sense,
Broken against false knowledge,
You who can know at first hand,
Hated, shut in, mistrusted:

Take thought:
I have weathered the storm,
I have beaten out my exile.

The Study in Aesthetics

The very small children in patched clothing,
Being smitten with an unusual wisdom,
Stopped in their play as she passed them
And cried up from their cobbles:

Guarda! Ahi, guarda! ch' è be' a!

But three years after this
I heard the young Dante, whose last name I do not know —
For there are, in Sirmione, twenty-eight young Dantes and thirty-four
Catulli;
And there had been a great catch of sardines,
And his elders
Were packing them in the great wooden boxes
For the market in Brescia, and he
Leapt about, snatching at the bright fish
And getting in both of their ways;
And in vain they commanded him to sta fermo!

And when they would not let him arrange
The fish in the boxes
He stroked those which were already arranged,
Murmuring for his own satisfaction
This identical phrase:

Ch' è be'a.

And at this I was mildly abashed.

Coda

O my songs,
Why do you look so eagerly and so curiously into
     people's faces,
Will you find your lost dead among them?

In a Station of the Metro

The apparition of these faces in the crowd;
Petals on a wet, black bough.

Ancient Wisdom, Rather Cosmic

So-shu dreamed,
And having dreamed that he was a bird, a bee, and a butterfly,
He was uncertain why he should try to feel like anything else,

Hence his contentment.

The Temperaments

Nine adulteries, 12 liaisons, 64 fornications and something approaching
    a rape
Rest nightly upon the soul of our delicate friend Florialis,
And yet the man is so quiet and reserved in demeanour
That he passes for both bloodless and sexless.
Bastidides, on the contrary, who both talks and writes of nothing save
    copulation,
Has become the father of twins,
But he accomplished this feat at some cost;
He had to be four times cuckold.

from Homage to Sextus Propertius

I

Shades of Callimachus, Coan ghosts of Philetas
It is in your grove I would walk,
I who come first from the clear font
Bringing the Grecian orgies into Italy,
　　　　　　　and the dance into Italy.
Who hath taught you so subtle a measure,
　　　　　　in what hall have you heard it;
What foot beat out your time-bar,
　　　what water has mellowed your whistles?

Out-weariers of Apollo will, as we know, continue their Martian
　　　　　　　　　　　　　　generalities,
　　　We have kept our erasers in order.
A new-fangled chariot follows the flower-hung horses:
A young Muse with young loves clustered about her
　　　ascends with me into the æther, . . .
And there is no high-road to the Muses.

Annalists will continue to record Roman reputations,
Celebrities from the Trans-Caucasus will belaud Roman celebrities
And expound the distentions of Empire,
But for something to read in normal circumstances?
For a few pages brought down from the forked hill unsullied?
I ask a wreath which will not crush my head.
　　　　　　　　And there is no hurry about it;
I shall have, doubtless, a boom after my funeral,
Seeing that long standing increases all things
　　　　　　　　　regardless of quality.
And who would have known the towers
　　　　　　　pulled down by a deal-wood horse;
Or of Achilles withstaying waters by Simois
Or of Hector spattering wheel-rims,
Or of Polydmantus, by Scamander, or Helenus and Deiphoibos?
Their door-yards would scarcely know them, or Paris.
Small talk O Ilion, and O Troad
　　　　　　　　twice taken by Oetian gods,
If Homer had not stated your case!

And I also among the later nephews of this city
　　　　　　　　shall have my dog's day,
With no stone upon my contemptible sepulchre;

My vote coming from the temple of Phoebus in Lycia, at Patara,
And in the mean time my songs will travel,
And the devirginated young ladies will enjoy them
              when they have got over the strangeness,
For Orpheus tamed the wild beasts —
              and held up the Threician river;
And Citharaon shook up the rocks by Thebes
       and danced them into a bulwark at his pleasure,
And you, O Polyphemus? Did harsh Galatea almost
Turn to your dripping horses, because of a tune, under Aetna?
We must look into the matter.
Bacchus and Apollo in favour of it,
There will be a crowd of young women doing homage to my palaver,
Though my house is not propped up by Taenarian columns from Laconia
            (associated with Neptune and Cerberus),
Though it is not stretched upon gilded beams:
My orchards do not lie level and wide
            as the forests of Phæcia,
            the luxurious and Ionian,
Nor are my caverns stuffed stiff with a Marcian vintage,
My cellar does not date from Numa Pompilius,
Nor bristle with wine jars,
Nor is it equipped with a frigidaire patent;
Yet the companions of the Muses
            will keep their collective nose in my books,
And weary with historical data, they will turn to my dance tune.

Happy who are mentioned in my pamphlets,
       the songs shall be a fine tomb-stone over their beauty.
       But against this?
Neither expensive pyramids scraping the stars in their route,
Nor houses modelled upon that of Jove in East Elis,
Nor the monumental effigies of Mausolus,
           are a complete elucidation of death.

Flame burns, rain sinks into the cracks
And they all go to rack ruin beneath the thud of the years.
Stands genius a deathless adornment,
          a name not to be worn out with the years.

Hugh Selwyn Mauberley

(*Life and Contacts*)

I
E. P. Ode pour l'élection de son sepulchre

For three years, out of key with his time,
He strove to resuscitate the dead art
Of poetry; to maintain "the sublime"
In the old sense. Wrong from the start —

No, hardly, but seeing he had been born
In a half savage country, out of date;
Bent resolutely on wringing lilies from the acorn;
Capaneus; trout for factitious bait;

Ἴδμεν γάρ τοι πάνθ' ὄσ' ἐνὶ Τροίῃ
Caught in the unstopped ear;
Giving the rocks small lee-way
The chopped seas held him, therefore, that year.

His true Penelope was Flaubert,
He fished by obstinate isles;
Observed the elegance of Circe's hair
Rather than the mottoes on sun-dials.

Unaffected by "the march of events,"
He passed from men's memory in *l'an trentuniesme
De son eage*; the case presents
No adjunct to the Muses' diadem.

II

The age demanded an image
Of its accelerated grimace,
Something for the modern stage,
Not, at any rate, an Attic grace;

Not, not certainly, the obscure reveries
Of the inward gaze;
Better mendacities
Than the classics in paraphrase!

The "age demanded" chiefly a mould in plaster,
Made with no loss of time,
A prose kinema, not, not assuredly, alabaster
Or the "sculpture" of rhyme.

III

The tea-rose tea-gown, etc.
Supplants the mousseline of Cos,
The pianola "replaces"
Sappho's barbitos.

Christ follows Dionysus,
Phallic and ambrosial
Made way for macerations;
Caliban casts out Ariel.

All things are a flowing,
Sage Heracleitus says;
But a tawdry cheapness
Shall outlast our days.

Even the Christian beauty
Defects — after Samothrace;
We see τὸ καλόν
Decreed in the market place.

Faun's flesh is not to us,
Nor the saint's vision.
We have the press for wafer;
Franchise for circumcision.

All men, in law, are equals.
Free of Pisistratus,
We choose a knave or an eunuch
To rule over us.

O bright Apollo,
τίν' ἄνδρα, τίν' ἥρωα, τινα θεόν,
What god, man, or hero
Shall I place a tin wreath upon!

IV

These fought in any case,
and some believing,
                    pro domo, in any case . . .

Some quick to arm,
some for adventure,
some from fear of weakness,
some from fear of censure,
some for love of slaughter, in imagination,
learning later . . .
some in fear, learning love of slaughter;

Died some, pro patria,
               non "dulce" non "et decor". . . .
walked eye-deep in hell
believing in old men's lies, then unbelieving
came home, home to a lie,
home to many deceits,
home to old lies and new infamy;
usury age-old and age-thick
and liars in public places.

Daring as never before, wastage as never before.
Young blood and high blood,
fair cheeks, and fine bodies;

fortitude as never before

frankness as never before,
disillusions as never told in the old days,
hysterias, trench confessions,
laughter out of dead bellies.

V

    There died a myriad,
    And of the best, among them,
    For an old bitch gone in the teeth,
    For a botched civilization,

    Charm, smiling at the good mouth,
    Quick eyes gone under earth's lid,

    For two gross of broken statues,
    For a few thousand battered books.

Yeux Glauques

Gladstone was still respected,
When John Ruskin produced
"Kings' Treasuries"; Swinburne
And Rossetti still abused.

Fœtid Buchanan lifted up his voice
When that faun's head of hers
Became a pastime for
Painters and adulterers.

The Burne-Jones cartons
Have preserved her eyes;
Still, at the Tate, they teach
Cophetua to rhapsodize;

Thin like brook-water,
With a vacant gaze.
The English Rubaiyat was still-born
In those days.

The thin, clear gaze, the same
Still darts out faun-like from the half-ruin'd face,
Questing and passive. . . .
"Ah, poor Jenny's case". . .

Bewildered that a world
Shows no surprise
At her last maquero's
Adulteries.

"Siena mi fe'; disfecemi maremma"

Among the pickled fœtuses and bottled bones,
Engaged in perfecting the catalogue,
I found the last scion of the
Senatorial families of Strasbourg, Monsieur Verog.

For two hours he talked of Galliffet;
Of Dowson; of the Rhymers' Club;
Told me how Johnson (Lionel) died
By falling from a high stool in a pub . . .

But showed no trace of alcohol
At the autopsy, privately performed —
Tissue preserved — the pure mind
Arose toward Newman as the whiskey warmed.

Dowson found harlots cheaper than hotels;
Headlam for uplift; Image impartially imbued
With raptures for Bacchus, Terpsichore and the Church.
So spoke the author of "The Dorian Mood,"

M. Verog, out of step with the decade,
Detached from his contemporaries,
Neglected by the young,
Because of these reveries.

Brennbaum

The sky-like limpid eyes,
The circular infant's face,
The stiffness from spats to collar
Never relaxing into grace;

The heavy memories of Horeb, Sinai and the forty years,
Showed only when the daylight fell
Level across the face
Of Brennbaum "The Impeccable."

Mr. Nixon

In the cream gilded cabin of his steam yacht
Mr. Nixon advised me kindly, to advance with fewer
Dangers of delay. "Consider
      Carefully the reviewer.

"I was as poor as you are;
 When I began I got, of course,
 Advance on royalties, fifty at first," said Mr. Nixon,
"Follow me, and take a column,
 Even if you have to work free.

"Butter reviewers. From fifty to three hundred
 I rose in eighteen months;
 The hardest nut I had to crack
 Was Dr. Dundas.

"I never mentioned a man but with the view
Of selling my own works.
The tip's a good one, as for literature
It gives no man a sinecure.

"And no one knows, at sight, a masterpiece.
And give up verse, my boy,
There's nothing in it."

. . . .

Likewise a friend of Blougram's once advised me:
Don't kick against the pricks,
Accept opinion. The "Nineties" tried your game
And died, there's nothing in it.

X

Beneath the sagging roof
The stylist has taken shelter,
Unpaid, uncelebrated,
At last from the world's welter

Nature receives him;
With a placid and uneducated mistress
He exercises his talents
And the soil meets his distress.

The haven from sophistications and contentions
Leaks through its thatch;
He offers succulent cooking;
The door has a creaking latch.

XI

"Conservatrix of Milésien"
Habits of mind and feeling,
Possibly. But in Ealing
With the most bank-clerkly of Englishmen?

No, "Milésian" is an exaggeration.
No instinct has survived in her
Older than those her grandmother
Told her would fit her station.

XII

"Daphne with her thighs in bark
Stretches toward me her leafy hands,"
Subjectively. In the stuffed-satin drawing-room
I await The Lady Valentine's commands,

Knowing my coat has never been
Of precisely the fashion
To stimulate, in her,
A durable passion;

Doubtful, somewhat, of the value
Of well-gowned approbation
Of literary effort,
But never of The Lady Valentine's vocation:

Poetry, her border of ideas,
The edge, uncertain, but a means of blending
With other strata
Where the lower and higher have ending;

A hook to catch the Lady Jane's attention,
A modulation toward the theatre,
Also, in the case of revolution,
A possible friend and comforter.

. . . .

Conduct, on the other hand, the soul
"Which the highest cultures have nourished"
To Fleet St. where
Dr. Johnson flourished;

Beside this thoroughfare
The sale of half-hose has
Long since superseded the cultivation
Of Pierian roses.

Envoi

Go, dumb-born book,
Tell her that sang me once that song of Lawes:
Hadst thou but song
As thou hast subjects known,

Then were there cause in thee that should condone
Even my faults that heavy upon me lie,
And build her glories their longevity.

Tell her that sheds
Such treasure in the air,
Recking naught else but that her graces give
Life to the moment,
I would bid them live
As roses might, in magic amber laid,
Red overwrought with orange and all made
One substance and one colour
Braving time.

Tell her that goes
With song upon her lips
But sings not out the song, nor knows
The maker of it, some other mouth,
May be as fair as hers,
Might, in new ages, gain her worshippers,
When our two dusts with Waller's shall be laid,
Siftings on siftings in oblivion,
Till change hath broken down
All things save Beauty alone.

Mauberley

I

Turned from the "eau-forte
Par Jacquemart"
To the strait head
Of Messalina:

"His true Penelope
Was Flaubert,"
And his tool
The engraver's.

Firmness,
Not the full smile,
His art, but an art
In profile;

Colourless
Pier Francesca,
Pisanello lacking the skill
To forge Achaia.

II

*Qu'est ce qu'ils savent de l'amour, et qu'est ce
qu'ils peuvent comprendre?*
*S'ils ne comprennent pas la poésie, s'ils ne
sentent pas la musique, qu'est ce qu'ils peuvent
comprendre de cette passion en comparaison avec
laquelle la rose est grossière et le parfum des
violettes un tonnerre?*   CAID ALI

For three years, diabolus in the scale,
He drank ambrosia,
All passes, ANANGKE prevails,
Came end, at last, to that Arcadia.

He had moved amid her phantasmagoria,
Amid her galaxies,
NUKTIS 'AGALMA

. . . .

Drifted . . . drifted precipitate,
Asking time to be rid of . . .
Of his bewilderment; to designate
His new found orchid. . . .

To be certain . . . certain . . .
(Amid ærial flowers) . . . time for arrangements —
Drifted on
To the final estrangement;

Unable in the supervening blankness
To sift TO AGATHON from the chaff
Until he found his sieve . . .
Ultimately, his seismograph:

— Given that is his "fundamental passion,"
This urge to convey the relation
Of eye-lid and cheek-bone
By verbal manifestation;
To present the series
Of curious heads in medallion —

He had passed, inconscient, full gaze,
The wide-branded irides
And botticellian sprays implied
In their diastasis:

Which anæsthesis, noted a year late,
And weighed, revealed his great affect,
(Orchid), mandate
Of Eros, a retrospect.

. . . .

Mouths biting empty air,
The still stone dogs,
Caught in metamorphosis, were
Left him as epilogues.

"The Age Demanded"

For this agility chance found
Him of all men, unfit
As the red-beaked steeds of
The Cytheræan for a chain bit.

The glow of porcelain
Brought no reforming sense
To his perception
Of the social inconsequence.

Thus, if her colour
Came against his gaze,
Tempered as if
It were through a perfect glaze

He made no immediate application
Of this to relation of the state
To the individual, the month was more temperate
Because this beauty had been.

> The coral isle, the lion-coloured sand
> Burst in upon the porcelain revery:
> Impetuous troubling
> Of his imagery.

Mildness, amid the neo-Nietzschean clatter,
His sense of graduations,
Quite out of place amid
Resistance to current exacerbations,

Invitation, mere invitation to perceptivity
Gradually led him to the isolation
Which these presents place
Under a more tolerant, perhaps, examination.

By constant elimination
The manifest universe
Yielded an armour
Against utter consternation,

A Minoan undulation,
Seen, we admit, amid ambrosial circumstances
Strengthened him against
The discouraging doctrine of chances,

And his desire for survival,
Faint in the most strenuous moods,
Became an Olympian *apathein*
In the presence of selected perceptions.

A pale gold, in the aforesaid pattern,
The unexpected palms
Destroying, certainly, the artist's urge,
Left him delighted with the imaginary
Audition of the phantasmal sea-surge,

Incapable of the least utterance or composition,
Emendation, conservation of the "better tradition,"
Refinement of medium, elimination of superfluities,
August attraction or concentration.

Nothing, in brief, but maudlin confession,
Irresponse to human aggression,
Amid the precipitation, down-float
Of insubstantial manna,
Lifting the faint susurrus
Of his subjective hosannah.

Ultimate affronts to
Human redundancies;

Non-esteem of self-styled "his betters"
Leading, as he well knew,
To his final
Exclusion from the world of letters.

IV

Scattered Moluccas
Not knowing, day to day
The first day's end, in the next noon;
The placid water
Unbroken by the Simoon;

Thick foliage
Placid beneath warm suns,
Tawn fore-shores
Washed in the cobalt of oblivions;

Or through dawn-mist
The grey and rose
Of the juridical
Flamingoes;

A consciousness disjunct,
Being but this overblotted
Series
Of intermittences;

Coracle of Pacific voyages,
The unforecasted beach;
Then on an oar
Read this:

"I was
And I no more exist;
Here drifted
An hedonist.

Medallion

Luini in porcelain!
The grand piano
Utters a profane
Protest with her clear soprano.

The sleek head emerges
From the gold-yellow frock
As Anadyomene in the opening
Pages of Reinach.

Honey-red, closing the face-oval.
A basket-work of braids which seem as if they were
Spun in King Minos' hall
From metal, or intractable amber;

The face-oval beneath the glaze,
Bright in its suave bounding-line, as,
Beneath half-watt rays,
The eyes turn topaz.

Monumentum Aere, Etc.

You say that I take a good deal upon myself;
That I strut in the robes of assumption.

In a few years no one will remember the *buffo*,
No one will remember the trivial parts of me,
The comic detail will be absent.
As for you, you will rot in the earth,
And it is doubtful if even your manure will be rich enough

To keep grass
Over your grave.

Canto II

Hang it all, Robert Browning,
 there can be but the one "Sordello."
But Sordello, and my Sordello?

Lo Sordels si fo di Mantovana.
So-shu churned in the sea.
Seal sports in the spray-whited circles of cliff-wash,
Sleek head, daughter of Lir,
　　　　　eyes of Picasso
Under the black fur-hood, lithe daughter of Ocean;
And the wave runs in the beach-groove:
"Eleanor, ἐλέναυς and ἐλέπτολις!"
　　　　　And poor old Homer blind, blind, as a bat,
Ear, ear for the sea-surge, murmur of old men's voices:
"Let her go back to the ships,
Back among Grecian faces, lest evil come on our own,
Evil and further evil, and a curse cursed on our children,
Moves, yes she moves like a goddess
And has the face of a god
　　　　　and the voice of Schoeney's daughters,
And doom goes with her in walking,
Let her go back to the ships,
　　　　　back among Grecian voices."
That by the beach-run, Tyro,
　　　　　Twisted arms of the sea-god,
Lithe sinews of water, gripping her, cross-hold,
And the blue-gray glass of the wave tents them,
Glare azure of water, cold-welter, close cover.
Quiet sun-tawny sand-stretch,
The gulls broad out their wings,
　　　　　nipping between the splay feathers;
Snipe come for their bath,
　　　　　bend out their wing-joints,
Spread wet wings to the sun-film,
And by Scios,
　　　　　to left of the Naxos passage,
Naviform rock overgrown,
　　　　　algæ cling to its edge,
There is a wine-red glow in the shallows,
　　　　　a tin flash in the sun-dazzle.

The ship landed in Scios,
　　　　　men wanting spring-water,
And by the rock-pool a young boy loggy with vine-must,
　　　　　"To Naxos? Yes, we'll take you to Naxos,
Cum' along lad." "Not that way!"
"Aye, that way is Naxos."

And I said: "It's a straight ship."
And an ex-convict out of Italy
  knocked me into the fore-stays,
(He was wanted for manslaughter in Tuscany)
  And the whole twenty against me,
Mad for a little slave money.
   And they took her out of Scios
And off her course . . .
   And the boy came to, again, with the racket,
And looked out over the bows,
   and to eastward, and to the Naxos passage.
God sleight then, god-sleight:
  Ship stock fast in sea-swirl,
Ivy upon the oars, King Pentheus,
  grapes with no seed but sea-foam,
Ivy in scupper-hole.
Aye, I, Acœtes, stood there,
  and the god stood by me,
Water cutting under the keel,
Sea-break from stern forrards,
  wake running off from the bow,
And where was gunwale, there now was vine-trunk,
And tenthril where cordage had been,
  grape-leaves on the rowlocks,
Heavy vine on the oarshafts,
And, out of nothing, a breathing,
  hot breath on my ankles,
Beasts like shadows in glass,
  a furred tail upon nothingness.
Lynx-purr, and heathery smell of beasts,
  where tar smell had been,
Sniff and pad-foot of beasts,
  eye-glitter out of black air.
The sky overshot, dry, with no tempest,
Sniff and pad-foot of beasts,
  fur brushing my knee-skin,
Rustle of airy sheaths,
  dry forms in the *æther*.
And the ship like a keel in ship-yard,
  slung like an ox in smith's sling,
Ribs stuck fast in the ways,
  grape-cluster over pin-rack,
  void aid taking pelt.

Lifeless air become sinewed,
        feline leisure of panthers,
Leopards sniffing the grape shoots by scupper-hole,
Crouched panthers by fore-hatch,
And the sea blue-deep about us,
        green-ruddy in shadows,
And Lyæus: "From now, Acœtes, my altars,
Fearing no bondage,
        Fearing no cat of the wood,
Safe with my lynxes,
        feeding grapes to my leopards,
Olibanum is my incense,
        the vines grow in my homage."
The back-swell now smooth in the rudder-chains,
Black snout of a porpoise
        where Lycabs had been,
Fish-scales on the oarsmen,
        And I worship.
I have seen what I have seen.
        When they brought the boy I said:
"He has a god in him,
        though I do not know which god."
And they kicked me into the fore-stays.
I have seen what I have seen:
        Medon's face like the face of a dory,
Arms shrunk into fins. And you, Pentheus,
Had as well listen to Tiresias, and to Cadmus,
        or your luck will go out of you.
Fish-scales over groin muscles,
        lynx-purr amid sea . . .
And of a later year,
        pale in the wine-red algæ,
If you will lean over the rock,
        the coral face under wave-tinge,
Rose-paleness under water-shift,
        Ileuthyeria, fair Dafne of sea-bords,
The swimmer's arms turned to branches,
Who will say in what year,
        fleeing what band of tritons,
The smooth brows, seen, and half seen,
        now ivory stillness.
So-shu churned in the sea, So-shu also,
        using the long moon for a churn-stick . . .

Lithe turning of water,
  sinews of Poseidon,
Black azure and hyaline,
  glass wave over Tyro,
Close cover, unstillness,
  bright welter of wave-cords,
Then quiet water,
  quiet in the buff sands,
Sea-fowl stretching wing-joints,
  splashing in rock-hollows and sand-hollows
In the wave-runs by the half-dune;
Glass-glint of wave in the tide-rips against sunlight,
  pallor of Hesperus,
Grey peak of the wave,
  wave, colour of grape's pulp,

Olive grey in the near,
  far, smoke grey of the rock-slide,
Salmon-pink wings of the fish-hawk
  cast grey shadows in water,
The tower like a one-eyed great goose
  cranes up out of the olive-grove,

And we have heard the fauns chiding Proteus
  in the smell of hay under the olive-trees.
And the frogs singing against the fauns
  in the half-light.
And . . .

Canto VII

Eleanor (she spoiled in a British climate)
Ἑλανδρος and Ελεπτολις, and
  poor old Homer blind,
  blind as a bat,
Ear, ear for the sea-surge;
  rattle of old men's voices.
And then the phantom of Rome,
  marble narrow for seats
"Si pulvis nullus" said Ovid,
"Erit, nullum tamen excute."
To file and candles, e li mestiers ecoutes;

Scene for the battle only, but still scene,
Pennons and standards y cavals armatz
Not mere succession of strokes, sightless narration,
To Dante's "ciocco," brand struck in the game.

Un peu moisi, plancher plus bas que le jardin.

"Contre le lambris, fauteuil de paille,
Un vieux piano, et sous le baromètre . . ."

The old men's voices, beneath the columns of false marble,
The modish and darkish walls,
Discreeter gilding, and the panelled wood
Suggested, for the leasehold is
Touched with an imprecision . . . about three squares;
The house too thick, the paintings
a shade too oiled.
And the great domed head, *con gli occhi onesti e tardi*
Moves before me, phantom with weighted motion,
Grave incessu, drinking the tone of things,
And the old voice lifts itself
            weaving an endless sentence.

We also made ghostly visits, and the stair
That knew us, found us again on the turn of it,
Knocking at empty rooms, seeking for buried beauty;
But the sun-tanned, gracious and well-formed fingers
Lift no latch of bent bronze, no Empire handle
Twists for the knocker's fall; no voice to answer.
A strange concierge, in place of the gouty-footed.
Sceptic against all this one seeks the living,
Stubborn against the fact. The wilted flowers
Brushed out a seven year since, of no effect.
Damn the partition! Paper, dark brown and stretched.
Flimsy and damned partition.
            Ione, dead the long year
My lintel, and Liu Ch'e's.
Time blacked out with the rubber.
            The Elysée carries a name on
And the bus behind me gives me a date for peg;
Low ceiling and the Erard and the silver,
These are in "time." Four chairs, the bow-front dresser,
The panier of the desk, cloth top sunk in.

"Beer-bottle on the statue's pediment!
That, Fritz, is the era, to-day against the past,
Contemporary." And the passion endures.
Against their action, aromas. Rooms, against chronicles.
Smaragdos, chrysolithos; De Gama wore striped pants in Africa
And "Mountains of the sea gave birth to troops";

Le vieux commode en acajou:
        beer-bottles of various strata,
But is she dead as Tyro? In seven years?
'Ελεναυς, ελανδρος, ελεπτολις
The sea runs in the beach-groove, shaking the floated pebbles,
Eleanor!
        The scarlet curtain throws a less scarlet shadow;
Lamplight at Buovilla, e quel remir,
        And all that day
Nicea moved before me
And the cold grey air troubled her not
For all her naked beauty, bit not the tropic skin,
And the long slender feet lit on the curb's marge
And her moving height went before me,
        We alone having being.
And all that day, another day:
        Thin husks I had known as men,
Dry casques of departed locusts
        speaking a shell of speech . . .
Propped between chairs and table . . .
Words like the locust-shells, moved by no inner being;
        A dryness calling for death;

Another day, between walls of a sham Mycenian,
"Toc" sphinxes, sham-Memphis columns,
And beneath the jazz a cortex, a stiffness or stillness,
        Shell of the older house.
Brown-yellow wood, and the no colour plaster,
Dry professorial talk . . .
        now stilling the ill beat music,
House expulsed by this house.

        Square even shoulders and the satin skin,
Gone cheeks of the dancing woman,
        Still the old dead dry talk, gassed out —
It is ten years gone, makes stiff about her a glass,

A petrefaction of air.
      The old room of the tawdry class asserts itself;
The young men, never!
      Only the husk of talk.

O voi che siete in piccioletta barca,
Dido choked up with sobs, for her Sicheus
Lies heavy in my arms, dead weight
      Drowning, with tears, new Eros,

And the life goes on, mooning upon bare hills;
Flame leaps from the hand, the rain is listless,
Yet drinks the thirst from our lips,
      solid as echo,
Passion to breed a form in shimmer of rain-blur;
But Eros drowned, drowned, heavy, half dead with tears
      For dead Sicheus.

Life to make mock of motion:
For the husks, before me, move,
      The words rattle: shells given out by shells.
The live man, out of lands and prisons,
      shakes the dry pods,
Probes for old wills and friendships, and the big locust-casques
Bend to the tawdry table,
Lift up their spoons to mouths, put forks in cutlets,
And make sound like the sound of voices.
      Lorenzaccio
Being more live than they, more full of flames and voices.
Ma se morisse!
      Credesse caduto da sè, ma se morisse.
And the tall indifference moves,
      a more living shell,
Drift in the air of fate, dry phantom, but intact.
O Alessandro, chief and thrice warned, watcher,
      Eternal watcher of things,
Of things, of men, of passions.
      Eyes floating in dry, dark air,
E biondo, with glass-grey iris, with an even side-fall of hair
The stiff, still features.

Canto XLV

With *Usura*
With usura hath no man a house of good stone
each block cut smooth and well fitting
that design might cover their face,
with usura
hath no man a painted paradise on his church wall
harpes et luthes
or where virgin receiveth message
and halo projects from incision,
with usura
seeth no man Gonzaga his heirs and his concubines
no picture is made to endure nor to live with
but it is made to sell and sell quickly
with usura, sin against nature,
is thy bread ever more of stale rags
is thy bread dry as paper,
with no mountain wheat, no strong flour
with usura the line grows thick
with usura is no clear demarcation
and no man can find site for his dwelling.
Stone cutter is kept from his stone
weaver is kept from his loom
WITH USURA
wool comes not to market
sheep bringeth no gain with usura
Usura is a murrain, usura
blunteth the needle in the maid's hand
and stoppeth the spinner's cunning. Pietro Lombardo
came not by usura
Duccio came not by usura
nor Pier della Francesca; Zuan Bellin' not by usura
nor was "La Calunnia" painted.
Came not by usura Angelico; came not Ambrogio Praedis,
Came no church of cut stone signed: *Adamo me fecit.*
Not by usura St Trophime
Not by usura Saint Hilaire,
Usura rusteth the chisel
It rusteth the craft and the craftsman
It gnaweth the thread in the loom
None learned to weave gold in her pattern;

Azure hath a canker by usura; cramoisi is unbroidered
Emerald findeth no Memling
Usura slayeth the child in the womb
It stayeth the young man's courting
It hath brought palsey to bed, lyeth
between the young bride and her bridegroom
                                    CONTRA NATURA
They have brought whores for Eleusis
Corpses are set to banquet
at behest of usura.

Canto LXXXI

Zeus lies in Ceres' bosom
Taishan is attended of loves
                 under Cythera, before sunrise
and he said: Hay aquí mucho catolicismo — (sounded catoli*th*ismo)
                 y muy poco reliHion"
and he said: Yo creo que los reyes desparecen"
(Kings will, I think, disappear)
That was Padre José Elizondo
                 in 1906 and in 1917
or about 1917
                 and Dolores said: Come pan, niño," eat bread, me lad
Sargent had painted her
                 before he descended
(i.e. if he descended
                 but in those days he did thumb sketches,
impressions of the Velasquez in the Museo del Prado
and books cost a peseta,
                 brass candlesticks in proportion,
hot wind came from the marshes
                 and death-chill from the mountains.
And later Bowers wrote: "but such hatred,
       I had never conceived such"
and the London reds wouldn't show up his friends
                 (i.e. friends of Franco
working in London) and in Alcazar
forty years gone, they said: go back to the station to eat
you can sleep here for a peseta"
                 goat bells tinkled all night
                 and the hostess grinned: Eso es luto, *haw!*

mi marido es muerto
        (it is mourning, my husband is dead)
when she gave me paper to write on
with a black border half an inch or more deep,
    say 5/8ths, of the locanda
"We call *all* foreigners frenchies"
and the egg broke in Cabranez' pocket,
        thus making history. Basil says
they beat drums for three days
till all the drumheads were busted
        (simple village fiesta)
and as for his life in the Canaries . . .
Possum observed that the local folk dance
was danced by the same dancers in divers localities
      in political welcome . . .
the technique of demonstration
        Cole studied that (not G.D.H., Horace)
"You will find" said old André Spire,
that every man on that board (Crédit Agricole)
has a brother-in-law
           "You the one, I the few"
          said John Adams
speaking of fears in the abstract
      to his volatile friend Mr Jefferson
(to break the pentameter, that was the first heave)
or as Jo Bard says: they never speak to each other,
if it is baker and concierge visibly
        it is La Rouchefoucauld and de Maintenon audibly.
"Te cavero le budelle"
          "La corata a te"
In less than a geological epoch
          said Henry Mencken
"Some cook, some do not cook
    some things cannot be altered"
"Ἰυγξ. . . . . ἐμὸν ποτί δῶμα τὸν ἄνδρα
What counts is the cultural level,
      thank Benin for this table ex packing box
"doan yu tell no one I made it"
         from a mask fine as any in Frankfurt
"It'll get you offn th' groun' "
          Light as the branch of Kuanon
And at first disappointed with shoddy
the bare ram-shackle quais, but then saw the

high buggy wheels
            and was reconciled,
George Santayana arriving in the port of Boston
and kept to the end of his life that faint *thethear*
of the Spaniard
            as a grace quasi imperceptible
as did Muss the *v* for *u* of Romagna
and said the grief was a full act
            repeated for each new condoleress
working up to a climax.
and George Horace said he wd/"get Beveridge" (Senator)
Beveridge wouldn't talk and he wouldn't write for the papers
but George got him by campin' in his hotel
and assailin' him at lunch breakfast an' dinner
            three articles
and my ole man went on hoein' corn
      while George was a-tellin' him,
come across a vacant lot
           where you'd occasionally see a wild rabbit
or mebbe only a loose one
      AOI!
    a leaf in the current
                at my grates no Althea
libretto   Yet
         Ere the season died a-cold
         Borne upon a zephyr's shoulder
         I rose through the aureate sky
                Lawes and Jenkyns guard thy rest
                Dolmetsch ever be the guest,
         Has he tempered the viol's wood
         To enforce both the grave and the acute?
         Has he curved us the bowl of the lute?
                Lawes and Jenkyns guard thy rest
                Dolmetsch ever be thy guest
        Hast 'ou fashioned so airy a mood
          To draw up leaf from the root?
        Hast 'ou found a cloud so light
          As seemed neither mist nor shade?

               Then resolve me, tell me aright
               If Waller sang or Dowland played,

Your eyen two wol sleye me sodenly
I may the beauté of hem nat susteyne

And for 180 years almost nothing.

Ed ascoltando al leggier mormorio
　　there came new subtlety of eyes into my tent,
whether of spirit or hypostasis,
　　but what the blindfold hides
or at carneval
　　　　　　　　　nor any pair showed anger
　　Saw but the eyes and stance between the eyes,
colour, diastasis,
　　careless or unaware it had not the
　whole tent's room
nor was place for the full 'Ειδὼs
interpass, penetrate
　　casting but shade beyond the other lights
　　　　sky's clear
　　　　night's sea
　　　　green of the mountain pool
　　　　shone from the unmasked eyes in half-mask's space
What thou lovest well remains,
　　　　　　　　　the rest is dross
What thou lov'st well shall not be reft from thee
What thou lov'st well is thy true heritage
Whose world, or mine or theirs
　　　　　　　　or is it of none?
First came the seen, then thus the palpable
　　Elysium, though it were in the halls of hell,
What thou lovest well is thy true heritage
What thou lov'st well shall not be reft from thee

The ant's a centaur in his dragon world.
Pull down thy vanity, it is not man
Made courage, or made order, or made grace,
　　Pull down thy vanity, I say pull down.
Learn of the green world what can be thy place
In scaled invention or true artistry,
Pull down thy vanity,
　　　　　　　　Paquin pull down!
The green casque has outdone your elegance.

"Master thyself, then others shall thee beare"

    Pull down thy vanity
Thou art a beaten dog beneath the hail,
A swollen magpie in a fitful sun,
Half black half white
Nor knowst 'ou wing from tail
Pull down thy vanity
         How mean thy hates
Fostered in falsity,
         Pull down thy vanity,
Rathe to destroy, niggard in charity,
Pull down thy vanity,
         I say pull down.

But to have done instead of not doing
         this is not vanity
To have, with decency, knocked
That a Blunt should open
    To have gathered from the air a live tradition
or from a fine old eye the unconquered flame
This is not vanity.
    Here error is all in the not done,
all in the diffidence that faltered.

H. D.
(HILDA DOOLITTLE)
1886–1961

Pear Tree

Silver dust,
lifted from the earth,
higher than my arms reach,
you have mounted,
O, silver,
higher than my arms reach,
you front us with great mass;

no flower ever opened
so staunch a white leaf,
no flower ever parted silver
from such rare silver;

O, white pear,
your flower-tufts
thick on the branch
bring summer and ripe fruits
in their purple hearts.

Oread

Whirl up, sea —
whirl your pointed pines,
splash your great pines
on our rocks,
hurl your green over us,
cover us with your pools of fir.

At Baia

I should have thought
in a dream you would have brought
some lovely, perilous thing,
orchids piled in a great sheath,
as who would say (in a dream),
"I send you this,
who left the blue veins
of your throat unkissed."

Why was it that your hands
(that never took mine),
your hands that I could see
drift over the orchid-heads
so carefully,
your hands, so fragile, sure to lift
so gently, the fragile flower-stuff —
ah, ah, how was it

You never sent (in a dream)
the very form, the very scent,
not heavy, not sensuous,
but perilous — perilous —
of orchids, piled in a great sheath,
and folded underneath on a bright scroll,
some word:

"Flower sent to flower;
for white hands, the lesser white,
less lovely of flower-leaf,"

or

"Lover to lover, no kiss,
no touch, but forever and ever this."

Helen

All Greece hates
the still eyes in the white face,
the lustre as of olives
where she stands,
and the white hands.

All Greece reviles
the wan face when she smiles,
hating it deeper still
when it grows wan and white,
remembering past enchantments
and past ills.

Greece sees, unmoved,
God's daughter, born of love,
the beauty of cool feet
and slenderest knees,
could love indeed the maid,
only if she were laid,
white ash amid funereal cypresses.

Stars Wheel in Purple

Stars wheel in purple, yours is not so rare
as Hesperus, nor yet so great a star
as bright Aldeboran or Sirius
nor yet the stained and brilliant one of War;

stars turn in purple, glorious to the sight;
yours is not gracious as the Pleiads are
nor as Orion's sapphires, luminous;

yet disenchanted, cold, imperious face,
when all the others blighted, reel and fall,
your star, steel-set, keeps lone and frigid tryst
to freighted ships, baffled in wind and blast.

The Mysteries Remain

The mysteries remain,
I keep the same
cycle of seed-time
and of sun and rain;
Demeter in the grass,
I multiply,
renew and bless
Iacchus in the vine;
I hold the law,
I keep the mysteries true,
the first of these
to name the living, dead;
I am red wine and bread.

I keep the law,
I hold the mysteries true,
I am the vine,
the branches, you
and you.

from Tribute to the Angels

4

Not in our time, O Lord,
the plowshare for the sword,

not in our time, the knife,
sated with life-blood and life,

to trim the barren vine;
no grape-leaf for the thorn,

no vine-flower for the crown;
not in our time, O King,

the voice to quell the re-gathering,
thundering storm.

from The Flowering of the Rod

4

Blue-geese, white-geese, you may say,
yes, I know this duality, this double nostalgia;

I know the insatiable longing
in winter, for palm shadow

and sand and burnt sea-drift;
but in the summer, as I watch

the wave till its edge of foam
touches the hot sand and instantly

vanishes like snow on the equator,
I would cry out, stay, stay;

then I remember delicate enduring frost
and its mid-winter dawn-pattern;

in the hot noon-sun, I think of the grey
opalescent winter-dawn; as the wave

burns on the shingle, I think,
you are less beautiful than frost;

but it is also true that I pray,
O, give me burning blue

and brittle burnt sea-weed
above the tide-line,

as I stand, still unsatisfied,
under the long shadow-on-snow of the pine.

from Good Frend

6

Time has an end, they say,
sea-walls are worn away
by wind and the sea-spray,
not the herb,
      rosemary.

Queens have died, I am told,
faded the cloth-of-gold,
no Caesar half so bold,
as the herb,
      rosemary.

Rooted within the grave,
spreading to heaven, save
us by the grace He gave
to the herb,
      rosemary.

from *Helen in Egypt*

I, 3

Her concern is with the past, with the anathema or curse.
But to the Greeks who perished on the long voyage out, or
who died imprecating her, beneath the Walls, she says,
"you are forgiven." They did not understand what she
herself can only dimly apprehend. She may perceive the
truth, but how explain it? Is it possible that it all
happened, the ruin — it would seem not only of Troy, but
of the "holocaust of the Greeks," of which she speaks
later — in order that two souls or two soul-mates should
meet? It almost seems so.

Alas, my brothers,
Helen did not walk
upon the ramparts,

she whom you cursed
was but the phantom and the shadow thrown
of a reflection;

you are forgiven for I know my own,
and God for his own purpose
wills it so, that I

stricken, forsaken draw to me,
through magic greater than the trial of arms,
your own invincible, unchallenged Sire,

Lord of your legions, King of Myrmidons,
unconquerable, a mountain and a grave,
Achilles;

few were the words we said,
nor knew each other,
nor asked, are you Spirit?

are you sister? are you brother?
are you alive?
are you dead?

the harpers will sing forever
of how Achilles met Helen
among the shades,

but we were not, we are not shadows;
as we walk, heel and sole
leave our sandal-prints in the sand,

though the wounded heel treads lightly
and more lightly follow,
the purple sandals.

. . .

II, 7

So Helen remembers her part in the greatest drama of
Greece and of all time. She seems almost to speak by rote,
she has grown into her part. But she breaks off, as it were,
from the recorded drama to remind us of the unrecorded
. . . her first meeting with Achilles, "on the ledge of a
desolate beach."

Another shout from the wharves;
I fight my way through the crowd,
but the gates are barred;

are the ramparts free?
I am an enemy in a beleaguered city;
I find my way to the Tower,

to the Tower-stairs,
do I run? do I fly?
what pity for Helen?

Hecuba's lordly son
has been slain by Achilles;
could I join the confusion below,

I would leap from the Walls,
but a sentry snatches my sleeves,
dragging me back — what curse

can equal his curse?
how answer his scorn?
"for this is Hector dead,

was Hector born to be conquered
by harlots and thieves,
stealing a prince's honour?

let Paris retrieve
the fate of Priam's city;
he is next to the king

in the Trojan hierarchy,
but we will have no decadent lover
for king, none sick of a fever,

a Grecian harlot brings
to weaken the fibre,
to melt the sinews of war

in a lascivious seven-year dallying";
was it seven years, was it a day?
I can not remember . . .

I only remember the shells,
whiter than bone,
on the ledge of a desolate beach.

ROBINSON JEFFERS
1887–1962

To the Stone-Cutters

Stone-cutters fighting time with marble, you foredefeated
Challengers of oblivion
Eat cynical earnings, knowing rock splits, records fall down,
The square-limbed Roman letters
Scale in the thaws, wear in the rain. The poet as well
Builds his monument mockingly;
For man will be blotted out, the blithe earth die, the brave sun
Die blind and blacken to the heart:
Yet stones have stood for a thousand years, and pained thoughts found
The honey of peace in old poems.

Night

The ebb slips from the rock, the sunken
Tide-rocks lift streaming shoulders
Out of the slack, the slow west
Sombering its torch; a ship's light
Shows faintly, far out,
Over the weight of the prone ocean
On the low cloud.

Over the dark mountain, over the dark pinewood,
Down the long dark valley along the shrunken river,
Returns the splendor without rays, the shining of shadow,
Peace-bringer, the matrix of all shining and quieter of shining.
Where the shore widens on the bay she opens dark wings
And the ocean accepts her glory. O soul worshipful of her
You like the ocean have grave depths where she dwells always,
And the film of waves above that takes the sun takes also
Her, with more love. The sun-lovers have a blond favorite,
A father of lights and noises, wars, weeping and laughter,
Hot labor, lust and delight and the other blemishes. Quietness
Flows from her deeper fountain; and he will die; and she is immortal.

Far off from here the slender
Flocks of the mountain forest
Move among stems like towers
Of the old redwoods to the stream,

No twig crackling; dip shy
Wild muzzles into the mountain water
Among the dark ferns.

O passionately at peace you being secure will pardon
The blasphemies of glowworms, the lamp in my tower, the fretfulness
Of cities, the cressets of the planets, the pride of the stars.
This August night in a rift of cloud Antares reddens,
The great one, the ancient torch, a lord among lost children,
The earth's orbit doubled would not girdle his greatness, one fire
Globed, out of grasp of the mind enormous; but to you O Night
What? Not a spark? What flicker of a spark in the faint far glimmer
Of a lost fire dying in the desert, dim coals of a sand-pit the Bedouins
Wandered from at dawn . . . Ah singing prayer to what gulfs tempted
Suddenly are you more lost? To us the near-hand mountain
Be a measure of height, the tide-worn cliff at the sea-gate a measure of
    continuance.

The tide, moving the night's
Vastness with lonely voices,
Turns, the deep dark-shining
Pacific leans on the land,
Feeling his cold strength
To the outmost margins: you Night will resume
The stars in your time.

O passionately at peace when will that tide draw shoreward?
Truly the spouting fountains of light, Antares, Arcturus,
Tire of their flow, they sing one song but they think silence.
The striding winter giant Orion shines, and dreams darkness.
And life, the flicker of men and moths and the wolf on the hill,
Though furious for continuance, passionately feeding, passionately
Remaking itself upon its mates, remembers deep inward
The calm mother, the quietness of the womb and the egg,
The primal and the latter silences: dear Night it is memory
Prophesies, prophecy that remembers, the charm of the dark.
And I and my people, we are willing to love the four-score years
Heartily; but as a sailor loves the sea, when the helm is for harbor.

Have men's minds changed,
Or the rock hidden in the deep of the waters of the soul
Broken the surface? A few centuries
Gone by, was none dared not to people

The darkness beyond the stars with harps and habitations.
But now, dear is the truth. Life is grown sweeter and lonelier,
And death is no evil.

Phenomena

Great-enough both accepts and subdues; the great frame takes all creatures;
From the greatness of their element they all take beauty.
Gulls; and the dingy freightship lurching south in the eye of a rain-wind;
The airplane dipping over the hill; hawks hovering
The white grass of the headland; cormorants roosting upon the guano-
Whitened skerries; pelicans awind; sea-slime
Shining at night in the wave-stir like drowned men's lanterns; smugglers signaling
A cargo to land; or the old Point Pinos lighthouse
Lawfully winking over dark water; the flight of the twilight herons,
Lonely wings and a cry; or with motor-vibrations
That hum in the rock like a new storm-tone of the ocean's to turn eyes westward
The navy's new-bought Zeppelin going by in the twilight,
Far out seaward; relative only to the evening star and the ocean
It slides into a cloud over Point Lobos.

Shine, Perishing Republic

While this America settles in the mould of its vulgarity, heavily thickening to empire,
And protest, only a bubble in the molten mass, pops and sighs out, and the mass hardens,

I sadly smiling remember that the flower fades to make fruit, the fruit rots to make earth.
Out of the mother; and through the spring exultances, ripeness and decadence; and home to the mother.

You making haste haste on decay: not blameworthy; life is good, be it stubbornly long or suddenly
A mortal splendor: meteors are not needed less than mountains: shine, perishing republic.

But for my children, I would have them keep their distance from the
thickening center; corruption
Never has been compulsory, when the cities lie at the monster's feet
there are left the mountains.

And boys, be in nothing so moderate as in love of man, a clever servant,
insufferable master.
There is the trap that catches noblest spirits, that caught — they say —
God, when he walked on earth.

Fawn's Foster-Mother

The old woman sits on a bench before the door and quarrels
With her meager pale demoralized daughter.
Once when I passed I found her alone, laughing in the sun
And saying that when she was first married
She lived in the old farmhouse up Garapatas Canyon.
(It is empty now, the roof has fallen
But the log walls hang on the stone foundation; the redwoods
Have all been cut down, the oaks are standing;
The place is now more solitary than ever before.)
"When I was nursing my second baby
My husband found a day-old fawn hid in a fern-brake
And brought it; I put its mouth to the breast
Rather than let it starve, I had milk enough for three babies.
Hey, how it sucked, the little nuzzler,
Digging its little hoofs like quills into my stomach.
I had more joy from that than from the others."
Her face is deformed with age, furrowed like a bad road
With market-wagons, mean cares and decay.
She is thrown up to the surface of things, a cell of dry skin
Soon to be shed from the earth's old eyebrows,
I see that once in her spring she lived in the streaming arteries,
The stir of the world, the music of the mountain.

Hurt Hawks

I

The broken pillar of the wing jags from the clotted shoulder,
The wing trails like a banner in defeat,
No more to use the sky forever but live with famine

And pain a few days: cat nor coyote
Will shorten the week of waiting for death, there is game without talons.
He stands under the oak-bush and waits
The lame feet of salvation; at night he remembers freedom
And flies in a dream, the dawns ruin it.
He is strong and pain is worse to the strong, incapacity is worse.
The curs of the day come and torment him
At distance, no one but death the redeemer will humble that head,
The intrepid readiness, the terrible eyes.
The wild God of the world is sometimes merciful to those
That ask mercy, not often to the arrogant.
You do not know him, you communal people, or you have forgotten him;
Intemperate and savage, the hawk remembers him;
Beautiful and wild, the hawks, and men that are dying, remember him.

II

I'd sooner, except the penalties, kill a man than a hawk; but the great
    redtail
Had nothing left but unable misery
From the bone too shattered for mending, the wing that trailed under
    his talons when he moved.
We had fed him six weeks, I gave him freedom,
He wandered over the foreland hill and returned in the evening, asking
    for death,
Not like a beggar, still eyed with the old
Implacable arrogance. I gave him the lead gift in the twilight. What
    fell was relaxed,
Owl-downy, soft feminine feathers; but what
Soared: the fierce rush: the night-herons by the flooded river cried fear
    at its rising
Before it was quite unsheathed from reality.

Apology for Bad Dreams

I

In the purple light, heavy with redwood, the slopes drop seaward,
Headlong convexities of forest, drawn in together to the steep ravine.
    Below, on the sea-cliff,
A lonely clearing; a little field of corn by the streamside; a roof under
    spared trees. Then the ocean
Like a great stone someone has cut to a sharp edge and polished to
    shining. Beyond it, the fountain

And furnace of incredible light flowing up from the sunk sun. In the
little clearing a woman
Is punishing a horse; she had tied the halter to a sapling at the edge of
the wood, but when the great whip
Clung to the flanks the creature kicked so hard she feared he would
snap the halter; she called from the house
The young man her son; who fetched a chain tie-rope, they working
together
Noosed the small rusty links round the horse's tongue
And tied him by the swollen tongue to the tree.
Seen from this height they are shrunk to insect size.
Out of all human relation. You cannot distinguish
The blood dripping from where the chain is fastened,
The beast shuddering; but the thrust neck and the legs
Far apart. You can see the whip fall on the flanks . . .
The gesture of the arm. You cannot see the face of the woman.
The enormous light beats up out of the west across the cloud-bars of
the trade-wind. The ocean
Darkens, the high clouds brighten, the hills darken together. Unbridled
and unbelievable beauty
Covers the evening world . . . not covers, grows apparent out of it, as
Venus down there grows out
From the lit sky. What said the prophet? "I create good: and I
create evil: I am the Lord."

II

This coast crying out for tragedy like all beautiful places,
(The quiet ones ask for quieter suffering: but here the granite cliff
the gaunt cypresses crown
Demands what victim? The dykes of red lava and black what Titan?
The hills like pointed flames
Beyond Soberanes, the terrible peaks of the bare hills under the sun,
what immolation?)
This coast crying out for tragedy like all beautiful places: and like the
passionate spirit of humanity
Pain for its bread: God's, many victims', the painful deaths, the hor-
rible transfigurements: I said in my heart,
"Better invent than suffer: imagine victims
Lest your own flesh be chosen the agonist, or you
Martyr some creature to the beauty of the place." And I said,
"Burn sacrifices once a year to magic
Horror away from the house, this little house here
You have built over the ocean with your own hands

Beside the standing boulders: for what are we,
The beast that walks upright, with speaking lips
And little hair, to think we should always be fed,
Sheltered, intact, and self-controlled? We sooner more liable
Than the other animals. Pain and terror, the insanities of desire; not
    accidents but essential,
And crowd up from the core:" I imagined victims for those wolves, I
    made them phantoms to follow,
They have hunted the phantoms and missed the house. It is not good
    to forget over what gulfs the spirit
Of the beauty of humanity, the petal of a lost flower blown seaward
    by the night-wind, floats to its quietness.

III

Boulders blunted like an old bear's teeth break up from the headland;
    below them
All the soil is thick with shells, the tide-rock feasts of a dead people.
Here the granite flanks are scarred with ancient fire, the ghosts of the
    tribe
Crouch in the nights beside the ghost of a fire, they try to remember
    the sunlight,
Light has died out of their skies. These have paid something for the
    future
Luck of the country, while we living keep old griefs in memory: though
    God's
Envy is not a likely fountain of ruin, to forget evils calls down
Sudden reminders from the cloud: remembered deaths be our re-
    deemers;
Imagined victims our salvation: white as the half moon at midnight
Someone flamelike passed me, saying, "I am Tamar Cauldwell, I have
    my desire,"
Then the voice of the sea returned, when she had gone by, the stars
    to their towers.
. . . Beautiful country burn again, Point Pinos down to the Sur Rivers
Burn as before with bitter wonders, land and ocean and the Carmel
    water.

IV

He brays humanity in a mortar to bring the savor
From the bruised root: a man having bad dreams, who invents victims,
    is only the ape of that God.
He washes it out with tears and many waters, calcines it with fire in
    the red crucible,

Deforms it, makes it horrible to itself: the spirit flies out and stands
    naked, he sees the spirit,
He takes it in the naked ecstasy; it breaks in his hand, the atom is
    broken, the power that massed it
Cries to the power that moves the stars, "I have come home to myself,
    behold me.
I bruised myself in the flint mortar and burnt me
In the red shell, I tortured myself, I flew forth,
Stood naked of myself and broke me in fragments,
And here am I moving the stars that are me."
I have seen these ways of God: I know of no reason
For fire and change and torture and the old returnings.
He being sufficient might be still. I think they admit no reason; they
    are the ways of my love.
Unmeasured power, incredible passion, enormous craft: no thought
    apparent but burns darkly
Smothered with its own smoke in the human brain-vault: no thought
    outside: a certain measure in phenomena:
The fountains of the boiling stars, the flowers on the foreland, the
    ever-returning roses of dawn.

Shane O'Neill's Cairn

To U. J.

When you and I on the Palos Verdes cliff
Found life more desperate than dear,
And when we hawked at it on the lake by Seattle,
In the west of the world, where hardly
Anything has died yet: we'd not have been sorry, Una,
But surprised, to foresee this gray
Coast in our days, the gray waters of the Moyle
Below us, and under our feet
The heavy black stones of the cairn of the lord of Ulster.
A man of blood who died bloodily
Four centuries ago: but death's nothing, and life,
From a high death-mark on a headland
Of this dim island of burials, is nothing either.
How beautiful are both these nothings.

Antrim

No spot of earth where men have so fiercely for ages of time
Fought and survived and cancelled each other,
Pict and Gael and Dane, McQuillan, Clandonnel, O'Neill,
Savages, the Scot, the Norman, the English,
Here in the narrow passage and the pitiless north, perpetual
Betrayals, relentless resultless fighting.
A random fury of dirks in the dark: a struggle for survival
Of hungry blind cells of life in the womb.
But now the womb has grown old, her strength has gone forth; a few
     red carts in a fog creak flax to the dubs,
And sheep in the high heather cry hungrily that life is hard; a plaintive
     peace; shepherds and peasants.

We have felt the blades meet in the flesh in a hundred ambushes
And the groaning blood bubble in the throat;
In a hundred battles the heavy axes bite the deep bone,
The mountain suddenly stagger and be darkened.
Generation on generation we have seen the blood of boys
And heard the moaning of women massacred,
The passionate flesh and nerves have flamed like pitch-pine and fallen
And lain in the earth softly dissolving.
I have lain and been humbled in all these graves, and mixed new flesh
     with the old and filled the hollow of my mouth
With maggots and rotten dust and ages of repose. I lie here and plot
     the agony of resurrection.

Rock and Hawk

Here is a symbol in which
Many high tragic thoughts
Watch their own eyes.

This gray rock, standing tall
On the headland, where the seawind
Lets no tree grow,

Earthquake-proved, and signatured
By ages of storms: on its peak
A falcon has perched.

I think, here is your emblem
To hang in the future sky;
Not the cross, not the hive,

But this; bright power, dark peace;
Fierce consciousness joined with final
Disinterestedness;

Life with calm death; the falcon's
Realist eyes and act
Married to the massive

Mysticism of stone,
Which failure cannot cast down
Nor success make proud.

Ave Caesar

No bitterness: our ancestors did it.
They were only ignorant and hopeful, they wanted freedom but wealth
    too.
Their children will learn to hope for a Caesar.
Or rather — for we are not aquiline Romans but soft mixed colonists —
Some kindly Sicilian tyrant who'll keep
Poverty and Carthage off until the Romans arrive.
We are easy to manage, a gregarious people,
Full of sentiment, clever at mechanics, and we love our luxuries.

The Purse-Seine

Our sardine fishermen work at night in the dark of the moon; daylight
    or moonlight
They could not tell where to spread the net, unable to see the phos-
    phorescence of the shoals of fish.
They work northward from Monterey, coasting Santa Cruz; off New
    Year's Point or off Pigeon Point
The look-out man will see some lakes of milk-color light on the sea's
    night-purple; he points, and the helmsman
Turns the dark prow, the motorboat circles the gleaming shoal and drifts
    out her seine-net. They close the circle
And purse the bottom of the net, then with great labor haul it in.

I cannot tell you
How beautiful the scene is, and a little terrible, then, when the crowded fish
Know they are caught, and wildly beat from one wall to the other of their closing destiny the phosphorescent
Water to a pool of flame, each beautiful slender body sheeted with flame, like a live rocket
A comet's tail wake of clear yellow flame; while outside the narrowing
Floats and cordage of the net great sea-lions come up to watch, sighing in the dark; the vast walls of night
Stand erect to the stars.

Lately I was looking from a night mountain-top
On a wide city, the colored splendor, galaxies of light: how could I help but recall the seine-net
Gathering the luminous fish? I cannot tell you how beautiful the city appeared, and a little terrible.
I thought, We have geared the machines and locked all together into interdependence; we have built the great cities; now
There is no escape. We have gathered vast populations incapable of free survival, insulated
From the strong earth, each person in himself helpless, on all dependent. The circle is closed, and the net
Is being hauled in. They hardly feel the cords drawing, yet they shine already. The inevitable mass-disasters
Will not come in our time nor in our children's, but we and our children
Must watch the net draw narrower, government take all powers — or revolution, and the new government
Take more than all, add to kept bodies kept souls — or anarchy, the mass-disasters.

These things are Progress;
Do you marvel our verse is troubled or frowning, while it keeps its reason? Or it lets go, lets the mood flow
In the manner of the recent young men into mere hysteria, splintered gleams, crackled laughter. But they are quite wrong.
There is no reason for amazement: surely one always knew that cultures decay, and life's end is death.

The Beaks of Eagles

An eagle's nest on the head of an old redwood on one of the precipice-
footed ridges
Above Ventana Creek, that jagged country which nothing but a falling
meteor will ever plow; no horseman
Will ever ride there, no hunter cross this ridge but the winged ones, no
one will steal the eggs from this fortress.
The she-eagle is old, her mate was shot long ago, she is now mated with
a son of hers.
When lightning blasted her nest she built it again on the same tree, in
the splinters of the thunderbolt.
The she-eagle is older than I; she was here when the fires of eighty-five
raged on these ridges,
She was lately fledged and dared not hunt ahead of them but ate
scorched meat. The world has changed in her time;
Humanity has multiplied, but not here; men's hopes and thoughts and
customs have changed, their powers are enlarged,
Their powers and their follies have become fantastic,
The unstable animal never has been changed so rapidly. The motor and
the plane and the great war have gone over him,
And Lenin has lived and Jehovah died: while the mother-eagle
Hunts her same hills, crying the same beautiful and lonely cry and is
never tired; dreams the same dreams,
And hears at night the rock-slides rattle and thunder in the throats of
these living mountains.
                        It is good for man
To try all changes, progress and corruption, powers, peace and anguish,
not to go down the dinosaur's way
Until all his capacities have been explored: and it is good for him
To know that his needs and nature are no more changed in fact in ten
thousand years than the beaks of eagles.

Shiva

There is a hawk that is picking the birds out of our sky.
She killed the pigeons of peace and security,
She has taken honesty and confidence from nations and men,
She is hunting the lonely heron of liberty.
She loads the arts with nonsense, she is very cunning,
Science with dreams and the state with powers to catch them at last.
Nothing will escape her at last, flying nor running.
This is the hawk that picks out the stars' eyes.

This is the only hunter that will ever catch the wild swan;
The prey she will take last is the wild white swan of the beauty of things.
Then she will be alone, pure destruction, achieved and supreme,
Empty darkness under the death-tent wings.
She will build a nest of the swan's bones and hatch a new brood,
Hang new heavens with new birds, all be renewed.

Watch the Lights Fade

Gray steel, cloud-shadow-stained,
The ocean takes the last lights of evening.
Loud is the voice and the foam lead-color,
And flood-tide devours the sands.

Here stand, like an old stone,
And watch the lights fade and hear the sea's voice.
Hate and despair take Europe and Asia,
And the sea-wind blows cold.

Night comes: night will claim all.
The world is not changed, only more naked:
The strong struggle for power, and the weak
Warm their poor hearts with hate.

Night comes: come into the house,
Try around the dial for a late news-cast.
These others are America's voices: naive and
Powerful, spurious, doom-touched.

How soon? Four years or forty?
Why should an old stone pick at the future?
Stand on your shore, old stone, be still while the
Sea-wind salts your head white.

The Eye

The Atlantic is a stormy moat; and the Mediterranean,
The blue pool in the old garden,
More than five thousand years has drunk sacrifice
Of ships and blood, and shines in the sun; but here the Pacific —
Our ships, planes, wars are perfectly irrelevant.

Neither our present blood-feud with the brave dwarfs
Nor any future world-quarrel of westering
And eastering man, the bloody migrations, greed of power, clash of
    faiths —
Is a speck of dust on the great scale-pan.
Here from this mountain shore, headland beyond stormy headland plung-
    ing like dolphins through the blue sea-smoke
Into pale sea — look west at the hill of water: it is half the planet: this
    dome, this half-globe, this bulging
Eyeball of water, arched over to Asia,
Australia and white Antarctica: those are the eyelids that never close;
    this is the staring unsleeping
Eye of the earth; and what it watches is not our wars.

But I Am Growing Old and Indolent

I have been warned. It is more than thirty years since I wrote —
Thinking of the narrative poems I made, which always
Ended in blood and pain, though beautiful enough — my pain, my blood,
They were my creatures — I understood, and wrote to myself:
"Make sacrifices once a year to magic
Horror away from the house" — for that hangs imminent
Over all men and all houses — "This little house here
You have built over the ocean with your own hands
Beside the standing sea-boulders . . ." So I listened
To my Demon warning me that evil would come
If my work ceased, if I did not make sacrifice
Of storied and imagined lives, Tamar and Cawdor
And Thurso's wife — "imagined victims be our redeemers" —
At that time I was sure of my fates and felt
My poems guarding the house, well-made watchdogs
Ready to bite.
                    But time sucks out the juice,
A man grows old and indolent.

Vulture

I had walked since dawn and lay down to rest on a bare hillside
Above the ocean. I saw through half-shut eyelids a vulture wheeling high
    up in heaven,
And presently it passed again, but lower and nearer, its orbit narrowing,
    I understood then

That I was under inspection. I lay death-still and heard the flight-feathers
Whistle above me and make their circle and come nearer.
I could see the naked red head between the great wings
Bear downward staring. I said, "My dear bird, we are wasting time here.
These old bones will still work; they are not for you." But how beautiful
   he looked, gliding down
On those great sails; how beautiful he looked, veering away in the sea-
   light over the precipice. I tell you solemnly
That I was sorry to have disappointed him. To be eaten by that beak and
   become part of him, to share those wings and those eyes —
What a sublime end of one's body, what an enskyment; what a life after
   death.

MARIANNE MOORE
1887–1972

Poetry

I, too, dislike it: there are things that are important beyond all this fiddle.
   Reading it, however, with a perfect contempt for it, one discovers in
   it after all, a place for the genuine.
      Hands that can grasp, eyes
      that can dilate, hair that can rise
         if it must, these things are important not because a

high-sounding interpretation can be put upon them but because they are
   useful. When they become so derivative as to become unintelligible,
   the same thing may be said for all of us, that we
      do not admire what
      we cannot understand: the bat
         holding on upside down or in quest of something to

eat, elephants pushing, a wild horse taking a roll, a tireless wolf under
   a tree, the immovable critic twitching his skin like a horse that feels
                        a flea, the base-
   ball fan, the statistician —
      nor is it valid
         to discriminate against "business documents and

school-books"; all these phenomena are important. One must make a
                                   distinction
   however: when dragged into prominence by half poets, the result is
                                 not poetry,

nor till the poets among us can be
  "literalists of
    the imagination" — above
      insolence and triviality and can present

for inspection, "imaginary gardens with real toads in them," shall we have
it. In the meantime, if you demand on the one hand,
  the raw material of poetry in
    all its rawness and
    that which is on the other hand
      genuine, you are interested in poetry.

Critics and Connoisseurs

There is a great amount of poetry in unconscious
  fastidiousness. Certain Ming
    products, imperial floor coverings of coach-
  wheel yellow, are well enough in their way but I have seen something
    that I like better — a
      mere childish attempt to make an imperfectly ballasted animal
                                                          stand up,
        similar determination to make a pup
          eat his meat from the plate.

I remember a swan under the willows in Oxford,
  with flamingo-colored, maple-
    leaflike feet. It reconnoitered like a battle-
  ship. Disbelief and conscious fastidiousness were
    ingredients in its
      disinclination to move. Finally its hardihood was
        not proof against its
      proclivity to more fully appraise such bits
        of food as the stream

bore counter to it; it made away with what I gave it
  to eat. I have seen this swan and
    I have seen you; I have seen ambition without
  understanding in a variety of forms. Happening to stand
    by an ant-hill, I have
      seen a fastidious ant carrying a stick north, south,
        east, west, till it turned on
      itself, struck out from the flower bed into the lawn,
        and returned to the point

from which it had started. Then abandoning the stick as
  useless and overtaxing its
  jaws with a particle of whitewash — pill-like but
heavy — it again went through the same course of procedure.
        What is
    there in being able
      to say that one has dominated the stream in an attitude of self-
                                defense;
     in proving that one has had the experience
      of carrying a stick?

A Grave

Man looking into the sea,
taking the view from those who have as much right to it as you have to
                              it yourself,
it is human nature to stand in the middle of a thing,
but you cannot stand in the middle of this;
the sea has nothing to give but a well excavated grave.
The firs stand in a procession, each with an emerald turkey foot at
                              the top,
reserved as their contours, saying nothing;
repression, however, is not the most obvious characteristic of the sea;
the sea is a collector, quick to return a rapacious look.
There are others besides you who have worn that look —
whose expression is no longer a protest; the fish no longer investigate
                              them
for their bones have not lasted:
men lower nets, unconscious of the fact that they are desecrating a grave,
and row quickly away — the blades of the oars
moving together like the feet of water spiders as if there were no such
                            thing as death.
The wrinkles progress among themselves in a phalanx — beautiful under
                          networks of foam,
and fade breathlessly while the sea rustles in and out of the seaweed;
the birds swim through the air at top speed, emitting catcalls as
                          heretofore —
the tortoise shell scourges about the feet of the cliffs, in motion beneath
                            them;
and the ocean, under the pulsation of lighthouses and noise of bell buoys,
advances as usual, looking as if it were not that ocean in which dropped
                        things are bound to sink —
in which if they turn and twist, it is neither with volition nor con-
                        sciousness.

Marriage

This institution,
perhaps one should say enterprise
out of respect for which
one says one need not change one's mind
about a thing one has believed in,
requiring public promises
of one's intention
to fulfil a private obligation:
I wonder what Adam and Eve
think of it by this time,
this fire-gilt steel
alive with goldenness;
how bright it shows —
"of circular traditions and impostures,
committing many spoils,"
requiring all one's criminal ingenuity
to avoid!
Psychology which explains everything
explains nothing,
and we are still in doubt.
Eve: beautiful woman —
I have seen her
when she was so handsome
she gave me a start,
able to write simultaneously
in three languages —
English, German, and French —
and talk in the meantime;
equally positive in demanding a commotion
and in stipulating quiet:
"I should like to be alone";
to which the visitor replies,
"I should like to be alone;
why not be alone together?"
Below the incandescent stars
below the incandescent fruit,
the strange experience of beauty;
its existence is too much;
it tears one to pieces
and each fresh wave of consciousness
is poison.

"See her, see her in this common world,"
the central flaw
in that first crystal-fine experiment,
this amalgamation which can never be more
than an interesting impossibility,
describing it
as "that strange paradise
unlike flesh, stones,
gold or stately buildings,
the choicest piece of my life:
the heart rising
in its estate of peace
as a boat rises
with the rising of the water";
constrained in speaking of the serpent —
shed snakeskin in the history of politeness
not to be returned to again —
that invaluable accident
exonerating Adam.
And he has beauty also;
it's distressing — the O thou
to whom from whom,
without whom nothing — Adam;
"something feline,
something colubrine" — how true!
a crouching mythological monster
in that Persian miniature of emerald mines,
raw silk — ivory white, snow white,
oyster white, and six others —
that paddock full of leopards and giraffes —
long lemon-yellow bodies
sown with trapezoids of blue.
Alive with words,
vibrating like a cymbal
touched before it has been struck,
he has prophesied correctly —
the industrious waterfall,
"the speedy stream
which violently bears all before it,
at one time silent as the air
and now as powerful as the wind."
"Treading chasms
on the uncertain footing of a spear,"

forgetting that there is in woman
a quality of mind
which as an instinctive manifestation
is unsafe,
he goes on speaking
in a formal customary strain,
of "past states, the present state,
seals, promises,
the evil one suffered,
the good one enjoys,
hell, heaven,
everything convenient
to promote one's joy."
In him a state of mind
perceives what it was not
intended that he should;
"he experiences a solemn joy
in seeing that he has become an idol."
Plagued by the nightingale
in the new leaves,
with its silence —
not its silence but its silences,
he says of it:
"It clothes me with a shirt of fire."
"He dares not clap his hands
to make it go on
lest it should fly off;
if he does nothing, it will sleep;
if he cries out, it will not understand."
Unnerved by the nightingale
and dazzled by the apple,
impelled by "the illusion of a fire
effectual to extinguish fire,"
compared with which
the shining of the earth
is but deformity — a fire
"as high as deep
as bright as broad
as long as life itself,"
he stumbles over marriage,
"a very trivial object indeed"
to have destroyed the attitude
in which he stood —

the ease of the philosopher
unfathered by a woman.
Unhelpful Hymen!
a kind of overgrown cupid
reduced to insignificance
by the mechanical advertising
parading as involuntary comment,
by that experiment of Adam's
with ways out but no way in —
the ritual of marriage,
augmenting all its lavishness;
its fiddlehead ferns,
lotus flowers, opuntias, white dromedaries,
its hippopotamus —
nose and mouth combined
in one magnificent hopper —
its snake and the potent apple.
He tells us
that "for love that will
gaze an eagle blind,
that is with Hercules
climbing the trees
in the garden of the Hesperides,
from forty-five to seventy
is the best age,"
commending it
as a fine art, as an experiment,
a duty or as merely recreation.
One must not call him ruffian
nor friction a calamity —
the fight to be affectionate:
"no truth can be fully known
until it has been tried
by the tooth of disputation."
The blue panther with black eyes,
the basalt panther with blue eyes,
entirely graceful —
one must give them the path —
the black obsidian Diana
who "darkeneth her countenance
as a bear doth,"
the spiked hand
that has an affection for one

and proves it to the bone,
impatient to assure you
that impatience is the mark of independence,
not of bondage.
"Married people often look that way" —
"seldom and cold, up and down,
mixed and malarial
with a good day and a bad."
We Occidentals are so unemotional,
self lost, the irony preserved
in "the Ahasuerus *tête-à-tête* banquet"
with its small orchids like snakes' tongues,
with its "good monster, lead the way,"
with little laughter
and munificence of humor
in that quixotic atmosphere of frankness
in which "four o'clock does not exist,
but at five o'clock
the ladies in their imperious humility
are ready to receive you";
in which experience attests
that men have power
and sometimes one is made to feel it.
He says, "What monarch would not blush
to have a wife
with hair like a shaving brush?"
The fact of woman
is "not the sound of the flute
but very poison."
She says, "Men are monopolists
of 'stars, garters, buttons
and other shining baubles' —
unfit to be the guardians
of another person's happiness."
He says, "These mummies
must be handled carefully —
'the crumbs from a lion's meal,
a couple of shins and the bit of an ear';
turn to the letter M
and you will find
that 'a wife is a coffin,'
that severe object
with the pleasing geometry

stipulating space not people,
refusing to be buried
and uniquely disappointing,
revengefully wrought in the attitude
of an adoring child
to a distinguished parent."
She says, "This butterfly,
this waterfly, this nomad
that has 'proposed
to settle on my hand for life' —
What can one do with it?
There must have been more time
in Shakespeare's day
to sit and watch a play.
You know so many artists who are fools."
He says, "You know so many fools
who are not artists."
The fact forgot
that "some have merely rights
while some have obligations,"
he loves himself so much,
he can permit himself
no rival in that love.
She loves herself so much,
she cannot see herself enough —
a statuette of ivory on ivory,
the logical last touch
to an expansive splendor
earned as wages for work done:
one is not rich but poor
when one can always seem so right.
What can one do for them —
these savages
condemned to disaffect
all those who are not visionaries
alert to undertake the silly task
of making people noble?
This model of petrine fidelity
who "leaves her peaceful husband
only because she has seen enough of him" —
that orator reminding you,
"I am yours to command."
"Everything to do with love is mystery;

it is more than a day's work
to investigate this science."
One sees that it is rare —
that striking grasp of opposites
opposed each to the other, not to unity,
which in cycloid inclusiveness
has dwarfed the demonstration
of Columbus with the egg —
a triumph of simplicity —
that charitive Euroclydon
of frightening disinterestedness
which the world hates,
admitting:

   "I am such a cow,
     if I had a sorrow
     I should feel it a long time;
     I am not one of those
     who have a great sorrow
     in the morning
     and a great joy at noon";

which says: "I have encountered it
among those unpretentious
protégés of wisdom,
where seeming to parade
as the debater and the Roman,
the statesmanship
of an archaic Daniel Webster
persists to their simplicity of temper
as the essence of the matter:

   'Liberty and union
     now and forever';

the Book on the writing table;
the hand in the breast pocket."

Silence

My father used to say,
"Superior people never make long visits,
have to be shown Longfellow's grave
or the glass flowers at Harvard.
Self-reliant like the cat —
    that takes its prey to privacy,
    the mouse's limp tail hanging like a shoelace from its mouth —
they sometimes enjoy solitude,
and can be robbed of speech
by speech which has delighted them.
The deepest feeling always shows itself in silence;
not in silence, but restraint."
Nor was he insincere in saying, "Make my house your inn."
Inns are not residences.

The Steeple-Jack

Dürer would have seen a reason for living
        in a town like this, with eight stranded whales
to look at; with the sweet sea air coming into your house
on a fine day, from water etched
        with waves as formal as the scales
on a fish.

One by one in two's and three's, the seagulls keep
        flying back and forth over the town clock,
or sailing around the lighthouse without moving their wings —
rising steadily with a slight
        quiver of the body — or flock
mewing where

a sea the purple of the peacock's neck is
        paled to greenish azure as Dürer changed
the pine green of the Tyrol to peacock blue and guinea
gray. You can see a twenty-five-
        pound lobster; and fish nets arranged
to dry. The

whirlwind fife-and-drum of the storm bends the salt
    marsh grass, disturbs stars in the sky and the
star on the steeple; it is a privilege to see so
much confusion. Disguised by what
    might seem the opposite, the sea-
side flowers and

trees are favored by the fog so that you have
    the tropics at first hand: the trumpet vine,
foxglove, giant snapdragon, a salpiglossis that has
spots and stripes; morning-glories, gourds,
    or moon-vines trained on fishing twine
at the back door:

cattails, flags, blueberries and spiderwort,
    striped grass, lichens, sunflowers, asters, daisies —
yellow and crab-claw ragged sailors with green bracts — toad-plant,
petunias, ferns; pink lilies, blue
    ones, tigers; poppies; black sweet-peas.
The climate

is not right for the banyan, frangipani, or
    jack-fruit trees; or for exotic serpent
life. Ring lizard and snakeskin for the foot, if you see fit;
but here they've cats, not cobras, to
    keep down the rats. The diffident
little newt

with white pin-dots on black horizontal spaced-
    out bands lives here; yet there is nothing that
ambition can buy or take away. The college student
named Ambrose sits on the hillside
    with his not-native books and hat
and sees boats

at sea progress white and rigid as if in
    a groove. Liking an elegance of which
the source is not bravado, he knows by heart the antique
sugar-bowl shaped summerhouse of
    interlacing slats, and the pitch
of the church

spire, not true, from which a man in scarlet lets
    down a rope as a spider spins a thread;
he might be part of a novel, but on the sidewalk a
sign says C. J. Poole, Steeple Jack,
    in black and white; and one in red
and white says

Danger. The church portico has four fluted
    columns, each a single piece of stone, made
modester by whitewash. This would be a fit haven for
waifs, children, animals, prisoners,
    and presidents who have repaid
sin-driven

senators by not thinking about them. The
    place has a schoolhouse, a post-office in a
store, fish-houses, hen-houses, a three-masted
    schooner on
the stocks. The hero, the student,
    the steeple jack, each in his way,
is at home.

It could not be dangerous to be living
    in a town like this, of simple people,
who have a steeple-jack placing danger signs by the church
while he is gilding the solid-
    pointed star, which on a steeple
stands for hope.

The Hero

Where there is personal liking we go.
    Where the ground is sour; where there are
    weeds of beanstalk height,
    snakes' hypodermic teeth, or
    the wind brings the "scarebabe voice"
    from the neglected yew set with
    the semiprecious cat's eyes of the owl —
awake, asleep, "raised ears extended to fine points," and so
on — love won't grow.

We do not like some things, and the hero
    doesn't; deviating headstones
    and uncertainty;
    going where one does not wish
    to go; suffering and not
    saying so; standing and listening where something
    is hiding. The hero shrinks
as what it is flies out on muffled wings, with twin yellow
eyes — to and fro —

with quavering water-whistle note, low,
    high, in basso-falsetto chirps
    until the skin creeps.
    Jacob when a-dying, asked
    Joseph: Who are these? and blessed
    both sons, the younger most, vexing Joseph. And
    Joseph was vexing to some.
Cincinnatus was; Regulus; and some of our fellow
men have been, although devout,

like Pilgrim having to go slow
    to find his roll; tired but hopeful —
    hope not being hope
    until all ground for hope has
    vanished; and lenient, looking
    upon a fellow creature's error with the
    feelings of a mother — a
woman or a cat. The decorous frock-coated Negro
by the grotto

answers the fearless sightseeing hobo
    who asks the man she's with, what's this,
    what's that, where's Martha
    buried, "Gen-ral Washington
    there; his lady, here"; speaking
    as if in a play — not seeing her; with a
    sense of human dignity
and reverence for mystery, standing like the shadow
of the willow.

Moses would not be grandson to Pharaoh.
  It is not what I eat that is
  my natural meat,
  the hero says. He's not out
  seeing a sight but the rock
  crystal thing to see — the startling El Greco
  brimming with inner light — that
covets nothing that it has let go. This then you may know
as the hero.

The Monkeys

winked too much and were afraid of snakes. The zebras, supreme in
  their abnormality; the elephants with their fog-colored skin
    and strictly practical appendages
      were there, the small cats; and the parakeet —
        trivial and humdrum on examination, destroying
      bark and portions of the food it could not eat.

I recall their magnificence, now not more magnificent
  than it is dim. It is difficult to recall the ornament,
    speech, and precise manner of what one might
      call the minor acquaintances twenty
        years back; but I shall not forget him — that Gilgamesh among
      the hairy carnivora — that cat with the

wedge-shaped, slate-gray marks on its forelegs and the resolute tail,
  astringently remarking, "They have imposed on us with their pale
    half-fledged protestations, trembling about
      in inarticulate frenzy, saying
        it is not for us to understand art; finding it
      all so difficult, examining the thing

as if it were inconceivably arcanic, as symmet-
  rically frigid as if it had been carved out of chrysoprase
    or marble — strict with tension, malignant
      in its power over us and deeper
        than the sea when it proffers flattery in exchange for hemp,
      rye, flax, horses, platinum, timber, and fur."

The Pangolin

Another armored animal — scale
    lapping scale with spruce-cone regularity until they
form the uninterrupted central
    tail-row! This near artichoke with head and legs and grit-equipped
                                        gizzard,
    the night miniature artist engineer is,
        yes, Leonardo da Vinci's replica —
            impressive animal and toiler of whom we seldom hear.
Armor seems extra. But for him,
    the closing ear-ridge —
        or bare ear lacking even this small
        eminence and similarly safe

contracting nose and eye apertures
    impenetrably closable, are not; a true ant-eater,
not cockroach-eater, who endures
    exhausting solitary trips through unfamiliar ground at night,
    returning before sunrise; stepping in the moonlight,
        on the moonlight peculiarly, that the outside
        edges of his hands may bear the weight and save the claws
    for digging. Serpentined about
        the tree, he draws
        away from danger unpugnaciously,
        with no sound but a harmless hiss; keeping

the fragile grace of the Thomas-
    of-Leighton Buzzard Westminster Abbey wrought-iron vine, or
rolls himself into a ball that has
    power to defy all effort to unroll it; strongly intailed, neat
head for core, on neck not breaking off, with curled-in feet.
        Nevertheless he has sting-proof scales; and nest
        of rocks closed with earth from inside, which he can thus
                                    darken.
    Sun and moon and day and night and man and beast
        each with a splendor
        which man in all his vileness cannot
        set aside; each with an excellence!

"Fearful yet to be feared," the armored
    ant-eater met by the driver-ant does not turn back, but
engulfs what he can, the flattened sword-
      edged leafpoint on the tail and artichoke set leg- and body-plates
    quivering violently when it retaliates
        and swarms on him. Compact like the furled fringed frill
          on the hat-brim of Gargallo's hollow iron head of a
    matador, he will drop and will
        then walk away
          unhurt, although if unintruded on,
          he cautiously works down the tree, helped

by his tail. The giant-pangolin-
    tail, graceful tool, as prop or hand or broom or ax, tipped like
an elephant's trunk with special skin,
    is not lost on this ant- and stone-swallowing uninjurable
    artichoke which simpletons thought a living fable
        whom the stones had nourished, whereas ants had done
          so. Pangolins are not aggressive animals; between
      dusk and day they have the not unchain-like machine-like
        form and frictionless creep of a thing
        made graceful by adversities, con-

versities. To explain grace requires
    a curious hand. If that which is at all were not forever,
why would those who graced the spires
    with animals and gathered there to rest, on cold luxurious
    low stone seats — a monk and monk and monk — between the thus
        ingenious roof supports, have slaved to confuse
          grace with a kindly manner, time in which to pay a debt,
      the cure for sins, a graceful use
        of what are yet
          approved stone mullions branching out across
          the perpendiculars? A sailboat

was the first machine. Pangolins, made
    for moving quietly also, are models of exactness,
on four legs; on hind feet plantigrade,
    with certain postures of a man. Beneath sun and moon, man slaving
to make his life more sweet, leaves half the flowers worth having,
        needing to choose wisely how to use his strength;
          a paper-maker like the wasp; a tractor of foodstuffs,
      like the ant; spidering a length

of web from bluffs
above a stream; in fighting, mechanicked
like the pangolin; capsizing in

disheartenment. Bedizened or stark
naked, man, the self, the being we call human, writing-
master to this world, griffons a dark
"Like does not like like that is obnoxious"; and writes error with four
r's. Among animals, *one* has a sense of humor.
Humor saves a few steps, it saves years. Unignorant,
modest and unemotional, and all emotion,
he has everlasting vigor,
power to grow,
though there are few creatures who can make one
breathe faster and make one erecter.

Not afraid of anything is he,
and then goes cowering forth, tread paced to meet an obstacle
at every step. Consistent with the
formula — warm blood, no gills, two pairs of hands and a few hairs
— that
is a mammal; there he sits in his own habitat,
serge-clad, strong-shod. The prey of fear, he, always
curtailed, extinguished, thwarted by the dusk, work partly
done,
says to the alternating blaze,
"Again the sun!
anew each day; and new and new and new,
that comes into and steadies my soul."

What Are Years?

What is our innocence,
what is our guilt? All are
naked, none is safe. And whence
is courage: the unanswered question,
the resolute doubt —
dumbly calling, deafly listening — that
is misfortune, even death,
encourages others
and in its defeat, stirs

the soul to be strong? He
sees deep and is glad, who
    accedes to mortality
and in his imprisonment rises
upon himself as
the sea in a chasm, struggling to be
free and unable to be,
    in its surrendering
    finds its continuing.

So he who strongly feels,
behaves. The very bird,
    grown taller as he sings, steels
his form straight up. Though he is captive,
his mighty singing
says, satisfaction is a lowly
thing, how pure a thing is joy.
    This is mortality,
    this is eternity.

Spenser's Ireland

has not altered; —
    a place as kind as it is green,
    the greenest place I've never seen.
Every name is a tune.
Denunciations do not affect
    the culprit; nor blows, but it
is torture to him to not be spoken to.
They're natural —
    the coat, like Venus'
mantle lined with stars,
buttoned close at the neck — the sleeves new from disuse.

If in Ireland
    they play the harp backward at need,
    and gather at midday the seed
of the fern, eluding
their "giants all covered with iron," might
    there be fern seed for unlearn-
ing obduracy and for reinstating
the enchantment?

Hindered characters
seldom have mothers
in Irish stories, but they all have grandmothers.

It was Irish;
    a match not a marriage was made
    when my great great grandmother'd said
with native genius for
disunion, "Although your suitor be
    perfection, one objection
is enough; he is not
Irish." Outwitting
    the fairies, befriending the furies,
whoever again
and again says, "I'll never give in," never sees

that you're not free
    until you've been made captive by
    supreme belief — credulity
you say? When large dainty
fingers tremblingly divide the wings
    of the fly for mid-July
with a needle and wrap it with peacock tail,
or tie wool and
    buzzard's wing, their pride,
like the enchanter's
is in care, not madness. Concurring hands divide

flax for damask
    that when bleached by Irish weather
    has the silvered chamois-leather
water-tightness of a
skin. Twisted torcs and gold new-moon-shaped
    lunulae aren't jewelry
like the purple-coral fuchsia-tree's. Eire —
the guillemot
    so neat and the hen
of the heath and the
linnet spinet-sweet — bespeak relentlessness? Then

they are to me
    like enchanted Earl Gerald who
    changed himself into a stag, to

a great green-eyed cat of
the mountain. Discommodity makes
    them invisible; they've dis-
appeared. The Irish say your trouble is their
trouble and your
      joy their joy? I wish
I could believe it;
I am troubled, I'm dissatisfied, I'm Irish.

Enough
Jamestown, 1607–1957

Some in the Godspeed, the Susan C.,
others in the Discovery,

found their too earthly paradise,
a paradise in which hope dies,

found pests and pestilence instead,
the living outnumbered by the dead.

The same reward for best and worst
doomed communism, tried at first.

Three acres each, initiative,
six bushels paid back, they could live.

Captain Dale became kidnaper —
the master — lawless when the spur

was desperation, even though
his victim had let her victim go —

Captain John Smith. Poor Powhatan
was forced to make peace, embittered man.

Then teaching — insidious recourse —
enhancing Pocahontas, flowered of course

in marriage. John Rolfe fell in love
with her and she — in rank above

what she became — renounced her name
yet found her status not too tame.

The crested moss rose casts a spell;
and bud of solid green as well;

old deep pink one with fragrant wings
imparting balsam scent that clings

where red-brown tanbark holds the sun —
path enticing beyond comparison.

Not to begin with. No select
artlessly perfect French effect

mattered at first. (Don't speak in rhyme
of maddened men in starving-time.)

Tested until so unnatural
that one became a cannibal.

Marriage, tobacco, and slavery
initiated liberty

when the Deliverance brought seed
of that now controversial weed —

a blameless plant Red-Ridinghood.
Blameless, but who knows what is good?

The victims of a search for gold
cast yellow soil into the hold.

With nothing but the feeble tower
to mark the site that did not flower,

could the most ardent have been sure
that they had done what would endure?

It was enough; it is enough
if present faith mend partial proof.

In the Public Garden

Boston has a festival —
compositely for all —
and nearby, cupolas of learning
(crimson, blue, and gold) that
have made education individual.

My first — an exceptional,
an almost scriptural —
taxi driver to Cambridge from Back Bay
said, as we went along, "They
make some fine young men at Harvard." I recall

the summer when Faneuil Hall
had its weathervane with gold ball
and grasshopper, gilded again by
a -leafer and -jack
till it glittered. Spring can be a miracle

there — a more than usual
bouquet of what is vernal —
"pear blossoms whiter than the clouds," pin-
oak leaves that barely show
when other trees are making shade, besides small

fairy iris suitable
for Dulcinea del
Toboso; O yes, and snowdrops
in the snow, that smell like
violets. Despite secular bustle,

let me enter King's Chapel
to hear them sing: "My work be praise while
others go and come. No more a stranger
or a guest but like a child
at home." A chapel or a festival

means giving what is mutual,
even if irrational:
black sturgeon eggs — a camel
from Hamadan, Iran;
a jewel, or, what is more unusual,

silence — after a word-waterfall of the banal —
as unattainable
as freedom. And what is freedom for?
For "self-discipline," as our
hardest-working citizen has said — a school;

it is for "freedom to toil"
with a feel for the tool.
Those in the trans-shipment camp must have
a skill. With hope of freedom hanging
by a thread — some gather medicinal

herbs which they can sell.
Ineligible if they ail.
Well?

There are those who will talk for an hour
without telling you why they have
come. And I? This is no madrigal —
no medieval gradual.
It is a grateful tale —
without that radiance which poets
are supposed to have —
unofficial, unprofessional. But still one need not fail

to wish poetry well
where intellect is habitual —
glad that the Muses have a home and swans —
that legend can be factual;
happy that Art, admired in general,
is always actually personal.

JOHN CROWE RANSOM
1888–1974

Bells for John Whiteside's Daughter

There was such speed in her little body,
And such lightness in her footfall,
It is no wonder her brown study
Astonishes us all.

Her wars were bruited in our high window.
We looked among orchard trees and beyond
Where she took arms against her shadow,
Or harried unto the pond

The lazy geese, like a snow cloud
Dripping their snow on the green grass,
Tricking and stopping, sleepy and proud,
Who cried in goose, Alas,

For the tireless heart within the little
Lady with rod that made them rise
From their noon apple-dreams and scuttle
Goose-fashion under the skies!

But now go the bells, and we are ready,
In one house we are sternly stopped
To say we are vexed at her brown study,
Lying so primly propped.

Judith of Bethulia

Beautiful as the flying legend of some leopard
She had not chosen yet her captain, nor Prince
Depositary to her flesh, and our defense;
A wandering beauty is a blade out of its scabbard.
You know how dangerous, gentlemen of threescore?
May you know it yet ten more.

Nor by process of veiling she grew less fabulous.
Grey or blue veils, we were desperate to study
The invincible emanations of her white body,
And the winds at her ordered raiment were ominous.
Might she walk in the market, sit in the council of soldiers?
Only of the extreme elders.

But a rare chance was the girl's then, when the Invader
Trumpeted from the South, and rumbled from the North,
Beleaguered the city from four quarters of the earth,
Our soldiery too craven and sick to aid her —
Where were the arms could countervail this horde?
Her beauty was the sword.

She sat with the elders, and proved on their blear visage
How bright was the weapon unrusted in her keeping,
While he lay surfeiting on their harvest heaping
Wasting the husbandry of their rarest vintage —
And dreaming of the broad-breasted dames for concubine?
These floated on his wine.

He was lapped with bay-leaves, and grass and fumiter weed,
And from under the wine-film encountered his mortal vision,
For even within his tent she accomplished his derision,
Loosing one veil and another, she stood unafraid;
So he perished. Nor brushed her with even so much as a daisy?
She found his destruction easy.

The heathen have all perished. The victory was furnished.
We smote them hiding in vineyards, barns, annexes,
And now their white bones clutter the holes of foxes,
And the chieftain's head, with grinning sockets, and varnished —
Is it hung on the sky with a hideous epitaphy?
No, the woman keeps the trophy.

May God send unto our virtuous lady her Prince!
It is stated she went reluctant to that orgy,
Yet a madness fevers our young men, and not the clergy
Nor the elders have turned them unto modesty since.
Inflamed by the thought of her nakedness with desire?
Yes, and chilled with fear and despair.

Winter Remembered

Two evils, monstrous either one apart,
Possessed me, and were long and loath at going:
A cry of Absence, Absence, in the heart,
And in the wood the furious winter blowing.

Think not, when fire was bright upon my bricks,
And past the tight boards hardly a wind could enter,
I glowed like them, the simple burning sticks,
Far from my cause, my proper heat and center.

Better to walk forth in the frozen air
And wash my wound in the snows; that would be healing;
Because my heart would throb less painful there,
Being caked with cold, and past the smart of feeling.

And where I walked, the murderous winter blast
Would have this body bowed, these eyeballs streaming,
And though I think this heart's blood froze not fast
It ran too small to spare one drop for dreaming.

Dear love, these fingers that had known your touch,
And tied our separate forces first together,
Were ten poor idiot fingers not worth much,
Ten frozen parsnips hanging in the weather.

Captain Carpenter

Captain Carpenter rose up in his prime
Put on his pistols and went riding out
But had got wellnigh nowhere at that time
Till he fell in with ladies in a rout.

It was a pretty lady and all her train
That played with him so sweetly but before
An hour she'd taken a sword with all her main
And twined him of his nose for evermore.

Captain Carpenter mounted up one day
And rode straightway into a stranger rogue
That looked unchristian but be that as may
The Captain did not wait upon prologue.

But drew upon him out of his great heart
The other swung against him with a club
And cracked his two legs at the shinny part
And let him roll and stick like any tub.

Captain Carpenter rode many a time
From male and female took he sundry harms
He met the wife of Satan crying "I'm
The she-wolf bids you shall bear no more arms."

Their strokes and counters whistled in the wind
I wish he had delivered half his blows
But where she should have made off like a hind
The bitch bit off his arms at the elbows.

And Captain Carpenter parted with his ears
To a black devil that used him in this wise
O Jesus ere his threescore and ten years
Another had plucked out his sweet blue eyes.

Captain Carpenter got up on his roan
And sallied from the gate in hell's despite
I heard him asking in the grimmest tone
If any enemy yet there was to fight?

"To any adversary it is fame
If he risk to be wounded by my tongue
Or burnt in two beneath my red heart's flame
Such are the perils he is cast among.

"But if he can he has a pretty choice
From an anatomy with little to lose
Whether he cut my tongue and take my voice
Or whether it be my round red heart he choose."

It was the neatest knave that ever was seen
Stepping in perfume from his lady's bower
Who at this word put in his merry mien
And fell on Captain Carpenter like a tower.

I would not knock old fellows in the dust
But there lay Captain Carpenter on his back
His weapons were the old heart in his bust
And a blade shook between rotten teeth alack.

The rogue in scarlet and grey soon knew his mind
He wished to get his trophy and depart
With gentle apology and touch refined
He pierced him and produced the Captain's heart.

God's mercy rest on Captain Carpenter now
I thought him Sirs an honest gentleman
Citizen husband soldier and scholar enow
Let jangling kites eat of him if they can.

But God's deep curses follow after those
That shore him of his goodly nose and ears
His legs and strong arms at the two elbows
And eyes that had not watered seventy years.

The curse of hell upon the sleek upstart
That got the Captain finally on his back
And took the red red vitals of his heart
And made the kites to whet their beaks clack clack.

Philomela

Procne, Philomela, and Itylus,
Your names are liquid, your improbable tale
Is recited in the classic numbers of the nightingale,
Ah, but our numbers are not felicitous,
It goes not liquidly for us.

Perched on a Roman ilex, and duly apostrophized,
The nightingale descanted unto Ovid;
She has even appeared to the Teutons, the swilled and gravid;
At Fontainebleau it may be the bird was gallicized;
Never was she baptized.

To England came Philomela with her pain,
Fleeing the hawk her husband; querulous ghost,
She wanders when he sits heavy on his roost,
Utters herself in the original again,
The untranslatable refrain.

Not to these shores she came! this other Thrace,
Environ barbarous to the royal Attic;
How could her delicate dirge run democratic,
Delivered in a cloudless boundless public place
To an inordinate race?

I pernoctated with the Oxford students once,
And in the quadrangles, in the cloisters, on the Cher,
Precociously knocked at antique doors ajar,
Fatuously touched the hems of the hierophants,
Sick of my dissonance.

I went out to Bagley Wood, I climbed the hill;
Even the moon had slanted off in a twinkling,
I heard the sepulchral owl and a few bells tinkling,
There was no more villainous day to unfulfil,
The diuturnity was still.

Out óf the darkness where Philomela sat,
Her fairy numbers issued. What then ailed me?
My ears are called capacious but they failed me,
Her classics registered a little flat!
I rose, and venomously spat.

Philomela, Philomela, lover of song,
I am in despair if we may make us worthy,
A bantering breed sophistical and swarthy;
Unto more beautiful, persistently more young,
Thy fabulous provinces belong.

Old Mansion

(After Henry James)

As an intruder I trudged with careful innocence
To mask in decency a meddlesome stare,
Passing the old house often on its eminence,
Exhaling my foreign weed on its weighted air.

Here age seemed newly imaged for the historian
After his monstrous châteaux on the Loire,
A beauty not for depicting by old vulgarian
Reiterations that gentle readers abhor.

It was a Southern manor. One hardly imagines
Towers, arcades, or forbidding fortress walls;
But sufficient state though its peacocks now were pigeons;
Where no courts kept, but grave rites and funerals.

Indeed, not distant, possibly not external
To the property, were tombstones, where the catafalque
Had carried their dead; and projected a note too charnel
But for the honeysuckle on its intricate stalk.

Stability was the character of its rectangle
Whose line was seen in part and guessed in part
Through trees. Decay was the tone of old brick and shingle.
Green shutters dragging frightened the watchful heart

To assert: Your mansion, long and richly inhabited,
Its porches and bowers suiting the children of men,
Will not forever be thus, O man, exhibited,
And one had best hurry to enter it if one can.

And at last, with my happier angel's own temerity,
Did I clang their brazen knocker against the door,
To beg their dole of a look, in simple charity,
Or crumbs of wisdom dropping from their great store.

But it came to nothing — and may so gross denial
Which has been deplored with a beating of the breast
Never shorten the tired historian, loyal
To acknowledge defeat and discover a new quest.

The old mistress was ill, and sent my dismissal
By one even more wrappered and lean and dark
Than that warped concierge and imperturbable vassal
Who had bid me begone from her master's Gothic park.

Emphatically, the old house crumbled; the ruins
Would litter, as already the leaves, this petted sward;
And no annalist went in to the lords or the peons;
The antiquary would finger the bits of shard.

But on retreating I saw myself in the token,
How loving from my dying weed the feather curled
On the languid air; and I went with courage shaken
To dip, alas, into some unseemlier world.

Piazza Piece

— I am a gentleman in a dustcoat trying
To make you hear. Your ears are soft and small
And listen to an old man not at all,
They want the young men's whispering and sighing.

But see the roses on your trellis dying
And hear the spectral singing of the moon;
For I must have my lovely lady soon,
I am a gentleman in a dustcoat trying.

— I am a lady young in beauty waiting
Until my truelove comes, and then we kiss.
But what grey man among the vines is this
Whose words are dry and faint as in a dream?
Back from my trellis, Sir, before I scream!
I am a lady young in beauty waiting.

Vision by Sweetwater

Go and ask Robin to bring the girls over
To Sweetwater, said my Aunt; and that was why
It was like a dream of ladies sweeping by
The willows, clouds, deep meadowgrass, and river.

Robin's sisters and my Aunt's lily daughter
Laughed and talked, and tinkled light as wrens
If there were a little colony all hens
To go walking by the steep turn of Sweetwater.

Let them alone, dear Aunt, just for one minute
Till I go fishing in the dark of my mind:
Where have I seen before, against the wind,
These bright virgins, robed and bare of bonnet,

Flowing with music of their strange quick tongue
And adventuring with delicate paces by the stream, —
Myself a child, old suddenly at the scream
From one of the white throats which it hid among?

The Equilibrists

Full of her long white arms and milky skin
He had a thousand times remembered sin.
Alone in the press of people traveled he,
Minding her jacinth, and myrrh, and ivory.

Mouth he remembered: the quaint orifice
From which came heat that flamed upon the kiss,
Till cold words came down spiral from the head,
Grey doves from the officious tower illsped.

Body: it was a white field ready for love,
On her body's field, with the gaunt tower above,
The lilies grew, beseeching him to take,
If he would pluck and wear them, bruise and break.

Eyes talking: Never mind the cruel words,
Embrace my flowers, but not embrace the swords.
But what they said, the doves came straightway flying
And unsaid: Honor, Honor, they came crying.

Importunate her doves. Too pure, too wise,
Clambering on his shoulder, saying, Arise,
Leave me now, and never let us meet,
Eternal distance now command thy feet.

Predicament indeed, which thus discovers
Honor among thieves, Honor between lovers.
O such a little word is Honor, they feel!
But the grey word is between them cold as steel.

At length I saw these lovers fully were come
Into their torture of equilibrium;
Dreadfully had forsworn each other, and yet
They were bound each to each, and they did not forget.

And rigid as two painful stars, and twirled
About the clustered night their prison world,
They burned with fierce love always to come near,
But Honor beat them back and kept them clear.

Ah, the strict lovers, they are ruined now!
I cried in anger. But with puddled brow
Devising for those gibbeted and brave
Came I descanting: Man, what would you have?

For spin your period out, and draw your breath,
A kinder sæculum begins with Death.
Would you ascend to Heaven and bodiless dwell?
Or take your bodies honorless to Hell?

In Heaven you have heard no marriage is,
No white flesh tinder to your lecheries,
Your male and female tissue sweetly shaped
Sublimed away, and furious blood escaped.

Great lovers lie in Hell, the stubborn ones
Infatuate of the flesh upon the bones;
Stuprate, they rend each other when they kiss,
The pieces kiss again, no end to this.

But still I watched them spinning, orbited nice.
Their flames were not more radiant than their ice.
I dug in the quiet earth and wrought the tomb
And made these lines to memorize their doom: —

EPITAPH

Equilibrists lie here; stranger, tread light;
Close, but untouching in each other's sight;
Mouldered the lips and ashy the tall skull.
Let them lie perilous and beautiful.

Painted Head

By dark severance the apparition head
Smiles from the air a capital on no
Column or a Platonic perhaps head
On a canvas sky depending from nothing;

Stirs up an old illusion of grandeur
By tickling the instinct of heads to be
Absolute and to try decapitation
And to play truant from the body bush;

But too happy and beautiful for those sorts
Of head (homekeeping heads are happiest)
Discovers maybe thirty unwidowed years
Of not dishonoring the faithful stem;

Is nameless and has authored for the evil
Historian headhunters neither book
Nor state and is therefore distinct from tart
Heads with crowns and guilty gallery heads;

Wherefore the extravagant device of art
Unhousing by abstraction this once head
Was capital irony by a loving hand
That knew the no treason of a head like this;

Makes repentance in an unlovely head
For having vinegarly traduced the flesh
Till, the hurt flesh recusing, the hard egg
Is shrunken to its own deathlike surface;

And an image thus. The body bears the head
(So hardly one they terribly are two)
Feeds and obeys and unto please what end?
Not to the glory of tyrant head but to

The estate of body. Beauty is of body.
The flesh contouring shallowly on a head
Is a rock-garden needing body's love
And best bodiness to colorify

The big blue birds sitting and sea-shell flats
And caves, and on the iron acropolis
To spread the hyacinthine hair and rear
The olive garden for the nightingales.

T. S. ELIOT
1888–1965

The Love Song of J. Alfred Prufrock

*S'io credessi che mia risposta fosse
a persona che mai tornasse al mondo,
questa fiamma staria senza più scosse.
Ma perciòche giammai di questo fondo
non tornò vivo alcun, s'i'odo il vero,
senza tema d'infamia ti rispondo.*

Let us go then, you and I,
When the evening is spread out against the sky
Like a patient etherised upon a table;
Let us go, through certain half-deserted streets,

The muttering retreats
Of restless nights in one-night cheap hotels
And sawdust restaurants with oyster-shells:
Streets that follow like a tedious argument
Of insidious intent
To lead you to an overwhelming question. . .
Oh, do not ask, "What is it?"
Let us go and make our visit.

In the room the women come and go
Talking of Michelangelo.

The yellow fog that rubs is back upon the window-panes,
The yellow smoke that rubs its muzzle on the window-panes,
Licked its tongue into the corners of the evening,
Lingered upon the pools that stand in drains,
Let fall upon its back the soot that falls from chimneys,
Slipped by the terrace, made a sudden leap,
And seeing that it was a soft October night,
Curled once about the house, and fell asleep.

And indeed there will be time
For the yellow smoke that slides along the street
Rubbing its back upon the window-panes;
There will be time, there will be time
To prepare a face to meet the faces that you meet;
There will be time to murder and create,
And time for all the works and days of hands
That lift and drop a question on your plate;
Time for you and time for me,
And time yet for a hundred indecisions,
And for a hundred visions and revisions,
Before the taking of a toast and tea.

In the room the women come and go
Talking of Michelangelo.

And indeed there will be time
To wonder, "Do I dare?" and, "Do I dare?"
Time to turn back and descend the stair,
With a bald spot in the middle of my hair —
(They will say: "How his hair is growing thin!")
My morning coat, my collar mounting firmly to the chin,

My necktie rich and modest, but asserted by a simple pin —
(They will say: "But how his arms and legs are thin!")
Do I dare
Disturb the universe?
In a minute there is time
For decisions and revisions which a minute will reverse.

    For I have known them all already, known them all —
Have known the evenings, mornings, afternoons,
I have measured out my life with coffee spoons;
I know the voices dying with a dying fall
Beneath the music from a farther room.
      So how should I presume?

    And I have known the eyes already, known them all —
The eyes that fix you in a formulated phrase,
And when I am formulated, sprawling on a pin,
When I am pinned and, wriggling on the wall,
Then how should I begin
To spit out all the butt-ends of my days and ways?
      And how should I presume?

    And I have known the arms already, known them all —
Arms that are braceleted and white and bare
(But in the lamplight, downed with light brown hair!)
Is it perfume from a dress
That makes me so digress?
Arms that lie along a table, or wrap about a shawl..
      And should I then presume?
      And how should I begin?

       · · · · ·

    Shall I say, I have gone at dusk through narrow streets
And watched the smoke that rises from the pipes
Of lonely men in shirt-sleeves, leaning out of windows? . . .

    I should have been a pair of ragged claws
Scuttling across the floors of silent seas.

       · · · · ·

And the afternoon, the evening, sleeps so peacefully!
Smoothed by long fingers,
Asleep . . . tired . . . or it malingers,
Stretched on the floor, here beside you and me.
Should I, after tea and cakes and ices,
Have the strength to force the moment to its crisis?
But though I have wept and fasted, wept and prayed,
Though I have seen my head (grown slightly bald)
   brought in upon a platter,
I am no prophet — and here's no great matter;
I have seen the moment of my greatness flicker,
And I have seen the eternal Footman hold my coat, and snicker,
And in short, I was afraid.

And would it have been worth it, after all,
After the cups, the marmalade, the tea,
Among the porcelain, among some talk of you and me,
Would it have been worth while,
To have bitten off the matter with a smile,
To have squeezed the universe into a ball
To roll it towards some overwhelming question,
To say: "I am Lazarus, come from the dead,
Come back to tell you all, I shall tell you all" —
If one, settling a pillow by her head,
   Should say: "That is not what I meant at all.
   That is not it, at all."

And would it have been worth it, after all,
Would it have been worth while,
After the sunsets and the dooryards and the sprinkled streets,
After the novels, after the teacups, after the skirts that trail along
   the floor —
And this, and so much more? —
It is impossible to say just what I mean!
But as if a magic lantern threw the nerves in patterns on a screen:
Would it have been worth while
If one, settling a pillow or throwing off a shawl,
And turning toward the window, should say:
   "That is not it at all,
   That is not what I meant, at all."

. . . . .

No! I am not Prince Hamlet, nor was meant to be;
Am an attendant lord, one that will do
To swell a progress, start a scene or two,
Advise the prince; no doubt, an easy tool,
Deferential, glad to be of use,
Politic, cautious, and meticulous;
Full of high sentence, but a bit obtuse;
At times, indeed, almost ridiculous —
Almost, at times, the Fool.

I grow old . . . I grow old . . .
I shall wear the bottoms of my trousers rolled.

Shall I part my hair behind? Do I dare to eat a peach?
I shall wear white flannel trousers, and walk upon the beach.
I have heard the mermaids singing, each to each.

I do not think that they will sing to me.

I have seen them riding seaward on the waves
Combing the white hair of the waves blown back
When the wind blows the water white and black.

We have lingered in the chambers of the sea
By sea-girls wreathed with seaweed red and brown
Till human voices wake us, and we drown.

Gerontion

*Thou hast nor youth nor age
But as it were an after dinner sleep
Dreaming of both.*

Here I am, an old man in a dry month,
Being read to by a boy, waiting for rain.
I was neither at the hot gates
Nor fought in the warm rain
Nor knee deep in the salt marsh, heaving a cutlass,
Bitten by flies, fought.
My house is a decayed house,
And the Jew squats on the window sill, the owner,
Spawned in some estaminet of Antwerp,
Blistered in Brussels, patched and peeled in London.

The goat coughs at night in the field overhead;
Rocks, moss, stonecrop, iron, merds.
The woman keeps the kitchen, makes tea,
Sneezes at evening, poking the peevish gutter.
                              I an old man,
A dull head among windy spaces.

Signs are taken for wonders. "We would see a sign!"
The word within a word, unable to speak a word,
Swaddled with darkness. In the juvescence of the year
Came Christ the tiger

In depraved May, dogwood and chestnut, flowering Judas,
To be eaten, to be divided, to be drunk
Among whispers; by Mr. Silvero
With caressing hands, at Limoges
Who walked all night in the next room;
By Hakagawa, bowing among the Titians;
By Madame de Tornquist, in the dark room
Shifting the candles; Fräulein von Kulp
Who turned in the hall, one hand on the door. Vacant shuttles
Weave the wind. I have no ghosts,
An old man in a draughty house
Under a windy knob.

After such knowledge, what forgiveness? Think now
History has many cunning passages, contrived corridors
And issues, deceives with whispering ambitions,
Guides us by vanities. Think now
She gives when our attention is distracted
And what she gives, gives with such supple confusions
That the giving famishes the craving. Gives too late
What's not believed in, or if still believed,
In memory only, reconsidered passion. Gives too soon
Into weak hands, what's thought can be dispensed with
Till the refusal propagates a fear. Think
Neither fear nor courage saves us. Unnatural vices
Are fathered by our heroism. Virtues
Are forced upon us by our impudent crimes.
These tears are shaken from the wrath-bearing tree.

The tiger springs in the new year. Us he devours. Think at last
We have not reached conclusion, when I
Stiffen in a rented house. Think at last
I have not made this show purposelessly
And it is not by any concitation
Of the backward devils.
I would meet you upon this honestly.
I that was near your heart was removed therefrom
To lose beauty in terror, terror in inquisition.
I have lost my passion: why should I need to keep it
Since what is kept must be adulterated?
I have lost my sight, smell, hearing, taste and touch:
How should I use them for your closer contact?

These with a thousand small deliberations
Protract the profit of their chilled delirium,
Excite the membrane, when the sense has cooled,
With pungent sauces, multiply variety
In a wilderness of mirrors. What will the spider do,
Suspend its operations, will the weevil
Delay? De Bailhache, Fresca, Mrs. Cammel, whirled
Beyond the circuit of the shuddering Bear
In fractured atoms. Gull against the wind, in the windy straits
Of Belle Isle, or running on the Horn.
White feathers in the snow, the Gulf claims,
And an old man driven by the Trades
To a sleepy corner.

                             Tenants of the house,
Thoughts of a dry brain in a dry season.

Whispers of Immortality

Webster was much possessed by death
And saw the skull beneath the skin;
And breastless creatures under ground
Leaned backward with a lipless grin.

Daffodil bulbs instead of balls
Stared from the sockets of the eyes!
He knew that thought clings round dead limbs
Tightening its lusts and luxuries.

Donne, I suppose, was such another
Who found no substitute for sense,
To seize and clutch and penetrate;
Expert beyond experience,

He knew the anguish of the marrow
The ague of the skeleton;
No contact possible to flesh
Allayed the fever of the bone.

.   .   .   .   .

Grishkin is nice: her Russian eye
Is underlined for emphasis;
Uncorseted, her friendly bust
Gives promise of pneumatic bliss.

The couched Brazilian jaguar
Compels the scampering marmoset
With subtle effluence of cat;
Grishkin has a maisonnette;

The sleek Brazilian jaguar
Does not in its arboreal gloom
Distil so rank a feline smell
As Grishkin in a drawing-room.

And even the Abstract Entities
Circumambulate her charm;
But our lot crawls between dry ribs
To keep our metaphysics warm.

Sweeney Among the Nightingales

ὤμοι, πέπληγμαι καιρίαν πληγὴν ἔσω.

Apeneck Sweeney spreads his knees
Letting his arms hang down to laugh,
The zebra stripes along his jaw
Swelling to maculate giraffe.

The circles of the stormy moon
Slide westward toward the River Plate,
Death and thĕ Raven drift above
And Sweeney guards the hornèd gate.

Gloomy Orion and the Dog
Are veiled; and hushed the shrunken seas;
The person in the Spanish cape
Tries to sit on Sweeney's knees

Slips and pulls the table cloth
Overturns a coffee-cup,
Reorganised upon the floor
She yawns and draws a stocking up;

The silent man in mocha brown
Sprawls at the window-sill and gapes;
The waiter brings in oranges
Bananas figs and hothouse grapes;

The silent vertebrate in brown
Contacts and concentrates, withdraws;
Rachel *née* Rabinovitch
Tears at the grapes with murderous paws;

She and the lady in the cape
Are suspect, thought to be in league;
Therefore the man with heavy eyes
Declines the gambit, shows fatigue,

Leaves the room and reappears
Outside the window, leaning in,
Branches of wistaria
Circumscribe a golden grin;

The host with someone indistinct
Converses at the door apart,
The nightingales are singing near
The Convent of the Sacred Heart,

And sang within the bloody wood
When Agamemnon cried aloud
And let their liquid siftings fall
To stain the stiff dishonoured shroud.

The Waste Land

"Nam Sibyllam quidem Cumis ego ipse oculis meis vidi in ampulla pendere, et cum illi pueri dicerent: Σίβνλλα τί θέλεις; respondebat illa: ἀποθανεῖν θέλω."

For Ezra Pound
il miglior fabbro.

I. The Burial of the Dead

April is the cruellest month, breeding
Lilacs out of the dead land, mixing
Memory and desire, stirring
Dull roots with spring rain.
Winter kept us warm, covering
Earth in forgetful snow, feeding
A little life with dried tubers.
Summer surprised us, coming over the Starnbergersee
With a shower of rain; we stopped in the colonnade,
And went on in sunlight, into the Hofgarten,   10
And drank coffee, and talked for an hour.
Bin gar keine Russin, stamm' aus Litauen, echt deutsch.
And when we were children, staying at the arch-duke's,
My cousin's, he took me out on a sled,
And I was frightened. He said, Marie,
Marie, hold on tight. And down we went.
In the mountains, there you feel free.
I read, much of the night, and go south in the winter.

What are the roots that clutch, what branches grow
Out of this stony rubbish? Son of man,   20
You cannot say, or guess, for you know only
A heap of broken images, where the sun beats,
And the dead tree gives no shelter, the cricket no relief,
And the dry stone no sound of water. Only
There is shadow under this red rock,
Come in under the shadow of this red rock),
And I will show you something different from either
Your shadow at morning striding behind you
Or your shadow at evening rising to meet you;
I will show you fear in a handful of dust.   30
     Frisch weht der Wind
     Der Heimat zu
     Mein Irisch Kind,
     Wo weilest du?

"You gave me hyacinths first a year ago;
They called me the hyacinth girl."
— Yet when we came back, late, from the hyacinth garden,
Your arms full, and your hair wet, I could not
Speak, and my eyes failed, I was neither
Living nor dead, and I knew nothing,
Looking into the heart of light, the silence.
Oed' und leer das Meer.

Madame Sosostris, famous clairvoyante,
Had a bad cold, nevertheless
Is known to be the wisest woman in Europe,
With a wicked pack of cards. Here, said she,
Is your card, the drowned Phoenician Sailor,
(Those are pearls that were his eyes. Look!)
Here is Belladonna, the Lady of the Rocks,
The lady of situations.
Here is the man with three staves, and here the Wheel,
And here is the one-eyed merchant, and this card,
Which is blank, is something he carries on his back,
Which I am forbidden to see. I do not find
The Hanged Man. Fear death by water.
I see crowds of people, walking round in a ring.
Thank you. If you see dear Mrs. Equitone,
Tell her I bring the horoscope myself:
One must be so careful these days.

Unreal City,
Under the brown fog of a winter dawn,
A crowd flowed over London Bridge, so many,
I had not thought death had undone so many.
Sighs, short and infrequent, were exhaled,
And each man fixed his eyes before his feet.
Flowed up the hill and down King William Street,
To where Saint Mary Woolnoth kept the hours
With a dead sound on the final stroke of nine.
There I saw one I knew, and stopped him, crying: "Stetson!
You who were with me in the ships at Mylae!
That corpse you planted last year in your garden,
Has it begun to sprout? Will it bloom this year?
Or has the sudden frost disturbed its bed?
O keep the Dog far hence, that's friend to men,
Or with his nails he'll dig it up again!
You! hypocrite lecteur! — mon semblable, — mon frère!"

II. A *Game of Chess*

The Chair she sat in, like a burnished throne,
Glowed on the marble, where the glass
Held up by standards wrought with fruited vines
From which a golden Cupidon peeped out   80
(Another hid his eyes behind his wing)
Doubled the flames of sevenbranched candelabra
Reflecting light upon the table as
The glitter of her jewels rose to meet it,
From satin cases poured in rich profusion.
In vials of ivory and coloured glass
Unstoppered, lurked her strange synthetic perfumes,
Unguent, powdered, or liquid — troubled, confused
And drowned the sense in odours; stirred by the air
That freshened from the window, these ascended   90
In fattening the prolonged candle-flames,
Flung their smoke into the laquearia,
Stirring the pattern on the coffered ceiling.
Huge sea-wood fed with copper
Burned green and orange, framed by the coloured stone,
In which sad light a carved dolphin swam.
Above the antique mantel was displayed
As though a window gave upon the sylvan scene
The change of Philomel, by the barbarous king
So rudely forced; yet there the nightingale   100
Filled all the desert with inviolable voice
And still she cried, and still the world pursues,
"Jug Jug" to dirty ears.
And other withered stumps of time
Were told upon the walls; staring forms
Leaned out, leaning, hushing the room enclosed.
Footsteps shuffled on the stair.
Under the firelight, under the brush, her hair
Spread out in fiery points
Glowed into words, then would be savagely still.   110

    "My nerves are bad to-night. Yes, bad. Stay with me.
Speak to me. Why do you never speak. Speak.
    What are you thinking of? What thinking? What?
I never know what you are thinking. Think."

I think we are in rats' alley
Where the dead men lost their bones.

"What is that noise?"
        The wind under the door.
"What is that noise now? What is the wind doing?"
        Nothing again nothing.
                    "Do
You know nothing? Do you see nothing? Do you remember
Nothing?"

    I remember
Those are pearls that were his eyes.
"Are you alive, or not? Is there nothing in your head?"
                    But
O O O O that Shakespeherian Rag —
It's so elegant
So intelligent
"What shall I do now? What shall I do?"
"I shall rush out as I am, and walk the street
With my hair down, so. What shall we do tomorrow?
What shall we ever do?"
              The hot water at ten.
And if it rains, a closed car at four.
And we shall play a game of chess,
Pressing lidless eyes and waiting for a knock upon the door.

    When Lil's husband got demobbed, I said —
I didn't mince my words, I said to her myself,
HURRY UP PLEASE ITS TIME
Now Albert's coming back, make yourself a bit smart.
He'll want to know what you done with that money he gave you
To get yourself some teeth. He did, I was there.
You have them all out, Lil, and get a nice set,
He said, I swear, I can't bear to look at you.
And no more can't I, I said, and think of poor Albert,
He's been in the army four years, he wants a good time,
And if you don't give it him, there's others will, I said.
Oh is there, she said. Something o' that, I said.
Then I'll know who to thank, she said, and give me a straight look.
HURRY UP PLEASE ITS TIME
If you don't like it you can get on with it, I said.
Others can pick and choose if you can't.
But if Albert makes off, it won't be for lack of telling.
You ought to be ashamed, I said, to look so antique.
(And her only thirty-one.)

I can't help it, she said, pulling a long face,
It's them pills I took, to bring it off, she said.
(She's had five already, and nearly died of young George.) 160
The chemist said it would be all right, but I've never been the same.
You *are* a proper fool, I said.
Well, if Albert won't leave you alone, there it is, I said,
What you get married for if you don't want children?
HURRY UP PLEASE ITS TIME
Well, that Sunday Albert was home, they had a hot gammon,
And they asked me in to dinner, to get the beauty of it hot —
HURRY UP PLEASE ITS TIME
HURRY UP PLEASE ITS TIME
Goonight Bill. Goonight Lou. Goonight May. Goonight. 170
Ta ta. Goonight. Goonight.
Good night, ladies, good night, sweet ladies, good night, good night.

III. *The Fire Sermon*

  The river's tent is broken; the last fingers of leaf
Clutch and sink into the wet bank. The wind
Crosses the brown land, unheard. The nymphs are departed.
Sweet Thames, run softly, till I end my song.
The river bears no empty bottles, sandwich papers,
Silk handkerchiefs, cardboard boxes, cigarette ends
Or other testimony of summer nights. The nymphs are departed.
And their friends, the loitering heirs of City directors; 180
Departed, have left no addresses.
By the waters of Leman I sat down and wept . . .
Sweet Thames, run softly till I end my song,
Sweet Thames, run softly, for I speak not loud or long.
But at my back in a cold blast I hear
The rattle of the bones, and chuckle spread from ear to ear.

A rat crept softly through the vegetation
Dragging its slimy belly on the bank
While I was fishing in the dull canal
On a winter evening round behind the gashouse 190
Musing upon the king my brother's wreck
And on the king my father's death before him.
White bodies naked on the low damp ground
And bones cast in a little low dry garret,
Rattled by the rat's foot only, year to year.

But at my back from time to time I hear
The sound of horns and motors, which shall bring
Sweeney to Mrs. Porter in the spring.
O the moon shone bright on Mrs. Porter
And on her daughter   20
They wash their feet in soda water
Et O ces voix d'enfants, chantant dans la coupole!

Twit twit twit
Jug jug jug jug jug jug
So rudely forc'd.
Tereu

   Unreal City
Under the brown fog of a winter noon
Mr. Eugenides, the Smyrna merchant
Unshaven, with a pocket full of currants   21
C.i.f. London: documents at sight,
Asked me in demotic French
To luncheon at the Cannon Street Hotel
Followed by a weekend at the Metropole.

   At the violet hour, when the eyes and back
Turn upward from the desk, when the human engine waits
Like a taxi throbbing waiting,
I Tiresias, though blind, throbbing between two lives,
Old man with wrinkled female breasts, can see
At the violet hour, the evening hour that strives   22
Homeward, and brings the sailor home from sea,
The typist home at teatime, clears her breakfast, lights
Her stove, and lays out food in tins.
Out of the window perilously spread
Her drying combinations touched by the sun's last rays,
On the divan are piled (at night her bed)
Stockings, slippers, camisoles, and stays.
I Tiresias, old man with wrinkled dugs
Perceived the scene, and foretold the rest —
I too awaited the expected guest.   2
He, the young man carbuncular, arrives,
A small house agent's clerk, with one bold stare,
One of the low on whom assurance sits
As a silk hat on a Bradford millionaire.

The time is now propitious, as he guesses,
The meal is ended, she is bored and tired,
Endeavours to engage her in caresses
Which still are unreproved, if undesired.
Flushed and decided, he assaults at once;
Exploring hands encounter no defence;   240
His vanity requires no response,
And makes a welcome of indifference.
(And I Tiresias have foresuffered all
Enacted on this same divan or bed;
I who have sat by Thebes below the wall
And walked among the lowest of the dead.)
Bestows one final patronising kiss,
And gropes his way, finding the stairs unlit . . .

        She turns and looks a moment in the glass,
Hardly aware of her departed lover;   250
Her brain allows one half-formed thought to pass:
"Well now that's done: and I'm glad it's over."
When lovely woman stoops to folly and
Paces about her room again, alone,
She smoothes her hair with automatic hand,
And puts a record on the gramophone.

"This music crept by me upon the waters"
And along the Strand, up Queen Victoria Street.
O City city, I can sometimes hear
Besides a public bar in Lower Thames Street,   260
The pleasant whining of a mandoline
And a clatter and a chatter from within
Where fishmen lounge at noon: where the walls
Of Magnus Martyr hold
Inexplicable splendour of Ionian white and gold.

            The river sweats
            Oil and tar
            The barges drift
            With the turning tide
            Red sails   270
            Wide
            To leeward, swing on the heavy spar.
            The barges wash
            Drifting logs

Down Greenwich reach
Past the Isle of Dogs.
>>Weialala leia
>>Wallala leialala

Elizabeth and Leicester
Beating oars
The stern was formed
A gilded shell
Red and gold
The brisk swell
Rippled both shores
Southwest wind
Carried down stream
The peal of bells
White towers
>>Weialala leia
>>Wallala leialala

"Trams and dusty trees.
Highbury bore me. Richmond and Kew
Undid me. By Richmond I raised my knees
Supine on the floor of a narrow canoe."

"My feet are at Moorgate, and my heart
Under my feet. After the event
He wept. He promised 'a new start.'
I made no comment. What should I resent?"

"On Margate Sands.
I can connect
Nothing with nothing.
The broken fingernails of dirty hands.
My people humble people who expect
Nothing."
>>la la

To Carthage then I came

Burning burning burning burning
O Lord Thou pluckest me out
O Lord Thou pluckest

burning

IV. *Death by Water*

Phlebas the Phoenician, a fortnight dead,
Forgot the cry of gulls, and the deep sea swell
And the profit and loss.
                                    A current under sea
Picked his bones in whispers. As he rose and fell
He passed the stages of his age and youth
Entering the whirlpool.
                                    Gentile or Jew
O you who turn the wheel and look to windward,   320
Consider Phlebas, who was once handsome and tall as you.

V. *What the Thunder said*

After the torchlight red on sweaty faces
After the frosty silence in the gardens
After the agony in stony places
The shouting and the crying
Prison and palace and reverberation
Of thunder of spring over distant mountains
He who was living is now dead
We who were living are now dying
With a little patience   330

Here is no water but only rock
Rock and no water and the sandy road
The road winding above among the mountains
Which are mountains of rock without water
If there were water we should stop and drink
Amongst the rock one cannot stop or think
Sweat is dry and feet are in the sand
If there were only water amongst the rock
Dead mountain mouth of carious teeth that cannot spit
Here one can neither stand nor lie nor sit   340
There is not even silence in the mountains
But dry sterile thunder without rain
There is not even solitude in the mountains
But red sullen faces sneer and snarl
From doors of mudcracked houses
                        If there were water
    And no rock
    If there were rock

And also water
And water
A spring
A pool among the rock
If there were the sound of water only
Not the cicada
And dry grass singing
But sound of water over a rock
Where the hermit-thrush sings in the pine trees
Drip drop drip drop drop drop drop
But there is no water

Who is the third who walks always beside you?
When I count, there are only you and I together
But when I look ahead up the white road
There is always another one walking beside you
Gliding wrapt in a brown mantle, hooded
I do not know whether a man or a woman
— But who is that on the other side of you?

What is that sound high in the air
Murmur of maternal lamentation
Who are those hooded hordes swarming
Over endless plains, stumbling in cracked earth
Ringed by the flat horizon only
What is the city over the mountains
Cracks and reforms and bursts in the violet air
Falling towers
Jerusalem Athens Alexandria
Vienna London
Unreal

A woman drew her long black hair out tight
And fiddled whisper music on those strings
And bats with baby faces in the violet light
Whistled, and beat their wings
And crawled head downward down a blackened wall
And upside down in air were towers
Tolling reminiscent bells, that kept the hours
And voices singing out of empty cisterns and exhausted wells.

In this decayed hole among the mountains
In the faint moonlight, the grass is singing
Over the tumbled graves, about the chapel
There is the empty chapel, only the wind's home.
It has no windows, and the door swings,   390
Dry bones can harm no one.
Only a cock stood on the rooftree
Co co rico co co rico
In a flash of lightning. Then a damp gust
Bringing rain

Ganga was sunken, and the limp leaves
Waited for rain, while the black clouds
Gathered far distant, over Himavant.
The jungle crouched, humped in silence.
Then spoke the thunder   400
DA
Datta: what have we given?
My friend, blood shaking my heart
The awful daring of a moment's surrender
Which an age of prudence can never retract
By this, and this only, we have existed
Which is not to be found in our obituaries
Or in memories draped by the beneficent spider
Or under seals broken by the lean solicitor
In our empty room   410
DA
Dayadhvam: I have heard the key
Turn in the door once and turn once only
We think of the key, each in his prison
Thinking of the key, each confirms a prison
Only at nightfall, aethereal rumours
Revive for a moment a broken Coriolanus
DA
Damyata: The boat responded
Gaily, to the hand expert with sail and oar   420
The sea was calm, your heart would have responded
Gaily, when invited, beating obedient
To controlling hands

I sat upon the shore
Fishing, with the arid plain behind me
Shall I at least set my lands in order?
London Bridge is falling down falling down falling down
Poi s'ascose nel foco che gli affina
Quando fiam uti chelidon — O swallow swallow
Le Prince d' Aquintaine à la tour abolie
These fragments I have shored against my ruins
Why then Ile fit you. Hieronymo's mad againe.
Datta. Dayadhvam. Damyata.
Shantih shantih shantih

Notes on the Waste Land

Not only the title, but the plan and a good deal of the incidental symbolism of the poem were suggested by Miss Jessie L. Weston's book on the Grail legend: *From Ritual to Romance* (Cambridge). Indeed, so deeply am I indebted, Miss Weston's book will elucidate the difficulties of the poem much better than my notes can do; and I recommend it (apart from the great interest of the book itself) to any who think such elucidation of the poem worth the trouble. To another work of anthropology I am indebted in general, one which has influenced our generation profoundly; I mean *The Golden Bough*; I have used especially the two volumes *Adonis, Attis, Osiris*. Anyone who is acquainted with these works will immediately recognize in the poem certain references to vegetation ceremonies.

I. The Burial of the Dead

Line 20. Cf. Ezekiel II, i.
23. Cf. Ecclesiastes XII, v.
31. V. Tristan und Isolde, I, verses 5–8.
42. Id. III, verse 24.
46. I am not familiar with the exact constitution of the Tarot pack of cards, from which I have obviously departed to suit my own convenience. The Hanged Man, a member of the traditional pack, fits my purpose in two ways: because he is associated in my mind with the Hanged God of Frazer, and because I associate him with the hooded figure in the passage of the disciples to Emmaus in Part V. The Phoenician Sailor and the Merchant appear later; also the "crowds of people," and Death by Water is executed in Part IV. The Man with Three Staves (an authentic member of the Tarot pack) I associate, quite arbitrarily, with the Fisher King himself.
60. Cf. Baudelaire:

"Fourmillante cité, cité pleine de rêves,
Où le spectre en plein jour raccroche le passant."
63. Cf. Inferno III, 55–57:
si lunga tratta
di gente, ch'io non averei creduto
che morte tanta n'avesse disfatta.
64. Cf. Inferno IV, 25–27:
Quivi, secondo che per ascoltare,
non avea piante mai che di sospiri
che l'aura eterna facevan tremare.
68. A phenomenon which I have often noticed.
74. Cf. the Dirge in Webster's *White Devil.*
76. V. Baudelaire, Preface to *Fleurs du Mal.*

II. A Game of Chess

77. Cf. *Antony and Cleopatra*, II, ii, l. 190.
92. Laquearia. V. *Aeneid*, I, 726:
dependent lychni laquearibus aureis
incensi, et noctem flammis funalia vincunt.
98. Sylvan scene. V. Milton, *Paradise Lost*, IV, 140.
99. V. Ovid, *Metamorphoses*, VI, Philomela.
100. Cf. Part III, l. 204.
115. Cf. Part III, l. 195.
118. Cf. Webster: "Is the wind in that door still?"
126. Cf. Part I, l. 37, 48.
138. Cf. the game of chess in Middleton's *Women beware Women.*

III. The Fire Sermon

176. V. Spenser, *Prothalamion.*
192. Cf. *The Tempest*, I, ii.
196. Cf. Marvell, *To His Coy Mistress*
197. Cf. Day, *Parliament of Bees*:
"When of the sudden, listening, you shall hear,
A noise of horns and hunting, which shall bring
Actaeon to Diana in the spring,
Where all shall see her naked skin . . ."
199. I do not know the origin of the ballad from which these lines are taken: it was reported to me from Sydney, Australia.
202. V. Verlaine, *Parsifal.*
210. The currants were quoted at a price "cost insurance and freight to London"; and the Bill of Lading, etc., were to be handed to the buyer upon payment of the sight draft.

218. Tiresias, although a mere spectator and not indeed a "character," is yet the most important personage in the poem, uniting all the rest. Just as the one-eyed merchant, seller of currants, melts into the Phoenician Sailor, and the latter is not wholly distinct from Ferdinand Prince of Naples, so all the women are one woman, and the two sexes meet in Tiresias. What Tiresias *sees*, in fact, is the substance of the poem. The whole passage from Ovid is of great anthropological interest:

> . . . Cum Iunone iocos et "major vestra profecto est
> Quam quae contingit maribus," dixisse, "voluptas."
> Illa negat; placuit quae sit sententia docti
> Quaerere Tiresiae: venus huic erat utraque nota.
> Nam duo magnorum viridi coeuntia silva
> Corpora serpentum baculi violaverat ictu
> Deque viro factus, mirabile, femina septem
> Egerat autumnos; octavo rursus eosdem
> Vidit et "est vestrae si tanta potentia plagae,"
> Dixit "ut auctoris sortem in contraria mutet,
> Nunc quoque vos feriam!" percussis anguibus isdem
> Forma prior rediit genetivaque venit imago.
> Arbiter hic igitur sumptus de lite iocosa
> Dicta Iovis firmat; gravius Saturnia iusto
> Nec pro materia fertur doluisse suique
> Iudicis aeterna damnavit lumina nocte,
> At pater omnipotens (neque enim licet inrita cuiquam
> Facta dei fecisse deo) pro lumine adempto
> Scire futura dedit poenamque levavit honore.

221. This may not appear as exact as Sappho's lines, but I had in mind the "longshore" or "dory" fisherman, who returns at nightfall.

253. V. Goldsmith, the song in *The Vicar of Wakefield*.

257. V. *The Tempest*, as above.

264. The interior of St. Magnus Martyr is to my mind one of the finest among Wren's interiors. See *The Proposed Demolition of Nineteen City Churches*: (P. S. King & Son, Ltd.).

266. The Song of the (three) Thames-daughters begins here. From line 292 to 306 inclusive they speak in turn. V. *Götterdämmerung*, III, i: the Rhine-daughters.

279. V. Froude, *Elizabeth*, Vol. I, ch. iv, letter of De Quadra to Philip of Spain:

"In the afternoon we were in a barge, watching the games on the river. (The Queen) was alone with Lord Robert and myself on the poop, when they began to talk nonsense, and went so far that Lord Robert at last said, as I was on the spot there was no reason why they should not be married if the queen pleased."

293. Cf. *Purgatorio*, V. 133:
> "Ricorditi di me, che son la Pia;
> Siena mi fe', disfecemi Maremma."

307. V. St. Augustine's *Confessions*: "to Carthage then I came, where a cauldron of unholy loves sang all about mine ears."

308. The complete text of the Buddha's Fire Sermon (which corresponds in importance to the Sermon on the Mount) from which these words are taken, will be found translated in the late Henry Clarke Warren's *Buddhism in Translation* (Harvard Oriental Series). Mr. Warren was one of the great pioneers of Buddhist studies in the Occident.

309. From St. Augustine's *Confessions* again. The collocation of these two representatives of eastern and western asceticism, as the culmination of this part of the poem, is not an accident.

V. *What the Thunder said*

In the first part of Part V three themes are employed: the journey to Emmaus, the approach to the Chapel Perilous (see Miss Weston's book) and the present decay of eastern Europe.

357. This is *Turdus aonalaschkae pallasii*, the hermit-thrush which I have heard in Quebec Province. Chapman says (*Handbook of Birds of Eastern North America*) "it is most at home in secluded woodland and thickety retreats. . . . Its notes are not remarkable for variety or volume, but in purity and sweetness of tone and exquisite modulation they are unequalled." Its "water-dripping song" is justly celebrated.

360. The following lines were stimulated by the account of one of the Antarctic expeditions (I forget which, but I think one of Shackleton's): it was related that the party of explorers, at the extremity of their strength, had the constant delusion that there was *one more member* than could actually be counted.

366–76. Cf. Hermann Hesse, *Blick ins Chaos*: "Schon ist halb Europa, schon ist zumindest der halbe Osten Europas auf dem Wege zum Chaos, fährt betrunken im heiligen Wahn am Abgrund entlang und singt dazu, singt betrunken und hymnisch wie Dmitri Karamasoff sang. Ueber diese Lieder lacht der Bürger beleidigt, der Heilige und Seher hört sie mit Tränen."

401. "Datta, dayadhvam, damyata" (Give, sympathise, control). The fable of the meaning of the Thunder is found in the *Brihadaranyaka —Upanishad*, 5, 1. A translation is found in Deussen's *Sechzig Upanishads des Veda*, p. 489.

407. Cf. Webster, *The White Devil*, V, vi:
> ". . . they'll remarry
> Ere the worm pierce your winding-sheet, ere the spider
> Make a thin curtain for your epitaphs."

411. Cf. *Inferno*, XXXIII, 46:
> "ed io senti chiavar l'uscio di sotto
> all' orribile torre."

Also F. H. Bradley, *Appearance and Reality*, p. 306.

"My external sensations are no less private to my self than are my thoughts or my feelings. In either case my experience falls within my own circle, a circle closed on the outside; and, with all its elements alike, every sphere is opaque to the others which surround it. . . In brief, regarded as an existence which appears in a soul, the whole world for each is peculiar and private to that soul."

424. V. Weston: *From Ritual to Romance*; chapter on the Fisher King.

427. V. *Purgatorio*, XXVI, 148.
> " 'Ara vos prec per aquella valor
> que vos condus al som de l'escalina,
> sovegna vos a temps de ma dolor.'
> Poi s'ascose nel foco che gli affina."

428. V. *Pervigilium Veneris*. Cf. Philomela in Parts II and III.

429. V. Gerard de Nerval, Sonnet *El Desdichado*.

431. V. Kyd's *Spanish Tragedy*.

433. Shantih. Repeated as here, a formal ending to an Upanishad. "The peace which passeth understanding" is our equivalent to this word.

from Ash-Wednesday

III

At the first turning of the second stair
I turned and saw below
The same shape twisted on the banister
Under the vapour in the fetid air
Struggling with the devil of the stairs who wears
The deceitful face of hope and of despair.

At the second turning of the second stair
I left them twisting, turning below;
There were no more faces and the stair was dark,
Damp, jaggèd, like an old man's mouth drivelling, beyond repair,
Or the toothed gullet of an agèd shark.

At the first turning of the third stair
Was a slotted window bellied like the fig's fruit
And beyond the hawthorn blossom and a pasture scene

The broadbacked figure drest in blue and green
Enchanted the maytime with an antique flute.
Blown hair is sweet, brown hair over the mouth blown,
Lilac and brown hair;
Distraction, music of the flute, stops and steps of the mind over the third
    stair,
Fading, fading; strength beyond hope and despair
Climbing the third stair.

Lord, I am not worthy
Lord, I am not worthy
        but speak the word only.

Little Gidding

I

Midwinter spring is its own season
Sempiternal though sodden towards sundown,
Suspended in time, between pole and tropic.
When the short day is brightest, with frost and fire,
The brief sun flames the ice, on pond and ditches,
In windless cold that is the heart's heat,
Reflecting in a watery mirror
A glare that is blindness in the early afternoon.
And glow more intense than blaze of branch, or brazier,
Stirs the dumb spirit: no wind, but pentecostal fire
In the dark time of the year. Between melting and freezing
The soul's sap quivers. There is no earth smell
Or smell of living things. This is the spring time
But not in time's covenant. Now the hedgerow
Is blanched for an hour with transitory blossom
Of snow, a bloom more sudden
Than that of summer, neither budding nor fading,
Not in the scheme of generation.
Where is the summer, the unimaginable
Zero summer?

      If you came this way,
Taking the route you would be likely to take
From the place you would be likely to come from,
If you came this way in may time, you would find the hedges
White again, in May, with voluptuary sweetness.

It would be the same at the end of the journey,
If you came at night like a broken king,
If you came by day not knowing what you came for,
It would be the same, when you leave the rough road
And turn behind the pig-sty to the dull façade
And the tombstone. And what you thought you came for
Is only a shell, a husk of meaning
From which the purpose breaks only when it is fulfilled
If at all. Either you had no purpose
Or the purpose is beyond the end you figured
And is altered in fulfillment. There are other places
Which also are the world's end, some at the sea jaws,
Or over a dark lake, in a desert or a city —
But this is the nearest, in place and time,
Now and in England.

        If you came this way,
Taking any route, starting from anywhere,
At any time or at any season,
It would always be the same: you would have to put off
Sense and notion. You are not here to verify,
Instruct yourself, or inform curiosity
Or carry report. You are here to kneel
Where prayer has been valid. And prayer is more
Than an order of words, the conscious occupation
Of the praying mind, or the sound of the voice praying.
And what the dead had no speech for, when living,
They can tell you, being dead: the communication
Of the dead is tongued with fire beyond the language of the living.
Here, the intersection of the timeless moment
Is England and nowhere. Never and always.

II

Ash on an old man's sleeve
Is all the ash the burnt roses leave.
Dust in the air suspended
Marks the place where a story ended.
Dust inbreathed was a house —
The wall, the wainscot and the mouse.
The death of hope and despair,
     This is the death of air.

There are flood and drouth
Over the eyes and in the mouth,
Dead water and dead sand
Contending for the upper hand.
The parched eviscerate soil
Gapes at the vanity of toil,
Laughs without mirth.
    This is the death of earth.

Water and fire succeed
The town, the pasture and the weed.
Water and fire deride
The sacrifice that we denied.
Water and fire shall rot
The marred foundations we forgot,
Of sanctuary and choir.
    This is the death of water and fire.

In the uncertain hour before the morning
   Near the ending of interminable night
   At the recurrent end of the unending
After the dark dove with the flickering tongue
   Had passed below the horizon of his homing
   While the dead leaves still rattled on like tin
Over the asphalt where no other sound was
   Between three districts whence the smoke arose
   I met one walking, loitering and hurried
As if blown towards me like the metal leaves
   Before the urban dawn wind unresisting.
   And as I fixed upon the down-turned face
That pointed scrutiny with which we challenge
   The first-met stranger in the waning dusk
   I caught the sudden look of some dead master
Whom I had known, forgotten, half recalled
   Both one and many; in the brown baked features
The eyes of a familiar compound ghost
   Both intimate and unidentifiable.
   So I assumed a double part, and cried
   And heard another's voice cry: "What! are *you* here?"
Although we were not. I was still the same,
   Knowing myself yet being someone other —
   And he a face still forming; yet the words sufficed

To compel the recognition they preceded.
    And so, compliant to the common wind,
    Too strange to each other for misunderstanding,
In concord at this intersection time
    Of meeting nowhere, no before and after,
    We trod the pavement in a dead patrol.
I said: "The wonder that I feel is easy,
    Yet ease is cause of wonder. Therefore speak:
    I may not comprehend, may not remember."
And he: "I am not eager to rehearse
    My thoughts and theory which you have forgotten.
    These things have served their purpose: let them be.
So with your own, and pray they be forgiven
    By others, as I pray you to forgive
    Both bad and good. Last season's fruit is eaten
And the fulfilled beast shall kick the empty pail.
    For last year's words belong to last year's language
    And next year's words await another voice.
But, as the passage now presents no hindrance
    To the spirit unappeased and peregrine
    Between two worlds become much like each other,
So I find words I never thought to speak
    In streets I never thought I should revisit
    When I left my body on a distant shore.
Since our concern was speech, and speech impelled us
    To purify the dialect of the tribe
    And urge the mind to aftersight and foresight,
Let me disclose the gifts reserved for age
    To set a crown upon your lifetime's effort.
    First, the cold friction of expiring sense
Without enchantment, offering no promise
    But bitter tastelessness of shadow fruit
    As body and soul begin to fall asunder.
Second, the conscious impotence of rage
    At human folly, and the laceration
    Of laughter at what ceases to amuse.
And last, the rending pain of re-enactment
    Of all that you have done, and been; the shame
    Of motives late revealed, and the awareness
Of things ill done and done to others' harm
    Which once you took for exercise of virtue.
    Then fools' approval stings, and honour stains.

From wrong to wrong the exasperated spirit
  Proceeds, unless restored by that refining fire
  Where you must move in measure, like a dancer."
The day was breaking. In the disfigured street
  He left me, with a kind of valediction,
  And faded on the blowing of the horn.

III

There are three conditions which often look alike
Yet differ completely, flourish in the same hedgerow:
Attachment to self and to things and to persons, detachment
From self and from things and from persons; and, growing
     between them, indifference
Which resembles the others as death resembles life,
Being between two lives — unflowering, between
The live and the dead nettle. This is the use of memory:
For liberation — not less of love but expanding
Of love beyond desire, and so liberation
From the future as well as the past. Thus, love of a country
Begins as attachment to our own field of action
And comes to find that action of little importance
Though never indifferent. History may be servitude,
History may be freedom. See, now they vanish,
The faces and places, with the self which, as it could, loved them,
To become renewed, transfigured, in another pattern.
Sin is Behovely, but
All shall be well, and
All manner of thing shall be well.
If I think, again, of this place,
And of people, not wholly commendable,
Of no immediate kin or kindness,
But some of peculiar genius,
All touched by a common genius,
United in the strife which divided them;
If I think of a king at nightfall,
Of three men, and more, on the scaffold
And a few who died forgotten
In other places, here and abroad,
And of one who died blind and quiet,
Why should we celebrate
These dead men more than the dying?
It is not to ring the bell backward

Nor is it an incantation
To summon the spectre of a Rose.
We cannot revive old factions
We cannot restore old policies
Or follow an antique drum.
These men, and those who opposed them
And those whom they opposed
Accept the constitution of silence
And are folded in a single party.
Whatever we inherit from the fortunate
We have taken from the defeated
What they had to leave us — a symbol:
A symbol perfected in death.
And all shall be well and
All manner of thing shall be well
By the purification of the motive
In the ground of our beseeching.

IV

The dove descending breaks the air
With flame of incandescent terror
Of which the tongues declare
The one discharge from sin and error.
The only hope, or else despair
 Lies in the choice of pyre or pyre —
 To be redeemed from fire by fire.

Who then devised the torment? Love.
Love is the unfamiliar Name
Behind the hands that wove
The intolerable shirt of flame
Which human power cannot remove.
 We only live, only suspire
 Consumed by either fire or fire.

V

What we call the beginning is often the end
And to make an end is to make a beginning.
The end is where we start from. And every phrase
And sentence that is right (where every word is at home,
Taking its place to support the others,
The word neither diffident nor ostentatious,
An easy commerce of the old and the new,

The common word exact without vulgarity,
The formal word precise but not pedantic,
The complete consort dancing together)
Every phrase and every sentence is an end and a beginning,
Every poem an epitaph. And any action
Is a step to the block, to the fire, down the sea's throat
Or to an illegible stone: and that is where we start.
We die with the dying:
See, they depart, and we go with them.
We are born with the dead:
See, they return, and bring us with them.
The moment of the rose and the moment of the yew-tree
Are of equal duration. A people without history
Is not redeemed from time, for history is a pattern
Of timeless moments. So, while the light fails
On a winter's afternoon, in a secluded chapel
History is now and England.

With the drawing of this Love and the voice of this Calling

We shall not cease from exploration
And the end of all our exploring
Will be to arrive where we started
And know the place for the first time.
Through the unknown, remembered gate
When the last of earth left to discover
Is that which was the beginning;
At the source of the longest river
The voice of the hidden waterfall
And the children in the apple-tree
Not known, because not looked for
But heard, half-heard, in the stillness
Between two waves of the sea.
Quick now, here, now, always —
A condition of complete simplicity
(Costing not less than everything)
And all shall be well and
All manner of thing shall be well
When the tongues of flame are in-folded
Into the crowned knot of fire
And the fire and the rose are one.

CONRAD AIKEN
1889–1973

from Discordants

I

Music I heard with you was more than music,
And bread I broke with you was more than bread;
Now that I am without you, all is desolate;
All that was once so beautiful is dead.

Your hands once touched this table and this silver,
And I have seen your fingers hold this glass.
These things do not remember you, belovèd, —
And yet your touch upon them will not pass.

For it was in my heart you moved among them,
And blessed them with your hands and with your eyes;
And in my heart they will remember always, —
They knew you once, O beautiful and wise.

from Priapus and the Pool

III

When trout swim down Great Ormond Street,
And sea-gulls cry above them lightly,
And hawthorns heave cold flagstones up
To blossom whitely,

Against old walls of houses there,
Gustily shaking out in moonlight
Their country sweetness on sweet air;
And in the sunlight,

By the green margin of that water,
Children dip white feet and shout,
Casting nets in the braided water
To catch the trout:

Then I shall hold my breath and die,
Swearing I never loved you; no,
"You were not lovely!" I shall cry,
"I never loved you so."

IV

This is the shape of the leaf, and this of the flower,
And this the pale bole of the tree
Which watches its bough in a pool of unwavering water
In a land we never shall see.

The thrush on the bough is silent, the dew falls softly,
In the evening is hardly a sound.
And the three beautiful pilgrims who come here together
Touch lightly the dust of the ground,

Touch it with feet that trouble the dust but as wings do,
Come shyly together, are still,
Like dancers who wait, in a pause of the music, for music
The exquisite silence to fill.

This is the thought of the first, and this of the second,
And this the grave thought of the third:
"Linger we thus for a moment, palely expectant,
And silence will end, and the bird

"Sing the pure phrase, sweet phrase, clear phrase in the twilight
To fill the blue bell of the world;
And we, who on music so leaflike have drifted together,
Leaflike apart shall be whirled

"Into what but the beauty of silence, silence forever?" . . .
. . . This is the shape of the tree,
And the flower, and the leaf, and the three pale beautiful pilgrims;
This is what you are to me.

The Room

Through that window — all else being extinct
Except itself and me — I saw the struggle
Of darkness against darkness. Within the room
It turned and turned, dived downward. Then I saw
How order might — if chaos wished — become:
And saw the darkness crush upon itself,
Contracting powerfully; it was as if
It killed itself: slowly: and with much pain.
Pain. The scene was pain, and nothing but pain.

What else, when chaos draws all forces inward
To shape a single leaf? . . .
                    For the leaf came,
Alone and shining in the empty room;
After a while the twig shot downward from it;
And from the twig a bough; and then the trunk,
Massive and coarse; and last the one black root.
The black root cracked the walls. Boughs burst the window:
The great tree took possession.
                    Tree of trees!
Remember (when time comes) how chaos died
To shape the shining leaf. Then turn, have courage,
Wrap arms and roots together, be convulsed
With grief, and bring back chaos out of shape.
I will be watching then as I watch now.
I will praise darkness now, but then the leaf.

Hatteras Calling

Southeast, and storm, and every weathervane
shivers and moans upon its dripping pin,
ragged on chimneys the cloud whips, the rain
howls at the flues and windows to get in,

the golden rooster claps his golden wings
and from the Baptist Chapel shrieks no more,
the golden arrow into the southeast sings
and hears on the roof the Atlantic Ocean roar.

Waves among wires, sea scudding over poles,
down every alley the magnificence of rain,
dead gutters live once more, the deep manholes
hollo in triumph a passage to the main.

Umbrellas, and in the Gardens one old man
hurries away along a dancing path,
listens to music on a watering-can,
observes among the tulips the sudden wrath,

pale willows thrashing to the needled lake,
and dinghies filled with water; while the sky
smashes the lilacs, swoops to shake and break,
till shattered branches shriek and railings cry.

Speak, Hatteras, your language of the sea:
scour with kelp and spindrift the stale street:
that man in terror may learn once more to be
child of that hour when rock and ocean meet.

Dear Uncle Stranger

All my shortcomings, in this year of grace,
preach, and at midnight, from my mirrored face,
the arrogant, strict dishonesty, that lies
behind the animal forehead and the eyes;

the bloodstream coiling with its own intent,
never from passion or from pleasure bent;
the mouth and nostrils eager for their food,
indifferent to god, or to man's good.

Oh, how the horror rises from that look,
which is an open, and a dreadful, book!
much evil, and so little kindness, done,
selfish the loves, yes all, the selfless none;

illness and pain, ignored; the poor, forgotten;
the letters to the dying man, not written —
the many past, or passing, great or small,
from whom I took, nor ever gave at all!

Dear Uncle stranger, Cousin known too late,
sweet wife unkissed, come, we will celebrate
in this thronged mirror the uncelebrated dead,
good men and women gone too soon to bed.

The Accomplices

A love I love whose lips I love
but conscience she has none
nor can I rest upon her breast
for faith's to her unknown
light-hearted to my bed she comes
but she is early gone.

This lady in the sunlight is
as magic as the sun
and in my arms and all night long
she seems and is my own
yet but a Monday love is she
and Tuesday she is gone.

Rare as charity is her hand
that rests my heart upon
but charity to so many kind
stays for a day with none
a spendthrift love she spends her love
and all will soon be gone.

Yet though my trust has been betrayed
reproaches have I none
no heart but is of treason made
or has not mischief done
and we could be together false
if she would but stay on.

Herman Melville

"My towers at last!" —
                              What meant the word
from what acknowledged circuit sprung
and in the heart and on the tongue
at sight of few familiar birds
when seaward his last sail unfurled
to leeward from the wheel once more
bloomed the pale crags of haunted shore
that once-more-visited notch of world:
and straight he knew as known before
the Logos in Leviathan's roar
he deepest sounding with his lead
who all had fathomed all had said.

Much-loving hero — towers indeed
were those that overhung your log
with entries of typhoon and fog
and thunderstone for Adam's breed:

man's warm Sargasso Sea of faith
dislimned in light by luck or fate
you for mankind set sail by hate
and weathered it, and with it death.
And now at world's end coasting late
in dolphined calms beyond the gate
which Hercules flung down, you come
to the grim rocks that nod you home.
Depth below depth this love of man:
among unnumbered and unknown
to mark and make his cryptic own
one landfall of all time began:
of all life's hurts to treasure one
and hug it to the wounded breast,
in this to dedicate the rest,
all injuries received or done.
Your towers again but towers now blest
your haven in a shoreless west
o mariner of the human soul
who in the landmark notched the Pole
and in the Item loved the Whole.

ARCHIBALD MACLEISH
b. 1892

L'An trentiesme de mon eage

And I have come upon this place
By lost ways, by a nod, by words,
By faces, by an old man's face
At Morlaix lifted to the birds,

By hands upon the tablecloth
At Aldebori's by the thin
Child's hands that opened to the moth
And let the flutter of the moonlight in,

By hands, by voices, by the voice
Of Mrs. Whitman on the stair,
By Margaret's "If we had the choice
To choose or not — " through her thick hair,

By voices, by the creak and fall
Of footsteps on the upper floor,
By silence waiting in the hall
Between the doorbell and the door,

By words, by voices, a lost way —
And here above the chimney stack
The unknown constellations sway —
And by what way shall I go back?

The End of the World

Quite unexpectedly as Vasserot
The armless ambidextrian was lighting
A match between his great and second toe
And Ralph the lion was engaged in biting
The neck of Madame Sossman while the drum
Pointed, and Teeny was about to cough
In waltz-time swinging Jocko by the thumb —
Quite unexpectedly the top blew off:

And there, there overhead, there, there, hung over
Those thousands of white faces, those dazed eyes,
There in the starless dark the poise, the hover,
There with vast wings across the canceled skies,
There in the sudden blackness the black pall
Of nothing, nothing, nothing — nothing at all.

Ars Poetica

A poem should be palpable and mute
As a globed fruit,

Dumb
As old medallions to the thumb,

Silent as the sleeve-worn stone
Of casement ledges where the moss has grown —

A poem should be wordless
As the flight of birds.

*

A poem should be motionless in time
As the moon climbs,

Leaving, as the moon releases
Twig by twig the night-entangled trees,

Leaving, as the moon behind the winter leaves,
Memory by memory the mind —

A poem should be motionless in time
As the moon climbs.

*

A poem should be equal to:
Not true.

For all the history of grief
An empty doorway and a maple leaf.

For love
The leaning grasses and two lights above the sea —

A poem should not mean
But be.

You, Andrew Marvell

And here face down beneath the sun
And here upon earth's noonward height
To feel the always coming on
The always rising of the night:

To feel creep up the curving east
The earthy chill of dusk and slow
Upon those under lands the vast
And ever climbing shadow grow

And strange at Ecbatan the trees
Take leaf by leaf the evening strange
The flooding dark about their knees
The mountains over Persia change

And now at Kermanshah the gate
Dark empty and the withered grass
And through the twilight now the late
Few travelers in the westward pass

And Baghdad darken and the bridge
Across the silent river gone
And through Arabia the edge
Of evening widen and steal on

And deepen on Palmyra's street
The wheel rut in the ruined stone
And Lebanon fade out and Crete
High through the clouds and overblown

And over Sicily the air
Still flashing with the landward gulls
And loom and slowly disappear
The sails above the shadowy hulls

And Spain go under and the shore
Of Africa the gilded sand
And evening vanish and no more
The low pale light across that land

Nor now the long light on the sea:

And here face downward in the sun
To feel how swift how secretly
The shadow of the night comes on . . .

Epistle to Be Left in the Earth

. . . It is colder now,
                    there are many stars,
                                        we are drifting
North by the Great Bear,
                    the leaves are falling,
The water is stone in the scooped rocks,
                                        to southward

626

Red sun grey air:
        the crows are
Slow on their crooked wings,
                the jays have left us:
Long since we passed the flares of Orion.
Each man believes in his heart he will die.
Many have written last thoughts and last letters.
None know if our deaths are now or forever:
None know if this wandering earth will be found.

We lie down and the snow covers our garments.
I pray you,
        you (if any open this writing)
Make in your mouths the words that were our names.
I will tell you all we have learned,
                  I will tell you everything:
The earth is round,
           there are springs under the orchards,
The loam cuts with a blunt knife,
              beware of
Elms in thunder,
          the lights in the sky are stars —
We think they do not see,
           we think also
The trees do not know nor the leaves of the grasses hear us:
The birds too are ignorant.
            Do not listen.
Do not stand at dark in the open windows.
We before you have heard this:
            they are voices:
They are not words at all but the wind rising.
Also none among us has seen God.
(... We have thought often
The flaws of sun in the late and driving weather
Pointed to one tree but it was not so.)
As for the nights I warn you the nights are dangerous:
The wind changes at night and the dreams come.

It is very cold,
          there are strange stars near Arcturus,

Voices are crying an unknown name in the sky

Lines for an Interment

Now it is fifteen years you have lain in the meadow:
The boards at your face have gone through: the earth is
Packed down and the sound of the rain is fainter:
The roots of the first grass are dead.

It's a long time to lie in the earth with your honor:
The world, Soldier, the world has been moving on.

The girls wouldn't look at you twice in the cloth cap:
Six years old they were when it happened:

It bores them even in books: "Soissons besieged!"
As for the gents they have joined the American Legion:

Belts and a brass band and the ladies' auxiliaries:
The Californians march in the OD silk.

We are all acting again like civilized beings:
People mention it at tea . . .

The Facts of Life we have learned are Economic:
You were deceived by the detonations of bombs:

You thought of courage and death when you thought of warfare.
Hadn't they taught you the fine words were unfortunate?

Now that we understand we judge without bias:
We feel of course for those who had to die:

Women have written us novels of great passion
Proving the useless death of the dead was a tragedy.

Nevertheless it is foolish to chew gall:
The foremost writers on both sides have apologized:

The Germans are back in the Midi with cropped hair:
The English are drinking the better beer in Bavaria.

You can rest now in the rain in the Belgian meadow —
Now that it's all explained and forgotten:
Now that the earth is hard and the wood rots:

Now you are dead . . .

Brave New World

But you, Thomas Jefferson,
You could not lie so still,
You could not bear the weight of stone
On the quiet hill,

You could not keep your green grown peace
Nor hold your folded hand
If you could see your new world now,
Your new sweet land.

There was a time, Tom Jefferson,
When freedom made free men.
The new found earth and the new freed mind
Were brothers then.

There was a time when tyrants feared
The new world of the free.
Now freedom is afraid and shrieks
At tyranny.

Words have not changed their sense so soon
Nor tyranny grown new.
The truths you held, Tom Jefferson,
Will still hold true.

What's changed is freedom in this age.
What great men dared to choose
Small men now dare neither win
Nor lose.

Freedom, when men fear freedom's use
But love its useful name,
Has cause and cause enough for fear
And cause for shame.

We fought a war in freedom's name
And won it in our own.
We fought to free a world and raised
A wall of stone.

Your countrymen who could have built
The hill fires of the free
To set the dry world all ablaze
With liberty —

To burn the brutal thorn in Spain
Of bigotry and hate
And the dead lie and the brittle weed
Beyond the Plate:

Who could have heaped the bloody straw,
The dung of time, to light
The Danube in a sudden flame
Of hope by night —

Your countrymen who could have hurled
Their freedom like a brand
Have cupped it to a candle spark
In a frightened hand.

Freedom that was a thing to use
They've made a thing to save
And staked it in and fenced it round
Like a dead man's grave.

You, Thomas Jefferson,
You could not lie so still,
You could not bear the weight of stone
On your green hill,

You could not hold your angry tongue
If you could see how bold
The old stale bitter world plays new —
And the new world old.

Ezry

Maybe you ranted in the Grove —
Maybe! — but you found the mark
That measures altitude above
Sea-level for a poet's work.

Mad if you were or fool instead
You found the bench-mark in the stone —
Horizon over arrow-head —
Alder and dock had overgrown.

These later and more cautious critics
Think themselves high if they look down
From Rome's or England's steeple — spit
On fools below them in the town:

Not you! Although the absolute sea
Is far down from the Muses' Wood,
You gauged the steep declivity,
Giddy with grandeur where you stood.

E. E. CUMMINGS
1894–1962

when god lets my body be

when god lets my body be

From each brave eye shall sprout a tree
fruit that dangles therefrom

the purpled world will dance upon
Between my lips which did sing

a rose shall beget the spring
that maidens whom passion wastes

will lay between their little breasts
My strong fingers beneath the snow

Into strenuous birds shall go
my love walking in the grass

their wings will touch with her face
and all the while shall my heart be

With the bulge and nuzzle of the sea

Buffalo Bill's

Buffalo Bill's
defunct
    who used to
    ride a watersmooth-silver
                stallion
and break onetwothreefourfive pigeonsjustlikethat
                        Jesus

he was a handsome man
               and what i want to know is
how do you like your blueeyed boy
Mister Death

the Cambridge ladies who live in furnished souls

the Cambridge ladies who live in furnished souls
are unbeautiful and have comfortable minds
(also, with the church's protestant blessings
daughters, unscented shapeless spirited)
they believe in Christ and Longfellow, both dead,
are invariably interested in so many things —
at the present writing one still finds
delighted fingers knitting for the is it Poles?
perhaps.   While permanent faces coyly bandy
scandal of Mrs. N and Professor D
. . . . the Cambridge ladies do not care, above
Cambridge if sometimes in its box of
sky lavender and cornerless, the
moon rattles like a fragment of angry candy

nobody loses all the time

nobody loses all the time

i had an uncle named
Sol who was a born failure and
nearly everybody said he should have gone
into vaudeville perhaps because my Uncle Sol could
sing McCann He Was A Diver on Xmas Eve like Hell Itself which
may or may not account for the fact that my Uncle

Sol indulged in that possibly most inexcusable
of all to use a highfalootin phrase
luxuries that is or to
wit farming and be
it needlessly
added

my Uncle Sol's farm
failed because the chickens
ate the vegetables so
my Uncle Sol had a
chicken farm till the
skunks ate the chickens when

my Uncle Sol
had a skunk farm but
the skunks caught cold and
died and so
my Uncle Sol imitated the
skunks in a subtle manner

or by drowning himself in the watertank
but somebody who'd given my Uncle Sol a Victor
Victrola and records while he lived presented to
him upon the auspicious occasion of his decease a
scrumptious not to mention splendiferous funeral with
tall boys in black gloves and flowers and everything and

i remember we all cried like the Missouri
when my Uncle Sol's coffin lurched because
somebody pressed a button
(and down went
my Uncle
Sol

and started a worm farm)

she being Brand

she being Brand

-new;and you
know consequently a
little stiff i was
careful of her and(having

thoroughly oiled the universal
joint tested my gas felt of
her radiator made sure her springs were O.

K.)i went right to it flooded-the-carburetor cranked her

up,slipped the
clutch(and then somehow got into reverse she
kicked what
the hell)next
minute i was back in neutral tried and

again slo-wly;bare,ly nudg.   ing(my

lev-er Right-
oh and her gears being in
 A 1 shape passed
from low through
second-in-to-high like
greasedlightning)just as we turned the corner of Divinity

avenue i touched the accelerator and give

her the juice,good

                (it
was the first ride and believe i we was
happy to see how nice she acted right up to
the last minute coming back down by the Public
Gardens i slammed on
the

internalexpanding
&
externalcontracting
brakes Bothatonce and

brought allofher tremB
-ling
to a:dead.

stand-
;Still)

a man who had fallen among thieves

a man who had fallen among thieves
lay by the roadside on his back
dressed in fifteenth-rate ideas
wearing a round jeer for a hat

fate per a somewhat more than less
emancipated evening
had in return for consciousness
endowed him with a changeless grin

whereon a dozen staunch and leal
citizens did graze at pause
then fired by hypercivic zeal
sought newer pastures or because

swaddled with a frozen brook
of pinkest vomit out of eyes
which noticed nobody he looked
as if he did not care to rise

one hand did nothing on the vest
its wideflung friend clenched weakly dirt
while the mute trouserfly confessed
a button solemnly inert.

Brushing from whom the stiffened puke
i put him all into my arms
and staggered banged with terror through
a million billion trillion stars

if i have made,my lady,intricate

if i have made,my lady,intricate
imperfect various things chiefly which wrong
your eyes(frailer than most deep dreams are frail)
songs less firm than your body's whitest song
upon my mind — if i have failed to snare
the glance too shy — if through my singing slips
the very skillful strangeness of your smile
the keen primeval silence of your hair

— let the world say "his most wise music stole
nothing from death" —
                                        you only will create
(who are so perfectly alive)my shame:
lady through whose profound and fragile lips
the sweet small clumsy feet of April came

into the ragged meadow of my soul.

i sing of Olaf glad and big

i sing of Olaf glad and big
whose warmest heart recoiled at war:
a conscientious object-or

his wellbelovéd colonel(trig
westpointer most succinctly bred)
took erring Olaf soon in hand;
but — though an host of overjoyed
noncoms(first knocking on the head
him)do through icy waters roll
that helplessness which others stroke
with brushes recently employed
anent this muddy toiletbowl,
while kindred intellects evoke
allegiance per blunt instruments —
Olaf(being to all intents
a corpse and wanting any rag
upon what God unto him gave)
responds, without getting annoyed
"I will not kiss your f.ing flag"

straightway the silver bird looked grave
(departing hurriedly to shave)

but — though all kinds of officers
(a yearning nation's blueeyed pride)
their passive prey did kick and curse
until for wear their clarion
voices and boots were much the worse,
and egged the firstclassprivates on
his rectum wickedly to tease
by means of skilfully applied
bayonets roasted hot with heat —
Olaf(upon what were once knees)
does almost ceaselessly repeat
"there is some s. I will not eat"

our president,being of which
assertions duly notified
threw the yellowsonofabitch
into a dungeon,where he died

Christ(of His mercy infinite)
i pray to see;and Olaf,too

preponderatingly because
unless statistics lie he was
more brave than me:more blond than you.

may i feel said he

may i feel said he
(i'll squeal said she
just once said he)
it's fun said she

(may i touch said he
how much said she
a lot said he)
why not said she

(let's go said he
not too far said she
what's too far said he
where you are said she)

may i stay said he
(which way said she
like this said he
if you kiss said she

may i move said he
is it love said she)
if you're willing said he
(but you're killing said she

but it's life said he
but your wife said she
now said he)
ow said she

(tiptop said he
don't stop said she
oh no said he)
go slow said she

(cccome?said he
ummm said she)
you're divine!said he
(you are Mine said she)

my specialty is living said

my specialty is living said
a man(who could not earn his bread
because he would not sell his head)

squads right impatiently replied
two billion pubic lice inside
one pair of trousers(which had died)

you shall above all things be
glad and young

you shall above all things be glad and young.
For if you're young,whatever life you wear

it will become you;and if you are glad
whatever's living will yourself become.
Girlboys may nothing more than boygirls need:
i can entirely her only love

whose any mystery makes every man's
flesh put space on;and his mind take off time

that you should ever think,may god forbid
and(in his mercy)your true lover spare:
for that way knowledge lies,the foetal grave
called progress,and negation's dead undoom.

I'd rather learn from one bird how to sing
than teach ten thousand stars how not to dance

flotsam and jetsam

flotsam and jetsam
are gentlemen poeds
urseappeal netsam
our spinsters and coeds)

thoroughly bretish
they scout the inhuman
itarian fetish
that man isn't wuman

vive the millenni
um three cheers for labor
give all things to enni
one bugger thy nabor

(neck and senecktie
are gentlemen ppoyds
even whose recktie
are covered by lloyd's

the way to hump a cow is not

the way to hump a cow is not
to get yourself a stool
but draw a line around the spot
and call it beautifool

to multiply because and why
dividing thens by nows
and adding and (i understand)
is hows to hump a cows

the way to hump a cow is not
to elevate your tool
but drop a penny in the slot
and bellow like a bool

to lay a wreath from ancient greath
on insulated brows
(while tossing boms at uncle toms)
is hows to hump a cows

the way to hump a cow is not
to push and then to pull
but practicing the art of swot
to preach the golden rull

to vote for me (all decent mem
and wonens will allows
which if they don't to hell with them)
is hows to hump a cows

as freedom is a breakfastfood

as freedom is a breakfastfood
or truth can live with right and wrong
or molehills are from mountains made
— long enough and just so long
will being pay the rent of seem
and genius please the talentgang
and water most encourage flame

as hatracks into peachtrees grow
or hopes dance best on bald men's hair
and every finger is a toe
and any courage is a fear
— long enough and just so long
will the impure think all things pure
and hornets wail by children stung

or as the seeing are the blind
and robins never welcome spring
nor flatfolk prove their world is round
nor dingsters die at break of dong
and common's rare and millstones float
— long enough and just so long
tomorrow will not be too late

worms are the words but joy's the voice
down shall go which and up come who
breasts will be breasts thighs will be thighs
deeds cannot dream what dreams can do
— time is a tree(this life one leaf)
but love is the sky and i am for you
just so long and long enough

anyone lived in a pretty how town

anyone lived in a pretty how town
(with up so floating many bells down)
spring summer autumn winter
he sang his didn't he danced his did.

Women and men(both little and small)
cared for anyone not at all
they sowed their isn't they reaped their same
sun moon stars rain

children guessed(but only a few
and down they forgot as up they grew
autumn winter spring summer)
that noone loved him more by more

when by now and tree by leaf
she laughed his joy she cried his grief
bird by snow and stir by still
anyone's any was all to her

someones married their everyones
laughed their cryings and did their dance
(sleep wake hope and then) they
said their nevers they slept their dream

stars rain sun moon
(and only the snow can begin to explain
how children are apt to forget to remember
with up so floating many bells down)

one day anyone died i guess
(and noone stooped to kiss his face)
busy folk buried them side by side
little by little and was by was

all by all and deep by deep
and more by more they dream their sleep
noone and anyone earth by april
wish by spirit and if by yes.

Women and men(both dong and ding)
summer autumn winter spring
reaped their sowing and went their came
sun moon stars rain

my father moved through dooms of love

my father moved through dooms of love
through sames of am through haves of give,
singing each morning out of each night
my father moved through depths of height

this motionless forgetful where
turned at his glance to shining here;
that if(so timid air is firm)
under his eyes would stir and squirm

newly as from unburied which
floats the first who,his april touch
drove sleeping selves to swarm their fates
woke dreamers to their ghostly roots

and should some why completely weep
my father's fingers brought her sleep:
vainly no smallest voice might cry
for he could feel the mountains grow.

Lifting the valleys of the sea
my father moved through griefs of joy;
praising a forehead called the moon
singing desire into begin

joy was his song and joy so pure
a heart of star by him could steer
and pure so now and now so yes
the wrists of twilight would rejoice

keen as midsummer's keen beyond
conceiving mind of sun will stand,
so strictly(over utmost him
so hugely)stood my father's dream

his flesh was flesh his blood was blood:
no hungry man but wished him food;
no cripple wouldn't creep one mile
uphill to only see him smile.

Scorning the pomp of must and shall
my father moved through dooms of feel;
his anger was as right as rain
his pity was as green as grain

septembering arms of year extend
less humbly wealth to foe and friend
than he to foolish and to wise
offered immeasurable is

proudly and(by octobering flame
beckoned)as earth will downward climb,
so naked for immortal work
his shoulders marched against the dark

his sorrow was as true as bread:
no liar looked him in the head;
if every friend became his foe
he'd laugh and build a world with snow.

My father moved through theys of we,
singing each new leaf out of each tree
(and every child was sure that spring
danced when she heard my father sing)

then let men kill which cannot share,
let blood and flesh be mud and mire,
scheming imagine,passion willed,
freedom a drug that's bought and sold

giving to steal and cruel kind,
a heart to fear,to doubt a mind,
to differ a disease of same,
conform the pinnacle of am

though dull were all we taste as bright,
bitter all utterly things sweet,
maggoty minus and dumb death
all we inherit,all bequeath

and nothing quite so least as truth
— i say though hate were why men breathe —
because my father lived his soul
love is the whole and more than all

plato told

plato told

him:he couldn't
believe it(jesus

told him;he
wouldn't believe
it)lao

tsze
certainly told
him,and general
(yes

mam)
sherman;
and even
(believe it
or

not)you
told him:i told
him;we told him
(he didn't believe it,no

sir)it took
a nipponized bit of
the old sixth

avenue
el;in the top of his head:to tell

him

pity this busy monster,manunkind

pity this busy monster,manunkind,

not.   Progress is a comfortable disease:
your victim(death and life safely beyond)

plays with the bigness of his littleness
— electrons deify one razorblade
into a mountainrange;lenses extend

unwish through curving wherewhen till unwish
returns on its unself.
                              A world of made
is not a world of born — pity poor flesh

and trees,poor stars and stones,but never this
fine specimen of hypermagical

ultraomnipotence.　We doctors know

a hopeless case if — listen:there's a hell
of a good universe next door;let's go

what if a much of a which
of a wind

what if a much of a which of a wind
gives the truth to summer's lie;
bloodies with dizzying leaves the sun
and yanks immortal stars awry?
Blow king to beggar and queen to seem
(blow friend to fiend:blow space to time)
— when skies are hanged and oceans drowned,
the single secret will still be man

what if a keen of a lean wind flays
screaming hills with sleet and snow:
strangles valleys by ropes of thing
and stifles forests in white ago?
Blow hope to terror;blow seeing to blind
(blow pity to envy and soul to mind)
— whose hearts are mountains,roots are trees,
it's they shall cry hello to the spring

what if a dawn of a doom of a dream
bites this universe in two,
peels forever out of his grave
and sprinkles nowhere with me and you?
Blow soon to never and never to twice
(blow life to isn't:blow death to was)
— all nothing's only our hugest home;
the most who die,the more we live

all ignorance toboggans into know

all ignorance toboggans into know
and trudges up to ignorance again:
but winter's not forever,even snow
melts;and if spring should spoil the game,what then?

all history's a winter sport or three:
but were it five,i'd still insist that all
history is too small for even me;
for me and you,exceedingly too small.

Swoop(shrill collective myth)into thy grave
merely to toil the scale to shrillerness
per every madge and mabel dick and dave
— tomorrow is our permanent address

and there they'll scarcely find us(if they do,
we'll move away still further:into now

maggie and milly and molly and may

maggie and milly and molly and may
went down to the beach(to play one day)

and maggie discovered a shell that sang
so sweetly she couldn't remember her troubles,and

milly befriended a stranded star
whose rays five languid fingers were;

and molly was chased by a horrible thing
which raced sideways while blowing bubbles:and

may came home with a smooth round stone
as small as a world and as large as alone.

For whatever we lose(like a you or a me)
it's always ourselves we find in the sea

in heavenly realms of hellas dwelt

in heavenly realms of hellas dwelt
two very different sons of zeus:
one,handsome strong and born to dare
— a fighter to his eyelashes —
the other,cunning ugly lame;
but as you'll shortly comprehend
a marvellous artificer

now Ugly was the husband of
(as happens every now and then
upon a merely human plane)
someone completely beautiful;
and Beautiful,who(truth to sing)
could never quite tell right from wrong,
took brother Fearless by the eyes
and did the deed of joy with him

then Cunning forged a web so subtle
air is comparatively crude;
an indestructible occult
supersnare of resistless metal:
and(stealing toward the blissful pair)
skilfully wafted over them-
selves this implacable unthing

next,our illustrious scientist
petitions the celestial host
to scrutinize his handiwork:
they(summoned by that savage yell
from shining realms of regions dark)
laugh long at Beautiful and Brave
— wildly who rage,vainly who strive;
and being finally released
flee one another like the pest

thus did immortal jealousy
quell divine generosity,
thus reason vanquished instinct and
matter became the slave of mind;

thus virtue triumphed over vice
and beauty bowed to ugliness
and logic thwarted life:and thus —
but look around you,friends and foes

my tragic tale concludes herewith:
soldier,beware of mrs smith

HART CRANE
1899–1932

My Grandmother's Love Letters

There are no stars to-night
But those of memory.
Yet how much room for memory there is
In the loose girdle of soft rain.

There is even room enough
For the letters of my mother's mother,
Elizabeth,
That have been pressed so long
Into a corner of the roof
That they are brown and soft,
And liable to melt as snow.

Over the greatness of such space
Steps must be gentle.
It is all hung by an invisible white hair.
It trembles as birch limbs webbing the air.

And I ask myself:

"Are your fingers long enough to play
Old keys that are but echoes:
Is the silence strong enough
To carry back the music to its source
And back to you again
As though to her?"

Yet I would lead my grandmother by the hand
Through much of what she would not understand;
And so I stumble. And the rain continues on the roof
With such a sound of gently pitying laughter.

Praise for an Urn

In memoriam: Ernest Nelson

It was a kind of northern face
That mingled in such exile guise
The everlasting eyes of Pierrot
And, of Gargantua, the laughter.

His thoughts, delivered to me
From the white coverlet and pillow,
I see now, were inheritances —
Delicate riders of the storm.

The slant moon on the slanting hill
Once moved us toward presentiments
Of what the dead keep, living still,
And such assessments of the soul

As, perched in the crematory lobby,
The insistent clock commented on,
Touching as well upon our praise
Of glories proper to the time.

Still, having in mind gold hair,
I cannot see that broken brow
And miss the dry sound of bees
Stretching across a lucid space.

Scatter these well-meant idioms
Into the smoky spring that fills
The suburbs, where they will be lost.
They are no trophies of the sun.

Chaplinesque

We make our meek adjustments,
Contented with such random consolations
As the wind deposits
In slithered and too ample pockets.

For we can still love the world, who find
A famished kitten on the step, and know
Recesses for it from the fury of the street,
Or warm torn elbow coverts.

We will sidestep, and to the final smirk
Dally the doom of that inevitable thumb
That slowly chafes its puckered index toward us,
Facing the dull squint with what innocence
And what surprise!

And yet these fine collapses are not lies
More than the pirouettes of any pliant cane;
Our obsequies are, in a way, no enterprise.
We can evade you, and all else but the heart:
What blame to us if the heart live on.

The game enforces smirks; but we have seen
The moon in lonely alleys make
A grail of laughter of an empty ash can,
And through all sound of gaiety and quest
Have heard a kitten in the wilderness.

In Shadow

Out in the late amber afternoon,
Confused among chrysanthemums,
Her parasol, a pale balloon,
Like a waiting moon, in shadow swims.

Her furtive lace and misty hair
Over the garden dial distill
The sunlight, — then withdrawing, wear
Again the shadows at her will.

Gently yet suddenly, the sheen
Of stars inwraps her parasol.
She hears my step behind the green
Twilight, stiller than shadows, fall.

"Come, it is too late, — too late
To risk alone the light's decline:
Nor has the evening long to wait," —
But her own words are night's and mine.

Repose of Rivers

The willows carried a slow sound,
A sarabande the wind mowed on the mead.
I could never remember
That seething, steady leveling of the marshes
Till age had brought me to the sea.

Flags, weeds. And remembrance of steep alcoves
Where cypresses shared the noon's
Tyranny; they drew me into hades almost.
And mammoth turtles climbing sulphur dreams
Yielded, while sun-silt rippled them
Asunder . . .

How much I would have bartered! the black gorge
And all the singular nestings in the hills
Where beavers learn stitch and tooth.
The pond I entered once and quickly fled —
I remember now its singing willow rim.

And finally, in that memory all things nurse;
After the city that I finally passed
With scalding unguents spread and smoking darts
The monsoon cut across the delta
At gulf gates . . . There, beyond the dykes

I heard wind flaking sapphire, like this summer,
And willows could not hold more steady sound.

Passage

Where the cedar leaf divides the sky
I heard the sea.
In sapphire arenas of the hills
I was promised an improved infancy.

Sulking, sanctioning the sun,
My memory I left in a ravine, —
Casual louse that tissues the buckwheat,
Aprons rocks, congregates pears
In moonlit bushels
And wakens alleys with a hidden cough.

Dangerously the summer burned
(I had joined the entrainments of the wind).
The shadows of boulders lengthened my back:
In the bronze gongs of my cheeks
The rain dried without odour.

"It is not long, it is not long;
See where the red and black
Vine-stanchioned valleys — ": but the wind
Died speaking through the ages that you know
And hug, chimney-sooted heart of man!

So was I turned about and back, much as your smoke
Compiles a too well-known biography.

The evening was a spear in the ravine
That throve through very oak. And had I walked
The dozen particular decimals of time?
Touching an opening laurel, I found
A thief beneath, my stolen book in hand.

"Why are you back here — smiling an iron coffin?"
"To argue with the laurel," I replied:
"Am justified in transience, fleeing
Under the constant wonder of your eyes — ."

He closed the book. And from the Ptolemies
Sand troughed us in a glittering abyss.
A serpent swam a vertex to the sun
— On unpaced beaches leaned its tongue and drummed.
What fountains did I hear? what icy speeches?
Memory, committed to the page, had broke.

The Wine Menagerie

Invariably when wine redeems the sight,
Narrowing the mustard scansions of the eyes,
A leopard ranging always in the brow
Asserts a vision in the slumbering gaze.

Then glozening decanters that reflect the street
Wear me in crescents on their bellies. Slow
Applause flows into liquid cynosures:
— I am conscripted to their shadows' glow.

Against the imitation onyx wainscoting
(Painted emulsion of snow, eggs, yarn, coal, manure)
Regard the forceps of the smile that takes her.
Percussive sweat is spreading to his hair. Mallets,
Her eyes, unmake an instant of the world . . .

What is it in this heap the serpent pries —
Whose skin, facsimile of time, unskeins
Octagon, sapphire transepts round the eyes;
— From whom some whispered carillon assures
Speed to the arrow into feathered skies?

Sharp to the window-pane guile drags a face,
And as the alcove of her jealousy recedes
An urchin who has left the snow
Nudges a cannister across the bar
While August meadows somewhere clasp his brow.

Each chamber, transept, coins some squint,
Remorseless line, minting their separate wills —
Poor streaked bodies wreathing up and out,
Unwitting the stigma that each turn repeals:
Between black tusks the roses shine!

New thresholds, new anatomies! Wine talons
Build freedom up about me and distill
This competence — to travel in a tear
Sparkling alone, within another's will.

Until my blood dreams a receptive smile
Wherein new purities are snared; where chimes
Before some flame of gaunt repose a shell
Tolled once, perhaps, by every tongue in hell.
— Anguished, the wit that cries out of me:

"Alas, — these frozen billows of your skill!
Invent new dominoes of love and bile . . .
Ruddy, the tooth implicit of the world
Has followed you. Though in the end you know
And count some dim inheritance of sand,
How much yet meets the treason of the snow.

"Rise from the dates and crumbs. And walk away,
Stepping over Holofernes' shins —
Beyond the wall, whose severed head floats by
With Baptist John's. Their whispering begins.

"— And fold your exile on your back again;
Petrushka's valentine pivots on its pin."

For the Marriage of Faustus and Helen

And so we may arrive by Talmud skill
And profane Greek to raise the building up
Of Helen's house against the Ismaelite,
King of Thogarma, and his habergeons
Brimstony, blue and fiery; and the force
Of King Abaddon, and the beast of Cittim;
Which Rabbi David Kimchi, Onkelos,
And Aben Ezra do interpret Rome.
THE ALCHEMIST

I

The mind has shown itself at times
Too much the baked and labeled dough
Divided by accepted multitudes.
Across the stacked partitions of the day —
Across the memoranda, baseball scores,
The stenographic smiles and stock quotations
Smutty wings flash out equivocations.

The mind is brushed by sparrow wings;
Numbers, rebuffed by asphalt, crowd
The margins of the day, accent the curbs,
Convoying divers dawns on every corner
To druggist, barber and tobacconist,
Until the graduate opacities of evening
Take them away as suddenly to somewhere
Virginal perhaps, less fragmentary, cool.

There is the world dimensional for
those untwisted by the love of things
irreconcilable . . .

And yet, suppose some evening I forgot
The fare and transfer, yet got by that way
Without recall, — lost yet poised in traffic.
Then I might find your eyes across an aisle,
Still flickering with those prefigurations —
Prodigal, yet uncontested now,
Half-riant before the jerky window frame.

There is some way, I think, to touch
Those hands of yours that count the nights
Stippled with pink and green advertisements.
And now, before its arteries turn dark,
I would have you meet this bartered blood.
Imminent in his dream, none better knows
The white wafer cheek of love, or offers words
Lightly as moonlight on the eaves meets snow.

Reflective conversion of all things
At your deep blush, when ecstasies thread
The limbs and belly, when rainbows spréad
Impinging on the throat and sides . . .
Inevitable, the body of the world
Weeps in inventive dust for the hiatus
That winks above it, bluet in your breasts.

The earth may glide diaphanous to death;
But if I lift my arms it is to bend
To you who turned away once, Helen, knowing
The press of troubled hands, too alternate
With steel and soil to hold you endlessly.
I meet you, therefore, in that eventual flame
You found in final chains, no captive then —
Beyond their million brittle, bloodshot eyes;
White, through white cities passed on to assume
That world which comes to each of us alone.

Accept a lone eye riveted to your plane,
Bent axle of devotion along companion ways
That beat, continuous, to hourless days —
One inconspicuous, glowing orb of praise.

II

Brazen hypnotics glitter here;
Glee shifts from foot to foot,
Magnetic to their tremolo.
This crashing opéra bouffe,
Blest excursion! this ricochet
From roof to roof —
Know, Olympians, we are breathless
While nigger cupids scour the stars!

A thousand light shrugs balance us
Through snarling hails of melody.
White shadows slip across the floor
Splayed like cards from a loose hand;
Rhythmic ellipses lead into canters
Until somewhere a rooster banters.

Greet naïvely — yet intrepidly
New soothings, new amazements
That cornets introduce at every turn —
And you may fall downstairs with me
With perfect grace and equanimity.
Or, plaintively scud past shores
Where, by strange harmonic laws
All relatives, serene and cool,
Sit rocked in patent armchairs.

O, I have known metallic paradises
Where cuckoos clucked to finches
Above the deft catastrophes of drums.
While titters hailed the groans of death
Beneath gyrating awnings I have seen
The incunabula of the divine grotesque.
This music has a reassuring way.

The siren of the springs of guilty song —
Let us take her on the incandescent wax
Striated with nuances, nervosities
That we are heir to: she is still so young,
We cannot frown upon her as she smiles,
Dipping here in this cultivated storm
Among slim skaters of the gardened skies.

III

Capped arbiter of beauty in this street
That narrows darkly into motor dawn, —
You, here beside me, delicate ambassador
Of intricate slain numbers that arise
In whispers, naked of steel;
                      religious gunman!
Who faithfully, yourself, will fall too soon,
And in other ways than as the wind settles
On the sixteen thrifty bridges of the city:
Let us unbind our throats of fear and pity.

                        We even,
Who drove speediest destruction
In corymbulous formations of mechanics, —
Who hurried the hill breezes, spouting malice
Plangent over meadows, and looked down
On rifts of torn and empty houses
Like old women with teeth unjubilant
That waited faintly, briefly and in vain:

We know, eternal gunman, our flesh remembers
The tensile boughs, the nimble blue plateaus,
The mounted, yielding cities of the air!
That saddled sky that shook down vertical
Repeated play of fire — no hypogeum
Of wave or rock was good against one hour.

We did not ask for that, but have survived,
And will persist to speak again before
All stubble streets that have not curved
To memory, or known the ominous lifted arm
That lowers down the arc of Helen's brow
To saturate with blessing and dismay.

A goose, tobacco and cologne —
Three-winged and gold-shod prophecies of heaven,
The lavish heart shall always have to leaven
And spread with bells and voices, and atone
The abating shadows of our conscript dust.

Anchises' navel, dripping of the sea, —
The hands Erasmus dipped in gleaming tides,
Gathered the voltage of blown blood and vine;
Delve upward for the new and scattered wine,
O brother-thief of time, that we recall.
Laugh out the meager penance of their days
Who dare not share with us the breath released,
The substance drilled and spent beyond repair
For golden, or the shadow of gold hair.

Distinctly praise the years, whose volatile
Blamed bleeding hands extend and thresh the height
The imagination spans beyond despair,
Outpacing bargain, vocable and prayer.

Voyages

I

Above the fresh ruffles of the surf
Bright striped urchins flay each other with sand.
They have contrived a conquest for shell shucks,
And their fingers crumble fragments of baked weed
Gaily digging and scattering.

And in answer to their treble interjections
The sun beats lightning on the waves,
The waves fold thunder on the sand;
And could they hear me I would tell them:

O brilliant kids, frisk with your dog,
Fondle your shells and sticks, bleached
By time and the elements; but there is a line
You must not cross nor ever trust beyond it
Spry cordage of your bodies to caresses
Too lichen-faithful from too wide a breast.
The bottom of the sea is cruel.

II

And yet this great wink of eternity,
Of rimless floods, unfettered leewardings,
Samite sheeted and processioned where
Her undinal vast belly moonward bends,
Laughing the wrapt inflections of our love;

Take this Sea, whose diapason knells
On scrolls of silver snowy sentences,
The sceptred terror of whose sessions rends
As her demeanors motion well or ill,
All but the pieties of lovers' hands.

And onward, as bells off San Salvador
Salute the crocus lustres of the stars,
In these poinsettia meadows of her tides, —
Adagios of islands, O my Prodigal,
Complete the dark confessions her veins spell.

Mark how her turning shoulders wind the hours,
And hasten while her penniless rich palms
Pass superscription of bent foam and wave, —
Hasten, while they are true, — sleep, death, desire,
Close round one instant in one floating flower.

Bind us in time, O Seasons clear, and awe.
O minstrel galleons of Carib fire,
Bequeath us to no earthly shore until
Is answered in the vortex of our grave
The seal's wide spindrift gaze toward paradise.

III

Infinite consanguinity it bears —
This tendered theme of you that light
Retrieves from sea plains where the sky
Resigns a breast that every wave enthrones;
While ribboned water lanes I wind
Are laved and scattered with no stroke
Wide from your side, whereto this hour
The sea lifts, also, reliquary hands.

And so, admitted through black swollen gates
That must arrest all distance otherwise, —
Past whirling pillars and lithe pediments,
Light wrestling there incessantly with light,
Star kissing star through wave on wave unto
Your body rocking!

and where death, if shed,
Presumes no carnage, but this single change, —
Upon the steep floor flung from dawn to dawn
The silken skilled transmemberment of song;

Permit me voyage, love, into your hands . . .

IV

Whose counted smile of hours and days, suppose
I know as spectrum of the sea and pledge
Vastly now parting gulf on gulf of wings
Whose circles bridge, I know, (from palms to the severe
Chilled albatross's white immutability)
No stream of greater love advancing now
Than, singing, this mortality alone
Through clay aflow immortally to you.

All fragrance irrefragibly, and claim
Madly meeting logically in this hour
And region that is ours to wreathe again,
Portending eyes and lips and making told
The chancel port and portion of our June —

Shall they not stem and close in our own steps
Bright staves of flowers and quills to-day as I
Must first be lost in fatal tides to tell?
In signature of the incarnate word
The harbor shoulders to resign in mingling
Mutual blood, transpiring as foreknown
And widening noon within your breast for gathering
All bright insinuations that my years have caught
For islands where must lead inviolably
Blue latitudes and levels of your eyes, —

In this expectant, still exclaim receive
The secret oar and petals of all love.

V

Meticulous, past midnight in clear rime,
Infrangible and lonely, smooth as though cast
Together in one merciless white blade —
The bay estuaries fleck the hard sky limits.

— As if too brittle or too clear to touch!
The cables of our sleep so swiftly filed,
Already hang, shred ends from remembered stars.
One frozen trackless smile . . . What words
Can strangle this deaf moonlight? For we

Are overtaken. Now no cry, no sword
Can fasten or deflect this tidal wedge,
Slow tyranny of moonlight, moonlight loved
And changed . . . "There's

Nothing like this in the world," you say,
Knowing I cannot touch your hand and look
Too, into that godless cleft of sky
Where nothing turns but dead sands flashing.

"— And never to quite understand!" No,
In all the argosy of your bright hair I dreamed
Nothing so flagless as this piracy.

                              But now
Draw in your head, alone and too tall here.
Your eyes already in the slant of drifting foam;
Your breath sealed by the ghosts I do not know:
Draw in your head and sleep the long way home.

VI

Where icy and bright dungeons lift
Of swimmers their lost morning eyes,
And ocean rivers, churning, shift
Green borders under stranger skies,

Steadily as a shell secretes
Its beating leagues of monotone,
Or as many waters trough the sun's
Red kelson past the cape's wet stone;

O rivers mingling toward the sky
And harbor of the phœnix' breast —
My eyes pressed black against the prow,
— Thy derelict and blinded guest

Waiting, afire, what name, unspoke,
I cannot claim: let thy waves rear
More savage than the death of kings,
Some splintered garland for the seer.

Beyond siroccos harvesting
The solstice thunders, crept away,
Like a cliff swinging or a sail
Flung into April's inmost day —

Creation's blithe and petalled word
To the lounged goddess when she rose
Conceding dialogue with eyes
That smile unsearchable repose —

Still fervid covenant, Belle Isle,
— Unfolded floating dais before
Which rainbows twine continual hair —
Belle Isle, white echo of the oar!

The imaged Word, it is, that holds
Hushed willows anchored in its glow.
It is the unbetrayable reply
Whose accent no farewell can know.

from The Bridge

To Brooklyn Bridge

How many dawns, chill from his rippling rest
The seagull's wings shall dip and pivot him,
Shedding white rings of tumult, building high
Over the chained bay waters Liberty —

Then, with inviolate curve, forsake our eyes
As apparitional as sails that cross
Some page of figures to be filed away;
— Till elevators drop us from our day . . .

I think of cinemas, panoramic sleights
With multitudes bent toward some flashing scene
Never disclosed, but hastened to again,
Foretold to other eyes on the same screen;

And Thee, across the harbor, silver-paced
As though the sun took step of thee, yet left
Some motion ever unspent in thy stride, —
Implicitly thy freedom staying thee!

Out of some subway scuttle, cell or loft
A bedlamite speeds to thy parapets,
Tilting there momently, shrill shirt ballooning,
A jest falls from the speechless caravan.

Down Wall, from girder into street noon leaks,
A rip-tooth of the sky's acetylene;
All afternoon the cloud-flown derricks turn . . .
Thy cables breathe the North Atlantic still.

And obscure as that heaven of the Jews,
Thy guerdon . . . Accolade thou dost bestow
Of anonymity time cannot raise:
Vibrant reprieve and pardon thou dost show.

O harp and altar, of the fury fused,
(How could mere toil align thy choiring strings!)
Terrific threshold of the prophet's pledge,
Prayer of pariah, and the lover's cry, —

Again the traffic lights that skim thy swift
Unfractioned idiom, immaculate sigh of stars,
Beading thy path — condense eternity:
And we have seen night lifted in thine arms.

Under thy shadow by the piers I waited;
Only in darkness is thy shadow clear.
The City's fiery parcels all undone,
Already snow submerges an iron year . . .

O Sleepless as the river under thee,
Vaulting the sea, the prairies' dreaming sod,
Unto us lowliest sometime sweep, descend
And of the curveship lend a myth to God.

.   .   .

Ave Maria

Venient annis, sæcula seris,
Quibus Oceanus vincula rerum
Laxet et ingens pateat tellus
Tiphysque novos detegat orbes
Nec sit terris ultima Thule.

SENECA

Be with me, Luis de San Angel, now —
Witness before the tides can wrest away
The word I bring, O you who reined my suit
Into the Queen's great heart that doubtful day;
For I have seen now what no perjured breath
Of clown nor sage can riddle or gainsay; —
To you, too, Juan Perez, whose counsel fear
And greed adjourned, — I bring you back Cathay!

Here waves climb into dusk on gleaming mail;
Invisible valves of the sea, — locks, tendons
Crested and creeping, troughing corridors
That fall back yawning to another plunge.
Slowly the sun's red caravel drops light
Once more behind us. . . . It is morning there —
O where our Indian emperies lie revealed,
Yet lost, all, let this keel one instant yield!

I thought of Genoa; and this truth, now proved,
That made me exile in her streets, stood me
More absolute than ever — biding the moon
Till dawn should clear that dim frontier, first seen
— The Chan's great continent. . . . Then faith, not fear
Nigh surged me witless. . . . Hearing the surf near —
I, wonder-breathing, kept the watch, — saw
The first palm chevron the first lighted hill.

And lowered. And they came out to us crying,
"The Great White Birds!" (O Madre Maria, still
One ship of these thou grantest safe returning;
Assure us through thy mantle's ageless blue!)
And record of more, floating in a casque,
Was tumbled from us under bare poles scudding;
And later hurricanes may claim more pawn. . . .
For here between two worlds, another, harsh,

Columbus, alone, gazing toward Spain, invokes the presence of two faithful partisans of his quest . . .

665

This third, of water, tests the word; lo, here
Bewilderment and mutiny heap whelming
Laughter, and shadow cuts sleep from the heart
Almost as though the Moor's flung scimitar
Found more than flesh to fathom in its fall.
Yet under tempest-lash and surfeitings,
Some inmost sob, half-heard, dissuades the abyss,
Merges the wind in measure to the waves,

Series on series, infinite, — till eyes
Starved wide on blackened tides, accrete — enclose
This turning rondure whole, this crescent ring
Sun-cusped and zoned with modulated fire
Like pearls that whisper through the Doge's hands
— Yet no delirium of jewels! O Fernando,
Take of that eastern shore, this western sea,
Yet yield thy God's, thy Virgin's charity!

— Rush down the plenitude, and you shall see
Isaiah counting famine on this lee!

*

An herb, a stray branch among salty teeth,
The jellied weeds that drag the shore, — perhaps
Tomorrow's moon will grant us Saltes Bar —
Palos again, — a land cleared of long war.
Some Angelus environs the cordage tree;
Dark waters onward shake the dark prow free.

*

O Thou who sleepest on Thyself, apart
Like ocean athwart lanes of death and birth,
And all the eddying breath between dost search
Cruelly with love thy parable of man, —
Inquisitor! incognizable Word
Of Eden and the enchained Sepulchre,
Into thy steep savannahs, burning blue,
Utter to loneliness the sail is true.

Who grindest oar, and arguing the mast
Subscribest holocaust of ships, O Thou
Within whose primal scan consummately
The glistening seignories of Ganges swim; —

666

Who sendest greeting by the corposant,
And Teneriffe's garnet — flamed it in a cloud,
Urging through night our passage to the Chan; —
Te Deum laudamus, for thy teeming span!

Of all that amplitude that time explores,
A needle in the sight, suspended north, —
Yielding by inference and discard, faith
And true appointment from the hidden shoal:
This disposition that thy night relates
From Moon to Saturn in one sapphire wheel:
The orbic wake of thy once whirling feet,
Elohim, still I hear thy sounding heel!

White toil of heaven's cordons, mustering
In holy rings all sails charged to the far
Hushed gleaming fields and pendant seething wheat
Of knowledge, — round thy brows unhooded now
— The kindled Crown! acceded of the poles
And biassed by full sails, meridians reel
Thy purpose — still one shore beyond desire!
The sea's green crying towers a-sway, Beyond

And kingdoms
                    naked in the
                                        trembling heart —
          Te Deum laudamus
                                        O Thou Hand of Fire
               .   .   .

The River

Stick your patent name on a signboard
brother — all over — going west — young man
Tintex — Japalac — Certain-teed Overalls ads
and lands sakes! under the new playbill ripped
in the guaranteed corner — see Bert Williams what?
Minstrels when you steal a chicken just
save me the wing for if it isn't
Erie it ain't for miles around a
Mazda — and the telegraphic night coming on Thomas

*. . . and past
the din and
slogans of
the year —*

667

a Ediford — and whistling down the tracks
a headlight rushing with the sound — can you
imagine — while an EXPRESS makes time like
SCIENCE — COMMERCE and the HOLYGHOST
RADIO ROARS IN EVERY HOME WE HAVE THE NORTHPOLE
WALLSTREET AND VIRGINBIRTH WITHOUT STONES OR
WIRES OR EVEN RUNning brooks connecting ears
and no more sermons windows flashing roar
Breathtaking — as you like it . . . eh?

    So the 20th Century — so
whizzed the Limited — roared by and left
three men, still hungry on the tracks, ploddingly
watching the tail lights wizen and converge, slip-
ping gimleted and neatly out of sight.

     *

The last bear, shot drinking in the Dakotas
Loped under wires that span the mountain stream.
Keen instruments, strung to a vast precision
Bind town to town and dream to ticking dream.
But some men take their liquor slow — and count
— Though they'll confess no rosary nor clue —
The river's minute by the far brook's year.
Under a world of whistles, wires and steam
Caboose-like they go ruminating through
Ohio, Indiana — blind baggage —
To Cheyenne tagging . . . Maybe Kalamazoo.

to those
whose
addresses are
never near

Time's rendings, time's blendings they construe
As final reckonings of fire and snow;
Strange bird-wit, like the elemental gist
Of unwalled winds they offer, singing low
My Old Kentucky Home and *Casey Jones,*
Some Sunny Day. I heard a road-gang chanting so.
And afterwards, who had a colt's eyes — one said,
"Jesus! Oh I remember watermelon days!" And sped
High in a cloud of merriment, recalled
"— And when my Aunt Sally Simpson smiled," he drawled —
"It was almost Louisiana, long ago."

"There's no place like Booneville though, Buddy,"
One said, excising a last burr from his vest,
"— For early trouting." Then peering in the can,
"— But I kept on the tracks." Possessed, resigned,
He trod the fire down pensively and grinned,
Spreading dry shingles of a beard. . . .

                                                     Behind
My father's cannery works I used to see
Rail-squatters ranged in nomad raillery,
The ancient men — wifeless or runaway
Hobo-trekkers that forever search
An empire wilderness of freight and rails.
Each seemed a child, like me, on a loose perch,
Holding to childhood like some termless play.
John, Jake or Charley, hopping the slow freight
— Memphis to Tallahassee — riding the rods,
Blind fists of nothing, humpty-dumpty clods.

Yet they touch something like a key perhaps.
From pole to pole across the hills, the states
but who have — They know a body under the wide rain;
touched her, Youngsters with eyes like fjords, old reprobates
knowing her With racetrack jargon, — dotting immensity
without name They lurk across her, knowing her yonder breast
Snow-silvered, sumac-stained or smoky blue —
Is past the valley-sleepers, south or west.
— As I have trod the rumorous midnights, too,

And past the circuit of the lamp's thin flame
(O Nights that brought me to her body bare!)
Have dreamed beyond the print that bound her name.
Trains sounding the long blizzards out — I heard
Wail into distances I knew were hers.
Papooses crying on the wind's long mane
Screamed redskin dynasties that fled the brain,
— Dead echoes! But I knew her body there,
Time like a serpent down her shoulder, dark,
And space, an eaglet's wing, laid on her hair.

Under the Ozarks, domed by Iron Mountain,
The old gods of the rain lie wrapped in pools

nor the
myths of her
fathers . . .

Where eyeless fish curvet a sunken fountain
And re-descend with corn from querulous crows.
Such pilferings make up their timeless eatage,
Propitiate them for their timber torn
By iron, iron — always the iron dealt cleavage!
They doze now, below axe and powder horn.

And Pullman breakfasters glide glistening steel
From tunnel into field — iron strides the dew —
Straddles the hill, a dance of wheel on wheel.
You have a half-hour's wait at Siskiyou,
Or stay the night and take the next train through.
Southward, near Cairo passing, you can see
The Ohio merging, — borne down Tennessee;
And if it's summer and the sun's in dusk
Maybe the breeze will lift the River's musk
— As though the waters breathed that you might know
Memphis Johnny, Steamboat Bill, Missouri Joe.
Oh, lean from the window, if the train slows down,
As though you touched hands with some ancient clown,
— A little while gaze absently below
And hum *Deep River* with them while they go.

Yes, turn again and sniff once more — look see,
O Sheriff, Brakeman and Authority —
Hitch up your pants and crunch another quid,
For you, too, feed the River timelessly.
And few evade full measure of their fate;
Always they smile out eerily what they seem.
I could believe he joked at heaven's gate —
Dan Midland — jolted from the cold brake-beam.

Down, down — born pioneers in time's despite,
Grimed tributaries to an ancient flow —
They win no frontier by their wayward plight,
But drift in stillness, as from Jordan's brow.

You will not hear it as the sea; even stone
Is not more hushed by gravity . . . But slow,
As loth to take more tribute — sliding prone
Like one whose eyes were buried long ago

The River, spreading, flows — and spends your dream.
What are you, lost within this tideless spell?
You are your father's father, and the stream —
A liquid theme that floating niggers swell.

Damp tonnage and alluvial march of days —
Nights turbid, vascular with silted shale
And roots surrendered down of moraine clays:
The Mississippi drinks the farthest dale.

O quarrying passion, undertowed sunlight!
The basalt surface drags a jungle grace
Ochreous and lynx-barred in lengthening might;
Patience! and you shall reach the biding place!

Over De Soto's bones the freighted floors
Throb past the City storied of three thrones.
Down two more turns the Mississippi pours
(Anon tall ironsides up from salt lagoons)

And flows within itself, heaps itself free.
All fades but one thin skyline 'round . . . Ahead
No embrace opens but the stinging sea;
The River lifts itself from its long bed,

Poised wholly on its dream, a mustard glow
Tortured with history, its one will — flow!
— The Passion spreads in wide tongues, choked and slow,
Meeting the Gulf, hosannas silently below.

To Emily Dickinson

You who desired so much — in vain to ask —
Yet fed your hunger like an endless task,
Dared dignify the labor, bless the quest —
Achieved that stillness ultimately best,

Being, of all, least sought for: Emily, hear!
O sweet, dead Silencer, most suddenly clear
When singing that Eternity possessed
And plundered momently in every breast;

— Truly no flower yet withers in your hand,
The harvest you descried and understand
Needs more than wit to gather, love to bind.
Some reconcilement of remotest mind —

Leaves Ormus rubyless, and Ophir chill.
Else tears heap all within one clay-cold hill.

The Broken Tower

The bell-rope that gathers God at dawn
Dispatches me as though I dropped down the knell
Of a spent day — to wander the cathedral lawn
From pit to crucifix, feet chill on steps from hell.

Have you not heard, have you not seen that corps
Of shadows in the tower, whose shoulders sway
Antiphonal carillons launched before
The stars are caught and hived in the sun's ray?

The bells, I say, the bells break down their tower;
And swing I know not where. Their tongues engrave
Membrane through marrow, my long-scattered score
Of broken intervals. . . . And I, their sexton slave!

Oval encyclicals in canyons heaping
The impasse high with choir. Banked voices slain!
Pagodas, campaniles with reveilles outleaping —
O terraced echoes prostrate on the plain! . . .

And so it was I entered the broken world
To trace the visionary company of love, its voice
An instant in the wind (I know not whither hurled)
But not for long to hold each desperate choice.

My word I poured. But was it cognate, scored
Of that tribunal monarch of the air
Whose thigh embronzes earth, strikes crystal Word
In wounds pledged once to hope — cleft to despair?

The steep encroachments of my blood left me
No answer (could blood hold such a lofty tower
As flings the question true?) — or is it she
Whose sweet mortality stirs latent power? —

And through whose pulse I hear, counting the strokes
My veins recall and add, revived and sure
The angelus of wars my chest evokes:
What I hold healed, original now, and pure . . .

And builds, within, a tower that is not stone
(Not stone can jacket heaven) — but slip
Of pebbles — visible wings of silence sown
In azure circles, widening as they dip

The matrix of the heart, lift down the eye
That shrines the quiet lake and swells a tower . . .
The commodious, tall decorum of the sky
Unseals her earth, and lifts love in its shower.

ALLEN TATE
b. 1899

Ode to the Confederate Dead

Row after row with strict impunity
The headstones yield their names to the element,
The wind whirrs without recollection;
In the riven troughs the splayed leaves
Pile up, of nature the casual sacrament
To the seasonal eternity of death;
Then driven by the fierce scrutiny
Of heaven to their election in the vast breath,
They sough the rumour of mortality.

Autumn is desolation in the plot
Of a thousand acres where these memories grow
From the inexhaustible bodies that are not
Dead, but feed the grass row after rich row.
Think of the autumns that have come and gone! —
Ambitious November with the humors of the year,
With a particular zeal for every slab,

Staining the uncomfortable angels that rot
On the slabs, a wing chipped here, an arm there:
The brute curiosity of an angel's stare
Turns you, like them, to stone,
Transforms the heaving air
Till plunged to a heavier world below
You shift your sea-space blindly
Heaving, turning like the blind crab.

   Dazed by the wind, only the wind
   The leaves flying, plunge

You know who have waited by the wall
The twilight certainty of an animal,
Those midnight restitutions of the blood
You know — the immitigable pines, the smoky frieze
Of the sky, the sudden call: you know the rage,
The cold pool left by the mounting flood,
Of muted Zeno and Parmenides.
You who have waited for the angry resolution
Of those desires that should be yours tomorrow,
You know the unimportant shrift of death
And praise the vision
And praise the arrogant circumstance
Of those who fall
Rank upon rank, hurried beyond decision —
Here by the sagging gate, stopped by the wall.

   Seeing, seeing only the leaves
   Flying, plunge and expire

Turn your eyes to the immoderate past,
Turn to the inscrutable infantry rising
Demons out of the earth — they will not last.
Stonewall, Stonewall, and the sunken fields of hemp,
Shiloh, Antietam, Malvern Hill, Bull Run.
Lost in that orient of the thick-and-fast
You will curse the setting sun.

   Cursing only the leaves crying
   Like an old man in a storm

You hear the shout, the crazy hemlocks point
With troubled fingers to the silence which
Smothers you, a mummy, in time.

                        The hound bitch
Toothless and dying, in a musty cellar
Hears the wind only.

                Now that the salt of their blood
Stiffens the saltier oblivion of the sea,
Seals the malignant purity of the flood,
What shall we who count our days and bow
Our heads with a commemorial woe
In the ribboned coats of grim felicity,
What shall we say of the bones, unclean,
Whose verdurous anonymity will grow?
The ragged arms, the ragged heads and eyes
Lost in these acres of the insane green?
The gray lean spiders come, they come and go;
In a tangle of willows without light
The singular screech-owl's tight
Invisible lyric seeds the mind
With the furious murmur of their chivalry.

  We shall say only the leaves
  Flying, plunge and expire

We shall say only the leaves whispering
In the improbable mist of nightfall
That flies on multiple wing;
Night is the beginning and the end
And in between the ends of distraction
Waits mute speculation, the patient curse
That stones the eyes, or like the jaguar leaps
For his own image in a jungle pool, his victim.
What shall we say who have knowledge
Carried to the heart? Shall we take the act
To the grave? Shall we, more hopeful, set up the grave
In the house? The ravenous grave?

Leave now
The shut gate and the decomposing wall:
The gentle serpent, green in the mulberry bush,
Riots with his tongue through the hush —
Sentinel of the grave who counts us all!

The Subway

Dark accurate plunger down the successive knell
Of arch on arch, where ogives burst a red
Reverberance of hail upon the dead
Thunder like an exploding crucible!
Harshly articulate, musical steel shell
Of angry worship, hurled religiously
Upon your business of humility
Into the iron forestries of hell:

Till broken in the shift of quieter
Dense altitudes tangential of your steel,
I am become geometries, and glut
Expansions like a blind astronomer
Dazed, while the wordless heavens bulge and reel
In the cold revery of an idiot.

Mr. Pope

When Alexander Pope strolled in the city
Strict was the glint of pearl and gold sedans.
Ladies leaned out more out of fear than pity
For Pope's tight back was rather a goat's than man's.

Often one thinks the urn should have more bones
Than skeletons provide for speedy dust,
The urn gets hollow, cobwebs brittle as stones
Weave to the funeral shell a frivolous rust.

And he who dribbled couplets like a snake
Coiled to a lithe precision in the sun
Is missing. The jar is empty; you may break
It only to find that Mr. Pope is gone.

What requisitions of a verity
Prompted the wit and rage between his teeth
One cannot say. Around a crooked tree
A moral climbs whose name should be a wreath.

The Paradigm

For when they meet, the tensile air
Like fine steel strains under the weight
Of messages that both hearts bear —
Pure passion once, now purest hate;

Till the taut air like a cold hand
Clasped to cold hand and bone to bone
Seals them up in their icy land
(A few square feet) where into stone

The two hearts turning quickly pass
Once more their impenetrable world;
So fades out each heart's looking-glass
Whose image is the surface hurled

By all the air; air, glass is not;
So is their fleeting enmity
Like a hard mirror crashed by what
The quality of air must be.

For in the air all lovers meet
After they've hated out their love;
Love's but the echo of retreat
Caught by the sunbeam stretched above

Their frozen exile from the earth
And lost. Each is the other's crime.
This is their equity in birth —
Hate is its ignorant paradigm.

The Wolves

There are wolves in the next room waiting
With heads bent low, thrust out, breathing
At nothing in the dark; between them and me
A white door patched with light from the hall
Where it seems never (so still is the house)
A man has walked from the front door to the stair.
It has all been forever. Beasts claw the floor.
I have brooded on angels and archfiends
But no man has ever sat where the next room's
Crowded with wolves, and for the honor of man
I affirm that never have I before. Now while
I have looked for the evening star at a cold window
And whistled when Arcturus spilt his light,
I've heard the wolves scuffle, and said: So this
Is man; so — what better conclusion is there —
The day will not follow night, and the heart
Of man has a little dignity, but less patience
Than a wolf's, and a duller sense that cannot
Smell its own mortality. (This and other
Meditations will be suited to other times
After dog silence howls his epitaph.)
Now remember courage, go to the door,
Open it and see whether coiled on the bed
Or cringing by the wall, a savage beast
Maybe with golden hair, with deep eyes
Like a bearded spider on a sunlit floor
Will snarl — and man can never be alone.

Last Days of Alice

Alice grown lazy, mammoth but not fat,
Declines upon her lost and twilight age;
Above in the dozing leaves the grinning cat
Quivers forever with his abstract rage:

Whatever light swayed on the perilous gate
Forever sways, nor will the arching grass,
Caught when the world clattered, undulate
In the deep suspension of the looking-glass.

Bright Alice! always pondering to gloze
The spoiled cruelty she had meant to say
Gazes learnedly down her airy nose
At nothing, nothing thinking all the day.

Turned absent-minded by infinity
She cannot move unless her double move,
The All-Alice of the world's entity
Smashed in the anger of her hopeless love,

Love for herself who, as an earthly twain,
Pouted to join her two in a sweet one;
No more the second lips to kiss in vain
The first she broke, plunged through the glass alone —

Alone to the weight of impassivity,
Incest of spirit, theorem of desire,
Without will as chalky cliffs by the sea,
Empty as the bodiless flesh of fire:

All space, that heaven is a dayless night,
A nightless day driven by perfect lust
For vacancy, in which her bored eyesight
Stares at the drowsy cubes of human dust.

— We too back to the world shall never pass
Through the shattered door, a dumb shade-harried crowd
Being all infinite, function depth and mass
Without figure, a mathematical shroud

Hurled at the air — blesséd without sin!
O God of our flesh, return us to Your wrath,
Let us be evil could we enter in
Your grace, and falter on the stony path!

Aeneas at Washington

I myself saw furious with blood
Neoptolemus, at his side the black Atridae,
Hecuba and the hundred daughters, Priam
Cut down, his filth drenching the holy fires.
In that extremity I bore me well,

A true gentleman, valorous in arms,
Disinterested and honourable. Then fled:
That was a time when civilization
Run by the few fell to the many, and
Crashed to the shout of men, the clang of arms:
Cold victualing I seized, I hoisted up
The old man my father upon my back,
In the smoke made by sea for a new world
Saving little — a mind imperishable
If time is, a love of past things tenuous
As the hesitation of receding love.

(To the reduction of uncitied littorals
We brought chiefly the vigor of prophecy,
Our hunger breeding calculation
And fixed triumphs.)

                     I saw the thirsty dove
In the glowing fields of Troy, hemp ripening
And tawny corn, the thickening Blue Grass
All lying rich forever in the green sun.
I see all things apart, the towers that men
Contrive I too contrived long, long ago.
Now I demand little. The singular passion
Abides its object and consumes desire
In the circling shadow of its appetite.
There was a time when the young eyes were slow,
Their flame steady beyond the firstling fire,
I stood in the rain, far from home at nightfall
By the Potomac, the great Dome lit the water,
The city my blood had built I knew no more
While the screech-owl whistled his new delight
Consecutively dark.

               Stuck in the wet mire
Four thousand leagues from the ninth buried city
I thought of Troy, what we had built her for.

Sonnets at Christmas

I

This is the day His hour of life draws near,
Let me get ready from head to foot for it
Most handily with eyes to pick the year
For small feed to reward a feathered wit.
Some men would see it an epiphany
At ease, at food and drink, others at chase;
Yet I, stung lassitude, with ecstasy
Unspent argue the season's difficult case
So: Man, dull creature of enormous head,
What would he look at in the coiling sky?
But I must kneel again unto the Dead
While Christmas bells of paper white and red,
Figured with boys and girls spilt from a sled,
Ring out the silence I am nourished by.

II

Ah, Christ, I love you rings to the wild sky
And I must think a little of the past:
When I was ten I told a stinking lie
That got a black boy whipped; but now at last
The going years, caught in an after-glow,
Reverse like balls englished upon green baize —
Let them return, let the round trumpets blow
The ancient crackle of the Christ's deep gaze.
Deafened and blind, with senses yet unfound,
Am I, untutored to the after-wit
Of knowledge, knowing a nightmare has no sound;
Therefore with idle hands and head I sit
In late December before the fire's daze
Punished by crimes of which I would be quit.

The Swimmers

Kentucky water, clear springs: a boy fleeing
 To water under the dry Kentucky sun,
 His four little friends in tandem with him, seeing

Long shadows of grapevine wriggle and run
 Over the green swirl; mullein under the ear
 Soft as Nausicaä's palm; sullen fun

Savage as childhood's thin harmonious tear:
  O fountain, bosom source undying-dead
  Replenish me the spring of love and fear

And give me back the eye that looked and fled
  When a thrush idling in the tulip tree
  Unwound the cold dream of the copperhead.

— Along the creek the road was winding; we
  Felt the quicksilver sky. I see again
  The shrill companions of that odyssey:

Bill Eaton, Charlie Watson, "Nigger" Layne
  The doctor's son, Harry Duèsler who played
  The flute; and Tate, with water on the brain.

Dog-days: the dusty leaves where rain delayed
  Hung low on poison-oak and scuppernong,
  And we were following the active shade

Of water, that bells and bickers all night long.
  "No more'n a mile," Layne said. All five stood still.
  Listening, I heard what seemed at first a song;

Peering, I heard the hooves come down the hill.
  The posse passed, twelve horse; the leader's face
  Was worn as limestone on an ancient sill.

Then, as sleepwalkers shift from a hard place
  In bed, and rising to keep a formal pledge
  Descend a ladder into empty space,

We scuttled down the bank below a ledge
  And marched stiff-legged in our common fright
  Along a hog-track by the riffle's edge:

Into a world where sound shaded the sight
  Dropped the dull hooves again; the horsemen came
  Again, all but the leader: it was night

Momently and I feared: eleven same
  Jesus-Christers unmembered and unmade,
  Whose Corpse had died again in dirty shame.

The bank then levelling in a speckled glade,
    We stopped to breathe above the swimming-hole;
    I gazed at its reticulated shade

Recoiling in blue fear, and felt it roll
    Over my ears and eyes and lift my hair
    Like seaweed tossing on a sunk atoll.

I rose again. Borne on the copper air
    A distant voice green as a funeral wreath
    Against a grave: "That dead nigger there."

The melancholy sheriff slouched beneath
    A giant sycamore; shaking his head
    He plucked a sassafras twig and picked his teeth:

"We come too late." He spoke to the tired dead
    Whose ragged shirt soaked up the viscous flow
    Of blood in which It lay discomfited.

A butting horse-fly gave one ear a blow
    And glanced off, as the sheriff kicked the rope
    Loose from the neck and hooked it with his toe

Away from the blood. — I looked back down the slope:
    The friends were gone that I had hoped to greet. —
    A single horseman came at a slow lope

And pulled up at the hanged man's horny feet;
    The sheriff noosed the feet, the other end
    The stranger tied to his pommel in a neat

Slip-knot. I saw the Negro's body bend
    And straighten, as a fish-line cast transverse
    Yields to the current that it must subtend.

The sheriff's Goddamn was a murmured curse
    Not for the dead but for the blinding dust
    That boxed the cortège in a cloudy hearse

And dragged it towards our town. I knew I must
    Not stay till twilight in that silent road;
    Sliding my bare feet into the warm crust,

I hopped the stonecrop like a panting toad
   Mouth open, following the heaving cloud
   That floated to the court-house square its load

Of limber corpse that took the sun for shroud.
   There were three figures in the dying sun
   Whose light were company where three was crowd.

My breath crackled the dead air like a shotgun
   As, sheriff and the stranger disappearing,
   The faceless head lay still. I could not run

Or walk, but stood. Alone in the public clearing
   This private thing was owned by all the town,
   Though never claimed by us within my hearing.

YVOR WINTERS
1900–1968

The Rows of Cold Trees

To be my own Messiah to the
burning end. Can one endure the
acrid, steeping darkness of
the brain, which glitters and is
dissipated? Night. The night is
winter and a dull man bending,
muttering above a freezing pipe;
and I, bent heavily on books; the
mountain iron in my sleep and
ringing; but the pipe has frozen, haired with
unseen veins, and cold is on the eyelids: who can
remedy this vision?

                        I have walked upon
the streets between the trees that
grew unleaved from asphalt in a night of
sweating winter in distracted silence.

                                        I have
walked among the tombs — the rushing of the air
in the rich pines above my head is that which
ceaseth not nor stirreth whence it is:
in this the sound of wind is like a flame.

It was the dumb decision of the
madness of my youth that left me with
this cold eye for the fact; that keeps me
quiet, walking toward a
stinging end: I am alone,
and, like the alligator cleaving timeless mud,
among the blessed who have Latin names.

The Slow Pacific Swell

Far out of sight forever stands the sea,
Bounding the land with pale tranquillity.
When a small child, I watched it from a hill
At thirty miles or more. The vision still
Lies in the eye, soft blue and far away:
The rain has washed the dust from April day;
Paint-brush and lupine lie against the ground;
The wind above the hill-top has the sound
Of distant water in unbroken sky;
Dark and precise the little steamers ply —
Firm in direction they seem not to stir.
That is illusion. The artificer
Of quiet, distance holds me in a vise
And holds the ocean steady to my eyes.

Once when I rounded Flattery, the sea
Hove its loose weight like sand to tangle me
Upon the washing deck, to crush the hull;
Subsiding, dragged flesh at the bone. The skull
Felt the retreating wash of dreaming hair.
Half drenched in dissolution, I lay bare.
I scarcely pulled myself erect; I came
Back slowly, slowly knew myself the same.
That was the ocean. From the ship we saw
Gray whales for miles: the long sweep of the jaw,
The blunt head plunging clean above the wave.

And one rose in a tent of sea and gave
A darkening shudder; water fell away;
The whale stood shining, and then sank in spray.

A landsman, I. The sea is but a sound.
I would be near it on a sandy mound,
And hear the steady rushing of the deep
While I lay stinging in the sand with sleep.
I have lived inland long. The land is numb.
It stands beneath the feet, and one may come
Walking securely, till the sea extends
Its limber margin, and precision ends.
By night a chaos of commingling power,
The whole Pacific hovers hour by hour.
The slow Pacific swell stirs on the sand,
Sleeping to sink away, withdrawing land,
Heaving and wrinkled in the moon, and blind;
Or gathers seaward, ebbing out of mind.

Orpheus

In memory of Hart Crane

Climbing from the Lethal dead,
Past the ruined waters' bed,
In the sleep his music cast
Tree and flesh and stone were fast —
As amid Dodona's wood
Wisdom never understood.

Till the shade his music won
Shuddered, by a pause undone —
Silence would not let her stay.
He could go one only way:
By the river, strong with grief,
Gave his flesh beyond belief.

Yet the fingers on the lyre
Spread like an avenging fire.
Crying loud, the immortal tongue,
From the empty body wrung,
Broken in a bloody dream,
Sang unmeaning down the stream.

On Teaching the Young

The young are quick of speech.
Grown middle-aged, I teach
Corrosion and distrust,
Exacting what I must.

A poem is what stands
When imperceptive hands,
Feeling, have gone astray.
It is what one should say.

Few minds will come to this.
The poet's only bliss
Is in cold certitude —
Laurel, archaic, rude.

Theseus: A Trilogy

For Henry Ramsey

I. The Wrath of Artemis

On the wet sand the queen emerged from forest,
Tall as a man, half naked, and at ease,
Leaned on her bow and eyed them. This, the priestess,
Who, with her savages, had harried Greece
From south to east, and now fought down from Thrace,
Her arrows cold as moonlight, and her flesh
Bright as her arrows, and her hatred still.
Heracles eyed the ground, and Theseus watched her.
Remote and thin as a bird-call over ice
From deep in the forest came the cry of her warriors,
Defiance from Artemis, the evasive daemon:
Hippolyta smiled, but Heracles moved softly
And seized her suddenly, bore her to the ship,
Bound her and left her vibrating like a deer,
Astounded beyond terror. And her women
Fell as they came, like water to dry earth,
An inundation of the living moon.

From out the close hold of the nervous galley
She heard the shouting muffled in soft blood;
She heard it thinning quietly away.

687

And anger seized her; mind exceeded body,
Invoked divinity and rose to godhead:
She prayed the goddess to avenge the dead.
Then, in the doorway, blackened with maiden death,
Appeared the Attic conqueror in fulfillment.
Theseus, inexorable with love and war,
And ignorant with youth, begot upon her
A son, created in her shuddering fury,
To be born in Attica, the naked land.
In Attica, the naked land, she strode,
Brooding upon the secrets of the goddess,
Upon the wet bark of the Scythian forest,
The wet turf under bare foot, and the night
Blue with insistence of the staring eye.
The son, conceived in hatred, grew implacably,
Beyond her slow death, which he saw in passing,
Insolent, slender, effeminate, and chill,
His muscles made for running down the stag,
Dodging the boar, which Theseus would have broken,
Keeping step with the moon's shadows, changing
From thought to thought with an unchanging face.
He, judging Theseus from his narrow wisdom,
Yet judged him, and exiled him from his quiet,
The wrath of Artemis grown part of Theseus,
A man of moonlight and intensive calm.

II. *Theseus and Ariadne*

After the mossy night and the wet stone,
The grappling with the wet hair of the beast,
After the slow and careful fingering
Of the pale linen on the cold return,
Theseus emerged. Ariadne awaited him,
Her face half hidden with black hair and shame.
And Theseus spoke:
                    The Minotaur is dead.
Pasiphaë the white will sin no more:
The daughter of the moon, who bore this ghast
And dripping horror has been long at rest.
The sin of your blood I have extinguished; yet
Think not you will go quit. Your body is mine,
By all these tokens; and the taint of hell
Has eaten through my skin. Minos contrived
The trembling blackness of that hall of vision;

The prisoned fiend, your brother, beat me down,
I drew him after, and his blood burned through me,
Stinging more wildly than your body.

She:

My mother's sin has poisoned you, and I
Was poisoned long ago. We share this crime,
And I am yours, I know not to what end.
Minos' vengeance is buried in our two bodies.
You had me from Minos, should you prevail,
And Minos is the will of Zeus, withdraws not.
I am motionless in the scales of Justice.
We go now to your ship; the carven wood
Will glide in quiet from the rocks of Crete,
That bloodstained island of the gods, and we
Shall set our feet in peace on lesser isles.
So Theseus took her by the hand, boarded
The limber galley, and the foam distended
Coldly above the crash on rock. The boat,
Quick on the heavy tumult, scoured the inlets
And found that island where he slew her, yet
Escaped not, took her sister, her for whom
Poseidon betrayed him, when he slew his son.

III.   *The Old Age of Theseus*

He gathered Phaedra, hard with childhood, small,
Shivering in arm and breast, into his arms.
He knew his age at last. Sin with this child
Was sin in solitude. Arms that had bound
The Heraclean bull, Phaea the sow,
That had fought side by side with Heracles
And beat their black way from the ice of Lethe,
Were hard with realized identity,
Beyond her comprehension, and he lay
Whole in the salty toughness of his age.

When he set foot in Attica, he found
Aegeus at rest, and he assumed the State.
Here were abstractions fitter for his years:
The calculation of corruption, thus
To balance evil against evil surely
And establish immitigable good.

                                                    He ruled
Hard in his certitude through Phaedra's death,
The betrayal of his son, that eccentricity
Of furious children. And he gathered up
The knowledge of his youth: the steady shame
Of tall Hippolyta; the calm of Aethra;
The quiet evil of the grave Medea;
The image of Pirithoüs in Hell,
Caught in the moving flesh among the shades —
Passion immovable! — the Orphic music
That swelled the measure of the Argo's oars
To a golden stride coëval with the Sun —
Gathered them slowly up and fed upon them,
Distilled from them the honey of calm wisdom —
The face of Ariadne dead, himself
Suddenly translated to another time.

Alone, he and the State. The State, established,
Exiled him into Scyros. Lycomedes,
The strange face of a king, was all that stood
Between him and himself. And Lycomedes,
The treacherous host, betrayed him to the State,
Which had betrayed him, to which he had been betrayed
By every movement of his flesh and spirit;
So cast him from the rock to solitude,
To the cold perfection of unending peace.

John Sutter

I was the patriarch of the shining land,
Of the blond summer and metallic grain;
Men vanished at the motion of my hand,
And when I beckoned they would come again.

The earth grew dense with grain at my desire;
The shade was deepened at the springs and streams;
Moving in dust that clung like pillared fire,
The gathering herds grew heavy in my dreams.

Across the mountains, naked from the heights,
Down to the valley broken settlers came,
And in my houses feasted through the nights,
Rebuilt their sinews and assumed a name.

In my clear rivers my own men discerned
The motive for the ruin and the crime —
Gold heavier than earth, a wealth unearned,
Loot, for two decades, from the heart of Time.

Metal, intrinsic value, deep and dense.
Preanimate, inimitable, still,
Real, but an evil with no human sense,
Dispersed the mind to concentrate the will.

Grained by alchemic change, the human kind
Turned from themselves to rivers and to rocks;
With dynamite broke metal unrefined;
Measured their moods by geologic shocks.

With knives they dug the metal out of stone;
Turned rivers back, for gold through ages piled,
Drove knives to hearts, and faced the gold alone;
Valley and river ruined and reviled;

Reviled and ruined me, my servant slew,
Strangled him from the figtree by my door.
When they had done what fury bade them do,
I was a cursing beggar, stripped and sore.

What end impersonal, what breathless age,
Incontinent of quiet and of years,
What calm catastrophe will yet assuage
This final drouth of penitential tears?

At the San Francisco Airport

To my daughter, 1954

This is the terminal: the light
Gives perfect vision, false and hard;
The metal glitters, deep and bright.
Great planes are waiting in the yard —
They are already in the night.

And you are here beside me, small,
Contained and fragile, and intent
On things that I but half recall —
Yet going whither you are bent.
I am the past, and that is all.

But you and I in part are one:
The frightened brain, the nervous will,
The knowledge of what must be done,
The passion to acquire the skill
To face that which you dare not shun.

The rain of matter upon sense
Destroys me momently. The score:
There comes what will come. The expense
Is what one thought, and something more —
One's being and intelligence.

This is the terminal, the break.
Beyond this point, on lines of air,
You take the way that you must take;
And I remain in light and stare —
In light, and nothing else, awake.

LANGSTON HUGHES
1902–1967

The Weary Blues

Droning a drowsy syncopated tune,
Rocking back and forth to a mellow croon,
   I heard a Negro play.
Down on Lenox Avenue the other night
By the pale dull pallor of an old gas light
   He did a lazy sway. . . .
   He did a lazy sway. . . .
To the tune o' those Weary Blues.
With his ebony hands on each ivory key
He made that poor piano moan with melody.
   O Blues!
Swaying to and fro on his rickety stool
He played that sad raggy tune like a musical fool.

Sweet Blues!
Coming from a black man's soul.
  O Blues!
In a deep song voice with a melancholy tone
I heard that Negro sing, that old piano moan —
  "Ain't got nobody in all this world,
  Ain't got nobody but ma self.
  I's gwine to quit ma frownin'
  And put ma troubles on the shelf."
Thump, thump, thump, went his foot on the floor.
He played a few chords then he sang some more —
  "I got the Weary Blues
  And I can't be satisfied.
  Got the Weary Blues
  And can't be satisfied —
  I ain't happy no mo'
  And I wish that I had died."
And far into the night he crooned that tune.
The stars went out and so did the moon.
The singer stopped playing and went to bed
While the Weary Blues echoed through his head.
He slept like a rock or a man that's dead.

Dream Variations

To fling my arms wide
In some place of the sun,
To whirl and to dance
Till the white day is done.
Then rest at cool evening
Beneath a tall tree
While night comes on gently,
  Dark like me —
That is my dream!

To fling my arms wide
In the face of the sun,
Dance! Whirl! Whirl!
Till the quick day is done.
Rest at pale evening . . .
A tall, slim tree . . .
Night coming tenderly
  Black like me.

The Negro Speaks of Rivers

I've known rivers:
I've known rivers ancient as the world and older than the flow of human
    blood in human veins.

My soul has grown deep like the rivers.

I bathed in the Euphrates when dawns were young.
I built my hut near the Congo and it lulled me to sleep.
I looked upon the Nile and raised the pyramids above it.
I heard the singing of the Mississippi when Abe Lincoln went down to
    New Orleans, and I've seen its muddy bosom turn all golden in the
    sunset.

I've known rivers:
Ancient, dusky rivers.

My soul has grown deep like the rivers.

Fire

Fire,
Fire, Lord!
Fire gonna burn ma soul!

I ain't been good,
I ain't been clean —
I been stinkin', low-down, mean.

Fire,
Fire, Lord!
Fire gonna burn ma soul!

Tell me, brother,
Do you believe
If you wanta go to heaben
Got to moan an' grieve?

Fire,
Fire, Lord!
Fire gonna burn ma soul!

I been stealin',
Been tellin' lies,
Had more women
Than Pharaoh had wives.

Fire,
Fire, Lord!
Fire gonna burn ma soul!
I means Fire, Lord!
Fire gonna burn ma soul!

50–50

I'm all alone in this world, she said,
Ain't got nobody to share my bed,
Ain't got nobody to hold my hand —
The truth of the matter's
I ain't got no man.

Big Boy opened his mouth and said,
Trouble with you is
You ain't got no head!
If you had a head and used your mind
You could have *me* with you
All the time.

She answered, Babe, what must I do?

He said, Share your bed —
And your money, too.

Stony Lonesome

They done took Cordelia
Out to stony lonesome ground.
Done took Cordelia
To stony lonesome,
Laid her down.
They done put Cordelia
Underneath that
Grassless mound.

Ay-Lord!
   Ay-Lord!
      Ay-Lord!
She done left po' Buddy
To struggle by his self.
Po' Buddy Jones,
Yes, he's done been left.
She's out in stony lonesome,
Lordy! Sleepin' by herself.
   Cordelia's
      In stony
         Lonesome
            Ground!

Ballad of the Landlord

Landlord, landlord,
My roof has sprung a leak.
Don't you 'member I told you about it
Way last week?

Landlord, landlord,
These steps is broken down.
When you come up yourself
It's a wonder you don't fall down.

Ten Bucks you say I owe you?
Ten Bucks you say is due?
Well, that's Ten Bucks more'n I'll pay you
Till you fix this house up new.

What? You gonna get eviction orders?
You gonna cut off my heat?
You gonna take my furniture and
Throw it in the street?

Um-huh! You talking high and mighty.
Talk on — till you get through.
You ain't gonna be able to say a word
If I land my fist on you.

Police! Police!
Come and get this man!
He's trying to ruin the government
And overturn the land!

Copper's whistle!
Patrol bell!
Arrest.

Precinct Station.
Iron cell.
Headlines in press:

MAN THREATENS LANDLORD

. .

TENANT HELD NO BAIL

. .

JUDGE GIVES NEGRO 90 DAYS IN COUNTY JAIL

Heaven

Heaven is
The place where
Happiness is
Everywhere.

Animals
And birds sing —
As does
Everything.

To each stone,
"How-do-you-do?"
Stone answers back,
"Well! And you?"

Personal

In an envelope marked:
Personal
God addressed me a letter.
In an envelope marked:
Personal
I have given my answer.

Madam and the Minister

Reverend Butler came by
My house last week.
He said, Have you got
A little time to speak?

He said, I am interested
In your soul.
Has it been saved,
Or is your heart stone-cold?

I said, Reverend,
I'll have you know
I was baptized
Long ago.

He said, What have you
Done since then?
I said, None of your
Business, friend.

He said, Sister
Have you back-slid?
I said, It felt good —
If I did!

He said, Sister,
Come time to die,
The Lord will surely
Ask you why!
I'm gonna pray
For you!
Goodbye!

I felt kinder sorry
I talked that way
After Rev. Butler
Went away —
So I ain't in no mood
For sin today.

Preference

I likes a woman
six or eight and ten years older'n myself.
I don't fool with these young girls.
Young girl'll say,
    Daddy, I want so-and-so.
    I needs this, that, and the other.
But a old woman'll say,
    Honey, what does YOU need?
    I just drawed my money tonight
    and it's all your'n.
That's why I likes a older woman
who can appreciate me:
When she conversations you
it ain't forever, *Gimme!*

Necessity

Work?
I don't have to work.
I don't have to do nothing
but eat, drink, stay black, and die.
This little old furnished room's
so small I can't whip a cat
without getting fur in my mouth
and my landlady's so old
her features is all run together
and God knows she sure can overcharge —
Which is why I reckon I *does*
have to work after all.

LANGSTON HUGHES

Theme for English B

The instructor said,

> Go home and write
> a page tonight.
> And let that page come out of you —
> Then, it will be true.

I wonder if it's that simple?
I am twenty-two, colored, born in Winston-Salem.
I went to school there, then Durham, then here
to this college on the hill above Harlem.
I am the only colored student in my class.
The steps from the hill lead down into Harlem,
through a park, then I cross St. Nicholas,
Eighth Avenue, Seventh, and I come to the Y,
the Harlem Branch Y, where I take the elevator
up to my room, sit down, and write this page:

It's not easy to know what is true for you or me
at twenty-two, my age. But I guess I'm what
I feel and see and hear, Harlem, I hear you:
hear you, hear me — we two — you, me, talk on this page.
(I hear New York, too.) Me — who?
Well, I like to eat, sleep, drink, and be in love.
I like to work, read, learn, and understand life.
I like a pipe for a Christmas present,
or records — Bessie, bop, or Bach.
I guess being colored doesn't make me *not* like
the same things other folks like who are other races.
So will my page be colored that I write?
Being me, it will not be white.
But it will be
a part of you, instructor.
You are white —
yet a part of me, as I am a part of you.
That's American.
Sometimes perhaps you don't want to be a part of me.
Nor do I often want to be a part of you.
But we are, that's true!
As I learn from you,

I guess you learn from me —
although you're older — and white —
and somewhat more free.

This is my page for English B.

ROBERT PENN WARREN
b. 1905

The Ballad of Billie Potts

Big Billie Potts was big and stout
In the land between the rivers.
His shoulders were wide and his gut stuck out
Like a croker of nubbins and his holler and shout
Made the bob-cat shiver and the black-jack leaves shake
In the section between the rivers.
He would slap you on your back and laugh.

Big Billie had a wife, she was dark and little
In the land between the rivers,
And clever with her wheel and clever with her kettle,
But she never said a word and when she sat
By the fire her eyes worked slow and narrow like a cat.
Nobody knew what was in her head.

They had a big boy with fuzz on his chin
So tall he ducked the door when he came in,
A clabber-headed bastard with snot in his nose
And big red wrists hanging out of his clothes
And a whicker when he laughed where his father had a bellow
In the section between the rivers.
They called him Little Billie.
He was their darling.

(It is not hard to see the land, what it was.
Low hills and oak. The fetid bottoms where
The slough uncoiled and in the tangled cane,
Where no sun comes, the muskrat's astute face
Was lifted to the yammering jay; then dropped.
A cabin where the shagbark stood and the
Magnificent tulip-tree; both now are gone.

But the land is there, and as you top a rise,
Beyond you all the landscape steams and simmers
— The hills, now gutted, red, cane-brake and black-jack yet.
The oak leaf steams under the powerful sun.
"Mister, is this the right road to Paducah?"
The red face, seamed and gutted like the hill,
Slow under time, and with the innocent savagery
Of Time, the bleared eyes rolling, answers from
Your dream: "They names it so, but I ain't bin.")

Big Billie was the kind who laughed but could spy
The place for a ferry where folks would come by.
He built an inn and folks bound West
Hitched their horses there to take their rest
And grease the gall and grease the belly
And jaw and spit under the trees
In the section between the rivers.
Big Billie said: "Git down, friend, and take yore ease!"
He would slap you on your back and set you at his table.

(Leaning and slow, you see them move
In massive passion colder than any love:
Their lips move but you do not hear the words,
Nor trodden twig nor fluted irony of birds,
Nor hear the rustle of the heart
That, heave and settle, gasp and start,
Heaves like a fish in the ribs' dark basket borne
West from the great water's depth whence it was torn.
Their names are like the leaves, but are forgot
— The slush and swill of the world's great pot
That foamed at the Appalachian lip, and spilled
Like quicksilver across green baize, the unfulfilled
Disparate glitter, gleam, wild symptom, seed
Flung in the long wind: silent, they proceed
Past meadow, salt-lick, and the lyric swale;
Enter the arbor, shadow of trees, fade, fail.)

Big Billie was sharp at swap and trade
And could smell the nest where the egg was laid.
He could read and cipher and they called him squire,
And he added up his money while he sat by the fire,
And sat in the shade while folks sweated and strove,

For he was the one who fatted and throve
In the section between the rivers.
"Thank you kindly, sir," Big Billie would say
When the man in the black coat paid him at streak of day
And swung to the saddle, was ready to go,
And rode away and didn't know
That he was already as good as dead,
For at midnight the message had been sent ahead:
"Man in black coat, riding bay mare with star."

(There was a beginning but you cannot see it.
There will be an end but you cannot see it.
They will not turn their faces to you though you call,
Who pace a logic merciless as light,
Whose law is their long shadow on the grass,
Sun at the back; who pace, pass,
And passing nod in that glacial delirium
While the tight sky shudders like a drum
And speculation rasps its idiot nails
Across the dry slate where you did the sum.

The answer is in the back of the book but the page is gone.
And Grandma told you to tell the truth but she is dead.
And heedless, their hairy faces fixed
Beyond your call or question now, they move
Under the infatuate weight of their wisdom,
Precious but for the preciousness of their burden,
Sainted and sad and sage as the hairy ass, these who bear
History like bound faggots, with stiff knees;
And breathe the immaculate climate where
The lucent leaf is lifted, lank beard fingered, by no breeze,
Rapt in the fabulous complacency of fresco, vase, or frieze:

And the testicles of the fathers hang down like old lace.)

Little Billie was full of vinegar
And full of sap as a maple tree
And full of tricks as a lop-eared pup,
So one night when the runner didn't show up,
Big Billie called Little and said, "Saddle up,"
And nodded toward the man who was taking his sup
With his belt unlatched and his feet to the fire.

Big Billie said, "Give Amos a try,
Fer this feller takes the South Fork and Amos'll be nigher
Than Baldy or Buster, and Amos is sly
And slick as a varmint, and I don't deny
I lak business with Amos, fer he's one you kin trust
In the section between the rivers,
And it looks lak they's mighty few.
Amos will split up fair and square."

Little Billie had something in his clabber-head
By way of brains, and he reckoned he knew
How to skin a cat or add two and two.
So long before the sky got red
Over the land between the rivers,
He hobbled his horse back in the swamp
And squatted on his hams in the morning dew and damp
And scratched his stomach and grinned to think
How Pap would be proud and Mammy glad
To know what a thriving boy they had.
He always was a good boy to his darling Mammy.

(Think of yourself riding away from the dawn,
Think of yourself and the unnamed ones who had gone
Before, riding, who rode away from *goodbye, goodbye,*
And toward *hello,* toward Time's unwinking eye;
And like the cicada had left, at cross-roads or square,
The old shell of self, thin, ghostly, translucent, light as air;
At dawn riding into the curtain of unwhispering green,
Away from the vigils and voices into the green
World, land of the innocent bough, land of the leaf.
Think of your face green in the submarine light of the leaf.

Or think of yourself crouched at the swamp-edge:
Dawn-silence past last owl-hoot and not yet at day-verge
First bird-stir, titmouse or drowsy warbler not yet.
You touch the grass in the dark and your hand is wet.
Then light: and you wait for the stranger's hoofs on the soft trace,
And under the green leaf's translucence the light bathes your face.

Think of yourself at dawn: Which one are you? What?)

Little Billie heard hoofs on the soft grass,
But squatted and let the rider pass,
For he wouldn't waste good lead and powder
Just to make the slough-fish and swamp-buzzards prouder
In the land between the rivers.
But he saw the feller's face and thanked his luck
It was the one Pap said was fit to pluck.
So he got on his horse and cantered up the trace.
Called, "Hi thar!" and the stranger watched him coming,
And sat his mare with a smile on his face,
Just watching Little Billie and smiling and humming.
Little Billie rode up and the stranger said,
"Why, bless my heart, if it ain't Little Billie!"

"Good mornen," said Billie, and said, "My Pap
Found somethen you left and knowed you'd be missen,
And Pap don't want nuthen not proper his'n."
But the stranger didn't do a thing but smile and listen
Polite as could be to what Billie said.
But he must have had eyes in the side of his head
As they rode along beside the slough
In the land between the rivers,
Or guessed what Billie was out to do,
For when Billie said, "Mister, I've brung it to you,"
And reached his hand for it down in his britches,
The stranger just reached his own hand, too.

"Boom!" Billie's gun said, and the derringer, "Bang!"
"Oh, I'm shot!" Billie howled and grabbed his shoulder.
"Not bad," said the stranger, "for you're born to hang,
But I'll save some rope 'fore you're a minute older
If you don't high-tail to your honest Pap
In the section between the rivers."
Oh, Billie didn't tarry and Billie didn't linger,
For Billie didn't trust the stranger's finger
And didn't admire the stranger's face
And didn't like the climate of the place,
So he turned and high-tailed up the trace,
With blood on his shirt and snot in his nose
And pee in his pants, for he'd wet his clothes,
And the stranger just sits and admires how he goes,
And says, "Why, that boy would do right well back on the Bardstown
    track!"

"You fool!" said his Pap, but his Mammy cried
To see the place where the gore-blood dried
Round the little hole in her darling's hide.
She wiped his nose and patted his head,
But Pappy barred the door and Pappy said,
"Two hundred in gold's in my money belt,
And take the roan and the brand-new saddle
And stop yore blubberen and skeedaddle,
And next time you try and pull a trick
Fer God's sake don't talk but do it quick."

So Little Billie took his leave
And left his Mammy there to grieve
And left his Pappy in Old Kaintuck
And headed West to try his luck,
For it was Roll, Missouri,
It was Roll, roll, Missouri.
And he was gone nigh ten long year
And never sent word to give his Pappy cheer
Nor wet pen in ink for his Mammy dear.
For Little Billie never was much of a hand with a pen-staff.

(There is always another country and always another place.
There is always another name and another face.
And the name and the face are you, and you
The name and the face, and the stream you gaze into
Will show the adoring face, show the lips that lift to you
As you lean with the implacable thirst of self,
As you lean to the image which is yourself,
To set the lip to lip, fix eye on bulging eye,
To drink not of the stream but of your deep identity,
But water is water and it flows,
Under the image on the water the water coils and goes
And its own beginning and its end only the water knows.

There are many countries and the rivers in them
— Cumberland, Tennessee, Ohio, Colorado, Pecos, Little Big Horn,
And Roll, Missouri, roll.
But there is only water in them.

And in the new country and in the new place
The eyes of the new friend will reflect the new face
And his mouth will speak to frame
The syllables of the new name
And the name is you and is the agitation of the air
And is the wind and the wind runs and the wind is everywhere.

The name and the face are you.
The name and the face are always new
And they are you.
Are new.

For they have been dipped in the healing flood.
For they have been dipped in the redeeming blood.
For they have been dipped in Time.
For Time is always the new place,
And no-place.
For Time is always the new name and the new face,
And no-name and no-face.

For Time is motion
For Time is innocence
For Time is West.)

Oh, who is coming along the trace,
Whistling along in the late sunshine,
With a big black hat above his big red face
And a long black coat that swings so fine?
Oh, who is riding along the trace
Back to the land between the rivers,
With a big black beard growing down to his guts
And silver mountings on his pistol-butts
And a belt as broad as a saddle-girth
And a look in his eyes like he owned the earth?
And meets a man riding up the trace
And squints right sharp and scans his face
And says, "Durn, if it ain't Joe Drew!"
"I reckin it's me," says Joe and gives a spit,
"But whupped if I figger how you knows it,
Fer if I'm Joe, then who air you?"
And the man with the black beard says: "Why, I'm Little Billie!"
And Joe Drew says: "Wal, I'll be whupped."

"Be whupped," Joe said, "and whar you goen?"
"Oh, just visiten back whar I done my growen
In the section between the rivers,
Fer I bin out West and taken my share
And I reckin my luck helt out fer fair,
So I done come home," Little Billie said,
"To see my folks if they ain't dead."
"Ain't dead," Joe answered, and shook his head,
"But that's the best a man kin say,
Fer it looked lak when you went away
You taken West yore Pappy's luck."
Little Billie jingled his pockets and said: "Ain't nuthen wrong with my
    luck."

And said: "Wal, I'll be gitten on home,
But after yore supper why don't you come
And we'll open a jug and you tell me the news
In the section between the rivers.
But not too early, fer it's my aim
To git me some fun 'fore they know my name,
And tease 'em and fun 'em, fer you never guessed
I was Little Billie what went out West."
And Joe Drew said: "Durn if you always wasn't a hand to git yore fun."

(Over the plain, over mountain and river, drawn,
Wanderer with slit-eyes adjusted to distance,
Drawn out of distance, drawn from the great plateau
Where the sky heeled in the unsagging wind and the cheek burned,
Who stood beneath the white peak that glimmered like a dream,
And spat, and it was morning and it was morning.
You lay among the wild plums and the kildees cried.
You lay in the thicket under the new leaves and the kildees cried,
For you all luck, for all the astuteness of your heart,
And would not stop and would not stop
And the clock ticked all night long in the furnished room
And would not stop
And the *El*-train passed on the quarters with a whish like a terrible
    broom
And would not stop
And there is always the sound of breathing in the next room
And it will not stop
And the waitress says, "Will that be all, sir, will that be all?"

And will not stop
For nothing is ever all and nothing is ever all,
For all your experience and your expertness of human vices and of valor
At the hour when the ways are darkened.

Though your luck held and the market was always satisfactory,
Though the letter always came and your lovers were always true,
Though you always received the respect due to your position,
Though your hand never failed of its cunning and your glands always
     thoroughly knew their business,
Though your conscience was easy and you were assured of your
     innocence,
You became gradually aware that something was missing from the
     picture,
And upon closer inspection exclaimed: "Why, I'm not in it at all!"
Which was perfectly true.

Therefore you tried to remember when you had last had
Whatever it was you had lost,
And you decided to retrace your steps from that point,
But it was a long way back.
It was, nevertheless, absolutely essential to make the effort,
And since you had never been a man to be deterred by difficult
     circumstances,
You came back.
For there is no place like home.)

He joked them and teased them and he had his fun
And they never guessed that he was the one
Had been Mammy's darling and Pappy's joy
When he was a great big whickering boy
In the land between the rivers.
He jingled his pockets and took his sop
And patted his belly which was full nigh to pop
And wiped the buttermilk out of his beard
And took his belch and up and reared
Back from the table and cocked his chair
And said: "Old man, ain't you got any fresh drinken water, this here
     ain't fresher'n a hoss puddle?"
And the old woman said: "Pappy, take the young gentleman down to the
     spring so he kin git it good and fresh?"
The old woman gave the old man a straight look.
She gave him the bucket but it was not empty but it was not water.

The stars are shining and the meadow is bright
But under the trees is dark and night
In the land between the rivers.
The leaves hang down in the dark of the trees,
And there is the spring in the dark of the trees,
And there is the spring as black as ink,
And one star in it caught through a chink
Of the leaves that hang down in the dark of the trees.
The star is there but it does not wink.
Little Billie gets down on his knees
And props his hands in the same old place
To sup the water at his ease;
And the star is gone but there is his face.
"Just help yoreself," Big Billie said;
Then set the hatchet in his head.
They went through his pockets and they buried him in the dark of the
        trees.
"I figgered he was a ripe 'un," the old man said.
"Yeah, but you wouldn't done nuthen hadn't bin fer me," the old woman
        said.

(The reflection is shadowy and the form not clear,
For the hour is late, and scarcely a glimmer comes here
Under the leaf, the bough, in its innocence dark;
And under your straining face you can scarcely mark
The darkling gleam of your face little less than the water dark.

But perhaps what you lost was lost in the pool long ago
When childlike you lost it and then in your innocence rose to go
After kneeling, as now, with your thirst beneath the leaves:
And years it lies here and dreams in the depth and grieves,
More faithful than mother or father in the light or dark of the leaves.

So, weary of greetings now and the new friend's smile,
Weary in art of the stranger, worn with your wanderer's wile,
Weary of innocence and the husks of Time,
You come, back to the homeland of no-Time,
To ask forgiveness and the patrimony of your crime;

And kneel in the untutored night as to demand
What gift — oh, father, father — from that dissevering hand?)

"And whar's Little Billie?" Joe Drew said.
"Air you crazy," said Big, "and plum outa yore head,
  Fer you knows he went West nigh ten long year?"
"Went West," Joe said, "but I seen him here
  In the section between the rivers,
  Riden up the trace as big as you please
  With a long black coat comen down to his knees
  And a big black beard comen down to his guts
  And silver mountens on his pistol-butts
  And he said out West how he done struck
  It rich and wuz bringen you back yore luck."
"I shore-God could use some luck," Big Billie said,
  But his woman wet her lips and craned her head,
  And said: "Come riden with a big black beard, you say?"
  And Joe: "Oh, it wuz Billie as big as day."
And the old man's eyes bugged out of a sudden and he croaked like a
    sick bull-frog and said: "Come riden with a long black coat?"

The night is still and the grease-lamp low
And the old man's breath comes wheeze and slow.
Oh, the blue flame sucks on the old rag wick
And the old woman's breath comes sharp and quick,
And there isn't a sound under the roof
But her breath's hiss and his breath's puff,
And there isn't a sound outside the door
As they hearken but cannot hear any more
The creak of saddle or the plop of hoof,
For a long time now Joe Drew's been gone
And left them sitting there alone
In the land between the rivers.
And so they sit and breathe and wait
And breathe while the night gets big and late,
And neither of them gives move or stir.
She won't look at him and he won't look at her.
He doesn't look at her but he says: "Git me the spade."

She grabbled with her hands and he dug with the spade
Where leaves let down the dark and shade
In the land between the rivers.
She grabbled like a dog in the hole they made,
But stopped of a sudden and then she said,
"My hand's on his face."

They light up a pine-knot and lean at the place
Where the man lies in the black coat slumbers and lies
With trash in his beard and dirt on his face;
And the torch-flame in his wide-open eyes.
Down the old man leans with the flickering flame
And moves his lips, says: "Tell me his name."

"Ain't Billie, ain't Billie," the old woman cries,
"Oh, it ain't my Billie, fer he wuz little
And helt to my skirt while I stirred the kittle
And called me Mammy and hugged me tight
And come in the house when it fell night."
But the old man leans down with the flickering flame
And croaks: "But tell me his name."

"Oh, he ain't got none, he just come riden
From some fer place whar he'd bin biden.
Ain't got a name and never had none —
But Billie, my Billie, he had one,
And it was Billie, it was his name."
But the old man croaked: "Tell me his name."
"Oh, he ain't got none and it's all the same,
But Billie had one, and he was little
And offen his chin I would wipe the spittle
And wiped the drool and kissed him thar
And counted his toes and kissed him whar
The little black mark was under his tit,
Shaped lak a clover under his left tit,
With a shape fer luck and I'd kiss it —"

The old man blinks in the pine-knot flare
And his mouth comes open like a fish for air,
Then he says right low, "I had nigh fergot."
"Oh, I kissed him on his little luck-spot
And I kissed and he'd laugh as lak as not —"
The old man said: "Git his shirt open."
The old woman opened the shirt and there was the birthmark under the
    left tit.
It was shaped for luck.

(The bee knows, and the eel's cold ganglia burn,
And the sad head lifting to the long return,
Through brumal deeps, in the great unsolsticed coil,

Carries its knowledge, navigator without star,
And under the stars, pure in its clamorous toil,
The goose hoots north where the starlit marshes are.
The salmon heaves at the fall, and, wanderer, you
Heave at the great fall of Time, and gorgeous, gleam
In the powerful arc, and anger and outrage like dew,
In your plunge, fling, and plunge to the thunderous stream:
Back to the silence, back to the pool, back
To the high pool, motionless, and the unmurmuring dream.
And you, wanderer, back,
Brother to pinion and the pious fin that cleave
Their innocence of air and the disinfectant flood
And wing and welter and weave
The long compulsion and the circuit hope
Back,
And bear through that limitless and devouring fluidity
The itch and humble promise which is home.

And the father waits for the son.

The hour is late,
The scene familiar even in shadow,
The transaction brief,
And you, wanderer, back,
After the striving and the wind's word,
To kneel
Here in the evening empty of wine or bird,
To kneel in the sacramental silence of evening
At the feet of the old man
Who is evil and ignorant and old,
To kneel
With the little black mark under your heart,
Which is your name,
Which is shaped for luck,
Which is your luck.)

Bearded Oaks

The oaks, how subtle and marine,
Bearded, and all the layered light
Above them swims; and thus the scene,
Recessed, awaits the positive night.

So, waiting, we in the grass now lie
Beneath the languorous tread of light:
The grasses, kelp-like, satisfy
The nameless motions of the air.

Upon the floor of light, and time,
Unmurmuring, of polyp made,
We rest; we are, as light withdraws,
Twin atolls on a shelf of shade.

Ages to our construction went,
Dim architecture, hour by hour:
And violence, forgot now, lent
The present stillness all its power.

The storm of noon above us rolled,
Of light the fury, furious gold,
The long drag troubling us, the depth:
Dark is unrocking, unrippling, still.

Passion and slaughter, ruth, decay
Descend, minutely whispering down,
Silted down swaying streams, to lay
Foundation for our voicelessness.

All our debate is voiceless here,
As all our rage, the rage of stone;
If hope is hopeless, then fearless is fear,
And history is thus undone.

Our feet once wrought the hollow street
With echo when the lamps were dead
At windows, once our headlight glare
Disturbed the doe that, leaping, fled.

I do not love you less that now
The caged heart makes iron stroke,
Or less that all that light once gave
The graduate dark should now revoke.

We live in time so little time
And we learn all so painfully,
That we may spare this hour's term
To practice for eternity.

ROBERT PENN WARREN

Two Pieces After Suetonius

I. Apology for Domitian

He was not bad, as emperors go, not really —
Not like Tiberius cruel, or poor Nero silly.
The trouble was only that omens said he would die,
So what could he, mortal, do? Not worse, however, than you might, or I.

Suppose from long back you had known the very hour —
"Fear the fifth hour" — and yet for all your power
Couldn't strike it out from the day, or the day from the year,
Then wouldn't you have to strike something at least? If you did, would
    it seem so queer?

Suppose you were proud of your beauty, but baldness set in?
Suppose your good leg were dwindling to spindly and thin?
Wouldn't you, like Domitian, try the classic bed-stunt
To prove immortality on what was propped to bear the imperial brunt?

Suppose you had dreamed a gold hump sprouted out of your back,
And such a prosperous burden oppressed you to breath-lack;
Suppose lightning scorched the sheets in your own bedroom;
And from your own statue a storm yanked the name plate and chucked
    it into a tomb —

Well, it happened to him. Therefore, there's little surprise
That for hours he'd lock himself up to pull wings from flies.
Fly or man, what odds? He would wander his hall of moonstone,
Mirror-bright so he needn't look over his shoulder to see if he was alone.

Let's stop horsing around — it's not Domitian, it's you
We mean, and the omens are bad, very bad, and it's true
That virtue comes hard in face of the assiduous clock,
And music, at sunset, faint as a dream, is heard from beyond the
    burdock,

And as for Domitian, the first wound finds the groin,
And he claws like a cat, but the blade continues to go in,
And the body is huddled forth meanly, and what ritual
It gets is at night, and from his old nurse, a woman poor, nonpolitical.

II. *Tiberius on Capri*

1

All is nothing, nothing all:
To tired Tiberius soft sang the sea thus,
Under his cliff-palace wall.
The sea, in soft approach and repulse,
Sings thus, and Tiberius,
Sea-sad, stares past the dusking sea-pulse
Yonder, where come,
One now by one, the lights, far off, of Surrentum.
He stares in the blue dusk-fall,
For all is nothing, nothing all.

Let darkness up from Asia tower.
On that darkening island behind him *spintriae* now stir.
In grot and scented bower,
They titter, yawn, paint lip, grease thigh,
And debate what role each would prefer
When they project for the Emperor's eye
Their expertise
Of his Eastern lusts and complex Egyptian fantasies.
But darkward he stares in that hour,
Blank now in totality of power.

2

There once, on that goat island, I,
As dark fell, stood and stared where Europe stank.
Many were soon to die —
From acedia snatched, from depravity, virtue,
Or frolic, not knowing the reason, in rank
On rank hurled, or in bed, or in church, or
Dishing up supper,
Or in a dark doorway, loosening the girl's elastic to tup her,
While high in the night sky,
The murderous tear dropped from God's eye;

And faintly forefeeling, forefearing, all
That to fulfill our time, and heart, would come,
I stood on the crumbling wall
Of that foul place, and my lungs drew in

Scent of dry gorse on the night air of autumn,
And I seized, in dark, a small stone from that ruin,
And I made outcry
At the paradox of powers that would grind us like grain, small and dry.
Dark down, the stone, in its fall,
Found the sea: I could do that much, after all.

from Mortmain

*I. After Night Flight Son Reaches Bedside of Already Unconscious Father,
Whose Right Hand Lifts in a Spasmodic Gesture, as Though Trying to
Make Contact: 1955*

In Time's concatenation and
Carnal conventicle, I,
Arriving, being flung through dark and
The abstract flight-grid of sky,
Saw rising from the sweated sheet and
Ruck of bedclothes ritualistically
Reordered by the paid hand
Of mercy — saw rising the hand —

Christ, start again! What was it I,
Standing there, travel-shaken, saw
Rising? What could it be that I,
Caught sudden in gut- or conscience-gnaw,
Saw rising out of the past, which I
Saw now as twisted bedclothes? Like law,
The hand rose cold from History
To claw at a star in the black sky,

But could not reach that far — oh, cannot!
And the star horribly burned, burns,
For in darkness the wax-white clutch could not
Reach it, and white hand on wrist-stem turns,
Lifts in last tension of tendon, but cannot
Make contact — *oh, oop-si-daisy,* churns
The sad heart, *oh, atta-boy, daddio's got
One more shot in the locker, peas-porridge hot —*

717

But no. Like an eyelid the hand sank, strove
Downward, and in that darkening roar,
All things — all joy and the hope that strove,
The failed exam, the admired endeavor,
Prizes and prinkings, and the truth that strove,
And back of the Capitol, boyhood's first whore —
Were snatched from me, and I could not move,
Naked in that black blast of his love.

THEODORE ROETHKE
1908–1963

Open House

My secrets cry aloud.
I have no need for tongue.
My heart keeps open house,
My doors are widely swung.
An epic of the eyes
My love, with no disguise.

My truths are all foreknown,
This anguish self-revealed.
I'm naked to the bone,
With nakedness my shield.
Myself is what I wear:
I keep the spirit spare.

The anger will endure,
The deed will speak the truth
In language strict and pure.
I stop the lying mouth:
Rage warps my clearest cry
To witless agony.

"Long Live the Weeds" Hopkins

Long live the weeds that overwhelm
My narrow vegetable realm!
The bitter rock, the barren soil
That force the son of man to toil;

All things unholy, marred by curse,
The ugly of the universe.
The rough, the wicked, and the wild
That keep the spirit undefiled.
With these I match my little wit
And earn the right to stand or sit,
Hope, love, create, or drink and die:
These shape the creature that is I.

Cuttings

Sticks-in-a-drowse droop over sugary loam,
Their intricate stem-fur dries;
But still the delicate slips keep coaxing up water;
The small cells bulge;

One nub of growth
Nudges a sand-crumb loose,
Pokes through a musty sheath
Its pale tendrilous horn.

Cuttings

later

This urge, wrestle, resurrection of dry sticks,
Cut stems struggling to put down feet,
What saint strained so much,
Rose on such lopped limbs to a new life?

I can hear, underground, that sucking and sobbing,
In my veins, in my bones I feel it, —
The small waters seeping upward,
The tight grains parting at last.
When sprouts break out,
Slippery as fish,
I quail, lean to beginnings, sheath-wet.

Frau Bauman, Frau Schmidt, and Frau Schwartze

Gone the three ancient ladies
Who creaked on the greenhouse ladders,
Reaching up white strings
To wind, to wind
The sweet-pea tendrils, the smilax,
Nasturtiums, the climbing
Roses, to straighten
Carnations, red
Chrysanthemums; the stiff
Stems, jointed like corn,
They tied and tucked, —
These nurses of nobody else.
Quicker than birds, they dipped
Up and sifted the dirt;
They sprinkled and shook;
They stood astride pipes,
Their skirts billowing out wide into tents,
Their hands twinkling with wet;
Like witches they flew along rows
Keeping creation at ease;
With a tendril for needle
They sewed up the air with a stem;
They tested out the seed that the cold kept asleep, —
All the coils, loops, and whorls.
They trellised the sun; they plotted for more than themselves.

I remember how they picked me up, a spindly kid,
Pinching and poking my thin ribs
Till I lay in their laps, laughing,
Weak as a whiffet;
Now, when I'm alone and cold in my bed,
They still hover over me,
These ancient leathery crones,
With their bandannas stiffened with sweat,
And their thorn-bitten wrists,
And their snuff-laden breath blowing lightly over me in my first sleep.

THEODORE ROETHKE

My Papa's Waltz

The whiskey on your breath
Could make a small boy dizzy;
But I hung on like death:
Such waltzing was not easy.

We romped until the pans
Slid from the kitchen shelf;
My mother's countenance
Could not unfrown itself.

The hand that held my wrist
Was battered on one knuckle;
At every step you missed
My right ear scraped a buckle.

You beat time on my head
With a palm caked hard by dirt,
Then waltzed me off to bed
Still clinging to your shirt.

The Minimal

I study the lives on a leaf: the little
Sleepers, numb nudgers in cold dimensions,
Beetles in caves, newts, stone-deaf fishes,
Lice tethered to long limp subterranean weeds,
Squirmers in bogs,
And bacterial creepers
Wriggling through wounds
Like elvers in ponds,
Their wan mouths kissing the warm sutures,
Cleaning and caressing,
Creeping and healing.

Four for Sir John Davies

1. The Dance

Is that dance slowing in the mind of man
That made him think the universe could hum?
The great wheel turns its axle when it can;
I need a place to sing, and dancing-room,
And I have made a promise to my ears
I'll sing and whistle romping with the bears.

For they are all my friends: I saw one slide
Down a steep hillside on a cake of ice, —
Or was that in a book? I think with pride:
A caged bear rarely does the same thing twice
In the same way: O watch his body sway! —
This animal remembering to be gay.

I tried to fling my shadow at the moon,
The while my blood leaped with a wordless song.
Though dancing needs a master, I had none
To teach my toes to listen to my tongue.
But what I learned there, dancing all alone,
Was not the joyless motion of a stone.

I take this cadence from a man named Yeats;
I take it, and I give it back again:
For other tunes and other wanton beats
Have tossed my heart and fiddled through my brain.
Yes, I was dancing-mad, and how
That came to be the bears and Yeats would know.

2. The Partner

Between such animal and human heat
I find myself perplexed. What is desire? —
The impulse to make someone else complete?
That woman would set sodden straw on fire.
Was I the servant of a sovereign wish,
Or ladle rattling in an empty dish?

We played a measure with commingled feet:
The lively dead had taught us to be fond.
Who can embrace the body of his fate?
Light altered light along the living ground.
She kissed me close, and then did something else.
My marrow beat as wildly as my pulse.

I'd say it to my horse: we live beyond
Our outer skin. Who's whistling up my sleeve?
I see a heron prancing in his pond;
I know a dance the elephants believe.
The living all assemble! What's the cue? —
Do what the clumsy partner wants to do!

Things loll and loiter. Who condones the lost?
This joy outleaps the dog. Who cares? Who cares?
I gave her kisses back, and woke a ghost.
O what lewd music crept into our ears!
The body and the soul know how to play
In that dark world where gods have lost their way.

3. The Wraith

Incomprehensible gaiety and dread
Attended what we did. Behind, before,
Lay all the lonely pastures of the dead;
The spirit and the flesh cried out for more.
We two, together, on a darkening day
Took arms against our own obscurity.

Did each become the other in that play?
She laughed me out, and then she laughed me in;
In the deep middle of ourselves we lay;
When glory failed, we danced upon a pin.
The valley rocked beneath the granite hill;
Our souls looked forth, and the great day stood still.

There was a body, and it cast a spell, —
God pity those but wanton to the knees, —
The flesh can make the spirit visible;
We woke to find the moonlight on our toes.
In the rich weather of a dappled wood
We played with dark and light as children should.

What shape leaped forward at the sensual cry? —
Sea-beast or bird flung toward the ravaged shore?
Did space shake off an angel with a sigh?
We rose to meet the moon, and saw no more.
It was and was not she, a shape alone,
Impaled on light, and whirling slowly down.

4. The Vigil

Dante attained the purgatorial hill,
Trembled at hidden virtue without flaw,
Shook with a mighty power beyond his will, —
Did Beatrice deny what Dante saw?
All lovers live by longing, and endure:
Summon a vision and declare it pure.

Though everything's astonishment at last,
Who leaps to heaven at a single bound?
The links were soft between us; still, we kissed;
We undid chaos to a curious sound:
The waves broke easy, cried to me in white;
Her look was morning in the dying light.

The visible obscures. But who knows when?
Things have their thought: they are the shards of me;
I thought that once, and thought comes round again;
Rapt, we leaned forth with what we could not see.
We danced to shining; mocked before the black
And shapeless night that made no answer back.

The world is for the living. Who are they?
We dared the dark to reach the white and warm.
She was the wind when wind was in my way;
Alive at noon, I perished in her form.
Who rise from flesh to spirit know the fall:
The word outleaps the world, and light is all.

The Waking

I wake to sleep, and take my waking slow.
I feel my fate in what I cannot fear.
I learn by going where I have to go.

We think by feeling. What is there to know?
I hear my being dance from ear to ear.
I wake to sleep, and take my waking slow.

Of those so close beside me, which are you?
God bless the Ground! I shall walk softly there,
And learn by going where I have to go.

Light takes the Tree; but who can tell us how?
The lowly worm climbs up a winding stair;
I wake to sleep, and take my waking slow.

Great Nature has another thing to do
To you and me; so take the lively air,
And, lovely, learn by going where to go.

This shaking keeps me steady. I should know.
What falls away is always. And is near.
I wake to sleep, and take my waking slow.
I learn by going where I have to go.

Words for the Wind

1

Love, love, a lily's my care,
She's sweeter than a tree.
Loving, I use the air
Most lovingly: I breathe;
Mad in the wind I wear
Myself as I should be,
All's even with the odd,
My brother the vine is glad.

Are flower and seed the same?
What do the great dead say?
Sweet Phoebe, she's my theme:
She sways whenever I sway.
"O love me while I am,
You green thing in my way!"
I cried, and the birds came down
And made my song their own.

Motion can keep me still:
She kissed me out of thought
As a lovely substance will;
She wandered; I did not:
I stayed, and light fell
Across her pulsing throat;
I stared, and a garden stone
Slowly became the moon.

The shallow stream runs slack;
The wind creaks slowly by;
Out of a nestling's beak
Comes a tremulous cry
I cannot answer back;
A shape from deep in the eye —
That woman I saw in a stone —
Keeps pace when I walk alone.

2

The sun declares the earth;
The stones leap in the stream;
On a wide plain, beyond
The far stretch of a dream,
A field breaks like the sea;
The wind's white with her name,
And I walk with the wind.

The dove's my will today.
She sways, half in the sun:
Rose, easy on a stem,
One with the sighing vine,
One to be merry with,
And pleased to meet the moon.
She likes wherever I am.

Passion's enough to give
Shape to a random joy:
I cry delight: I know
The root, the core of a cry.
Swan-heart, arbutus-calm,
She moves when time is shy:
Love has a thing to do.

A fair thing grows more fair;
The green, the springing green
Makes an intenser day
Under the rising moon;
I smile, no mineral man;
I bear, but not alone,
The burden of this joy.

3

Under a southern wind,
The birds and fishes move
North, in a single stream;
The sharp stars swing around;
I get a step beyond
The wind, and there I am,
I'm odd and full of love.

Wisdom, where is it found? —
Those who embrace, believe.
Whatever was, still is,
Says a song tied to a tree.
Below, on the ferny ground,
In rivery air, at ease,
I walk with my true love.

What time's my heart? I care.
I cherish what I have
Had of the temporal:
I am no longer young
But the winds and waters are;
What falls away will fall;
All things bring me to love.

4

The breath of a long root,
The shy perimeter
Of the unfolding rose,
The green, the altered leaf,
The oyster's weeping foot,
And the incipient star —
Are part of what she is.
She wakes the ends of life.

Being myself, I sing
The soul's immediate joy.
Light, light, where's my repose?
A wind wreathes round a tree.
A thing is done: a thing
Body and spirit know
When I do what she does:
Creaturely creature, she! —

I kiss her moving mouth,
Her swart hilarious skin;
She breaks my breath in half;
She frolicks like a beast;
And I dance round and round,
A fond and foolish man,
And see and suffer myself
In another being, at last.

I Knew a Woman

I knew a woman, lovely in her bones,
When small birds sighed, she would sigh back at them;
Ah, when she moved, she moved more ways than one:
The shapes a bright container can contain!
Of her choice virtues only gods should speak,
Or English poets who grew up on Greek
(I'd have them sing in chorus, cheek to cheek).

How well her wishes went! She stroked my chin,
She taught me Turn, and Counter-turn, and Stand;
She taught me Touch, that undulant white skin;
I nibbled meekly from her proffered hand;
She was the sickle; I, poor I, the rake,
Coming behind her for her pretty sake
(But what prodigious mowing we did make).

Love likes a gander, and adores a goose:
Her full lips pursed, the errant note to seize;
She played it quick, she played it light and loose;
My eyes, they dazzled at her flowing knees;
Her several parts could keep a pure repose,
Or one hip quiver with a mobile nose
(She moved in circles, and those circles moved).

Let seed be grass, and grass turn into hay:
I'm martyr to a motion not my own;
What's freedom for? To know eternity.
I swear she cast a shadow white as stone.
But who would count eternity in days?
These old bones live to learn her wanton ways:
(I measure time by how a body sways).

Snake

I saw a young snake glide
Out of the mottled shade
And hang, limp on a stone:
A thin mouth, and a tongue
Stayed, in the still air.

It turned; it drew away;
Its shadow bent in half;
It quickened, and was gone.

I felt my slow blood warm.
I longed to be that thing,
The pure, sensuous form.

And I may be, some time.

from Meditations of an Old Woman
First Meditation

1

On love's worst ugly day,
The weeds hiss at the edge of the field,
The small winds make their chilly indictments.
Elsewhere, in houses, even pails can be sad;
While stones loosen on the obscure hillside,
And a tree tilts from its roots,
Toppling down an embankment.

The spirit moves, but not always upward,
While animals eat to the north,
And the shale slides an inch in the talus,
The bleak wind eats at the weak plateau,
And the sun brings joy to some.
But the rind, often, hates the life within.

How can I rest in the days of my slowness?
I've become a strange piece of flesh,
Nervous and cold, bird-furtive, whiskery,
With a cheek soft as a hound's ear.
What's left is light as a seed;
I need an old crone's knowing.

2

Often I think of myself as riding —
Alone, on a bus through western country.
I sit above the back wheels, where the jolts are hardest,
And we bounce and sway along toward the midnight,
The lights tilting up, skyward, as we come over a little rise,
Then down, as we roll like a boat from a wave-crest.

All journeys, I think, are the same:
The movement is forward, after a few wavers,
And for a while we are all alone,
Busy, obvious with ourselves,
The drunken soldier, the old lady with her peppermints;
And we ride, we ride, taking the curves
Somewhat closer, the trucks coming
Down from behind the last ranges,
Their black shapes breaking past;
And the air claps between us,
Blasting the frosted windows,
And I seem to go backward,
Backward in time:

  Two song sparrows, one within a greenhouse,
  Shuttling its throat while perched on a wind-vent,
  And another, outside, in the bright day,
  With a wind from the west and the trees all in motion.
  One sang, then the other,
  The songs tumbling over and under the glass,

And the men beneath them wheeling in dirt to the cement benches,
The laden wheelbarrows creaking and swaying,
And the up-spring of the plank when a foot left the runway.

Journey within a journey:
The ticket mislaid or lost, the gate
Inaccessible, the boat always pulling out
From the rickety wooden dock,
The children waving;
Or two horses plunging in snow, their lines tangled,
A great wooden sleigh careening behind them,
Swerving up a steep embankment.
For a moment they stand above me,
Their black skins shuddering:
Then they lurch forward,
Lunging down a hillside.

3

As when silt drifts and sifts down through muddy pond-water,
Settling in small beads around weeds and sunken branches,
And one crab, tentative, hunches himself before moving along the bottom,
Grotesque, awkward, his extended eyes looking at nothing in particular,
Only a few bubbles loosening from the ill-matched tentacles,
The tail and smaller legs slipping and sliding slowly backward —
So the spirit tries for another life,
Another way and place in which to continue;
Or a salmon, tired, moving up a shallow stream,
Nudges into a back-eddy, a sandy inlet,
Bumping against sticks and bottom-stones, then swinging
Around, back into the tiny maincurrent, the rush of brownish-white water,
Still swimming forward —
So, I suppose, the spirit journeys.

4

I have gone into the waste lonely places
Behind the eye; the lost acres at the edge of smoky cities.
What's beyond never crumbles like an embankment,
Explodes like a rose, or thrusts wings over the Caribbean.
There are no pursuing forms, faces on walls:
Only the motes of dust in the immaculate hallways,
The darkness of falling hair, the warnings from lint and spiders,
The vines graying to a fine powder.
There is no riven tree, or lamb dropped by an eagle.

There are still times, morning and evening:
The cerulean, high in the elm,
Thin and insistent as a cicada,
And the far phoebe, singing,
The long plaintive notes floating down,
Drifting through leaves, oak and maple,
Or the whippoorwill, along the smoky ridges,
A single bird calling and calling;
A fume reminds me, drifting across wet gravel;
A cold wind comes over stones;
A flame, intense, visible,
Plays over the dry pods,
Runs fitfully along the stubble,
Moves over the field,
Without burning.
   In such times, lacking a god,
   I am still happy.

What Can I Tell My Bones?

1

Beginner,
Perpetual beginner,
The soul knows not what to believe,
In its small folds, stirring sluggishly,
In the least place of its life,
A pulse beyond nothingness,
A fearful ignorance.

     Before the moon draws back,
     Dare I blaze like a tree?

In a world always late afternoon,
In the circular smells of a slow wind,
I listen to the weeds' vesperal whine,
Longing for absolutes that never come.
And shapes make me afraid:
The dance of natural objects in the mind,
The immediate sheen, the reality of straw,
The shadows, crawling down a sunny wall.

A bird sings out in solitariness
A thin harsh song. The day dies in a child.
How close we are to the sad animals!
I need a pool; I need a puddle's calm.

O my bones,
Beware those perpetual beginnings,
Thinning the soul's substance;
The swan's dread of the darkening shore,
Or these insects pulsing near my skin,
The songs from a spiral tree.

Fury of wind, and no apparent wind,
A gust blowing the leaves suddenly upward,
A vine lashing in dry fury,
A man chasing a cat,
With a broken umbrella,
Crying softly.

2

It is difficult to say all things are well,
When the worst is about to arrive;
It is fatal to woo yourself,
However graceful the posture.

Loved heart, what can I say?
When I was a lark, I sang;
When I was a worm, I devoured.

The self says, I am;
The heart says, I am less;
The spirit says, you are nothing.

Mist alters the rocks. What can I tell my bones?
My desire's a wind trapped in a cave.
The spirit declares itself to these rocks.
I'm a small stone, loose in the shale.
Love is my wound.

The wide streams go their way,
The pond lapses back into a glassy silence.
The cause of God in me — has it gone?
Do these bones live? Can I live with these bones?

Mother, mother of us all, tell me where I am!
O to be delivered from the rational into the realm of pure song,
My face on fire, close to the points of a star,
A learned nimble girl,
Not drearily bewitched,
But sweetly daft.

To try to become like God
Is far from becoming God.
O, but I seek and care!

I rock in my own dark,
Thinking, God has need of me.
The dead love the unborn.

3

Weeds turn toward the wind weed-skeletons.
How slowly all things alter.
Existence dares perpetuate a soul,
A wedge of heaven's light, autumnal song.
I hear a beat of birds, the plangent wings
That disappear into a waning moon;
The barest speech of light among the stones.

To what more vast permission have I come?
When I walk past a vat, water joggles,
I no longer cry for green in the midst of cinders,
Or dream of the dead, and their holes.
Mercy has many arms.

Instead of a devil with horns, I prefer a serpent with scales;
In temptation, I rarely seek counsel;
A prisoner of smells, I would rather eat than pray.
I'm released from the dreary dance of opposites.
The wind rocks with my wish; the rain shields me;
I live in light's extreme; I stretch in all directions;
Sometimes I think I'm several.

The sun! The sun! And all we can become!
And the time ripe for running to the moon!
In the long fields, I leave my father's eye;
And shake the secrets from my deepest bones;
My spirit rises with the rising wind;

I'm thick with leaves and tender as a dove,
I take the liberties a short life permits —
I seek my own meekness;
I recover my tenderness by long looking.
By midnight I love everything alive.
Who took the darkness from the air?
I'm wet with another life.
Yea, I have gone and stayed.

What came to me vaguely is now clear,
As if released by a spirit,
Or agency outside me.
Unprayed-for,
And final.

The Rose

1

There are those to whom place is unimportant,
But this place, where sea and fresh water meet,
Is important —
Where the hawks sway out into the wind,
Without a single wingbeat,
And the eagles sail low over the fir trees,
And the gulls cry against the crows
In the curved harbors,
And the tide rises up against the grass
Nibbled by sheep and rabbits.

A time for watching the tide,
For the heron's hieratic fishing,
For the sleepy cries of the towhee,
The morning birds gone, the twittering finches,
But still the flash of the kingfisher, the wingbeat of the scoter,
The sun a ball of fire coming down over the water,
The last geese crossing against the reflected afterlight,
The moon retreating into a vague cloud-shape
To the cries of the owl, the eerie whooper.
The old log subsides with the lessening waves,
And there is silence.

I sway outside myself
Into the darkening currents,
Into the small spillage of driftwood,
The waters swirling past the tiny headlands.
Was it here I wore a crown of birds for a moment
While on a far point of the rocks
The light heightened,
And below, in a mist out of nowhere,
The first rain gathered?

2

As when a ship sails with a light wind —
The waves less than the ripples made by rising fish,
The lacelike wrinkles of the wake widening, thinning out,
Sliding away from the traveler's eye,
The prow pitching easily up and down,
The whole ship rolling slightly sideways,
The stern high, dipping like a child's boat in a pond —
Our motion continues.

But this rose, this rose in the sea-wind,
Stays,
Stays in its true place,
Flowering out of the dark,
Widening at high noon, face upward,
A single wild rose, struggling out of the white embrace of the morning-
    glory,
Out of the briary hedge, the tangle of matted underbrush,
Beyond the clover, the ragged hay,
Beyond the sea pine, the oak, the wind-tipped madrona,
Moving with the waves, the undulating driftwood,
Where the slow creek winds down to the black sand of the shore
With its thick grassy scum and crabs scuttling back into their glistening
    craters.

And I think of roses, roses,
White and red, in the wide six-hundred-foot greenhouses,
And my father standing astride the cement benches,
Lifting me high over the four-foot stems, the Mrs. Russells, and his own
    elaborate hybrids,
And how those flowerheads seemed to flow toward me, to beckon me, only
    a child, out of myself.

What need for heaven, then,
With that man, and those roses?

3

What do they tell us, sound and silence?
I think of American sounds in the silence:
On the banks of the Tombstone, the wind-harps having their say,
The thrush singing alone, that easy bird,
The killdeer whistling away from me,
The mimetic chortling of the catbird
Down in the corner of the garden, among the raggedy lilacs,
The bobolink skirring from a broken fencepost,
The bluebird, lover of holes in old wood, lilting its light song,
And that thin cry, like a needle piercing the ear, the insistent cicada,
And the ticking of snow around oil drums in the Dakotas,
The thin whine of telephone wires in the wind of a Michigan winter,
The shriek of nails as old shingles are ripped from the top of a roof,
The bulldozer backing away, the hiss of the sandblaster,
And the deep chorus of horns coming up from the streets in early
    morning.
I return to the twittering of swallows above water,
And that sound, that single sound,
When the mind remembers all,
And gently the light enters the sleeping soul,
A sound so thin it could not woo a bird,

Beautiful my desire, and the place of my desire.

I think of the rock singing, and light making its own silence,
At the edge of ripening meadow, in early summer,
The moon lolling in the close elm, a shimmer of silver,
Or that lonely time before the breaking of morning
When the slow freight winds along the edge of the ravaged hillside,
And the wind tries the shape of a tree,
While the moon lingers,
And a drop of rain water hangs at the tip of a leaf
Shifting in the wakening sunlight
Like the eye of a new-caught fish.

4

I live with the rocks, their weeds,
Their filmy fringes of green, their harsh
Edges, their holes

Cut by the sea-slime, far from the crash
Of the long swell,
The oily, tar-laden walls
Of the toppling waves,
Where the salmon ease their way into the kelp beds,
And the sea rearranges itself among the small islands.

Near this rose, in this grove of sun-parched, wind-warped madronas,
Among the half-dead trees, I came upon the true ease of myself,
As if another man appeared out of the depths of my being,
And I stood outside myself,
Beyond becoming and perishing,
A something wholly other,
As if I swayed out on the wildest wave alive,
And yet was still.
And I rejoiced in being what I was:
In the lilac change, the white reptilian calm,
In the bird beyond the bough, the single one
With all the air to greet him as he flies,
The dolphin rising from the darkening waves;

And in this rose, this rose in the sea-wind,
Rooted in stone, keeping the whole of light,
Gathering to itself sound and silence —
Mine and the sea-wind's.

In a Dark Time

In a dark time, the eye begins to see,
I meet my shadow in the deepening shade;
I hear my echo in the echoing wood —
A lord of nature weeping to a tree.
I live between the heron and the wren,
Beasts of the hill and serpents of the den.

What's madness but nobility of soul
At odds with circumstance? The day's on fire!
I know the purity of pure despair,
My shadow pinned against a sweating wall.
That place among the rocks — is it a cave,
Or winding path? The edge is what I have.

A steady storm of correspondences!
A night flowing with birds, a ragged moon,
And in broad day the midnight come again!
A man goes far to find out what he is —
Death of the self in a long, tearless night,
All natural shapes blazing unnatural light.

Dark, dark my light, and darker my desire.
My soul, like some heat-maddened summer fly,
Keeps buzzing at the sill. Which I is I?
A fallen man, I climb out of my fear.
The mind enters itself, and God the mind,
And one is One, free in the tearing wind.

CHARLES OLSON
1910–1970

The Kingfishers

I

1
What does not change / is the will to change

He woke, fully clothed, in his bed. He
remembered only one thing, the birds, how
when he came in, he had gone around the rooms
and got them back in their cage, the green one first,
she with the bad leg, and then the blue,
the one they had hoped was a male

Otherwise? Yes, Fernand, who had talked lispingly of Albers & Angkor
Vat.
He had left the party without a word. How he got up, got into his coat,
I do not know. When I saw him, he was at the door, but it did not
matter,
he was already sliding along the wall of the night, losing himself
in some crack of the ruins. That it should have been he who said, "The
kingfishers?
who cares
for their feathers
now?"

His last words had been, "The pool is slime." Suddenly everyone,
ceasing their talk, sat in a row around him, watched
they did not so much hear, or pay attention, they
wondered, looked at each other, smirked, but listened,
he repeated and repeated, could not go beyond his thought
"The pool   the kingfishers' feathers were wealth   why
did the export stop?"

It was then he left

2
I though of the E on the stone, and of what Mao said
la lumiere"
                but the kingfisher
de l'aurore"
                but the kingfisher flew west
est devant nous!
                he got the color of his breast
                from the heat of the setting sun!

The features are, the feebleness of the feet (syndactylism of the 3rd &
                                                          4th digit)
the bill, serrated, sometimes a pronounced beak, the wings
where the color is, short and round, the tail
inconspicuous.

But not these things were the factors. Not the birds.
The legends are
legends. Dead, hung up indoors, the kingfisher
will not indicate a favoring wind,
or avert the thunderbolt. Nor, by its nesting,
still the waters, with the new year, for seven days.
It is true, it does nest with the opening year, but not on the waters.
It nests at the end of a tunnel bored by itself in a bank. There,
six or eight white and translucent eggs are laid, on fishbones
not on bare clay, on bones thrown up in pellets by the birds.

                                On these rejectamenta
(as they accumulate they form a cup-shaped structure) the young are
                                                          born.
And, as they are fed and grow, this nest of excrement and decayed fish
                                                          becomes
                                a dripping, fetid mass

Mao concluded:
> nous devons
>> nous lever
>>> et agir!

3
When the attentions change / the jungle
leaps in
> even the stones are split
>> they rive

Or,
enter
that other conqueror we more naturally recognize
he so resembles ourselves

But the E
cut so rudely on that oldest stone
sounded otherwise,
was differently heard

as, in another time, were treasures used:

(and, later, much later, a fine ear thought
a scarlet coat)

> "of green feathers   feet, beaks and eyes
>   of gold

> "animals likewise,
>   resembling snails

> "a large wheel, gold, with figures of unknown four-foots,
>   and worked with tufts of leaves, weight
>   3800 ounces

> "last, two birds, of thread and featherwork, the quills
>   gold, the feet
>   gold, the two birds perched on two reeds
>   gold, the reeds arising from two embroidered mounds,
>   one yellow, the other
>   white.

"And from each reed hung
seven feathered tassels.

In this instance, the priests
(in dark cotton robes, and dirty,
their dishevelled hair matted with blood, and flowing wildly
over their shoulders)
rush in among the people, calling on them
to protect their gods

And all now is war
where so lately there was peace,
and the sweet brotherhood, the use
of tilled fields.

4
Not one death but many,
not accumulation but change, the feed-back proves, the feed-back is
the law

      Into the same river no man steps twice
      When fire dies air dies
      No one remains, nor is, one

Around an appearance, one common model, we grow up
many. Else how is it,
if we remain the same,
we take pleasure now
in what we did not take pleasure before? love
contrary objects? admire and/or find fault? use
other words, feel other passions, have
nor figure, appearance, disposition, tissue
the same?

      To be in different states without a change
      is not a possibility

We can be precise. The factors are
in the animal and/or the machine the factors are
communication and/or control, both involve
the message. And what is the message? The message is
a discrete or continuous sequence of measurable events distributed in
                                                      time

is the birth of air, is
the birth of water, is
a state between
the origin and
the end, between
birth and the beginning of
another fetid nest

is change, presents
nor more than itself

And the too strong grasping of it,
when it is pressed together and condensed,
loses it

This very thing you are

II

They buried their dead in a sitting posture
serpent   cane   razor   ray of the sun

And she sprinkled water on the head of the child, crying
"Cioa-coatl! Cioa-coatl!"
with her face to the west

Where the bones are found, in each personal heap
with what each enjoyed, there is always
the Mongolian louse

The light is in the east. Yes. And we must rise, act. Yet
in the west, despite the apparent darkness (the whiteness
which covers all), if you look, if you can bear, if you can, long enough

as long as it was necessary for him, my guide
to look into the yellow of that longest-lasting rose

so you must, and, in that whiteness, into that face, with what candor,

look

and, considering the dryness of the place
the long absence of an adequate race

(of the two who first came, each a conquistador, one healed,
the other
tore the eastern idols down, toppled
the temple walls, which, says the excuser
were black from human gore)

hear
hear, where the dry blood talks
where the old appetite walks

la piu saporita et migliore
che si possa truovar al mondo

where it hides, look
in the eye how it runs
in the flesh / chalk

but under these petals
in the emptiness
regard the light, contemplate
the flower

whence it arose

with what violence benevolence is bought
what cost in gesture justice brings
what wrongs domestic rights involve
what stalks
this silence

what pudor pejorocracy affronts
how awe, night-rest and neighborhood can rot
what breeds where dirtiness is law
what crawls
below

III
I am no Greek, hath not th'advantage.
And of course, no Roman:
he can take no risk that matters,
the risk of beauty least of all.

But I have my kin, if for no other reason than
(as he said, next of kin) I commit myself, and,
given my freedom, I'd be a cad
if I didn't. Which is most true.

It works out this way, despite the disadvantage.
I offer, in explanation, a quote:
si j'ai du goût, ce n'est guère
que pour la terre et les pierres

Despite the discrepancy (an ocean   courage   age)
this is also true: if I have any taste
it is only because I have interested myself
in what was slain in the sun

     I pose you your question:

shall you uncover honey / where maggots are?

     I hunt among stones

The Ring of

   it was the west wind caught her up, as
   she rose
   from the genital
   wave, and bore her from the delicate
   foam, home
   to her isle

   and those lovers
   of the difficult, the hours
   of the golden day welcomed her, clad her, were
   as though they had made her, were wild
   to bring this new thing born
   of the ring of the sea pink
   & naked, this girl, brought her
   to the face of the gods, violets
   in her hair

Beauty, and she
said no to zeus & them all, all were not or
was it she chose the ugliest
to bed with, or was it straight
and to expiate the nature of beauty, was it?

knowing hours, anyway,
she did not stay long, or the lame
was only one part, & the handsome
mars had her   And the child
had that name, the arrow of
as the flight of, the move of
his mother who adorneth

with myrtle the dolphin and words
they rise, they do who
are born of like
elements

from The Maximus Poems

I, Maximus of Gloucester, to You
(in part)

> Off-shore, by islands hidden in the blood
> jewels & miracles, I, Maximus
> a metal hot from boiling water, tell you
> what is a lance, who obeys the figures of
> the present dance

1

the thing you're after
may lie around the bend
of the nest (second, time slain, the bird! the bird!

And there! (strong) thrust, the mast! flight
(of the bird
o kylix, o
Antony of Padua
sweep low, o bless

the roofs, the old ones, the gentle steep ones
on whose ridge-poles the gulls sit, from which they depart,

                                        And the flake-racks

of my city!

                            2
love is form, and cannot be without
important substance (the weight
say, 58 carats each one of us, perforce
our goldsmith's scale

                        feather to feather added
                        (and what is mineral, what
                        is curling hair, the string
                        you carry in your nervous beak, these

                        make bulk, these, in the end, are
                        the sum

                        (o my lady of good voyage
                        in whose arm, whose left arm rests
no boy but a carefully carved wood, a painted face, a schooner!
a delicate mast, as bow-sprit for

                            forwarding

                        3
the underpart is, though stemmed, uncertain
is, as sex is, as moneys are, facts!
facts, to be dealt with, as the sea is, the demand
that they be played by, that they only can be, that they must
be played by, said he, coldly, the
ear!

By ear, he sd.
But that which matters, that which insists, that which will last,
that! o my people, where shall you find it, how, where, where shall you
        listen
when all is become billboards, when, all, even silence, is spray-gunned?

747

when even our bird, my roofs,
cannot be heard

when even you, when sound itself is neoned in?

when, on the hill, over the water
where she who used to sing,
when the water glowed,
black, gold, the tide
outward, at evening

when bells came like boats
over the oil-slicks, milkweed
hulls

And a man slumped,
attentionless,
against pink shingles

o sea city)

4

one loves only form,
and form only comes
into existence when
the thing is born

        born of yourself, born
        of hay and cotton struts,
        of street-pickings, wharves, weeds
        you carry in, my bird

                of a bone of a fish
                of a straw, or will
                of a color, of a bell
                of yourself, torn

.   .   .

Maximus, to Himself

I have had to learn the simplest things
last. Which made for difficulties.
Even at sea I was slow, to get the hand out, or to cross
a wet deck.

The sea was not, finally, my trade.
But even my trade, at it, I stood estranged
from that which was most familiar. Was delayed,
and not content with the man's argument
that such postponement
is now the nature of
obedience,
>   that we are all late
>   in a slow time,
>   that we grow up many
>   And the single
>   is not easily
>   known

It could be, though the sharpness (the *achiote*)
I note in others,
makes more sense
than my own distances. The agilities

>   they show daily
>   who do the world's
>   businesses
>   And who do nature's
>   as I have no sense
>   I have done either

I have made dialogues,
have discussed ancient texts,
have thrown what light I could, offered
what pleasures
doceat allows

>   But the known?
This, I have had to be given,
a life, love, and from one man
the world.

>   Tokens.
>   But sitting here
>   I look out as a wind
>   and water man, testing
>   And missing
>   some proof

I know the quarters
of the weather, where it comes from,
where it goes. But the stem of me,
this I took from their welcome,
or their rejection, of me

       And my arrogance
       was neither diminished
       nor increased,
       by the communication

2
It is undone business
I speak of, this morning,
with the sea
stretching out
from my feet

Maximus to Gloucester, Letter 27

I come back to the geography of it,
the land falling off to the left
where my father shot his scabby golf
and the rest of us played baseball
into the summer darkness until no flies
could be seen and we came home
to our various piazzas where the women
buzzed

To the left the land fell to the city,
to the right, it fell to the sea

I was so young my first memory
is of a tent spread to feed lobsters
to Rexall conventioneers, and my father,
a man for kicks, came out of the tent roaring
with a bread-knife in his teeth to take care of
a druggist they'd told him had made a pass at
my mother, she laughing, so sure, as round
as her face, Hines pink and apple,
under one of those frame hats women then

This, is no bare incoming
of novel abstract form, this

is no welter or the forms
of those events, this,

Greeks, is the stopping
of the battle

        It is the imposing
of all those antecedent predecessions, the precessions

of me, the generation of those facts
which are my words, it is coming

from all that I no longer am, yet am,
the slow westward motion of

more than I am

There is no strict personal order

for my inheritance.

        No Greek will be able

to discriminate my body.

        An American

is a complex of occasions,

themselves a geometry

of spatial nature.

        I have this sense,

that I am one

with my skin

        Plus this — plus this:

that forever the geography

which leans in

on me I compell

backwards I compell Gloucester

to yield, to

change

      Polis

is this

Variations Done for Gerald Van de Wiele

I. Le Bonheur

dogwood flakes
what is green

the petals   *
from the apple
blow on the road

mourning doves
mark the sway
of the afternoon, bees
dig the plum blossoms

the morning
stands up straight, the night
is blue from the full of the April moon

iris and lilac, birds
birds, yellow flowers
white flowers, the Diesel
does not let up dragging
the plow

as the whippoorwill,
the night's tractor, grinds
his song

and no other birds but us
are as busy (O saisons, o chateaux!

Délires!

What soul
is without fault?

Nobody studies
happiness

Every time the cock crows
I salute him

I have no longer any excuse
for envy. My life

has been given its orders: the seasons
seize

the soul and the body, and make mock
of any dispersed effort. The hour of death

is the only trespass

II. *The Charge*

dogwood flakes
the green

the petals from the apple-trees
fall for the feet to walk on

the birds are so many they are
loud, in the afternoon

they distract, as so many bees do
suddenly all over the place

With spring one knows today to see
that in the morning each thing

is separate but by noon
they have melted into each other

and by night only crazy things
like the full moon and the whippoorwill

and us, are busy. We are busy
if we can get by that whiskered bird,

that nightjar, and get across, the moon
is our conversation, she will say

what soul
isn't in default?

can you afford not to make
the magical study

which happiness is? do you hear
the cock when he crows? do you know the charge,

that you shall have no envy, that your life
has its orders, that the seasons

seize you too, that no body and soul are one
if they are not wrought

in this retort? that otherwise efforts
are efforts? And that the hour of your flight

will be the hour of your death?

III. The Spring

The dogwood
lights up the day.

The April moon
flakes the night.

Birds, suddenly,
are a multitude

The flowers are ravined
by bees, the fruit blossoms

are thrown to the ground, the wind
the rain forces everything. Noise —

even the night is drummed
by whippoorwills, and we get

as busy, we plow, we move,
we break out, we love. The secret

which got lost neither hides
nor reveals itself, it shows forth

tokens. And we rush
to catch up. The body

whips the soul. In its great desire
it demands the elixir

In the roar of spring,
transmutations. Envy

drags herself off. The fault of the body and the soul
— that they are not one —

the matutinal cock clangs
and singleness: we salute you

season of no bungling

ELIZABETH BISHOP
b. 1911

The Map

Land lies in water; it is shadowed green.
Shadows, or are they shallows, at its edges
showing the line of long sea-weeded ledges
where weeds hang to the simple blue from green.

ELIZABETH BISHOP

Or does the land lean down to lift the sea from under,
drawing it unperturbed around itself?
Along the fine tan sandy shelf
is the land tugging at the sea from under?

The shadow of Newfoundland lies flat and still.
Labrador's yellow, where the moony Eskimo
has oiled it. We can stroke these lovely bays,
under a glass as if they were expected to blossom,
or as if to provide a clean cage for invisible fish.
The names of seashore towns run out to sea,
the names of cities cross the neighboring mountains
— the printer here experiencing the same excitement
as when emotion too far exceeds its cause.
These peninsulas take the water between thumb and finger
like women feeling for the smoothness of yard-goods.

Mapped waters are more quiet than the land is,
lending the land their waves' own conformation:
and Norway's hare runs south in agitation,
profiles investigate the sea, where land is.
Are they assigned, or can the countries pick their colors?
— What suits the character or the native waters best.
Topography displays no favorites; North's as near as West.
More delicate than the historians' are the map-makers' colors.

The Man-Moth*

Here, above,
cracks in the buildings are filled with battered moonlight.
The whole shadow of Man is only as big as his hat.
It lies at his feet like a circle for a doll to stand on,
and he makes an inverted pin, the point magnetized to the moon.
He does not see the moon; he observes only her vast properties,
feeling the queer light on his hands, neither warm nor cold,
of a temperature impossible to record in thermometers.

But when the Man-Moth
pays his rare, although occasional, visits to the surface,
the moon looks rather different to him. He emerges

* Newspaper misprint for "mammoth."

from an opening under the edge of one of the sidewalks
and nervously begins to scale the faces of the buildings.
He thinks the moon is a small hole at the top of the sky,
proving the sky quite useless for protection.
He trembles, but must investigate as high as he can climb.

Up the façades,
his shadow dragging like a photographer's cloth behind him,
he climbs fearfully, thinking that this time he will manage
to push his small head through that round clean opening
and be forced through, as from a tube, in black scrolls on the light.
(Man, standing below him, has no such illusions.)
But what the Man-Moth fears most he must do, although
he fails, of course, and falls back scared but quite unhurt.

Then he returns
to the pale subways of cement he calls his home. He flits,
he flutters, and cannot get aboard the silent trains
fast enough to suit him. The doors close swiftly.
The Man-Moth always seats himself facing the wrong way
and the train starts at once at its full, terrible speed,
without a shift in gears or a gradation of any sort.
He cannot tell the rate at which he travels backwards.

Each night he must
be carried through artificial tunnels and dream recurrent dreams.
Just as the ties recur beneath his train, these underlie
his rushing brain. He does not dare look out the window,
for the third rail, the unbroken draught of poison,
runs there beside him. He regards it as a disease
he has inherited the susceptibility to. He has to keep
his hands in his pockets, as others must wear mufflers.

If you catch him,
hold up a flashlight to his eye. It's all dark pupil,
an entire night itself, whose haired horizon tightens
as he stares back, and closes up the eye. Then from the lids
one tear, his only possession, like the bee's sting, slips.
Slyly he palms it, and if you're not paying attention
he'll swallow it. However, if you watch, he'll hand it over,
cool as from underground springs and pure enough to drink.

757

The Monument

Now can you see the monument? It is of **wood**
built somewhat like a box. No. Built
like several boxes in descending sizes
one above the other.
Each is turned half-way round so that
its corners point toward the sides
of the one below and the angles alternate.
Then on the topmost cube is set
a sort of fleur-de-lys of weathered wood,
long petals of board, pierced with odd holes,
four-sided, stiff, ecclesiastical.
From it four thin, warped poles spring out,
(slanted like fishing-poles or flag poles)
and from them jig-saw work hangs down,
four lines of vaguely whittled ornament
over the edges of the boxes
to the ground.
The monument is one-third set against
a sea; two-thirds against a sky.
The view is geared
(that is, the view's perspective)
so low there is no "far away,"
and we are far away within the view.
A sea of narrow, horizontal boards
lies out behind our lonely monument,
its long grains alternating right and left
like floor-boards — spotted, swarming-still,
and motionless. A sky runs parallel,
and it is palings, coarser than the sea's:
splintery sunlight and long-fibred clouds.
"Why does that strange sea make no sound?
Is it because we're far away?
Where are we? Are we in Asia Minor,
or in Mongolia?"
                    An ancient promontory,
an ancient principality whose artist-prince
might have wanted to build a monument
to mark a tomb or boundary, or make
a melancholy or romantic scene of it . . .
"But that queer sea looks made of wood,
half-shining, like a driftwood sea.

And the sky looks wooden, grained with cloud.
It's like a stage-set; it is all so flat!
Those clouds are full of glistening splinters!
What is that?"
                    It is the monument.
"It's piled-up boxes,
outlined with shoddy fret-work, half-fallen off,
cracked and unpainted. It looks old."
— The strong sunlight, the wind from the sea,
all the conditions of its existence,
may have flaked off the paint, if ever it was painted,
and made it homelier than it was.
"Why did you bring me here to see it?
A temple of crates in cramped and crated scenery,
what can it prove?
I am tired of breathing this eroded air,
this dryness in which the monument is cracking."
It is an artifact
of wood. Wood holds together better
than sea or cloud or sand could by itself,
much better than real sea or sand or cloud.
It chose that way to grow and not to move.
The monument's an object, yet those decorations,
carelessly nailed, looking like nothing at all,
give it away as having life, and wishing;
wanting to be a monument, to cherish something.
The crudest scroll-work says "commemorate,"
while once each day the light goes around it
like a prowling animal,
or the rain falls on it, or the wind blows into it.
It may be solid, may be hollow.
The bones of the artist-prince may be inside
or far away on even drier soil.
But roughly but adequately it can shelter
what is within (which after all
cannot have been intended to be seen).
It is the beginning of a painting,
a piece of sculpture, or poem, or monument,
and all of wood. Watch it closely.

The Fish

I caught a tremendous fish
and held him beside the boat
half out of water, with my hook
fast in a corner of his mouth.
He didn't fight.
He hadn't fought at all.
He hung a grunting weight,
battered and venerable
and homely. Here and there
his brown skin hung in strips
like ancient wallpaper,
and its pattern of darker brown
was like wallpaper;
shapes like full-blown roses
stained and lost through age.
He was speckled with barnacles,
fine rosettes of lime,
and infested
with tiny white sea-lice,
and underneath two or three
rags of green weed hung down.
While his gills were breathing in
the terrible oxygen
— the frightening gills,
fresh and crisp with blood,
that can cut so badly —
I thought of the coarse white flesh
packed in like feathers,
the big bones and the little bones,
the dramatic reds and blacks
of his shiny entrails,
and the pink swim-bladder
like a big peony.
I looked into his eyes
which were far larger than mine
but shallower, and yellowed,
the irises backed and packed
with tarnished tinfoil
seen through the lenses
of old scratched isinglass.

They shifted a little, but not
to return my stare.
— It was more like the tipping
of an object toward the light.
I admired his sullen face,
the mechanism of his jaw,
and then I saw
that from his lower lip
— if you could call it a lip —
grim, wet, and weaponlike,
hung five old pieces of fish-line,
or four and a wire leader
with the swivel still attached,
with all their five big hooks
grown firmly in his mouth.
A green line, frayed at the end
where he broke it, two heavier lines,
and a fine black thread
still crimped from the strain and snap
when it broke and he got away.
Like medals with their ribbons
frayed and wavering,
a five-haired beard of wisdom
trailing from his aching jaw.
I stared and stared
and victory filled up
the little rented boat,
from the pool of bilge
where oil had spread a rainbow
around the rusted engine
to the bailer rusted orange,
the sun-cracked thwarts,
the oarlocks on their strings,
the gunnels — until everything
was rainbow, rainbow, rainbow!
And I let the fish go.

Questions of Travel

There are too many waterfalls here; the crowded streams
hurry too rapidly down to the sea,
and the pressure of so many clouds on the mountaintops

makes them spill over the sides in soft slow-motion,
turning to waterfalls under our very eyes.
— For if those streaks, those mile-long, shiny, tearstains,
aren't waterfalls yet,
in a quick age or so, as ages go here,
they probably will be.
But if the streams and clouds keep travelling, travelling,
the mountains look like the hulls of capsized ships,
slime-hung and barnacled.

Think of the long trip home.
Should we have stayed at home and thought of here?
Where should we be today?
Is it right to be watching strangers in a play
in this strangest of theatres?
What childishness is it that while there's a breath of life
in our bodies, we are determined to rush
to see the sun the other way around?
The tiniest green hummingbird in the world?
To stare at some inexplicable old stonework,
inexplicable and impenetrable,
at any view,
instantly seen and always, always delightful?
Oh, must we dream our dreams
and have them, too?
And have we room
for one more folded sunset, still quite warm?

But surely it would have been a pity
not to have seen the trees along this road,
really exaggerated in their beauty,
not to have seen them gesturing
like noble pantomimists, robed in pink.
— Not to have had to stop for gas and heard
the sad, two-noted, wooden tune
of disparate wooden clogs
carelessly clacking over
a grease-stained filling-station floor.
(In another country the clogs would all be tested.
Each pair there would have identical pitch.)
— A pity not to have heard
the other, less primitive music of the fat brown bird
who sings above the broken gasoline pump

in a bamboo church of Jesuit baroque:
three towers, five silver crosses.
— Yes, a pity not to have pondered,
blurr'dly and inconclusively,
on what connection can exist for centuries
between the crudest wooden footwear
and, careful and finicky,
the whittled fantasies of wooden cages.
— Never to have studied history in
the weak calligraphy of songbird's cages.
— And never to have had to listen to rain
so much like politicians' speeches:
two hours of unrelenting oratory
and then a sudden golden silence
in which the traveller takes a notebook, writes:

*"Is it lack of imagination that makes us come
to imagined places, not just stay at home?
Or could Pascal have been not entirely right
about just sitting quietly in one's room?*

*Continent, city, country, society:
the choice is never wide and never free.
And here, or there . . . No. Should we have stayed at home,
wherever that may be?"*

The Armadillo
For Robert Lowell

This is the time of year
when almost every night
the frail, illegal fire balloons appear.
Climbing the mountain height,

rising toward a saint
still honored in these parts,
the paper chambers flush and fill with light
that comes and goes, like hearts.

Once up against the sky it's hard
to tell them from the stars —
planets, that is — the tinted ones:
Venus going down, or Mars,

763

or the pale green one. With a wind,
they flare and falter, wobble and toss;
but if it's still they steer between
the kite sticks of the Southern Cross,

receding, dwindling, solemnly
and steadily forsaking us,
or, in the downdraft from a peak,
suddenly turning dangerous.

Last night another big one fell.
It splattered like an egg of fire
against the cliff behind the house.
The flame ran down. We saw the pair

of owls who nest there flying up
and up, their whirling black-and-white
stained bright pink underneath, until
they shrieked up out of sight.

The ancient owls' nest must have burned.
Hastily, all alone,
a glistening armadillo left the scene,
rose-flecked, head down, tail down,

and then a baby rabbit jumped out,
short-eared, to our surprise.
So soft! — a handful of intangible ash
with fixed, ignited eyes.

Too pretty, dreamlike mimicry!
O falling fire and piercing cry
and panic, and a weak mailed fist
clenched ignorant against the sky!

First Death in Nova Scotia

In the cold, cold parlor
my mother laid out Arthur
beneath the chromographs:
Edward, Prince of Wales,
with Princess Alexandra,

and King George with Queen Mary.
Below them on the table
stood a stuffed loon
shot and stuffed by Uncle
Arthur, Arthur's father.

Since Uncle Arthur fired
a bullet into him,
he hadn't said a word.
He kept his own counsel
on his white, frozen lake,
the marble-topped table.
His breast was deep and white,
cold and caressable;
his eyes were red glass,
much to be desired.

"Come," said my mother,
"Come and say goodbye
to your little cousin Arthur."
I was lifted up and given
one lily of the valley
to put in Arthur's hand.
Arthur's coffin was
a little frosted cake,
and the red-eyed loon eyed it
from his white, frozen lake.

Arthur was very small.
He was all white, like a doll
that hadn't been painted yet.
Jack Frost had started to paint him
the way he always painted
the Maple Leaf (Forever).
He had just begun on his hair,
a few red strokes, and then
Jack Frost had dropped the brush
and left him white, forever.

The gracious royal couples
were warm in red and ermine;
their feet were well wrapped up
in the ladies' ermine trains.

They invited Arthur to be
the smallest page at court.
But how could Arthur go,
clutching his tiny lily,
with his eyes shut up so tight
and the roads deep in snow?

In the Waiting Room

In Worcester, Massachusetts,
I went with Aunt Consuelo
to keep her dentist's appointment
and sat and waited for her
in the dentist's waiting room.
It was winter. It got dark
early. The waiting room
was full of grown-up people,
arctics and overcoats,
lamps and magazines.
My aunt was inside
what seemed like a long time
and while I waited I read
the *National Geographic*
(I could read) and carefully
studied the photographs:
The inside of a volcano,
black, and full of ashes;
then it was spilling over
in rivulets of fire.
Osa and Martin Johnson
dressed in riding breeches,
laced boots, and pith helmets.
A dead man slung on a pole
— "Long Pig," the caption said.
Babies with pointed heads
wound round and round with string;
black, naked women with necks
wound round and round with wire
like the necks of light bulbs.
Their breasts were horrifying.
I read it right straight through.
I was too shy to stop.

And then I looked at the cover:
the yellow margins, the date.

Suddenly, from inside,
came an *oh!* of pain
— Aunt Consuelo's voice —
not very loud or long.
I wasn't at all surprised;
even then I knew she was
a foolish, timid woman.
I might have been embarrassed,
but wasn't. What took me
completely by surprise
was that it was *me:*
my voice, in my mouth.
Without thinking at all
I was my foolish aunt,
I — we — were falling, falling,
our eyes glued to the cover
of the *National Geographic,*
February, 1918.

I said to myself: three days
and you'll be seven years old.
I was saying it to stop
the sensation of falling off
the round, turning world
into cold, blue-black space.
But I felt: you are an *I*,
you are an *Elizabeth*,
you are one of *them.*
Why should you be one, too?
I scarcely dared to look
to see what it was I was.
I gave a sidelong glance
— I couldn't look any higher —
at shadowy gray knees,
trousers and skirts and boots
and different pairs of hands
lying under the lamps.
I knew that nothing stranger
had ever happened, that nothing
stranger could ever happen.

Why should I be my aunt,
or me, or anyone?
What similarities —
boots, hands, the family voice
I felt in my throat, or even
the *National Geographic*
and those awful hanging breasts —
held us all together
or made us all just one?
How — I didn't know any
word for it — how "unlikely" . . .
How had I come to be here,
like them, and overhear
a cry of pain that could have
got loud and worse but hadn't?

The waiting room was bright
and too hot. It was sliding
beneath a big black wave,
another, and another.

Then I was back in it.
The War was on. Outside,
in Worcester, Massachusetts,
were night and slush and cold,
and it was still the fifth
of February, 1918.

DELMORE SCHWARTZ
1913–1966

In the Naked Bed, in Plato's Cave

In the naked bed, in Plato's cave,
Reflected headlights slowly slid the wall,
Carpenters hammered under the shaded window,
Wind troubled the window curtains all night long,
A fleet of trucks strained uphill, grinding,
Their freights covered, as usual.
The ceiling lightened again, the slanting diagram
Slid slowly forth.

Hearing the milkman's chop,
His striving up the stair, the bottle's chink,
I rose from bed, lit a cigarette,
And walked to the window. The stony street
Displayed the stillness in which buildings stand,
The street-lamp's vigil and the horse's patience.
The winter sky's pure capital
Turned me back to bed with exhausted eyes.
Strangeness grew in the motionless air. The loose
Film grayed. Shaking wagons, hooves' waterfalls,
Sounded far off, increasing, louder and nearer.
A car coughed, starting. Morning, softly
Melting the air, lifted the half-covered chair
From underseas, kindled the looking-glass,
Distinguished the dresser and the white wall.
The bird called tentatively, whistled, called,
Bubbled and whistled, so! Perplexed, still wet
With sleep, affectionate, hungry and cold. So, so,
O son of man, the ignorant night, the travail
Of early morning, the mystery of beginning
Again and again,
        while History is unforgiven.

The Heavy Bear Who Goes With Me

the withness of the body

The heavy bear who goes with me,
A manifold honey to smear his face,
Clumsy and lumbering here and there,
The central ton of every place,
The hungry beating brutish one
In love with candy, anger, and sleep,
Crazy factotum, dishevelling all,
Climbs the building, kicks the football,
Boxes his brother in the hate-ridden city.

Breathing at my side, that heavy animal,
That heavy bear who sleeps with me,
Howls in his sleep for a world of sugar,
A sweetness intimate as the water's clasp,

Howls in his sleep because the tight-rope
Trembles and shows the darkness beneath.
— The strutting show-off is terrified,
Dressed in his dress-suit, bulging his pants,
Trembles to think that his quivering meat
Must finally wince to nothing at all.

That inescapable animal walks with me,
Has followed me since the black womb held,
Moves where I move, distorting my gesture,
A caricature, a swollen shadow,
A stupid clown of the spirit's motive,
Perplexes and affronts with his own darkness,
The secret life of belly and bone,
Opaque, too near, my private, yet unknown,
Stretches to embrace the very dear
With whom I would walk without him near,
Touches her grossly, although a word
Would bare my heart and make me clear,
Stumbles, flounders, and strives to be fed
Dragging me with him in his mouthing care,
Amid the hundred million of his kind,
The scrimmage of appetite everywhere.

RANDALL JARRELL
1914–1965

90 North

At home, in my flannel gown, like a bear to its floe,
I clambered to bed; up the globe's impossible sides
I sailed all night — till at last, with my black beard,
My furs and my dogs, I stood at the northern pole.

There in the childish night my companions lay frozen,
The stiff furs knocked at my starveling throat,
And I gave my great sigh: the flakes came huddling,
Were they really my end? In the darkness I turned to my rest.

— Here, the flag snaps in the glare and silence
Of the unbroken ice. I stand here,
The dogs bark, my beard is black, and I stare
At the North Pole . . .
                                    And now what? Why, go back.

Turn as I please, my step is to the south.
The world — my world spins on this final point
Of cold and wretchedness: all lines, all winds
End in this whirlpool I at last discover.

And it is meaningless. In the child's bed
After the night's voyage, in that warm world
Where people work and suffer for the end
That crowns the pain — in that Cloud-Cuckoo-Land

I reached my North and it had meaning.
Here at the actual pole of my existence,
Where all that I have done is meaningless,
Where I die or live by accident alone —

Where, living or dying, I am still alone;
Here where North, the night, the berg of death
Crowd me out of the ignorant darkness,
I see at last that all the knowledge

I wrung from the darkness — that the darkness flung me —
Is worthless as ignorance: nothing comes from nothing,
The darkness from the darkness. Pain comes from the darkness
And we call it wisdom. It is pain.

The Death of the Ball Turret Gunner

From my mother's sleep I fell into the State,
And I hunched in its belly till my wet fur froze.
Six miles from earth, loosed from its dream of life,
I woke to black flak and the nightmare fighters.
When I died they washed me out of the turret with a hose.

Eighth Air Force

If, in an odd angle of the hutment,
A puppy laps the water from a can
Of flowers, and the drunk sergeant shaving
Whistles O Paradiso! — shall I say that man
Is not as men have said: a wolf to man?

The other murderers troop in yawning;
Three of them play Pitch, one sleeps, and one
Lies counting missions, lies there sweating
Till even his heart beats: One; One; One.
O murderers! . . . Still, this is how it's done:

This is a war. . . . But since these play, before they die,
Like puppies with their puppy; since, a man,
I did as these have done, but did not die —
I will content the people as I can
And give up these to them: Behold the man!

I have suffered, in a dream, because of him,
Many things; for this last saviour, man,
I have lied as I lie now. But what is lying?
Men wash their hands, in blood, as best they can:
I find no fault in this just man.

The Range in the Desert

Where the lizard ran to its little prey
And a man on a horse rode by in a day
They set their hangars: a continent
Taught its conscripts its unloved intent
In the scrawled fire, the singing lead —
Protocols of the quick and dead.
The wounded gunner, his missions done,
Fired absently in the range's sun;
And, chained with cartridges, the clerk
Sat sweating at his war-time work.
The cold flights bombed — again, again —
The craters of the lunar plain. . . .

All this was priceless: men were paid
For these rehearsals of the raids
That used up cities at a rate
That left the coals without a State
To call another's; till the worse
Ceded at last, without remorse,
Their conquests to their conquerors.
The equations were without two powers.

Profits and death grow marginal:
Only the mourning and the mourned recall
The wars we love, the wars we win;
And the world is — what it has been.

The lizard's tongue licks angrily
The shattered membranes of the fly.

A Girl in a Library

An object among dreams, you sit here with your shoes off
And curl your legs up under you; your eyes
Close for a moment, your face moves toward sleep . . .
You are very human.
                   But my mind, gone out in tenderness,
Shrinks from its object with a thoughtful sigh.
This is a waist the spirit breaks its arm on.
The gods themselves, against you, struggle in vain.
This broad low strong-boned brow; these heavy eyes;
These calves, grown muscular with certainties;
This nose, three medium-sized pink strawberries
— But I exaggerate. In a little you will leave:
I'll hear, half squeal, half shriek, your laugh of greeting —
Then, *decrescendo*, bars of that strange speech
In which each sound sets out to seek each other,
Murders its own father, marries its own mother,
And ends as one grand transcendental vowel.

(Yet for all I know, the Egyptian Helen spoke so.)
As I look, the world contracts around you:
I see Brünnhilde had brown braids and glasses
She used for studying; Salome straight brown bangs,
A calf's brown eyes, and sturdy light-brown limbs
Dusted with cinnamon, an apple-dumpling's . . .

Many a beast has gnawn a leg off and got free,
Many a dolphin curved up from Necessity —
The trap has closed about you, and you sleep.
If someone questioned you, *What doest thou here?*
You'd knit your brows like an orangoutang
(But not so sadly; not so thoughtfully)
And answer with a pure heart, guilelessly:
I'm studying. . . .
         If only you were not!
Assignments,
      recipes,
          the *Official Rulebook*
Of Basketball — ah, let them go; you needn't mind.
The soul has no assignments, neither cooks
Nor referees: it wastes its time.
              It wastes its time.
Here in this enclave there are centuries
For you to waste: the short and narrow stream
Of Life meanders into a thousand valleys
Of all that was, or might have been, or is to be.
The books, just leafed through, whisper endlessly . . .
Yet it is hard. One sees in your blurred eyes
The "uneasy half-soul" Kipling saw in dogs'.
One sees it, in the glass, in one's own eyes.
In rooms alone, in galleries, in libraries,
In tears, in searchings of the heart, in staggering joys
We memorize once more our old creation,
Humanity: with what yawns the unwilling
Flesh puts on its spirit, O my sister!

So many dreams! And not one troubles
Your sleep of life? no self stares shadowily
From these worn hexahedrons, beckoning
With false smiles, tears? . . .
          Meanwhile Tatyana
Larina (gray eyes nickel with the moonlight
That falls through the willows onto Lensky's tomb;
Now young and shy, now old and cold and sure)
Asks, smiling: "But what is she dreaming of, fat thing?"
I answer: She's not fat. She isn't dreaming.
She purrs or laps or runs, all in her sleep;
Believes, awake, that she is beautiful;
She never dreams.

Those sunrise-colored clouds
Around man's head — that inconceivable enchantment
From which, at sunset, we come back to life
To find our graves dug, families dead, selves dying:
Of all this, Tanya, she is innocent.
For nineteen years she's faced reality:
They look alike already.
                They say, man wouldn't be
The best thing in this world — and isn't he? —
If he were not too good for it. But she
— She's good enough for it.
              And yet sometimes
Her sturdy form, in its pink strapless formal,
Is as if bathed in moonlight — modulated
Into a form of joy, a Lydian mode;
This Wooden Mean's a kind, furred animal
· That speaks, in the Wild of things, delighting riddles
To the soul that listens, trusting . . .
                 Poor senseless Life:
When, in the last light sleep of dawn, the messenger
Comes with his message, you will not awake.
He'll give his feathery whistle, shake you hard,
You'll look with wide eyes at the dewy yard
And dream, with calm slow factuality:
"Today's Commencement. My bachelor's degree
In Home Ec., my doctorate of philosophy
In Phys. Ed.
        [Tanya, they won't even *scan*]
Are waiting for me. . . ."
            Oh, Tatyana,
The Angel comes: better to squawk like a chicken
Than to say with truth, "But I'm a *good* girl,"
And Meet his Challenge with a last firm strange
Uncomprehending smile; and — then, then! — see
The blind date that has stood you up: your life.
(For all this, if it isn't, perhaps, life,
Has yet, at least, a language of its own
Different from the books'; worse than the books'.)
And yet, the ways we miss our lives are life.
Yet . . . yet . . .
        to have one's life add up to *yet!*

You sigh a shuddering sigh. Tatyana murmurs,
"Don't cry, little peasant"; leaves us with a swift
"Good-bye, good-bye . . . Ah, don't think ill of me . . ."
Your eyes open: you sit here thoughtlessly.

I love you — and yet — and yet — I love you.

Don't cry, little peasant. Sit and dream.
One comes, a finger's width beneath your skin,
To the braided maidens singing as they spin;
There sound the shepherd's pipe, the watchman's rattle
Across the short dark distance of the years.
I am a thought of yours: and yet, you do not think . . .
The firelight of a long, blind, dreaming story
Lingers upon your lips; and I have seen
Firm, fixed forever in your closing eyes,
The Corn King beckoning to his Spring Queen.

The Orient Express

One looks from the train
Almost as one looked as a child. In the sunlight
What I see still seems to me plain,
I am safe; but at evening
As the lands darken, a questioning
Precariousness comes over everything.

Once after a day of rain
I lay longing to be cold; and after a while
I was cold again, and hunched shivering
Under the quilt's many colors, gray
With the dull ending of the winter day.
Outside me there were a few shapes
Of chairs and tables, things from a primer;
Outside the window
There were the chairs and tables of the world. . . .
I saw that the world
That had seemed to me the plain
Gray mask of all that was strange
Behind it — all of that *was* — was all.

But it is beyond belief.
One thinks, "Behind everything
An unforced joy, an unwilling
Sadness (a willing sadness, a forced joy)
Moves changelessly"; one looks from the train
And there is something, the same thing
Behind everything: all these little villages,
A passing woman, a field of grain,
The man who says good-bye to his wife —
A path through a wood full of lives, and the train
Passing, after all unchangeable
And not now ever to stop, like a heart —

It is like any other work of art.
It is and never can be changed.
Behind everything there is always
The unknown unwanted life.

Well Water

What a girl called "the dailiness of life"
(Adding an errand to your errand. Saying,
"Since you're up . . ." Making you a means to
A means to a means to) is well water
Pumped from an old well at the bottom of the world.
The pump you pump the water from is rusty
And hard to move and absurd, a squirrel-wheel
A sick squirrel turns slowly, through the sunny
Inexorable hours. And yet sometimes
The wheel turns of its own weight, the rusty
Pump pumps over your sweating face the clear
Water, cold, so cold! you cup your hands
And gulp from them the dailiness of life.

Woman

"All things become thee, being thine," I think sometimes
As I think of you. I think: "How many faults
In thee have seemed a virtue!" While your taste is on my tongue
The years return, blessings innumerable
As the breaths that you have quickened, gild my flesh.
Lie there in majesty!

When, like Disraeli, I murmur
That you are more like a mistress than a wife,
More like an angel than a mistress; when, like Satan,
I hiss in your ear some vile suggestion,
Some delectable abomination,
You smile at me indulgently: "Men, men!"

You smile at mankind, recognizing in it
The absurd occasion of your fall.
For men — as your soap operas, as your *Home Journals*,
As your hearts whisper — men are only children.
And you believe them. Truly, you are children.

Should I love you so dearly if you weren't?
If I weren't?
                O morning star,
Each morning my dull heart goes out to you
And rises with the sun, but with the sun
Sets not, but all the long night nests within your eyes.

Men's share of grace, of all that can make bearable,
Lovable almost, the apparition, Man,
Has fallen to you. Erect, extraordinary
As a polar bear on roller skates, he passes
On into the Eternal . . .
                    From your pedestal, you watch
Admiringly, when you remember to.

Let us form, as Freud has said, "a group of two."
You are the best thing that this world can offer —
He said so. Or I remember that he said so;
If I am mistaken it's a Freudian error,
An error nothing but a man would make.
Women can't bear women. Cunningly engraved
On many an old wife's dead heart is "Women,
Beware women!" And yet it was a man
Sick of too much sweetness — of a life
Rich with a mother, wife, three daughters. a wife's sister,
An abyss of analysands — who wrote: "I cannot
Escape the notion (though I hesitate
To give it expression) that for women
The level of what is ethically normal
Is different from what it is in men.

778

Their superego" — he goes on without hesitation —
"Is never so inexorable, so impersonal,
So independent of its emotional
Origins as we require it in a man."

Did not the angel say to Abraham
That he would spare the cities of the plain
If there were found in them ten unjust women?
— That is to say, merciful; that is to say,
Extravagant; that is to say, unjust as judges
Who look past judgment, always, to the eyes
(Long-lashed, a scapegoat's, yearning sheepishly)
Under the curly-yarned and finger-tickling locks
Of that dear-wooled, inconsequential head.

You save him and knit an afghan from his hair.
And in the cold tomb, save for you, and afghanless,
He leaves you to wage wars, build bridges, visit women
Who like to run their fingers through his hair.
He complains of you to them, describing you
As "the great love of my life." What pains it took
To win you, a mere woman! — "worst of all,"
He ends, "a woman who was not my type."

But then, a woman never is a man's type.
Possessed by that prehistoric unforgettable
Other One, who never again is equaled
By anyone, he searches for his ideal,
The Good Whore who reminds him of his mother.
The realities are too much one or the other,
Too much like Mother or too bad . . . Too bad!
He resigns himself to them — as "they are, after all,
The best things that are offered in that line";
And should he not spare Nineveh, that city
Wherein are more than sixscore thousand women
Who cannot tell their left hand from their right,
But smile up hopefully at the policeman?

Are you as mercenary as the surveys show?
What a way to put it! Let us write instead
That you are realists; or as a realist might say,
Naturalists. It's in man's future — woman's nature
To want the best, and to be careless how it comes.

And what have we all to sell except ourselves?
Poor medlar, no sooner ripe than rotten!
You must be seized today, or stale tomorrow
Into a wife, a mother, a homemaker,
An Elector of the League of Women Voters.
Simply by your persistence, you betray
Yourselves and all that was yours, you momentary
And starry instances; are falling, falling
Into the sagging prison of your flesh,
Residuary legatees of earth, grandmothers
And legal guardians of the tribes of men.
If all Being showered down on you in gold
Would you not murmur, with averted breasts: "Not now"?

When he looks upon your nakedness he is blinded.
Your breasts and belly are one incandescence
Like the belly of an idol: how can a man go in that fire
And come out living? "The burnt child dreads the fire,"
He says later, warming his hands before the fire.
Last — last of all — he says that there are three things sure:
"That the Dog returns to his Vomit and the Sow returns to her Mire,
And the burnt Fool's bandaged finger goes wabbling back to the Fire."

Part of himself is shocked at part of himself
As, beside the remnants of a horrible
Steak, a little champagne, he confesses
Candidly to you: "In the beginning
There was a baby boy that loved his mother,
There was a baby girl that loved its mother.
The boy grew up and got to love a woman,
The girl grew up and had to love a man.
Because isn't that what's wrong with women? Men?
Isn't that the reason you're the way you are?
Why *are* you the way you are?"
                                        You say: "Because."

When you float with me through the Tunnel of Love
Or Chamber of Horrors — one of those concessions —
And a great hand, dripping, daggered, reaches out for you
And you scream, and it misses, and another hand,
Soiled, hairy, lustful, reaches out for you

And you faint, and it misses: when you come to,
You say, looking up weakly: "Did you notice?
The second one had on a wedding ring."

May the Devil fly away with the roof of the house
That you and I aren't happy in, you angel!
And yet, how quickly the bride's veils evaporate!
A girl hesitates a moment in mid-air
And settles to the ground a wife, a mother.
Each evening a tired spirit visits
Her full house; wiping his feet upon a mat
Marked *Women and Children First,* the husband looks
At this grown woman. She stands there in slacks
Among the real world's appliances,
Women, and children; kisses him hello
Just as, that morning, she kissed him goodbye,
And he sits down, till dinner, with the paper.
This home of theirs is haunted by a girl's
Ghost. At sunset a woodpecker knocks
At a tree by the window, asking their opinion
Of life. The husband answers, "Life is life,"
And when his wife calls to him from the kitchen
He tells her who it was, and what he wanted.
Beating the whites of seven eggs, the beater
Asks her her own opinion; she says, "Life
Is life." "See how it sounds to say it isn't,"
The beater tempts her. "Life is not life,"
She says. It sounds the same. Putting her cake
Into the oven, she is satisfied
Or else dissatisfied: it sounds the same.
With knitted brows, with care's swift furrows nightly
Smoothed out with slow care, and come again with care
Each morning, she lives out her gracious life.

But you should gush out over being like a spring
The drinker sighs to lift his mouth from: a dark source
That brims over, with its shining, every cup
That is brought to it in shadow, filled there, broken there.
You look at us out of sunlight and of shade,
Dappled, inexorable, the last human power.

All earth is the labyrinth along whose ways
You walk mirrored: rosy-fingered, many-breasted
As Diana of the Ephesians, strewing garments
Before the world's eyes narrowed in desire.
Now, naked on my doorstep, in the sun
Gold-armed, white-breasted, pink-cheeked, and black-furred,
You call to me, "Come"; and when I come say, "Go,"
Smiling your soft contrary smile . . .
                    He who has these
Is secure from the other sorrows of the world.
While you are how am I alone? Your voice
Soothes me to sleep, and finds fault with my dreams,
Till I murmur in my sleep: "Man is the animal
That finds fault."
           And you say: "Who said that?"

But be, as you have been, my happiness;
Let me sleep beside you, each night, like a spoon;
When, starting from my dreams, I groan to you,
May your *I love you* send me back to sleep.
At morning bring me, grayer for its mirroring,
The heavens' sun perfected in your eyes.

Thinking of the Lost World

This spoonful of chocolate tapioca
Tastes like — like peanut butter, like the vanilla
Extract Mama told me not to drink.
Swallowing the spoonful, I have already traveled
Through time to my childhood. It puzzles me
That age is like it.
           Come back to that calm country
Through which the stream of my life first meandered,
My wife, our cat, and I sit here and see
Squirrels quarreling in the feeder, a mockingbird
Copying our chipmunk, as our end copies
Its beginnings.
           Back in Los Angeles, we missed
Los Angeles. The sunshine of the Land
Of Sunshine is a gray mist now, the atmosphere
Of some factory planet: when you stand and look
You see a block or two, and your eyes water.

The orange groves are all cut down . . . My bow
Is lost, all my arrows are lost or broken,
My knife is sunk in the eucalyptus tree
Too far for even Pop to get it out,
And the tree's sawed down. It and the stair-sticks
And the planks of the tree house are all firewood
Burned long ago; its gray smoke smells of Vicks.

Twenty Years After, thirty-five years after, .
Is as good as ever — better than ever,
Now that D'Artagnan is no longer old —
Except that it is unbelievable.
I say to my old self: "I believe. Help thou
Mine unbelief."
            I believe the dinosaur
Or pterodactyl's married the pink sphinx
And lives with those Indians in the undiscovered
Country between California and Arizona
That the mad girl told me she was princess of —
Looking at me with the eyes of a lion,
Big, golden, without human understanding,
As she threw paper-wads from the back seat
Of the car in which I drove her with her mother
From the jail in Waycross to the hospital
In Daytona. If I took my eyes from the road
And looked back into her eyes, the car would — I'd be —

Or if only I could find a crystal set
Sometimes, surely, I could still hear their chief
Reading to them from Dumas or *Amazing Stories*;
If I could find in some Museum of Cars
Mama's dark blue Buick, Lucky's electric,
Couldn't I be driven there? Hold out to them,
The paraffin half picked out, Tawny's dewclaw —
And have walk to me from among their wigwams
My tall brown aunt, to whisper to me: "Dead?
They told you I was dead?"
                As if you could die!
If I never saw you, never again
Wrote to you, even, after a few years,
How often you've visited me, having put on,
As a mermaid puts on her sealskin, another face
And voice, that don't fool me for a minute —

That are yours for good . . . All of them are gone
Except for me; and for me nothing is gone —
The chicken's body is still going round
And round in widening circles, a satellite
From which, as the sun sets, the scientist bends
A look of evil on the unsuspecting earth.
Mama and Pop and Dandeen are still there
In the Gay Twenties.
                                   The Gay Twenties! You say
The Gay Nineties . . . But it's all right: they *were* gay,
O so gay! A certain number of years after,
Any time is Gay, to the new ones who ask:
"Was that the first World War or the second?"
Moving between the first world and the second,
I hear a boy call, now that my beard's gray:
"Santa Claus! Hi, Santa Claus!" It *is* miraculous
To have the children call you Santa Claus.
I wave back. When my hand drops to the wheel,
It is brown and spotted, and its nails are ridged
Like Mama's. Where's my own hand? My smooth
White bitten-fingernailed one? I seem to see
A shape in tennis shoes and khaki riding-pants
Standing there empty-handed; I reach out to it
Empty-handed, my hand comes back empty,
And yet my emptiness is traded for its emptiness,
I have found that Lost World in the Lost and Found
Columns whose gray illegible advertisements
My soul has memorized world after world:
LOST — NOTHING. STRAYED FROM NOWHERE. NO REWARD.
I hold in my own hands, in happiness,
Nothing: the nothing for which there's no reward.

JOHN BERRYMAN
1914–1972

The Ball Poem

What is the boy now, who has lost his ball,
What, what is he to do? I saw it go
Merrily bouncing, down the street, and then
Merrily over — there it is in the water!
No use to say "O there are other balls":

An ultimate shaking grief fixes the boy
As he stands rigid, trembling, staring down
All his young days into the harbour where
His ball went. I would not intrude on him,
A dime, another ball, is worthless. Now
He senses first responsibility
In a world of possessions. People will take balls,
Balls will be lost always, little boy,
And no one buys a ball back. Money is external.
He is learning, well behind his desperate eyes,
The epistemology of loss, how to stand up
Knowing what every man must one day know
And most know many days, how to stand up.
And gradually light returns to the street,
A whistle blows, the ball is out of sight,
Soon part of me will explore the deep and dark
Floor of the harbour . . I am everywhere,
I suffer and move, my mind and my heart move
With all that move me, under the water
Or whistling, I am not a little boy.

A Professor's Song

(. . rabid or dog-dull.) Let me tell you how
The Eighteenth Century couplet ended. Now
Tell me. Troll me the sources of that Song —
Assigned last week — by Blake. Come, come along,
Gentlemen. (Fidget and huddle, do. Squint soon.)
I want to end these fellows all by noon.

"That deep romantic chasm" — an early use;
The word is from the French, by our abuse
Fished out a bit. (Red all your eyes. O when?)
"A poet is a man speaking to men":
But I am then a poet, am I not? —
Ha ha. The radiator, please. Well, what?

Alive now — no — Blake would have written prose,
But movement following movement crisply flows,
So much the better, better the much so,
As burbleth Mozart. Twelve. The class can go.
Until I meet you, then, in Upper Hell
Convulsed, foaming immortal blood: farewell.

JOHN BERRYMAN

A Winter-piece to a Friend Away

Your letter came. — Glutted the earth & cold
With rains long heavy, follows intense frost;
      Snow howls and hides the world
We workt awhile to build; all the roads are lost;
Icy spiculae float, filling strange air;
No voice goes far; one is alone whirling since where,
      And when was it one crossed?
      You have been there.

I too the breaking blizzard's eddies bore
One year, another year; tempted to drop
      At my own feet forlorn
Under the warm fall, frantic more to chop
Wide with the gale until my thought ran numb
Clenching the blue skin tight against what white spikes come,
      And the sick brain estop.
      Your pendulum

Mine, not stilled wholly, has been sorry for,
Weeps from, and wonder instruct . . Unless I lied
      What word steadies that cord?
Glade grove & ghyll of antique childhood glide
Off; from our grown grief, weathers that appal,
The massive sorrow of the mental hospital,
      Friends & our good friends hide.
      They came to call.

Hardly theirs, moment when the tempest gains,
Loose heart convulses. Their hearts bend off dry,
      Their fruit dangles and fades.
— Solicitudes of the orchard heart, comply
A little with my longing, a little sing
Our sorrow among steel & glass, our stiffening,
      That hers may modify:
      O trembling Spring. —

Immortal risks our sort run, to a house
Reported in a wood . . mould upon bread
      And brain, breath giving out,
From farms we go by, barking, and shaken head,

786

The shrunk pears hang, Hölderlin's weathercock
Rattles to tireless wind, the fireless landscape rock,
　　Artists insane and dead
　　Strike like a clock:

If the fruit is dead, fast. Wait. Chafe your left wrist.
All these too lie, whither a true form strays.
　　Sweet when the lost arrive.
Foul sleet ices the twigs, the vision frays,
Festoons all signs; still as I come to name
My joy to you my joy springs up again the same, —
　　The thaw alone delays, —
　　Your letter came!

from Homage to Mistress Bradstreet

1

The Governor your husband lived so long
moved you not, restless, waiting for him? Still,
you were a patient woman —
I seem to see you pause here still:
Sylvester, Quarles, in moments odd you pored
before a fire at, bright eyes on the Lord,
all the children still.
"Simon . ." Simon will listen while you read a Song.

2

Outside the New World winters in grand dark
white air lashing high thro' the virgin stands
foxes down foxholes sigh,
surely the English heart quails, stunned.
I doubt if Simon than this blast, that sea,
spares from his rigour for your poetry
more. We are on each other's hands
who care. Both of our worlds unhanded us. Lie stark,

3

thy eyes look to me mild. Out of maize & air
your body's made, and moves. I summon, see,
from the centuries it.
I think you won't stay. How do we

linger, diminished, in our lovers' air,
implausibly visible, to whom, a year,
years, over interims; or not;
to a long stranger; or not; shimmer and disappear.

4
Jaw-ript, rot with its wisdom, rending then;
then not. When the mouth dies, who misses you?
Your master never died,
Simon ah thirty years past you —
Pockmarkt & westward staring on a haggard deck
it seems I find you, young. I come to check,
I come to stay with you,
and the Governor, & Father, & Simon, & the huddled men.

. . .

34
I trundle the bodies, on the iron bars,
over that fire backward & forth; they burn;
bits fall. I wonder if
I killed them. Women serve my turn.
— Dreams! You are good. — No. — Dense with hardihood
the wicked are dislodged, and lodged the good.
In green space we are safe.
God awaits us (but I am yielding) who Hell wars.

35
— I cannot feel myself God waits. He flies
nearer a kindly world; or he is flown.
One Saturday's rescue
won't show. Man is entirely alone
may be. I am a man of griefs & fits
trying to be my friend. And the brown smock splits,
down the pale flesh a gash
broadens and Time holds up your heart against my eyes.

36
— Hard and divided heaven! creases me. Shame
is failing. My breath is scented, and I throw
hostile glances towards God.
Crumpling plunge of a pestle, bray:

sin cross & opposite, wherein I survive
nightmares of Eden. Reaches foul & live
he for me, this soul
to crunch, a minute tangle of eternal flame.

37
I fear Hell's hammer-wind. But fear does wane.
Death's blossoms grain my hair; I cannot live.
A black joy clashes
joy, in twilight. The Devil said
"I will deal toward her softly, and her enchanting cries
will fool the horns of Adam." Father of lies,
a male great pestle smashes
small women swarming towards the mortar's rim in vain.

. . .

57
O all your ages at the mercy of my loves
together lie at once, forever or
so long as I happen.
In the rain of pain & departure, still
Love has no body and presides the sun,
and elfs from silence melody. I run.
Hover, utter, still,
a sourcing   whom my lost candle like the firefly loves.

from 77 Dream Songs

Life, friends, is boring. We must not say so (14)

Life, friends, is borning. We must not say so.
After all, the sky flashes, the great sea yearns,
we ourslves flash and yearn,
and moreover my mother told me as a boy
(repeatedly) "Ever to confess you're bored
means you have no

Inner Resources." I conclude now I have no
inner resources, because I am heavy bored.
Peoples bore me,
literature bores me, especially great literature,
Henry bores me, with his plights & gripes
as bad as achilles,

who loves people and valiant art, which bores me.
And the tranquil hills, & gin, look like a drag
and somehow a dog
has taken itself & its tail considerably away
into mountains or sea or sky, leaving
behind: me, wag.

. . .

A *Strut for Roethke*

Westward, hit a low note, for a roarer lost
across the Sound but north from Bremerton,
hit a way down note.
And never cadenza again of flowers, or cost.
Him who could really do that cleared his throat
& staggered on.

The bluebells, pool-shallows, saluted his over-needs,
while the clouds growled, heh-heh, & snapped, & crashed.

No stunt he'll ever unflinch once more will fail
(O lucky fellow, eh Bones?) — drifted off upstairs,
downstairs, somewheres.
No more daily, trying to hit the head on the nail:
thirstless: without a think in his head:
back from wherever, with it said.

Hit a high long note, for a lover found
needing a lower into friendlier ground
to bug among worms no more
around um jungles where ah blurt "What for?"
Weeds, too, he favoured as   most men don't favour men.
The Garden Master's gone.

from His Toy, His Dream, His Rest

A *Thurn* (126)

Among them marble where the man may lie
lie chieftains grand in final phase, or pause,
"O rare Ben Jonson",
dictator too, & the thinky other Johnson,
dictator too, backhanders down of laws,
men of fears, weird & sly.

Not of these least is borne to rest.
If grandeur & mettle prompted his lone journey
neither oh crowded shelves
nor this slab I celebrates attest
his complex slow fame forever (more or less).
I imagine the Abbey

among their wonders will be glad of him
whom some are sorry for   his griefs across the world
grievously understated
and grateful for that bounty, for bright whims
of heavy mind across the tiresome world
which the tiresome world debated, complicated.

.   .   .

Again, his friend's death
made the man sit still (127)

Again, his friend's death made the man sit still
and freeze inside — his daughter won first prize —
his wife scowled over at him —
It seemed to be Hallowe'en.
His friend's death had been adjudged suicide,
which dangles a trail

longer than Henry's chill, longer than his loss
and longer than the letter that he wrote
that day to the widow
to find out what the hell had happened thus.
All souls converge upon a hopeless mote
tonight, as though

the throngs of souls in hopeless pain rise up
to say they cannot care, to say they abide
whatever is to come.
My air is flung with souls which will not stop
and among them hangs a soul that has not died
and refuses to come home.

.   .   .

Henry's mind grew blacker
the more he thought (147)

Henry's mind grew blacker the more he thought.
He looked onto the world like the act of an aged whore.
Delmore, Delmore.
He flung to pieces and they hit the floor.
Nothing was true but what Marcus Aurelius taught,
"All that is foul smell & blood in a bag."

He lookt on the world like the leavings of a hag.
Almost his love died from him, any more.
His mother & William
were vivid in the same mail Delmore died.
The world is lunatic. This is the last ride.
Delmore, Delmore.

High in the summer branches the poet sang.
His throat ached, and he could sing no more.
All ears closed
across the heights where Delmore & Gertrude sprang
so long ago, in the goodness of which it was composed.
Delmore, Delmore!

. . .

This world is gradually becoming a place (149)

This world is gradually becoming a place
where I do not care to be any more. Can Delmore die?
I don't suppose
in all them years a day went ever by
without a loving thought for him. Welladay.
In the brightness of his promise,

unstained, I saw him thro' the mist of the actual
blazing with insight, warm with gossip
thro' all our Harvard years
when both of us were just becoming known
I got him out of a police-station once, in Washington, the world is *tref*
and grief too astray for tears.

I imagine you have heard the terrible news,
that Delmore Schwartz is dead, miserably & alone,
in New York: he sang me a song
"I am the Brooklyn poet Delmore Schwartz
Harms & the child I sing, two parents' torts"
when he was young & gift-strong.

. . .

So Long? Stevens (219)

He lifted up, among the actuaries,
a grandee crow. Ah ha & he crowed good.
That funny money-man.
Mutter we all must as well as we can.
He mutter spiffy. He make wonder Henry's
wits, though, with a odd

. . . something . . . something . . . not there in his flourishing art.
O veteran of death, you will not mind
a counter-mutter.
What was it missing, then, at the man's heart
so that he does not wound? It is our kind
to wound, as well as utter

a fact of happy world. That metaphysics
he hefted up until we could not breathe
the physics. *On our side,*
monotonous (or ever-fresh) — it sticks
in Henry's throat to judge — brilliant, he seethe;
better than us; less wide.

Henry's Understanding

He was reading late, at Richard's, down in Maine,
aged 32? Richard & Helen long in bed,
my good wife long in bed.
All I had to do was strip & get into my bed,
putting the marker in the book, & sleep,
& wake to a hot breakfast.

Off the coast was an island, P'tit Manaan,
the bluff from Richard's lawn was almost sheer.
A chill at four o'clock.
It only takes a few minutes to make a man.
A concentration upon now & here.
Suddenly, unlike Bach,

& horribly, unlike Bach, it occurred to me
that *one* night, instead of warm pajamas,
I'd take off all my clothes
& cross the damp cold lawn & down the bluff
into the terrible water & walk forever
under it out toward the island.

JEAN GARRIGUE
1914–1972

From Venice Was That Afternoon

From Venice was that afternoon
Though it was our land's canal we viewed.
There willows clove the bluish heat
By dropping leaf or two, gold green
And every tuft of hill beyond
Stood bright, distinct, as if preserved
By glass that sealed out light but not
Its gold or influence.
And floated on the speckled stream
A child of brilliant innocence
Where on the docks of green we stood
Naming it Love for its perfection.
This seemed to be . . .
But the current carried the leaves swiftly,
So flowed that child away from us,
So stared we sternly at the water's empty face.
Ah, in the greenhouse of that hour
Waited in the tare and sorrel
The mouth of fleshliness that stopped:
The leaves that dappled on that breast
The five-sensed image of our pleasance
Have now destroyed its lineaments.

For the waters of that afternoon
Flowed through Negation's glassy land
Where, in this civil, gate-closed hour
The verges of those waters now
Drown that joy that was our power.
What tyranny imposed this pride
That caused love's gift to be denied
And our destroying features to
Cast perpetually on its brow
The glass accepting no leaves now?
In rages of the intellect
We gave to heaven abstinence
Who said our love must issue from
No cisterns of the ruddy sun
But like the artifice of fountains
Leap from cold, infertile sources.
And our destroying features thus
Cast from that land its beingness
And strewed upon the green-fleshed hills
Sands of our darkening great ills.

The Stranger

Now upon this piteous year
I sit in Denmark beside the quai
And nothing that the fishers say
Or the children carrying boats
Can recall me from that place
Where sense and wish departed me
Whose very shores take on
The whiteness of anon.
For I beheld a stranger there
Who moved ahead of me
So tensile and so dancer made
That like a thief I followed her
Though my heart was so alive
I thought it equal to that beauty.
But when at last a turning came
Like the branching of a river
And I saw if she walked on
She would be gone forever,

Fear, then, so wounded me
As fell upon my ear
The voice a blind man dreams
And broke on me the smile
I dreamed as deaf men hear,
I stood there like a spy,
My tongue and eyelids taken
In such necessity.
Now upon this piteous year
The rains of Autumn fall.
Where may she be?
I suffered her to disappear
Who hunger in the prison of my fear.
That lean and brown, that stride,
That cold and melting pride,
For whom the river like a clear
Melodic line and the distant carrousel
Where lovers on their beasts of play
Rose and fell,
That wayfare where the swan adorned
With every wave and eddy
The honor of his sexual beauty,
Create her out of sorrow
That, never perishing,
Is a stately thing.

Forest

There is the star bloom of the moss
And the hairy chunks of light between the conifers;
There are alleys of light where the green leads to a funeral
Down the false floor of needles.
There are rocks and boulders that jut, saw-toothed and urine-yellow.
Other stones in a field look in the distance like sheep grazing,
Grey trunk and trunklike legs and lowered head.
There are short-stemmed forests so close to the ground
You would pity a dog lost there in the spore-budding
Blackness where the sun has never struck down.
There are dying ferns that glow like a gold mine
And weeds and sumac extend the Sodom of color.
Among the divisions of stone and the fissures of branch
Lurk the abashed resentments of the ego.

Do not say this is pleasurable!
Bats, skittering on wires over the lake,
And the bug on the water, bristling in light as he measures forward his
    leaps,
The hills holding back the sun by their notched edges
(What volcanoes lie on the other side
Of heat, light, burning up even the angels)
And the mirror of forests and hills drawing nearer
Till the lake is all forests and hills made double,
Do not say this is kindly, convenient,
Warms the hands, crosses the senses with promise,
Harries our fear.
Uneasy, we bellow back at the tree frogs
And, night approaching like the entrance of a tunnel,
We would turn back and cannot, we
Surprise our natures; the woods lock us up
In the secret crimes of our intent.

Primer of Plato

All endeavor to be beautiful:
The loved and the loveless as well:
All women rob from duty's time
To pitch adornment to its prime.
The lion in his golden coat
Begets his joy by that; his mate
Beneath that fiery mane repeats
The fury of each sudden sense.
The swan reflecting on the stream
The opposite feathers of the swan-
Webbed dream is like the fox at night
Who glows as in original delight.
Not least, the sun in tedious round
Bestows on rock and land
Principles that all creation
Imitates in adoration.

I never knew this till I
Chanced to see how your bright cheek
Brightened from the gaze of one
Whose spirit swam a Hellespont.

I saw then that beauty was
Both for lover and beloved a feast,
The lover mirroring by his joy
That flush beauty brings, in
His eye her actual face globed small,
And beauty flattered by that glass
Pitched to its highest comeliness,
Doubled and increased until
All would seem
Derived back into first essence.
Both animals and men dwell
In such a mirror of the real
Until a sudden ecstasy
They break the boundaries of that glass
To be the image each first was.

ROBERT LOWELL
b. 1917

As a Plane Tree by the Water

Darkness has called to darkness, and disgrace
Elbows about our windows in this planned
Babel of Boston where our money talks
And multiplies the darkness of a land
Of preparation where the Virgin walks
And roses spiral her enamelled face
Or fall to splinters on unwanted streets.
Our Lady of Babylon, go by, go by,
I was once the apple of your eye;
Flies, flies are on the plane tree, on the streets.

The flies, the flies, the flies of Babylon
Buzz in my ear-drums while the devil's long
Dirge of the people detonates the hour
For floating cities where his golden tongue
Enchants the masons of the Babel Tower
To raise tomorrow's city to the sun
That never sets upon these hell-fire streets
Of Boston, where the sunlight is a sword
Striking at the withholder of the Lord:
Flies, flies are on the plane tree, on the streets.

Flies strike the miraculous waters of the iced
Atlantic and the eyes of Bernadette
Who saw Our Lady standing in the cave
At Massabielle, saw her so squarely that
Her vision put out reason's eyes. The grave
Is open-mouthed and swallowed up in Christ.
O walls of Jericho! And all the streets
To our Atlantic wall are singing: "Sing,
Sing for the resurrection of the King."
Flies, flies are on the plane tree, on the streets.

The Quaker Graveyard in Nantucket

(For Warren Winslow, dead at sea)

*Let man have dominion over the fishes of the sea and the
fowls of the air and the beasts and the whole earth, and
every creeping creature that moveth upon the earth.*

I

A brackish reach of shoal off Madaket, —
The sea was still breaking violently and night
Had steamed into our North Atlantic Fleet,
When the drowned sailor clutched the drag-net. Light
Flashed from his matted head and marble feet,
He grappled at the net
With the coiled, hurdling muscles of his thighs:
The corpse was bloodless, a botch of reds and whites,
Its open, staring eyes
Were lustreless dead-lights
Or cabin-windows on a stranded hulk
Heavy with sand. We weight the body, close
Its eyes and heave it seaward whence it came,
Where the heel-headed dogfish barks its nose
On Ahab's void and forehead; and the name
Is blocked in yellow chalk.
Sailors, who pitch this portent at the sea
Where dreadnoughts shall confess
Its heel-bent deity,
When you are powerless
To sand-bag this Atlantic bulwark, faced
By the earth-shaker, green, unwearied, chaste

In his steel scales: ask for no Orphean lute
To pluck life back. The guns of the steeled fleet
Recoil and then repeat
The hoarse salute.

II

All you recovered from Poseidon died
With you, my cousin, and the harrowed brine
Is fruitless on the blue beard of the god,
Stretching beyond us to the castles in Spain,
Nantucket's westward haven. To Cape Cod
Guns, cradled on the tide,
Blast the eelgrass about a waterclock
Of bilge and backwash, roil the salt and sand
Lashing earth's scaffold, rock
Our warships in the hand
Of the great God, where time's contrition blues
Whatever it was these Quaker sailors lost
In the mad scramble of their lives. They died
When time was open-eyed,
Wooden and childish; only bones abide
There, in the nowhere, where their boats were tossed
Sky-high, where mariners had fabled news
Of IS, the whited monster. What it cost
Them is their secret. In the sperm-whale's slick
I see the Quakers drown and hear their cry:
"If God himself had not been on our side,
If God himself had not been on our side,
When the Atlantic rose against us, why,
Then it had swallowed us up quick."

III

When the whale's viscera go and the roll
Of its corruption shall overrun this world,
Beyond tree-swept Nantucket and Wood's Hole
And Martha's Vineyard, Sailor, will your sword
Whistle and fall and sink into the fat?
In the great ash-pit of Jehoshaphat
The bones cry for the blood of the white whale,
The fat flukes and whack about its ears,
The death-lance churns into the sanctuary, tears
The gun-blue swingle, heaving like a flail,
And hacks the coiling life out: it works and drags

And rips the sperm-whale's midriff into rags,
Gobbets of blubber spill to wind and weather,
Sailor, and gulls go round the stoven timbers
Where the morning stars sing out together
And thunder shakes the white surf and dismembers
The red flag hammered in the mast-head. Hide,
Our steel, Jonas Messias, in Thy side.

IV

You could cut the brackish winds with a knife
Here in Nantucket, and cast up the time
When the Lord God formed man from the sea's slime
And breathed into his face the breath of life,
And blue-lung'd combers lumbered to the kill.
The Lord survives the rainbow of His will.

The Drunken Fisherman

Wallowing in this bloody sty,
I cast for fish that pleased my eye
(Truly Jehovah's bow suspends
No pots of gold to weight its ends);
Only the blood-mouthed rainbow trout
Rose to my bait. They flopped about . . .

A calendar to tell the day;
A handkerchief to wave away
The gnats; a couch unstuffed with storm
Pouching a bottle in one arm;
A whisky bottle full of worms . . .

Once fishing was a rabbit's foot —
O wind blow cold, O wind blow hot,
Let suns stay in or suns step out:
Life danced a jig on the sperm whale's spout . . .

Now the hot river, ebbing, hauls
Its bloody waters into holes;
A grain of sand inside my shoe
Mimics the moon that might undo
Man and Creation too.

Is there no way to cast my hook
Out of this dynamited brook?

I will catch Christ with a greased worm,
And when the Prince of Darkness stalks
My bloodstream to its Stygian term . . .
On water the Man-Fisher walks.

At the Indian Killer's Grave

Here, also, are the veterans of King Philip's War who
burned villages and slaughtered young and old, with pious
fierceness, while the godly souls throughout the land were
helping them with prayer.　　　　　HAWTHORNE

Behind King's Chapel what the earth has kept
Whole from the jerking noose of time extends
Its dark enigma to Jehoshaphat;
Or will King Philip plait
The just man's scalp in the wailing valley! Friends,
Blacker than these black stones the subway bends
About the dirty elm roots and the well
For the unchristened infants in the waste
Of the great garden rotten to its roots;
Death, the engraver, puts forward his bone foot
And Grace-with-wings and Time-on-wings compel
All this antique abandon of the disgraced
To face Jehovah's buffets and his ends.

The dusty leaves and frizzled lilacs gear
This garden of the elders with baroque
And prodigal embellishments but smoke,
Settling upon the pilgrims and their grounds,
Espouses and confounds
Their dust with the off-scourings of the town:
The libertarian crown
Of England built their mausoleum. Here
A clutter of Bible and weeping willows guards
The stern Colonial magistrates and wards
Of Charles the Second, and the clouds
Weep on the just and unjust as they will, —
For the poor dead cannot see Easter crowds
On Boston Common or the Beacon Hill

Where strangers hold the golden Statehouse dome
For good and always. Where they live is home:
A common with an iron railing: here
Frayed cables wreathe the spreading cenotaph
Of John and Mary Winslow and the laugh
Of Death is hacked in sandstone, in their year.

When we go down this man-hole to the drains,
The doorman barricades us in and out;
We wait upon his pleasure. All about
The pale, sand-coloured, treeless chains
Of T-squared buildings strain
To curb the spreading of the braced terrain;
When you go down this hole, perhaps your pains
Will be rewarded well; no rough-cast house
Will bed and board you in King's Chapel. Here
A public servant putters with a knife
And paints the railing red
Forever, as a mouse
Cracks walnuts by the headstones of the dead
Whose chiselled angels peer
At you, as if their art were long as life.

I ponder on the railing at this park:
Who was the man who sowed the dragon's teeth,
That fabulous or fancied patriarch
Who sowed so ill for his descent, beneath
King's Chapel in this underworld and dark?
John, Matthew, Luke and Mark,
Gospel me to the Garden, let me come
Where Mary twists the warlock with her flowers —
Her soul a bridal chamber fresh with flowers
And her whole body an ecstatic womb,
As through the trellis peers the sudden Bridegroom.

In the Cage

The lifers file into the hall,
According to their houses — twos
Of laundered denim. On the wall
A colored fairy tinkles blues

And titters by the balustrade;
Canaries beat their bars and scream.
We come from tunnels where the spade
Pick-axe and hod for plaster steam
In mud and insulation. Here
The Bible-twisting Israelite
Fasts for his Harlem. It is night,
And it is vanity, and age
Blackens the heart of Adam. Fear,
The yellow chirper, beaks its cage.

Mr. Edwards and the Spider

I saw the spiders marching through the air,
Swimming from tree to tree that mildewed day
     In latter August when the hay
     Came creaking to the barn. But where
          The wind is westerly,
     Where gnarled November makes the spiders fly
     Into the apparitions of the sky,
     They purpose nothing but their ease and die
Urgently beating east to sunrise and the sea;

What are we in the hands of the great God?
It was in vain you set up thorn and briar
     In battle array against the fire
     And treason cracking in your blood;
          For the wild thorns grow tame
     And will do nothing to oppose the flame;
     Your lacerations tell the losing game
     You play against a sickness past your cure.
How will the hands be strong? How will the heart endure?

A very little thing, a little worm,
Or hourglass-blazoned spider, it is said,
     Can kill a tiger. Will the dead
     Hold up his mirror and affirm
          Against the four winds the smell
     And flash of his authority? It's well
     If God who holds you to the pit of hell,
     Much as one holds a spider, will destroy,
Baffle and dissipate your soul. As a small boy

On Windsor Marsh, I saw the spider die
When thrown into the bowels of fierce fire:
　　There's no long struggle, no desire
　　To get up on its feet and fly —
　　　　It stretches out its feet
　　And dies. This is the sinner's last retreat;
　　Yes, and no strength exerted on the heat
Then sinews the abolished will, when sick
And full of burning, it will whistle on a brick.

But who can plumb the sinking of that soul?
Josiah Hawley, picture yourself cast
　　Into a brick-kiln where the blast
　　Fans your quick vitals to a coal —
　　　　If measured by a glass,
　　How long would it seem burning! Let there pass
　　A minute, ten, ten trillion; but the blaze
Is infinite, eternal: this is death,
To die and know it. This is the Black Widow, death.

Beyond the Alps

*(On the train from Rome to Paris, 1950, the year when Pius
XII defined the dogma of Mary's bodily assumption.)*

Reading how even the Swiss had thrown the sponge
in once again and Everest was still
unscaled, I watched our Paris pullman lunge
mooning across the fallow Alpine snow.
O bella Roma! I saw our stewards go
forward on tiptoe banging on their gongs.
Man changed to landscape. Much against my will,
I left the City of God where it belongs.
There the skirt-mad Mussolini unfurled
the eagle of Caesar. He was one of us
only, pure prose. I envy the conspicuous
waste of our grandparents on their grand tours —
long-haired Victorian sages accepted the universe,
while breezing on their trust funds through the world.

When the Vatican made Mary's Assumption dogma,
the crowds at San Pietro screamed *Papa.*
The Holy Father dropped his shaving glass,

and listened. His electric razor purred,
his pet canary chirped on his left hand.
The lights of science couldn't hold a candle
to Mary risen — at one miraculous stroke,
angel-wing'd, gorgeous as a jungle bird!
But who believed this? Who could understand?
Pilgrims still kissed Saint Peter's brazen sandal.
The Duce's lynched, bare, booted skull still spoke.
God herded his people to the *coup de grâce* —
the costumed Switzers sloped their pikes to push,
O Pius, through the monstrous human crush. . . .

I thought of Ovid. For in Caesar's eyes
that tomcat had the Number of the Beast,
and now where Turkey faces the red east,
and the twice-stormed Crimean spit, he lies.
Rome asked for poets. At her beck and call,
came Lucan, Tacitus and Juvenal,
the *black republicans* who tore the tits
and bowels of the Mother Wolf to bits.
Killer and army-commander waved the rod
of empire over the Caesars' salvaged bog . . .
"Imperial Tiber, Oh my yellow dog,
black earth by the black Roman sea, I lie
with the boy-crazy daughter of the God.
il duce Augusto. I shall never die."

Our mountain-climbing train had come to earth.
Tired of the querulous hush-hush of the wheels,
the blear-eyed ego kicking in my berth
lay still, and saw Apollo plant his heels
on terra firma through the morning's thigh . . .
each backward, wasted Alp, a Parthenon,
fire-branded socket of the Cyclop's eyes.
There are no tickets for that altitude
once held by Hellsa, when the Goddess stood,
prince, pope, philosopher and golden bough,
pure mind and murder at the scything prow —
Minerva, the miscarriage of the brain.

Now Paris, our black classic, breaking up
like killer kings on an Etruscan cup.

Memories of West Street and Lepke

Only teaching on Tuesdays, book-worming
in pajamas fresh from the washer each morning,
I hog a whole house on Boston's
"hardly passionate Marlborough Street",
where even the man
scavenging filth in the back alley trash cans,
has two children, a beach wagon, a helpmate,
and is "a young Republican."
I have a nine months' daughter,
young enough to be my granddaughter.
Like the sun she rises in her flame-flamingo infants' wear.

These are the tranquillized *Fifties*,
and I am forty. Ought I to regret my seedtime?
I was a fire-breathing Catholic C.O.,
and made my manic statement,
telling off the state and president, and then
sat waiting sentence in the bull pen
beside a negro boy with curlicues
of marijuana in his hair.

Given a year,
I walked on the roof of the West Street Jail, a short
enclosure like my school soccer court,
and saw the Hudson River once a day
through sooty clothesline entanglements
and bleaching khaki tenements.
Strolling, I yammered metaphysics with Abramowitz,
a jaundice-yellow ("it's really tan")
and fly-weight pacifist,
so vegetarian,
he wore rope shoes and preferred fallen fruit.
He tried to convert Bioff and Brown,
the Hollywood pimps, to his diet.
Hairy, muscular, suburban,
wearing chocolate double-breasted suits,
they blew their tops and beat him black and blue.

I was so out of things, I'd never heard
of the Jehovah's Witnesses.
"Are you a C.O.?" I asked a fellow jailbird.

"No," he answered, "I'm a J.W."
He taught me the hospital "tuck,"
and pointed out the T-shirted back
of *Murder Incorporated's* Czar Lepke,
there piling towels on a rack,
or dawdling off to his little segregated cell full
of things forbidden the common man:
a portable radio, a dresser, two toy American
flags tied together with a ribbon of Easter palm.
Flabby, bald, lobotomized,
he drifted in a sheepish calm,
where no agonizing reappraisal
jarred his concentration on the electric chair —
hanging like an oasis in his air
of lost connections . . .

Skunk Hour

(For Elizabeth Bishop)

Nautilus Island's hermit
heiress still lives through winter in her Spartan cottage;
her sheep still graze above the sea.
Her son's a bishop. Her farmer
is first selectman in our village,
she's in her dotage.

Thirsting for
the hierarchic privacy
of Queen Victoria's century,
she buys up all
the eyesores facing her shore,
and lets them fall.

The season's ill —
we've lost our summer millionaire,
who seemed to leap from an L. L. Bean
catalogue. His nine-knot yawl
was auctioned off to lobstermen.
A red fox stain covers Blue Hill.

And now our fairy
decorator brightens his shop for fall,
his fishnet's filled with orange cork,
orange, his cobbler's bench and awl,
there is no money in his work,
he'd rather marry.

One dark night,
my Tudor Ford climbed the hill's skull,
I watched for love-cars. Lights turned down,
they lay together, hull to hull,
where the graveyard shelves on the town. . . .
My mind's not right.

A car radio bleats,
"Love, O careless Love . . ." I hear
my ill-spirit sob in each blood cell,
as if my hand were at its throat . . .
I myself am hell,
nobody's here —

only skunks, that search
in the moonlight for a bite to eat.
They march on their soles up Main Street:
white stripes, moonstruck eyes' red fire
under the chalk-dry and spar spire
of the Trinitarian Church.

I stand on top
of our back steps and breathe the rich air —
a mother skunk with her column of kittens swills the garbage pail
She jabs her wedge head in a cup
of sour cream, drops her ostrich tail,
and will not scare.

Water

It was a Maine lobster town —
Each morning boatloads of hands
pushed off for granite
quarries on the islands,

and left dozens of bleak
white frame houses stuck
like oyster shells
on a hill of rock,

and below us, the sea lapped
the raw little match-stick
mazes of a weir
where the fish for bait were trapped.

Remember? We sat on a slab of rock.
From this distance in time,
it seems the color
of iris, rotting and turning purpler,

but it was only
the usual gray rock
turning the usual green
when drenched by the sea.

The sea drenched the rock
at our feet all day,
and kept tearing away
flake after flake.

One night you dreamed
you were a mermaid clinging to a wharf-pile,
and trying to pull
off the barnacles with your hands.
We wished our two souls
might return like gulls
to the rock. In the end,
the water was too cold for us.

The Old Flame

My old flame, my wife!
Remember our lists of birds?
One morning last summer, I drove
by our house in Maine. It was still
on top of its hill —

Now a red ear of Indian maize
was splashed on the door.
Old Glory with thirteen stripes
hung on a pole. The clapboard
was old-red schoolhouse red.

Inside, a new landlord,
a new wife, a new broom!
Atlantic seaboard antique shop
pewter and plunder
shone in each room.

A new frontier!
No running next door
now to phone the sheriff
for his taxi to Bath
and the State Liquor Store!

No one saw your ghostly
imaginary lover
stare through the window,
and tighten
the scarf at his throat.

Health to the new people,
health to their flag, to their old
restored house on the hill!
Everything had been swept bare,
furnished, garnished and aired.

Everything's changed for the best —
how quivering and fierce we were,
there snowbound together,
simmering like wasps
in our tent of books!

Poor ghost, old love, speak
with your old voice
of flaming insight
that kept us awake all night.
In one bed and apart,

we heard the plow
groaning up hill —
a red light, then a blue,
as it tossed off the snow
to the side of the road.

For the Union Dead

"Relinquunt Omnia Servare Rem Publicam."

The old South Boston Aquarium stands
in a Sahara of snow now. Its broken windows are boarded.
The bronze weathervane cod has lost half its scales.
The airy tanks are dry.

Once my nose crawled like a snail on the glass;
my hand tingled
to burst the bubbles
drifting from the noses of the cowed, compliant fish.

My hand draws back. I often sigh still
for the dark downward and vegetating kingdom
of the fish and reptile. One morning last March,
I pressed against the new barbed and galvanized

fence on the Boston Common. Behind their cage,
yellow dinosaur steamshovels were grunting
as they cropped up tons of mush and grass
to gouge their underworld garage.

Parking spaces luxuriate like civic
sandpiles in the heart of Boston.
A girdle of orange, Puritan-pumpkin colored girders
braces the tingling Statehouse,

shaking over the excavations, as it faces Colonel Shaw
and his bell-cheeked Negro infantry
on St. Gaudens' shaking Civil War relief,
propped by a plank splint against the garage's earthquake.

Two months after marching through Boston,
half the regiment was dead;
at the dedication,
William James could almost hear the bronze Negroes breathe.

Their monument sticks like a fishbone
in the city's throat.
Its Colonel is as lean
as a compass-needle.

He has an angry wrenlike vigilance,
a greyhound's gentle tautness;
he seems to wince at pleasure,
and suffocate for privacy.

He is out of bounds now. He rejoices in man's lovely,
peculiar power to choose life and die —
when he leads his black soldiers to death,
he cannot bend his back.

On a thousand small town New England greens,
the old white churches hold their air
of sparse, sincere rebellion; frayed flags
quilt the graveyards of the Grand Army of the Republic.

The stone statues of the abstract Union Soldier
grow slimmer and younger each year —
wasp-wasted, they doze over muskets
and muse through their sideburns . . .

Shaw's father wanted no monument
except the ditch,
where his son's body was thrown
and lost with his "niggers."

The ditch is nearer.
There are no statues for the last war here;
on Boylston Street, a commercial photograph
shows Hiroshima boiling

over a Mosler Safe, the "Rock of Ages"
that survived the blast. Space is nearer.
When I crouch to my television set,
the drained faces of Negro school-children rise like balloons.

Colonel Shaw
is riding on his bubble,
he waits
for the blesséd break.

The Aquarium is gone. Everywhere,
giant finned cars nose forward like fish;
a savage servility
slides by on grease.

Waking Early Sunday Morning

O to break loose, like the chinook
salmon jumping and falling back,
nosing up to the impossible
stone and bone-crushing waterfall —
raw-jawed, weak-fleshed there, stopped by ten
steps of the roaring ladder, and then
to clear the top on the last try,
alive enough to spawn and die.

Stop, back off. The salmon breaks
water, and now my body wakes
to feel the unpolluted joy
and criminal leisure of a boy —
no rainbow smashing a dry fly
in the white run is free as I,
here squatting like a dragon on
time's hoard before the day's begun!

Vermin run for their unstopped holes;
in some dark nook a fieldmouse rolls
a marble, hours on end, then stops;
the termite in the woodwork sleeps —
listen, the creatures of the night
obsessive, casual, sure of foot,
go on grinding, while the sun's
daily remorseful blackout dawns.

Fierce, fireless mind, running downhill.
Look up and see the harbor fill:
business as usual in eclipse
goes down to the sea in ships —
wake of refuse, dacron rope,
bound for Bermuda or Good Hope,
all bright before the morning watch
the wine-dark hulls of yawl and ketch.

I watch a glass of water wet
with a fine fuzz of icy sweat,
silvery colors touched with sky,
serene in their neutrality —
yet if I shift, or change my mood,
I see some object made of wood,
background behind it of brown grain,
to darken it, but not to stain.

O that the spirit could remain
tinged but untarnished by its strain!
Better dressed and stacking birch,
or lost with the Faithful at Church —
anywhere, but somewhere else!
And now the new electric bells,
clearly chiming, "Faith of our fathers,"
and now the congregation gathers.

O Bible chopped and crucified
in hymns we hear but do not read,
none of the milder subtleties
of grace or art will sweeten these
stiff quatrains shovelled out four-square —
they sing of peace, and preach despair;
yet they gave darkness some control,
and left a loophole for the soul.

No, put old clothes on, and explore
the corners of the woodshed for
its dregs and dreck: tools with no handle,
ten candle-ends not worth a candle,
old lumber banished from the Temple,
damned by Paul's precept and example,
cast from the kingdom, banned in Israel,
the wordless sign, the tinkling cymbal.

When will we see Him face to face?
Each day, He shines through darker glass —
In this small town where everything
is known, I see His vanishing
emblems, His white spire and flag-
pole sticking out above the fog,
like old white china doorknobs, sad,
slight, useless things to calm the mad.

Hammering military splendor,
top-heavy Goliath in full armor —
little redemption in the mass
liquidations of their brass,
elephant and phalanx moving
with the times and still improving,
when that kingdom hit the crash:
a million foreskins stacked like trash . . .

Sing softer! But what if a new
diminuendo brings no true
tenderness, only restlessness,
excess, the hunger for success,
sanity of self-deception
fixed and kicked by reckless caution,
while we listen to the bells —
anywhere, but somewhere else!

O to break loose. All life's grandeur
is something with a girl in summer . . .
elated as the President
girdled by his establishment
this Sunday morning, free to chaff
his own thoughts with his bear-cuffed staff,
swimming nude, unbuttoned, sick
of his ghost-written rhetoric!

No weekends for the gods now. Wars
flicker, earth licks its open sores,
fresh breakage, fresh promotions, chance
assassinations, no advance.
Only man thinning out his kind
sounds through the Sabbath noon, the blind
swipe of the pruner and his knife
busy about the tree of life . . .

Pity the planet, all joy gone
from this sweet volcanic cone;
peace to our children when they fall
in small war on the heels of small
war — until the end of time
to police the earth, a ghost
orbiting forever lost
in our monotonous sublime.

Near the Ocean

(For E.H.L.)

The house is filled. The last heartthrob
thrills through her flesh. The hero stands,
stunned by the applauding hands,
and lifts her head to please the mob . . .
No, young and starry-eyed, the brother
and sister wait before their mother,
old iron-bruises, powder, "Child,
these breasts . . ." He knows. And if she's killed

his treadmill heart will never rest —
his wet mouth pressed to some slack breast,
or shifting over on his back . . .
The severed radiance filters back,
athirst for nightlife — gorgon head,
fished up from the Aegean dead,
with all its stranded snakes uncoiled,
here beheaded and despoiled.

We hear the ocean. Older seas
and deserts give asylum, peace
to each abortion and mistake.
Lost in the Near Eastern dreck,
the tyrant and tyrannicide
lie like the bridegroom and the bride;
the battering ram, abandoned, prone,
beside the apeman's phallic stone.

Betrayals! Was it the first night?
They stood against a black and white
inland New England backdrop. No dogs
there, horse or hunter, only frogs
chirring from the dark trees and swamps.
Elms watching like extinguished lamps.
Knee-high hedges of black sheep
encircling them at every step.

Some subway-green coldwater flat,
its walls tattooed with neon light,
then high delirious squalor, food
burned down with vodka . . . menstrual blood
caking the covers, when they woke
to the dry, childless Sunday walk,
saw cars on Brooklyn Bridge descend
through steel and coal dust to land's end.

Was it years later when they met,
and summer's coarse last-quarter drought
had dried the hardveined elms to bark —
lying like people out of work,
dead sober, cured, recovered, on
the downslope of some gritty green,
all access barred with broken glass;
and dehydration browned the grass?

Is it this shore? Their eyes worn white
as moons from hitting bottom? Night,
the sandfleas scissoring their feet,
the sandbed cooling to concrete,
one borrowed blanket, lights of cars
shining down at them like stars? . . .
Sand built the lost Atlantis . . . sand,
Atlantic ocean, condoms, sand.

Sleep, sleep. The ocean, grinding stones,
can only speak the present tense;
nothing will age, nothing will last,
or take corruption from the past.
A hand, your hand then! I'm afraid
to touch the crisp hair on your head —
Monster loved for what you are,
till time, that buries us, lay bare.

Dolphin

My Dolphin, you only guide me by surprise,
a captive as Racine, the man of craft,
drawn through his maze of iron composition
by the incomparable wandering voice of Phèdre.
When I was troubled in mind, you made for my body
caught in its hangman's-knot of sinking lines,
the glassy bowing and scraping of my will. . . .
I have sat and listened to too many
words of the collaborating muse,
and plotted perhaps too freely with my life,
not avoiding injury to others,
not avoiding injury to myself —
to ask compassion . . . this book, half fiction,
an eelnet made by man for the eel fighting —

my eyes have seen what my hand did.

T. S. Eliot

Caught between two streams of traffic, in the gloom
of Memorial Hall and Harvard's war-dead. . . . And he:
"Don't you loathe to be compared with your relatives?
I do. I've just found two of mine reviewed by Poe.
He wiped the floor with them . . . and I was *delighted*."
Then on with warden's pace across the Yard,
talking of Pound, "It's balls to say he only
pretends to be Ezra. . . . He's better though. This year,
he no longer wants to rebuild the Temple at Jerusalem.
Yes, he's better. 'You speak,' he said, when he'd talked two hours.
By then I had absolutely nothing to *say*."
Ah Tom, one muse, one music, had one your luck —
lost in the dark night of the brilliant talkers,
humor and honor from the everlasting dross!

Ezra Pound

Horizontal on a deckchair in the ward
of the criminal mad. . . . A man without shoestrings clawing
the Social Credit broadside from your table, you saying,
". . . here with a black suit and black briefcase; in the brief,

an abomination, Possum's *hommage* to Milton."
Then sprung; Rapallo, and the decade gone;
and three years later, Eliot dead, you saying,
"Who's left alive to understand my jokes?
My old Brother in the arts . . . besides, he was a smash of a poet."
You showed me your blotched, bent hands, saying, "Worms.
When I talked that nonsense about Jews on the Rome
wireless, Olga knew it was shit, and still loved me."
And I, "Who else has been in Purgatory?"
You, "I began with a swelled head and end with swelled feet."

For John Berryman I

I feel I know what you have worked through, you
know what I have worked through — we are words;
John, we used the language as if we made it.
Luck threw up the coin, and the plot swallowed,
monster yawning for its mess of potage.
Ah privacy, as if we had preferred mounting
some rock by a mossy stream and counting the sheep . . .
to fame that renews the soul but not the heart.
The out-tide flings up wonders: rivers, linguini,
beercans, mussels, bloodstreams; how gaily they gallop
to catch the ebb — Herbert, Thoreau, Pascal,
born to die with the enlarged hearts of athletes at forty —
Abraham sired with less expectancy,
heaven his friend, the earth his follower.

Last Things, Black Pines at 4 a.m.

Imperfect enough once for all at thirty,
in his last days Van Gogh painted as if
he were hurling everything he had: clothes,
bed and furniture against the door
to keep out a robber — he would have roughened
my black pines imperceptibly withdrawing
from the blue back cold of morning sky,
black pines disengaging from blue ice —
for imperfection is the language of art.
Even the best writer in his best lines

820

is incurably imperfect, crying for truth, knowledge,
honesty, inspiration he cannot have —
after a show of effort, Valéry
and Trollope the huntsman are happy to drop out.

GWENDOLYN BROOKS
b. 1917

A Song in the Front Yard

I've stayed in the front yard all my life.
I want a peek at the back
Where it's rough and untended and hungry weed grows.
A girl gets sick of a rose.

I want to go in the back yard now
And maybe down the alley,
To where the charity children play.
I want a good time today.

They do some wonderful things.
They have some wonderful fun.
My mother sneers, but I say it's fine
How they don't have to go in at quarter to nine.
My mother, she tells me that Johnnie Mae
Will grow up to be a bad woman.
That George'll be taken to Jail soon or late
(On account of last winter he sold our back gate).

But I say it's fine. Honest, I do.
And I'd like to be a bad woman, too,
And wear the brave stockings of night-black lace
And strut down the streets with paint on my face.

Sadie and Maud

Maud went to college.
Sadie stayed at home.
Sadie scraped life
With a fine-tooth comb.

She didn't leave a tangle in.
Her comb found every strand.
Sadie was one of the livingest chits
In all the land.

Sadie bore two babies
Under her maiden name.
Maud and Ma and Papa
Nearly died of shame.

When Sadie said her last so-long
Her girls struck out from home.
(Sadie had left as heritage
Her fine-tooth comb.)

Maud, who went to college,
Is a thin brown mouse.
She is living all alone
In this old house.

Of De Witt Williams
on His Way to Lincoln Cemetery

He was born in Alabama.
He was bred in Illinois.
He was nothing but a
Plain black boy.

Swing low swing low sweet sweet chariot.
Nothing but a plain black boy.

Drive him past the Pool Hall.
Drive him past the Show.
Blind within his casket,
But maybe he will know.

Down through Forty-seventh Street:
Underneath the L,
And Northwest Corner, Prairie,
That he loved so well.

Don't forget the Dance Halls —
Warwick and Savoy,
Where he picked his women, where
He drank his liquid joy.

Born in Alabama.
Bred in Illinois.
He was nothing but a
Plain black boy.

Swing low swing low sweet sweet chariot.
Nothing but a plain black boy.

The Vacant Lot

Mrs. Coley's three-flat brick
Isn't here any more.
All done with seeing her fat little form
Burst out of the basement door;
And with seeing her African son-in-law
(Rightful heir to the throne)
With his great white strong cold squares of teeth
And his little eyes of stone;
And with seeing the squat fat daughter
Letting in the men
When majesty has gone for the day —
And letting them out again.

The Lovers of the Poor

        arrive. The Ladies from the Ladies' Betterment
  League
Arrive in the afternoon, the late light slanting
In diluted gold bars across the boulevard brag
Of proud, seamed faces with mercy and murder hinting
Here, there, interrupting, all deep and debonair,
The pink paint on the innocence of fear;
Walk in a gingerly manner up the hall.
Cutting with knives served by their softest care,
Served by their love, so barbarously fair.
Whose mothers taught: You'd better not be cruel!

You had better not throw stones upon the wrens!
Herein they kiss and coddle and assault
Anew and dearly in the innocence
With which they baffle nature. Who are full,
Sleek, tender-clad, fit, fiftyish, a-glow, all
Sweetly abortive, hinting at fat fruit,
Judge it high time that fifytish fingers felt
Beneath the lovelier planes of enterprise.
To resurrect. To moisten with milky chill.
To be a random hitching-post or plush.
To be, for wet eyes, random and handy hem.
          Their guild is giving money to the poor.
The worthy poor. The very very worthy
And beautiful poor. Perhaps just not too swarthy?
Perhaps just not too dirty nor too dim
Nor — passionate. In truth, what they could wish
Is — something less than derelict or dull.
Not staunch enough to stab, though, gaze for gaze!
God shield them sharply from the beggar-bold!
The noxious needy ones whose battle's bald
Nonetheless for being voiceless, hits one down.
          But it's all so bad! and entirely too much for them.
The stench; the urine, cabbage, and dead beans,
Dead porridges of assorted dusty grains,
The old smoke, *heavy* diapers, and, they're told,
Something called chitterlings. The darkness: Drawn
Darkness, or dirty light. The soil that stirs.
The soil that looks the soil of centuries.
And for that matter the general oldness. Old
Wood. Old marble. Old tile. Old old old.
Not homekind Oldness! Not Lake Forest, Glencoe.
Nothing is sturdy, nothing is majestic,
There is no quiet drama, no rubbed glaze, no
Unkillable infirmity of such
A tasteful turn as lately they have left,
Glencoe, Lake Forest, and to which their cars
Must presently restore them. When they're done
With dullards and distortions of this fistic
Patience of the poor and put-upon.
          They've never seen such a make-do-ness as
Newspaper rugs before! In this, this "flat,"
Their hostess is gathering up the oozed, the rich
Rugs of the morning (tattered! the bespattered. . . .)

.

Readies to spread clean rugs for afternoon.
Here is a scene for you. The Ladies look,
In horror, behind a substantial citizeness
Whose trains clank out across her swollen heart.
Who, arms akimbo, almost fills a door.
All tumbling children, quilts dragged to the floor
And tortured thereover, potato peelings, soft-
Eyed kitten, hunched-up, haggard, to-be-hurt.
           Their League is allotting largesse to the Lost.
But to put their clean, their pretty money, to put
Their money collected from delicate rose-fingers
Tipped with their hundred flawless rose-nails seems . . .
           They own Spode, Lowestoft, candelabra,
Mantels, and hostess gowns, and sunburst clocks,
Turtle soup, Chippendale, red satin "hangings,"
Aubussons and Hattie Carnegie. They Winter
In Palm Beach; cross the Water in June; attend,
When suitable, the nice Art Institute;
Buy the right books in the best bindings; saunter
On Michigan, Easter mornings, in sun or wind.
Oh Squalor! This sick four-story hulk, this fibre
With fissures everywhere! Why, what are bringings
Of loathe-love largesse? What shall peril hungers
So old old, what shall flatter the desolate?
Tin can, blocked fire escape and chitterling
And swaggering seeking youth and the puzzled wreckage
Of the middle passage, and urine and stale shames
And, again, the porridges of the underslung
And children children children. Heavens! That
Was a rat, surely, off there, in the shadows? Long
And long-tailed? Gray? The Ladies from the Ladies'
Betterment League agree it will be better
To achieve the outer air that rights and steadies,
To hie to a house that does not holler, to ring
Bells elsetime, better presently to cater
To no more Possibilities, to get
Away. Perhaps the money can be posted.
Perhaps they two may choose another Slum!
Some serious sooty half-unhappy home! —
Where loathe-love likelier may be invested.
           Keeping their scented bodies in the center
Of the hall as they walk down the hysterical hall,
They allow their lovely skirts to graze no wall,

Are off at what they manage of a canter,
And, resuming all the clues of what they were,
Try to avoid inhaling the laden air.

Of Robert Frost

There is a little lightning in his eyes.
Iron at the mouth.
His brows ride neither too far up nor down.

He is splendid. With a place to stand.

Some glowing in the common blood.
Some specialness within.

The Sermon on the Warpland

The fact that we are black is our ultimate reality.
RON KARENGA

And several strengths from drowsiness campaigned
but spoke in Single Sermon on the warpland.

And went about the warpland saying No.
"My people, black and black, revile the River.
Say that the River turns, and turn the River.

Say that our Something in doublepod contains
seeds for the coming hell and health together.
Prepare to meet
(sisters, brothers) the brash and terrible weather;
the pains;
the bruising; the collapse of bestials, idols.
But then oh then! — the stuffing of the hulls!
the seasoning of the perilously sweet!
the health! the heralding of the clear obscure!

Build now your Church, my brothers, sisters. Build
never with brick nor Corten nor with granite.
Build with lithe love. With love like lion-eyes.
With love like morningrise.
With love like black, our black —
luminously indiscreet;
complete; continuous."

The Second Sermon on the Warpland

For Walter Bradford

1

This is the urgency: Live!
and have your blooming in the noise of the whirlwind.

2

Salve salvage in the spin.
Endorse the splendor splashes;
stylize the flawed utility;
prop a malign or failing light —
but know the whirlwind is our commonwealth.
Not the easy man, who rides above them all,
not the jumbo brigand,
not the pet bird of poets, that sweetest sonnet,
shall straddle the whirlwind.
Nevertheless, live.

3

All about are the cold places,
all about are the pushmen and jeopardy, theft —
all about are the stormers and scramblers but
what must our Season be, which starts from Fear?
Live and go out.
Define and
medicate the whirlwind.

4

The time
cracks into furious flower. Lifts its face
all unashamed. And sways in wicked grace.
Whose half-black hands assemble oranges
is tom-tom hearted
(goes in bearing oranges and boom).
And there are bells for orphans —
and red and shriek and sheen.
A garbageman is dignified
as any diplomat.
Big Bessie's feet hurt like nobody's business,
but she stands — bigly — under the unruly scrutiny, stands in the wild
    weed.

In the wild weed
she is a citizen,
and is a moment of highest quality; admirable.

It is lonesome, yes. For we are the last of the loud.
Nevertheless, live.

Conduct your blooming in the noise and whip of the whirlwind.

ROBERT DUNCAN
b. 1919

The Temple of the Animals

The temple of the animals has fallen into disrepair.
The pad of feet has faded.
The panthers flee the shadows of the day.
The smell of musk has faded but lingers there . . .
lingers, lingers. Ah, bitterly in my room.
Tired, I recall the animals of last year —
the altars of the bear, tribunals of the ape,
solitudes of elephantine gloom, rare
zebra-striped retreats, prophecies of dog,
sanctuaries of the pygmy deer.

Were there rituals I had forgotten? animal calls
to which those animal voices replied,
calld and calld until the jungle stirrd?
Were there voices that I heard?
Love was the very animal made his lair,
slept out his winter in my heart.
Did he seek my heart or ever
sleep there?

I have seen the animals depart,
forgotten their voices, or barely remembered
— like the last speech when the company goes
or the beloved face that the heart knows,
forgets and knows —
I have heard the dying footsteps fall.
The sound has faded, but lingers here.
Ah, bitterly I recall
the animals of last year.

Often I am Permitted to Return to a Meadow

as if it were a scene made-up by the mind,
that is not mine, but is a made place,

that is mine, it is so near to the heart,
an eternal pasture folded in all thought
so that there is a hall therein

that is a made place, created by light
wherefrom the shadows that are forms fall.

Wherefrom fall all architectures I am
I say are likenesses of the First Beloved
whose flowers are flames lit to the Lady.

She it is Queen Under The Hill
whose hosts are a disturbance of words within words
that is a field folded.

It is only a dream of the grass blowing
east against the source of the sun
in an hour before the sun's going down

whose secret we see in a children's game
of ring a round of roses told.

Often I am permitted to return to a meadow
as if it were a given property of the mind
that certain bounds hold against chaos,

that is a place of first permission,
everlasting omen of what is.

This Place Rumord to have been Sodom

   might have been.
Certainly these ashes might have been pleasures.
Pilgrims on their way to the Holy Places remark
this place. Isn't it plain to all
that these mounds were palaces? This was once
a city among men, a gathering together of spirit.
It was measured by the Lord and found wanting.

It was measured by the Lord and found wanting,
destroyd by the angels that inhabit longing.
Surely this is Great Sodom where such cries
as if men were birds flying up from the swamp
ring in our ears, where such fears that were once
desires walk, almost spectacular,
stalking the desolate circles, red eyed.

This place rumord to have been a City surely was,
separated from us by the hand of the Lord.
The devout have laid out gardens in the desert,
drawn water from springs where the light was blighted.
How tenderly they must attend these friendships
or all is lost. All *is* lost.
Only the faithful hold this place green.

Only the faithful hold this place green
where the crown of fiery thorns descends.
Men that once lusted grow listless. A spirit
wrappd·in a cloud, ashes more than ashes,
fire more than fire, ascends.
Only these new friends gather joyous here,
where the world like Great Sodom lies under fear.

The world like Great Sodom lies under Love
and knows not the hand of the Lord that moves.
This the friends teach where such cries
as if men were birds fly up from the crowds
gatherd and howling in the heat of the sun.
In the Lord Whom the friends have named at last Love
the images and loves of the friends never die.
This place rumord to have been Sodom is blessd
in the Lord's eyes.

The Ballad of Mrs Noah

Mrs Noah in the Ark
wove a great nightgown out of the dark,
did Mrs Noah,

had her own hearth in the Holy Boat,
two cats, two books, two cooking pots,
had Mrs Noah,

two pints of porter, two pecks of peas,
and a stir in her stew of memories.

Oh, that was a town, said Mrs Noah,
that the Lord in His wrath
did up and drown!

I liked its windows and I liked its trees.
Save me a little, Lord, I prayd on my knees.
And now, Lord save me, I've two of each!
apple, apricot, cherry and peach.

How shall I manage it? I've two of them all —
hairy, scaly, leathery, slick,
fluttery, buttery, thin and thick,
shaped like a stick, shaped like a ball,
too tiny to see, and much too tall.

I've all that I askd for and more and more,
windows and chimneys, and a great store
of needles and pins, of outs and ins,
and a regular forgive-us for some of my sins.

　　She wove a great nightgown out of the dark
　　decorated like a Sunday Park
　　with clouds of black thread to remember her grief
　　sewn about with bright flowers to give relief,

and, in a grim humor, a border all round
with the little white bones of the wicked drownd.

　　Tell me, Brother, what do you see?
　　said Mrs Noah to the Lowly Worm.

O Mother, the Earth is black, black.
To my crawlly bride and lowly me
the Earth is bitter as can be
where the Dead lie down and never come back,
said the blind Worm.

Tell me, Brother, what do *you* see?
said Mrs Noah to the sleeping Cat.

O Mother, the weather is dreadful wet.
I'll keep house for you wherever you'll be.
I'll sit by the fireside and be your pet.
And as long as I'm dry I'll purr for free,
said snug-loving Cat.

Tell me, Brother, has the Flood gone?
said Mrs Noah to the searching Crow.

No. No. No home in sight.
I fly thru the frightful waste alone,
said the carrion Crow.
The World is an everlasting Night.

Now that can't be true, Noah, Old Noah,
said the good Housewife to her good Spouse.
How long must we go in this floating House?
growing old and hope cold,
Husband, without new land?

And then Glory-Be with a Rainbow to-boot!
the Dove returnd with an Olive Shoot.

Tell me, Brother, what have we here,
my Love? to the Dove said Mrs Noah.

It's a Branch of All-Cheer
you may wear on your nightgown all the long year
as a boa, Mrs Noah, said the Dove,
with God's Love!

    Then out from the Ark
    in her nightgown all dark
    with only her smile to betoken the Day
    and a wreath-round of olive leaves

Mrs Noah stepped down
into the same old wicked repenting
Lord-Will-We-Ever recently recoverd
comfortable World-Town.

O where have you been, Mother Noah, Mother Noah?

I've had a great Promise for only Tomorrow.
In the Ark of Sleep I've been on a sail
over the wastes of the world's sorrow.

And the Promise? the Tomorrow? Mother Noah, Mother Noah?

Ah! the Rainbow's awake
and we will not fail!

Poetry, a Natural Thing

    Neither our vices nor our virtues
further the poem. "They came up
     and died
just like they do every year
    on the rocks."

    The poem
feeds upon thought, feeling, impulse,
    to breed   itself,
a spiritual urgency at the dark ladders leaping.

This beauty is an inner persistence
    toward the source
striving against (within) down-rushet of the river,
    a call we heard and answer
in the lateness of the world
    primordial bellowings
from which the youngest world might spring,

salmon not in the well where the
    hazelnut falls
but at the falls battling, inarticulate,
    blindly making it.

This is one picture apt for the mind.

A second: a moose painted by Stubbs,
where last year's extravagant antlers
    lie on the ground.
The forlorn moosey-faced poem wears
    new antler-buds,
    the same,

*

"a little heavy, a little contrived,"

his only beauty to be
all moose.

Persephone

"We have passed the great Trauma.
These wounds disclose our loss."

memory: farfields of morning,
      maimd winter, wheel and hoofhammerd weeds,
bare patches of earth. We heard rumor of the rape
among the women who wait at the wells with dry urns,
talk among leaves and among the old men
who sift tin cans and seashells searching for driftwood
to make fires on cold hearthstones. Stone hearts
and arteries hardend to stone.
        This sound of our mourning, wailing of reeds,
comes over the ice and the grey wastes of water.
We listen: it shrieks thru the ruins of cities,
whistles in shellholes
and freezes like ether in our lungs.

Shades falling under the oakshadow . . . shade upon shade
intent with their sorrow. The lust of such sorrow
listless, moving over the leafmold,
footmolded and hoofmolded, spoors of past violence.
From such clay our roots writhe, sucking the life
from corpsemold and footclay
and mold of the skull rooting.

Spore-spotted Onan, baldheaded, trickling with seed,
moved among us, or troops of swift women
    pursuing the leopard
passd. The quiet unbroken, dark beneath dark
branches spotted with light; or a flute in the morning
made truce, awakening the leaves like birds.
We shot green from the bark to flute music,
moving out from the trunk in a dream.

The sun was like gold on my body,
roots in the cold dark below me and arms
from the slender trunk showerd in gold light and shadows,
fingers green seeking the sun.

Lost, lost such peace, and Persephone lost.
Last dream brought silence,
silent thread of death-threatening dream.

We remember in symbols such violence:
the splintering of rock, the shock of the trauma,
in which she was taken from us. Shade
falls under the shadow . . . shade upon shade.
Spotted with bonewhite, splinter of driftwood,
the bark wet with terror, no sleep,
only waiting. Only we wait, our wounds barely heald
for the counterattack before sunrise.

Passage Over Water

We have gone out in boats upon the sea at night,
lost, and the vast waters close traps of fear about us.
The boats are driven apart, and we are alone at last
under the incalculable sky, listless, diseased with stars.

Let the oars be idle, my love, and forget at this time
our love like a knife between us
defining the boundaries that we can never cross
nor destroy as we drift into the heart of our dream,
cutting the silence, slyly, the bitter rain in our mouths
and the dark wound closed in behind us.

Forget depth-bombs, death and promises we made,
gardens laid waste, and, over the wastelands westward,
the rooms where we had come together bombd.

But even as we leave, your love turns back. I feel
your absence like the ringing of bells silenced. And salt
over your eyes and the scales of salt between us. Now,
you pass with ease into the destructive world.
There is a dry crash of cement. The light fails,
falls into the ruins of cities upon the distant shore
and within the indestructible night I am alone.

Homage and Lament for Ezra Pound in Captivity
May 12, 1944

Apprehension this spring . . . the leaves, the leaves,
still, as still as everness returnd,
defining distances with green. The space between
alive with each upon each barely in motion.
Coming into a room from hidden windows, light
reflects in shade a spotted shade of spring
having almost sound upon the ear. Four voices
— violin, viola, cello and bass, appear and reappear
upon a warp and woof of distances
unified in light and sense of leaves, of Venus
sea-ambulant among the boughs. The numerous leaves
are still, as still as the heart in seeing, in hearing
— a melody within an edifice of sound, as sound
as Brzeska's head in solid stone made, as lasting
in the heart though the particular stone be crackt.
Iconoclasts may never break that stone once seen,
once heard in the returning everness of mind.
The numerous leaves are still in seeing, in hearing.
The numerous leaves await in knowing
apprehension this spring like some crackt voice,
fanatic dryad among the boughs, the melodies
of mind.   Ezra, this time of year,
this deceptive real we fear lest hunting voices
overtake the hunted. Torn by wild upon the wild
evasive beauty, a mocking face recalls to mind
among the leaves, the lights, an enemy.
Far down — I hang in qualms of deep —
an old man stumbles,
mutters maledictions upon the hounds.

In this place, before Hell's door, anger-blind,
leaves rehearse crimes. Human figures in a frieze
rehearse remembered faces. Universities, the damnd,
seas of human faces go down like wolves
behind the eyes to fill these distances with fire.
The desire, for all its leaves, for all of violin,
of solid stone, turns a human hurt and damnd
toward outrage's Hell. Desire has crackt
crosst eyes to see a Hell's door Heaven.

Hell's door's Heaven will never change as leaves
may change and fall like wolves
upon the human flesh and bone. Universities,
the damnd, that turn upon the damnd
with passive righteousness — another hell,
more treacherous than fire or wolves.
Far down — I voice in the wrong beauty
better than no beauty — to see a still world still
hopping mad among its calm of leaves.

*

We have not less to fear or hate. Old man, early
devoted voice, this afternoon as light falls down
it leaves one shining sill, promising, illusive.
The room is filld, enters in the mind, with this,
an architecture to house the mind in Heaven —
apprehending in a single phrase of Mozart
a universe, the tones, the tones like leaves of light
to fall, to reappear, establishing distances
upon the warp and woof of person not to fall.
A single window upon another scene,
upon a painted Mediterranean blueness in the room,
gives possession of a world by love.
Against some Mediterranean scene an old man
stumbles, mutters maledictions, sees that blue,
as Joyce once saw a sea, tighten scrotum,
mock at an old man's heart.

He screams abominations, curses, seeing a gull
fly up upon the wind, seeing an early eagerness
falter and drift to be toucht by usury.
What still and wondrous knowledge
avails then? to know as leaves, as sea of soul
gives out, no longer capable to eager green,
to see each upon each barely in motion
as still as everness returnd. Apprehension this spring
. . . the leaves, the leaves,
still, as still as everness returning.

Tribal Memories   *Passages* 1

And to Her-Without-Bounds I send,
wherever She wanders,   by what
        campfire at evening,

among tribes setting each the City where
                we Her people are
at the end of a day's reaches   here
        the Eternal
lamps lit, here   the wavering human
     sparks of heat and light
glimmer, go out, and reappear.

For this is the company of the living
and the poet's voice speaks from no
        crevice in the ground between
        mid-earth and underworld
breathing fumes of what is deadly to know,
                news larvae in tombs
                and twists of time do feed upon,

but from the hearth stone, the lamp light,
                the heart of the matter where the

                                house is held

yet here, the warning light at the edge of town!

The City will go out in time, will go out
        into time, hiding even its embers.
And we were scatterd thruout the countries and times of man

for we took alarm in ourselves,
                rumors of the enemy
spread among the feathers of the wing that covered us.

Mnemosyne, they named her, the
                Mother with the whispering
        feathered wings.   Memory,
the great speckled bird who broods over the
                nest of souls, and her egg,
        the dream in which all things are living,
I return to, leaving my self.

838

I am beside myself with this
    thought of the One in the World-Egg,
enclosed,   in a shell of murmurings,

        rimed round,
        sound-chambered child.

It's that first!   The forth-going to be
        bursts into green as the spring
    winds blow watery from the south
and the sun returns north.   He hides

    fire among words in his mouth

and comes racing out of the zone of dark and storm

        towards us.

I sleep in the afternoon, retreating from work,
reading and dropping away from the reading,
as if I were only a seed of myself,
    unawakend,   unwilling
        to sleep or wake.

    What I Saw   *Passages 3*

The white peacock roosting
might have been Christ,

    feathered robe of Osiris,

the radiant bird, a sword-flash,

    percht in the tree

and the other,   the fumed-glass slide

    — were like night and day,

the slit of an eye opening in

    time

vertical to the horizon

RICHARD WILBUR
b. 1921

Cigales

You know those windless summer evenings, swollen to stasis
by too-substantial melodies, rich as a
running-down record, ground round
to full quiet. Even the leaves
have thick tongues.

And if the first crickets quicken then,
other inhabitants, at window or door
or rising from table, feel in the lungs
a slim false-freshness, by this
trick of the ear.

Chanters of miracles took for a simple sign
the Latin cigale, because of his long waiting
and sweet change in daylight, and his singing
all his life, pinched on the ash leaf,
heedless of ants.

Others made morals; all were puzzled and joyed
by this gratuitous song. Such a plain thing
morals could not surround, nor listening:
not "chirr" nor "cri-cri." There is no straight
way of approaching it.

This thin uncomprehended song it is
springs healing questions into binding air.
Fabre, by firing all the municipal cannon
under a piping tree, found out
cigales cannot hear.

My Father Paints the Summer

A smoky rain riddles the ocean plains,
Rings on the beaches' stones, stomps in the swales,
Batters the panes
Of the shore hotel, and the hoped-for summer chills and fails.
The summer people sigh,
"Is this July?"

They talk by the lobby fire but no one hears
For the thrum of the rain. In the dim and sounding halls,
Din at the ears,
Dark at the eyes well in the head, and the ping-pong balls
Scatter their hollow knocks
Like crazy clocks.

But up in his room by artificial light
My father paints the summer, and his brush
Tricks into sight
The prosperous sleep, the girdling stir and clear steep hush
Of a summer never seen,
A granted green.

Summer, luxuriant Sahara, the orchard spray
Gales in the Eden trees, the knight again
Can cast away
His burning mail, Rome is at Anzio: but the rain
For the ping-pong's optative bop
Will never stop.

Caught Summer is always an imagined time.
Time gave it, yes, but time out of any mind.
There must be prime
In the heart to beget that season, to reach past rain and find
Riding the palest days
Its perfect blaze.

"A World without Objects is a Sensible Emptiness"

The tall camels of the spirit
Steer for their deserts, passing the last groves loud
With the sawmill shrill of the locust, to the whole honey of the arid
Sun. They are slow, proud,

And move with a stilted stride
To the land of sheer horizon, hunting Traherne's
Sensible emptiness, there where the brain's lantern-slide
Revels in vast returns.

O connoisseurs of thirst,
Beasts of my soul who long to learn to drink
Of pure mirage, those prosperous islands are accurst
That shimmer on the brink

Of absence; auras, lustres,
And all shinings need to be shaped and borne.
Think of those painted saints, capped by the early masters
With bright, jauntily-worn

Aureate plates, or even
Merry-go-round rings. Turn, O turn
From the fine sleights of the sand, from the long empty oven
Where flames in flamings burn

Back to the trees arrayed
In bursts of glare, to the halo-dialling run
Of the country creeks, and the hills' bracken tiaras made
Gold in the sunken sun,

Wisely watch for the sight
Of the supernova burgeoning over the barn,
Lampshine blurred in the steam of beasts, the spirit's right
Oasis, light incarnate.

The Pardon

My dog lay dead five days without a grave
In the thick of summer, hid in a clump of pine
And a jungle of grass and honeysuckle-vine.
I who had loved him while he kept alive

Went only close enough to where he was
To sniff the heavy honeysuckle-smell
Twined with another odour heavier still
And hear the flies' intolerable buzz.

Well, I was ten and very much afraid.
In my kind world the dead were out of range
And I could not forgive the sad or strange
In beast or man. My father took the spade

And buried him. Last night I saw the grass
Slowly divide (it was the same scene
But now it glowed a fierce and mortal green)
And saw the dog emerging. I confess

I felt afraid again, but still he came
In the carnal sun, clothed in a hymn of flies,
And death was breeding in his lively eyes.
I started in to cry and call his name,

Asking forgiveness of his tongueless head.
. . . I dreamt the past was never past redeeming:
But whether this was false or honest dreaming
I beg death's pardon now. And mourn the dead.

Epistemology

I
Kick at the rock, Sam Johnson, break your bones:
But cloudy, cloudy is the stuff of stones.

II
We milk the cow of the world, and as we do
We whisper in her ear, "You are not true."

Grasse: The Olive Trees
For Marcelle and Ferdinand Springer

Here luxury's the common lot. The light
Lies on the rain-pocked rocks like yellow wool
And around the rocks the soil is rusty bright
From too much wealth of water, so that the grass
Mashes under the foot, and all is full
Of heat and juice and a heavy jammed excess.

Whatever moves moves with the slow complete
Gestures of statuary. Flower smells
Are set in the golden day, and shelled in heat,
Pine and columnar cypress stand. The palm
Sinks its combs in the sky. This whole South swells
To a soft rigour, a rich and crowded calm.

Only the olive contradicts. My eye,
Travelling slopes of rust and green, arrests
And rests from plenitude where olives lie
Like clouds of doubt against the earth's array.
Their faint dishevelled foliage divests
The sunlight of its colour and its sway.

Not that the olive spurns the sun; its leaves
Scatter and point to every part of the sky,
Like famished fingers waving. Brilliance weaves
And sombres down among them, and among
The anxious silver branches, down to the dry
And twisted trunk, by rooted hunger wrung.

Even when seen from near, the olive shows
A hue of far away. Perhaps for this
The dove brought olive back, a tree which grows
Unearthly pale, which ever dims and dries,
And whose great thirst, exceeding all excess,
Teaches the South it is not paradise.

A Voice from under the Table

To Robert and Jane Brooks

How shall the wine be drunk, or the woman known?
I take this world for better or for worse,
But seeing rose carafes conceive the sun
My thirst conceives a fierier universe:
And then I toast the birds in the burning trees
That chant their holy lucid drunkenness;
I swallowed all the phosphorus of the seas
Before I fell into this low distress.

You upright people all remember how
Love drove you first to the woods, and there you heard
The loose-mouthed wind complaining *Thou* and *Thou*;
My gawky limbs were shuddered by the word.
Most of it since was nothing but charades
To spell that hankering out and make an end,
But the softest hands against my shoulder-blades
Only increased the crying of the wind.

For this the goddess rose from the midland sea
And stood above the famous wine-dark wave,
To ease our drouth with clearer mystery
And be a South to all our flights of love.
And down by the selfsame water I have seen
A blazing girl with skin like polished stone
Splashing until a far-out breast of green
Arose and with a rose contagion shone.

"A myrtle-shoot in hand, she danced; her hair
Cast on her back and shoulders a moving shade."
Was it some hovering light that showed her fair?
Was it of chafing dark that light was made?
Perhaps it was Archilochus' fantasy,
Or that his saying sublimed the thing he said.
All true enough; and true as well that she
Was beautiful, and danced, and is now dead.

Helen was no such high discarnate thought
As men in dry symposia pursue,
But was as bitterly fugitive, not to be caught
By what men's arms in love or fight could do.
Groan in your cell; rape Troy with sword and flame;
The end of thirst exceeds experience.
A devil told me it was all the same
Whether to fail by spirit or by sense.

God keep me a damned fool, nor charitably
Receive me into his shapely resignations.
I am a sort of martyr, as you see,
A horizontal monument to patience.
The calves of waitresses parade about
My helpless head upon this sodden floor.
Well, I am down again, but not yet out.
O sweet frustrations, I shall be back for more.

All These Birds

Agreed that all these birds,
Hawk or heavenly lark or heard-of nightingale,
Perform upon the kitestrings of our sight
In a false distance, that the day and night

Are full of wingèd words
                              gone rather stale,
        That nothing is so worn
        As Philomel's bosom-thorn,

        That it is, in fact, the male
Nightingale which sings, and that all these creatures wear
        Invisible armour such as Hébert beheld
        His water-ousel through, as, wrapped or shelled
        In a clear bellying veil
                              or bubble of air,
        It bucked the flood to feed
        At the stream-bottom. Agreed

        That the sky is a vast claire
In which the gull, despite appearances, is not
        Less claustral than the oyster in its beak
        And dives like nothing human; that we seek
        Vainly to know the heron
                              (but can plot
        What angle of the light
        Provokes its northern flight).

        Let them be polyglot
And wordless then, those boughs that spoke with Solomon
        In Hebrew canticles, and made him wise;
        And let a clear and bitter wind arise
        To storm into the hotbeds
                              of the sun,
        And there, beyond a doubt,
        Batter the Phoenix out.

        Let us, with glass or gun,
Watch (from our clever blinds) the monsters of the sky
        Dwindle to habit, habitat, and song,
        And tell the imagination it is wrong
        Till, lest it be undone,
                              it spin a lie
        So fresh, so pure, so rare
        As to possess the air.

Why should it be more shy
Than chimney-nesting storks, or sparrows on a wall?
Oh, let it climb wherever it can cling
Like some great trumpet-vine, a natural thing
To which all birds that fly
     come natural.
Come, stranger, sister, dove:
Put on the reins of love.

A Hole in the Floor

For René Magritte

The carpenter's made a hole
In the parlor floor, and I'm standing
Staring down into it now
At four o'clock in the evening,
As Schliemann stood when his shovel
Knocked on the crowns of Troy.

A clean-cut sawdust sparkles
On the grey, shaggy laths,
And here is a cluster of shavings
From the time when the floor was laid.
They are silvery-gold, the color
Of Hesperian apple-parings.

Kneeling, I look in under
Where the joists go into hiding.
A pure street, faintly littered
With bits and strokes of light,
Enters the long darkness
Where its parallels will meet.

The radiator-pipe
Rises in middle distance
Like a shuttered kiosk, standing
Where the only news is night.
Here it's not painted green,
As it is in the visible world.

For God's sake, what am I after?
Some treasure, or tiny garden?
Or that untrodden place,
The house's very soul,
Where time has stored our footbeats
And the long skein of our voices?

Not these, but the buried strangeness
Which nourishes the known:
That spring from which the floor-lamp
Drinks now a wilder bloom,
Inflaming the damask love-seat
And the whole dangerous room.

On the Marginal Way

For J. C. P.

Another cove of shale,
But the beach here is rubbed with strange rock
  That is sleek, fluent, and taffy-pale.
I stare, reminded with a little shock
How, by a shore in Spain, George Borrow saw
A hundred women basking in the raw.

They must have looked like this,
That catch of bodies on the sand, that strew
  Of rondure, crease, and orifice,
Lap, flank, and knee — a too abundant view
Which, though he'd had the lenses of a fly,
Could not have waked desire in Borrow's eye.

Has the light altered now?
The rocks flush rose and have the melting shape
  Of bodies fallen anyhow.
It is a Géricault of blood and rape,
Some desert town despoiled, some caravan
Pillaged, its people murdered to a man,

And those who murdered them
Galloping off, a rumpling line of dust
   Like the wave's white, withdrawing hem.
But now the vision of a colder lust
Clears, as the wind goes chill and all is greyed
By a swift cloud that drags a carrion shade.

   If these are bodies still,
Theirs is a death too dead to look asleep,
   Like that of Auschwitz' final kill,
Poor slaty flesh abandoned in a heap
And then, like sea-rocks buried by a wave,
Bulldozed at last into a common grave.

   It is not tricks of sense
But the time's fright within me which distracts
   Least fancies into violence
And makes my thought take cover in the facts,
As now it does, remembering how the bed
Of layered rock two miles above my head

   Hove ages up and broke
Soundless asunder, when the shrinking skin
   Of Earth, blacked out by steam and smoke,
Gave passage to the muddled fire within,
Its crannies flooding with a sweat of quartz,
And lathered magmas out of deep retorts

   Welled up, as here, to fill
With tumbled rockmeal, stone-fume, lithic spray,
   The dike's brief chasm and the sill.
Weathered until the sixth and human day
By sanding winds and water, scuffed and brayed
By the slow glacier's heel, these forms were made

   That now recline and burn
Comely as Eve and Adam, near a sea
   Transfigured by the sun's return.
And now three girls lie golden in the lee
Of a great arm or thigh, and are as young
As the bright boulders that they lie among.

Though, high above the shore
On someone's porch, spread wings of newsprint flap
  The tidings of some dirty war,
It is a perfect day: the waters clap
Their hands and kindle, and the gull in flight
Loses himself at moments, white in white,

  And like a breaking thought
Joy for a moment floods into the mind,
  Blurting that all things shall be brought
To the full state and stature of their kind,
By what has found the manhood of this stone.
May that vast motive wash and wash our own.

Playboy

High on his stockroom ladder like a dunce
The stock-boy sits, and studies like a sage
The subject matter of one glossy page,
As lost in curves as Archimedes once.

Sometimes, without a glance, he feeds himself.
The left hand, like a mother-bird in flight,
Brings him a sandwich for a sidelong bite,
And then returns it to a dusty shelf.

What so engrosses him? The wild décor
Of this pink-papered alcove into which
A naked girl has stumbled, with its rich
Welter of pelts and pillows on the floor,

Amidst which, kneeling in a supple pose,
She lifts a goblet in her farther hand,
As if about to toast a flower-stand
Above which hovers an exploding rose

Fired from a long-necked crystal vase that rests
Upon a tasseled and vermilion cloth
One taste of which would shrivel up a moth?
Or is he pondering her perfect breasts?

Nothing escapes him of her body's grace
Or of her floodlit skin, so sleek and warm
And yet so strangely like a uniform,
But what now grips his fancy is her face,

And how the cunning picture holds her still
At just that smiling instant when her soul,
Grown sweetly faint, and swept beyond control,
Consents to his inexorable will.

ANTHONY HECHT
b. 1923

The Dover Bitch

A *Criticism of Life*
For Andrews Wanning

So there stood Matthew Arnold and this girl
With the cliffs of England crumbling away behind them,
And he said to her, "Try to be true to me,
And I'll do the same for you, for things are bad
All over, etc., etc."
Well now, I knew this girl. It's true she had read
Sophocles in a fairly good translation
And caught that bitter allusion to the sea,
But all the time he was talking she had in mind
The notion of what his whiskers would feel like
On the back of her neck. She told me later on
That after a while she got to looking out
At the lights across the channel, and really felt sad,
Thinking of all the wine and enormous beds
And blandishments in French and the perfumes.
And then she got really angry. To have been brought
All the way down from London, and then be addressed
As sort of a mournful cosmic last resort
Is really tough on a girl, and she was pretty.
Anyway, she watched him pace the room
And finger his watch-chain and seem to sweat a bit,
And then she said one or two unprintable things.
But you mustn't judge her by that. What I mean to say is,
She's really all right. I still see her once in a while

And she always treats me right. We have a drink
And I give her a good time, and perhaps it's a year
Before I see her again, but there she is,
Running to fat, but dependable as they come,
And sometimes I bring her a bottle of *Nuit d'Amour.*

Birdwatchers of America

*I suffer now continually from vertigo, and today, 23rd of
January, 1862, I received a singular warning: I felt the
wind of the wing of madness pass over me.*
BAUDELAIRE, *Journals*

It's all very well to dream of a dove that saves,
Picasso's or the Pope's,
The one that annually coos in Our Lady's ear
Half the world's hopes,
And the other one that shall cunningly engineer
The retirement of all businessmen to their graves,
And when this is brought about
Make us the loving brothers of every lout —

But in our part of the country a false dusk
Lingers for hours; it steams
From the soaked hay, wades in the cloudy woods,
Engendering other dreams.
Formless and soft beyond the fence it broods
Or rises as a faint and rotten musk
Out of a broken stalk.
There are some things of which we seldom talk;

For instance, the woman next door, whom we hear at night,
Claims that when she was small
She found a man stone dead near the cedar trees
After the first snowfall.
The air was clear. He seemed in ultimate peace
Except that he had no eyes. Rigid and bright
Upon the forehead, furred
With a light frost, crouched an outrageous bird.

"More Light! More Light!"

For Heinrich Blücher and Hannah Arendt

Composed in the Tower before his execution
These moving verses, and being brought at that time
Painfully to the stake, submitted, declaring thus:
"I implore my God to witness that I have made no crime."

Nor was he forsaken of courage, but the death was horrible,
The sack of gunpowder failing to ignite.
His legs were blistered sticks on which the black sap
Bubbled and burst as he howled for the Kindly Light.

And that was but one, and by no means one of the worst;
Permitted at least his pitiful dignity;
And such as were by made prayers in the name of Christ,
That shall judge all men, for his soul's tranquillity.

We move now to outside a German wood.
Three men are there commanded to dig a hole
In which the two Jews are orderd to lie down
And be buried alive by the third, who is a Pole.

Not light from the shrine at Weimar beyond the hill
Nor light from heaven appeared. But he did refuse.
A Lüger settled back deeply in its glove.
He was ordered to change places with the Jews.

Much casual death had drained away their souls.
The thick dirt mounted toward the quivering chin.
When only the head was exposed the order came
To dig him out again and to get back in.

No light, no light in the blue Polish eye.
When he finished a riding boot packed down the earth.
The Lüger hovered lightly in its glove.
He was shot in the belly and in three hours bled to death.

No prayers or incense rose up in those hours
Which grew to be years, and every day came mute
Ghosts from the ovens, sitting through crisp air,
And settled upon his eyes in a black soot.

"It Out-Herods Herod. Pray You, Avoid It."

Tonight my children hunch
Toward their Western, and are glad
As, with a Sunday punch,
The Good casts out the Bad.

And in their fairy tales
The warty giant and witch
Get sealed in doorless jails
And the match-girl strikes it rich.

I've made myself a drink.
The giant and witch are set
To bust out of the clink
When my children have gone to bed.

All frequencies are loud
With signals of despair;
In flash and morse they crowd
The rondure of the air.

For the wicked have grown strong,
Their numbers mock at death,
Their cow brings forth its young,
Their bull engendereth.

Their very fund of strength,
Satan, bestrides the globe;
He stalks its breadth and length
And finds out even Job.

Yet by quite other laws
My children make their case;
Half God, half Santa Claus,
But with my voice and face,

A hero comes to save
The poorman, beggarman, thief,
And make the world behave
And put an end to grief.

And that their sleep be sound
I say this childermas
Who could not, at one time,
Have saved them from the gas.

JAMES DICKEY
b. 1923

The Underground Stream

I lay at the edge of a well,
And thought how to bury my smile
Under the thorn, where the leaf,
At the sill of oblivion safe,
Put forth its instant green
In a flow from underground.
I sought how the spirit could fall
Down this moss-feathered well:
The motion by which my face
Could descend through structureless grass,
Dreaming of love, and pass
Through solid earth, to rest
On the unseen water's breast,
Timelessly smiling, and free
Of the world, of light, and of me.
I made and imagined that smile
To float there, mile on mile
Of streaming, unknowable wonder,
Overhearing a silence like thunder
Possess every stone of the well
Forever, where my face fell
From the upper, springtime world,
And my odd, living mouth unfurled
An eternal grin, while I
In the bright and stunned grass lay
And turned to air without age.
My first love fingered a page
And sang with Campion.
The heart in my breast turned green;
I entered the words afresh,
At one with her singing flesh.
But all the time I felt
The secret triumph melt
Down through the rooted thorn,
And the smile I filtered through stone
Motionless lie, not murmuring
But listening only, and hearing
My image of joy flow down.
I turned from the girl I had found

In a song once sung by my mother,
And loved my one true brother,
The tall cadaver, who
Either grew or did not grow,
But smiled, with the smile of singing,
Or a smile of incredible longing
To rise through a circle of stone,
Gazing up at a sky, alone
Visible, at the top of a well,
And seeking for years to deliver
His mouth from the endless river
Of my oil-on-the-water smile,
And claim his own grave face
That mine might live in its place.
I lay at the edge of a well;
And then I smiled, and fell.

The Performance

The last time I saw Donald Armstrong
He was staggering oddly off into the sun,
Going down, of the Philippine Islands.
I let my shovel fall, and put that hand
Above my eyes, and moved some way to one side
That his body might pass through the sun,

And I saw how well he was not
Standing there on his hands,
On his spindle-shanked forearms balanced,
Unbalanced, with his big feet looming and waving
In the great, untrustworthy air
He flew in each night, when it darkened.

Dust fanned in scraped puffs from the earth
Between his arms, and blood turned his face inside out,
To demonstrate its suppleness
Of veins, as he perfected his role.
Next day, he toppled his head off
On an island beach to the south,

And the enemy's two-handed sword
Did not fall from anyone's hands
At that miraculous sight,
As the head rolled over upon
Its wide-eyed face, and fell
Into the inadequate grave

He had dug for himself, under pressure.
Yet I put my flat hand to my eyebrows
Months later, to see him again
In the sun, when I learned how he died,
And imagined him, there,
Come, judged, before his small captors,

Doing all his lean tricks to amaze them —
The back somersault, the kip-up —
And at last, the stand on his hands,
Perfect, with his feet together,
His head down, evenly breathing,
As the sun poured up from the sea

And the headsman broke down
In a blaze of tears, in that light
Of the thin, long human frame
Upside down in its own strange joy,
And, if some other one had not told him,
Would have cut off the feet

Instead of the head,
And if Armstrong had not presently risen
In kingly, round-shouldered attendance,
And then knelt down in himself
Beside his hacked, glittering grave, having done
All things in this life that he could.

The Heaven of Animals

Here they are. The soft eyes open.
If they have lived in a wood
It is a wood.
If they have lived on plains
It is grass rolling
Under their feet forever.

Having no souls, they have come,
Anyway, beyond their knowing.
Their instincts wholly bloom
And they rise.
The soft eyes open.

To match them, the landscape flowers,
Outdoing, desperately
Outdoing what is required:
The richest wood,
The deepest field.

For some of these,
It could not be the place
It is, without blood.
These hunt, as they have done,
But with claws and teeth grown perfect,

More deadly than they can believe.
They stalk more silently,
And crouch on the limbs of trees,
And their descent
Upon the bright backs of their prey

May take years
In a sovereign floating of joy.
And those that are hunted
Know this as their life,
Their reward: to walk

Under such trees in full knowledge
Of what is in glory above them,
And to feel no fear,
But acceptance, compliance.
Fulfilling themselves without pain

At the cycle's center,
They tremble, they walk
Under the tree,
They fall, they are torn,
They rise, they walk again.

A Birth

Inventing a story with grass,
I find a young horse deep inside it.
I cannot nail wires around him;
My fence posts fail to be solid,

And he is free, strangely, without me.
With his head still browsing the greenness,
He walks slowly out of the pasture
To enter the sun of his story.

My mind freed of its own creature,
I find myself deep in my life
In a room with my child and my mother,
When I feel the sun climbing my shoulder

Change, to include a new horse.

Buckdancer's Choice

So I would hear out those lungs,
The air split into nine levels,
Some gift of tongues of the whistler

In the invalid's bed: my mother,
Warbling all day to herself
The thousand variations of one song;

It is called Buckdancer's Choice.
For years, they have all been dying
Out, the classic buck-and-wing men

Of traveling minstrel shows;
With them also an old woman
Was dying of breathless angina,

Yet still found breath enough
To whistle up in my head
A sight like a one-man band,

Freed black, with cymbals at heel,
An ex-slave who thrivingly danced
To the ring of his own clashing light

Through the thousand variations of one song
All day to my mother's prone music,
The invalid's warbler's note,

While I crept close to the wall
Sock-footed, to hear the sounds alter,
Her tongue like a mockingbird's break

Through stratum after stratum of a tone
Proclaiming what choices there are
For the last dancers of their kind,

For ill women and for all slaves
Of death, and children enchanted at walls
With a brass-beating glow underfoot,

Not dancing but nearly risen
Through barnlike, theatrelike houses
On the wings of the buck and wing.

The Sheep Child

Farm boys wild to couple
With anything   with soft-wooded trees
With mounds of earth   mounds
Of pinestraw   will keep themselves off
Animals by legends of their own:
In the hay-tunnel dark
And dung of barns, they will
Say   I have heard tell

That in a museum in Atlanta
Way back in a corner somewhere
There's this thing that's only half
Sheep   like a woolly baby
Pickled in alcohol   because
Those things can't live   his eyes
Are open   but you can't stand to look
I heard from somebody who . . .

But this is now almost all
Gone. The boys have taken
Their own true wives in the city,
The sheep are safe in the west hill
Pasture   but we who were born there
Still are not sure. Are we,
Because we remember, remembered
In the terrible dust of museums?

Merely with his eyes, the sheep-child may

Be saying   saying

> I am here, in my father's house.
> I who am half of your world, came deeply
> To my mother in the long grass
> Of the west pasture, where she stood like moonlight
> Listening for foxes. It was something like love
> From another world that seized her
> From behind, and she gave, not lifting her head
> Out of dew, without ever looking, her best
> Self to that great need. Turned loose, she dipped her face
> Farther into the chill of the earth, and in a sound
> Of sobbing   of something stumbling
> Away, began, as she must do,
> To carry me. I woke, dying,
>
> In the summer sun of the hillside, with my eyes
> Far more than human. I saw for a blazing moment
> The great grassy world from both sides,
> Man and beast in the round of their need,
> And the hill wind stirred in my wool,
> My hoof and my hand clasped each other,
> I ate my one meal
> Of milk, and died
> Staring. From dark grass I came straight
>
> To my father's house, whose dust
> Whirls up in the halls for no reason
> When no one comes   piling deep in a hellish mild corner,
> And, through my immortal waters,
> I meet the sun's grains eye
> To eye, and they fail at my closet of glass.

Dead, I am most surely living
In the minds of farm boys: I am he who drives
Them like wolves from the hound bitch and calf
And from the chaste ewe in the wind.
They go into woods   into bean fields   they go
Deep into their known right hands. Dreaming of me,
They groan   they wait   they suffer
Themselves, they marry, they raise their kind.

LOUIS SIMPSON
b. 1923

Carentan O Carentan

Trees in the old days used to stand
And shape a shady lane
Where lovers wandered hand in hand
Who came from Carentan.

This was the shining green canal
Where we came two by two
Walking at combat-interval.
Such trees we never knew.

The day was early June, the ground
Was soft and bright with dew.
Far away the guns did sound,
But here the sky was blue.

The sky was blue, but there a smoke
Hung still above the sea
Where the ships together spoke
To towns we could not see.

Could you have seen us through a glass
You would have said a walk
Of farmers out to turn the grass,
Each with his own hay-fork.

The watchers in their leopard suits
Waited till it was time,
And aimed between the belt and boot
And let the barrel climb.

I must lie down at once, there is
A hammer at my knee.
And call it death or cowardice,
Don't count again on me.

Everything's alright, Mother,
Everyone gets the same
At one time or another.
It's all in the game.

I never strolled, nor ever shall,
Down such a leafy lane.
I never drank in a canal,
Nor ever shall again.

There is a whistling in the leaves
And it is not the wind,
The twigs are falling from the knives
That cut men to the ground.

Tell me, Master-Sergeant,
The way to turn and shoot.
But the Sergeant's silent
That taught me how to do it.

O Captain, show us quickly
Our place upon the map.
But the Captain's sickly
And taking a long nap.

Lieutenant, what's my duty,
My place in the platoon?
He too's a sleeping beauty,
Charmed by that strange tune.

Carentan O Carentan
Before we met with you
We never yet had lost a man
Or known what death could do.

To the Western World

A siren sang, and Europe turned away
From the high castle and the shepherd's crook.
Three caravels went sailing to Cathay
On the strange ocean, and the captains shook
Their banners out across the Mexique Bay.

And in our early days we did the same.
Remembering our fathers in their wreck
We crossed the sea from Palos where they came
And saw, enormous to the little deck,
A shore in silence waiting for a name.

The treasures of Cathay were never found.
In this America, this wilderness
Where the axe echoes with a lonely sound,
The generations labor to possess
And grave by grave we civilize the ground.

The Troika

Troika, troika! The snow moon
whirls through the forest.

Where lamplight like a knife
gleams through a door, I see two graybeards bending.
They're playing chess, it seems. And then one rises
and stands in silence. Does he hear me passing?

Troika, troika! In the moonlight
his spirit hears my spirit passing.

I whip the horses on. The houses vanish.
The moon looks over fields
littered with debris. And there in trenches
the guardsmen stand, wind fluttering their rags.

And there were darker fields without a moon.
I walk across a field, bound on an errand.
The errand's forgotten — something depended on it.
A nightmare! I have lost my father's horses!

And then a white bird rises
and goes before me, hopping through the forest.

I held the bird — it vanished with a cry,
and on a branch a girl sat sideways, combing
her long black hair. The dew
shone on her lips; her breasts were white as roses.

Troika, troika! Three white horses,
a whip of silver, and my father's sleigh . . .

When morning breaks, the sea
gleams through the branches,
and the white bird, enchanted,
is flying through the world, across the sea.

My Father in the Night Commanding No

My father in the night commanding No
Has work to do. Smoke issues from his lips;
    He reads in silence.
The frogs are croaking and the streetlamps glow.

And then my mother winds the gramophone;
The Bride of Lammermoor begins to shriek —
    Or reads a story
About a prince, a castle, and a dragon.

The moon is glittering above the hill.
I stand before the gateposts of the King —
    So runs the story —
Of Thule, at midnight when the mice are still.

And I have been in Thule! It has come true —
The journey and the danger of the world,
    All that there is
To bear and to enjoy, endure and do.

Landscapes, seascapes . . . where have I been led?
The names of cities — Paris, Venice, Rome —
    Held out their arms.
A feathered god, seductive, went ahead.

865

Here is my house. Under a red rose tree
A child is swinging; another gravely plays.
    They are not surprised
That I am here; they were expecting me.

And yet my father sits and reads in silence,
My mother sheds a tear, the moon is still,
    And the dark wind
Is murmuring that nothing ever happens.

Beyond his jurisdiction as I move
Do I not prove him wrong? And yet, it's true
    They will not change
There, on the stage of terror and of love.

The actors in that playhouse always sit
In fixed positions — father, mother, child
    With painted eyes.
How sad it is to be a little puppet!

Their heads are wooden. And you once pretended
To understand them! Shake them as you will,
    They cannot speak.
Do what you will, the comedy is ended.

Father, why did you work? Why did you weep,
Mother? Was the story so important?
    "Listen!" the wind
Said to the children, and they fell asleep.

American Poetry

Whatever it is, it must have
A stomach that can digest
Rubber, coal, uranium, moons, poems.

Like the shark, it contains a shoe.
It must swim for miles through the desert
Uttering cries that are almost human.

Dvonya

In the town of Odessa
there is a garden
and Dvonya is there,
Dvonya whom I love
though I have never been in Odessa.

I love her black hair, and eyes
as green as a salad
that you gather in August
between the roots of alder,
her skin with an odor of wildflowers.

We understand each other perfectly.
We are cousins twice removed.
In the garden we drink our tea,
discussing the plays of Chekhov
as evening falls and the lights begin to twinkle.

But this is only a dream.
I am not there
with my citified speech,
and the old woman is not there
peering between the curtains.

We are only phantoms, bits of ash,
like yesterday's newspaper
or the smoke of chimneys.
All that passed long ago
on a summer night in Odessa.

The Country House

You always know what to expect
in a novel by L. V. Kalinin. . . .

"One morning in June, in the provincial town
of X, had you been observant,
you might have seen a stranger
alighting at the railroad station."

From there it moves to a country house,
introduction of the principal characters —
a beautiful girl, a youth
on fire with radical ideas.

There are drawing-room discussions,
picnics at the lake, or a mountain,
if there is one in the vicinity.

Then some misunderstanding —
the young man banished from the house
by the angry father. Tears.

All this with the most meticulous attention
to the "spirit of the times,"
bearing in mind the classical saying,
"Don't be the first to try anything, or the last."

*

The tone of his letters was quite different:

"The Polish girl I told you about, who is living with us,
has a wart. Two days ago, the idiot
tried to remove it with lye.
For hours on end the house has been filled with howling,
and I can't think or write."

The Climate of Paradise

A story about Indians,
the tribe that claimed Mt. Shasta. . . .

Five lawyers said, "It's ridiculous!
What possible use can they have for the mountain?"

The interpreter said, "Your Honor,
they say that their gods live there."

*

How different this is from the Buzzy Schofields,
people I met in Pasadena.

Green lawns, imposing villas —
actually, these are caves inhabited

by Pufendorf's dwarfs and Vico's
Big Feet, the "abandoned by God."

Thought, says Vico, begins in caves —
but not the Buzzy Schofields'.

They're haunted by Red China —
bugles — a sky lit with artillery.

They're terrified they'll be brainwashed.
They can see themselves breaking under torture . . .

"Stop! I'm on your side!
You're making a terrible mistake!"

O even in Paradise
the mind would make its own winter.

DENISE LEVERTOV
b. 1923

Illustrious Ancestors

The Rav
of Northern White Russia declined,
in his youth, to learn the
language of birds, because
the extraneous did not interest him; nevertheless
when he grew old it was found
he understood them anyway, having
listened well, and as it is said, "prayed
                    with the bench and the floor." He used
what was at hand — as did
Angel Jones of Mold, whose meditations
were sewn into coats and britches.
                    Well, I would like to make,
thinking some line still taut between me and them,
poems direct as what the birds said,
hard as a floor, sound as a bench,
mysterious as the silence when the tailor
would pause with his needle in the air.

Pleasures

I like to find
what's not found
at once, but lies

within something of another nature,
in repose, distinct.
Gull feathers of glass, hidden

in white pulp: the bones of squid
which I pull out and lay
blade by blade on the draining board —

    tapered as if for swiftness, to pierce
    the heart, but fragile, substance
    belying design.   Or a fruit, *mamey*,

cased in rough brown peel, the flesh
rose-amber, and the seed:
the seed a stone of wood, carved and

polished, walnut-colored, formed
like a brazilnut, but large,
large enough to fill
the hungry palm of a hand.

I like the juicy stem of grass that grows
within the coarser leaf folded round,
and the butteryellow glow

in the narrow flute from which the morning-glory
opens blue and cool on a hot morning.

The Goddess

    She in whose lipservice
    I passed my time,
    whose name I knew, but not her face,
    came upon me where I lay in Lie Castle!

    Flung me across the room, and
    room after room (hitting the walls, re-
    bounding — to the last

sticky wall — wrenching away from it
pulled hair out!)
till I lay
outside the outer walls!

There in cold air
lying still where her hand had thrown me,
I tasted the mud that splattered my lips:
the seeds of a forest were in it,
asleep and growing! I tasted
her power!

The silence was answering my silence,
a forest was pushing itself
out of sleep between my submerged fingers.

I bit on a seed and it spoke on my tongue
of day that shone already among stars
in the water-mirror of low ground,
and a wind rising ruffled the lights:
she passed near me returning from the encounter,
she who plucked me from the close rooms,

without whom nothing
flowers, fruits, sleeps in season,
without whom nothing
speaks in its own tongue, but returns
lie for lie!

Matins

i

The authentic! Shadows of it
sweep past in dreams, one could say imprecisely,
evoking the almost-silent
ripping apart of giant
sheets of cellophane. No.
It thrusts up close. Exactly in dreams
it has you off-guard, you
recognize it before you have time.
For a second before waking
the alarm bell is a red conical hat, it
takes form.

ii

The authentic! I said
rising from the toilet seat.
The radiator in rhythmic knockings
spoke of the rising steam.
The authentic, I said
breaking the handle of my hairbrush as I
brushed my hair in
rhythmic strokes: That's it,
that's joy, it's always
a recognition, the known
appearing fully itself, and
more itself than one knew.

iii

The new day rises
as heat rises,
knocking in the pipes
with rhythms it seizes for its own
to speak of its invention —
the real, the new-laid
egg whose speckled shell
the poet fondles and must break
if he will be nourished.

iv

A shadow painted where
yes, a shadow must fall.
The cow's breath
not forgotten in the mist, in the
words. Yes,
verisimilitude draws up
heat in us, zest
to follow through,
follow through,
follow
transformations of day
in its turning, in its becoming.

v

Stir the holy grains, set
the bowls on the table and
call the child to eat.

While we eat we think,
as we think an undercurrent
of dream runs through us
faster than thought
towards recognition.

Call the child to eat,
send him off, his mouth
tasting of toothpaste, to go down
into the ground, into a roaring train
and to school.

His cheeks are pink
his black eyes hold his dreams, he has left
forgetting his glasses.

Follow down the stairs at a clatter
to give them to him and save
his clear sight.

Cold air
comes in at the street door.

vi

The authentic! It rolls
just out of reach, beyond
running feet and
stretching fingers, down
the green slope and into
the black waves of the sea.
Speak to me, little horse, beloved,
tell me
how to follow the iron ball,
how to follow through to the country
beneath the waves
to the place where I must kill you and you step out
of your bones and flystrewn meat
tall, smiling, renewed,
formed in your own likeness.

vii

Marvelous Truth, confront us
at every turn,
in every guise, iron ball,
egg, dark horse, shadow,
cloud
of breath on the air,

dwell
in our crowded hearts
our steaming bathrooms, kitchens full of
things to be done, the
ordinary streets.

Thrust close your smile
that we know you, terrible joy.

The Ache of Marriage

The ache of marriage:

thigh and tongue, beloved,
are heavy with it,
it throbs in the teeth

We look for communion
and are turned away, beloved,
each and each

It is leviathan and we
in its belly
looking for joy, some joy
not to be known outside it

two by two in the ark of
the ache of it.

Losing Track

Long after you have swung back
away from me
I think you are still with me:

you come in close to the shore
on the tide
and nudge me awake the way

a boat adrift nudges the pier:
am I a pier
half-in half-out of the water?

- and in the pleasure of that communion
I lose track,
the moon I watch goes down, the

tide swings you away before
I know I'm
alone again long since,

mud sucking at gray and black
timbers of me,
a light growth of green dreams drying.

The Earth Worm

The worm artist
out of soil, by passage
of himself
constructing.
Castles of metaphor!
Delicate
            dungeon turrets!
He throws off
artifacts as he
contracts and expands the
muscle of his being,
ringed in himself,
tilling. He
is homage to
earth, aerates
the ground of his living.

The Cat as Cat

The cat on my bosom
sleeping and purring
— fur-petalled chrysanthemum,
squirrel-killer —

is a metaphor only if I
force him to be one,
looking too long in his pale, fond,
dilating, contracting eyes

that reject mirrors, refuse
to observe what bides
stockstill.
        Likewise

flex and reflex of claws
gently pricking through sweater to skin
gently sustains their own tune,
not mine. I-Thou, cat, I-Thou.

The Mutes

Those groans men use
passing a woman on the street
or on the steps of the subway

to tell her she is a female
and their flesh knows it,

are they a sort of tune,
an ugly enough song, sung
by a bird with a slit tongue

but meant for music?

Or are they the muffled roaring
of deafmutes trapped in a building that is
slowly filling with smoke?

Perhaps both.

Such men most often
look as if groan were all they could do,
yet a woman, in spite of herself,

knows it's a tribute:
if she were lacking all grace
they'd pass her in silence:

so it's not only to say she's
a warm hole. It's a word

in grief-language, nothing to do with
primitive, not an ur-language;
language stricken, sickened, cast down

in decrepitude. She wants to
throw the tribute away, dis-
gusted, and can't,

it goes on buzzing in her ear,
it changes the pace of her walk,
the torn posters in echoing corridors

spell it out, it
quakes and gnashes as the train comes in.
Her pulse sullenly

had picked up speed,
but the cars slow down and
jar to a stop while her understanding

keeps on translating:
"Life after life after life goes by

without poetry,
without seemliness,
without love."

What Wild Dawns There Were

What wild dawns there were
in our first years here
when we would run outdoors naked

877

to pee in the long grass behind the house
        and see over the hills such streamers,
        such banners of fire and blue (the blue
        that is Lilith to full day's honest Eve) —
What feathers of gold under the morning star
    we saw from dazed eyes before
stumbling back to bed chilled with dew
to sleep till the sun was high!

Now if we wake early
    we don't go outdoors — or I don't —
    and you if you do go
    rarely call me to see the day break.
I watch the dawn through glass: this year
        only cloudless flushes of light, paleness
        slowly turning to rose,
        and fading subdued.
We have not spoken of these tired
risings of the sun.

Relearning the Alphabet

For G. who could not help it, I. who saw me, R. who
read me, and M. for everything.

*"The treasure . . . lies buried. There is no need to seek it
in a distant country . . . It is behind the stove, the center
of the life and warmth that rule our existence, if only we
knew how to unearth it. And yet — there is this strange
and persistent fact, that it is only after . . . a journey in
a distant region, in a new land, that . . . the inner voice
. . . can make itself understood by us. And to this strange
and persistent fact is added another: that he who reveals
to us the meaning of our . . . inward pilgrimage must be
himself a stranger . . ."*   HEINRICH ZIMMER

A

Joy — a beginning.   Anguish, ardor.
To relearn the ah! of knowing in unthinking
joy: the belovéd stranger lives.
Sweep up anguish as with a wing-tip,
brushing the ashes back to the fire's core.

B
To be. To love an other only for being.

C
Clear, cool? Not those evasions. The seeing
that burns through, comes through to
the fire's core.

D
In the beginning was delight. A depth
stirred as one stirs fire unthinking.
Dark dark dark . And the blaze illumines
dream.

E
Endless
returning, endless
revolution of dream to ember, ember to anguish,
anguish to flame, flame to delight,
delight to dark and dream, dream to ember

F
that the mind's fire may not fail.
The *vowels of affliction,* of unhealed
not to feel it, uttered,
transformed in utterance
to song.
        Not farewell, not farewell, but faring

G
forth into the grace of transformed
continuance, the green meadows
of Grief-Dale where joy grew, flowering
close to the ground, old tales recount,

H
and may be had yet for the harvesting.

I, J
Into the world of continuance, to find
I-who-I-am again, who wanted
to enter a life not mine,
        to leap a wide, deep, swift river.

At the edge, I stand yet. No, I am moving away,
walking away from the unbridged rush of waters towards
"Imagination's holy forest," meaning to thread its ways, that are dark,
and come to my own clearing, where "dreamy, gloomy,
friendly trees" grow, one by one — but
        I'm not looking where I'm going,
        my head's turned back, to see
           whom I called "jester": someone dreamed
           on the far bank: not dreamed, seen
in epiphany, as Picasso's bronze *Head of a Jester*
was seen.
        I go stumbling
              (head turned)
                        back to my origins:
(if that's where I'm going)
               to joy, my Jerusalem.
Weeping, gesturing,
I'm a small figure in mind's eye,
diminishing in the sweep of rain or gray tears
that cloud the far shore as jealous rage
clouds love and changes it, changes vision.

K

Caritas is what I must travel to.
Through to the fire's core,
an alchemy:
         caritas, claritas.
But find my face clenched
when I wake at night
           in limbo.

L

Back there forgetting, among the
letters   folded and put away.
Not uttered.
      "The feel of
not to feel it
was never said . . ." Keats said.
"Desolation . . . Absence an absolute
presence
        calling forth . . ." the jester said
from the far shore ("gravely, ringing his bells,
a tune of sorrow." I dance to it?)

DENISE LEVERTOV

"You are offhand. The trouble
is concealed?" Isak said,
calling me forth.

I am called forth
from time to time.

I was in the time
of desolation.
What light is it
waking me?
        Absence has not become
a presence.
        Lost in the alphabet
        I was looking for
        the word I can't now say
(love)
        and am called forth
        unto the twelfth letter
        by the love in a question.

           M
Honest man, I wanted
        the moon and went
        out to sea to touch
        the moon and

        down a lane of bright
        broken vanishing
        curled pyramids of
        moonwater
        moving
        towards the moon
        and touched
        the luminous dissolving
        half moon
        cold
I am
come back,
humbled, to warm myself,
honest man,

our bed is
          upon the earth
your soul is
          in your body
your mouth
          has found
my mouth once more
— I'm home.

                    N
Something in me that wants to cling
to *never*,
          wants to have been
          wounded deeper
          burned by the cold moon to cinder,

shrinks as the disk
dwindles to vision
                    numb not to continuance
                    but to that source
                    of mind's fire

                    waning now,
                    no doubt to wax again —

                    yet I perhaps not be there
                    in its light.

                    O
Hostile.   Ordinary.   Home.
Order.   Alone.   Other.

Hostile longing.   Ordinary rose, omnivorous.
                    Home, solitude.

Somnolence grotto.
Caught. Lost. Orient almost,
volition.
Own.   Only.   `

Pain recedes, rising from heart to head
and out.

Apple thunder, rolling over the
attic floor.

Yet I would swear
there had been savage light
moments before.

P, Q

In childhood dream-play I was always
the knight or squire, not
the lady:
quester, petitioner, win or lose, not
she who was sought.
The initial of quest or question
branded itself long since on the flank
of my Pegasus.
Yet he flies always
home to the present.

R

Released through bars of sorrow
as if not a gate had opened but I
grown intangible had passed through, shadowy,
from dark of yearning into
a soft day, western March;

a thrust of birdsong
parts the gold flowers thickbranching
that roof the path over.

Arms enfold me
tenderly. I am trusted, I trust
the real that transforms me.
And relinquish
in grief
the seeing that burns through, comes through
to fire's core: transformation, continuance,
as acts of magic I would perform, are no longer
articles of faith.

S

Or no: it
slowly becomes known to me:
articles of faith are indeed
rules of the will — graceless,
                          faithless.
The door I flung my weight against
was constructed to open   out
                          towards me.

In-seeing
to candleflame's
blue ice-cavern, measureless,

may not be forced by sharp
desire.
            The Prince
            turns in the wood: "Retrace
                          thy steps, seek out
            the hut you passed, impatient,
            the day you lost your quarry.

            There dwells
            a secret. Restore to it
            its life.
            You will not recognize
            your desire until
            thou hast it fast, it goeth
            aside, it hath
            the cunning of quicksilver."

I turn in the forest,
About me the tree-multitudes
twist their roots in earth
to rip it, draw
hidden rivers up into
branch-towers.
Their crowns in the light sway
green beyond vision
                    All utterance
takes me step by hesitant step towards

T

— yes, to continuance: into
                      that life beyond the dead-end where
(in a desert time of
dry strange heat, of dust
that tinged mountain clouds with copper,
turn of the year impending unnoticed,
the cactus shadows brittle thornstars,
time of
desolation)   I was lost.

The forest is holy.
The sacred paths are of stone.
A clearing.
The altars are shifting deposits of pineneedles,
            hidden waters,
              streets of choirwood,
not what the will
thinks to construct for its testimonies.

U

Relearn the alphabet,
relearn the world, the world
understood anew only in doing, under-
stood only as
looked-up-into out of earth,
the heart an eye looking,
the heart a root
planted in earth.
Transmutation is not
under the will's rule.

V

Vision sets out
journeying somewhere,
walking the dreamwaters:
arrives
not on the far shore but upriver,
a place not evoked, discovered.

W

Heart breaks but mends
like good bone.

It's the vain will
wants to have been wounded deeper,
burned by the cold moon to cinder.

Wisdom's a stone
dwells in forgotten pockets —
lost, refound, exiled —
revealed again
in the palm of
mind's hand, moonstone
of wax and wane, stone pulse.

Y

Vision will not be used.
Yearning will not be used.
Wisdom will not be used.
Only the vain will
strives to use and be used,
comes not to fire's core
but cinder.

Z

Sweep up
anguish as with a wing-tip:

the blaze addresses
a different darkness:
absence has not become
the transformed presence the will
looked for,
but other: the present,

that which was poised already in the ah! of praise.

A. R. AMMONS
b. 1926

So I Said I Am Ezra

So I said I am Ezra
and the wind whipped my throat
gaming for the sounds of my voice
I listened to the wind

go over my head and up into the night
Turning to the sea I said
   I am Ezra
but there were no echoes from the waves
The words were swallowed up
  in the voice of the surf
or leaping over swells
lost themselves oceanward
  Over the bleached and broken fields
I moved my feet and turning from the wind
  that ripped sheets of sand
  from the beach and threw them
  like seamists across the dunes
swayed as if the wind were taking me away
and said
   I am Ezra
As a word too much repeated
falls out of being
so I Ezra went out into the night
like a drift of sand
and splashed among the windy oats
that clutch the dunes
of unremembered seas

Unsaid

Have you listened for the things I have left out?
I am nowhere near the end yet and already
  hear
  the hum of omissions,
the chant of vacancies, din of

silences:

there is the other side of matter, antimatter,
  the antiproton:
  we
have measured the proton: it has mass: we
have measured the antiproton: it has negative mass:

you will not

hear me completely even at this early point
unless you hear my emptiness:
      go back:
      how can I
tell you what I have not said: you must look for it

yourself: that

side has weight, too, though words cannot bear it
out: listen for the things I have left out:
      I am
      aware
of them, as you must be, or you will miss

the non-song

in my singing: it is not that words *cannot* say
what is missing: it is only that what is missing
      cannot
      be missed if
spoken: read the parables of my unmaking:

feel the ris-

ing bubble's trembling walls: rush into the domes
these wordy arches shape: hear
      me
      when I am
silent: gather the boundaried vacancies.

Triphammer Bridge

I wonder what to mean by *sanctuary*, if a real or
apprehended place, as of a bell rung in a gold
surround, or as of silver roads along the beaches

of clouds seas don't break or black mountains
overspill; jail: ice here's shapelier than anything,
on the eaves massive, jawed along gorge ledges, solid

in the plastic blue boat fall left water in: if I
think the bitterest thing I can think of that seems like
reality, slickened back, hard, shocked by rip-high wind:

sanctuary, sanctuary, I say it over and over and the
word's sound is the one place to dwell: that's it, just
the sound, and the imagination of the sound — a place.

Coon Song

I got one good look
    in the raccoon's eyes
        when he fell from the tree
came to his feet
    and perfectly still
        seized the baying hounds
in his dull fierce stare,
    in that recognition all
        decision lost,
choice irrelevant, before the
    battle fell
        and the unwinding
of his little knot of time began:

        Dostoevsky would think
it important if the coon
    could choose to
        be back up the tree:
or if he could choose to be
    wagging by a swamp pond,
        dabbling at scuttling
crawdads: the coon may have
    dreamed in fact of curling
        into the holed-out gall
of a fallen oak some squirrel
    had once brought
        high into the air
clean leaves to: but

        reality can go to hell
is what the coon's eyes said to me:
    and said how simple
        the solution to my
problem is: it needs only
    not to be: I thought the raccoon
        felt no anger,

saw none; cared nothing for cowardice,
        bravery; was in fact
            bored at
knowing what would ensue:
        the unwinding, the whirling growls,
            exposed tenders,
the wet teeth — a problem to be
        solved, the taut-coiled vigor
            of the hunt
ready to snap loose:

            you want to know what happened,
you want to hear me describe it,
        to placate the hound's-mouth
            slobbering in your own heart:
I will not tell you: actually the coon
        possessing secret knowledge
            pawed dust on the dogs
and they disappeared, yapping into
        nothingness, and the coon went
            down to the pond
and washed his face and hands and beheld
        the world: maybe he didn't:
            I am no slave that I
should entertain you, say what you want
        to hear, let you wallow in
            your silt: one two three four five:
one two three four five six seven eight nine ten:

        (all this time I've been
            counting spaces
while you were thinking of something else)
        mess in your own sloppy silt:
            the hounds disappeared
yelping (the way you would at extinction)
        into — the order
            breaks up here — immortality:
I know that's where you think the brave
        little victims should go:
            I do not care what
you think: I do not care what you think:
        I do not care what you
            think: one two three four five

six seven eight nine ten: here we go
   round the here-we-go-round, the
      here-we-go-round, the here-we-
go-round: coon will end in disorder at the
   teeth of hounds: the situation
   will get him:
spheres roll, cubes stay put: now there
   one two three four five
   are two philosophies:
here we go round the mouth-wet of hounds:

      what I choose
      is youse:
      baby

The Yucca Moth

   The yucca clump
is blooming,
   tall sturdy spears
spangling into bells of light,
   green
in the white blooms
   faint as
a memory of mint:

I raid
   a bloom,
spread the hung petals out,
   and, surprised he is not
a bloom-part, find
   a moth inside, the exact color,
the bloom his daylight port or cove:

though time comes
   and goes and troubles
are unlessened,
   the yucca is lifting temples
of bloom: from the night
   of our dark flights, can
we go in to heal, live
   out in white-green shade
the radiant, white, hanging day?

Corsons Inlet

I went for a walk over the dunes again this morning
to the sea,
then turned right along
  the surf

              rounded a naked headland
              and returned

  along the inlet shore:

it was muggy sunny, the wind from the sea steady and high,
crisp in the running sand,
    some breakthroughs of sun
  but after a bit

continuous overcast:

the walk liberating, I was released from forms,
from the perpendiculars,
    straight lines, blocks, boxes, binds
of thought
into the hues, shadings, rises, flowing bends and blends
          of sight:

              I allow myself eddies of meaning:
yield to a direction of significance
running
like a stream through the geography of my work:
  you can find
in my sayings
              swerves of action
              like the inlet's cutting edge:
      there are dunes of motion,
organizations of grass, white sandy paths of remembrance
in the overall wandering of mirroring mind:

but Overall is beyond me: is the sum of these events
I cannot draw, the ledger I cannot keep, the accounting
beyond the account:

in nature there are few sharp lines: there are areas of
primrose
    more or less dispersed;

disorderly orders of bayberry; between the rows
of dunes,
irregular swamps of reeds,
though not reeds alone, but grass, bayberry, yarrow, all . . .
predominantly reeds:

I have reached no conclusions, have erected no boundaries,
shutting out and shutting in, separating inside
       from outside: I have
       drawn no lines:
       as

manifold events of sand
change the dune's shape that will not be the same shape
tomorrow,

so I am willing to go along, to accept
the becoming
thought, to stake off no beginnings or ends, establish
       no walls:

by transitions the land falls from grassy dunes to creek
to undercreek: but there are no lines, though
     change in that transition is clear
     as any sharpness: but "sharpness" spread out,
allowed to occur over a wider range
than mental lines can keep:

the moon was full last night: today, low tide was low:
black shoals of mussels exposed to the risk
of air
and, earlier, of sun,
waved in and out with the waterline, waterline inexact,
caught always in the event of change:
     a young mottled gull stood free on the shoals
     and ate
to vomiting: another gull, squawking possession, cracked a crab,
picked out the entrails, swallowed the soft-shelled legs, a ruddy
turnstone running in to snatch leftover bits:

risk is full: every living thing in
siege: the demand is life, to keep life: the small
white blacklegged egret, how beautiful, quietly stalks and spears

the shallows, darts to shore
            to stab — what? I couldn't
see against the black mudflats — a frightened
fiddler crab?

            the news to my left over the dunes and
reeds and bayberry clumps was
            fall: thousands of tree swallows
            gathering for flight:
            an order held
            in constant change: a congregation
rich with entropy: nevertheless, separable, noticeable
            as one event,
                  not chaos: preparations for
flight from winter,
cheet, cheet, cheet, cheet, wings rifling the green clumps,
beaks
at the bayberries
      a perception full of wind, flight, curve,
      sound:
      the possibility of rule as the sum of rulelessness:
the "field" of action
with moving, incalculable center:

in the smaller view, order tight with shape:
blue tiny flowers on a leafless weed: carapace of crab:
snail shell:
            pulsations of order
            in the bellies of minnows: orders swallowed,
broken down, transferred through membranes
to strengthen larger orders: but in the large view, no
lines or changeless shapes: the working in and out, together
            and against, of millions of events: this,
                  so that I make
                  no form
                  formlessness:

orders as summaries, as outcomes of actions override
or in some way result, not predictably (seeing me gain
the top of a dune,
the swallows
could take flight — some other fields of bayberry
            could enter fall
            berryless) and there is serenity:

no arranged terror: no forcing of image, plan,
or thought:
no propaganda, no humbling of reality to precept:

terror pervades but is not arranged, all possibilities
of escape open: no route shut, except in
   the sudden loss of all routes:

     I see narrow orders, limited tightness, but will
not run to that easy victory:
     still around the looser, wider forces work:
     I will try
   to fasten into order enlarging grasps of disorder, widening
scope, but enjoying the freedom that
Scope eludes my grasp, that there is no finality of vision,
that I have perceived nothing completely,
     that tomorrow a new walk is a new walk.

Apologia pro Vita Sua

I started picking up the stones
throwing them into one place
and by sunrise I was going far away
for the large ones
always turning to see never lost
the cairn's height
lengthening my radial reach:

the sun watched with deep concentration
and the heap through the hours grew
and became by nightfall
distinguishable from all the miles around
of slate and sand:

during the night the wind falling
turned earthward its lofty freedom and speed
and the sharp blistering sound muffled
toward dawn and the blanket was
drawn up over a breathless face:

even so you can see in full dawn
the ground there lifts
a foreign thing desertless in origin.

Laser

An image comes
and the mind's light, confused
as that on surf
or ocean shelves,
gathers up,
parallelizes, focuses
and in a rigid beam illuminates the image:

the head seeks in itself
fragments of left-over light
to cast a new
direction,
any direction,
to strike and fix
a random, contradicting image:

but any found image falls
back to darkness or
the lesser beams splinter and
go out:
the mind tries to
dream of diversity, of mountain
rapids shattered with sound and light,

of wind fracturing brush or
bursting out of order against a mountain
range: but the focused beam
folds all energy in:
the image glares filling all space:
the head falls and
hangs and cannot wake itself.

Cascadilla Falls

I went down by Cascadilla
Falls this
evening, the
stream below the falls,
and picked up a
handsized stone
kidney-shaped, testicular, and

thought all its motions into it,
the 800 mph earth spin,
the 190-million-mile yearly
displacement around the sun,
the overriding
grand
haul

of the galaxy with the 30,000
mph of where
the sun's going:
thought all the interweaving
motions
into myself: dropped

the stone to dead rest:
the stream from other motions
broke
rushing over it:
shelterless,
I turned

to the sky and stood still:
Oh
I do
not know where I am going
that I can live my life
by this single creek.

Classic

I sat by a stream in a
perfect — except for willows —
emptiness
and the mountain that
was around,

scraggly with brush &
rock
said
I see you're scribbling again:

accustomed to mountains,
their cumbersome intrusions,
I said

well, yes, but in a fashion very
like the water here
uncapturable and vanishing:

but that
said the mountain does not
excuse the stance
or diction

and next if you're not careful
you'll be
arriving at ways
water survives its motions.

Periphery

One day I complained about the periphery
that it was thickets hard to get around in
    or get around for
an older man: it's like keeping charts

of symptoms, every reality a symptom
where the ailment's not nailed down:
    much knowledge, precise enough,
but so multiple it says this man is alive

or isn't: it's like all of a body answering
all of pharmacopoeia, a too
    adequate relationship:
so I complained and said maybe I'd brush

deeper and see what was pushing all this
periphery, so difficult to make any sense
    out of, out:
with me, decision brings its own

hesitation: a symptom, no doubt, but open
and meaningless enough without paradigm:
    but hesitation
can be all right, too: I came on a spruce

thicket full of elk, gushy snow-weed,
nine species of lichen, four pure white
    rocks and
several swatches of verbena near bloom.

Upland

Certain presuppositions are altered
by height: the inversion to
sky-well a peak
in a desert makes: the welling

from clouds down the boulder fountains:
it is always a
surprise out west there —
the blue ranges loose and aglide

with heat and then come close
on slopes leaning up into green:
a number of other phenomena might
be summoned —

take the Alleghenies for example,
some quality in the air
of summit stones lying free and loose
out among the shrub trees: every

exigency seems prepared for that might
roll, bound, or give flight
to stone: that is, the stones are
prepared: they are round and ready.

The Unifying Principle

Ramshackles, archipelagoes, loose constellations
are less fierce, subsidiary centers, with the
attenuations of interstices, roughing the salience,

jarring the outbreak of too insistent commonalty:
a board, for example, not surrendering the rectitude
of its corners, the island of the oaks an

admonishment to pines, underfigurings (as of the Bear)
that take identity on: this motion is against
the grinding oneness of seas, hallows distinction

into the specific: but less lovely, too, for how
is the mass to be amassed, by what sanction
neighbor touch neighbor, island bear resemblance,

how are distinction's hard lines to be dissolved
(and preserved): what may all the people turn to,
the old letters, the shaped, characteristic peak

generations of minds have deflected and kept:
a particular tread that sometimes unweaves, taking
more shape on, into dance: much must be

tolerated as out of timbre, out of step, as being not
in its time or mood (the hiatus of the unconcerned)
and much room provided for the wretched to find caves

to ponder way off in: what then can lift the people
and only when they choose to rise or what can make
them want to rise, though business prevents: the

unifying principle will be a
phrase shared, an old cedar long known, general
wind-shapes in a usual sand: those objects single,

single enough to be uninterfering, multiple by
the piling on of shared sight, touch, saying:
when it's found the people live the small wraths of ease.

The City Limits

When you consider the radiance, that it does not withhold
itself but pours its abundance without selection into every
nook and cranny not overhung or hidden; when you consider

that birds' bones make no awful noise against the light but
lie low in the light as in a high testimony; when you consider
the radiance, that it will look into the guiltiest

swervings of the weaving heart and bear itself upon them,
not flinching into disguise or darkening; when you consider
the abundance of such resource as illuminates the glow-blue

bodies and gold-skeined wings of flies swarming the dumped
guts of a natural slaughter or the coil of shit and in no
way winces from its storms of generosity; when you consider

that air or vacuum, snow or shale, squid or wolf, rose or lichen,
each is accepted into as much light as it will take, then
the heart moves roomier, the man stands and looks about, the

leaf does not increase itself above the grass, and the dark
work of the deepest cells is of a tune with May bushes
and fear lit by the breadth of such calmly turns to praise.

JAMES MERRILL
b. 1926

An Urban Convalescence

Out for a walk, after a week in bed,
I find them tearing up part of my block
And, chilled through, dazed and lonely, join the dozen
In meek attitudes, watching a huge crane
Fumble luxuriously in the filth of years.
Her jaws dribble rubble. An old man
Laughs and curses in her brain,
Bringing to mind the close of *The White Goddess*.

As usual in New York, everything is torn down
Before you have had time to care for it.
Head bowed, at the shrine of noise, let me try to recall
What building stood here. Was there a building at all?
I have lived on this same street for a decade.

Wait. Yes. Vaguely a presence rises
Some five floors high, of shabby stone
— Or am I confusing it with another one
In another part of town, or of the world? —
And over its lintel into focus vaguely
Misted with blood (my eyes are shut)
A single garland sways, stone fruit, stone leaves,
Which years of grit had etched until it thrust
Roots down, even into the poor soil of my seeing.
When did the garland become part of me?
I ask myself, amused almost,
Then shiver once from head to toe,

Transfixed by a particular cheap engraving of garlands
Bought for a few francs long ago,
All calligraphic tendril and cross-hatched rondure,
Ten years ago, and crumpled up to stanch
Boughs dripping, whose white gestures filled a cab,
And thought of neither then nor since.
Also, to clasp them, the small, red-nailed hand
Of no one I can place. Wait. No. Her name, her features
Lie toppled underneath that year's fashions.
The words she must have spoken, setting her face
To fluttering like a veil, I cannot hear now,
Let alone understand.

So that I am already on the stair,
As it were, of where I lived,
When the whole structure shudders at my tread
And soundlessly collapses, filling
The air with motes of stone.
Onto the still erect building next door
Are pressed levels and hues —
Pocked rose, streaked greens, brown whites.
Who drained the pousse-café?
Wires and pipes, snapped off at the roots, quiver.

Well, that is what life does. I stare
A moment longer, so. And presently
The massive volume of the world
Closes again.

Upon that book I swear
To abide by what it teaches:
Gospels of ugliness and waste,
Of towering voids, of soiled gusts,
Of a shrieking to be faced
Full into, eyes astream with cold —

With cold?
All right then. With self-knowledge.

Indoors at last, the pages of *Time* are apt
To open, and the illustrated mayor of New York,
Given a glimpse of how and where I work,
To note yet one more house that can be scrapped.

Unwillingly I picture
My walls weathering in the general view.
It is not even as though the new
Buildings did very much for architecture.

Suppose they did. The sickness of our time requires
That these as well be blasted in their prime.
You would think the simple fact of having lasted
Threatened our cities like mysterious fires.

There are certain phrases which to use in a poem
Is like rubbing silver with quicksilver. Bright
But facile, the glamour deadens overnight.
For instance, how "the sickness of our time"

Enhances, then debases, what I feel.
At my desk I swallow in a glass of water
No longer cordial, scarcely wet, a pill
They had told me not to take until much later.

With the result that back into my imagination
The city glides, like cities seen from the air,
Mere smoke and sparkle to the passenger
Having in mind another destination

Which now is not that honey-slow descent
Of the Champs-Elysées, her hand in his,
But the dull need to make some kind of house
Out of the life lived, out of the love spent.

After Greece

Light into the olive entered
And was oil. Rain made the huge pale stones
Shine from within. The moon turned his hair white
Who next stepped from between the columns,
Shielding his eyes. All through
The countryside were old ideas
Found lying open to the elements.
Of the gods' houses only
A minor premise here and there
Would be balancing the heaven of fixed stars
Upon a Doric capital. The rest
Lay spilled, their fluted drums half sunk in cyclamen
Or deep in water's biting clarity
Which just barely upheld me
The next week, when I sailed for home.
But where is home — these walls?
These limbs? The very spaniel underfoot
Races in sleep, toward what?
It is autumn. I did not invite
Those guests, windy and brittle, who drink my liquor.
Returning from a walk I find
The bottles filled with spleen, my room itself
Smeared by reflection onto the far hemlocks.
I some days flee in dream
Back to the exposed porch of the maidens
Only to find my great-great-grandmothers
Erect there, peering
Into a globe of red Bohemian glass.
As it swells and sinks, I call up
Graces, Furies, Fates, removed
To my country's warm, lit halls, with rivets forced
Through drapery, and nothing left to bear.
They seem anxious to know
What holds up heaven nowadays.
I start explaining how in that vast fire
Were other irons — well, Art, Public Spirit,
Ignorance, Economics, Love of Self,
Hatred of Self, a hundred more,
Each burning to be felt, each dedicated
To sparing us the worst; how I distrust them
As I should have done those ladies; how I want

Essentials: salt, wine, olive, the light, the scream —
No! I have scarcely named you,
And look, in a flash you stand full-grown before me,
Row upon row, Essentials,
Dressed like your sister caryatids
Or tombstone angels jealous of their dead,
With undulant coiffures, lips weathered, cracked by grime,
And faultless eyes gone blank beneath the immense
Zinc and gunmetal northern sky . . .
Stay then. Perhaps the system
Calls for spirits. This first glass I down
To the last time
I ate and drank in that old world. May I
Also survive its meanings, and my own.

The Parrot Fish

The shadow of the little fishing launch
Discreetly, inch by inch,
Crept after us on its belly over
The reef's uneven floor.

The motor gasped out drowsy vapor.
Seconds went by before
Anyone thought to interpret
The jingling of Inez's bracelet.

Chalk-violet, olive, all veils and sequins, a
Priestess out of the next Old Testament extravaganza,
With round gold eyes and minuscule buck-teeth,
Up flaunted into death

The parrot fish. And for a full hour beat
Irregular, passionate
Tattoos from its casket lined with zinc.
Finally we understood, I think.

Ashore, the warm waves licked our feet.
One or two heavy chords the heat
Struck, set the white beach vibrating.
And throwing back its head the sea began to sing.

The Furnished Room

Blue boughs, green fruit —
That was our wallpaper.
Two doors, both shut;
Two windows, a mirror.

Against the walls
Table and divan stood,
Odd animals,
One pine, one cherry wood.

One bore the book, the bowl,
The lamp. Its four
Legs shook. Its soul
Slid out like an empty drawer.

The other: claw-foot, soft
Belly, striped hide.
Glad in its hug we laughed.
Time howled outside.

But central heat
Hissed back and kept us warm.
Come dusk, lamplight
Lit out into a storm

Determined, all that week,
To fill us with
What no one else could wreak
On the room's myth.

The Broken Home

Crossing the street,
I saw the parents and the child
At their window, gleaming like fruit
With evening's mild gold leaf.

In a room on the floor below,
Sunless, cooler — a brimming
Saucer of wax, marbly and dim —
I have lit what's left of my life.

I have thrown out yesterday's milk
And opened a book of maxims.
The flame quickens. The word stirs.

Tell me, tongue of fire,
That you and I are as real
At least as the people upstairs.

My father, who had flown in World War I,
Might have continued to invest his life
In cloud banks well above Wall Street and wife.
But the race was run below, and the point was to win.

Too late now, I make out in his blue gaze
(Through the smoked glass of being thirty-six)
The soul eclipsed by twin black pupils, sex
And business; time was money in those days.

Each thirteenth year he married. When he died
There were already several chilled wives
In sable orbit — rings, cars, permanent waves.
We'd felt him warming up for a green bride.

He could afford it. He was "in his prime"
At three score ten. But money was not time.

When my parents were younger this was a popular act:
A veiled woman would leap from an electric, wine-dark car
To the steps of no matter what — the Senate or the Ritz Bar —
And bodily, at newsreel speed, attack

No matter whom — Al Smith or José Maria Sert
Or Clemenceau — veins standing out on her throat
As she yelled *War mongerer! Pig! Give us the vote!*,
And would have to be hauled away in her hobble skirt.

What had the man done? Oh, made history.
Her business (he had implied) was giving birth,
Tending the house, mending the socks.

Always that same old story —
Father Time and Mother Earth,
A marriage on the rocks.

One afternoon, red, satyr-thighed
Michael, the Irish setter, head
Passionately lowered, led
The child I was to a shut door. Inside,

Blinds beat sun from the bed.
The green-gold room throbbed like a bruise.
Under a sheet, clad in taboos
Lay whom we sought, her hair undone, outspread,

And of a blackness found, if ever now, in old
Engravings where the acid bit.
I must have needed to touch it
Or the whiteness — was she dead?
Her eyes flew open, startled strange and cold.
The dog slumped to the floor. She reached for me. I fled.

Tonight they have stepped out onto the gravel.
The party is over. It's the fall
Of 1931. They love each other still.

She: Charlie, I can't stand the pace.
He: Come on, honey — why, you'll bury us all!

A lead soldier guards my windowsill:
Khaki rifle, uniform, and face.
Something in me grows heavy, silvery, pliable.

How intensely people used to feel!
Like metal poured at the close of a proletarian novel,
Refined and glowing from the crucible,
I see those two hearts, I'm afraid,
Still. Cool here in the graveyard of good and evil,
They are even so to be honored and obeyed.

. . . Obeyed, at least, inversely. Thus
I rarely buy a newspaper, or vote.
To do so, I have learned, is to invite
The tread of a stone guest within my house.

Shooting this rusted bolt, though, against him,
I trust I am no less time's child than some
Who on the heath impersonate Poor Tom
Or on the barricades risk life and limb.

Nor do I try to keep a garden, only
An avocado in a glass of water —
Roots pallid, gemmed with air. And later,

When the small gilt leaves have grown
Fleshy and green, I let them die, yes, yes,
And start another. I am earth's no less.

A child, a red dog roam the corridors,
Still, of the broken home. No sound. The brilliant
Rag runners halt before wide-open doors.
My old room! Its wallpaper — cream, medallioned
With pink and brown —brings back the first nightmares,
Long summer colds, and Emma, sepia-faced,
Perspiring over broth carried upstairs
Aswim with golden fats I could not taste.

The real house became a boarding-school.
Under the ballroom ceiling's allegory
Someone at last may actually be allowed
To learn something; or, from my window, cool
With the unstiflement of the entire story,
Watch a red setter stretch and sink in cloud.

The Mad Scene

Again last night I dreamed the dream called Laundry.
In it, the sheets and towels of a life we were going to share,
The milk-stiff bibs, the shroud, each rag to be ever
Trampled or soiled, bled on or groped for blindly,
Came swooning out of an enormous willow hamper
Onto moon-marbly boards. We had just met. I watched
From outer darkness. I had dressed myself in clothes
Of a new fiber that never stains or wrinkles, never
Wears thin. The opera house sparkled with tiers
And tiers of eyes, like mine enlarged by belladonna,
Trained inward. There I saw the cloud-clot, gust by gust,
Form, and the lightning bite, and the roan mane unloosen.
Fingers were running in panic over the flute's nine gates.
Why did I flinch? I loved you. And in the downpour laughed
To have us wrung white, gnarled together, one
Topmost mordent of wisteria,
As the lean tree burst into grief.

A Preface to the Memoirs

Angrier than my now occasional
Rum-blossom, to adolescence come
Deep buds of pain. The blood-stained butcher-boy
And Laure at the clavier who would not smile
Were sufferers no less than the Sun King
Spots on whose countenance, the theory goes,
Must answer for that August
Of dry electric storms, of leaves'
Incendiary pamphlets fluttering.
History's lesson? What is young and burns,
Complexion of the boy, the star, the age,
Invites disfigurement. Too late
The shepherdess, her peach-bloom criminal,
Was recognized as queen. Too soon
The cleaver glittered and the chord was struck,
And in the dark that mercifully fell
You had arisen, gibbous moon,
Lit by such laws as exile both of us
From the eruptions of a court whose pageants
These deeply-pitted features chronicle.

Matinees

For David Kalstone

A gray maidservant lets me in
To Mrs Livingston's box. It's already begun!
The box is full of grownups. She sits me down
Beside her. Meanwhile a ravishing din

Swells from below — Scene One
Of *Das Rheingold*. The entire proscenium
Is covered with a rippling azure scrim.
The three sopranos dart hither and yon

On invisible strings. Cold lights
Cling to bare arms, fair tresses. Flat
And natural aglitter like paillettes
Upon the great green sonorous depths float

Until with pulsing wealth the house is filled,
No one believing, everybody thrilled.

Lives of the Great Composers make it sound
Too much like cooking: "Sore beset,
He put his heart's blood into that quintet . . ."
So let us try the figure turned around

As in some Lives of Obscure Listeners:
"The strains of Cimarosa and Mozart
Flowed through his veins, and fed his solitary heart.
Long beyond adolescence [One infers

Your elimination, sweet Champagne
Drunk between acts!] the aria's remote
Control surviving his worst interval,

Tissue of sound and tissue of the brain
Would coalesce, and what the Masters wrote
Itself compose his features sharp and small."

Hilariously Dr Scherer took the guise
Of a bland smoothshaven Alberich whose ageold
Plan had been to fill my tooth with gold.
Another whiff of laughing gas,

And the understanding was implicit
That we must guard each other, this gold and I,
Against amalgamation by
The elemental pit.

Vague as to what dentist and tooth "stood for,"
One patient dreamer gathered something more.
A voice said in the speech of birds,

"My father having tampered with your mouth,
From now on, metal, music, myth
Will seem to taint its words."

We love the good, said Plato? He was wrong.
We love as well the wicked and the weak.
Flesh hugs its shaved plush. Twenty-four-hour-long
Galas fill the hulk of the Comique.

Flesh knows by now what dishes to avoid,
Tries not to brood on bomb or heart attack.
Anatomy is destiny, said Freud.
Soul is the brilliant hypochondriac.

Soul will cough blood and sing, and softer sing,
Drink poison, breathe her joyous last, a waltz
Rubato from his arms who sobs and stays

Behind, death after death, who fairly melts
Watching her turn from him, restored, to fling
Kisses into the furnace roaring praise.

The fallen cake, the risen price of meat,
Staircase run ten times up and down like scales
(Greek proverb: He who has no brain has feet) —
One's household opera never palls or fails.

The pipes' aubade. Recitatives. — Come back!
— I'm out of pills! — We'd love to! — What? — *Nothing,*
Let me be! — No, no, I'll drink it black . . .
The neighbors' chorus. The quick darkening

In which a prostrate figure must inquire
With every earmark of its being meant
Why God in Heaven harries him/her so.

The love scene (often cut). The potion. The tableau:
Sleepers folded in a magic fire,
Tongues flickering up from humdrum incident.

When Jan Kiepura sang His Handsomeness
Of Mantua those high airs light as lust
Attuned one's bare throat to the dagger-thrust.
Living for them would have been death no less.

Or Lehmann's Marschallin! — heartbreak so shrewd,
So ostrich-plumed, one ached to disengage
Oneself from a last love, at center stage,
To the beloved's dazzled gratitude.

What havoc certain Saturday afternoons
Wrought upon a bright young person's morals
I now leave to the public to condemn.

The point thereafter was to arrange for one's
Own chills and fever, passions and betrayals,
Chiefly in order to make song of them.

You and I, caro, seldom
Risk the real thing any more.
It's all too silly or too solemn.
Enough to know the score

From records or transcription
For our four hands. Old beauties, some
In advanced stages of decomposition,

Float up through the sustaining
Pedal's black and fluid medium.
Days like today

Even recur (wind whistling themes
From *Lulu*, and sun shining
On the rough Sound) when it seems
Kinder to remember than to play.

Dear Mrs Livingston,
I want to say that I am still in a daze
From yesterday afternoon.
I will treasure the experience always —

My very first Grand Opera! It was very
Thoughtful of you to invite
Me and am so sorry
That I was late, and for my coughing fit.

I play my record of the Overture
Over and over. I pretend
I am still sitting in the theatre.

I also wrote a poem which my Mother
Says I should copy out and send.
Ever gratefully, Your little friend . . .

ROBERT CREELEY
b. 1926

I Know a Man

As I sd to my
friend, because I am
always talking, — John, I

sd, which was not his
name, the darkness sur-
rounds us, what

can we do against
it, or else, shall we &
why not, buy a goddamn big car,

drive, he sd, for
christ's sake, look
out where yr going.

The Death of Venus

I dreamt her sensual proportions
had suffered sea-change,

that she was a porpoise, a
sea-beast rising lucid from the mist.

The sound of waves killed speech
but there were gestures —

of my own, it was to call her closer,
of hers, she snorted and filled her lungs with water,

then sank, to the bottom,
and looking down, clear it was, like crystal,

there I saw her.

Wait for Me

. . . give a man his
I said to her,

manliness: provide
what you want I

creature comfort
want only

for him and herself:
more so. You

preserve essential
think marriage is

hypocrisies —
everything?

in short, make a
Oh well,

home for herself.
I said.

Naughty Boy

When he brings home a whale,
she laughs and says, that's not for real.

And if he won the Irish sweepstakes,
she would say, where were you last night?

Where are you now, for that matter? Am
I always (she says) to be looking

at you? She says,
If I thought it would get any better I

would shoot you, you
nut, you. Then pats her hair

into place, and waits
for Uncle Jim's deep-fired, all-fat, real gone

whale steaks.

If You

If you were going to get a pet
what kind of animal would you get.

A soft bodied dog, a hen —
feathers and fur to begin it again.

When the sun goes down and it gets dark
I saw an animal in a park.

Bring it home, to give it to you.
I have seen animals break in two.

You were hoping for something soft
and loyal and clean and wondrously careful —

a form of otherwise vicious habit
can have long ears and be called a rabbit.

Dead. Died. Will die. Want.
Morning, midnight. I asked you

if you were going to get a pet
what kind of animal would you get.

Heroes

In all those stories the hero
is beyond himself into the next
thing, be it those labors
of Hercules, or Aeneas going into death.

I thought the instant of the one humanness
in Virgil's plan of it
was that it was of course human enough to die,
yet to come back, as he said, *hoc opus, hic labor est.*

That was the Cumaean Sibyl speaking.
This is Robert Creeley, and Virgil
is dead now two thousand years, yet Hercules
and the *Aeneid*, yet all that industrious wis-

dom lives in the way the mountains
and the desert are waiting
for the heroes, and death also
can still propose the old labors.

The Gift

He hands
down the gift
as from a great
height, his

precious
understanding clothed
in miraculous
fortitude. This

is the present
of the ages, all
rewards
in itself.

But the lady —
she, disdain-
ful, all
in white for

this occasion — cries
out petulantly, is
that all, is
that all.

For Love

For Bobbie

Yesterday I wanted to
speak of it, that sense above
the others to me
important because all

that I know derives
from what it teaches me.
Today, what is it that
is finally so helpless,

different, despairs of its own
statement, wants to
turn away, endlessly
to turn away.

If the moon did not . . .
no, if you did not
I wouldn't either, but
what would I not

do, what prevention, what
thing so quickly stopped.
That is love yesterday
or tomorrow, not

now. Can I eat
what you give me. I
have not earned it. Must
I think of everything

as earned. Now love also
becomes a reward so
remote from me I have
only made it with my mind.

Here is tedium,
despair, a painful
sense of isolation and
whimsical if pompous

self-regard. But that image
is only of the mind's
vague structure, vague to me
because it is my own.

Love, what do I think
to say. I cannot say it.
What have you become to ask,
what have I made you into,

companion, good company,
crossed legs with skirt, or
soft body under
the bones of the bed.

Nothing says anything
but that which it wishes
would come true, fears
what else might happen in

some other place, some
other time not this one.
A voice in my place, an
echo of that only in yours.

Let me stumble into
not the confession but
the obsession I begin with
now. For you

also (also)
some time beyond place, or
place beyond time, no
mind left to

say anything at all,
that face gone, now.
Into the company of love
it all returns.

The Fire

Oh flame falling, as shaken, as the stories
my daughter sees in the light, forming, seeing
the simple burning as an action which to speak of
now I complicate, with my own burning, her story.

Then it all goes, saying, here they were, and are,
and will be again, as I used to think, to remember,
then they were here, and now, again, they are.

What in the light's form finds her face,
makes of her eyes the simple grace.

The Window

Position is where you
put it, where it is,
did you, for example, that

large tank there, silvered,
with the white church along-
side, lift

all that, to what
purpose? How
heavy the slow

world is with
everything put
in place. Some

man walks by, a
car beside him on
the dropped

road, a leaf of
yellow color is
going to

fall. It
all drops into
place. My

face is heavy
with the sight. I can
feel my eye breaking.

Fancy

Do you know what
the truth is,
what's rightly
or wrongly said,

what is wiseness,
or rightness, what
wrong, or well-
done if it is,

or is not, done.
I thought.
I thought and
thought and thought.

In a place
I was sitting,
and there
it was, a little

faint thing
hardly felt, a
kind of small
nothing.

Here

What
has happened
makes

the world.
Live
on the edge,

looking.

ALLEN GINSBERG
b. 1926

A Supermarket in California

What thoughts I have of you tonight, Walt Whitman, for I walked down the sidestreets under the trees with a headache self-conscious looking at the full moon.

In my hungry fatigue, and shopping for images, I went into the neon fruit supermarket, dreaming of your enumerations!.

What peaches and what penumbras! Whole families shopping at night! Aisles full of husbands! Wives in the avocados, babies in the tomatoes! — and you, Garcia Lorca, what were you doing down by the watermelons?

I saw you, Walt Whitman, childless, lonely old grubber, poking among the meats in the refrigerator and eyeing the grocery boys.

I heard you asking questions of each: Who killed the pork chops? What price bananas? Are you my Angel?

I wandered in and out of the brilliant stacks of cans following you, and followed in my imagination by the store detective.

We strode down the open corridors together in our solitary fancy tasting artichokes, possessing every frozen delicacy, and never passing the cashier.

Where are we going, Walt Whitman? The doors close in an hour. Which way does your beard point tonight?

(I touch your book and dream of our odyssey in the supermarket and feel absurd.)

Will we walk all night through solitary streets? The trees add shade to shade, lights out in the houses, we'll both be lonely.

Will we stroll dreaming of the lost America of love past blue automobiles in driveways, home to our silent cottage?

Ah, dear father, graybeard, lonely old courage-teacher, what America did you have when Charon quit poling his ferry and you got out on a smoking bank and stood watching the boat disappear on the black waters of Lethe?

Sunflower Sutra

I walked on the banks of the tincan banana dock and sat down under the huge shade of a Southern Pacific locomotive to look at the sunset over the box house hills and cry.

Jack Kerouac sat beside me on a busted rusty iron pole, companion, we thought the same thoughts of the soul, bleak and blue and sad-eyed, surrounded by the gnarled steel roots of trees of machinery.

The oily water on the river mirrored the red sky, sun sank on top of final Frisco peaks, no fish in that stream, no hermit in those mounts, just ourselves rheumy-eyed and hungover like old bums on the riverbank, tired and wily.

Look at the Sunflower, he said, there was a dead gray shadow against the sky, big as a man, sitting dry on top of a pile of ancient sawdust —

— I rushed up enchanted — it was my first sunflower, memories of Blake — my visions — Harlem

and Hells of the Eastern rivers, bridges clanking Joes Greasy Sandwiches, dead baby carriages, black treadless tires forgotten and unretreaded, the poem of the riverbank, condoms & pots, steel knives, nothing stainless, only the dank muck and the razor sharp artifacts passing into the past —

and the gray Sunflower poised against the sunset, crackly bleak and dusty with the smut and smog and smoke of olden locomotives in its eye —

corolla of bleary spikes pushed down and broken like a battered crown, seeds fallen out of its face, soon-to-be-toothless mouth of sunny air, sunrays obliterated on its hairy head like a dried wire spiderweb,

leaves stuck out like arms out of the stem, gestures from the sawdust root, broke pieces of plaster fallen out of the black twigs, a dead fly in its ear,

Unholy battered old thing you were, my sunflower O my soul, I loved you then!

The grime was no man's grime but death and human locomotives,

all that dress of dust, that veil of darkened railroad skin, that smog of cheek, that eyelid of black mis'ry, that sooty hand or phallus or protuberance of artificial worse-than-dirt — industrial — modern — all that civilization spotting your crazy golden crown —

and those blear thoughts of death and dusty loveless eyes and ends and withered roots below, in the home-pile of sand and sawdust, rubber dollar bills, skin of machinery, the guts and innards of the weeping coughing car, the empty lonely tincans with their rusty tongues alack, what more could I name, the smoked ashes of some cock cigar, the cunts of wheelbarrows and the milky breasts of cars, wornout asses out of chairs & sphincters of dynamos — all these

entangled in your mummied roots — and you there standing before me in the sunset, all your glory in your form!

A perfect beauty of a sunflower! a perfect excellent lovely sunflower existence! a sweet natural eye to the new hip moon, woke up alive and excited grasping in the sunset shadow sunrise golden monthly breeze!

How many flies buzzed round you innocent of your grime, while you cursed the heavens of the railroad and your flower soul?

Poor dead flower? when did you forget you were a flower? when did you look at your skin and decide you were an impotent dirty old locomotive? the ghost of a locomotive? the specter and shade of a once powerful mad American locomotive?

You were never no locomotive, Sunflower, you were a sunflower!

And you Locomotive, you are a locomotive, forget me not!

So I grabbed up the skeleton thick sunflower and stuck it at my side like a scepter,

and deliver my sermon to my soul, and Jack's soul too, and anyone who'll listen,

— We're not our skin of grime, we're not our dread bleak dusty imageless locomotive, we're all beautiful golden sunflowers inside, we're blessed by our own seed & golden hairy naked accomplishment-bodies growing into mad black formal sunflowers in the sunset, spied on by our eyes under the shadow of the mad locomotive riverbank sunset Frisco hilly tincan evening sitdown vision.

from Kaddish
For
Naomi Ginsberg 1894–1956

I

Strange now to think of you, gone without corsets & eyes, while I walk on the sunny pavement of Greenwich Village.

downtown Manhattan, clear winter noon, and I've been up all night, talking, talking, reading the Kaddish aloud, listening to Ray Charles blues shout blind on the phonograph

the rhythm the rhythm — and your memory in my head three years after — And read Adonais' last triumphant stanzas aloud — wept, realizing how we suffer —

And how Death is that remedy all singers dream of, sing, remember, prophesy as in the Hebrew Anthem, or the Buddhist Book of Answers — and my own imagination of a withered leaf — at dawn —

Dreaming back thru life, Your time — and mine accelerating toward Apocalypse,

the final moment — the flower burning in the Day — and what comes after,

looking back on the mind itself that saw an American city

a flash away, and the great dream of Me or China, or you and a phantom Russia, or a crumpled bed that never existed —

like a poem in the dark — escaped back to Oblivion —

No more to say, and nothing to weep for but the Beings in the Dream, trapped in its disappearance,

sighing, screaming with it, buying and selling pieces of phantom, worshipping each other,

worshipping the God included in it all — longing or inevitability? — while it lasts, a Vision — anything more?

It leaps about me, as I go out and walk the street, look back over my shoulder, Seventh Avenue, the battlements of window office buildings shouldering each other high, under a cloud, tall as the sky an instant — and the sky above — an old blue place.

or down the Avenue to the South, to — as I walked toward the Lower East Side — where you walked 50 years ago, little girl — from Russia, eating the first poisonous tomatoes of America — frightened on the dock —

then struggling in the crowds of Orchard Street toward what? — toward Newark —

toward candy store, first home-made sodas of the century, hand-churned ice cream in backroom on musty brownfloor boards —

Toward education marriage nervous breakdown, operation, teaching school, and learning to be mad, in a dream — what is this life?

Toward the Key in the window — and the great Key lays its head of light on top of Manhattan, and over the floor, and lays down on the sidewalk — in a single vast beam, moving, as I walk down First toward the Yiddish Theater — and the place of poverty

you knew, and I know, but without caring now — Strange to have moved thru Paterson, and the West, and Europe and here again,

with the cries of Spaniards now in the doorstoops doors and dark boys on the street, fire escapes old as you
— Tho you're not old now, that's left here with me —
Myself, anyhow, maybe as old as the universe — and I guess that dies with us — enough to cancel all that comes — What came is gone forever every time —
That's good! That leaves it open for no regret — no fear radiators, lacklove, torture even toothache in the end —
Though while it comes it is a lion that eats the soul — and the lamb, the soul, in us, alas, offering itself in sacrifice to change's fierce hunger — hair and teeth — and the roar of bonepain, skull bare, break rib, rot-skin, braintricked Implacability.
Ai! ai! we do worse! We are in a fix! And you're out, Death let you out, Death had the Mercy, you're done with your century, done with God, done with the path thru it — Done with yourself at last — Pure — Back to the Babe dark before your Father, before us all — before the world —
There, rest. No more suffering for you. I know where you've gone, it's good.
No more flowers in the summer fields of New York, no joy now, no more fear of Louis,
and no more of his sweetness and glasses, his high school decades, debts, loves, frightened telephone calls, conception beds, relatives, hands —
No more of sister Elanor, — she gone before you — we kept it secret — you killed her — or she killed herself to bear with you — an arthritic heart — But Death's killed you both — No matter —
Nor your memory of your mother, 1915 tears in silent movies weeks and weeks — forgetting, agrieve watching Marie Dressler address humanity, Chaplin dance in youth,
or Boris Godinov, Chaliapin's at the Met, halling his voice of a weeping Czar — by standing room with Elanor & Max — watching also the Capitalists take seats in Orchestra, white furs, diamonds,
with the YPSL's hitch-hiking thru Pennsylvania, in black baggy gym skirts pants, photograph of 4 girls holding each other round the waste, and laughing eye, too coy, virginal solitude of 1920
all girls grown old, or dead, now, and that long hair in the grave — lucky to have husbands later —
You made it — I came too — Eugene my brother before (still grieving now and will gream on to his last stiff hand, as he goes thru his cancer — or kill — later perhaps — soon he will think —)
And it's the last moment I remember, which I see them all, thru myself, now — tho not you

I didn't foresee what you felt — what more hideous gape of bad mouth
came first — to you — and were you prepared?

To go where? In that Dark — that — in that God? a radiance? A Lord
in the Void? Like an eye in the black cloud in a dream? Adonoi at
last, with you?

Beyond my remembrance! Incapable to guess! Not merely the yellow skull
in the grave, or a box of worm dust, and a stained ribbon —
Deathshead with Halo? can you believe it?

Is it only the sun that shines once for the mind, only the flash
of existence, than none ever was?

Nothing beyond what we have — what you had — that so pitiful — yet
Triumph,

to have been here, and changed, like a tree, broken, or flower — fed to
the ground — but mad, with its petals, colored, thinking Great
Universe, shaken, cut in the head, leaf stript, hid in an egg crate
hospital, cloth wrapped, sore — freaked in the moon brain,
Naughtless.

No flower like that flower, which knew itself in the garden, and fought
the knife — lost

Cut down by an idiot Snowman's icy — even in the Spring — strange
ghost thought — some Death — Sharp icicle in his hand — crowned
with old roses — a dog in his eyes — cock of a sweatshop — heart
of electric irons.

All the accumulations of life, that wear us out — clocks, bodies,
consciousness, shoe, breasts — begotten sons — your Communism
— "Paranoia" into hospitals.

You once kicked Elanor in the leg, she died of heart failure later. You of
stroke. Asleep? within a year, the two of you, sisters in death. Is
Elanor happy?

Max grieves alive in an office on Lower Broadway, lone large mustache
over midnight Accountings, not sure. His life passes — as he sees —
and what does he doubt now? Still dream of making money, or that
might have made money, hired nurse, had children, found even your
Immortality, Naomi?

I'll see him soon. Now I've got to cut through — to talk to you — as I
didn't when you had a mouth.

Forever. And we're bound for that, Forever — like Emily Dickinson's
horses — headed to the End.

They know the way — These Steeds — run faster than we think — it's
our own life they cross — and take with them.

Magnificent, mourned no more, marred of heart, mind behind,
married dreamed, mortal changed — Ass and face done with murder.

In the world, given, flower maddened, made no Utopia, shut under pine, almed in Earth, balmed in Lone, Jehovah, accept.

Nameless, One Faced, Forever beyond me, beginningless, endless, Father in death. Tho I am not there for this Prophecy, I am unmarried, I'm hymnless, I'm Heavenless, headless in blisshood I would still adore

Thee, Heaven, after Death, only One blessed in Nothingness, not light or darkness, Dayless Eternity —

Take this, this Psalm, from me, burst from my hand in a day, some of my Time, now given to Nothing — to praise Thee — But Death

This is the end, the redemption from Wilderness, way for the Wonderer, House sought for All, black handkerchief washed clean by weeping — page beyond Psalm — Last change of mine and Naomi — to God's perfect Darkness — Death, stay thy phantoms!

Hymmnn

In the world which He has created according to his will Blessed Praised Magnified Lauded Exalted the Name of the Holy One Blessed is He!
In the house in Newark Blessed is He! In the madhouse Blessed is He! In the house of Death Blessed is He!
Blessed be He in homosexuality! Blessed be He in Paranoia! Blessed be He in the city! Blessed be He in the Book!
Blessed be He who dwells in the shadow! Blessed be He! Blessed be He!
Blessed be you Naomi in tears! Blessed be you Naomi in fears! Blessed Blessed Blessed in sickness!
Blessed be you Naomi in Hospitals! Blessed be you Naomi in solitude! Blest be your triumph! Blest be your bars! Blest be your last years' loneliness!
Blest be your failure! Blest be your stroke! Blest be the close of your eye! Blest be the gaunt of your cheek! Blest be your withered thighs!
Blessed be Thee Naomi in Death! Blessed be Death! Blessed be Death!
Blessed be He Who leads all sorrow to Heaven! Blessed be He in the end!
Blessed be He who builds Heaven in Darkness! Blessed Blessed Blessed be He! Blessed be He! Blessed be Death on us All!

My Alba

Now that I've wasted
five years in Manhattan
life decaying
talent a blank

talking disconnected
patient and mental
sliderule and number
machine on a desk

autographed triplicate
synopsis and taxes
obedient prompt
poorly paid

stayed on the market
youth of my twenties
fainted in offices
wept on typewriters

deceived multitudes
in vast conspiracies
deodorant battleships
serious business industry

every six weeks whoever
drank my blood bank
innocent evil now
part of my system

five years unhappy labor
22 to 27 working
not a dime in the bank
to show for it anyway

dawn breaks it's only the sun
the East smokes O my bedroom
I am damned to Hell what
alarmclock is ringing

On Burroughs' Work

The method must be purest meat
and no symbolic dressing,
actual visions & actual prisons
as seen then and now.

Prisons and visions presented
    with rare descriptions
corresponding exactly to those
    of Alcatraz and Rose.

A naked lunch is natural to us,
    we eat reality sandwiches.
But allegories are so much lettuce.
Don't hide the madness.

Dream Record: June 8, 1955

A drunken night in my house with a
boy, San Francisco : I lay asleep :
darkness :
            I went back to Mexico City
and saw Joan Burroughs leaning
forward in a garden-chair, arms
on her knees. She studied me with
clear eyes and downcast smile, her
face restored to a fine beauty
tequila and salt had made strange
before the bullet in her brow.

We talked of the life since then.
Well, what's Burroughs doing now?
Bill on earth, he's in North Africa.
Oh, and Kerouac? Jack still jumps
with the same beat genius as before,
notebooks filled with Buddha.
I hope he makes it, she laughed.
Is Huncke still in the can? No,
last time I saw him on Times Square.
And how is Kenney? Married, drunk
and golden in the East. You? New
loves in the West —
            Then I knew
she was a dream : and questioned her
— Joan, what kind of knowledge have
the dead? can you still love
your mortal acquaintances?
What do you remember of us?

                                        She
faded in front of me — The next instant
I saw her rain-stained tombstone
rear an illegible epitaph
under the gnarled branch of a small
tree in the wild grass
of an unvisited garden in Mexico.

Wales Visitation

White fog lifting & falling on mountain-brow
          Trees moving in rivers of wind
                              The clouds arise
     as on a wave, gigantic eddy lifting mist
          above teeming ferns exquisitely swayed
                              along a green crag
          glimpsed thru mullioned glass in valley rain —

Bardic, O Self, Visitacione, tell naught
     but what seen by one man in a vale in Albion,
          of the folk, whose physical sciences end in Ecology,
                    the wisdom of earthly relations,
          of mouths & eyes interknit ten centuries visible
                    orchards of mind language manifest human,
     of the satanic thistle that raises its horned symmetry
     flowering above sister grass-daisies' pink tiny
                    bloomlets angelic as lightbulbs —

Remember 160 miles from London's symmetrical thorned tower
          & network of TV pictures flashing bearded your Self
     the lambs on the tree-nooked hillside this day bleating
     heard in Blake's old ear, & the silent thought of Wordsworth in
                              eld Stillness
          clouds passing through skeleton arches of Tintern Abbey —
          Bard Nameless as the Vast, babble to Vastness!

All the Valley quivered, one extended motion, wind
                    undulating on mossy hills
     a giant wash that sank white fog delicately down red runnels
                    on the mountainside
     whose leaf-branch tendrils moved asway
                    in granitic undertow down —

and lifted the floating Nebulous upward, and lifted the arms of the trees
    and lifted the grasses an instant in balance
      and lifted the lambs to hold still
    and lifted the green of the hill, in one solemn wave

A solid mass of Heaven, mist-infused, ebbs thru the vale,
    a wavelet of Immensity, lapping gigantic through Llanthony Valley,
the length of all England, valley upon valley under Heaven's ocean
        tonned with cloud-hang,
    Heaven balanced on a grassblade —
Roar of the mountain wind slow, sigh of the body,
    One Being on the mountainside stirring gently
      Exquisite scales trembling everywhere in balance,
one motion thru the cloudy sky-floor shifting on the million
      feet of daisies,
one Majesty the motion that stirred wet grass quivering
    to the farthest tendril of white fog poured down
      through shivering flowers on the mountain's
      head —

No imperfection in the budded mountain,
    Valleys breathe, heaven and earth move together,
    daisies push inches of yellow air, vegetables tremble,
      green atoms shimmer in grassy mandalas,
sheep speckle the mountainside, revolving their jaws with empty eyes,
      horses dance in the warm rain,
    tree-lined canals network through live farmland,
      blueberries fringe stone walls
    on hill breasts nippled with hawthorn,
    pheasants croak up meadow-bellies haired with fern —

Out, out on the hillside, into the ocean sound, into delicate
      gusts of wet air,
Fall on the ground, O great Wetness, O Mother, No harm on thy body!
Stare close, no imperfection in the grass,
    each flower Buddha-eye, repeating the story,
      the myriad-formed soul
Kneel before the foxglove raising green buds, mauve bells drooped
    doubled down the stem trembling antennae,
      & look in the eyes of the branded lambs that stare
    breathing stockstill under dripping hawthorn —
I lay down mixing my beard with the wet hair of the mountainside,
    smelling the brown vagina-moist ground, harmless,

        tasting the violet thistle-hair, sweetness —
One being so balanced, so vast, that its softest breath
       moves every floweret in the stillness on the valley floor,
   trembles lamb-hair hung gossamer rain-beaded in the grass,
lifts trees on their roots, birds in the great draught
        hiding their strength in the rain, bearing same weight,

Groan thru breast and neck, a great Oh! to earth heart
               Calling our Presence together
     The great secret is no secret
     Senses fit the winds,
          Visible is visible,
          rain-mist curtains wave through the bearded vale,
          grey atoms wet the wind's Kaballah

Crosslegged on a rock in dusk rain,
        rubber booted in soft grass, mind moveless,
   breath trembles in white daisies by the roadside,
        Heaven breath and my own symmetric
     Airs wavering thru antlered green fern
drawn in my navel, same breath as breathes thru Capel-Y-Ffn,
       Sounds of Aleph and Aum
            through forests of gristle,
     my skull and Lord Hereford's Knob equal,
            All Albion one.

What did I notice? Particulars! The
       vision of the great One is myriad —
   smoke curls upward from ash tray,
       house fire burned low,
The night, still wet & moody black heaven
           starless
upward in motion with wet wind.

FRANK O'HARA
1926–1966

Poem

**At night Chinamen jump
on Asia with a thump**

while in our willful way
we, in secret, play

affectionate games and bruise
our knees like China's shoes.

The birds push apples through
grass the moon turns blue,

these apples roll beneath
our buttocks like a heath

full of Chinese thrushes
flushed from China's bushes.

As we love at night
birds sing out of sight,

Chinese rhythms beat
through us in our heat,

the apples and the birds
move us like soft words,

we couple in the grace
of that mysterious race.

Poem

The eager note on my door said "Call me,
call when you get in!" so I quickly threw
a few tangerines into my overnight bag,
straightened my eyelids and shoulders, and

headed straight for the door. It was autumn
by the time I got around the corner, oh all
unwilling to be either pertinent or bemused, but
the leaves were brighter than grass on the sidewalk!

Funny, I thought, that the lights are on this late
and the hall door open; still up at this hour, a
champion jai-alai player like himself? Oh fie!
for shame! What a host, so zealous! And he was

there in the hall, flat on a sheet of blood that
ran down the stairs. I did appreciate it. There are few
hosts who so thoroughly prepare to greet a guest
only casually invited, and that several months ago.

Chez Jane

The white chocolate jar full of petals
swills odds and ends around in a dizzying eye
of four o'clocks now and to come. The tiger,
marvellously striped and irritable, leaps
on the table and without disturbing a hair
of the flowers' breathless attention, pisses
into the pot, right down its delicate spout.
A whisper of steam goes up from that porcelain
urethra. "Saint-Saëns!" it seems to be whispering,
curling unerringly around the furry nuts
of the terrible puss, who is mentally flexing.
Ah be with me always, spirit of noisy
contemplation in the studio, the Garden
of Zoos, the eternally fixed afternoons!
There, while music scratches its scrofulous
stomach, the brute beast emerges and stands,
clear and careful, knowing always the exact peril
at this moment caressing his fangs with
a tongue given wholly to luxurious usages;
which only a moment before dropped aspirin
in this sunset of roses, and now throws a chair
in the air to aggravate the truly menacing.

To the Film Industry in Crisis

Not you, lean quarterlies and swarthy periodicals
with your studious incursions toward the pomposity of ants,
nor you, experimental theatre in which Emotive Fruition
is wedding Poetic Insight perpetually, nor you,
promenading Grand Opera, obvious as an ear (though you
are close to my heart), but you, Motion Picture Industry,
it's you I love!

In times of crisis, we must all decide again and again whom we love.
And give credit where it's due: not to my starched nurse, who taught me
how to be bad and not bad rather than good (and has lately availed
herself of this information), not to the Catholic Church
which is at best an oversolemn introduction to cosmic entertainment,
not to the American Legion, which hates everybody, but to you,
glorious Silver Screen, tragic Technicolor, amorous Cinemascope,
stretching Vistavision and startling Stereophonic Sound, with all
your heavenly dimensions and reverberations and iconoclasms! To
Richard Barthelmess as the "tol'able" boy barefoot and in pants,
Jeanette MacDonald of the flaming hair and lips and long, long neck,
Sue Carroll as she sits for eternity on the damaged fender of a car
and smiles, Ginger Rogers with her pageboy bob like a sausage
on her shuffling shoulders, peach-melba-voiced Fred Astaire of the feet,
Eric von Stroheim, the seducer of mountain-climbers' gasping spouses,
the Tarzans, each and every one of you (I cannot bring myself to prefer
Johnny Weissmuller to Lex Barker, I cannot!), Mae West in a furry sled,
her bordello radiance and bland remarks, Rudolph Valentino of the
        moon,
its crushing passions, and moonlike, too, the gentle Norma Shearer,
Miriam Hopkins dropping her champagne glass off Joel McCrea's yacht
and crying into the dappled sea, Clark Gable rescuing Gene Tierney
from Russia and Allan Jones rescuing Kitty Carlisle from Harpo Marx,
Cornel Wilde coughing blood on the piano keys while Merle Oberon
        berates,
Marilyn Monroe in her little spike heels reeling through Niagara Falls,
Joseph Cotten puzzling and Orson Welles puzzled and Dolores del Rio
eating orchids for lunch and breaking mirrors, Gloria Swanson reclining,
and Jean Harlow reclining and wiggling, and Alice Faye reclining
and wiggling and singing, Myrna Loy being calm and wise, William
        Powell
in his stunning urbanity, Elizabeth Taylor blossoming, yes, to you

and to all you others, the great, the near-great, the featured, the extras
who pass quickly and return in dreams saying your one or two lines,
my love!
Long may you illumine space with your marvellous appearances, delays
and enunciations, and may the money of the world glitteringly cover you
as you rest after a long day under the kleig lights with your faces
in packs for our edification, the way the clouds come often at night
but the heavens operate on the star system. It is a divine precedent
you perpetuate! Roll on, reels of celluloid, as the great earth rolls on!

The Day Lady Died

It is 12:20 in New York a Friday
three days after Bastille day, yes
it is 1959 and I go get a shoeshine
because I will get off the 4:19 in Easthampton
at 7:15 and then go straight to dinner
and I don't know the people who will feed me

I walk up the muggy street beginning to sun
and have a hamburger and a malted and buy
an ugly NEW WORLD WRITING to see what the poets
in Ghana are doing these days
                              I go on to the bank
and Miss Stillwagon (first name Linda I once heard)
doesn't even look up my balance for once in her life
and in the GOLDEN GRIFFIN I get a little Verlaine
for Patsy with drawings by Bonnard although I do
think of Hesiod, trans. Richmond Lattimore or
Brendan Behan's new play or *Le Balcon* or *Les Nègres*
of Genet, but I don't, I stick with Verlaine
after practically going to sleep with quandariness

and for Mike I just stroll into the PARK LANE
Liquor Store and ask for a bottle of Strega and
then I go back where I came from to 6th Avenue
and the tobacconist in the Ziegfeld Theatre and
casually ask for a carton of Gauloises and a carton
of Picayunes, and a NEW YORK POST with her face on it

and I am sweating a lot by now and thinking of
leaning on the john door in the 5 SPOT
while she whispered a song along the keyboard
to Mal Waldron and everyone and I stopped breathing

Why I Am Not a Painter

I am not a painter, I am a poet.
Why? I think I would rather be
a painter, but I am not. Well,

937

for instance, Mike Goldberg
is starting a painting. I drop in.
"Sit down and have a drink" he
says. I drink; we drink. I look
up. "You have SARDINES in it."
"Yes, it needed something there."
"Oh." I go and the days go by
and I drop in again. The painting
is going on, and I go, and the days
go by. I drop in. The painting is
finished. "Where's SARDINES?"
All that's left is just
letters, "It was too much," Mike says.

But me? One day I am thinking of
a color: orange. I write a line
about orange. Pretty soon it is a
whole page of words, not lines.
Then another page. There should be
so much more, not of orange, of
words, of how terrible orange is
and life. Days go by. It is even in
prose, I am a real poet. My poem
is finished and I haven't mentioned
orange yet. It's twelve poems, I call
it ORANGES. And one day in a gallery
I see Mike's painting, called SARDINES.

Autobiographia Literaria

When I was a child
I played by myself in a
corner of the schoolyard
all alone.

I hated dolls and I
hated games, animals were
not friendly and birds
flew away.

If anyone was looking
for me I hid behind a
tree and cried out "I am
an orphan."

And here I am, the
center of all beauty!
writing these poems!
Imagine!

Les Luths

Ah nuts! It's boring reading French newspapers
in New York as if I were a Colonial waiting for my gin
somewhere beyond this roof a jet is making a sketch of the sky
where is Gary Snyder I wonder if he's reading under a dwarf pine
stretched out so his book and his head fit under the lowest branch
while the sun of the Orient rolls calmly not getting through to him
not caring particularly because the light in Japan respects poets

while in Paris Monsieur Martory and his brother Jean the poet
are reading a piece by Matthieu Galey and preparing to send a *pneu*
everybody here is running around after dull pleasantries and
wondering if *The Hotel Wentley Poems* is as great as I say it is
and I am feeling particularly testy at being separated from
the one I love by the most dreary of practical exigencies money
when I want only to lean on my elbow and stare into space feeling
the one warm beautiful thing in the world breathing upon my right rib

what are lutes they make ugly twangs and rest on knees in cafés
I want to hear only your light voice running on about Florida
as we pass the changing traffic light and buy grapes for wherever
we will end up praising the mattressless sleigh-bed and the
Mexican egg and the clock that will not make me know
   how to leave you

ROBERT BLY

b. 1926

Waking from Sleep

Inside the veins there are navies setting forth,
Tiny explosions at the water lines,
And seagulls weaving in the wind of the salty blood.

It is the morning. The country has slept the whole winter.
Window seats were covered with fur skins, the yard was full
Of stiff dogs, and hands that clumsily held heavy books.

Now we wake, and rise from bed, and eat breakfast! —
Shouts rise from the harbor of the blood,
Mist, and masts rising, the knock of wooden tackle in the sunlight.

Now we sing, and do tiny dances on the kitchen floor.
Our whole body is like a harbor at dawn;
We know that our master has left us for the day.

Poem in Three Parts

I

Oh, on an early morning I think I shall live forever!
I am wrapped in my joyful flesh,
As the grass is wrapped in its clouds of green.

II

Rising from a bed, where I dreamt
Of long rides past castles and hot coals,
The sun lies happily on my knees,
I have suffered and survived the night
Bathed in dark water, like any blade of grass.

III

The strong leaves of the box-elder tree,
Plunging in the wind, call us to disappear
Into the wilds of the universe,
Where we shall sit at the foot of a plant,
And live forever, like the dust.

Poem Against the Rich

Each day I live, each day the sea of light
Rises, I seem to see
The tear inside the stone
As if my eyes were gazing beneath the earth.
The rich man in his red hat
Cannot hear
The weeping in the pueblos of the lily,
Or the dark tears in the shacks of the corn.
Each day the sea of light rises
I hear the sad rustle of the darkened armies,
Where each man weeps, and the plaintive
Orisons of the stones.
The stones bow as the saddened armies pass.

Snowfall in the Afternoon

I

The grass is half-covered with snow.
It was the sort of snowfall that starts in late afternoon,
And now the little houses of the grass are growing dark.

II

If I reached my hands down, near the earth,
I could take handfuls of darkness!
A darkness was always there, which we never noticed.

III

As the snow grows heavier, the cornstalks fade farther away,
And the barn moves nearer to the house.
The barn moves all alone in the growing storm.

IV

The barn is full of corn, and moving toward us now,
Like a hulk blown toward us in a storm at sea;
All the sailors on deck have been blind for many years.

Come with Me

Come with me into those things that have felt this despair for so long —
Those removed Chevrolet wheels that howl with a terrible loneliness,
Lying on their backs in the cindery dirt, like men drunk, and naked,
Staggering off down a hill at night to drown at last in the pond.
Those shredded inner tubes abandoned on the shoulders of thruways,
Black and collapsed bodies, that tried and burst,
And were left behind;
And the curly steel shavings, scattered about on garage benches,
Sometimes still warm, gritty when we hold them,
Who have given up, and blame everything on the government,
And those roads in South Dakota that feel around in the darkness . . .

Sleet Storm on the Merritt Parkway

I look out at the white sleet covering the still streets
As we drive through Scarsdale —
The sleet began falling as we left Connecticut,
And the winter leaves swirled in the wet air after cars
Like hands suddenly turned over in a conversation.
Now the frost has nearly buried the short grass of March.
Seeing the sheets of sleet untouched on the wide streets,
I think of the many comfortable homes stretching for miles,
Two and three stories, solid, with polished floors,
With white curtains in the upstairs bedrooms,
And small perfume flagons of black glass on the window sills,
And warm bathrooms with guest towels, and electric lights —
What a magnificent place for a child to grow up!
And yet the children end in the river of price-fixing,
Or in the snowy field of the insane asylum.
The sleet falls — so many cars moving toward New York —
Last night we argued about the Marines invading Guatemala in 1947,
The United Fruit Company had one water spigot for 200 families,
And the ideals of America, our freedom to criticize,
The slave systems of Rome and Greece, and no one agreed.

Johnson's Cabinet Watched by Ants

1

It is a clearing deep in a forest: overhanging boughs
Make a low place. Here the citizens we know during the day,
The ministers, the department heads,
Appear changed: the stockholders of large steel companies
In small wooden shoes: here are the generals dressed as gamboling lambs.

2

Tonight they burn the rice-supplies; tomorrow
They lecture on Thoreau; tonight they move around the trees,
Tomorrow they pick the twigs from their clothes;
Tonight they throw the fire-bombs, tomorrow
They read the Declaration of Independence; tomorrow they are in
church.

3

Ants are gathered around an old tree.
In a choir they sing, in harsh and gravelly voices,
Old Etruscan songs on tyranny.
Toads nearby clap their small hands, and join
The fiery songs, their five long toes trembling in the soaked earth.

Romans Angry about the Inner World

What shall the world do with its children?
There are lives the executives
Know nothing of,
A leaping of the body,
The body rolling — and I have felt it —
And we float
Joyfully on the dark places;
But the executioners
Move toward Drusia. They tie her legs
On the iron horse. "Here is a woman
Who has seen our mother
In the other world!" Next they warm
The hooks. The two Romans had put their trust
In the outer world. Irons glowed
Like teeth. They wanted her
To assure them. She refused. Finally they took burning

Pine sticks, and pushed them
Into her sides. Her breath rose
And she died. The executioners
Rolled her off onto the ground.
A light snow began to fall
And covered the mangled body,
And the executives, astonished, withdrew.
The other world is like a thorn
In the ear of a tiny beast!
The fingers of the executives are too thick
To pull it out!
It is like a jagged stone
Flying toward them out of the darkness.

When the Dumb Speak

There is a joyful night in which we lose
Everything, and drift
Like a radish
Rising and falling, and the ocean
At last throws us into the ocean,
And on the water we are sinking
As if floating on darkness.
The body raging
And driving itself, disappearing in smoke,
Walks in large cities late at night,
Or reading the Bible in Christian Science windows,
Or reading a history of Bougainville.
Then the images appear:
Images of death,
Images of the body shaken in the grave,
And the graves filled with seawater;
Fires in the sea,
The ships smoldering like bodies,
Images of wasted life,
Life lost, imagination ruined,
The house fallen,
The gold sticks broken,
Then shall the talkative be silent,
And the dumb shall speak.

Looking at Some Flowers

Light is around the petals, and behind them:
Some petals are living on the other side of the light.
Like sunlight drifting onto the carpet
Where the casket stands, not knowing which world it is in.
And fuzzy leaves, hair growing from some animal
Buried in the green trenches of the plant.
Or the ground this house is on,
Only free of the sea for five or six thousand years.

Looking into a Face

Conversation brings us so close! Opening
The surfs of the body,
Bringing fish up near the sun,
And stiffening the backbones of the sea!

I have wandered in a face, for hours,
Passing through dark fires.
I have risen to a body
Not yet born,
Existing like a light around the body,
Through which the body moves like a sliding moon.

Evolution from the Fish

This grandson of fishes holds inside him
A hundred thousand small black stones.
This nephew of snails, six feet long, lies naked on a bed
With a smiling woman, his head throws off light
Under marble, he is moving toward his own life
Like fur, walking. And when the frost comes, he is
Fur, mammoth fur, growing longer
And silkier, passing the woman's dormitory,
Kissing a stomach, leaning against a pillar,
He moves toward the animal, the animal with furry head!

What a joy to smell the flesh of a new child!
Like new grass! And this long man with the student girl,
Coffee cups, her pale waist, the spirit moving around them,
Moves, dragging a great tail into the darkness.

In the dark we blaze up, drawing pictures
Of spiny fish, we throw off the white stones!
Serpents rise from the ocean floor with spiral motions,
A man goes inside a jewel, and sleeps. Do
Not hold my hands down! Let me raise them!
A fire is passing up through the soles of my feet!

JOHN ASHBERY
b. 1927

The Instruction Manual

As I sit looking out of a window of the building
I wish I did not have to write the instruction manual on the uses of a
new metal.
I look down into the street and see people, each walking with an inner
peace,
And envy them — they are so far away from me!
Not one of them has to worry about getting out this manual on schedule.
And, as my way is, I begin to dream, resting my elbows on the desk and
leaning out of the window a little,
Of dim Guadalajara! City of rose-colored flowers!
City I wanted most to see, and most did not see, in Mexico!
But I fancy I see, under the press of having to write the instruction
manual,
Your public square, city, with its elaborate little bandstand!
The band is playing *Scheherazade* by Rimsky-Korsakov.
Around stand the flower girls, handing out rose- and lemon-colored
flowers,
Each attractive in her rose-and-blue striped dress (Oh! such shades of
rose and blue),
And nearby is the little white booth where women in green serve you
green and yellow fruit.
The couples are parading; everyone is in a holiday mood.
First, leading the parade, is a dapper fellow
Clothed in deep blue. On his head sits a white hat
And he wears a mustache, which has been trimmed for the occasion.
His dear one, his wife, is young and pretty; her shawl is rose, pink, and
white.
Her slippers are patent leather, in the American fashion,
And she carries a fan, for she is modest, and does not want the crowd to
see her face too often.

But everybody is so busy with his wife or loved one
I doubt they would notice the mustachioed man's wife.
Here come the boys! They are skipping and throwing little things on
the sidewalk
Which is made of gray tile. One of them, a little older, has a toothpick
in his teeth.
He is silenter than the rest, and affects not to notice the pretty young
girls in white.
But his friends notice them, and shout their jeers at the laughing girls.
Yet soon all this will cease, with the deepening of their years,
And love bring each to the parade grounds for another reason.
But I have lost sight of the young fellow with the toothpick.
Wait — there he is — on the other side of the bandstand,
.Secluded from his friends, in earnest talk with a young girl
Of fourteen or fifteen. I try to hear what they are saying
But it seems they are just mumbling something — shy words of love,
probably.
She is slightly taller than he, and looks quietly down into his sincere eyes.
She is wearing white. The breeze ruffles her long fine black hair against
her olive cheek.
Obviously she is in love. The boy, the young boy with the toothpick, he
is in love too;
His eyes show it. Turning from this couple,
I see there is an intermission in the concert.
The paraders are resting and sipping drinks through straws
(The drinks are dispensed from a large glass crock by a lady in dark
blue),
And the musicians mingle among them, in their creamy white uniforms,
and talk
About the weather, perhaps, or how their kids are doing at school.

Let us take this opportnuity to tiptoe into one of the side streets.
Here you may see one of those white houses with green trim
That are so popular here. Look — I told you!
It is cool and dim inside, but the patio is sunny.
An old woman in gray sits there, fanning herself with a palm leaf fan.
She welcomes us to her patio, and offers us a cooling drink.
"My son is in Mexico City," she says. "He would welcome you too
If he were here. But his job is with a bank there.
Look, here is a photograph of him."
And a dark-skinned lad with pearly teeth grins out at us from the worn
leather frame.

947

We thank her for her hospitality, for it is getting late
And we must catch a view of the city, before we leave, from a good high place.
That church tower will do — the faded pink one, there against the fierce blue of the sky. Slowly we enter.
The caretaker, an old man dressed in brown and gray, asks us how long we have been in the city, and how we like it here.
His daughter is scrubbing the steps — she nods to us as we pass into the tower.
Soon we have reached the top, and the whole network of the city extends before us.
There is the rich quarter, with its houses of pink and white, and its crumbling, leafy terraces.
There is the poorer quarter, its homes a deep blue.
There is the market, where men are selling hats and swatting flies.
And there is the public library, painted several shades of pale green and beige.
Look! There is the square we just came from, with the promenaders.
There are fewer of them, now that the heat of the day has increased,
But the young boy and girl still lurk in the shadows of the bandstand.
And there is the home of the little old lady —
She is still sitting in the patio, fanning herself.
How limited, but how complete withal, has been our experience of Guadalajara!
We have seen young love, married love, and the love of an aged mother for her son.
We have heard the music, tasted the drinks, and looked at colored houses.
What more is there to do, except stay? And that we cannot do.
And as a last breeze freshens the top of the weathered old tower, I turn my gaze
Back to the instruction manual which has made me dream of Guadalajara.

The Painter

Sitting between the sea and the buildings
He enjoyed painting the sea's portrait.
But just as children imagine a prayer
Is merely silence, he expected his subject
To rush up the sand, and, seizing a brush,
Plaster its own portrait on the canvas.

So there was never any paint on his canvas
Until the people who lived in the buildings
Put him to work: "Try using the brush
As a means to an end. Select, for a portrait,
Something less angry and large, and more subject
To a painter's moods, or, perhaps, to a prayer."

How could he explain to them his prayer
That nature, not art, might usurp the canvas?
He chose his wife for a new subject,
Making her vast, like ruined buildings,
As if, forgetting itself, the portrait
Had expressed itself without a brush.

Slightly encouraged, he dipped his brush
In the sea, murmuring a heartfelt prayer:
"My soul, when I paint this next portrait
Let it be you who wrecks the canvas."
The news spread like wildfire through the buildings:
He had gone back to the sea for his subject.

Imagine a painter crucified by his subject!
Too exhausted even to lift his brush,
He provoked some artists leaning from the buildings
To malicious mirth: "We haven't a prayer
Now, of putting ourselves on canvas,
Or getting the sea to sit for a portrait!"

Others declared it a self-portrait.
Finally all indications of a subject
Began to fade, leaving the canvas
Perfectly white. He put down the brush.
At once a howl, that was also a prayer,
Arose from the overcrowded buildings.

They tossed him, the portrait, from the tallest of the buildings;
And the sea devoured the canvas and the brush
As though his subject had decided to remain a prayer.

Rivers and Mountains

On the secret map the assassins
Cloistered, the Moon River was marked
Near the eighteen peaks and the city
Of humiliation and defeat — wan ending
Of the trail among dry, papery leaves
Gray-brown quills like thoughts
In the melodious but vast mass of today's
Writing through fields and swamps
Marked, on the map, with little bunches of weeds.
Certainly squirrels lived in the woods
But devastation and dull sleep still
Hung over the land, quelled
The rioters turned out of sleep in the peace of prisons
Singing on marble factory walls
Deaf consolation of minor tunes that pack
The air with heavy invisible rods
Pent in some sand valley from
Which only quiet walking ever instructs.
The bird flew over and
Sat — there was nothing else to do.
Do not mistake its silence for pride or strength
Or the waterfall for a harbor
Full of light boats that is there
Performing for thousands of people
In clothes some with places to go
Or games. Sometimes over the pillar
Of square stones its impact
Makes a light print.

So going around cities
To get to other places you found
It all on paper but the land
Was made of paper processed
To look like ferns, mud or other
Whose sea unrolled its magic
Distances and then rolled them up
Its secret was only a pocket
After all but some corners are darker
Than these moonless nights spent as on a raft
In the seclusion of a melody heard
As though through trees

And you can never ignite their touch
Long but there were homes
Flung far out near the asperities
Of a sharp, rocky pinnacle
And other collective places
Shadows of vineyards whose wine
Tasted of the forest floor
Fisheries and oyster beds
Tides under the pole
Seminaries of instruction, public
Places for electric light
And the major tax assessment area
Wrinkled on the plan
Of election to public office
Sixty-two years old bath and breakfast
The formal traffic, shadows
To make it not worth joining
After the ox had pulled away the cart.

Your plan was to separate the enemy into two groups
With the razor-edged mountains between.
It worked well on paper
But their camp had grown
To be the mountains and the map
Carefully peeled away and not torn
Was the light, a tender but tough bark
On everything. Fortunately the war was solved
In another way by isolating the two sections
Of the enemy's navy so that the mainland
Warded away the big floating ships.
Light bounced off the ends
Of the small gray waves to tell
Them in the observatory
About the great drama that was being won
To turn off the machinery
And quietly move among the rustic landscape
Scooping snow off the mountains rinsing
The coarser ones that love had
Slowly risen in the night to overflow
Wetting pillow and petal
Determined to place the letter
On the unassassinated president's desk
So that a stamp could reproduce all this

In detail, down to the last autumn leaf
And the affliction of June ride
Slowly out into the sun-blackened landscape.

Spring Day

The immense hope, and forbearance
Trailing out of night, to sidewalks of the day
Like air breathed into a paper city, exhaled
As night returns bringing doubts

That swarm around the sleeper's head
But are fended off with clubs and knives, so that morning
Installs again in cold hope
The air that was yesterday, is what you are,

In so many phases the head slips from the hand.
The tears ride freely, laughs or sobs:
What do they matter? There is free giving and taking;
The giant body relaxed as though beside a stream

Wakens to the force of it and has to recognize
The secret sweetness before it turns into life —
Sucked out of many exchanges, torn from the womb,
Disinterred before completely dead — and heaves

Its mountain-broad chest. "They were long in coming,
Those others, and mattered so little that it slowed them
To almost nothing. They were presumed dead,
Their names honorably grafted on the landscape

To be a memory to men. Until today
We have been living in their shell.
Now we break forth like a river breaking through a dam,
Pausing over the puzzled, frightened plain,

And our further progress shall be terrible,
Turning fresh knives in the wounds
In that gulf of recreation, that bare canvas
As matter-of-fact as the traffic and the day's noise."

The mountain stopped shaking; its body
Arched into its own contradiction, its enjoyment,
As far from us lights were put out, memories of boys and girls
Who walked here before the great change,

Before the air mirrored us,
Taking the opposite shape of our effort,
Its inseparable comment and corollary
But casting us further and further out.

Wha — what happened? You are with
The orange tree, so that its summer produce
Can go back to where we got it wrong, then drip gently
Into history, if it wants to. A page turned; we were

Just now floundering in the wind of its colossal death.
And whether it is Thursday, or the day is stormy,
With thunder and rain, or the birds attack each other,
We have rolled into another dream.

No use charging the barriers of that other:
It no longer exists. But you,
Gracious and growing thing, with those leaves like stars,
We shall soon give all our attention to you.

Years of Indiscretion

Whatever your eye alights on this morning is yours:
Dotted rhythms of colors as they fade to the color,
A gray agate, translucent and firm, with nothing
Beyond its purifying reach. It's all there.
These are things offered to your participation.

These pebbles in a row are the seasons.
This is a house in which you may wish to live.
There are more than any of us to choose from
But each must live its own time.

And with the urging of the year each hastens onward separately
In strange sensations of emptiness, anguish, romantic
Outbursts, visions and wraiths. One meeting
Cancels another. "The seven-league boot
Gliding hither and thither of its own accord"
Salutes these forms for what they now are:

Fables that time invents
To explain its passing. They entertain
The very young and the very old, and not
One's standing up in them to shoulder
Task and vision, vision in the form of a task
So that the present seems like yesterday
And yesterday the place where we left off a little while ago.

Worsening Situation

Like a rainstorm, he said, the braided colors
Wash over me and are no help. Or like one
At a feast who eats not, for he cannot choose
From among the smoking dishes. This severed hand
Stands for life, and wander as it will,
East or west, north or south, it is ever
A stranger who walks beside me. O seasons,
Booths, chaleur, dark-hatted charlatans
On the outskirts of some rural fete,
The name you drop and never say is mine, mine!
Some day I'll claim to you how all used up
I am because of you but in the meantime the ride
Continues. Everyone is along for the ride,
It seems. Besides, what else is there?
The annual games? True, there are occasions
For white uniforms and a special language
Kept secret from the others. The limes
Are duly sliced. I know all this
But can't seem to keep it from affecting me,
Every day, all day. I've tried recreation,
Reading until late at night, train rides
And romance.
          One day a man called while I was out
And left this message: "You got the whole thing wrong

From start to finish. Luckily, there's still time
To correct the situation, but you must act fast.
See me at your earliest convenience. And please
Tell no one of this. Much besides your life depends on it."
I thought nothing of it at the time. Lately
I've been looking at old-fashioned plaids, fingering
Starched white collars, wondering whether there's a way
To get them really white again. My wife
Thinks I'm in Oslo — Oslo, France, that is.

The One Thing That Can Save America

Is anything central?
Orchards flung out on the land,
Urban forests, rustic plantations, knee-high hills?
Are place names central?
Elm Grove, Adcock Corner, Story Book Farm?
As they concur with a rush at eye level
Beating themselves into eyes which have had enough
Thank you, no more thank you.
And they come on like scenery mingled with darkness
The damp plains, overgrown suburbs,
Places of known civic pride, of civil obscurity.

These are connected to my version of America
But the juice is elsewhere.
This morning as I walked out of your room
After breakfast crosshatched with
Backward and forward glances, backward into light,
Forward into unfamiliar light,
Was it our doing, and was it
The material, the lumber of life, or of lives
We were measuring, counting?
A mood soon to be forgotten
In crossed girders of light, cool downtown shadow
In this morning that has seized us again?

I know that I braid too much my own
Snapped-off perceptions of things as they come to me.
They are private and always will be.
Where then are the private turns of event

955

Destined to boom later like golden chimes
Released over a city from a highest tower?
The quirky things that happen to me, and I tell you,
And you instantly know what I mean?
What remote orchard reached by winding roads
Hides them? Where are these roots?

It is the lumps and trials
That tell us whether we shall be known
And whether our fate can be exemplary, like a star.
All the rest is waiting
For a letter that never arrives,
Day after day, the exasperation
Until finally you have ripped it open not knowing what it is
The two envelope halves lying on a plate.
The message was wise, and seemingly
Dictated a long time ago.
Its truth is timeless, but its time has still
Not arrived, telling of danger, and the mostly limited
Steps that can be taken against danger
Now and in the future, in cool yards,
In quiet small houses in the country,
Our country, in fenced areas, in cool shady streets.

Tenth Symphony

I have not told you
About the riffraff at the boat show.
But seeing the boats coast by
Just now on their truck:
All red and white and blue and red
Prompts me to, wanting to get in your way.

You've never told me about a lot of things:
Why you love me, why we love you, and just exactly
What sex is. When people speak of it
As happens increasingly, are they always
Referring to the kind where sexual organs are brought in —
Diffident, vague, hard to imagine as they are to a blind person?
I find that thinking these things divides us,
Brings us together. As on last Thanksgiving
Nobody could finish what was on his plate,

And gave thanks. Means more
To some than me I guess.
But again I'm not sure of that.

There is some connexion
(I like the way the English spell it
They're so clever about some things
Probably smarter generally than we are
Although there is supposed to be something
We have that they don't — don't ask me
What it is. And please no talk of openness.
I would pick Francis Thompson over Bret Harte
Any day, if I had to)
Among this. It connects up,
Not *to* anything, but kind of like
Closing the ranks so as to leave them open.
You can "stop and shop." Self service
And the honor system prevail, resulting in
Tremendous amounts of spare time,
A boon to some, to others more of a problem
That only points a way around it.
Sitting in the living room this afternoon I saw
How to use it. My vision remained etched in the
Buff wall a long time, an elective
Cheshire cat. Unable to cancel,
The message is received penultimately.

So over these past years —
A little puttering around,
Some relaxing, a lot of plans and ideas.
Hope to have more time to tell you about
The latter in the foreseeable future.

Märchenbilder

Es war einmal . . . No, it's too heavy
To be said. Besides, you aren't paying attention any more.
How shall I put it?
"The rain thundered on the uneven red flagstones.

The steadfast tin soldier gazed beyond the drops
Remembering the hat-shaped paper boat, that soon . . ."
That's not it either.
Think about the long summer evenings of the past, the queen anne's
    lace.

Sometimes a musical phrase would perfectly sum up
The mood of a moment. One of those lovelorn sonatas
For wind instruments was riding past on a solemn white horse.
Everybody wondered who the new arrival was.

Pomp of flowers, decorations
Junked next day. Now look out of the window.
The sky is clear and bland. The wrong kind of day
For business or games, or betting on a sure thing.

The trees weep drops
Into the water at night. Slowly couples gather.
She looks into his eyes. "It would not be good
To be left alone." He: "I'll stay

As long as the night allows." This was one of those night rainbows
In negative color. As we advance, it retreats; we see
We are now far into a cave, must be. Yet there seem to be
Trees all around, and a wind lifts their leaves, slightly.

I want to go back, out of the bad stories,
But there's always the possibility that the next one . . .
No, it's another almond tree, or a ring-swallowing frog . . .
Yet they are beautiful as we people them

With ourselves. They are empty as cupboards.
To spend whole days drenched in them, waiting for the next whisper,
For the word in the next room. This is how the princes must have
    behaved,
Lying down in the frugality of sleep.

GALWAY KINNELL
b. 1927

The Supper after the Last

1

The desert moves out on half the horizon
Rimming the illusory water which, among islands,
Bears up the sky. The sea scumbles in
From its own inviolate border under the sky.
A dragon-fly floating on six legs on the sand
Lifts its green-yellow tail, declines its wings
A little, flutters them a little, and lays
On dazzled sand the shadow of its wings. Near shore
A bather wades through his shadow in the water.
He tramples and kicks it; it recomposes.

2

Outside the open door
Of the whitewashed house,
Framed in its doorway, a chair,
Vacant, waits in the sunshine.

A jug of fresh water stands
Inside the door. In the sunshine
The chair waits, less and less vacant.
The host's plan is to offer water, then stand aside.

3

They eat *rosé* and chicken. The chicken head
Has been tucked under the shelter of the wing.
Under the table a red-backed, passionate dog
Cracks chicken bones on the blood and gravel floor.

No one else but the dog and the blind
Cat watching it knows who is that bearded
Wild man guzzling overhead, the wreck of passion
Emptying his eyes, who has not yet smiled,

Who stares at the company, where he is company,
Turns them to sacks of appalled, grinning skin,
Forks the fowl-eye out from under
The large, makeshift, cooked lid, evaporates the wine,

Jellies the sunlit table and spoons, floats
The deluxe grub down the intestines of the Styx,
Devours all but the cat and the dog, to whom he slips scraps,
The red-backed accomplice busy grinding gristle.

4

When the bones of the host
Crack in the hound's jaw
The wild man rises. Opening
His palms he announces:
I came not to astonish
But to destroy you. Your
Jug of cool water? Your
Hanker after wings? Your
Lech for transcendence?
I came to prove you are
Intricate and simple things
As you are, created
In the image of nothing,
Taught of the creator
By your images in dirt —
As mine, for which you set
A chair in the sunshine,
Mocking me with water!
As pictures of wings,
Not even iridescent,
That clasp the sand
And that cannot perish, you swear,
Having once been evoked!

5

The witnesses back off; the scene begins to float in water;
Far out in that mirage the Saviour sits whispering to the world,
Becoming a mirage. The dog turns into a smear on the sand.
The cat grows taller and taller as it flees into space.

From the hot shine where he sits his whispering drifts:
You struggle from flesh into wings; the change exists.
But the wings that live gripping the contours of the dirt
Are all at once nothing, flesh and light lifted away.

You are the flesh; I am the resurrection, because I am the light.
I cut to your measure the creeping piece of darkness
That haunts you in the dirt. Step into light —
I make you over. I breed the shape of your grave in the dirt.

For Robert Frost

1

Why do you talk so much
Robert Frost? One day
I drove up to Ripton to ask,

I stayed the whole day
And never got the chance
To put the question.

I drove off at dusk
Worn out and aching
In both ears. Robert Frost,

Were you shy as a boy?
Do you go on making up
For some long stint of solitude?

Is it simply that talk
Doesn't have to be metered and rhymed?
Or is gab distracting from something worse?

2

I saw you once on the TV,
Unsteady at the lectern,
The flimsy white leaf
Of hair standing straight up
In the wind, among top hats,
Old farmer and son
Of worse winters than this,
Stopped in the first dazzle

Of the District of Columbia,
Suddenly having to pay
For the cheap onionskin,
The worn-out ribbon, the eyes

Wrecked from writing poems
For us — stopped,
Lonely before millions,
The paper jumping in your grip,

And as the Presidents
Also on the platform
Began flashing nervously
Their Presidential smiles
For the harmless old guy,
And poets watching on the TV
Started thinking, Well that's
The end of that tradition,

And the managers of the event
Said, Boys this is it,
This sonofabitch poet
Is gonna croak,
Putting the paper aside
You drew forth
From your great faithful heart
The poem.

3

Once, walking in winter in Vermont,
In the snow, I followed a set of footprints
That aimed for the woods. At the verge
I could make out, "far in the pillared dark,"
An old creature in a huge, clumsy overcoat,
Lifting his great boots through the drifts,
Going as if to die among "those dark trees"
Of his own country. I watched him go,

Past a house, quiet, warm and light,
A farm, a countryside, a woodpile in its slow
Smokeless burning, alder swamps ghastly white,
Tumultuous snows, blanker whitenesses,
Into the pathless wood, one eye weeping,
The dark trees, for which no saying is dark enough,
Which mask the gloom and lead on into it,
The bare, the withered, the deserted.

There were no more cottages.
Soft bombs of dust falling from the boughs,
The sun shining no warmer than the moon,
He had outwalked the farthest city light,
And there, clinging to the perfect trees,
A last leaf. What was it?
What was that whiteness? — white, uncertain —
The night too dark to know.

4

He turned. *Love,*
Love of things, duty, he said,
And made his way back to the shelter
No longer sheltering him, the house
Where everything real was turning to words,

Where he would think on the white wave,
Folded back, that rides in place on the obscure
Pouring of this life to the sea —
And invent on the broken lips of darkness
The seal of form and the *mot juste.*

5

Poet of the country of white houses,
Of clearings going out to the dark wall of woods
Frayed along the skyline, you who nearly foreknew
The next lines of poems you suddenly dropped,
Who dwelt in access to that which other men
Have burnt all their lives to get near, who heard
The high wind, in gusts, seething
From far off, headed through the trees exactly
To this place where it must happen, who spent
Your life on the point of giving away your heart
To the dark trees, the dissolving woods,
Into which you go at last, heart in hand, deep in:
When we think of a man who was cursed
Neither with the mystical all-lovingness of Walt Whitman
Nor with Melville's anguish to know and to suffer,
And yet cursed . . . A man, what shall I say,
Vain, not fully convinced he was dying, whose calling
Was to set up in the wilderness of his country,
At whatever cost, a man, who would be his own man.
We think of you. And from the same doorway

At which you lived, between the house and the woods,
We see your old footprints going away across
The great Republic, Frost, up memorized slopes,
Down hills floating by heart on the bulldozed land.

Flower Herding on Mount Monadnock

1

I can support it no longer.
Laughing ruefully at myself
For all I claim to have suffered
I get up. Damned nightmarer!

It is New Hampshire out there,
It is nearly the dawn.
The song of the whippoorwill stops
And the dimension of depth seizes everything.

2

The song of a peabody bird goes overhead
Like a needle pushed five times through the air,
It enters the leaves, and comes out little changed.

The air is so still
That as they go off through the trees
The love songs of birds do not get any fainter.

3

The last memory I have
Is of a flower which cannot be touched,

Through the bloom of which, all day,
Fly crazed, missing bees.

4

As I climb sweat gets up my nostrils,
For an instant I think I am at the sea,

One summer off Cape Ferrat we watched a black seagull
Straining for the dawn, we stood in the surf,

Grasshoppers splash up where I step,
The mountain laurel crashes at my thighs.

5

There is something joyous in the elegies
Of birds. They seem
Caught up in a formal delight,
Though the mourning dove whistles of despair.

But at last in the thousand elegies
The dead rise in our hearts,
On the brink of our happiness we stop
Like someone on a drunk starting to weep.

6

I kneel at a pool,
I look through my face
At the bacteria I think
I see crawling through the moss.

My face sees me,
The water stirs, the face,
Looking preoccupied,
Gets knocked from its bones.

7

I weighed eleven pounds
At birth, having stayed on
Two extra weeks in the womb.
Tempted by room and fresh air
I came out big as a policeman
Blue-faced, with narrow red eyes.
It was eight days before the doctor
Would scare my mother with me.

Turning and craning in the vines
I can make out through the leaves
The old, shimmering nothingness, the sky.

8

Green, scaly moosewoods ascend,
Tenants of the shaken paradise,

At every wind last night's rain
Comes splattering from the leaves,

It drops in flurries and lies there,
The footsteps of some running start.

9

From a rock
A waterfall
A single trickle like a strand of wire
Breaks into beads halfway down.

I know
The birds fly off
But the hug of the earth wraps
With moss their graves and the giant boulders.

10

In the forest I discover a flower.

The invisible life of the thing
Goes up in flames that are invisible
Like cellophane burning in the sunlight.

It burns up. Its drift is to be nothing.

In its covertness it has a way
Of uttering itself in place of itself,
Its blossoms claim to float in the Empyrean,

A wrathful presence on the blur of the ground.

The appeal to heaven breaks off.
The petals begin to fall, in self-forgiveness.
It is a flower. On this mountainside it is dying.

The Correspondence School Instructor Says Goodbye to his Poetry Students

Goodbye, lady in Bangor, who sent me
snapshots of yourself, after definitely hinting
you were beautiful; goodbye,
Miami Beach urologist, who enclosed plain
brown envelopes for the return of your *very*
"Clinical Sonnets"; goodbye, manufacturer

of brassieres on the Coast, whose eclogues
give the fullest treatment in literature yet
to the sagging breast motif; goodbye, you in San Quentin,
who wrote, "Being German my hero is Hitler,"
instead of "Sincerely yours," at the end of long,
neat-scripted letters demolishing
the pre-Raphaelites:

I swear to you, it was just my way
of cheering myself up, as I licked
the stamped, self-addressed envelopes,
the game I had
of trying to guess which one of you, this time,
had poisoned his glue. I did care.
I did read each poem entire.
I did say what I thought was the truth
in the mildest words I knew. And now,
in this poem, or chopped prose, not any better,
I realize, than those troubled lines
I kept sending back to you,
I have to say I am relieved it is over:
at the end I could feel only pity
for that urge toward more life
your poems kept smothering in words, the smell
of which, days later, would tingle
in your nostrils as new, God-given impulses
to write.

Goodbye,
you who are, for me, the postmarks again
of shattered towns — Xenia, Burnt Cabins, Hornell —
their loneliness
given away in poems, only their solitude kept.

The Porcupine

1

Fatted
on herbs, swollen on crabapples,
puffed up on bast and phloem, ballooned
on willow flowers, poplar catkins, first
leafs of aspen and larch,

the porcupine
drags and bounces his last meal through ice,
mud, roses and goldenrod, into the stubbly high fields.

2

In character
he resembles us in seven ways:
he puts his mark on outhouses,
he alchemizes by moonlight,
he shits on the run,
he uses his tail for climbing,
he chuckles softly to himself when scared,
he's overcrowded if there's more than one of him per five acres,
his eyes have their own inner redness.

3

Digger of
goings across floors, of hesitations
at thresholds, of
handprints of dread
at doorpost or window jamb, he would
gouge the world
empty of us, hack and crater
it
until it is nothing, if that
could rinse it of all our sweat and pathos.

Adorer of ax
handles aflow with grain, of arms
of Morris chairs, of hand
crafted objects
steeped in the juice of fingertips,
of surfaces wetted down
with fist grease and elbow oil,
of clothespins that have
grabbed our body-rags by underarm and crotch . . .

Unimpressed — bored —
by the whirl of the stars, by *these*
he's astonished, ultra-
Rilkean angel!

for whom the true
portion of the sweetness of earth
is one of those bottom-heavy, glittering, saccadic
bits
of salt water that splash down
the haunted ravines of a human face.

4

A farmer shot a porcupine three times
as it dozed on a tree limb. On
the way down it tore open its belly
on a broken
branch, hooked its gut,
and went on falling. On the ground
it sprang to its feet, and
paying out gut heaved
and spartled through a hundred feet of goldenrod
before
the abrupt emptiness.

5

The Avesta
puts porcupine killers
into hell for nine generations, sentencing them
to gnaw out
each other's hearts for the
salts of desire.

I roll
this way and that in the great bed, under
the quilt
that mimics this country of broken farms and woods,
the fatty sheath of the man
melting off,
the self-stabbing coil
of bristles reversing, blossoming outward —
a red-eyed, hard-toothed, arrow-stuck urchin
tossing up mattress feathers,
pricking the
woman beside me until she cries.

6

In my time I have
crouched, quills erected,
Saint
Sebastian of the
scared heart, and been
beat dead with a locust club
on the bare snout.
And fallen from high places
I have fled, have
jogged
over fields of goldenrod,
terrified, seeking home,
and among flowers
I have come to myself empty, the rope
strung out behind me
in the fall sun
suddenly glorified with all my blood.

7

And tonight I think I prowl broken
skulled or vacant as a
sucked egg in the wintry meadow, softly chuckling, blank
template of myself, dragging
a starved belly through the lichflowered acres,
where
burdock looses the arks of its seed
and thistle holds up its lost blooms
and rosebushes in the wind scrape their dead limbs
for the forced-fire
of roses.

The Dead Shall Be Raised Incorruptible

1

A piece of flesh gives off
smoke in the field —

carrion,
caput mortuum,
orts,
pelf,

fenks,
sordes,
gurry dumped from hospital trashcans.

Lieutenant!
This corpse will not stop burning!

2

"That you Captain? Sure,
sure I remember — I still hear you
lecturing at me on the intercom, *Keep your guns up, Burnsie!*
and then screaming, *Stop shooting, for crissake, Burnsie,*
those are friendlies! But crissake, Captain,
I'd already started, burst
after burst, little black pajamas jumping
and falling . . . and remember that pilot
who'd bailed out over the North,
how I shredded him down to catgut on his strings?
one of his slant eyes, a piece
of his smile, sail past me
every night right after the sleeping pill . . .

"It was only
that I loved the *sound*
of them. I guess I just loved
the *feel* of them sparkin' off my hands . . ."

3

On the television screen:

Do you have a body that sweats?
Sweat that has odor?
False teeth clanging into your breakfast?
Case of the dread?
Headache so perpetual it may outlive you?
Armpits sprouting hair?
Piles so huge you don't need a chair to sit at a table?

We shall not all sleep, but we shall be changed . . .

971

4

In the Twentieth Century of my trespass on earth,
having exterminated one billion heathens,
heretics, Jews, Moslems, witches, mystical seekers,
black men, Asians, and Christian brothers,
every one of them for his own good,

a whole continent of red men for living in unnatural community
and at the same time having relations with the land,
one billion species of animals for being sub-human,
and ready to take on the bloodthirsty creatures from the other planets,
I, Christian man, groan out this testament of my last will.

I give my blood fifty parts polystyrene,
twenty-five parts benzene, twenty-five parts good old gasoline,
to the last bomber pilot aloft, that there shall be one acre
in the dull world where the kissing flower may bloom,
which kisses you so long your bones explode under its lips.

My tongue goes to the Secretary of the Dead
to tell the corpses, "I'm sorry, fellows,
the killing was just one of those things
difficult to pre-visualize — like a cow,
say, getting hit by lightning."

My stomach, which has digested
four hundred treaties giving the Indians
eternal right to their land, I give to the Indians,
I throw in my lungs which have spent four hundred years
sucking in good faith on peace pipes.

My soul I leave to the bee
that he may sting it and die, my brain
to the fly, his back the hysterical green color of slime,
that he may suck on it and die, my flesh to the advertising man,
the anti-prostitute, who loathes human flesh for money.

I assign my crooked backbone
to the dice maker, to chop up into dice,
for casting lots as to who shall see his own blood
on his shirt front and who his brother's,
for the race isn't to the swift but to the crooked.

To the last man surviving on earth
I give my eyelids worn out by fear, to wear
in his long nights of radiation and silence,
so that his eyes can't close, for regret
is like tears seeping through closed eyelids.

I give the emptiness my hand: the pinkie picks no more noses,
slag clings to the black stick of the ring finger,
a bit of flame jets from the tip of the fuck-you finger,
the first finger accuses the heart, which has vanished,
on the thumb stump wisps of smoke ask a ride into the emptiness.

In the Twentieth Century of my nightmare
on earth, I swear on my chromium testicles
to this testament
and last will
of my iron will, my fear of love, my itch for money, and my madness.

5

In the ditch
snakes crawl cool paths
over the rotted thigh, the toe bones
twitch in the smell of burnt rubber,
the belly
opens like a poison nightflower,
the tongue has evaporated,
the nostril
hairs sprinkle themselves with yellowish-white dust,
the five flames at the end
of each hand have gone out, a mosquito
sips a last meal from this plate of serenity.

And the fly,
the last nightmare, hatches himself.

6

I ran
my neck broken I ran
holding my head up with both hands I ran
thinking the flames
the flames may burn the oboe
but listen buddy boy they can't touch the notes!

7

A few bones
lie about in the smoke of bones.

Membranes,
effigies pressed into grass,
mummy windings,
desquamations,
sags incinerated mattresses gave back to the world,
memories left in mirrors on whorehouse ceilings,
angle's wings
flagged down into the snows of yesteryear,

kneel
on the scorched earth
in the shapes of men and animals:

do not let this last hour pass,
do not remove this last, poison cup from our lips.

And a wind holding
the cries of love-making from all our nights and days
moves among the stones, hunting
for two twined skeletons to blow its last cry across.

Lieutenant!
This corpse will not stop burning!

The Path Among the Stones

1

On the path winding
upward, toward the high valley
of waterfalls and flooded, hoof-shattered
meadows of spring,
where fish-roots boil
in the last grails of light on the water,
and vipers pimpled with urges to fly
drape the black stones hissing *pheet! pheet!* — land
of quills
and inkwells of skulls filled with black water —

I come to a field
glittering with the thousand sloughed skins
of arrowheads, stones
which shuddered and leapt forth
to give themselves into the broken hearts
of the living,
who gave themselves back, broken, to the stone.

2

I close my eyes:
on the heat-rippled beaches
where the hills came down to the sea,
the luminous
beach dust pounded out of funeral shells,
I can see
them living without me, dying
without me, the wing
and egg
shaped stones, broken
war-shells of slain fighting conches,
dog-eared immortality shells
in which huge constellations of slime, by the full moon,
writhed one more
coat of invisibility on a speck of sand,

and the agates knocked
from circles scratched into the dust
with the click
of a wishbone breaking, inward-swirling
globes biopsied out of sunsets never to open again,

and that wafer-stone
which skipped ten times across
the water, suddenly starting to run as it went under,
and the zeroes it left,
that met
and passed into each other, they themselves
smoothing themselves from the water . . .

3

I walk out from myself,
among the stones of the field,
each sending up its ghost-bloom
into the starlight, to float out
over the trees, seeking to be one
with the unearthly fires kindling and dying

in space — and falling back, knowing
the sadness of the wish
to alight
back among the glitter of bruised ground,
the stones holding between pasture and field,
the great, granite nuclei,
glimmering, even they, with ancient inklings of madness and war.

4

A way opens
at my feet. I go down
the night-lighted mule-steps into the earth,
the footprints behind me
filling already with pre-sacrificial trills
of canaries, go down
into the unbreathable goaf
of everything I ever craved and lost.

An old man, a stone
lamp at his forehead, squats
by his hell-flames, stirs into
his pot
chopped head
of crow, strings of white light,
opened tail of peacock, dressed
body of canary, robin breast
dragged through the mud of battlefields, wrung-out
blossom of caput mortuum flower — salts
it all down with sand
stolen from the upper bells of hourglasses . . .

Nothing.
Always nothing. Ordinary blood
boiling away in the glare of the brow lamp.

5

And yet, no,
perhaps not nothing. Perhaps
not ever nothing. In clothes
woven out of the blue spittle
of snakes, I crawl up: I find myself alive
in the whorled
archway of the fingerprint of all things,
skeleton groaning,
blood-strings wailing the wail of all things.

6

The witness trees heal
their scars at the flesh fire,
the flame
rises off the bones,
the hunger
to be new lifts off
my soul, an eerie blue light blooms
on all the ridges of the world. Somewhere
in the legends of blood sacrifice
the fatted calf
takes the bonfire into his arms, and *he*
burns *it*.

7

As above: the last scattered stars
kneel down in the star-form of the Aquarian age:
a splash
on the top of the head,
on the grass of this earth even the stars love, splashes of the sacred
    waters . . .

So below: in the graveyard
the lamps start lighting up, one for each of us,
in all the windows
of stone.

W. S. MERWIN
b. 1927

Ballad of John Cable and Three Gentlemen

He that had come that morning,
One after the other,
Over seven hills,
Each of a new color,

Came now by the last tree,
By the red-colored valley,
To a gray river
Wide as the sea.

There at the shingle
A listing wherry
Awash with dark water;
What should it carry?

There on the shelving,
Three dark gentlemen.
Might they direct him?
Three gentlemen.

"Cable, friend John, John Cable,"
When they saw him they said,
"Come and be company
As far as the far side."

"Come follow the feet," they said,
"Of your family,
Of your old father
That came already this way."

But Cable said, "First I must go
Once to my sister again;
What will she do come spring
And no man on her garden?

She will say 'Weeds are alive
From here to the Stream of Friday;
I grieve for my brother's plowing,'
Then break and cry."

978

"Lose no sleep," they said, "for that fallow:
She will say before summer,
'I can get me a daylong man,
Do better than a brother.' "

Cable said, "I think of my wife:
Dearly she needs consoling;
I must go back for a little
For fear she dies of grieving."

"Cable," they said, "John Cable,
Ask no such wild favor;
Still, if you fear she die soon,
The boat might wait for her."

But Cable said, "I remember:
Out of charity let me
Go shore up my poorly mother,
Cries all afternoon."

They said, "She is old and far,
Far and rheumy with years,
And, if you like, we shall take
No note of her tears."

But Cable said, "I am neither
Your hired man nor maid,
Your dog nor shadow
Nor your ape to be led."

He said, "I must go back:
Once I heard someone say
That the hollow Stream of Friday
Is a rank place to lie;

And this word, now I remember,
Makes me sorry: have you
Thought of my own body
I was always good to?

The frame that was my devotion
And my blessing was,
The straight bole whose limbs
Were long as stories —

Now, poor thing, left in the dirt
By the Stream of Friday
Might not remember me
Half tenderly."

They let him nurse no worry;
They said, "We give you our word:
Poor thing is made of patience;
Will not say a word."

"Cable, friend John, John Cable,"
After this they said,
"Come with no company
To the far side.

To a populous place,
A dense city
That shall not be changed
Before much sorrow dry."

Over shaking water
Toward the feet of his father,
Leaving the hills' color
And his poorly mother

And his wife at grieving
And his sister's fallow
And his body lying
In the rank hollow,

Now Cable is carried
On the dark river;
Not even a shadow
Followed him over.

On the wide river
Gray as the sea
Flags of white water
Are his company.

Song of Three Smiles

Let me call a ghost,
Love, so it be little:
In December we took
No thought for the weather.

Whom now shall I thank
For this wealth of water?
Your heart loves harbors
Where I am a stranger.

Where was it we lay
Needing no other
Twelve days and twelve nights
In each other's eyes?

Or was it at Babel
And the days too small
We spoke our own tongue
Needing no other?

If a seed grow green
Set a stone upon it
That it learn thereby
Holy charity.

If you must smile
Always on that other,
Cut me from ear to ear
And we all smile together.

Leviathan

This is the black sea-brute bulling through wave-rack,
Ancient as ocean's shifting hills, who in sea-toils
Travelling, who furrowing the salt acres
Heavily, his wake hoary behind him,
Shoulders spouting, the fist of his forehead
Over wastes gray-green crashing, among horses unbroken
From bellowing fields, past bone-wreck of vessels,
Tide-ruin, wash of lost bodies bobbing

No longer sought for, and islands of ice gleaming,
Who ravening the rank flood, wave-marshalling,
Overmastering the dark sea-marches, finds home
And harvest. Frightening to foolhardiest
Mariners, his size were difficult to describe:
The hulk of him is like hills heaving,
Dark, yet as crags of drift-ice, crowns cracking in thunder,
Like land's self by night black-looming, surf churning and trailing
Along his shores' rushing, shoal-water boding
About the dark of his jaws; and who should moor at his edge
And fare on afoot would find gates of no gardens,
But the hill of dark underfoot diving,
Closing overhead, the cold deep, and drowning.
He is called Leviathan, and named for rolling,
First created he was of all creatures,
He has held Jonah three days and nights,
He is that curling serpent that in ocean is,
Sea-fright he is, and the shadow under the earth.
Days there are, nonetheless, when he lies
Like an angel, although a lost angel
On the waste's unease, no eye of man moving,
Bird hovering, fish flashing, creature whatever
Who after him came to herit earth's emptiness.
Froth at flanks seething soothes to stillness,
Waits; with one eye he watches
Dark of night sinking last, with one eye dayrise
As at first it was, is the hand not yet contented
Though that light is a breath. The sea curling,
Star-climbed, wind-combed, cumbered with itself still
As at first it was, is the hand not yet contented
Of the Creator. And he waits for the world to begin.

Birds Waking

I went out at daybreak and stood on Primrose Hill.
It was April: a white haze over the hills of Surrey
Over the green haze of the hills above the dark green
Of the park trees, and over it all the light came up clear,
The sky like deep porcelain paling and paling,
With everywhere under it the faces of the buildings
Where the city slept, gleaming white and quiet,
St Paul's and the water tower taking the gentle gold.

And from the hill chestnuts and the park trees
There was such a clamour rose as the birds woke,
Such uncontainable tempest of whirled
Singing flung upward and upward into the new light,
Increasing still as the birds themselves rose
From the black trees and whirled in a rising cloud,
Flakes and water-spouts and hurled seas and continents of them
Rising, dissolving, streamering out, always
Louder and louder singing, shrieking, laughing.
Sometimes one would break from the cloud but from the song never,
And would beat past my ear dinning his deafening note.
I thought I had never known the wind
Of joy to be so shrill, so unanswerable,
With such clouds of winged song at its disposal, and I thought
Oh Voice that my demand is the newest name for,
There are many ways we may end, and one we must,
Whether burning, or the utter cold descending in darkness,
Explosion of our own devising, collision of planets, all
Violent, however silent they at last may seem;
Oh let it be by this violence, then, let it be now,
Now when in their sleep, unhearing, unknowing,
Most faces must be closest to innocence,
When the light moves unhesitating to fill the sky with clearness
And no dissent could be heard above the din of its welcome,
Let the great globe well up and dissolve like its last birds,
With the bursting roar and uprush of song!

Odysseus

For George Kirstein

Always the setting forth was the same,
Same sea, same dangers waiting for him
As though he had got nowhere but older.
Behind him on the receding shore
The identical reproaches, and somewhere
Out before him, the unravelling patience
He was wedded to. There were the islands
Each with its woman and twining welcome
To be navigated, and one to call "home."
The knowledge of all that he betrayed
Grew till it was the same whether he stayed

Or went. Therefore he went. And what wonder
If sometimes he could not remember
Which was the one who wished on his departure
Perils that he could never sail through,
And which, improbable, remote, and true,
Was the one he kept sailing home to?

The Room

I think all this is somewhere in myself
The cold room unlit before dawn
Containing a stillness such as attends death
And from a corner the sounds of a small bird trying
From time to time to fly a few beats in the dark
You would say it was dying it is immortal

For the Anniversary of My Death

Every year without knowing it I have passed the day
When the last fires will wave to me   '
And the silence will set out
Tireless traveller
Like the beam of a lightless star

Then I will no longer
Find myself in life as in a strange garment
Surprised at the earth
And the love of one woman
And the shamelessness of men
As today writing after three days of rain
Hearing the wren sing and the falling cease
And bowing not knowing to what

In the Winter of My Thirty-Eighth Year

It sounds unconvincing to say *When I was young*
Though I have long wondered what it would be like
To be me now
No older at all it seems from here
As far from myself as ever

Waking in fog and rain and seeing nothing
I imagine all the clocks have died in the night
Now no one is looking I could choose my age
It would be younger I suppose so I am older
It is there at hand I could take it
Except for the things I think I would do differently
They keep coming between they are what I am
They have taught me little I did not know when I was young

There is nothing wrong with my age now probably
It is how I have come to it
Like a thing I kept putting off as I did my youth

There is nothing the matter with speech
Just because it lent itself
To my uses

Of course there is nothing the matter with the stars
It is my emptiness among them
While they drift farther away in the invisible morning

The Asians Dying

When the forests have been destroyed their darkness remains
The ash the great walker follows the possessors
Forever
Nothing they will come to is real
Nor for long
Over the watercourses
Like ducks in the time of the ducks
The ghosts of the villages trail in the sky
Making a new twilight

Rain falls into the open eyes of the dead
Again again with its pointless sound
When the moon finds them they are the color of everything

The nights disappear like bruises but nothing is healed
The dead go away like bruises
The blood vanishes into the poisoned farmlands
Pain the horizon

Remains
Overhead the seasons rock
They are paper bells
Calling to nothing living

The possessors move everywhere under Death their star
Like columns of smoke they advance into the shadows
Like thin flames with no light
They with no past
And fire their only future

Looking for Mushrooms at Sunrise

For Jean and Bill Arrowsmith

When it is not yet day
I am walking on centuries of dead chestnut leaves
In a place without grief
Though the oriole
Out of another life warns me
That I am awake

In the dark while the rain fell
The gold chanterelles pushed through a sleep that was not mine
Waking me
So that I came up the mountain to find them

Where they appear it seems I have been before
I recognize their haunts as though remembering
Another life

Where else am I walking even now
Looking for me

The Approaches

The glittering rises in flocks
suddenly in the afternoon
and hangs
voiceless above the broken
houses
the cold in the doorways

and at the silent station
the hammers
out of hearts
laid in rows in the grass

The water is asleep
as they say
everywhere
cold cold
and at night the sky
is in many
pieces in the dark
the stars set out
and leave their light

When I wake
I say I may never
get there but should get
closer and hear the sound
seeing figures I go toward them waving
they make off
birds
no one to guide me
afraid
to the warm ruins
Canaan
where the fighting is

The Distances

When you think of the distances
you recall
that we are immortal

you think of them setting out from us
all of them setting out
from us
and none dies and none is forgotten

and all over the world there are dams
lying on their backs
thinking of the sea

The Old Boast

Listen natives of a dry place
from the harpist's fingers
rain

Surf-Casting

It has to be the end of the day
the hour of one star
the beach has to be a naked slab

and you have to have practised a long time
with the last moments of fish
sending them to look for the middle of the sea
until your fingers
can play back whole voyages

then you send out one
of your toes for bait
hoping it's the right evening

you have ten chances

the moon rises from the surf
your hands listen
if only the great Foot is running

if only it will strike
and you can bring it to shore

in two strides it will take you
to the emperor's palace
stamp stamp the gates will open
he will present you with half of his kingdom
and his only daughter

and the next night you will come back
to fish for the Hand

Exercise

First forget what time it is
for an hour
do it regularly every day

then forget what day of the week it is
do this regularly for a week
then forget what country you are in
and practise doing it in company
for a week
then do them together
for a week
with as few breaks as possible

follow these by forgetting how to add
or to subtract
it makes no difference
you can change them around
after a week
both will help you later
to forget how to count

forget how to count
starting with your own age
starting with how to count backward
starting with even numbers
starting with Roman numerals
starting with fractions of Roman numerals
starting with the old calendar
going on to the old alphabet
going on to the alphabet
until everything is continuous again

JAMES WRIGHT
b. 1927

Complaint

She's gone. She was my love, my moon or more.
She chased the chickens out and swept the floor,
Emptied the bones and nut-shells after feasts,
And smacked the kids for leaping up like beasts.

Now morbid boys have grown past awkwardness;
The girls let stitches out, dress after dress,
To free some swinging body's riding space
And form the new child's unimagined face.
Yet, while vague nephews, spitting on their curls,
Amble to pester winds and blowsy girls,
What arm will sweep the room, what hand will hold
New snow against the milk to keep it cold?
And who will dump the garbage, feed the hogs,
And pitch the chickens' heads to hungry dogs?
Not my lost hag who dumbly bore such pain:
Childbirth and midnight sassafras and rain.
New snow against her face and hands she bore,
And now lies down, who was my moon or more.

Evening

I called him to come in,
The wide lawn darkened so.
Laughing, he held his chin
And hid beside a bush.
The light gave him a push,
Shadowy grass moved slow.
He crept on agile toes
Under a sheltering rose.

His mother, still beyond
The bare porch and the door,
Called faintly out of sound,
And vanished with her voice.
I caught his curious eyes
Measuring me, and more —
The light dancing behind
My shoulder in the wind.

Then, struck beyond belief
By the child's voice I heard,
I saw his hair turn leaf,
His dancing toes divide
To hooves on either side,
One hand become a bird.
Startled, I held my tongue
To hear what note he sang.

Where was the boy gone now?
I stood on the grass, alone.
Swung from the apple bough
The bees ignored my cry.
A dog roved past, and I
Turned up a sinking stone,
But found beneath no more
Than grasses dead last year.

Suddenly lost and cold,
I knew the yard lay bare.
I longed to touch and hold
My child, my talking child,
Laughing or tame or wild —
Solid in light and air,
The supple hands, the face
To fill that barren place.

Slowly, the leaves descended,
The birds resolved to hands;
Laugh, and the charm was ended,
The hungry boy stepped forth.
He stood on the hard earth,
Like one who understands
Fairy and ghost — but less
Our human loneliness.

Then, on the withering lawn,
He walked beside my arm.
Trees and the sun were gone,
Everything gone but us.
His mother sang in the house,
And kept our supper warm,
And loved us, God knows how,
The wide earth darkened so.

A Breath of Air

I walked, when love was gone,
Out of the human town,
For an easy breath of air.
Beyond a break in the trees,

Beyond the hangdog lives
Of old men, beyond girls:
The tall stars held their peace.
Looking in vain for lies
I turned, like earth, to go.
An owl's wings hovered, bare
On the moon's hills of snow.

And things were as they were.

Saint Judas

When I went out to kill myself, I caught
A pack of hoodlums beating up a man.
Running to spare his suffering, I forgot
My name, my number, how my day began,
How soldiers milled around the garden stone
And sang amusing songs; how all that day
Their javelins measured crowds; how I alone
Bargained the proper coins, and slipped away.

Banished from heaven, I found this victim beaten,
Stripped, kneed, and left to cry. Dropping my rope
Aside, I ran, ignored the uniforms:
Then I remembered bread my flesh had eaten,
The kiss that ate my flesh. Flayed without hope,
I held the man for nothing in my arms.

Lying in a Hammock at William Duffy's Farm in Pine Island, Minnesota

Over my head, I see the bronze butterfly,
Asleep on the black trunk,
Blowing like a leaf in green shadow.
Down the ravine behind the empty house,
The cowbells follow one another
Into the distances of the afternoon.
To my right,
In a field of sunlight between two pines,
The droppings of last year's horses
Blaze up into golden stones.

JAMES WRIGHT

I lean back, as the evening darkens and comes on.
A chicken hawk floats over, looking for home.
I have wasted my life.

A Blessing

Just off the highway to Rochester, Minnesota,
Twilight bounds softly forth on the grass.
And the eyes of those two Indian ponies
Darken with kindness.
They have come gladly out of the willows
To welcome my friend and me.
We step over the barbed wire into the pasture
Where they have been grazing all day, alone.
They ripple tensely, the can hardly contain their happiness
That we have come.
They bow shyly as wet swans. They love each other.
There is no loneliness like theirs.
At home once more,
They begin munching the young tufts of spring in the darkness.
I would like to hold the slenderer one in my arms,
For she has walked over to me
And nuzzled my left hand.
She is black and white,
Her mane falls wild on her forehead,
And the light breeze moves me to caress her long ear
That is delicate as the skin over a girl's wrist.
Suddenly I realize
That if I stepped out of my body I would break
Into blossom.

Milkweed

While I stood here, in the open, lost in myself,
I must have looked a long time
Down the corn rows, beyond grass,
The small house,
White walls, animals lumbering toward the barn.
I look down now. It is all changed.
Whatever it was I lost, whatever I wept for
Was a wild, gentle thing, the small dark eyes

993

Loving me in secret.
It is here. At a touch of my hand,
The air fills with delicate creatures
From the other world.

To Flood Stage Again

In Fargo, North Dakota, a man
Warned me the river might rise
To flood stage again.
On the bridge, a girl hurries past me, alone,
Unhappy face.
Will she pause in wet grass somewhere?
Behind my eyes she stands tiptoe, yearning for confused sparrows
To fetch a bit of string and dried wheatbeard
To line her outstretched hand.
I open my eyes and gaze down
At the dark water.

Three Sentences for a Dead Swan

1

There they are now,
The wings,
And I heard them beginning to starve
Between two cold white shadows,
But I dreamed they would rise
Together,
My black Ohioan swan.

2

Now one after another I let the black scales fall
From the beautiful black spine
Of this lonesome dragon that is born on the earth at last,
My black fire,
Ovoid of my darkness,
Machine-gunned and shattered hillsides of yellow trees
In the autumn of my blood where the apples
Purse their wild lips and smirk knowingly
That my love is dead.

3
Here, carry his splintered bones
Slowly, slowly
Back into the
Tar and chemical strangled tomb,
The strange water, the
Ohio river, that is no tomb to
Rise from the dead
From.

Written in a Copy of Swift's Poems, for Wayne Burns

I promised once if I got hold of
This book, I'd send it on to you.
These are the songs that Roethke told of,
The curious music loved by few.
I think of lanes in Laracor
Where Brinsley MacNamara wrote
His lovely elegy, before
The Yahoos got the Dean by rote.

Only, when Swift-men are all gone
Back to their chosen fields by train
And the drunk Chairman snores alone,
Swift is alive in secret, Wayne:
Singing for Stella's happiest day,
Charming a charming man, John Gay,
And greeting, now their bones are lost,
Pope's beautiful, electric ghost.

Here are some songs he lived in, kept
Secret from almost everyone
And laid away, while Stella slept,
Before he slept, and died, alone.
Gently, listen, the great shade passes,
Magnificent, who still can bear,
Beyond the range of horses' asses,
Nobilities, light, light and air.

PHILIP LEVINE
b. 1928

Above It All

Strapped to my seat, I turn
to the thin Air Force major
and ask how far to L.A.
He lifts his sunglasses, stares
down at the ocean slipping
beneath, and says, "50 minutes."
We've left the land behind us,
the stump-pocked crests, the creased hills
of Vandenberg Missile Base
where nothing moved, nothing breathed
except one lone steam engine
pulling nothing, and the waves
which came at the shore as though
they mattered, row after row.

The major reads; his lips move
soundlessly, wordlessly
like a lunatic's in love,
he reads that they're making us
get out of our cars to be
counted, they're getting tough
and we're getting tougher back,
he passes over the small
blurred photo of Jean Cocteau,
the names of the champions
Cerdan, LaMotta, Piaf,
for whom there are no poems.
If I shut my eyes I know
I'll be in a private home
for the blind where things are worse.

My good neighbor, the major,
looks at me. His eyes are young,
placid, and light blue as though
unused, and he offers me
half his newspaper, offers
his window seat — for he's seen
it all — offers a comment
on the weather but not on

the night which seems to be
gathering at the margins
of sight or the bottom
of the ocean or in
the twin periods marking
the dead centers of our eyes.

To a Child Trapped in a Barber Shop

You've gotten in through the transom
     and you can't get out
till Monday morning or, worse,
     till the cops come.

That six-year-old red face
     calling for mama
is yours; it won't help you
     because your case

is closed forever, hopeless.
     So don't drink
the Lucky Tiger, don't
     fill up on grease

because that makes it a lot worse,
     that makes it a crime
against property and the state
     and that costs time.

We've all been here before,
     we took our turn
under the electric storm
     of the vibrator

and stiffened our wills to meet
     the close clippers
and heard the true blade mowing
     back and forth

on a strip of dead skin,
     and we stopped crying.
You think your life is over?
     It's just begun.

The Lost Angel

Four little children
in winged costumes —
it has something to do

with raising money.
Children are hungry
the one says, the one

who can talk.
And they go down the drive
in the driving rain, and there's

no car
to collect them, no
one waiting, and the bills

and coins spill
from his trailing hand
and float like pieces of light.

Wait! Wait!
I yell, and run
to gather what I can,

and he turns,
the one who can talk,
holding his empty fists

as offerings,
two shaking hammers,
and gives me back my life.

Animals are Passing from our Lives

It's wonderful how I jog
on four honed-down ivory toes
my massive buttocks slipping
like oiled parts with each light step.

I'm to market. I can smell
the sour, grooved block, I can smell
the blade that opens the hole
and the pudgy white fingers

that shake out the intestines
like a hankie. In my dreams
the snouts drool on the marble,
suffering children, suffering flies,

suffering the consumers
who won't meet their steady eyes
for fear they could see. The boy
who drives me along believes

that any moment I'll fall
on my side and drum my toes
like a typewriter or squeal
and shit like a new housewife

discovering television,
or that I'll turn like a beast
cleverly to hook his teeth
with my teeth. No. Not this pig.

Salami

Stomach of goat, crushed
sheep balls, soft full
pearls of pig eyes,
snout gristle, fresh earth,
worn iron of trotter, slate
of Zaragoza, dried cat heart,
cock claws. She grinds
them with one hand and
with the other fists
mountain thyme, basil,
paprika, and knobs of garlic.
And if a tooth of stink thistle
pulls blood from the round
blue marbled hand
all the better for

999

this ruby of Pamplona,
this bright jewel of Vich,
this stained crown
of Solsona, this
salami.
   The daughter
of mismatched eyes,
36 year old infant smelling
of milk. Mama, she cries, mama,
but mama is gone,
and the old stone cutter
must wipe the drool
from her jumper. His puffed fingers
unbutton and point her
to toilet. Ten, twelve hours
a day, as long as the winter sun
holds up he rebuilds
the unvisited church
of San Martin. Cheep cheep
of the hammer high above
the town, sparrow cries
lost in the wind or lost
in the mind. At dusk he leans
to the coal dull wooden Virgin
and asks for blessings on
the slow one and peace
on his grizzled head, asks
finally and each night
for the forbidden, for
the knowledge of every
mysterious stone, and
the words go out on
the overwhelming incense
of salami.
   A single crow
passed high over the house,
I wakened out of nightmare.
The winds had changed,
the Tremontana was tearing
out of the Holy Mountains
to meet the sea winds
in my yard, burning and
scaring the young pines.

The single poplar wailed
in terror. With salt,
with guilt, with the need
to die, the vestments
of my life flared, I
was on fire, a stranger
staggering through my house
butting walls and falling
over furniture, looking
for a way out. In the last room
where moonlight slanted
through a broken shutter
I found my smallest son
asleep or dead, floating
on a bed of colorless light.
When I leaned closer
I could smell the small breaths
going and coming, and each
bore its prayer for me,
the true and earthy prayer
of salami.

They Feed They Lion

Out of burlap sacks, out of bearing butter,
Out of black bean and wet slate bread,
Out of the acids of rage, the candor of tar,
Out of creosote, gasoline, drive shafts, wooden dollies,
They Lion grow.
        Out of the gray hills
Of industrial barns, out of rain, out of bus ride,
West Virginia to Kiss My Ass, out of buried aunties,
Mothers hardening like pounded stumps, out of stumps,
Out of the bones' need to sharpen and the muscles' to stretch,
They Lion grow.
        Earth is eating trees, fence posts,
Gutted cars, earth is calling in her little ones,
"Come home, Come home!" From pig balls,
From the ferocity of pig driven to holiness,
From the furred ear and the full jowl come
The repose of the hung belly, from the purpose
They Lion grow.

From the sweet glues of the trotters
Come the sweet kinks of the fist, from the full flower
Of the hams the thorax of caves,
From "Bow Down" come "Rise Up,"
Come they Lion from the reeds of shovels,
The grained arm that pulls the hands,
They Lion grow.
From my five arms and all my hands,
From all my white sins forgiven, they feed,
From my car passing under the stars,
They Lion, from my children inherit,
From the oak turned to a wall, they Lion,
From they sack and they belly opened
And all that was hidden burning on the oil-stained earth
They feed they Lion and he comes.

The Way Down

On the way down
blue lupin at the roadside,
red bud scattered
down the mountain, tiny
white jump-ups hiding
underfoot, the first push
of wild oats like froth
at the field's edge. The wind blows
through everything, the crowned
peaks above us, the soft floor
of the valley below,
the humps of rock
walking down the world.

On the way down
from the trackless snow fields
where a blackbird
eyed me from
a solitary pine, knowing
I would go back the way
I came, shaking my head,
and the blue glitter of ice
was like the darkness
of winter nights, deepening

before it could change,
and the only voice
my own saying
Goodbye.

Can you hear me?
the air says. I hold
my breath and listen
and a finger of dirt thaws,
a river drains
from a snow drop
and rages down
my cheeks, our father
the wind hums
a prayer through my mouth
and answers in the oat,
and now the tight rows of seed
bow to the earth
and hold on and hold on.

EDWARD DORN
b. 1929

From Gloucester Out

It has all
come back today.
That memory for me is nothing
there ever was,
                That man

so long,
when stretched out
and so bold
            on his ground
and so much
lonely anywhere.

But never to forget
                that moment

when we came out of the tavern
and wandered through the carnival.
They were playing
the washington post march
but I mistook it for manhattan beach
for all around were the colored lights
of delirium
          to the left the boats
of Italians
and ahead of us, past the shoulders
of St. Peter, the magician of those fishermen

the bay
stood, and immediately is it the silent
inclined pole where tomorrow the young men
of this colony
so dangerous on the street
will fall harmlessly
into the water.

They are not the solid
but are the solidly built
citizens, and they are about us
as we walk across
          the square
with their black provocative
women
slender, like whips of
sex in the sousa filled night.

Where edged
by that man in the music
of a transplanted time and
enough of drunkenness
to make you senseless of all
but virtue
          (there is never
no, there is never a small complaint)
(that all things shit poverty,
and Life, one wars on with
many embraces) oh it was a time that was **perfect**
but for my own hesitating
to know all I had not known.

Pure existence, even in the crowds
I love
will never be possible for me
even with the men I love
                            This is
the guilt
that kills me
                My adulterated presence

but please believe with all men
I love to be

That memory
of how he lay out
on the floor in his great length
and when morning came,
late,
we lingered
in the vastest of all cities
in this hemisphere
                        and all other movement
stopped, nowhere
else was there a stirring known to us

yet that morning I stood
by the window up 3 levels
and watched a game
of stick ball, thinking of going away,
and wondering what would befall that man
when he returned to his territory.
The street as you could guess
was thick with their running
and cars,
themselves, paid that activity
such respect I thought a ritual
in the truest sense,
where all time and all motion
part around the space of men
in that act
as does a river flow past
the large rock.

And he slept
in the next room, waiting
in an outward slumber
                    for the time

we climbed into the car, accepting all things
from love, the currency of which is
parting, and glancing.

Then went
out of that city to jersey
where instantly we could not find our way
and the maze of the outlands west
starts that quick
where you may touch
your finger to liberty
and look so short a space
to the columnar bust
of New York
and know those people exist
as a speck in your own lonely heart
who will shortly depart,
taking a conveyance for the
radial stretches
past girls on corners
past drugstores, tired hesitant
creatures who I also love
in all their alienation were it not so
past all equipment of country side
to temporary homes
where the wash of sea and other
populations come
once more to whisper only one thing
for all people: a late and far-away
night yearning for
and when he gets there
I want him to stay away
from the taverns of familiarity
I want him to walk by the seashore alone
in all height
which is nothing more than
a mountain. Or the hailing of a mast
with big bright eyes.

So rushing,
            all the senses
come to him
as a swarm of golden bees
and their sting is the power
he uses as parts of
the oldest brain. He hears
the delicate thrush
of the water attacking
He hears the cries, falling gulls
and watches silently the gesture of grey
bygone people. He hears their cries
and messages, he never

ignores any sound.
As they come to him he places them
puts clothes upon them
and gives them their place
in their new explanation, there is never
a lost time, nor any inhabitant
of that time to go split by prisms or unplaced
and unattended,
                    that you may believe

is the breath he gives
the great already occurred and nightly beginning world.
So with the populace of his mind
you think his nights? are not
lonely. My God. Of his
loves, you know nothing and of his
false beginning
you can know nothing,
                    but this thing to be marked
again
      only

he who worships the gods with his strictness
can be of their company
the cat and the animals, the bird he took
from the radiator
of my car saying it had died
a natural death, rarely seen in a bird.

To play, as areal particulars can out of the span
of Man, and of all, this man
does not
          he, does, he
     walks
          by the sea
in my memory

and sees all things and to him
are presented at night
the whispers of the most flung shores
from Gloucester out

Thesis

          Only the Illegitimate are beautiful
               and only the Good
          proliferate only the Illegitimate
          Oh Aklavik only you are beautiful
     Ah Aklavik your main street is dead
          only the blemished are beautiful only
               the deserted have life made
                    of whole, unsurpassable night
               only Aklavik is life inside life inside
itself.
                    They have gone who walk stiltedly
               on the legs of life. All life is
     in the northern hemisphere turning around
     the radicals of gross pain and great joy
          the poles of pure life move
                    into the circle of
               our north, oh Aklavik only
                    the outcast and ab
          andoned to the night are faultless
     only the faultless have fallen only
          the fallen are the pure Children of the Sun
     only they move West, only they are expected,
               in the virgin heat
               by those who wait intensively
               for the creatures from the East, only
          Aklavik, our Aklavik, is North
               and lovely, always abandoned

always dark, whose warp is light.
Simple fear compels Inuvik, her liquor store
lifts the darkness
by the rotation of a false summer.
The Children of the Sun never go
to Inuvik, on bloody feet, half starved,
or suffering the absolute intrusion
of any food oh Aklavik they vomit
on your remote and insupportably obscure streets
which run antiseptically into the wilderness
and if blackflies inhabit with the insistence
of castanets the delta of Inuvik in you Aklavik
around you Aklavik they form a core
and critical shell of inflexible lust, only
in the permafrost
is the new home of the Children
of the Sun in whose nakedness
is the desire not desire
in whose beauty is the flame of red
permafrost a thousand feet deep in whose
frail buildings
the shudder of total winter in whose
misshapened sun the Children bathe

from Oxford

Part III

Comforted by Limestone

The blocks
which are the buildings and walls
All Souls
come from lower Oolite
the upper Oolite
the portland beds
and Corallian
are for burning lime, placed
between the two, fallen from
the north Oxford is cut off from
the Chilterns
the massive chalk which ends

its arc

in a thin lip eastward from
King's Lynn and upon
an edge
Cambridge sits,
snagged on the Cretaceous bank
as the land flows
towards the Wash
and the Lynn Deeps

from Gunslinger

An Idle Visitation

The cautious Gunslinger
of impeccable personal smoothness
and slender leather encased hands
folded casually
to make his knock,
will show you his map.
There is your domain.
Is it the domicile it looks to be
or simply a retinal block
of seats in, yes of course
he will supply the phrase
the theater of impatience.

If it is all you have,
the footstep in the flat above, in a foreign land
or any shimmer the city
sends you
the prompt sounds
of a metropolitan nearness
he doesn't have to unroll the map of love.
The knock responds
to its own smile, where
I ask him is my heart
not this pump
artificial already and duty bound
he says, touching me
with his leathern finger
as the queen of hearts burns
from his gauntlet into my eyes.

Globes of fire
he says there will be.
This is for your sadly missing heart
or when two persons meet
it is the grove of Gethsemane
no matter where they are
it is the girl you left
in Juarez, the blank
political days press her now
in the narrow alleys
or in the confines of the river town
her dress is torn
by the misadventure of
                her gothic search
by omission behind carpentered doors
        the mission
bells are ringing in Kansas
Have you left something out?
Negative, says my Gunslinger,
no *thing* is omitted.

I held the reins of his horse
while he went off into the desert
to pee. *Yes,* he sd
when he returned, that's better.
How long, he asked
have you been in this territory.
Four years I sd. Four years.
Then you will no doubt know where we can have
a cold drink before sunset and then a bed
will be my desire if you can find one
for me, I have no wish to continue
my debate with men,
my mare lathers with tedium
her hooves are dry
Look they are covered with the alkali
of the enormous space
between here and formerly.
Need I repeat, we have come
without sleep from Nuevo Laredo

And why do you have a female horse
Gunslinger? I asked. Don't move
he replied
the sun rests deliberately
on the rim of the sierra.

And where will you now I asked.
Five days northeast of here
depending of course on whether one's horse
is of iron or flesh
there is a city called Boston
and in that city there is a hotel
whose second floor has been let
to an inscrutable Texan named Hughes
Howard? I asked
The very same.
And what do you mean by inscrutable,
                    oh Gunslinger?
I mean to say that he
has not been seen since 1832.
But when you have found him my Gunslinger
what will you do, oh what will you do?
You would not know
that the souls of old Texans
are in jeopardy in a way not common
to other men, young man.

You would not know
of the long plains night
where they carry on
and arrange their genetic duels
with men of other states —
so there is a longhorn bull half mad
half deity
who awaits an account from me
back of the sun you nearly disturbed
just then. Here hold my mare
I must visit the cactus once more
and then, we'll have that drink.

ADRIENNE RICH
b. 1929

The Afterwake

Nursing your nerves
to rest, I've roused my own; well,
now for a few bad hours!
Sleep sees you behind closed doors.
Alone, I slump in his front parlor.
You're safe inside. Good. But I'm
like a midwife who at dawn
has all in order: bloodstains
washed up, teapot on the stove,
and starts her five miles home
walking, the birthyell still
exploding in her head.

Yes, I'm with her now: here's
the streaked, livid road
edged with shut houses
breathing night out and in.
Legs tight with fatigue,
we move under morning's coal-blue star,
colossal as this load
of unexpired purpose, which drains
slowly, till scissors of cockcrow snip the air.

Necessities of Life

Piece by piece I seem
to re-enter the world: I first began

a small, fixed dot, still see
that old myself, a dark-blue thumbtack

pushed into the scene,
a hard little head protruding

from the pointillist's buzz and bloom.
After a time the dot

begins to ooze. Certain heats
melt it.
        Now I was hurriedly

blurring into ranges
of burnt red, burning green,

whole biographies swam up and
swallowed me like Jonah.

Jonah! I was Wittgenstein,
Mary Wollstonecraft, the soul

of Louis Jouvet, dead
in a blown-up photograph.

Till, wolfed almost to shreds,
I learned to make myself

unappetizing. Scaly as a dry bulb
thrown into a cellar

I used myself, let nothing use me.
Like being on a private dole,

sometimes more like kneading bricks in Egypt.
What life was there, was mine,

now and again to lay
one hand on a warm brick

and touch the sun's ghost
with economical joy,

now and again to name
over the bare necessities.

So much for those days. Soon
practice may make me middling-perfect, I'll

dare inhabit the world
trenchant in motion as an eel, solid

as a cabbage-head. I have invitations:
a curl of mist steams upward

from a field, visible as my breath,
houses along a road stand waiting

like old women knitting, breathless
to tell their tales.

The Trees

The trees inside are moving out into the forest,
the forest that was empty all these days
where no bird could sit
no insect hide
no sun bury its feet in shadow
the forest that was empty all these nights
will be full of trees by morning.

All night the roots work
to disengage themselves from the cracks
in the veranda floor.
The leaves strain toward the glass
small twigs stiff with exertion
long-cramped boughs shuffling under the roof
like newly discharged patients
half-dazed, moving
to the clinic doors.

I sit inside, doors open to the veranda
writing long letters
in which I scarcely mention the departure
of the forest from the house.
The night is fresh, the whole moon shines
in a sky still open
the smell of leaves and lichen
still reaches like a voice into the rooms.
My head is full of whispers
which tomorrow will be silent.

Listen. The glass is breaking.
The trees are stumbling forward
into the night. Winds rush to meet them.
The moon is broken like a mirror,
its pieces flash now in the crown
of the tallest oak.

Two Songs

1

Sex, as they harshly call it,
I fell into this morning
at ten o'clock, a drizzling hour
of traffic and wet newspapers.
I thought of him who yesterday
clearly didn't
turn me to a hot field
ready for plowing,
and longing for that young man
piercéd me to the roots
bathing every vein, etc.
All day he appears to me
touchingly desirable,
a prize one could wreck one's peace for.
I'd call it love if love
didn't take so many years
but lust too is a jewel
a sweet flower and what
pure happiness to know
all our high-toned questions
breed in a lively animal.

2

That "old last act"!
And yet sometimes
all seems post coitum triste
and I a mere bystander.
Somebody else is going off,
getting shot to the moon.
Or, a moon-race!
Split seconds after
my opposite number lands

I make it —
we lie fainting together
at a crater-edge
heavy as mercury in our moonsuits
till he speaks —
in a different language
yet one I've picked up
through cultural exchanges . . .
we murmur the first moonwords:
Spasibo. Thanks. O.K.

"*I Am in Danger — Sir —*"

"Half-cracked" to Higginson, living,
afterward famous in garbled versions,
your hoard of dazzling scraps a battlefield,
now your old snood

mothballed at Harvard
and you in your variorum monument
equivocal to the end —
who are you?

Gardening the day-lily,
wiping the wine-glass stems,
your thought pulsed on behind
a forehead battered paper-thin,

you, woman, masculine
in single-mindedness,
for whom the word was more
than a symptom —

a condition of being.
Till the air buzzing with spoiled language
sang in your ears
of Perjury

and in your half-cracked way you chose
silence for entertainment,
chose to have it out at last
on your own premises.

5:30 A.M.

Birds and periodic blood.
Old recapitulations.
The fox, panting, fire-eyed,
gone to earth in my chest.
How beautiful we are,
he and I, with our auburn
pelts, our trails of blood,
our miracle escapes,
our whiplash panic flogging us on
to new miracles!
They've supplied us with pills
for bleeding, pills for panic.
Wash them down the sink.
This is truth, then:
dull needle groping in the spinal fluid,
weak acid in the bottom of the cup,
foreboding, foreboding.
No one tells the truth about truth,
that it's what the fox
sees from his scuffled burrow:
dull-jawed, onrushing
killer, being that
inanely single-minded
will have our skins at last.

Planetarium

(Thinking of Caroline Herschel, 1750-1848, astronomer,
sister of William;   and others)

A woman in the shape of a monster
a monster in the shape of a woman
the skies are full of them

a woman   "in the snow
among the Clocks and instruments
or measuring the ground with poles"

in her 98 years to discover
8 comets

she whom the moon ruled
like us
levitating into the night sky
riding the polished lenses

Galaxies of women, there
doing penance for impetuousness
ribs chilled
in those spaces   of the mind

An eye,
          "virile, precise and absolutely certain"
          from the mad webs of Uranisborg
                              encountering the NOVA

every impulse of light exploding
from the core
as life flies out of us

          Tycho whispering at last
          "Let me not seem to have lived in vain"

What we see, we see
and seeing is changing

the light that shrivels a mountain
and leaves a man alive

Heartbeat of the pulsar
heart sweating through my body

The radio impulse
pouring in from Taurus

          I am bombarded yet   I stand

I have been standing all my life in the
direct path of a battery of signals
the most accurately transmitted most
untranslateable language in the universe
I am a galactic cloud so deep   so invo-
luted that a light wave could take 15
years to travel through me   And has

taken   I am an instrument in the shape
of a woman trying to translate pulsations
into images   for the relief of the body
and the reconstruction of the mind.

Diving into the Wreck

First having read the book of myths,
and loaded the camera,
and checked the edge of the knife-blade,
I put on
the body-armor of black rubber
the absurd flippers
the grave and awkward mask.
I am having to do this
not like Cousteau with his
assiduous team
aboard the sun-flooded schooner
but here alone.

There is a ladder.
The ladder is always there
hanging innocently
close to the side of the schooner.
We know what it is for,
we who have used it.
Otherwise
it's a piece of maritime floss
some sundry equipment.

I go down.
Rung after rung and still
the oxygen immerses me
the blue light
the clear atoms
of our human air.
I go down.
My flippers cripple me,
I crawl like an insect down the ladder
and there is no one
to tell me when the ocean
will begin.

First the air is blue and then
it is bluer and then green and then
black I am blacking out and yet
my mask is powerful
it pumps my blood with power
the sea is another story
the sea is not a question of power
I have to learn alone
to turn my body without force
in the deep element.

And now: it is easy to forget
what I came for
among so many who have always
lived here
swaying their crenellated fans
between the reefs
and besides
you breathe differently down here.

I came to explore the wreck.
The words are purposes.
The words are maps.
I came to see the damage that was done
and the treasures that prevail.
I stroke the beam of my lamp
slowly along the flank
of something more permanent
than fish or weed

the thing I came for:
the wreck and not the story of the wreck
the thing itself and not the myth
the drowned face always staring
toward the sun
the evidence of damage
worn by salt and sway into this threadbare beauty
the ribs of the disaster
curving their assertion
among the tentative haunters.

This is the place.
And I am here, the mermaid whose dark hair
streams black, the merman in his armored body
We circle silently
about the wreck
we dive into the hold.
I am she: I am he

whose drowned face sleeps with open eyes
whose breasts still bear the stress
whose silver, copper, vermeil cargo lies
obscurely inside barrels
half-wedged and left to rot
we are the half-destroyed instruments .
that once held to a course
the water-eaten log
the fouled compass

We are, I am, you are
by cowardice or courage
the one who find our way
back to this scene
carrying a knife, a camera
a book of myths
in which
our names do not appear.

Merced

Fantasies of old age:
they have rounded us up
in a rest-camp for the outworn.
Somewhere in some dustbowl
a barbed-wire cantonment
of low-cost dustcolored prefab
buildings, smelling of shame
and hopeless incontinence
identical clothes of disposable
paper, identical rations
of chemically flavored food
Death in order, by gas,
hypodermics daily

to neutralize despair
So I imagine my world
in my seventieth year alive
and outside the barbed wire
a purposeless exchange
of consciousness for the absence
of pain. We will call this life.

Yet only last summer I
burned my feet in the sand
of that valley traced by the thread
of the cold quick river Merced
watered by plummets of white
When I swam, my body ached
from the righteous cold
when I lay back floating the jays
flittered from pine to pine
and the shade moved hour by hour
across El Capitan
Our wine cooled in the water
and I watched my sons, half-men
half-children, testing their part
in a world almost archaic
so precious by this time
that merely to step in pure water
or stare into clear air
is to feel a spasm of pain.

For weeks now a rage
has possessed my body, driving
now out upon men and women
now inward upon myself
Walking Amsterdam Avenue
I find myself in tears
without knowing which thought
forced water to my eyes
To speak to another human
becomes a risk
I think of Norman Morrison
the Buddhists of Saigon
the black teacher last week
who put himself to death
to waken guilt in hearts

GARY SNYDER

too numb to get the message
in a world masculinity made
unfit for women or men
Taking off in a plane
I look down at the city
which meant life to me, not death
and think that somewhere there
a cold center, composed
of pieces of human beings
metabolized, restructured
by a process they do not feel
is spreading in our midst
and taking over our minds
a thing that feels neither guilt
nor rage: that is unable
to hate, therefore to love.

GARY SNYDER
b. 1930

Piute Creek

One granite ridge
A tree, would be enough
Or even a rock, a small creek,
A bark shred in a pool.
Hill beyond hill, folded and twisted
Tough trees crammed
In thin stone fractures
A huge moon on it all, is too much.
The mind wanders. A million
Summers, night air still and the rocks
Warm. Sky over endless mountains.
All the junk that goes with being human
Drops away, hard rock wavers
Even the heavy present seems to fail
This bubble of a heart.
Words and books
Like a small creek off a high ledge
Gone in the dry air.

A clear, attentive mind
Has no meaning but that
Which sees is truly seen.
No one loves rock, yet we are here.
Night chills. A flick
In the moonlight
Slips into Juniper shadow:
Back there unseen
Cold proud eyes
Of Cougar or Coyote
Watch me rise and go.

Riprap

Lay down these words
Before your mind like rocks.
         placed solid, by hands
In choice of place, set
Before the body of the mind
         in space and time:
Solidity of bark, leaf, or wall
         riprap of things:
Cobble of milky way.
         straying planets,
These poems, people,
         lost ponies with
Dragging saddles —
         and rocky sure-foot trails.
The worlds like an endless
         four-dimensional
Game of Go.
         ants and pebbles
In the thin loam, each rock a word
         a creek-washed stone
Granite: ingrained
         with torment of fire and weight
Crystal and sediment linked hot
         all change, in thoughts,
As well as things.

from Logging

3

"Lodgepole Pine: the wonderful reproductive
power of this species on areas over which its
stand has been killed by fire is dependent upon
the ability of the closed cones to endure a fire
which kills the tree without injuring its seed.
After fire, the cones open and shed their seeds
on the bared ground and a new growth springs up."

Stood straight
holding the choker high
As the Cat swung back the arch
piss-firs falling,
Limbs snapping on the tin hat
bright D caught on
Swinging butt-hooks
ringing against cold steel.

Hsü Fang lived on leeks and pumpkins.
Goosefoot,
wild herbs,
fields lying fallow!

But it's hard to farm
Between the stumps:
The cows get thin, the milk tastes funny,
The kids grow up and go to college
They don't come back
the little fir-trees do

Rocks the same blue as sky
Only icefields, a mile up,
are the mountain
Hovering over ten thousand acres
Of young fir.

GARY SNYDER

from Hunting

1

first shaman song

In the village of the dead,
Kicked loose bones
    ate pitch of a drift log
    (whale fat)
Nettles and cottonwood. Grass smokes
                    in the sun
Logs turn in the river
    sand scorches the feet.

Two days without food, trucks roll past
    in dust and light, rivers
    are rising.
Thaw in the high meadows. Move west in July.

Soft oysters rot now, between tides
            the flats stink.

I sit without thoughts by the log-road
Hatching a new myth
Watching the waterdogs
            the last truck gone.

· · ·

6

this poem is for bear

"As for me I am a child of the god of the mountains."

A bear down under the cliff.
She is eating huckleberries.
They are ripe now
Soon it will snow, and she
Or maybe he, will crawl into a hole
And sleep. You can see
Huckleberries in bearshit if you
Look, this time of year
If I sneak up on the bear
It will grunt and run

The others had all gone down
From the blackberry brambles, but one girl
Spilled her basket, and was picking up her
Berries in the dark.
A tall man stood in the shadow, took her arm,
Led her to his home. He was a bear.
In a house under the mountain
She gave birth to slick dark children
With sharp teeth, and lived in the hollow
Mountain many years.
              snare a bear: call him out:
honey-eater
forest apple
light-foot
Old man in the fur coat, Bear! come out!
Die of your own choice!
Grandfather black-food!
                this girl married a bear
Who rules in the mountains, Bear!
          you have eaten many berries
          you have caught many fish
          you have frightened many people

Twelve species north of Mexico
Sucking their paws in the long winter
Tearing the high-strung caches down
Whining, crying, jacking off
(Odysseus was a bear)

Bear-cubs gnawing the soft tits
Teeth gritted, eyes screwed tight
              but she let them.

Til her brothers found the place
Chased her husband up the gorge
Cornered him in the rocks.
Song of the snared bear:
      "Give me my belt.
      "I am near death.
      "I came from the mountain caves
      "At the headwaters,
      "The small streams there
      "Are all dried up.

— I think I'll go hunt bears.
             "hunt bears?
Why shit Snyder.
You couldn't hit a bear in the ass
            with a handful of rice!"

        .   .   .

8

this poem is for deer

"I dance on all the mountains
On five mountains, I have a dancing place
When they shoot at me I run
To my five mountains"

Missed a last shot
At the Buck, in twilight
So we came back sliding
On dry needles through cold pines.
Scared out a cottontail
Whipped up the winchester
Shot off its head.
The white body rolls and twitches
In the dark ravine
As we run down the hill to the car.

                  deer foot down scree
Picasso's fawn, Issa's fawn,
Deer on the autumn mountain
Howling like a wise man
Stiff springy jumps down the snowfields
Head held back, forefeet out,
Balls tight in a tough hair sack
Keeping the human soul from care
              on the autumn mountain
Standing in late sun, ear-flick
Tail-flick, gold mist of flies
Whirling from nostril to eyes.

Home by night
            drunken eye
Still picks out Taurus
Low, and growing high:

four-point buck
Dancing in the headlights
              on the lonely road
A mile past the mill-pond,
With the car stopped, shot
That wild silly blinded creature down.

Pull out the hot guts
              with hard bare hands
While night-frost chills the tongue
              and eye
The cold horn-bones.
The hunter's belt
              just below the sky
Warm blood in the car trunk.
Deer-smell,
              the limp tongue.

Deer don't want to die for me.
              I'll drink sea-water
Sleep on beach pebbles in the rain
Until the deer come down to die
              in pity for my pain.

from Burning

1

second shaman song

Squat in swamp shadows.
              mosquitoes sting;
              high light in cedar above.
Crouched in a dry vain frame
              — thirst for cold snow
              — green slime of bone marrow
Seawater fills each eye

Quivering in nerve and muscle
Hung in the pelvic cradle
Bones propped against roots
A blind flicker of nerve

Still hand moves out alone
Flowering and leafing
   turning to quartz
Streaked rock congestion of karma
The long body of the swamp.
A mud-streaked thigh.

Dying carp biting air
   in the damp grass,
River recedes. No matter.

Limp fish sleep in the weeds
The sun dries me as I dance

   . . .

8

John Muir on Mt. Ritter:

After scanning its face again and again,
I began to scale it, picking my holds
With intense caution. About half-way
To the top, I was suddenly brought to
A dead stop, with arms outspread
Clinging close to the face of the rock
Unable to move hand or foot
Either up or down. My doom
Appeared fixed. I MUST fall.
There would be a moment of
Bewilderment, and then,
A lifeless rumble down the cliff
To the glacier below.
My mind seemed to fill with a
Stifling smoke. This terrible eclipse
Lasted only a moment, when life blazed
Forth again with preternatural clearness.
I seemed suddenly to become possessed
Of a new sense. My trembling muscles
Became firm again, every rift and flaw in
The rock was seen as through a microscope,
My limbs moved with a positiveness and precision
With which I seemed to have
Nothing at all to do.

The Snow on Saddle Mountain

The only thing that can be relied on
is the snow on Kurakake Mountain.
fields and woods
thawing, freezing, and thawing,
totally untrustworthy.
it's true, a great fuzzy windstorm
like yeast up there today, still
the only faint source of hope
is the snow on Kurakake mountain.

A Walk

Sunday the only day we don't work:
Mules farting around the meadow,
                            Murphy fishing,
The tent flaps in the warm
Early sun: I've eaten breakfast and I'll
                            take a walk
To Benson Lake. Packed a lunch,
Goodbye. Hopping on creekbed boulders
Up the rock throat three miles
                            Piute Creek —
In steep gorge glacier-slick rattlesnake country
Jump, land by a pool, trout skitter,
The clear sky. Deer tracks.
Bad place by a falls, boulders big as houses,
Lunch tied to belt,
I stemmed up a crack and almost fell
But rolled out safe on a ledge
                            and ambled on.
Quail chicks freeze underfoot, color of stone
Then run cheep! away, hen quail fussing.
Craggy west end of Benson Lake — after edging
Past dark creek pools on a long white slope —
Lookt down in the ice-black lake
                            lined with cliff
From far above: deep shimmering trout.
A lone duck in a gunsightpass
                            steep side hill
Through slide-aspen and talus, to the east end,

Down to grass, wading a wide smooth stream
Into camp. At last.
        By the rusty three-year-
Ago left-behind cookstove
Of the old trail crew,
Stoppt and swam and ate my lunch.

A Heifer Clambers Up

a heifer clambers up
    nighthawk goes out
        horses
trail back to the barn.
    spider gleams in his
        new web
dew on the shingles, on the car,
    on the mailbox —
the mole, the onion, and the beetle
    cease their wars.
        worlds tip
into the sunshine, men and women
    get up, babies crying
children grab their lunches
        and leave for school.
the radio announces
    in the milking barn
        in the car bound for work
"tonight all the countries
    will get drunk and have a party"
russia, america, china,
        singing with their poets,
pregnant and gracious,
    sending flowers and dancing bears
        to all the capitals
fat
    with the baby happy land

GARY SNYDER

Four Poems for Robin

Siwashing it out once in Siuslaw Forest

I slept under   rhododendron
All night   blossoms fell
Shivering on   a sheet of cardboard
Feet stuck   in my pack
Hands deep   in my pockets
Barely able   to sleep.
I remembered   when we were in school
Sleeping together   in a big warm bed
We were   the youngest lovers
When we broke up   we were still nineteen.
Now our   friends are married
You teach   school back east
I dont mind   living this way
Green hills   the long blue beach
But sometimes   sleeping in the open
I think back   when I had you.

A spring night in Shokoku-ji

Eight years ago this May
We walked under cherry blossoms
At night in an orchard in Oregon.
All that I wanted then
Is forgotten now, but you.
Here in the night
In a garden of the old capital
I feel the trembling ghost of Yugao
I remember your cool body
Naked under a summer cotton dress.

An autumn morning in Shokoku-ji

Last night watching the Pleiades,
Breath smoking in the moonlight,
Bitter memory like vomit
Choked my throat.
I unrolled a sleeping bag
On mats on the porch
Under thick autumn stars.

In dream you appeared
(Three times in nine years)
Wild, cold, and accusing.
I woke shamed and angry:
The pointless wars of the heart.
Almost dawn. Venus and Jupiter.
The first time I have
Ever seen them close.

December at Yase

You said, that October,
In the tall dry grass by the orchard
When you chose to be free,
"Again someday, maybe ten years."

After college I saw you
One time. You were strange.
And I was obsessed with a plan.

Now ten years and more have
Gone by: I've always known
          where you were —
I might have gone to you
Hoping to win your love back.
You still are single.

I didn't.
I thought I must make it alone. I
Have done that.

Only in dream, like this dawn,
Does the grave, awed intensity
Of our young love
Return to my mind, to my flesh.

We had what the others
All crave and seek for;
We left it behind at nineteen

I feel ancient, as though I had
Lived many lives.

And may never now know
If I am a fool
Or have done what my
        karma demands.

Long Hair

Hunting season:

Once every year, the Deer catch human beings. They
do various things which irresistibly draw men near them;
each one selects a certain man. The Deer shoots the man,
who is then compelled to skin it and carry its meat home
and eat it. Then the Deer is inside the man. He waits
and hides in there, but the man doesn't know it. When
enough Deer have occupied enough men, they will strike
all at once. The men who don't have Deer in them will
also be taken by surprise, and everything will change
some. This is called "takeover from inside."

Deer trails:

Deer trails run on the side hills
        cross country access roads
        dirt ruts to bone-white
        board house ranches,
        tumbled down.

Waist high through manzanita,
Through sticky, prickly, crackling
        gold dry summer grass.

Deer trails lead to water,
Lead sidewise all ways
Narrowing down to one best path —
And split —
And fade away to nowhere.

Deer trails slide under freeways
        slip into cities
        swing back and forth in crops and orchards
        run up the sides of schools!

Deer spoor and crisscross dusty tracks
Are in the house: and coming out the walls:

And deer bound through my hair.

Pine Tree Tops

In the blue night
frost haze, the sky glows
with the moon
pine tree tops
bend snow-blue, fade
into sky, frost, starlight.
The creak of boots.
Rabbit tracks, deer tracks,
what do we know.

SYLVIA PLATH
1932–1963

The Colossus

I shall never get you put together entirely,
Pieced, glued, and properly jointed.
Mule-bray, pig-grunt and bawdy cackles
Proceed from your great lips.
It's worse than a barnyard.

Perhaps you consider yourself an oracle,
Mouthpiece of the dead, or of some god or other.
Thirty years now I have laboured
To dredge the silt from your throat.
I am none the wiser.

Scaling little ladders with gluepots and pails of lysol
I crawl like an ant in mourning
Over the weedy acres of your brow
To mend the immense skull-plates and clear
The bald, white tumuli of your eyes.

A blue sky out of the Oresteia
Arches above us. O father, all by yourself
You are pithy and historical as the Roman Forum.
I open my lunch on a hill of black cypress.
Your fluted bones and acanthine hair are littered

In their old anarchy to the horizon-line.
It would take more than a lightning-stroke
To create such a ruin.
Nights, I squat in the cornucopia
Of your left ear, out of the wind.

Counting the red stars and those of plum-colour.
The sun rises under the pillar of your tongue.
My hours are married to shadow.
No longer do I listen for the scrape of a keel
On the blank stones of the landing.

Morning Song

Love set you going like a fat gold watch.
The midwife slapped your footsoles, and your bald cry
Took its place among the elements.

Our voices echo, magnifying your arrival. New statue.
In a drafty museum, your nakedness
Shadows our safety. We stand round blankly as walls.

I'm no more your mother
Than the cloud that distils a mirror to reflect its own slow
Effacement at the wind's hand.

All night your moth-breath
Flickers among the flat pink roses. I wake to listen:
A far sea moves in my ear.

One cry, and I stumble from bed, cow-heavy and floral
In my Victorian nightgown.
Your mouth opens clean as a cat's. The window square

Whitens and swallows its dull stars. And now you try
Your handful of notes;
The clear vowels rise like balloons.

The Applicant

First, are you our sort of a person?
Do you wear
A glass eye, false teeth or a crutch,
A brace or a hook,
Rubber breasts or a rubber crotch,

Stitches to show something's missing? No, no? Then
How can we give you a thing?
Stop crying.
Open your hand.
Empty? Empty. Here is a hand

To fill it and willing
To bring teacups and roll away headaches
And do whatever you tell it.
Will you marry it?
It is guaranteed

To thumb shut your eyes at the end
And dissolve of sorrow.
We make new stock from the salt.
I notice you are stark naked.
How about this suit ——

Black and stiff, but not a bad fit.
Will you marry it?
It is waterproof, shatterproof, proof
Against fire and bombs through the roof.
Believe me, they'll bury you in it.

Now your head, excuse me, is empty.
I have the ticket for that.
Come here, sweetie, out of the closet.
Well, what do you think of *that?*
Naked as paper to start

But in twenty-five years she'll be silver,
In fifty, gold.
A living doll, everywhere you look.
It can sew, it can cook,
It can talk, talk, talk.

It works, there is nothing wrong with it.
You have a hole, it's a poultice.
You have an eye, it's an image.
My boy, it's your last resort.
Will you marry it, marry it, marry it.

Lady Lazarus

I have done it again.
One year in every ten
I manage it ——

A sort of walking miracle, my skin
Bright as a Nazi lampshade,
My right foot

A paperweight,
My face a featureless, fine
Jew linen.

Peel off the napkin
O my enemy.
Do I terrify? ——

The nose, the eye pits, the full set of teeth?
The sour breath
Will vanish in a day.

Soon, soon the flesh
The grave cave ate will be
At home on me

And I a smiling woman.
I am only thirty.
And like the cat I have nine times to die.

This is Number Three.
What a trash
To annihilate each decade.

What a million filaments.
The peanut-crunching crowd
Shoves in to see

Them unwrap me hand and foot ——
The big strip tease.
Gentleman, ladies,

These are my hands,
My knees.
I may be skin and bone,

Nevertheless, I am the same, identical woman.
The first time it happened I was ten.
It was an accident.

The second time I meant
To last it out and not come back at all.
I rocked shut

As a seashell.
They had to call and call
And pick the worms off me like sticky pearls.

Dying
Is an art, like everything else.
I do it exceptionally well.

I do it so it feels like hell.
I do it so it feels real.
I guess you could say I've a call.

It's easy enough to do it in a cell.
It's easy enough to do it and stay put.
It's the theatrical

Comeback in broad day
To the same place, the same face, the same brute
Amused shout:

"A miracle!"
That knocks me out.
There is a charge

For the eyeing of my scars, there is a charge
For the hearing of my heart ——
It really goes.

And there is a charge, a very large charge,
For a word or a touch
Or a bit of blood

Or a piece of my hair or my clothes.
So, so, Herr Doktor.
So, Herr Enemy.

I am your opus,
I am your valuable,
The pure gold baby

That melts to a shriek.
I turn and burn.
Do not think I underestimate your great concern.

Ash, ash —
You poke and stir.
Flesh, bone, there is nothing there ——

A cake of soap,
A wedding ring,
A gold filling.

Herr God, Herr Lucifer,
Beware
Beware.

Out of the ash
I rise with my red hair
And I eat men like air.

Elm

For Ruth Fainlight

I know the bottom, she says. I know it with my great tap root:
It is what you fear.
I do not fear it: I have been there.

Is it the sea you hear in me,
Its dissatisfactions?
Or the voice of nothing, that was your madness?

Love is a shadow.
How you lie and cry after it.
Listen: these are its hooves: it has gone off, like a horse.

All night I shall gallop thus, impetuously,
Till your head is a stone, your pillow a little turf,
Echoing, echoing.

Or shall I bring you the sound of poisons?
This is rain now, this big hush.
And this is the fruit of it: tin-white, like arsenic.

I have suffered the atrocity of sunsets.
Scorched to the root
My red filaments burn and stand, a hand of wires.

Now I break up in pieces that fly about like clubs.
A wind of such violence
Will tolerate no bystanding: I must shriek.

The moon, also, is merciless: she would drag me
Cruelly, being barren.
Her radiance scathes me. Or perhaps I have caught her.

I let her go. I let her go
Diminished and flat, as after radical surgery.
How your bad dreams possess and endow me.

I am inhabited by a cry.
Nightly it flaps out
Looking, with its hooks, for something to love.

I am terrified by this dark thing
That sleeps in me;
All day I feel its soft, feathery turnings, its malignity.

Clouds pass and disperse.
Are those the faces of love, those pale irretrievables?
Is it for such I agitate my heart?

I am incapable of more knowledge.
What is this, this face
So murderous in its strangle of branches? ——

Its snaky acids kiss.
It petrifies the will. These are the isolate, slow faults
That kill, that kill, that kill.

Ariel

Stasis in darkness.
Then the substanceless blue
Pour of tor and distances.

God's lioness,
How one we grow,
Pivot of heels and knees! — The furrow

Splits and passes, sister to
The brown arc
Of the neck I cannot catch,

Nigger-eye
Berries cast dark
Hooks ——

Black sweet blood mouthfuls,
Shadows.
Something else

Hauls me through air ——
Thighs, hair;
Flakes from my heels,

White
Godiva, I unpeel —
Dead hands, dead stringencies.

And now I
Foam to wheat, a glitter of seas.
The child's cry

Melts in the wall.
And I
Am the arrow,

The dew that flies
Suicidal, at one with the drive
Into the red

Eye, the cauldron of morning.

Gulliver

Over your body the clouds go
High, high and icily
And a little flat, as if they

Floated on a glass that was invisible.
Unlike swans,
Having no reflections;

Unlike you,
With no strings attached.
All cool, all blue. Unlike you ——

You, there on your back,
Eyes to the sky.
The spider-men have caught you,

Winding and twining their petty fetters,
Their bribes ——
So many silks.

How they hate you.
They converse in the valley of your fingers, they are inchworms.
They would have you sleep in their cabinets,

This toe and that toe, a relic.
Step off!
Step off seven leagues, like those distances

That revolve in Crivelli, untouchable.
Let this eye be an eagle,
The shadow of this lip, an abyss.

Daddy

You do not do, you do not do
Any more, black shoe
In which I have lived like a foot
For thirty years, poor and white,
Barely daring to breathe or Achoo.

Daddy, I have had to kill you.
You died before I had time ——
Marble-heavy, a bag full of God,
Ghastly statue with one grey toe
Big as a Frisco seal

And a head in the freakish Atlantic
Where it pours bean green over blue
In the waters off beautiful Nauset.
I used to pray to recover you.
Ach, du.

In the German tongue, in the Polish town
Scraped flat by the roller
Of wars, wars, wars.
But the name of the town is common.
My Polack friend

Says there are a dozen or two.
So I never could tell where you
Put your foot, your root,
I never could talk to you.
The tongue stuck in my jaw.

It stuck in a barb wire snare.
Ich, ich, ich, ich,
I could hardly speak.
I thought every German was you.
And the language obscene

An engine, an engine
Chuffing me off like a Jew.
A Jew to Dachau, Auschwitz, Belsen.
I began to talk like a Jew.
I think I may well be a Jew.

The snows of the Tyrol, the clear beer of Vienna
Are not very pure or true.
With my gypsy ancestress and my weird luck
And my Taroc pack and my Taroc pack
I may be a bit of a Jew.

I have always been scared of *you*,
With your Luftwaffe, your gobbledygoo.
And your neat moustache
And your Aryan eye, bright blue.
Panzer-man, panzer-man, O You ———

Not God but a swastika
So black no sky could squeak through.
Every woman adores a Fascist,
The boot in the face, the brute
Brute heart of a brute like you.

You stand at the blackboard, daddy,
In the picture I have of you,
A cleft in your chin instead of your foot
But no less a devil for that, no not
Any less the black man who

Bit my pretty red heart in two.
I was ten when they buried you.
At twenty I tried to die
And get back, back, back to you.
I thought even the bones would do.

But they pulled me out of the sack,
And they stuck me together with glue.
And then I knew what to do.
I made a model of you,
A man in black with a Meinkampf look

And a love of the rack and the screw.
And I said I do, I do.
So daddy, I'm finally through.
The black telephone's off at the root,
The voices just can't worm through.

If I've killed one man, I've killed two ——
The vampire who said he was you
And drank my blood for a year,
Seven years, if you want to know.
Daddy, you can lie back now.

There's a stake in your fat black heart
And the villagers never liked you.
They are dancing and stamping on you.
They always *knew* it was you.
Daddy, daddy, you bastard, I'm through.

Fever 103°

Pure? What does it mean?
The tongues of hell
Are dull, dull as the triple

Tongues of dull, fat Cerberus
Who wheezes at the gate. Incapable
Of licking clean

The aguey tendon, the sin, the sin.
The tinder cries.
The indelible smell

Of a snuffed candle!
Love, love, the low smokes roll
From me like Isadora's scarves, I'm in a fright

One scarf will catch and anchor in the wheel.
Such yellow sullen smokes
Make their own element. They will not rise,

But trundle round the globe
Choking the aged and the meek,
The weak

Hothouse baby in its crib,
The ghastly orchid
Hanging its hanging garden in the air,

Devilish leopard!
Radiation turned it white
And killed it in an hour.

Greasing the bodies of adulterers
Like Hiroshima ash and eating in.
The sin. The sin.

Darling, all night
I have been flickering, off, on, off, on.
The sheets grow heavy as a lecher's kiss.

Three days. Three nights.
Lemon water, chicken
Water, water make me retch.

I am too pure for you or anyone.
Your body
Hurts me as the world hurts God. I am a lantern ———

My head a moon
Of Japanese paper, my gold beaten skin
Infinitely delicate and infinitely expensive.

Does not my heat astound you. And my light.
All by myself I am a huge camellia
Glowing and coming and going, flush on flush.

I think I am going up,
I think I may rise ———
The beads of hot metal fly, and I, love, I

Am a pure acetylene
Virgin
Attended by roses,

By kisses, by cherubim,
By whatever these pink things mean.

Not you, nor him

Not him, nor him
(My selves dissolving, old whore petticoats) ———
To Paradise.

Blackberrying

Nobody in the lane, and nothing, nothing but blackberries,
Blackberries on either side, though on the right mainly,
A blackberry alley, going down in hooks, and a sea
Somewhere at the end of it, heaving. Blackberries
Big as the ball of my thumb, and dumb as eyes
Ebon in the hedges, fat
With blue-red juices. These they squander on my fingers.
I had not asked for such a blood sisterhood; they must love me.
They accommodate themselves to my milkbottle, flattening their sides.

Overhead go the choughs in black, cacophonous flocks —
Bits of burnt paper wheeling in a blown sky.
Theirs is the only voice, protesting, protesting.
I do not think the sea will appear at all.
The high, green meadows are glowing, as if lit from within.
I come to one bush of berries so ripe it is a bush of flies,
Hanging their bluegreen bellies and their wing panes in a Chinese screen.
The honey-feast of the berries has stunned them; they believe in heaven.
One more hook, and the berries and bushes end.

The only thing to come now is the sea.
From between two hills a sudden wind funnels at me,
Slapping its phantom laundry in my face.
These hills are too green and sweet to have tasted salt.
I follow the sheep path between them. A last hook brings me
To the hills' northern face, and the face is orange rock
That looks out on nothing, nothing but a great space
Of white and pewter lights, and a din like silversmiths
Beating and beating at an intractable metal.

Event

How the elements solidify! —
The moonlight, that chalk cliff
In whose rift we lie

Back to back. I hear an owl cry
From its cold indigo.
Intolerable vowels enter my heart.

The child in the white crib revolves and sighs,
Opens its mouth now, demanding.
His little face is carved in pained, red wood.

Then there are the stars — ineradicable, hard.
One touch: it burns and sickens.
I cannot see your eyes.

Where apple bloom ices the night
I walk in a ring,
A groove of old faults, deep and bitter.

Love cannot come here.
A black gap discloses itself.
On the opposite lip

A small white soul is waving, a small white maggot.
My limbs, also, have left me.
Who has dismembered us?

The dark is melting. We touch like cripples.

Love Letter

Not easy to state the change you made.
If I'm alive now, then I was dead,
Though, like a stone, unbothered by it,
Staying put according to habit.
You didn't just toe me an inch, no —
Nor leave me to set my small bald eye
Skyward again, without hope, of course,
Of apprehending blueness, or stars.

That wasn't it. I slept, say: a snake
Masked among black rocks as a black rock
In the white hiatus of winter —
Like my neighbours, taking no pleasure
In the million perfectly-chiselled
Cheeks alighting each moment to melt
My cheek of basalt. They turned to tears,
Angels weeping over dull natures,
But didn't convince me. Those tears froze.
Each dead head had a visor of ice.

And I slept on like a bent finger.
The first thing I saw was sheer air
And the locked drops rising in a dew
Limpid as spirits. Many stones lay
Dense and expressionless round about.
I didn't know what to make of it.
I shone, mica-scaled, and unfolded
To pour myself out like a fluid
Among bird feet and the stems of plants.
I wasn't fooled. I knew you at once.

Tree and stone glittered, without shadows.
My finger-length grew lucent as glass.
I started to bud like a March twig:
An arm and a leg, an arm, a leg.
From stone to cloud, so I ascended.
Now I resembled a sort of god
Floating through the air in my soul-shift
Pure as a pane of ice. It's a gift.

A Life

Touch it: it won't shrink like an eyeball,
This egg-shaped bailiwick, clear as a tear.
Here's yesterday, last year —
Palm-spear and lily distinct as flora in the vast
Windless threadwork of a tapestry.

Flick the glass with your fingernail:
It will ping like a Chinese chime in the slightest air stir
Though nobody in there looks up or bothers to answer.
The inhabitants are light as cork,
Every one of them permanently busy.

At their feet, the sea waves bow in single file,
Never trespassing in bad temper:
Stalling in midair,
Short-reined, pawing like paradeground horses.
Overhead, the clouds sit tasselled and fancy

As Victorian cushions. This family
Of valentine-faces might please a collector:
They ring true, like good china.

Elsewhere the landscape is more frank.
The light falls without letup, blindingly.

A woman is dragging her shadow in a circle
About a bald, hospital saucer.
It resembles the moon, or a sheet of blank paper
And appears to have suffered a sort of private blitzkrieg.
She lives quietly.

With no attachments, like a foetus in a bottle,
The obsolete house, the sea, flattened to a picture
She has one too many dimensions to enter.
Grief and anger, exorcized,
Leave her alone now.

The future is a grey seagull
Tattling in its cat-voice of departure, departure.
Age and terror, like nurses, attend her,
And a drowned man, complaining of the great cold,
Crawls up out of the sea.

IMAMU AMIRI BARAKA
(LeRoi Jones)
b. 1934

For Hettie

My wife is left-handed.
which implies a fierce de-
termination. A complete other
worldliness. ITS WEIRD, BABY.
The way some folks
are always trying to be
different. A sin & a shame.

But then, she's been a bohemian
all of her life . . . black stockings
refusing to take orders. I sit
patiently, trying to tell her
whats right. TAKE THAT DAMN
PENCIL OUTTA THAT HAND. YOU'RE
RITING BACKWARDS. & such. But
to no avail. & it shows

in her work. Left-handed coffee,
Left-handed eggs; when she comes
in at night . . . it's her left hand
offered for me to kiss. Damm.

& now her belly droops over the seat.
They say it's a child. But
I ain't quite so sure.

A Poem Some People Will Have to Understand

Dull unwashed windows of eyes
and buildings of industry. What
industry do I practice? A slick
colored boy, 12 miles from his
home. I practice no industry.
I am no longer a credit
to my race. I read a little,
scratch against silence slow spring
afternoons.
                    I had thought, before, some years ago
that I'd come to the end of my life.
                    Watercolor ego. Without the preciseness
a violent man could propose.
                    But the wheel, and the wheels,
wont let us alone. All the fantasy
                    and justice, and dry charcoal winters
All the pitifully intelligent citizens
                    I've forced myself to love.

                    We have awaited the coming of a natural
                    phenomenon. Mystics and romantics, knowledgeable
                    workers
                    of the land.
                    But none has come.
                    (Repeat)
                            but none has come.

Will the machinegunners please step forward?

IMAMU AMIRI BARAKA (LEROI JONES)

Legacy

(For Blues People)

In the south, sleeping against
the drugstore, growling under
the trucks and stoves, stumbling
through and over the cluttered eyes
of early mysterious night. Frowning
drunk waving moving a hand or lash.
Dancing kneeling reaching out, letting
a hand rest in shadows. Squatting
to drink or pee. Stretching to climb
pulling themselves onto horses near
where there was sea (the old songs
lead you to believe). Riding out
from this town, to another, where
it is also black. Down a road
where people are asleep. Towards
the moon or the shadows of houses.
Towards the songs' pretended sea.

I Substitute For The Dead Lecturer

> *What is most precious, because
> it is lost. What is lost,
> because it is most
> precious.*

They have turned, and say that I am dying. That
I have thrown
my life
away. They
have left me alone, where
there is no one, nothing
save who I am. Not a note
nor a word.

      Cold air batters
the poor (and their minds
turn open
like sores). What kindness

What wealth
can I offer? Except
what is, for me,
ugliest. What is
for me, shadows, shrieking
phantoms. Except
they have need
of life. Flesh
at least,
        should be theirs.

The Lord has saved me
to do this. The Lord
has made me strong. I
am as I must have
myself. Against all
thought, all music, all
my soft loves.

            For all these wan roads
I am pushed to follow, are
my own conceit. A simple muttering
elegance, slipped in my head
pressed on my soul, is my heart's
worth. And I am frightened
that the flame of my sickness
will burn off my face. And leave
the bones, my stewed black skull,
an empty cage of failure.

A Poem For Speculative Hipsters

He had got, finally,
to the forest
of motives. There were no
owls, or hunters. No Connie Chatterleys
resting beautifully
on their backs, having casually
brought socialism
to England.
        Only ideas,
and their opposites.

Like,
he was *really*
nowhere.

The Liar

What I thought was love
in me, I find a thousand instances
as fear. (Of the tree's shadow
winding around the chair, a distant music
of frozen birds rattling
in the cold.
　　　　　　Where ever I go to claim
my flesh, there are entrances
of spirit. And even its comforts
are hideous uses I strain
to understand.
　　　　　　Though I am a man
Who is loud
on the birth
of his ways. Publicly redefining
each change in my soul, as if I had predicted
them,
　　　　and profited, biblically, even tho
　　　　their chanting weight,
　　　　　　　　　　erased familiarity
　　　　　　　　　　from my face.
　　　　　　　　　　　　A question I think,
an answer; whatever sits
counting the minutes
till you die.

　　　　When they say, "It is Roi
　　　　who is dead?" I wonder
　　　　who will they mean?

Evil Nigger Waits for Lightnin'

Alone, at night, with all the world
not watching, around me,
who for the understanding
intended, the love
withheld,

1057

would be lost in the blackness
of self-nights
howling like something
or scurrying behind iceboxes
like something
would be them things
in my conscious
ness, or waddlegirls
full of invisible demands
they are children the world will tell you
only children, lost dreams, that you should love
if you can, from the tower of Headlust, you they moan
should always adore them, lost feeling, should love and
take yrself through any change to understand their blankness.

Alone at night the world disappears breathing over my head weeping it
is lost or unappreciated. It says I do not love it. And sends its dopey
messengers to touch me right. The world, the world says, is full of love
can you find it, can you enter, and remain, grow strong with it beautiful
thing
in the rain, the world,
these sent things whisper
mice, fucked ladies, whisps of cloud
still visible four oclock in the nighttime
for the expanding or retracting dying or just coming
thing
we will always
be.

The Astronomers,
The Philosophers,
The Crowd, of them,
Things, These dangerous feelers, for understanding,
now that I am alone so much I can manage to
hear another thing
singing through my face
describing the arc
and the constant
return . . .

      way out now,
      describing its own voice
      its
      reason

W. W.

Back home the black women are all beautiful
and the white ones fall back, cutoff from 1000
years stacked booty, and Charles of the Ritz
where jooshladies turn into billy burke in blueglass
kicks. With wings, and jingly bew-teeful things.
The black women in Newark are fine. Even with all that grease
in their heads. I mean even the ones where the wigs
slide around, and they coming at you 75degrees off course.
I could talk to them. Bring them around. To something.
Some kind of quick course, on the sidewalk, like Hey baby
why don't you take that thing off yo' haid. You look like
Miss Muffett in a runaway ugly machine. I mean. Like that.

Numbers, Letters

If you're not home, where
are you? Where'd you go? What
were you doing when gone? When
you come back, better make it good.
What was you doing down there, freakin' off
with white women, hangin' out
with Queens, say it straight to be
understood straight, put it flat and real
in the street where the sun comes and the
moon comes and the cold wind in winter
waters your eyes. Say what you mean, dig
it out put it down, and be strong
about it.

I cant say who I am
unless you agree I'm real

I cant be anything I'm not
Except these words pretend
to life not yet explained,
so here's some feeling for you
see how you like it, what it
reveals, and that's me.

Unless you agree I'm real
that I can feel
whatever beats hardest
at our black souls

I am real, and I can't say who
I am. Ask me if I know, I'll say
yes, I might say no. Still, ask.

I'm Everett LeRoi Jones, 30 yrs old.
A black nigger in the universe. A long breath singer,
wouldbe dancer, strong from years of fantasy
and study. All this time then, for what's happening
now. All that spilling of white ether, clocks in ghostheads
lips drying and rewet, eyes opening and shut, mouths churning.

I am a meditative man. And when I say something it's all of me
saying, and all the things that make me, have formed me, colored me
this brilliant reddish night. I will say nothing that I feel is
lie, or unproven by the same ghostclocks, by the same riders
always move so fast with the word slung over their backs or
in saddlebags, charging down Chinese roads. I carry some words,
some feeling, some life in me. My heart is large as my mind
this is a messenger calling, over here, over here, open your eyes
and your ears and your souls; today is the history we must learn
to desire. There is no guilt in love

INDEX

INDEX

INDEX

By fate, not option, frugal Nature gave, 76
By some derision of wild circumstance, 389
By the road to the contagious hospital, 468
By the rude bridge that arched the flood, 78

Call the roller of big cigars, 446
Calm as that second summer which precedes, 317
Cambridge ladies who live in furnished souls, the, 632
Canto II, 517
Canto VII, 521
Canto XLV, 525
Canto LXXXI, 526
Captain Carpenter, 578
Captain Carpenter rose up in his prime, 578
Carentan O Carentan, 862
Cascadilla Falls, 896
Cat as Cat, The, 876
Catholic Bells, The, 475
Caught between two streams of traffic, in the gloom, 819
Certain presuppositions are altered, 899
Chambered Nautilus, The, 139
Chaplinesque, 650
Charleston, 317
Chaucer, 96
Chez Jane, 935
Chicago, 422
Chieftain Iffucan of Azcan in caftan, 446
Cigales, 840
City in the Sea, The, 149
City Limits, The, 900
Classic, 897
Climate of Paradise, The, 868
Climbing from the Lethal dead, 686
Clouded Morning, The, 170
Coda [Pound], 502
Coda [Williams], 490
Coliseum, The, 153
Colossus, The, 1037
Columbine, The, 168
Come In, 416
Come, Said My Soul, 206
Come with Me, 942
Come with me into those things that have felt this despair for so long, 942
Comforted by Limestone, 1009
Compensation, 83
Complacencies of the peignoir, and late, 442
Complaint, 989
Composed in the Tower before his execution, 853
Concord Hymn, 78
Conflict of Convictions, The, 299
Congo, The, 432
Conqueror Worm, The, 155
Constantly near you, I never in my entire, 488
contend in a sea which the land partly encloses, 474

Conversation brings us so close! Opening, 945
Cool Tombs, 423
Coon Song, 889
Correspondence School Instructor Says Goodbye to his Poetry Students, The, 966
Corsons Inlet, 892
Country House, The, 867
Courtin', The, 193
Crane, Hart, 649
Crane, Stephen, 389
Creeley, Robert, 914
Cricket, The, 314
Critics and Connoisseurs, 553
Crossing Brooklyn Ferry, 266
Crossing the street, 906
Cross of Snow, The, 97
Crowning a bluff where gleams the lake below, 307
Crumbling is not an instant's Act (997), 346
Cummings, E.E., 631
Cuttings, 719
Cuttings, later, 719

Daddy, 1046
Damn it all! all this our South stinks peace, 494
Dance, The [Roethke], 722
Dance, The [Williams], 478
Dance of the Macabre Mice, 447
Danse Russe, 466
Dante attained the purgatorial hill, 724
Dark accurate plunger down the successive knell, 676
Darkness has called to darkness, and disgrace, 798
Daughters of Time, the hypocritic Days, 84
Day is Done, The, 85
Day Lady Died, The, 937
Day of Denial, The, 173
Days, 84
Deacon's Masterpiece, The, 136
Dead, The, 168
Dead Shall be Raised Incorruptible, The, 970
Dear Uncle Stranger, 621
Death of the Ball Turret Gunner, The, 771
Death of Venus, The, 914
December at Yase, 1035
Departmental, 412
Desert Places, 413
Design, 414
Dickey, James, 855
Dickinson, Emily, 322
Did Our Best Moment last (393), 332
Directive, 419
Discordants, 618
Distances, The, 987
Diving into the Wreck, 1020
dogwood flakes, 752
Dolphin, 819
Do not weep, maiden, for war is kind, 390

INDEX

INDEX

INDEX

INDEX

INDEX